SUPERMAN VS. DARKSEID

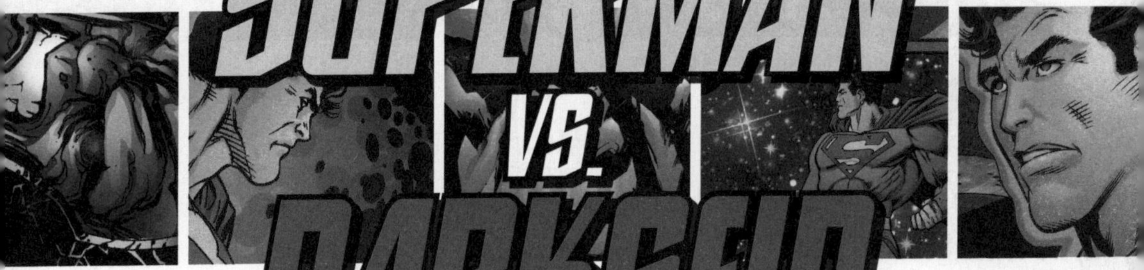

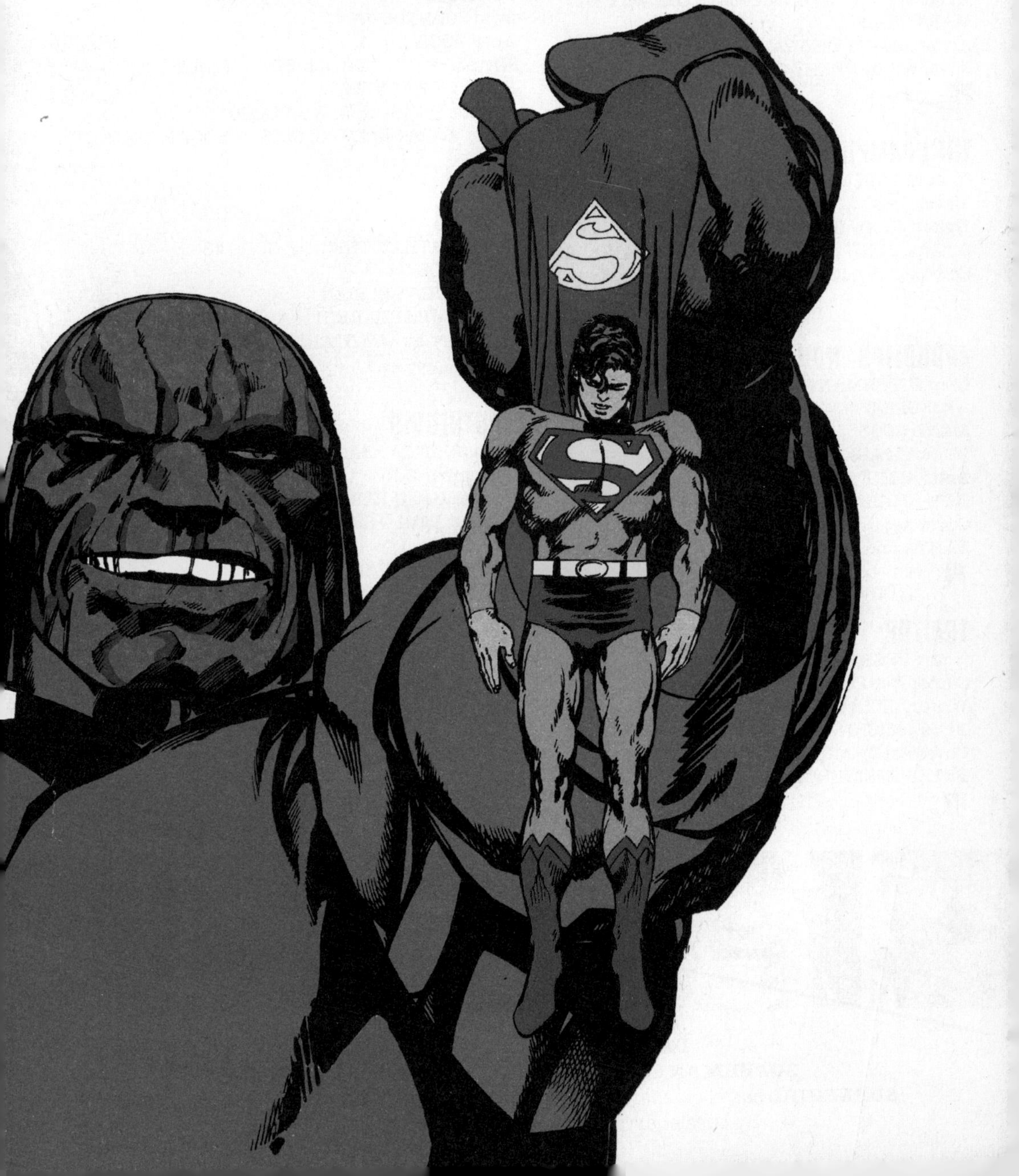

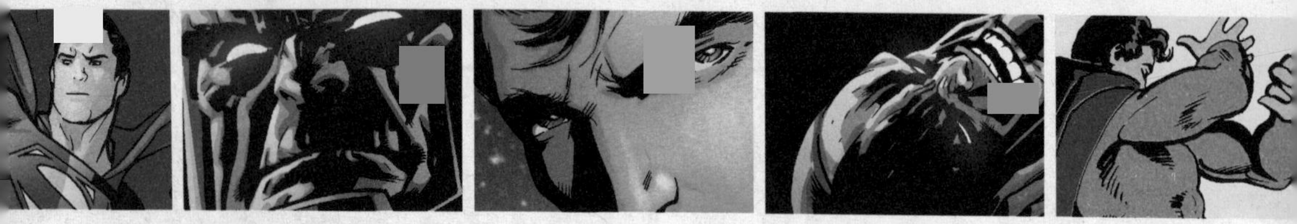

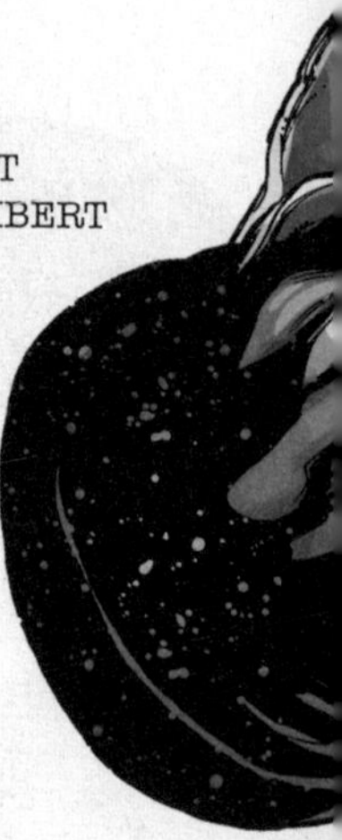

ADAM KUBERT & EDGAR DELGADO
Collection Cover Artists

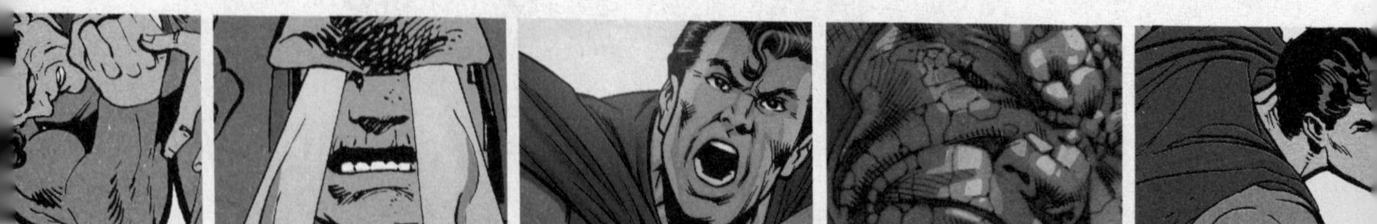

DARKSEID created by **JACK KIRBY**
SUPERMAN created by **JERRY SIEGEL** & **JOE SHUSTER**
SUPERGIRL based on characters created by **JERRY SIEGEL** & **JOE SHUSTER**
By special arrangement with the Jerry Siegel family

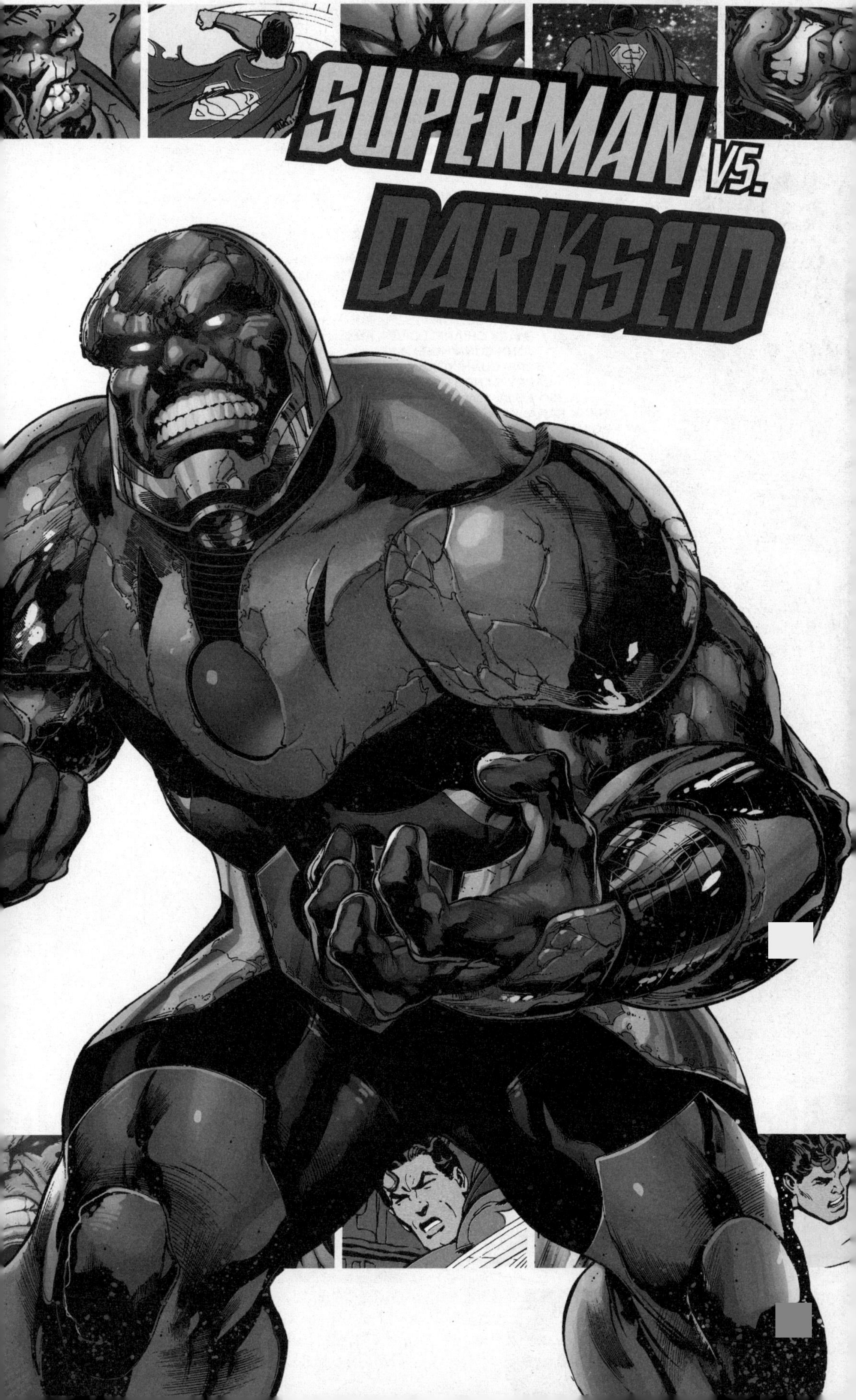
SUPERMAN VS. DARKSEID

SUPERMAN VS. DARKSEID

Published by DC Comics. Compilation Copyright © 2015 DC Comics.
All Rights Reserved.

Originally published in single magazine form in SUPERMAN 3, ADVENTURES OF
SUPERMAN 426, ACTION COMICS 586, SUPERMAN VS DARKSEID: APOKOLIPS
NOW! 1, SUPERMAN/BATMAN 12, 13; COUNTDOWN 2, 3; DEATH OF THE NEW
GODS 8, JUSTICE LEAGUE 23.1 © 1987, 2003, 2004, 2008, 2013 DC Comics.
All Rights Reserved. All characters, their distinctive likenesses and related
elements featured in this publication are trademarks of DC Comics. The stories,
characters and incidents featured in this publication are entirely fictional. DC
Comics does not read or accept unsolicited ideas, stories or artwork.

DC Comics, 1700 Broadway, New York, NY 10019
A Warner Bros. Entertainment Company.
Printed by RR Donnelley, Salem, VA, USA. 3/20/15 First Printing.
ISBN: 978-1-4012-5543-5

Library of Congress Cataloging-in-Publication Data

Superman vs. Darkseid / John Byrne , author.
    pages cm
    ISBN 978-1-4012-5543-5 (pbk.)
    1. Graphic novels. I. Byrne, John II. Title.

PN6728.S9S949 2013
741.5'973—dc23

2013030641

SUSTAINABLE FORESTRY INITIATIVE
Certified Sourcing
www.sfiprogram.org
SFI-01042
APPLIES TO TEXT STOCK ONLY

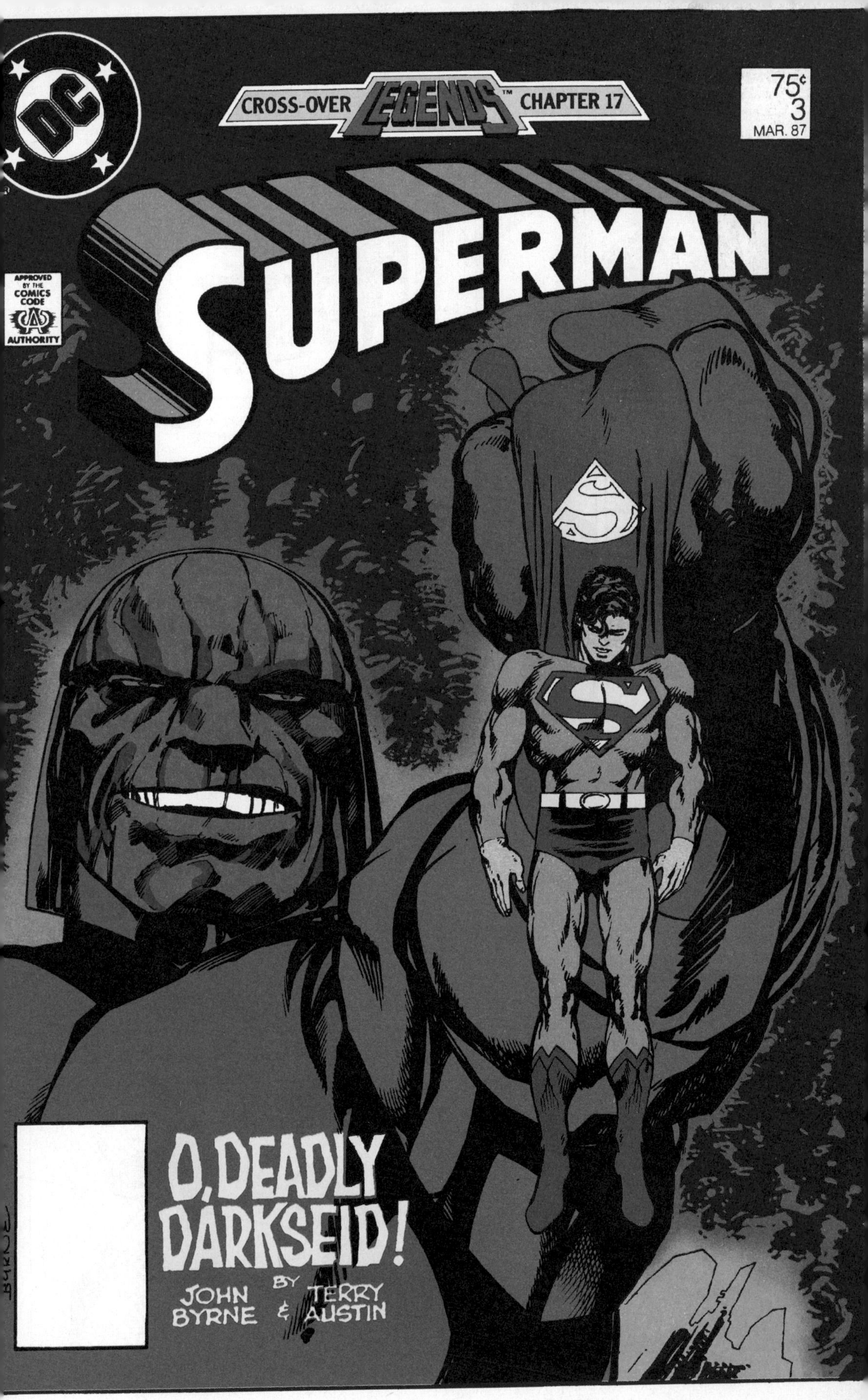
DC
CROSS-OVER LEGENDS™ CHAPTER 17
75¢
3
MAR. 87
SUPERMAN
APPROVED BY THE COMICS CODE AUTHORITY
O, DEADLY DARKSEID!
BY
JOHN BYRNE & TERRY AUSTIN

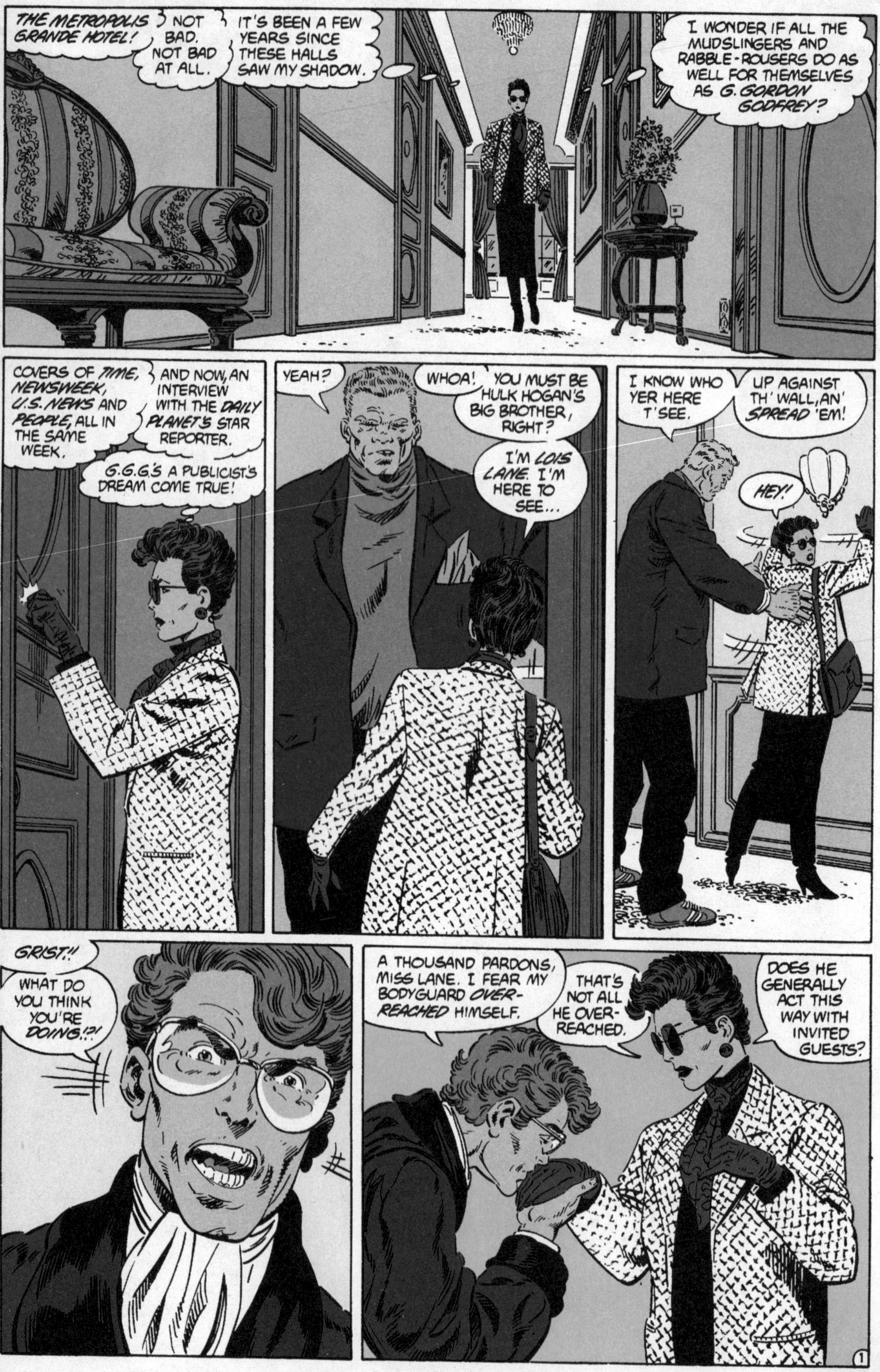

THE METROPOLIS GRANDE HOTEL!
NOT BAD. NOT BAD AT ALL.
IT'S BEEN A FEW YEARS SINCE THESE HALLS SAW MY SHADOW.
I WONDER IF ALL THE MUDSLINGERS AND RABBLE-ROUSERS DO AS WELL FOR THEMSELVES AS G. GORDON GODFREY?
COVERS OF TIME, NEWSWEEK, U.S. NEWS AND PEOPLE, ALL IN THE SAME WEEK.
AND NOW, AN INTERVIEW WITH THE DAILY PLANET'S STAR REPORTER.
G.G.G.'S A PUBLICIST'S DREAM COME TRUE!
YEAH?
WHOA!
YOU MUST BE HULK HOGAN'S BIG BROTHER, RIGHT?
I'M LOIS LANE. I'M HERE TO SEE...
I KNOW WHO YER HERE T'SEE.
UP AGAINST TH' WALL, AN' SPREAD 'EM!
HEY!
GRIST!!
WHAT DO YOU THINK YOU'RE DOING!?!
A THOUSAND PARDONS, MISS LANE. I FEAR MY BODYGUARD OVER-REACHED HIMSELF.
THAT'S NOT ALL HE OVER-REACHED.
DOES HE GENERALLY ACT THIS WAY WITH INVITED GUESTS?
1

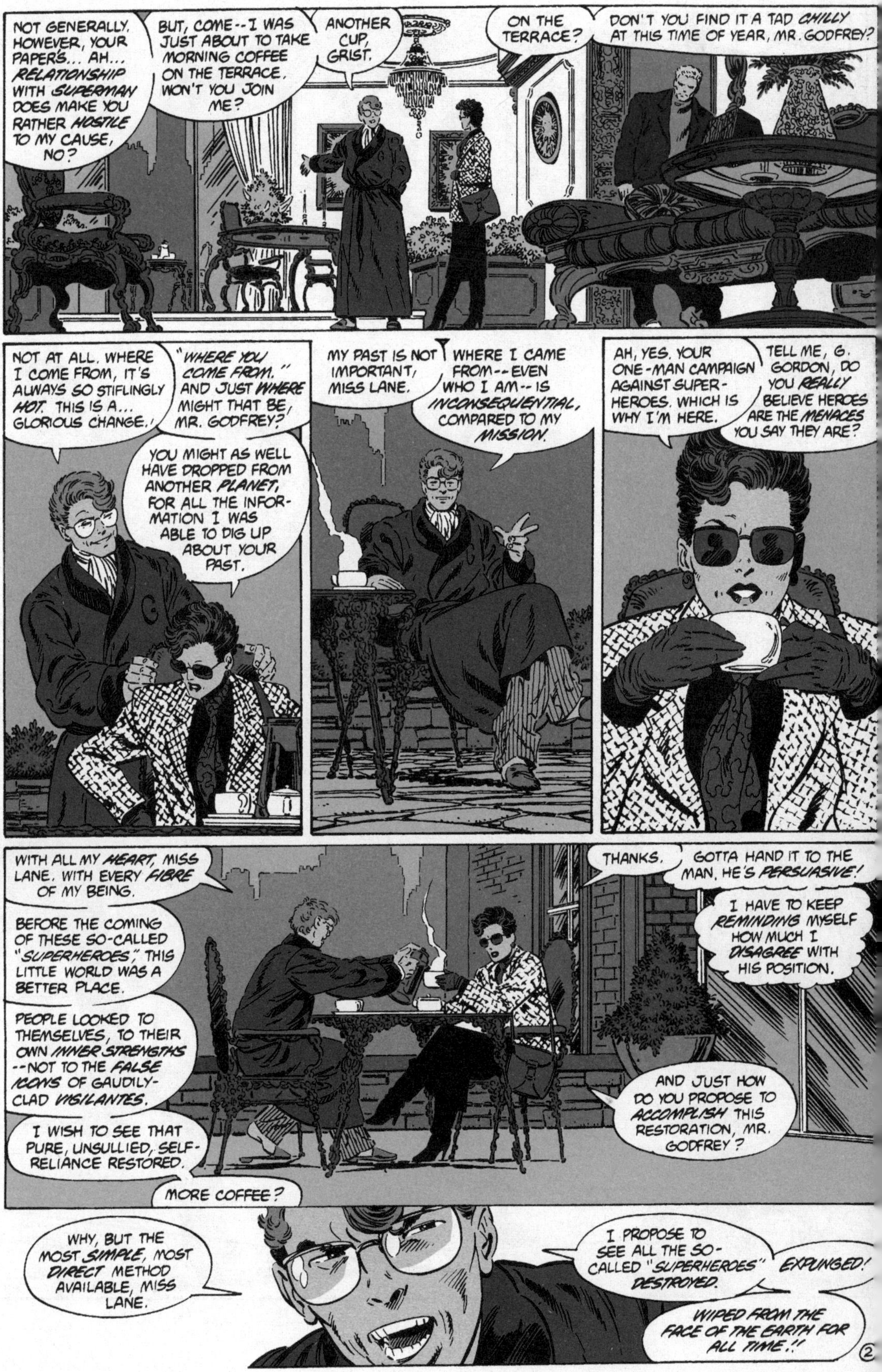
NOT GENERALLY. HOWEVER, YOUR PAPER'S... AH... RELATIONSHIP WITH SUPERMAN DOES MAKE YOU RATHER HOSTILE TO MY CAUSE, NO?
BUT, COME--I WAS JUST ABOUT TO TAKE MORNING COFFEE ON THE TERRACE. WON'T YOU JOIN ME?
ANOTHER CUP, GRIST.
ON THE TERRACE?
DON'T YOU FIND IT A TAD CHILLY AT THIS TIME OF YEAR, MR. GODFREY?
NOT AT ALL. WHERE I COME FROM, IT'S ALWAYS SO STIFLINGLY HOT. THIS IS A... GLORIOUS CHANGE.
"WHERE YOU COME FROM." AND JUST WHERE MIGHT THAT BE, MR. GODFREY?
YOU MIGHT AS WELL HAVE DROPPED FROM ANOTHER PLANET, FOR ALL THE INFORMATION I WAS ABLE TO DIG UP ABOUT YOUR PAST.
MY PAST IS NOT IMPORTANT, MISS LANE.
WHERE I CAME FROM--EVEN WHO I AM--IS INCONSEQUENTIAL, COMPARED TO MY MISSION.
AH, YES. YOUR ONE-MAN CAMPAIGN AGAINST SUPER-HEROES. WHICH IS WHY I'M HERE.
TELL ME, G. GORDON, DO YOU REALLY BELIEVE HEROES ARE THE MENACES YOU SAY THEY ARE?
WITH ALL MY HEART, MISS LANE. WITH EVERY FIBRE OF MY BEING.
BEFORE THE COMING OF THESE SO-CALLED "SUPERHEROES," THIS LITTLE WORLD WAS A BETTER PLACE.
PEOPLE LOOKED TO THEMSELVES, TO THEIR OWN INNER STRENGTHS --NOT TO THE FALSE ICONS OF GAUDILY-CLAD VIGILANTES.
I WISH TO SEE THAT PURE, UNSULLIED, SELF-RELIANCE RESTORED.
MORE COFFEE?
THANKS.
GOTTA HAND IT TO THE MAN, HE'S PERSUASIVE!
I HAVE TO KEEP REMINDING MYSELF HOW MUCH I DISAGREE WITH HIS POSITION.
AND JUST HOW DO YOU PROPOSE TO ACCOMPLISH THIS RESTORATION, MR. GODFREY?
WHY, BUT THE MOST SIMPLE, MOST DIRECT METHOD AVAILABLE, MISS LANE.
I PROPOSE TO SEE ALL THE SO-CALLED "SUPERHEROES" DESTROYED.
EXPUNGED!
WIPED FROM THE FACE OF THE EARTH FOR ALL TIME!!
2

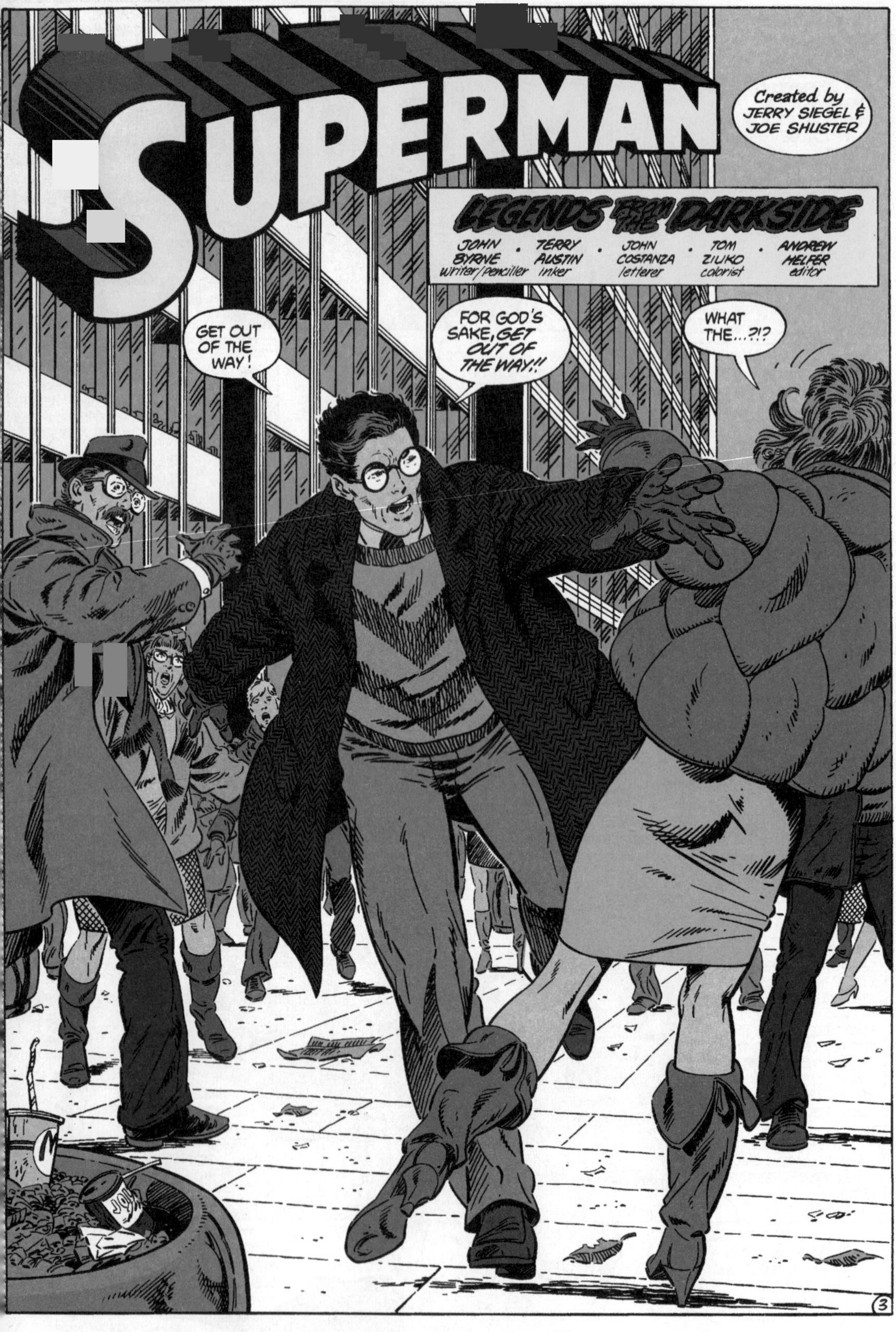
SUPERMAN
Created by JERRY SIEGEL & JOE SHUSTER
LEGENDS FROM THE DARKSIDE
JOHN BYRNE writer/penciller • TERRY AUSTIN inker • JOHN COSTANZA letterer • TOM ZIUKO colorist • ANDREW HELFER editor
GET OUT OF THE WAY!
FOR GOD'S SAKE, GET OUT OF THE WAY!!
WHAT THE...?!?
3

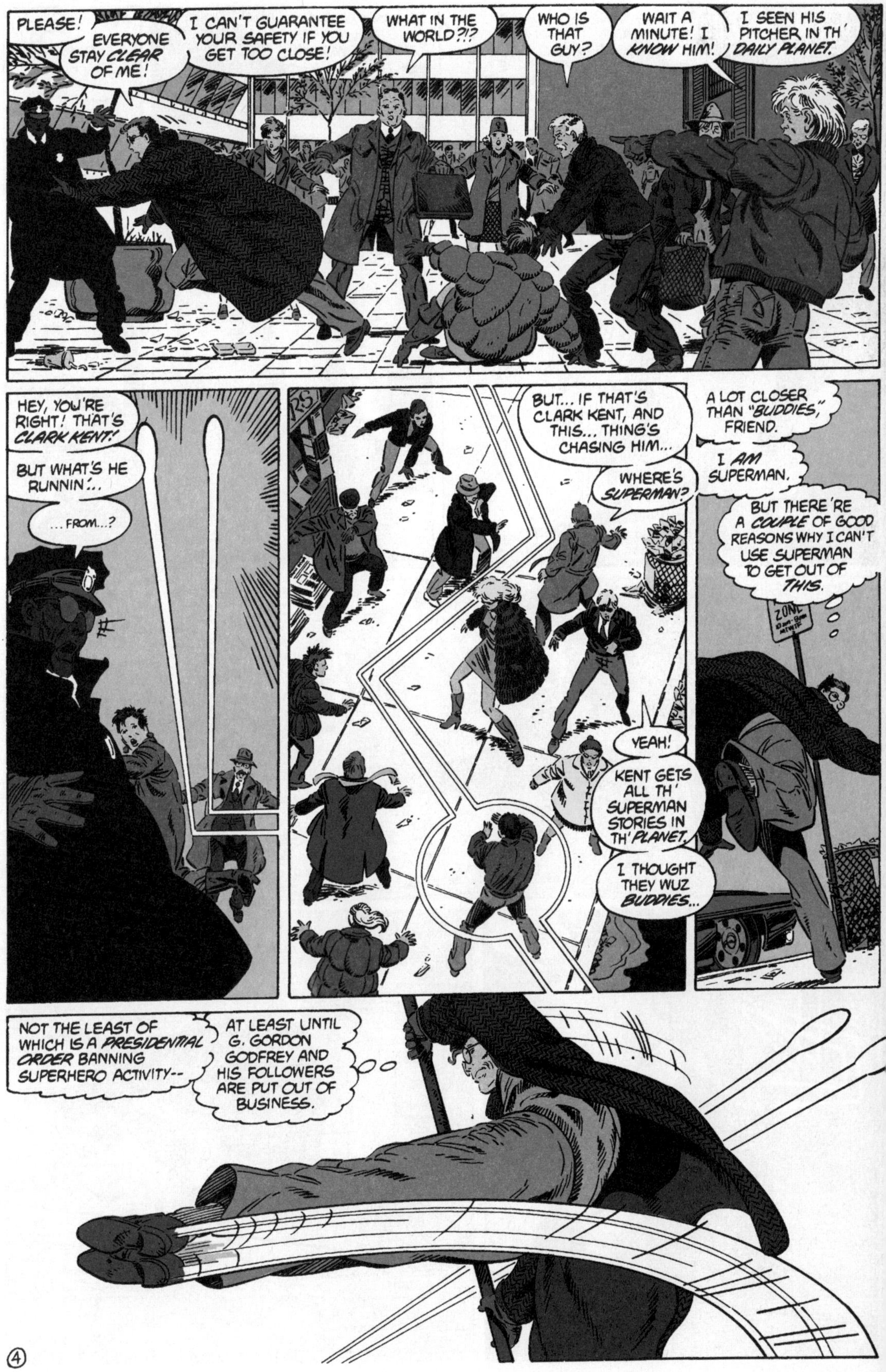
PLEASE!
EVERYONE STAY CLEAR OF ME!
I CAN'T GUARANTEE YOUR SAFETY IF YOU GET TOO CLOSE!
WHAT IN THE WORLD?!?
WHO IS THAT GUY?
WAIT A MINUTE! I KNOW HIM!
I SEEN HIS PITCHER IN TH' DAILY PLANET.
HEY, YOU'RE RIGHT! THAT'S CLARK KENT!
BUT WHAT'S HE RUNNIN'...
...FROM...?
BUT... IF THAT'S CLARK KENT, AND THIS... THING'S CHASING HIM...
WHERE'S SUPERMAN?
YEAH!
KENT GETS ALL TH' SUPERMAN STORIES IN TH' PLANET.
I THOUGHT THEY WUZ BUDDIES...
A LOT CLOSER THAN "BUDDIES," FRIEND.
I AM SUPERMAN.
BUT THERE'RE A COUPLE OF GOOD REASONS WHY I CAN'T USE SUPERMAN TO GET OUT OF THIS.
NOT THE LEAST OF WHICH IS A PRESIDENTIAL ORDER BANNING SUPERHERO ACTIVITY--
AT LEAST UNTIL G. GORDON GODFREY AND HIS FOLLOWERS ARE PUT OUT OF BUSINESS.
4

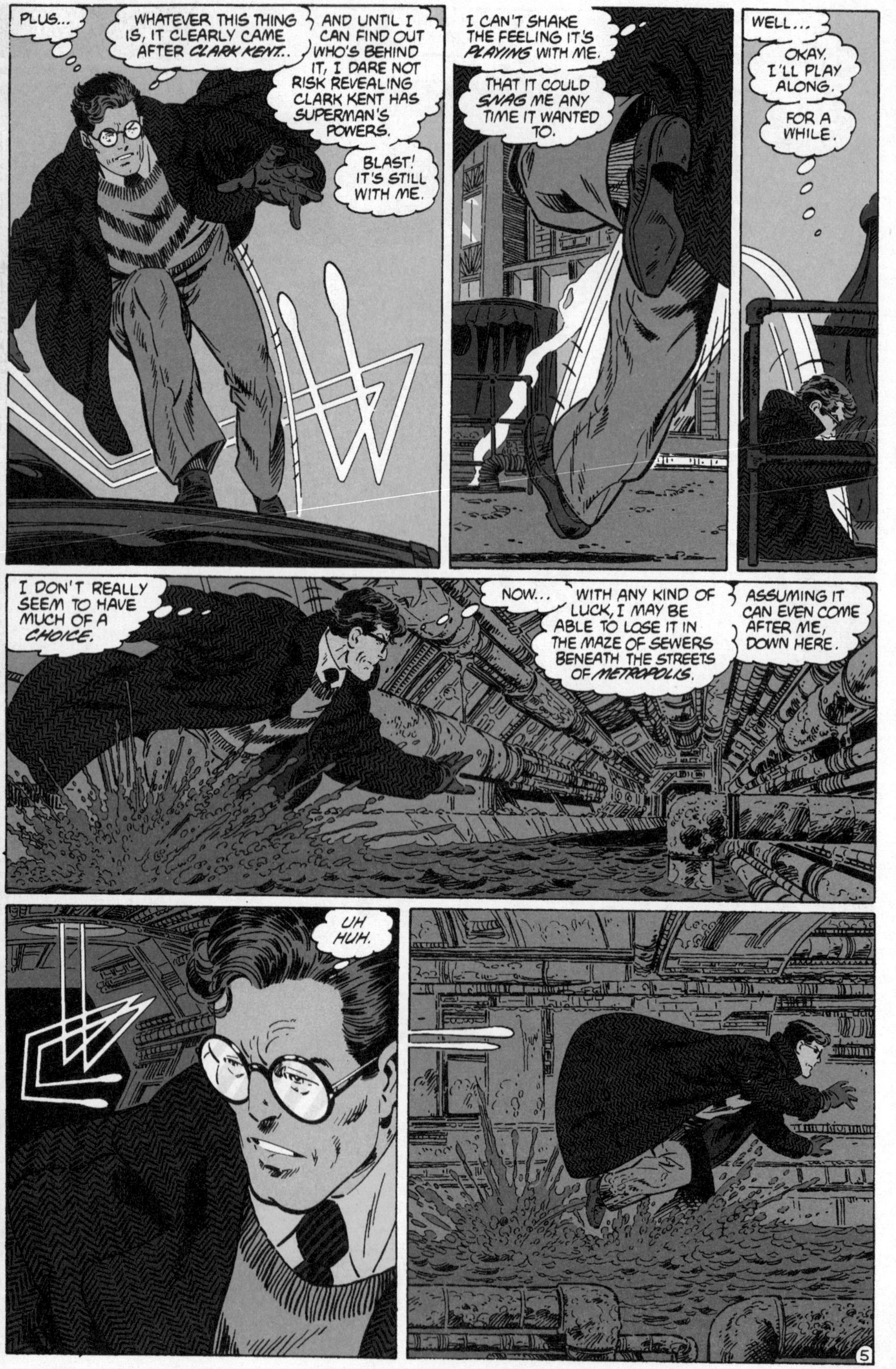
PLUS...
WHATEVER THIS THING IS, IT CLEARLY CAME AFTER CLARK KENT...
AND UNTIL I CAN FIND OUT WHO'S BEHIND IT, I DARE NOT RISK REVEALING CLARK KENT HAS SUPERMAN'S POWERS.
BLAST! IT'S STILL WITH ME.
I CAN'T SHAKE THE FEELING IT'S PLAYING WITH ME.
THAT IT COULD SNAG ME ANY TIME IT WANTED TO.
WELL...
OKAY. I'LL PLAY ALONG.
FOR A WHILE.
I DON'T REALLY SEEM TO HAVE MUCH OF A CHOICE.
NOW...
WITH ANY KIND OF LUCK, I MAY BE ABLE TO LOSE IT IN THE MAZE OF SEWERS BENEATH THE STREETS OF METROPOLIS.
ASSUMING IT CAN EVEN COME AFTER ME, DOWN HERE.
UH HUH.
5

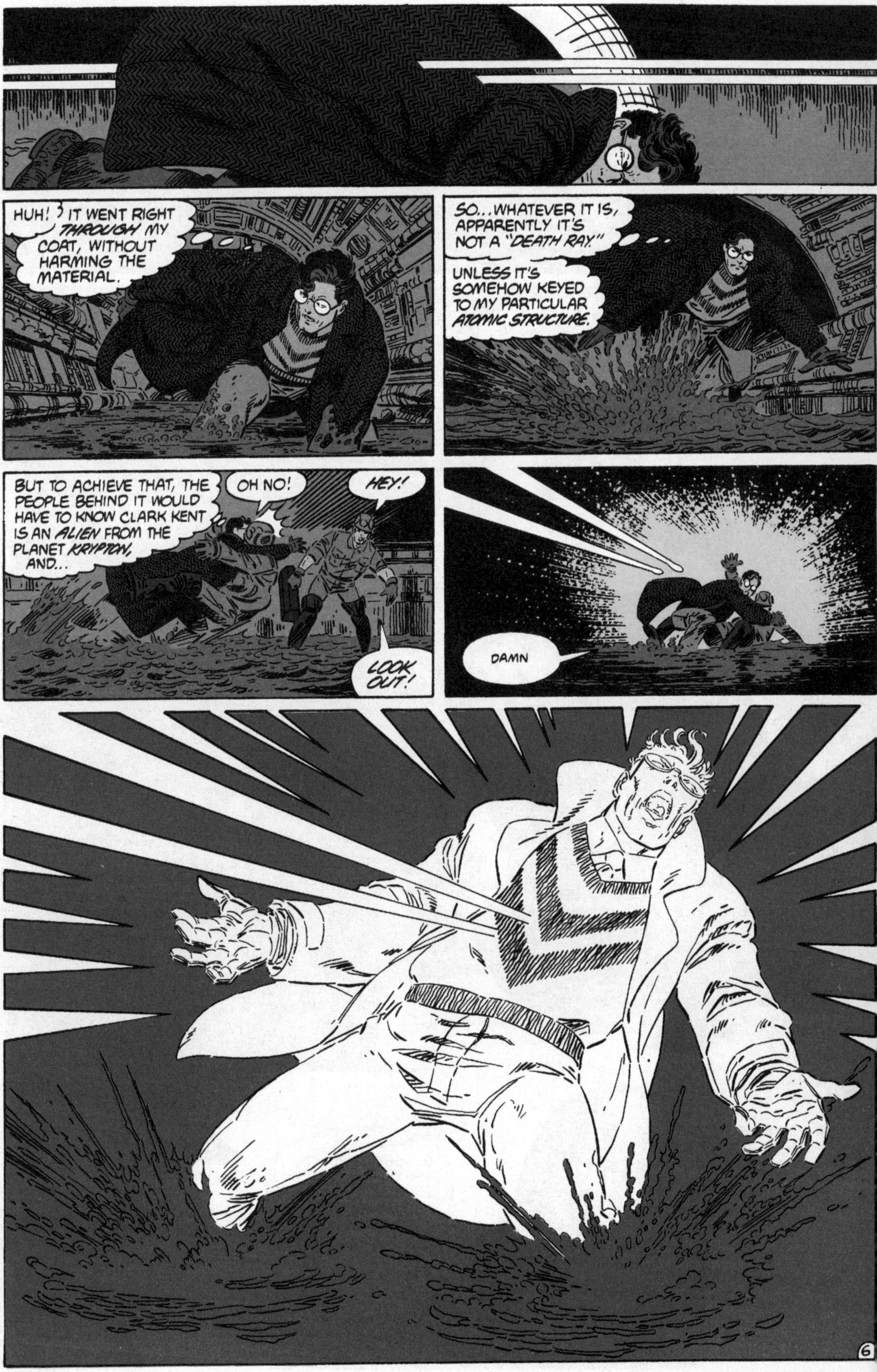
HUH! IT WENT RIGHT THROUGH MY COAT, WITHOUT HARMING THE MATERIAL.
SO...WHATEVER IT IS, APPARENTLY IT'S NOT A "DEATH RAY."
UNLESS IT'S SOMEHOW KEYED TO MY PARTICULAR ATOMIC STRUCTURE.
BUT TO ACHIEVE THAT, THE PEOPLE BEHIND IT WOULD HAVE TO KNOW CLARK KENT IS AN ALIEN FROM THE PLANET KRYPTON, AND...
OH NO!
HEY!
LOOK OUT!
DAMN
6

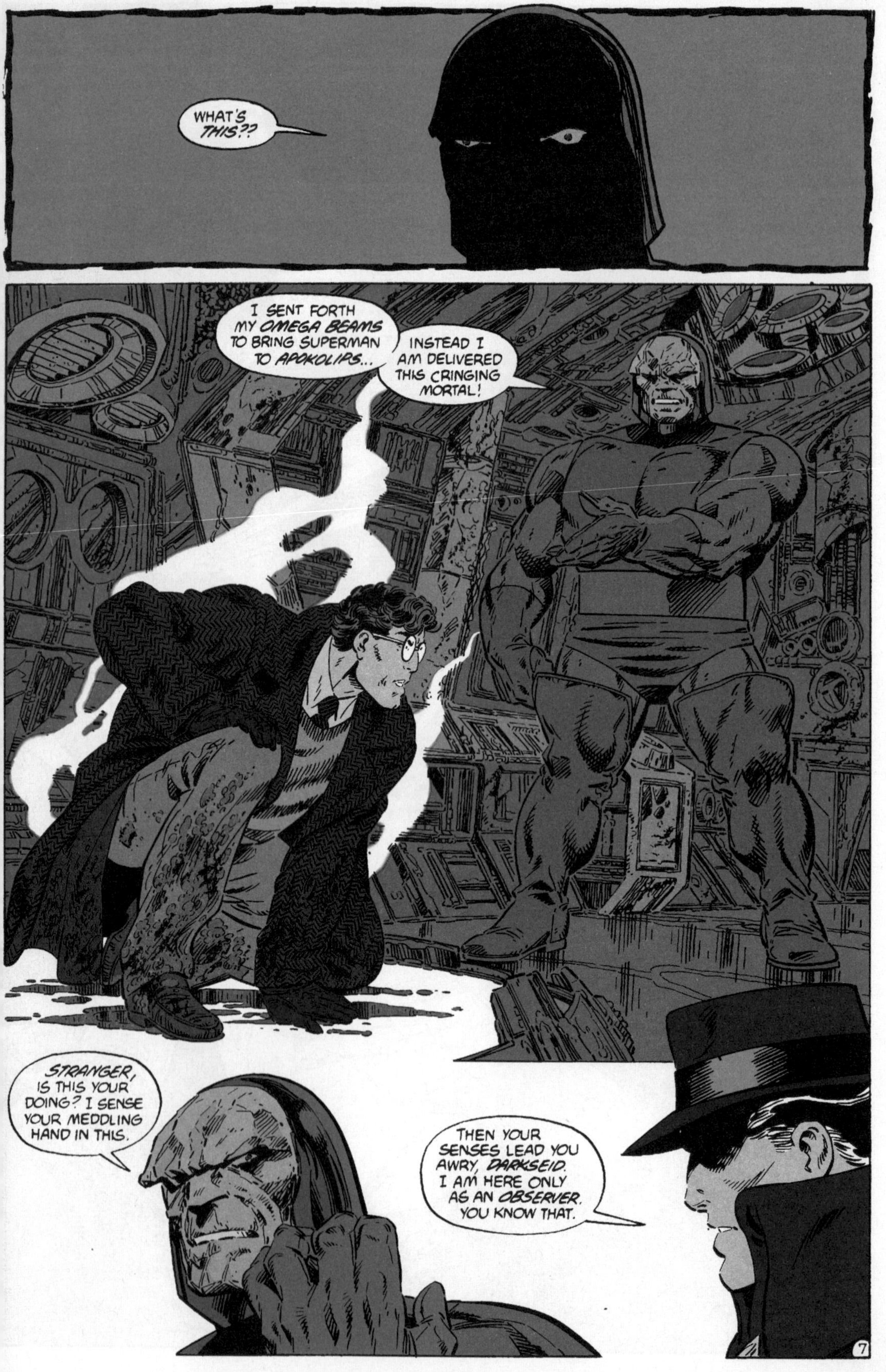
WHAT'S THIS??
I SENT FORTH MY OMEGA BEAMS TO BRING SUPERMAN TO APOKOLIPS...
INSTEAD I AM DELIVERED THIS CRINGING MORTAL!
STRANGER, IS THIS YOUR DOING? I SENSE YOUR MEDDLING HAND IN THIS.
THEN YOUR SENSES LEAD YOU AWRY, DARKSEID. I AM HERE ONLY AS AN OBSERVER. YOU KNOW THAT.
7

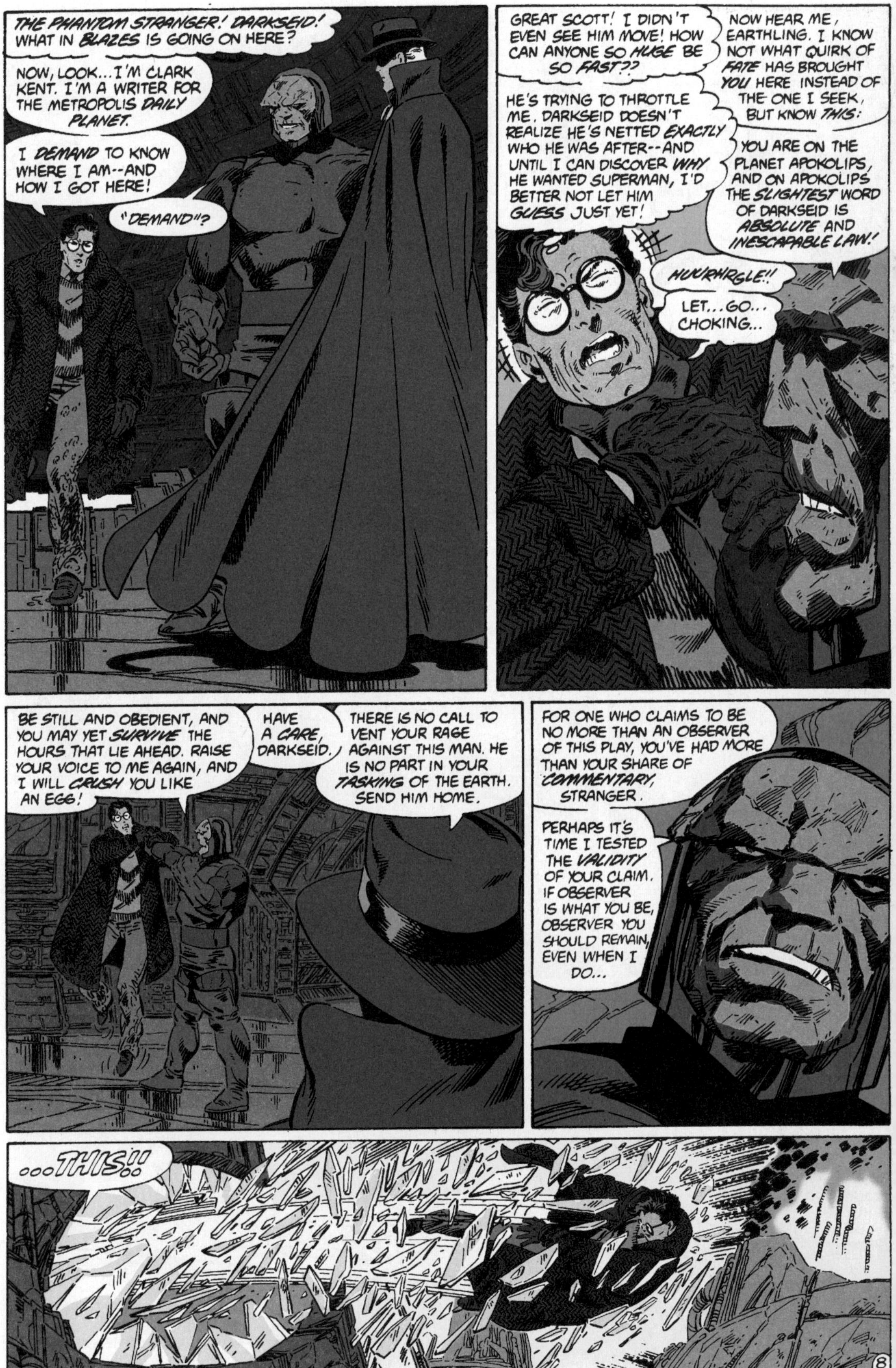
THE PHANTOM STRANGER! DARKSEID! WHAT IN BLAZES IS GOING ON HERE?
NOW, LOOK... I'M CLARK KENT. I'M A WRITER FOR THE METROPOLIS DAILY PLANET.
I DEMAND TO KNOW WHERE I AM--AND HOW I GOT HERE!
"DEMAND"?
GREAT SCOTT! I DIDN'T EVEN SEE HIM MOVE! HOW CAN ANYONE SO HUGE BE SO FAST??
HE'S TRYING TO THROTTLE ME. DARKSEID DOESN'T REALIZE HE'S NETTED EXACTLY WHO HE WAS AFTER--AND UNTIL I CAN DISCOVER WHY HE WANTED SUPERMAN, I'D BETTER NOT LET HIM GUESS JUST YET!
NOW HEAR ME, EARTHLING. I KNOW NOT WHAT QUIRK OF FATE HAS BROUGHT YOU HERE INSTEAD OF THE ONE I SEEK, BUT KNOW THIS:
YOU ARE ON THE PLANET APOKOLIPS, AND ON APOKOLIPS THE SLIGHTEST WORD OF DARKSEID IS ABSOLUTE AND INESCAPABLE LAW!
HUKRHRGLE!!
LET... GO... CHOKING...
BE STILL AND OBEDIENT, AND YOU MAY YET SURVIVE THE HOURS THAT LIE AHEAD. RAISE YOUR VOICE TO ME AGAIN, AND I WILL CRUSH YOU LIKE AN EGG!
HAVE A CARE, DARKSEID.
THERE IS NO CALL TO VENT YOUR RAGE AGAINST THIS MAN. HE IS NO PART IN YOUR TASKING OF THE EARTH. SEND HIM HOME.
FOR ONE WHO CLAIMS TO BE NO MORE THAN AN OBSERVER OF THIS PLAY, YOU'VE HAD MORE THAN YOUR SHARE OF COMMENTARY, STRANGER.
PERHAPS IT'S TIME I TESTED THE VALIDITY OF YOUR CLAIM. IF OBSERVER IS WHAT YOU BE, OBSERVER YOU SHOULD REMAIN, EVEN WHEN I DO...
...THIS!!
8

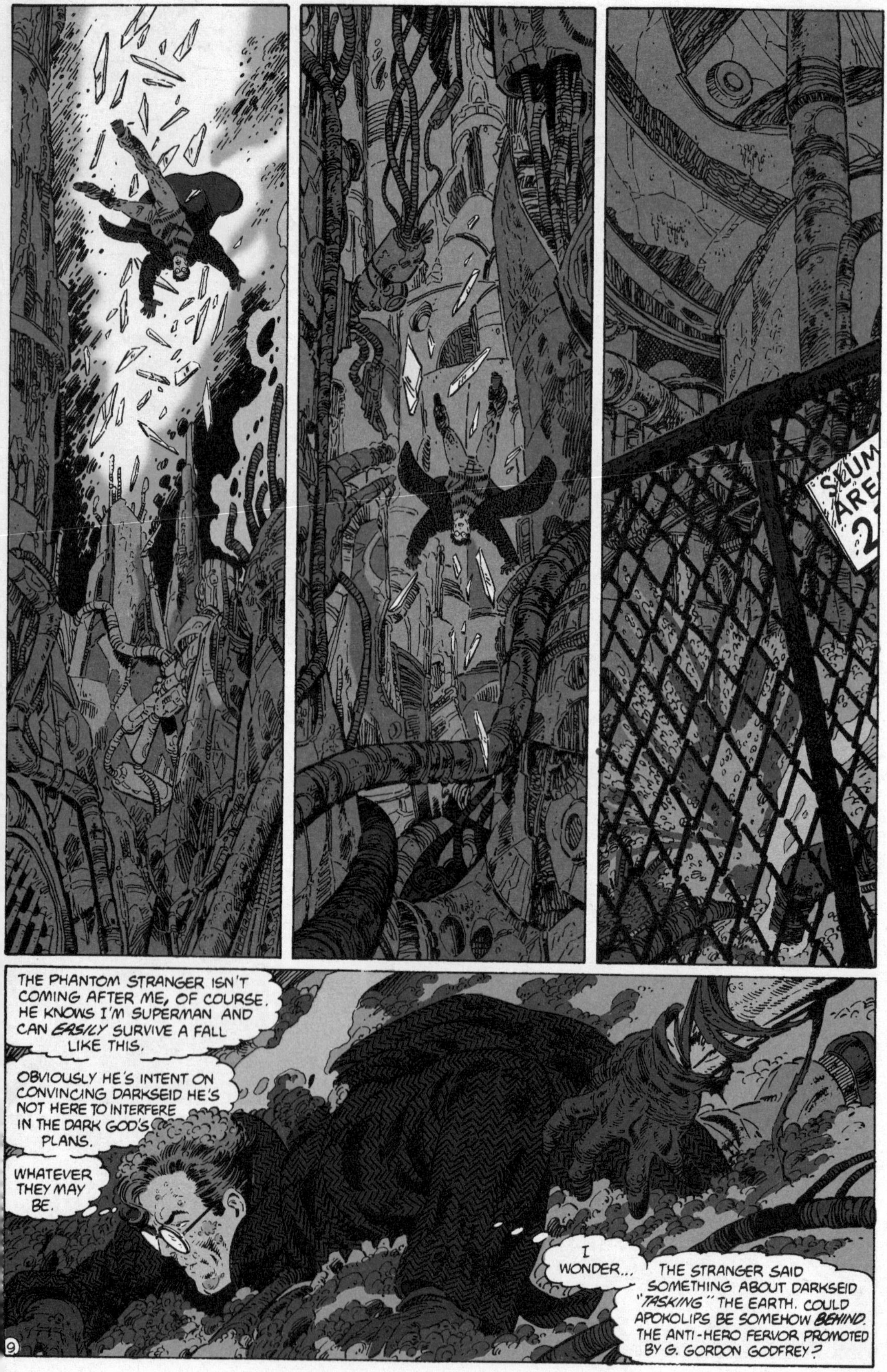
SLUM AREA 2
THE PHANTOM STRANGER ISN'T COMING AFTER ME, OF COURSE. HE KNOWS I'M SUPERMAN AND CAN EASILY SURVIVE A FALL LIKE THIS.
OBVIOUSLY HE'S INTENT ON CONVINCING DARKSEID HE'S NOT HERE TO INTERFERE IN THE DARK GOD'S PLANS.
WHATEVER THEY MAY BE.
I WONDER...
THE STRANGER SAID SOMETHING ABOUT DARKSEID "TASKING" THE EARTH. COULD APOKOLIPS BE SOMEHOW BEHIND THE ANTI-HERO FERVOR PROMOTED BY G. GORDON GODFREY?
9

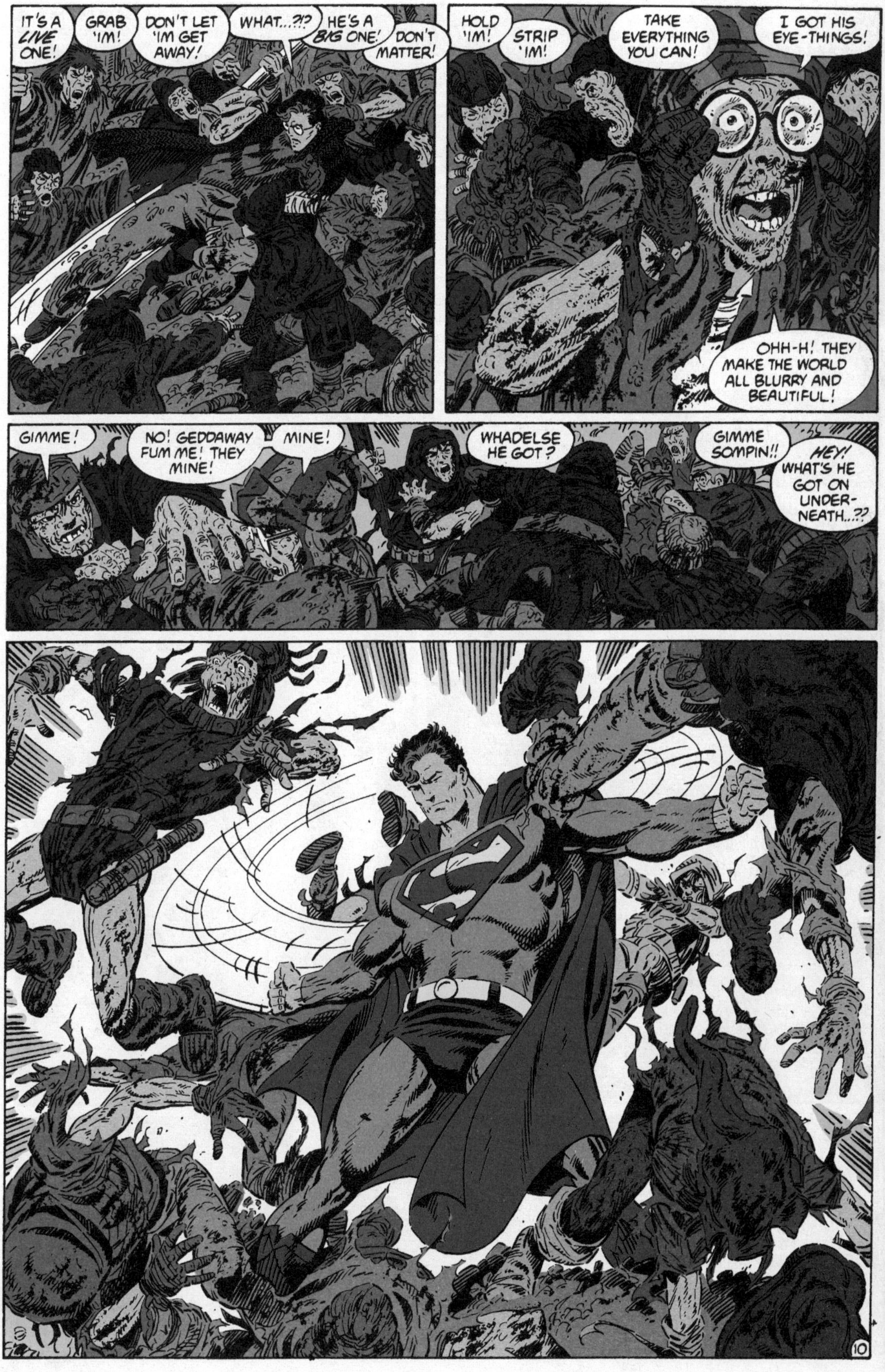

IT'S A *LIVE* ONE!
GRAB 'IM!
DON'T LET 'IM GET AWAY!
WHAT...?!?
HE'S A *BIG* ONE!
DON'T MATTER!
HOLD 'IM!
STRIP 'IM!
TAKE EVERYTHING YOU CAN!
I GOT HIS EYE-THINGS!
OHH-H! THEY MAKE THE WORLD ALL BLURRY AND BEAUTIFUL!
GIMME!
NO! GEDDAWAY FUM ME! THEY MINE!
MINE!
WHADELSE HE GOT?
GIMME SOMPIN!!
HEY! WHAT'S HE GOT ON UNDER-NEATH...??
10

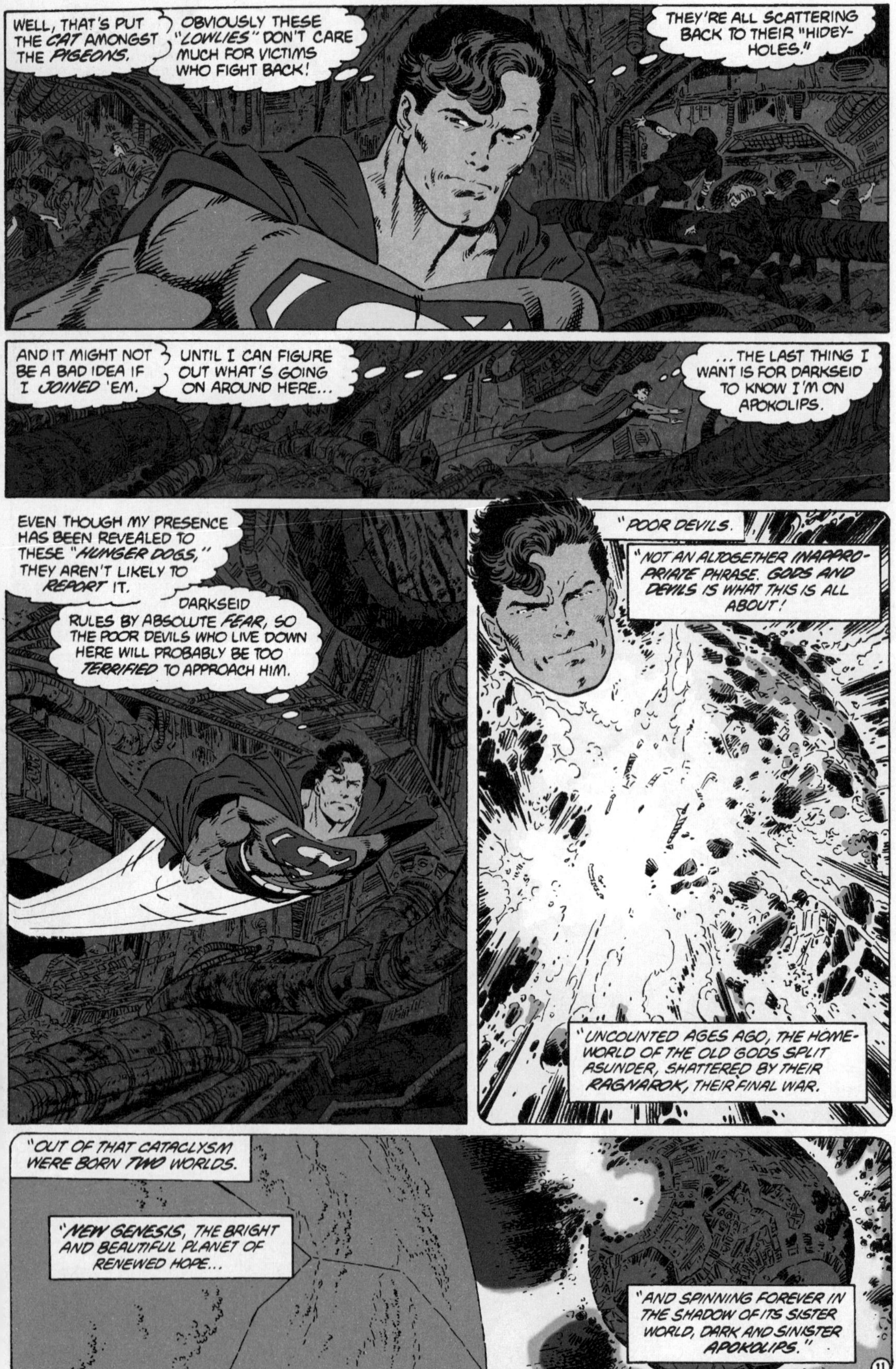
WELL, THAT'S PUT THE CAT AMONGST THE PIGEONS.
OBVIOUSLY THESE "LOWLIES" DON'T CARE MUCH FOR VICTIMS WHO FIGHT BACK!
THEY'RE ALL SCATTERING BACK TO THEIR "HIDEY-HOLES."
AND IT MIGHT NOT BE A BAD IDEA IF I JOINED 'EM.
UNTIL I CAN FIGURE OUT WHAT'S GOING ON AROUND HERE...
...THE LAST THING I WANT IS FOR DARKSEID TO KNOW I'M ON APOKOLIPS.
EVEN THOUGH MY PRESENCE HAS BEEN REVEALED TO THESE "HUNGER DOGS," THEY AREN'T LIKELY TO REPORT IT.
DARKSEID RULES BY ABSOLUTE FEAR, SO THE POOR DEVILS WHO LIVE DOWN HERE WILL PROBABLY BE TOO TERRIFIED TO APPROACH HIM.
"POOR DEVILS.
"NOT AN ALTOGETHER INAPPROPRIATE PHRASE. GODS AND DEVILS IS WHAT THIS IS ALL ABOUT!
"UNCOUNTED AGES AGO, THE HOMEWORLD OF THE OLD GODS SPLIT ASUNDER, SHATTERED BY THEIR RAGNAROK, THEIR FINAL WAR.
"OUT OF THAT CATACLYSM WERE BORN TWO WORLDS.
"NEW GENESIS, THE BRIGHT AND BEAUTIFUL PLANET OF RENEWED HOPE...
"AND SPINNING FOREVER IN THE SHADOW OF ITS SISTER WORLD, DARK AND SINISTER APOKOLIPS."
11

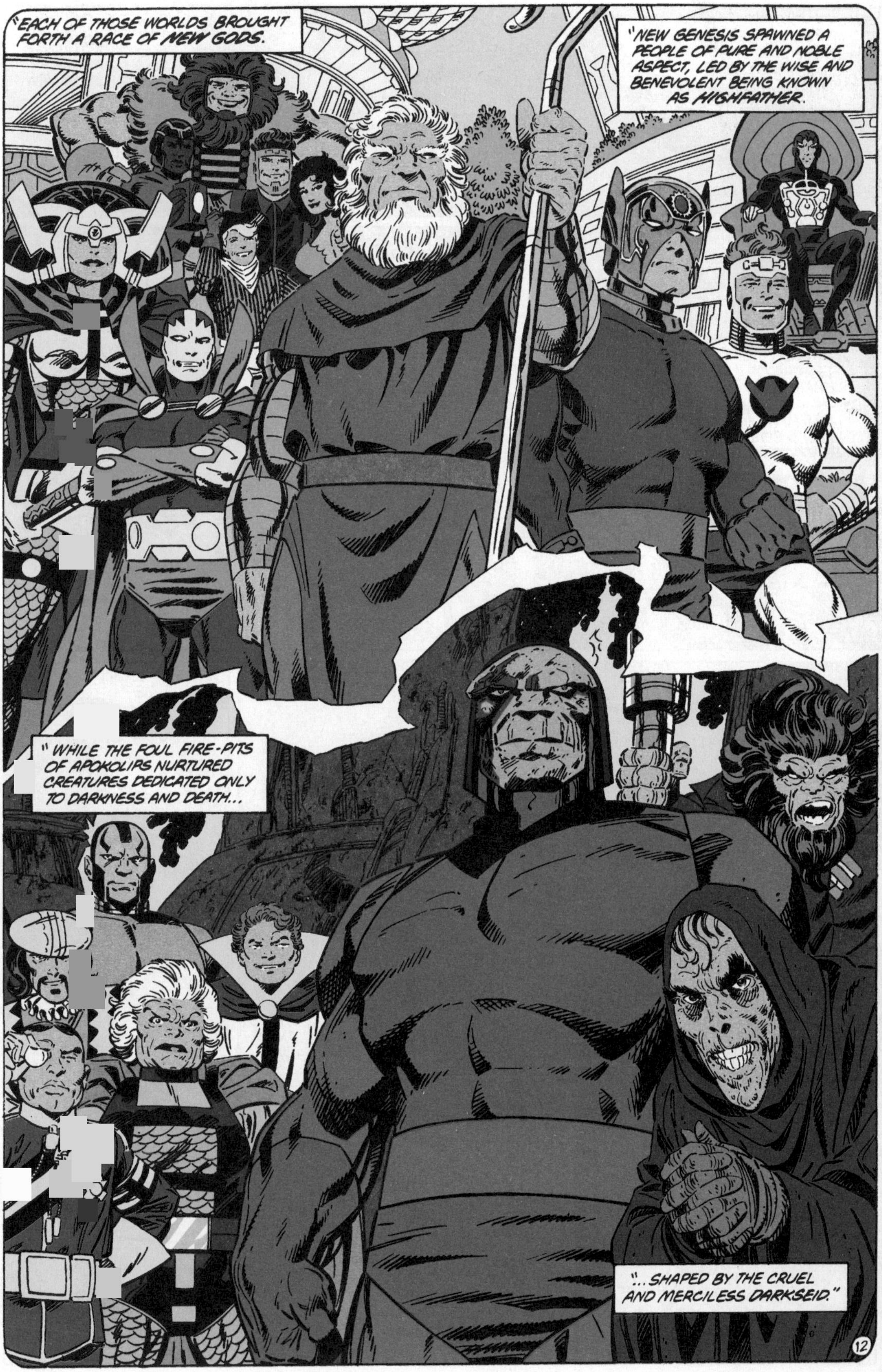
"EACH OF THOSE WORLDS BROUGHT FORTH A RACE OF NEW GODS.
"NEW GENESIS SPAWNED A PEOPLE OF PURE AND NOBLE ASPECT, LED BY THE WISE AND BENEVOLENT BEING KNOWN AS HIGHFATHER.
"WHILE THE FOUL FIRE-PITS OF APOKOLIPS NURTURED CREATURES DEDICATED ONLY TO DARKNESS AND DEATH...
"...SHAPED BY THE CRUEL AND MERCILESS DARKSEID."
12

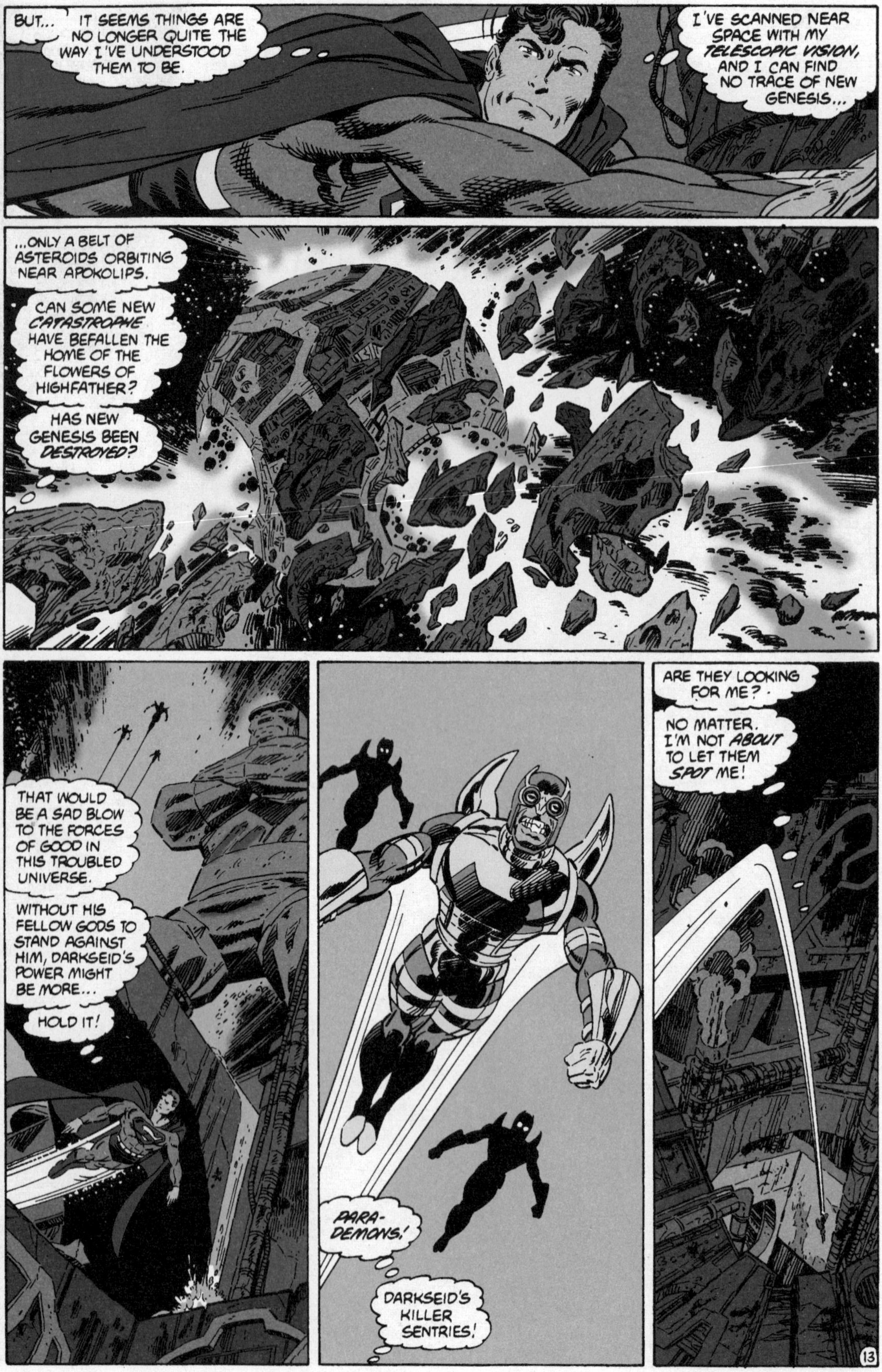
BUT... IT SEEMS THINGS ARE NO LONGER QUITE THE WAY I'VE UNDERSTOOD THEM TO BE.
I'VE SCANNED NEAR SPACE WITH MY TELESCOPIC VISION, AND I CAN FIND NO TRACE OF NEW GENESIS...
...ONLY A BELT OF ASTEROIDS ORBITING NEAR APOKOLIPS.
CAN SOME NEW CATASTROPHE HAVE BEFALLEN THE HOME OF THE FLOWERS OF HIGHFATHER?
HAS NEW GENESIS BEEN DESTROYED?
THAT WOULD BE A SAD BLOW TO THE FORCES OF GOOD IN THIS TROUBLED UNIVERSE.
WITHOUT HIS FELLOW GODS TO STAND AGAINST HIM, DARKSEID'S POWER MIGHT BE MORE...
HOLD IT!
PARA-DEMONS!
DARKSEID'S KILLER SENTRIES!
ARE THEY LOOKING FOR ME?
NO MATTER. I'M NOT ABOUT TO LET THEM SPOT ME!
13

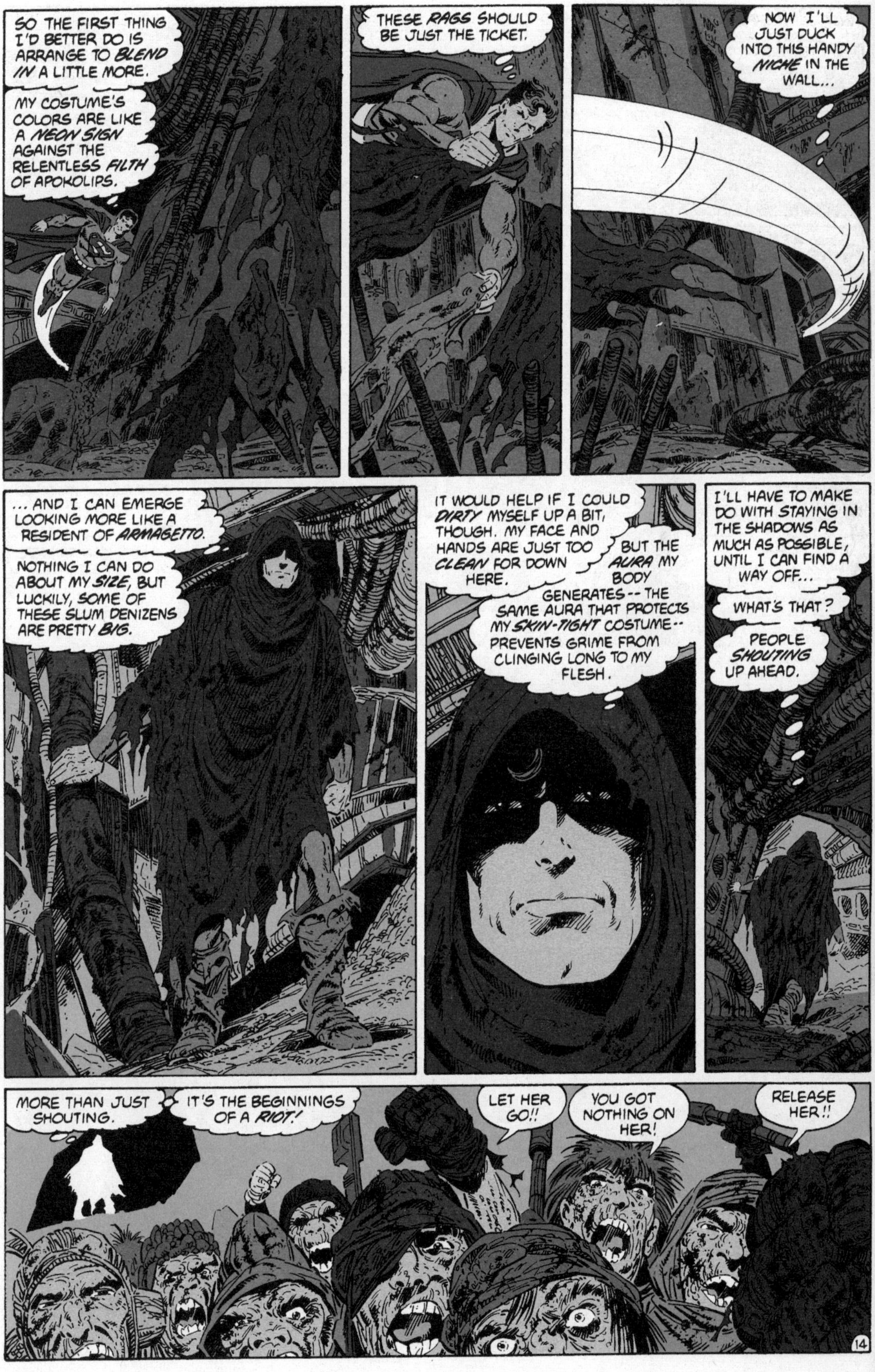

SO THE FIRST THING I'D BETTER DO IS ARRANGE TO BLEND IN A LITTLE MORE.
MY COSTUME'S COLORS ARE LIKE A NEON SIGN AGAINST THE RELENTLESS FILTH OF APOKOLIPS.
THESE RAGS SHOULD BE JUST THE TICKET.
NOW I'LL JUST DUCK INTO THIS HANDY NICHE IN THE WALL...
... AND I CAN EMERGE LOOKING MORE LIKE A RESIDENT OF ARMAGETTO.
NOTHING I CAN DO ABOUT MY SIZE, BUT LUCKILY, SOME OF THESE SLUM DENIZENS ARE PRETTY BIG.
IT WOULD HELP IF I COULD DIRTY MYSELF UP A BIT, THOUGH. MY FACE AND HANDS ARE JUST TOO CLEAN FOR DOWN HERE.
BUT THE AURA MY BODY GENERATES -- THE SAME AURA THAT PROTECTS MY SKIN-TIGHT COSTUME -- PREVENTS GRIME FROM CLINGING LONG TO MY FLESH.
I'LL HAVE TO MAKE DO WITH STAYING IN THE SHADOWS AS MUCH AS POSSIBLE, UNTIL I CAN FIND A WAY OFF...
WHAT'S THAT?
PEOPLE SHOUTING UP AHEAD.
MORE THAN JUST SHOUTING.
IT'S THE BEGINNINGS OF A RIOT!
LET HER GO!!
YOU GOT NOTHING ON HER!
RELEASE HER!!
14

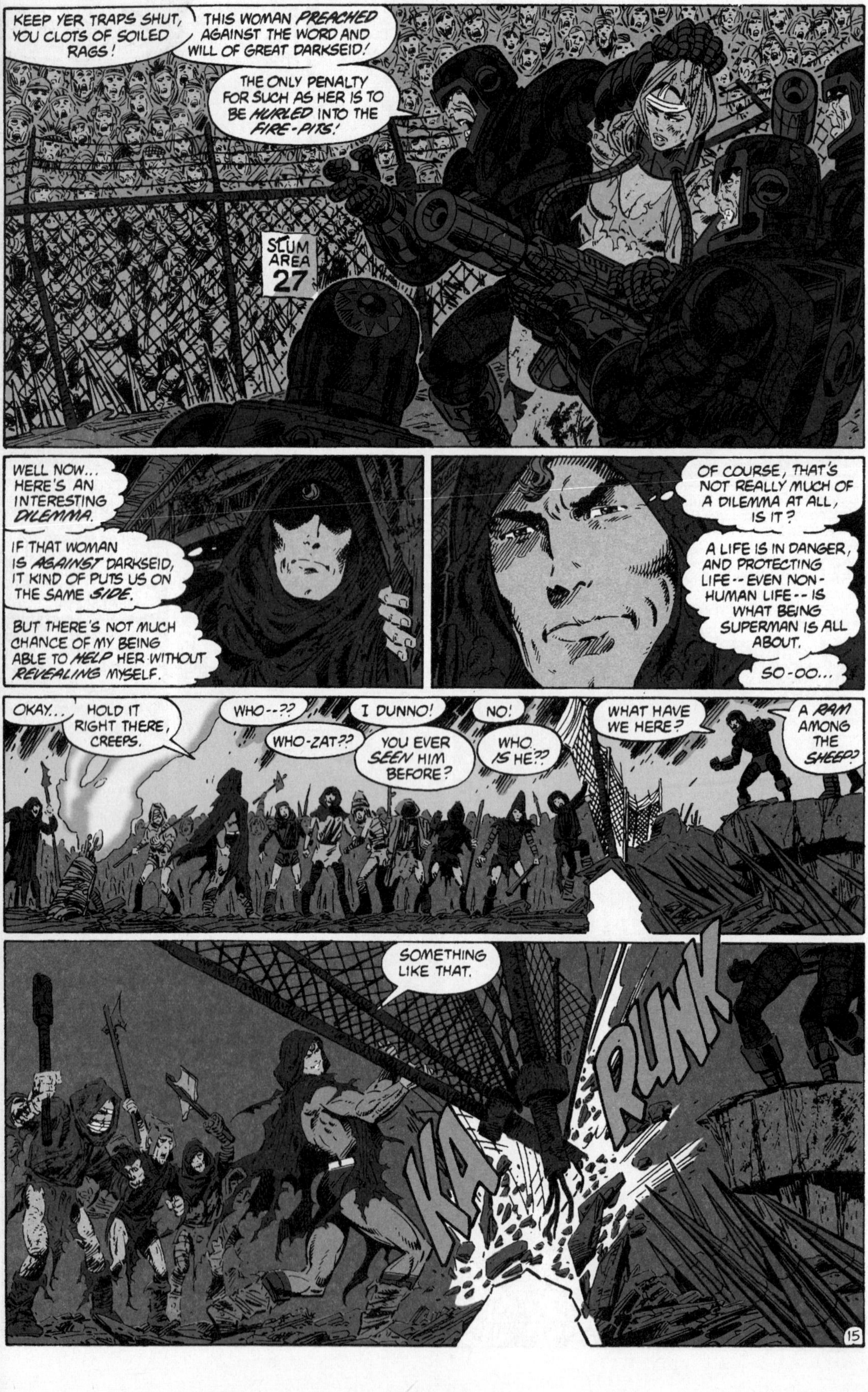

KEEP YER TRAPS SHUT, YOU CLOTS OF SOILED RAGS!
THIS WOMAN PREACHED AGAINST THE WORD AND WILL OF GREAT DARKSEID!
THE ONLY PENALTY FOR SUCH AS HER IS TO BE HURLED INTO THE FIRE-PITS!
SLUM AREA 27
WELL NOW... HERE'S AN INTERESTING DILEMMA.
IF THAT WOMAN IS AGAINST DARKSEID, IT KIND OF PUTS US ON THE SAME SIDE.
BUT THERE'S NOT MUCH CHANCE OF MY BEING ABLE TO HELP HER WITHOUT REVEALING MYSELF.
OF COURSE, THAT'S NOT REALLY MUCH OF A DILEMMA AT ALL, IS IT?
A LIFE IS IN DANGER, AND PROTECTING LIFE -- EVEN NON-HUMAN LIFE -- IS WHAT BEING SUPERMAN IS ALL ABOUT.
SO-OO...
OKAY...
HOLD IT RIGHT THERE, CREEPS.
WHO--??
WHO-ZAT??
I DUNNO!
YOU EVER SEEN HIM BEFORE?
NO!
WHO IS HE??
WHAT HAVE WE HERE?
A RAM AMONG THE SHEEP?
SOMETHING LIKE THAT.
KA-RUNK
15

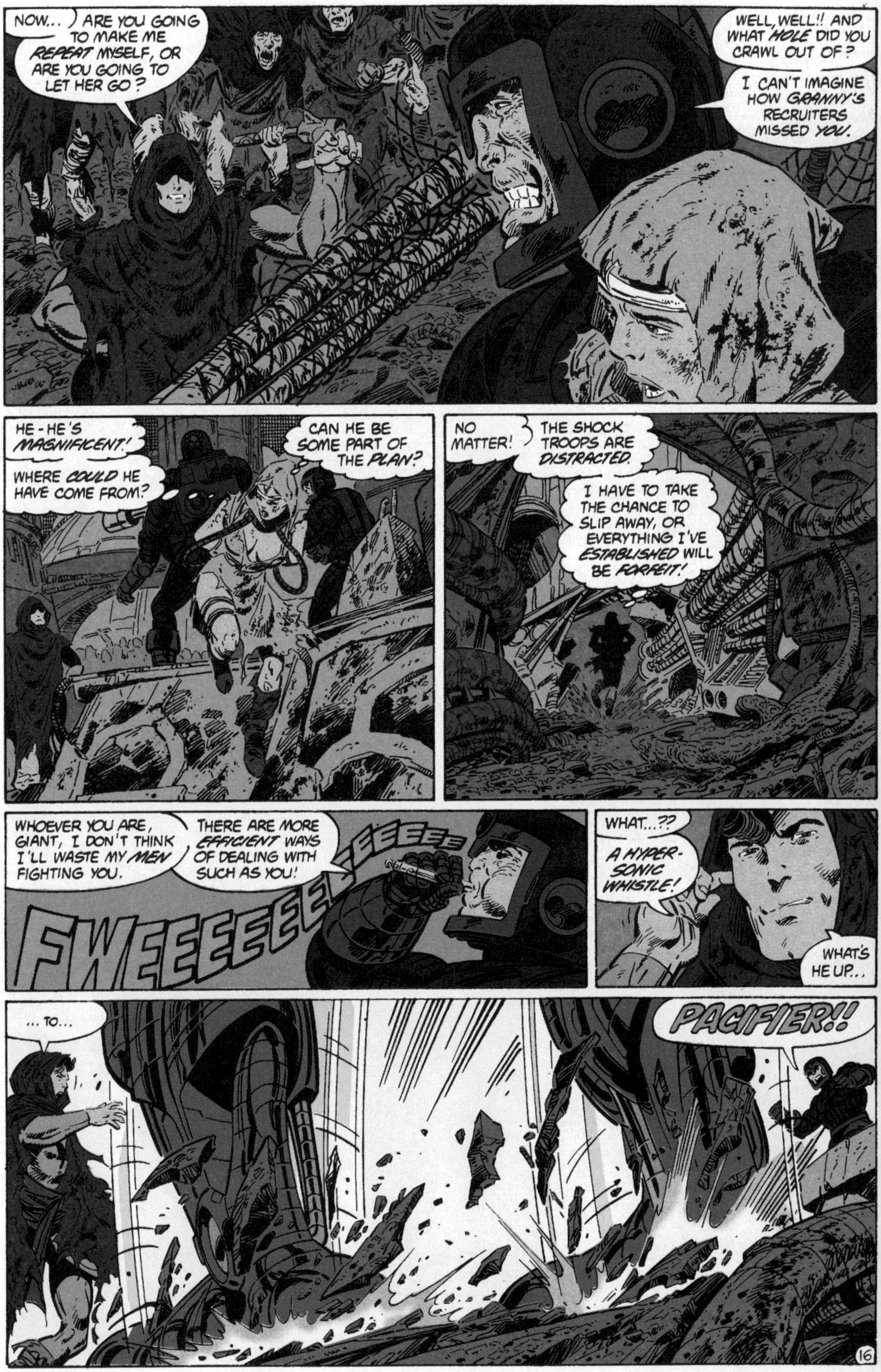
NOW...
ARE YOU GOING TO MAKE ME REPEAT MYSELF, OR ARE YOU GOING TO LET HER GO?
WELL, WELL!! AND WHAT HOLE DID YOU CRAWL OUT OF?
I CAN'T IMAGINE HOW GRANNY'S RECRUITERS MISSED YOU.
HE-HE'S MAGNIFICENT!
WHERE COULD HE HAVE COME FROM?
CAN HE BE SOME PART OF THE PLAN?
NO MATTER!
THE SHOCK TROOPS ARE DISTRACTED.
I HAVE TO TAKE THE CHANCE TO SLIP AWAY, OR EVERYTHING I'VE ESTABLISHED WILL BE FORFEIT!
WHOEVER YOU ARE, GIANT, I DON'T THINK I'LL WASTE MY MEN FIGHTING YOU.
THERE ARE MORE EFFICIENT WAYS OF DEALING WITH SUCH AS YOU!
FWEEEEEEEEEEEEEE
WHAT...??
A HYPER-SONIC WHISTLE!
WHAT'S HE UP...
... TO...
PACIFIER!!
16

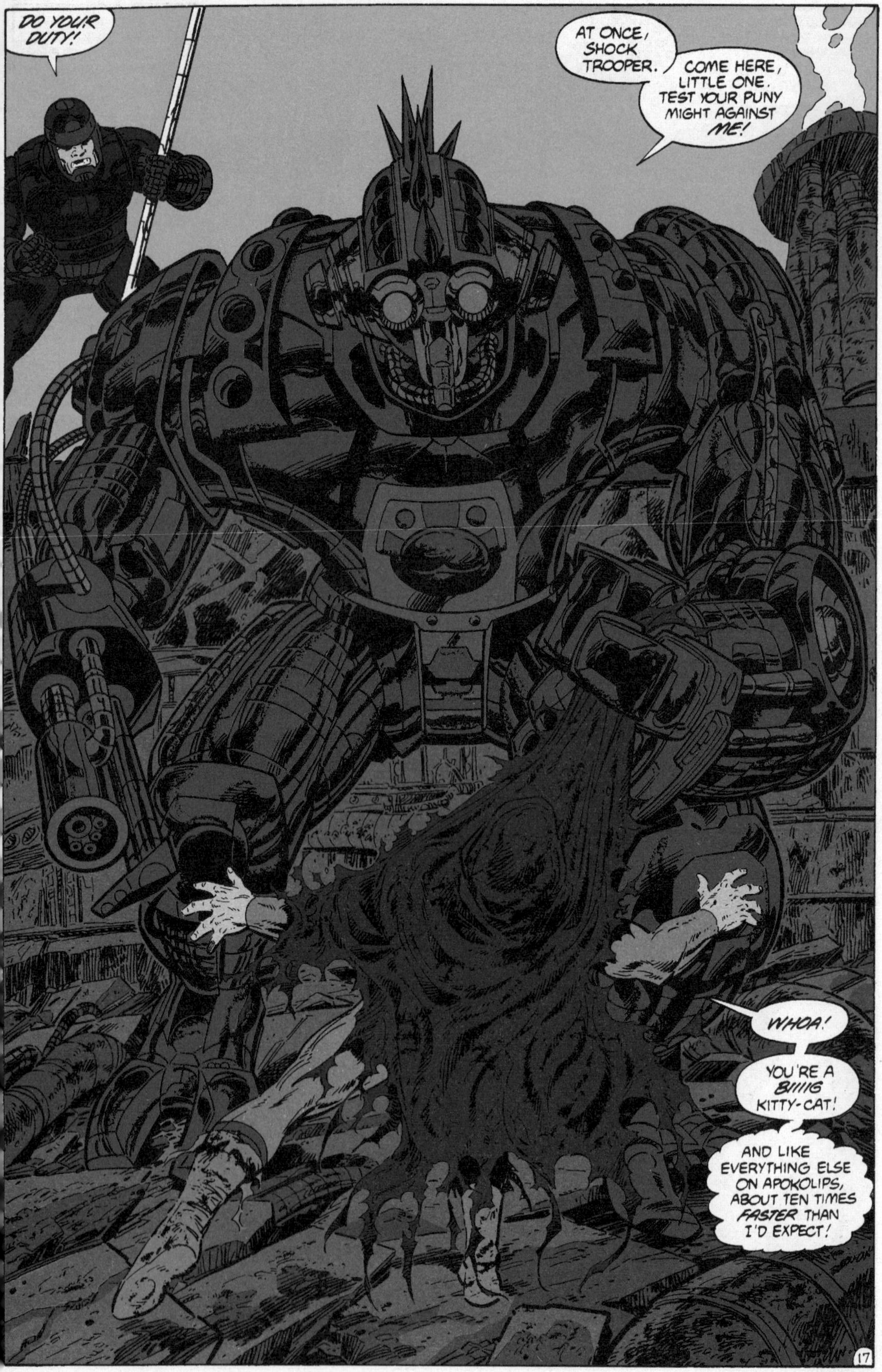

DO YOUR DUTY!
AT ONCE, SHOCK TROOPER.
COME HERE, LITTLE ONE. TEST YOUR PUNY MIGHT AGAINST ME!
WHOA!
YOU'RE A BIIIIG KITTY-CAT!
AND LIKE EVERYTHING ELSE ON APOKOLIPS, ABOUT TEN TIMES FASTER THAN I'D EXPECT!
17

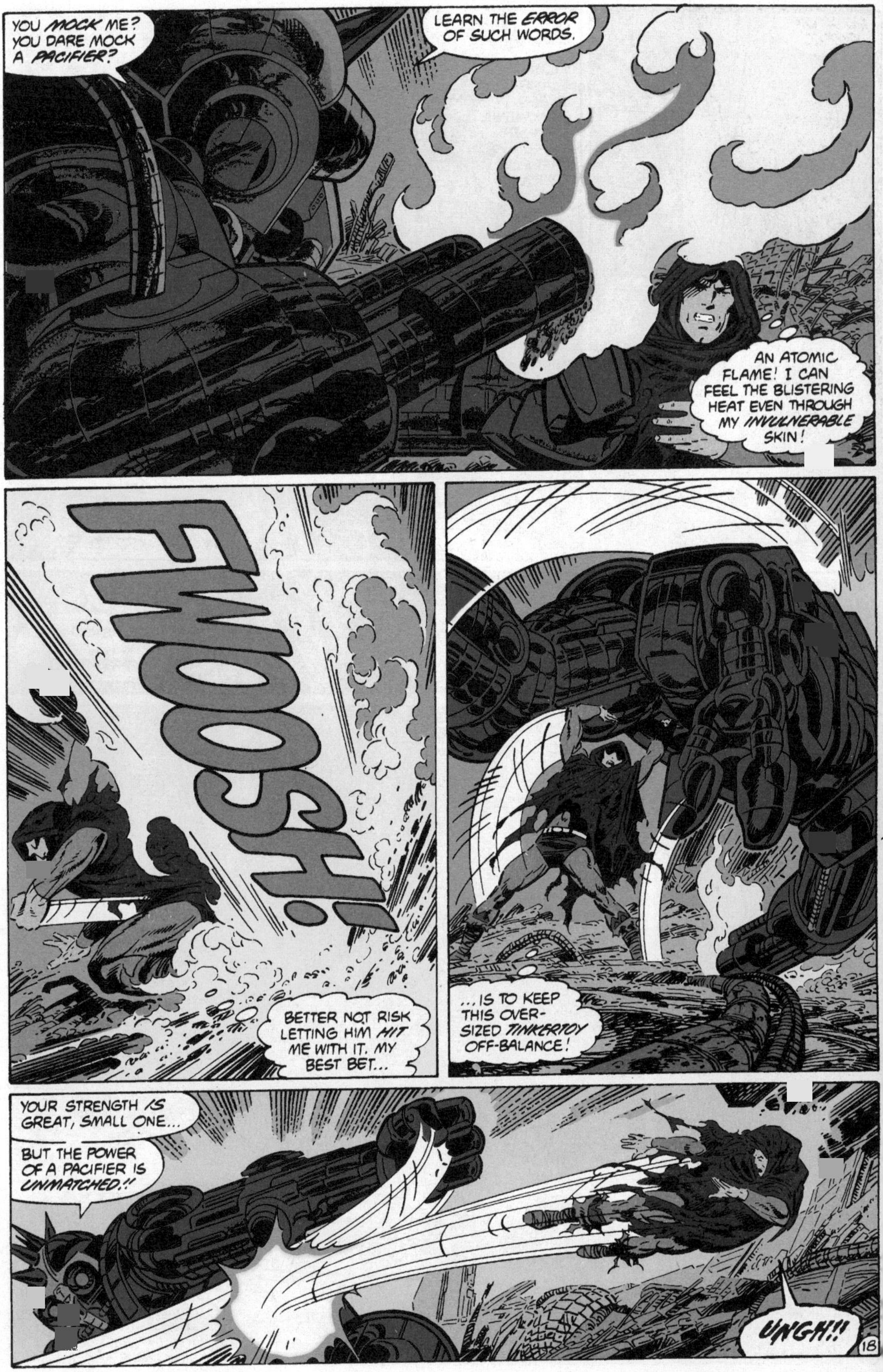
YOU MOCK ME? YOU DARE MOCK A PACIFIER?
LEARN THE ERROR OF SUCH WORDS.
AN ATOMIC FLAME! I CAN FEEL THE BLISTERING HEAT EVEN THROUGH MY INVULNERABLE SKIN!
FWOOSH!
BETTER NOT RISK LETTING HIM HIT ME WITH IT. MY BEST BET...
...IS TO KEEP THIS OVER-SIZED TINKERTOY OFF-BALANCE!
YOUR STRENGTH IS GREAT, SMALL ONE...
BUT THE POWER OF A PACIFIER IS UNMATCHED!!
UNGH!!
18

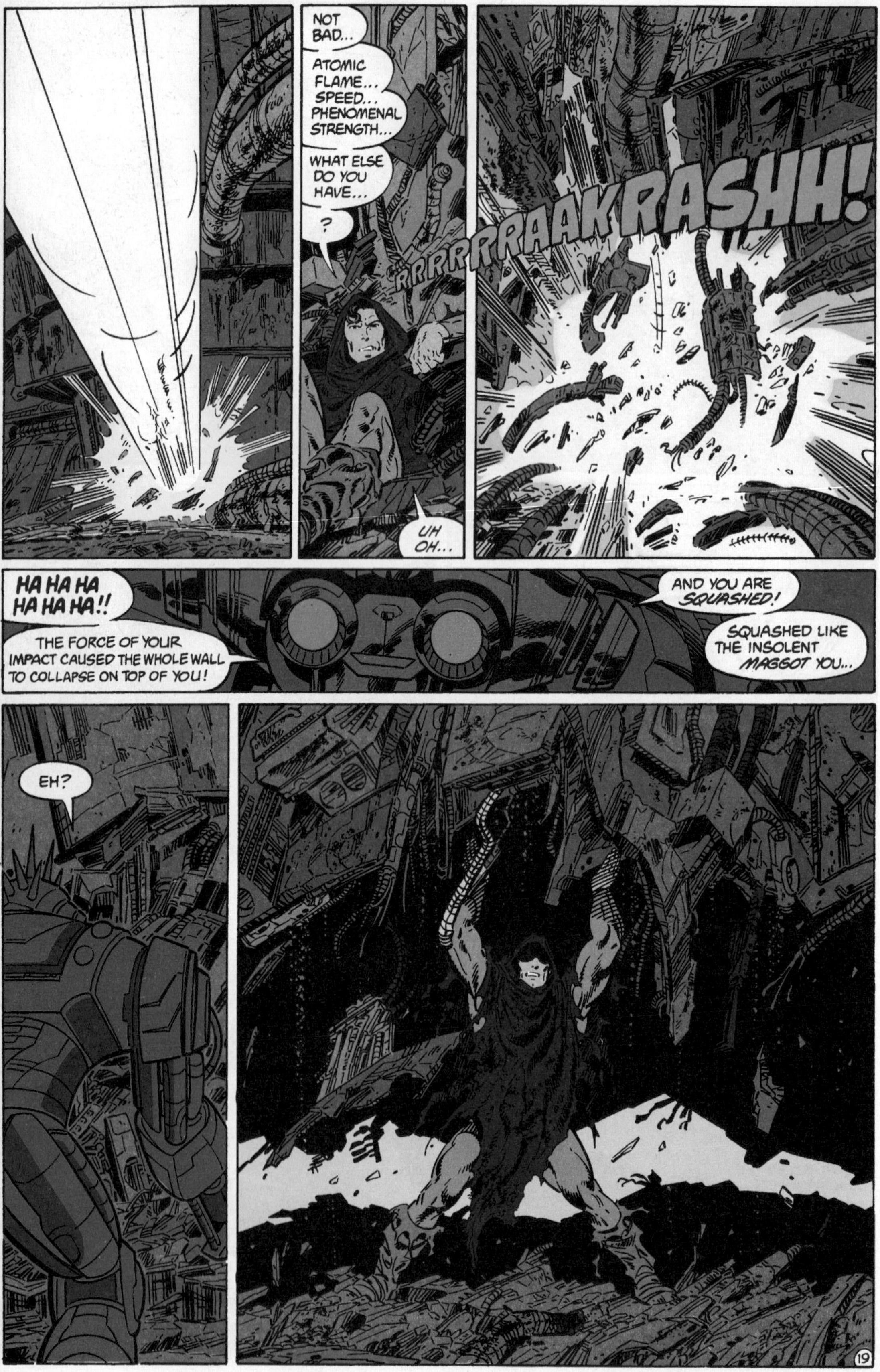
NOT BAD...
ATOMIC FLAME... SPEED... PHENOMENAL STRENGTH...
WHAT ELSE DO YOU HAVE...
?
UH OH...
RRRRRRAAKRASHH!
HA HA HA HA HA HA!!
THE FORCE OF YOUR IMPACT CAUSED THE WHOLE WALL TO COLLAPSE ON TOP OF YOU!
AND YOU ARE SQUASHED!
SQUASHED LIKE THE INSOLENT MAGGOT YOU...
EH?
19

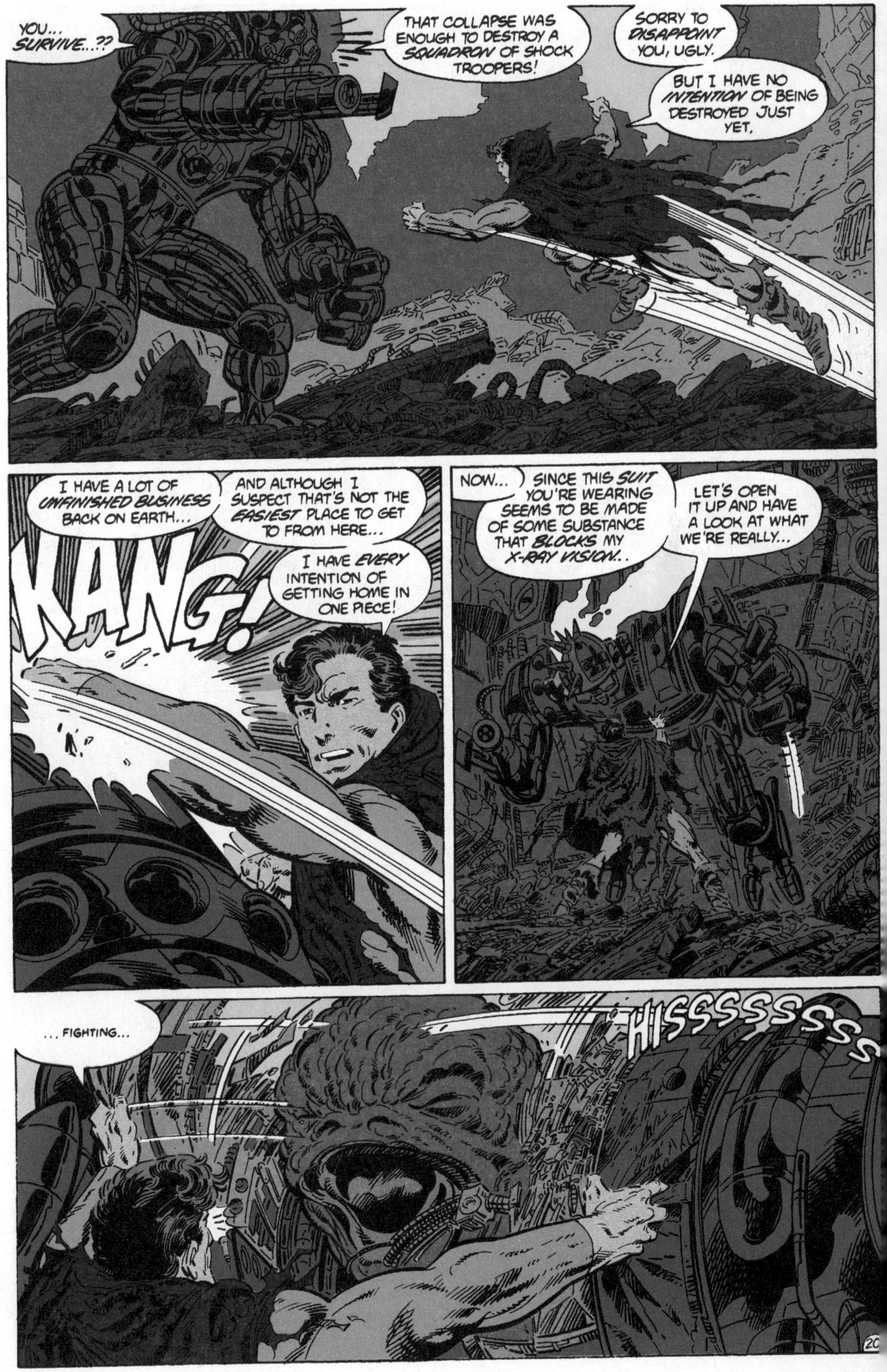
YOU... SURVIVE...??
THAT COLLAPSE WAS ENOUGH TO DESTROY A SQUADRON OF SHOCK TROOPERS!
SORRY TO DISAPPOINT YOU, UGLY.
BUT I HAVE NO INTENTION OF BEING DESTROYED JUST YET.
I HAVE A LOT OF UNFINISHED BUSINESS BACK ON EARTH...
AND ALTHOUGH I SUSPECT THAT'S NOT THE EASIEST PLACE TO GET TO FROM HERE...
KANG!
I HAVE EVERY INTENTION OF GETTING HOME IN ONE PIECE!
NOW...
SINCE THIS SUIT YOU'RE WEARING SEEMS TO BE MADE OF SOME SUBSTANCE THAT BLOCKS MY X-RAY VISION...
LET'S OPEN IT UP AND HAVE A LOOK AT WHAT WE'RE REALLY...
... FIGHTING...
HISSSSSSSSS
20

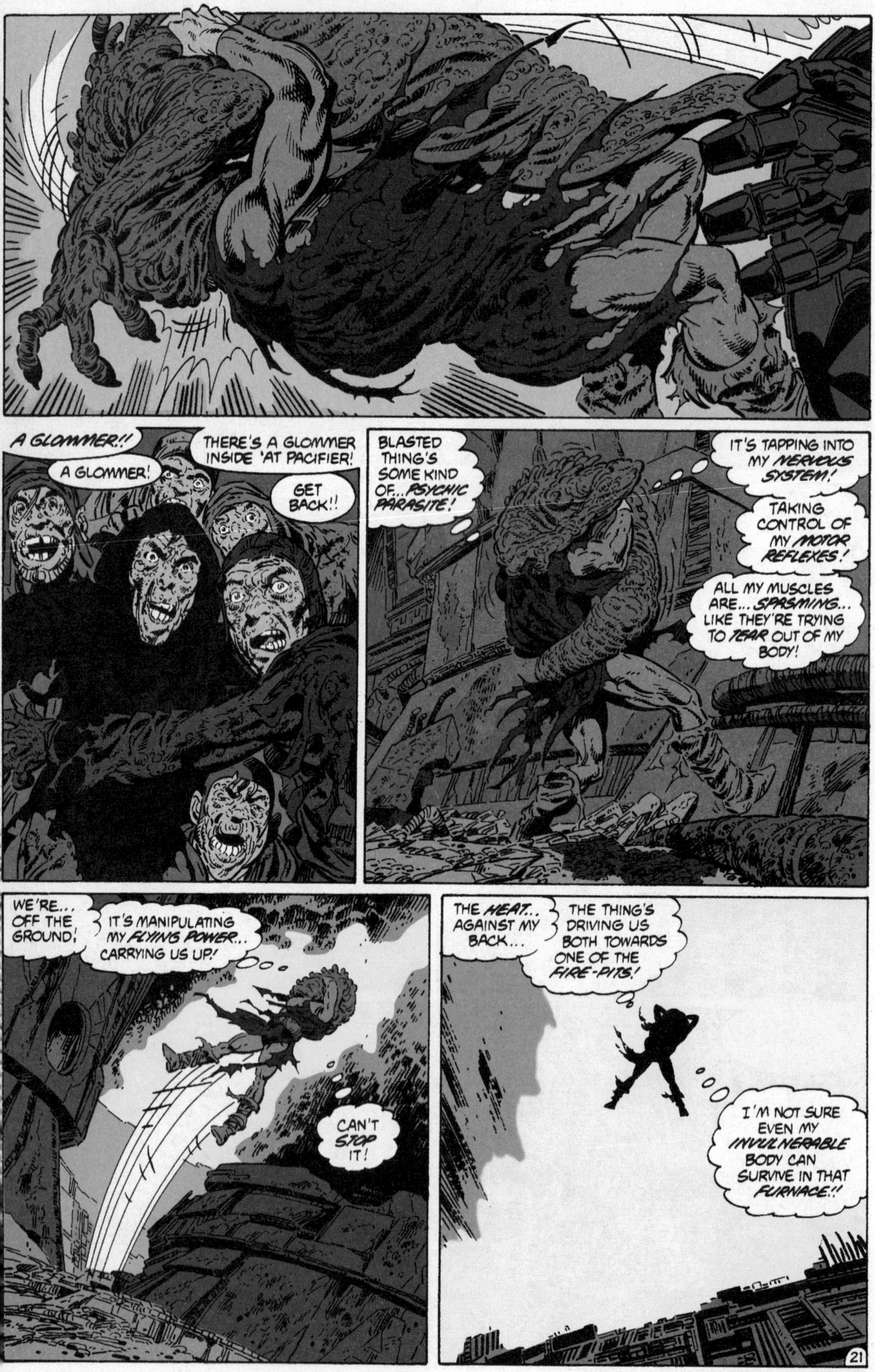
A GLOMMER!!
THERE'S A GLOMMER INSIDE 'AT PACIFIER!
A GLOMMER!
GET BACK!!
BLASTED THING'S SOME KIND OF... PSYCHIC PARASITE!
IT'S TAPPING INTO MY NERVOUS SYSTEM!
TAKING CONTROL OF MY MOTOR REFLEXES!
ALL MY MUSCLES ARE... SPASMING... LIKE THEY'RE TRYING TO TEAR OUT OF MY BODY!
WE'RE... OFF THE GROUND!
IT'S MANIPULATING MY FLYING POWER... CARRYING US UP!
CAN'T STOP IT!
THE HEAT... AGAINST MY BACK...
THE THING'S DRIVING US BOTH TOWARDS ONE OF THE FIRE-PITS!
I'M NOT SURE EVEN MY INVULNERABLE BODY CAN SURVIVE IN THAT FURNACE!!
21

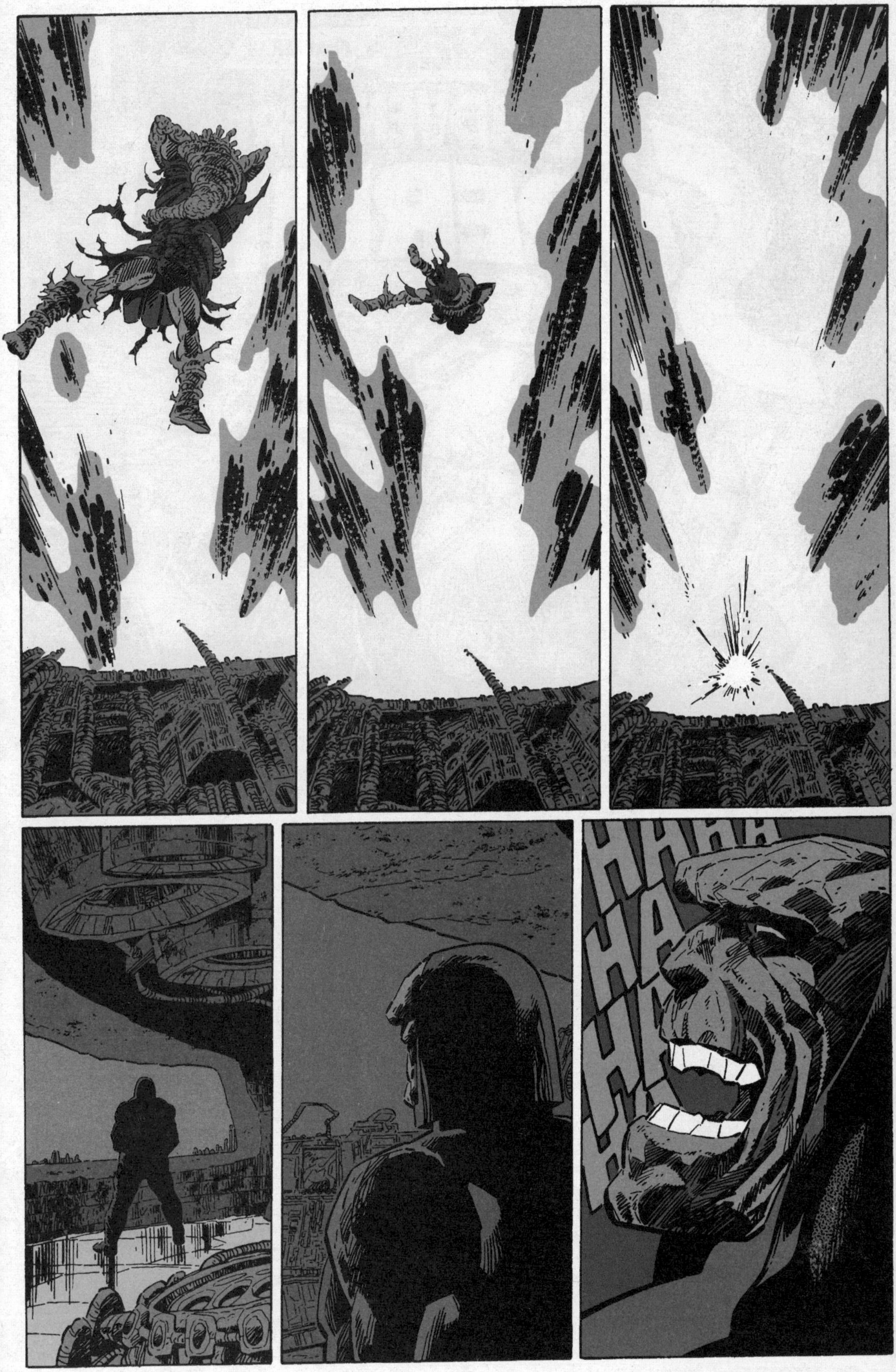
HAHAHA

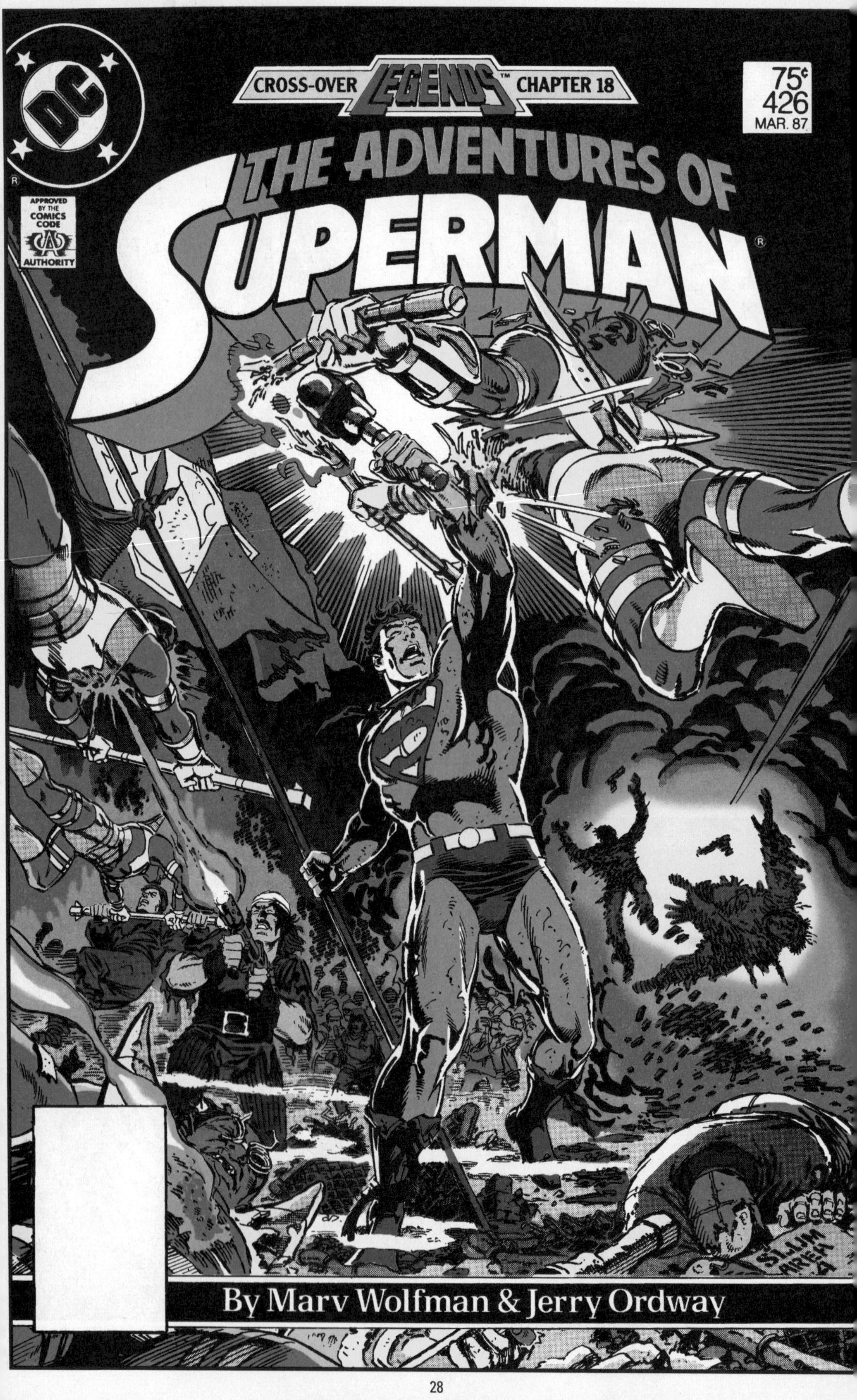
CROSS-OVER LEGENDS™ CHAPTER 18
75¢
426
MAR. 87
APPROVED BY THE COMICS CODE AUTHORITY
THE ADVENTURES OF SUPERMAN®
SLUM AREA 4
By Marv Wolfman & Jerry Ordway

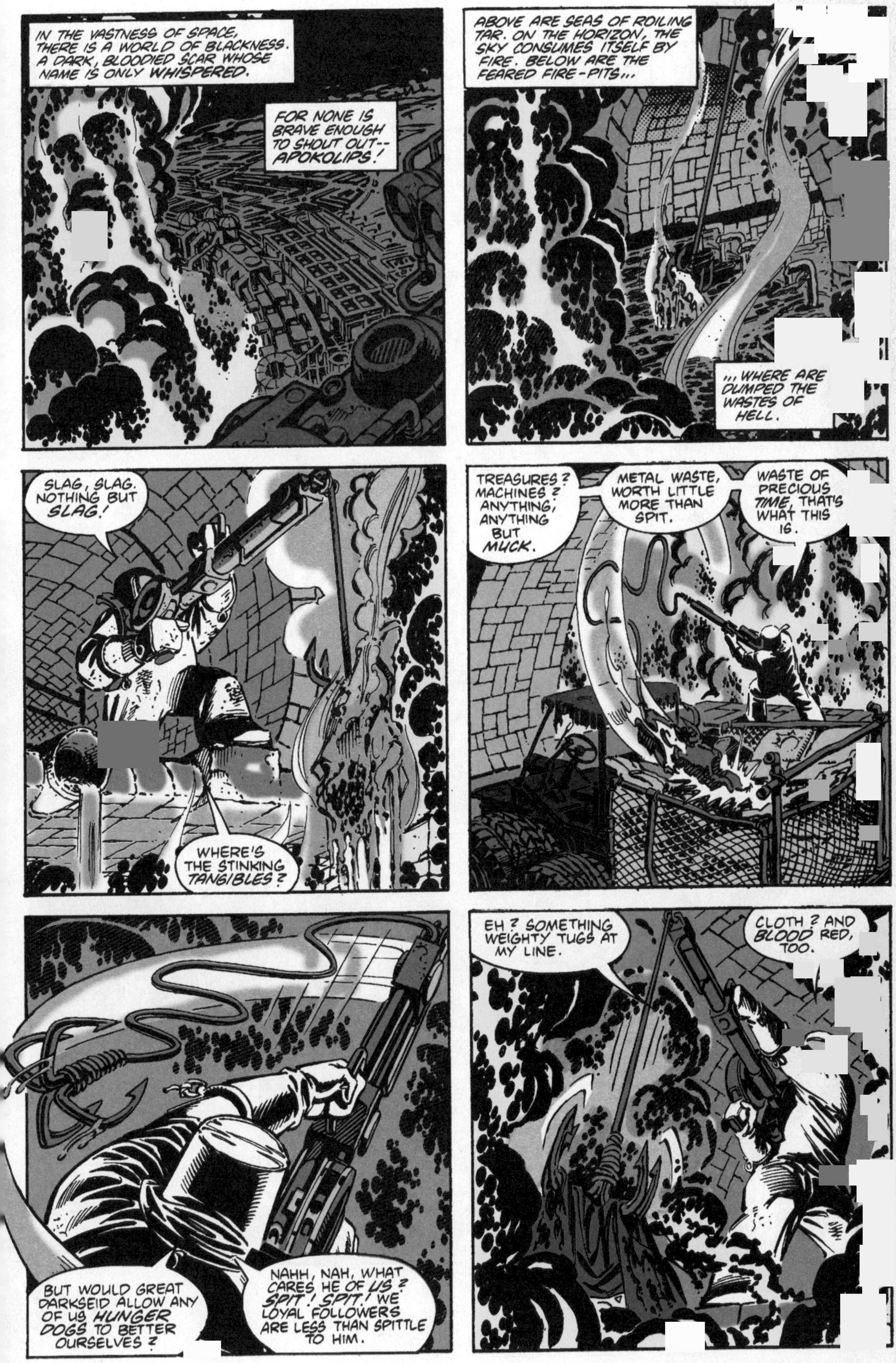
IN THE VASTNESS OF SPACE, THERE IS A WORLD OF BLACKNESS. A DARK, BLOODIED SCAR WHOSE NAME IS ONLY WHISPERED.
FOR NONE IS BRAVE ENOUGH TO SHOUT OUT-- APOKOLIPS!
ABOVE ARE SEAS OF ROILING TAR. ON THE HORIZON, THE SKY CONSUMES ITSELF BY FIRE. BELOW ARE THE FEARED FIRE-PITS...
...WHERE ARE DUMPED THE WASTES OF HELL.
SLAG, SLAG. NOTHING BUT SLAG!
WHERE'S THE STINKING TANGIBLES?
TREASURES? MACHINES? ANYTHING, ANYTHING BUT MUCK.
METAL WASTE, WORTH LITTLE MORE THAN SPIT.
WASTE OF PRECIOUS TIME, THAT'S WHAT THIS IS.
BUT WOULD GREAT DARKSEID ALLOW ANY OF US HUNGER DOGS TO BETTER OURSELVES?
NAHH, NAH, WHAT CARES HE OF US? SPIT! SPIT! WE LOYAL FOLLOWERS ARE LESS THAN SPITTLE TO HIM.
EH? SOMETHING WEIGHTY TUGS AT MY LINE.
CLOTH? AND BLOOD RED, TOO.

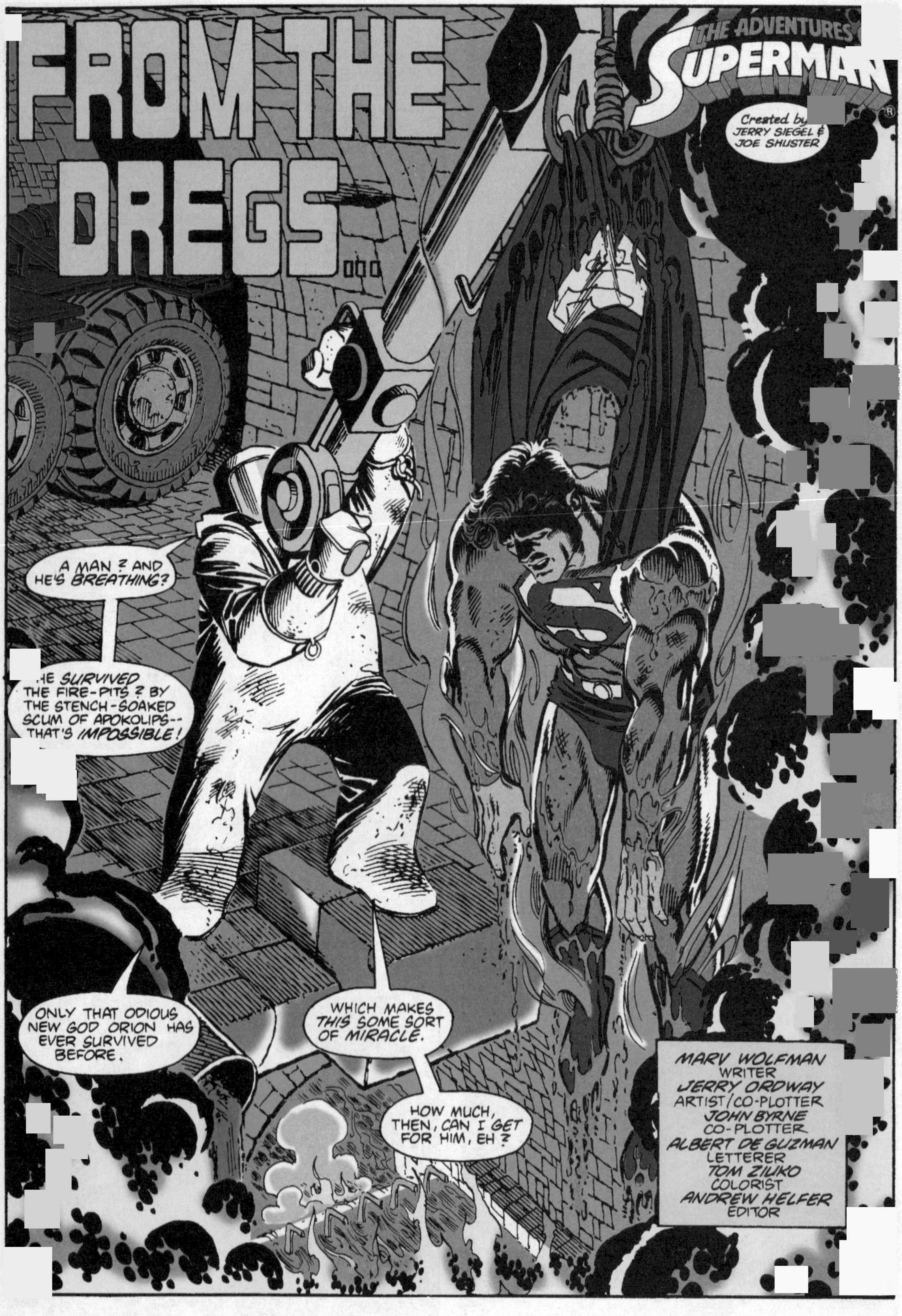
FROM THE DREGS...
THE ADVENTURES OF SUPERMAN
Created by JERRY SIEGEL & JOE SHUSTER
A MAN? AND HE'S BREATHING?
HE SURVIVED THE FIRE-PITS? BY THE STENCH-SOAKED SCUM OF APOKOLIPS--THAT'S IMPOSSIBLE!
ONLY THAT ODIOUS NEW GOD ORION HAS EVER SURVIVED BEFORE.
WHICH MAKES THIS SOME SORT OF MIRACLE.
HOW MUCH, THEN, CAN I GET FOR HIM, EH?
MARV WOLFMAN WRITER
JERRY ORDWAY ARTIST/CO-PLOTTER
JOHN BYRNE CO-PLOTTER
ALBERT DE GUZMAN LETTERER
TOM ZIUKO COLORIST
ANDREW HELFER EDITOR

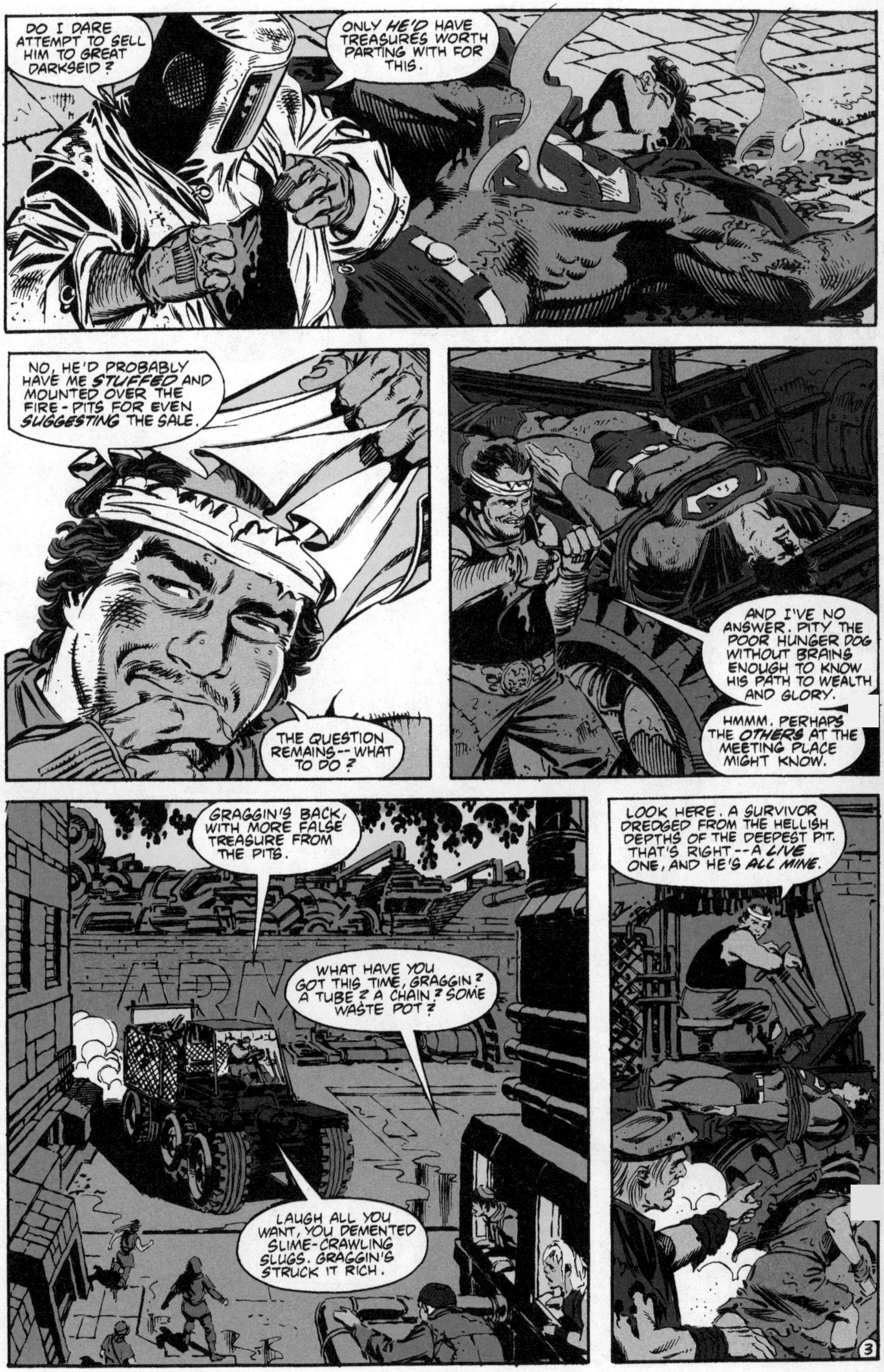
DO I DARE ATTEMPT TO SELL HIM TO GREAT DARKSEID?
ONLY HE'D HAVE TREASURES WORTH PARTING WITH FOR THIS.
NO, HE'D PROBABLY HAVE ME STUFFED AND MOUNTED OVER THE FIRE-PITS FOR EVEN SUGGESTING THE SALE.
THE QUESTION REMAINS--WHAT TO DO?
AND I'VE NO ANSWER. PITY THE POOR HUNGER DOG WITHOUT BRAINS ENOUGH TO KNOW HIS PATH TO WEALTH AND GLORY.
HMMM. PERHAPS THE OTHERS AT THE MEETING PLACE MIGHT KNOW.
GRAGGIN'S BACK, WITH MORE FALSE TREASURE FROM THE PITS.
WHAT HAVE YOU GOT THIS TIME, GRAGGIN? A TUBE? A CHAIN? SOME WASTE POT?
LAUGH ALL YOU WANT, YOU DEMENTED SLIME-CRAWLING SLUGS. GRAGGIN'S STRUCK IT RICH.
LOOK HERE. A SURVIVOR DREDGED FROM THE HELLISH DEPTHS OF THE DEEPEST PIT. THAT'S RIGHT--A LIVE ONE, AND HE'S ALL MINE.
3

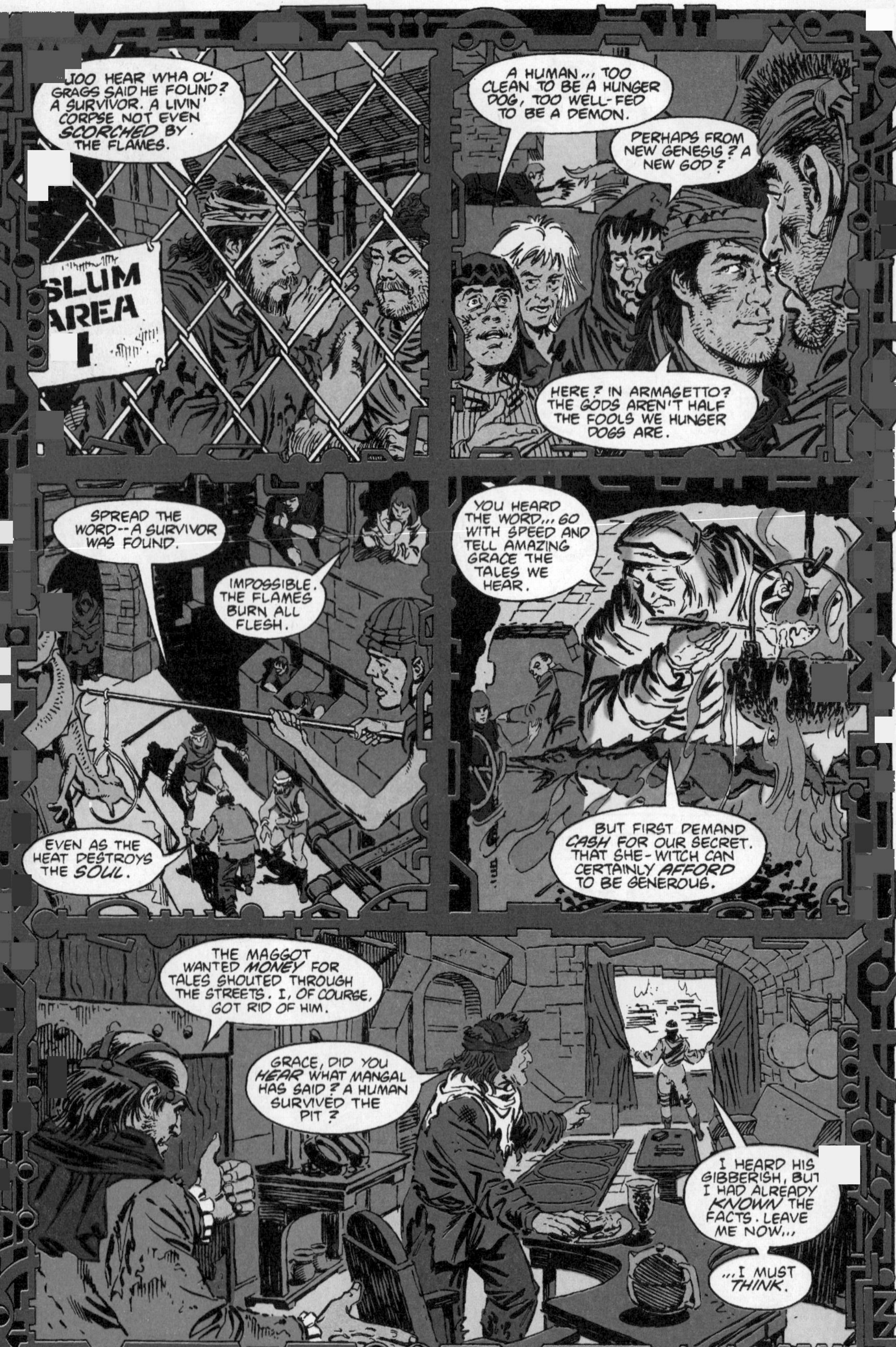
JOO HEAR WHA OL' GRAGS SAID HE FOUND? A SURVIVOR. A LIVIN' CORPSE NOT EVEN SCORCHED BY THE FLAMES.
SLUM AREA 4
A HUMAN... TOO CLEAN TO BE A HUNGER DOG, TOO WELL-FED TO BE A DEMON.
PERHAPS FROM NEW GENESIS? A NEW GOD?
HERE? IN ARMAGETTO? THE GODS AREN'T HALF THE FOOLS WE HUNGER DOGS ARE.
SPREAD THE WORD--A SURVIVOR WAS FOUND.
IMPOSSIBLE. THE FLAMES BURN ALL FLESH.
EVEN AS THE HEAT DESTROYS THE SOUL.
YOU HEARD THE WORD... GO WITH SPEED AND TELL AMAZING GRACE THE TALES WE HEAR.
BUT FIRST DEMAND CASH FOR OUR SECRET. THAT SHE-WITCH CAN CERTAINLY AFFORD TO BE GENEROUS.
THE MAGGOT WANTED MONEY FOR TALES SHOUTED THROUGH THE STREETS. I, OF COURSE, GOT RID OF HIM.
GRACE, DID YOU HEAR WHAT MANGAL HAS SAID? A HUMAN SURVIVED THE PIT?
I HEARD HIS GIBBERISH, BUT I HAD ALREADY KNOWN THE FACTS. LEAVE ME NOW...
...I MUST THINK.

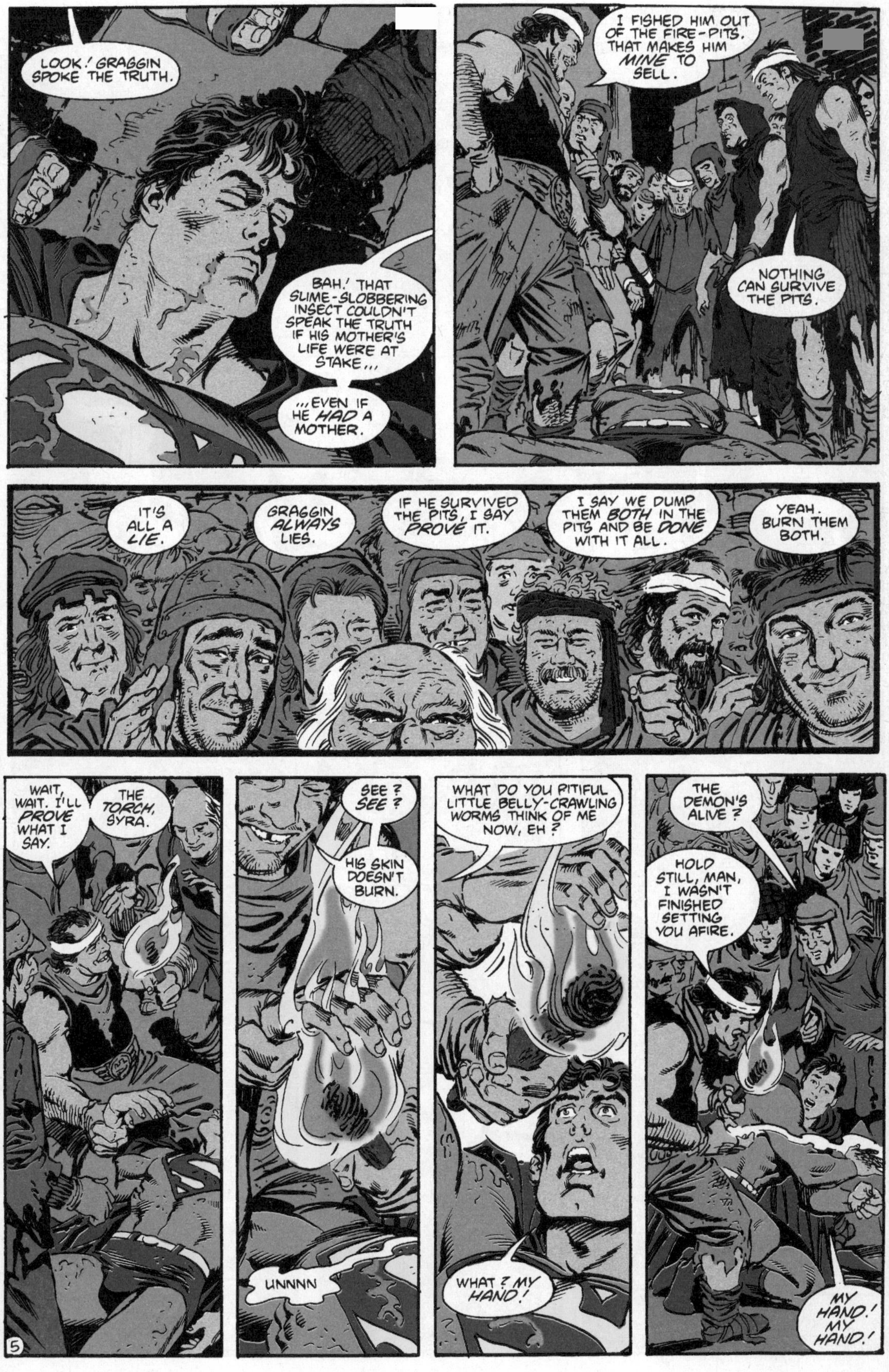

LOOK! GRAGGIN SPOKE THE TRUTH.
BAH! THAT SLIME-SLOBBERING INSECT COULDN'T SPEAK THE TRUTH IF HIS MOTHER'S LIFE WERE AT STAKE...
...EVEN IF HE *HAD* A MOTHER.
I FISHED HIM OUT OF THE FIRE-PITS. THAT MAKES HIM *MINE* TO SELL.
NOTHING CAN SURVIVE THE PITS.
IT'S ALL A *LIE*.
GRAGGIN *ALWAYS* LIES.
IF HE SURVIVED THE PITS, I SAY *PROVE* IT.
I SAY WE DUMP THEM *BOTH* IN THE PITS AND BE *DONE* WITH IT ALL.
YEAH. BURN THEM BOTH.
WAIT, WAIT. I'LL *PROVE* WHAT I SAY.
THE *TORCH*, SYRA.
5
SEE? *SEE*?
HIS SKIN DOESN'T BURN.
UNNNN
WHAT DO YOU PITIFUL LITTLE BELLY-CRAWLING WORMS THINK OF ME NOW, EH?
WHAT? MY *HAND*!
THE DEMON'S ALIVE?
HOLD STILL, MAN, I WASN'T FINISHED SETTING YOU AFIRE.
MY *HAND*! MY *HAND*!

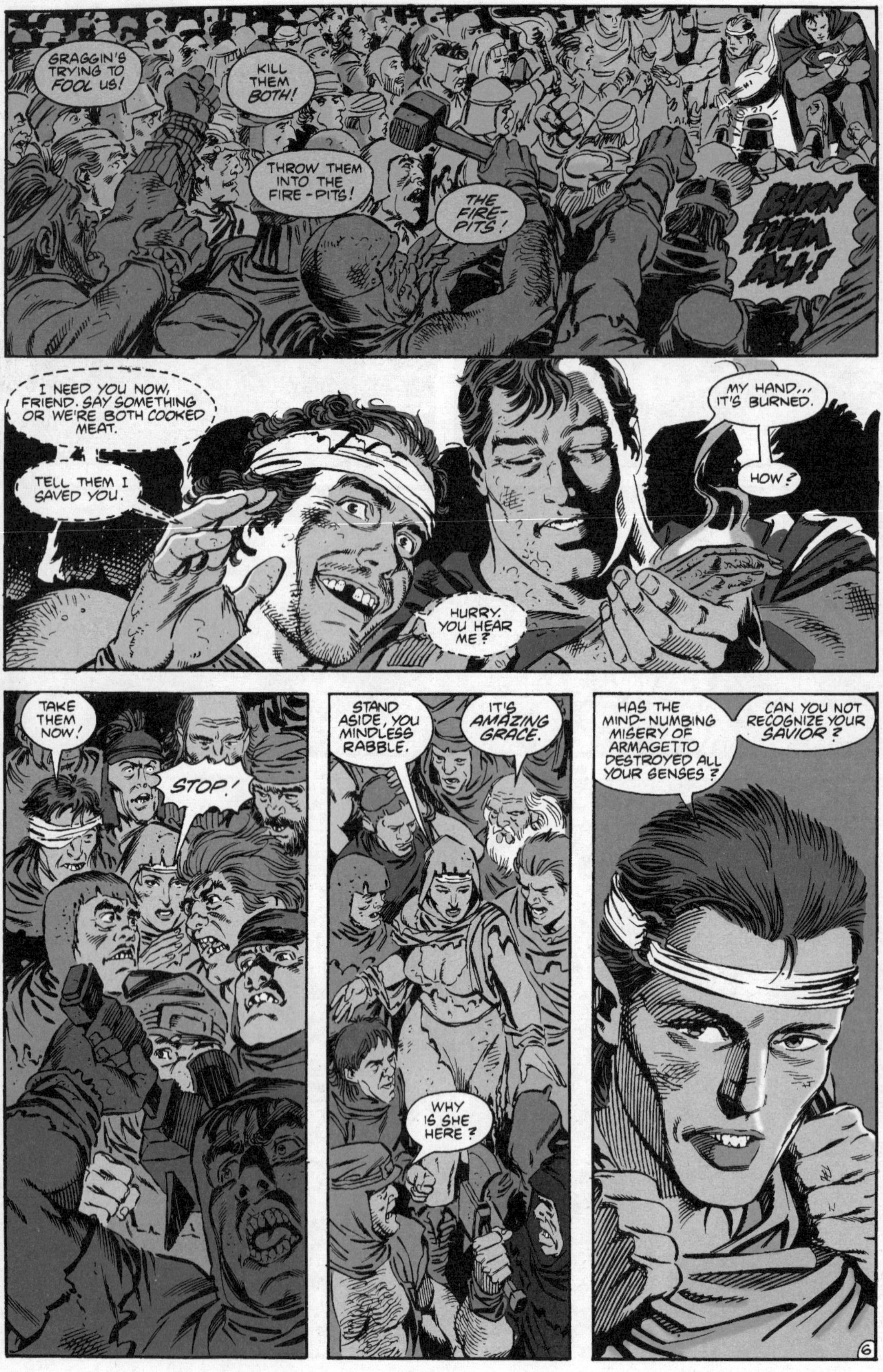
GRAGGIN'S TRYING TO FOOL US!
KILL THEM BOTH!
THROW THEM INTO THE FIRE-PITS!
THE FIRE-PITS!
BURN THEM ALL!
I NEED YOU NOW, FRIEND. SAY SOMETHING OR WE'RE BOTH COOKED MEAT.
TELL THEM I SAVED YOU.
HURRY. YOU HEAR ME?
MY HAND... IT'S BURNED.
HOW?
TAKE THEM NOW!
STOP!
STAND ASIDE, YOU MINDLESS RABBLE.
IT'S AMAZING GRACE.
WHY IS SHE HERE?
HAS THE MIND-NUMBING MISERY OF ARMAGETTO DESTROYED ALL YOUR SENSES?
CAN YOU NOT RECOGNIZE YOUR SAVIOR?
6

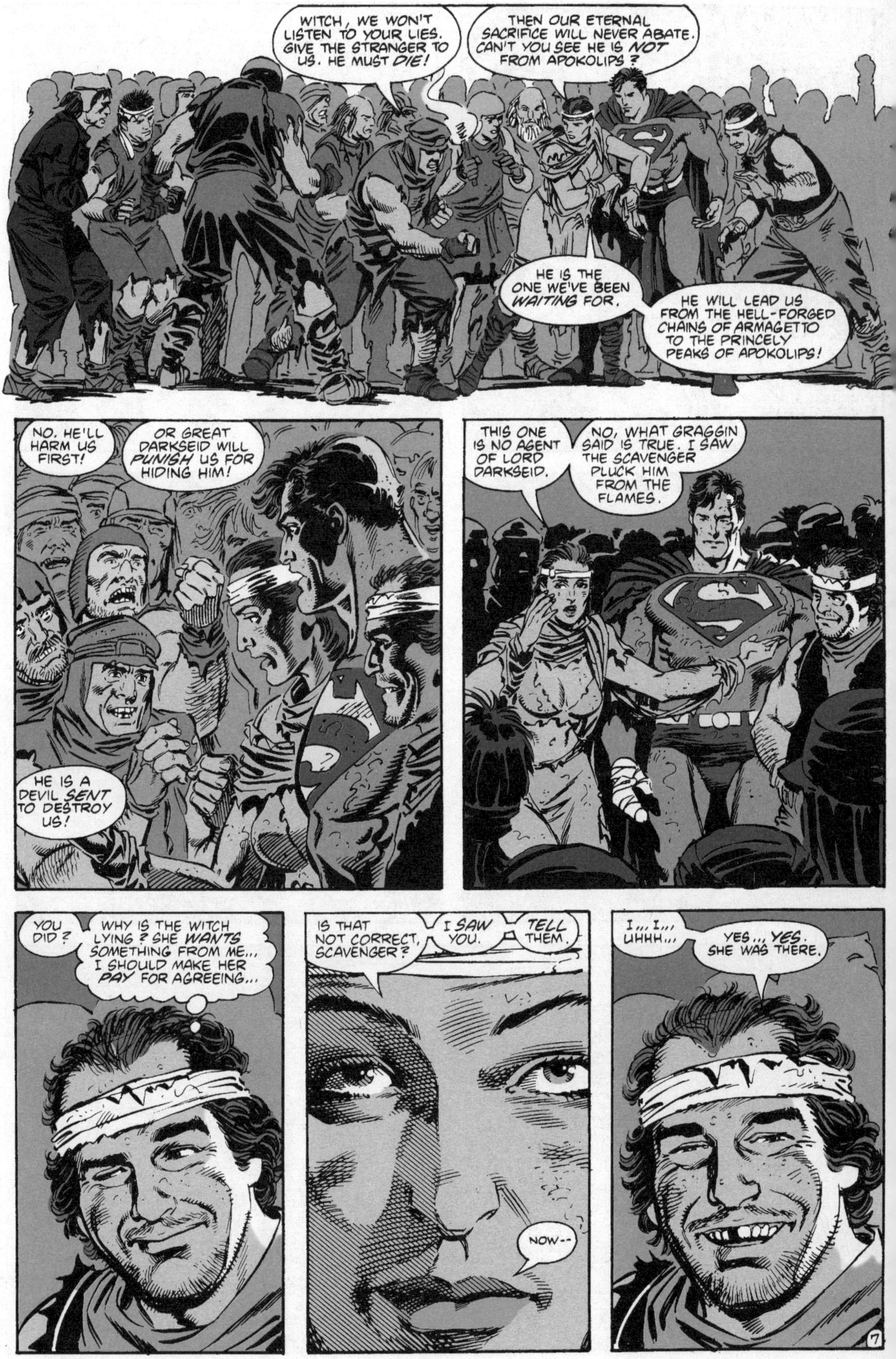
WITCH, WE WON'T LISTEN TO YOUR LIES. GIVE THE STRANGER TO US. HE MUST DIE!
THEN OUR ETERNAL SACRIFICE WILL NEVER ABATE. CAN'T YOU SEE HE IS NOT FROM APOKOLIPS?
HE IS THE ONE WE'VE BEEN WAITING FOR.
HE WILL LEAD US FROM THE HELL-FORGED CHAINS OF ARMAGETTO TO THE PRINCELY PEAKS OF APOKOLIPS!
NO. HE'LL HARM US FIRST!
OR GREAT DARKSEID WILL PUNISH US FOR HIDING HIM!
HE IS A DEVIL SENT TO DESTROY US!
THIS ONE IS NO AGENT OF LORD DARKSEID.
NO, WHAT GRAGGIN SAID IS TRUE. I SAW THE SCAVENGER PLUCK HIM FROM THE FLAMES.
YOU DID?
WHY IS THE WITCH LYING? SHE WANTS SOMETHING FROM ME... I SHOULD MAKE HER PAY FOR AGREEING...
IS THAT NOT CORRECT, SCAVENGER?
I SAW YOU.
TELL THEM.
NOW--
I... I... UHHH...
YES... YES. SHE WAS THERE.
7

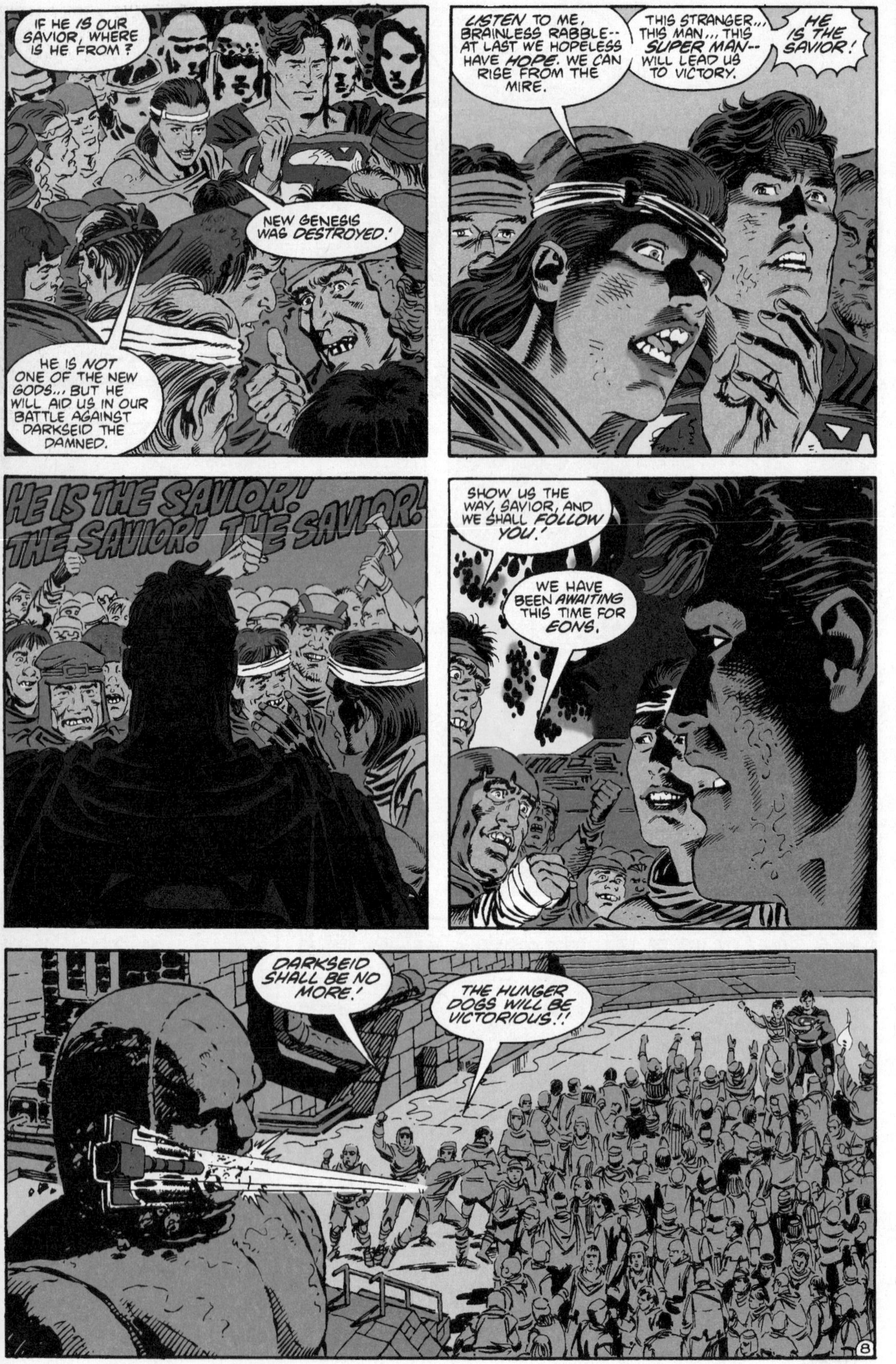
IF HE IS OUR SAVIOR, WHERE IS HE FROM?
NEW GENESIS WAS DESTROYED!
HE IS NOT ONE OF THE NEW GODS... BUT HE WILL AID US IN OUR BATTLE AGAINST DARKSEID THE DAMNED.
LISTEN TO ME, BRAINLESS RABBLE-- AT LAST WE HOPELESS HAVE HOPE. WE CAN RISE FROM THE MIRE.
THIS STRANGER... THIS MAN... THIS SUPER MAN-- WILL LEAD US TO VICTORY.
HE IS THE SAVIOR!
HE IS THE SAVIOR! THE SAVIOR! THE SAVIOR!
SHOW US THE WAY, SAVIOR, AND WE SHALL FOLLOW YOU!
WE HAVE BEEN AWAITING THIS TIME FOR EONS.
DARKSEID SHALL BE NO MORE!
THE HUNGER DOGS WILL BE VICTORIOUS!!
8

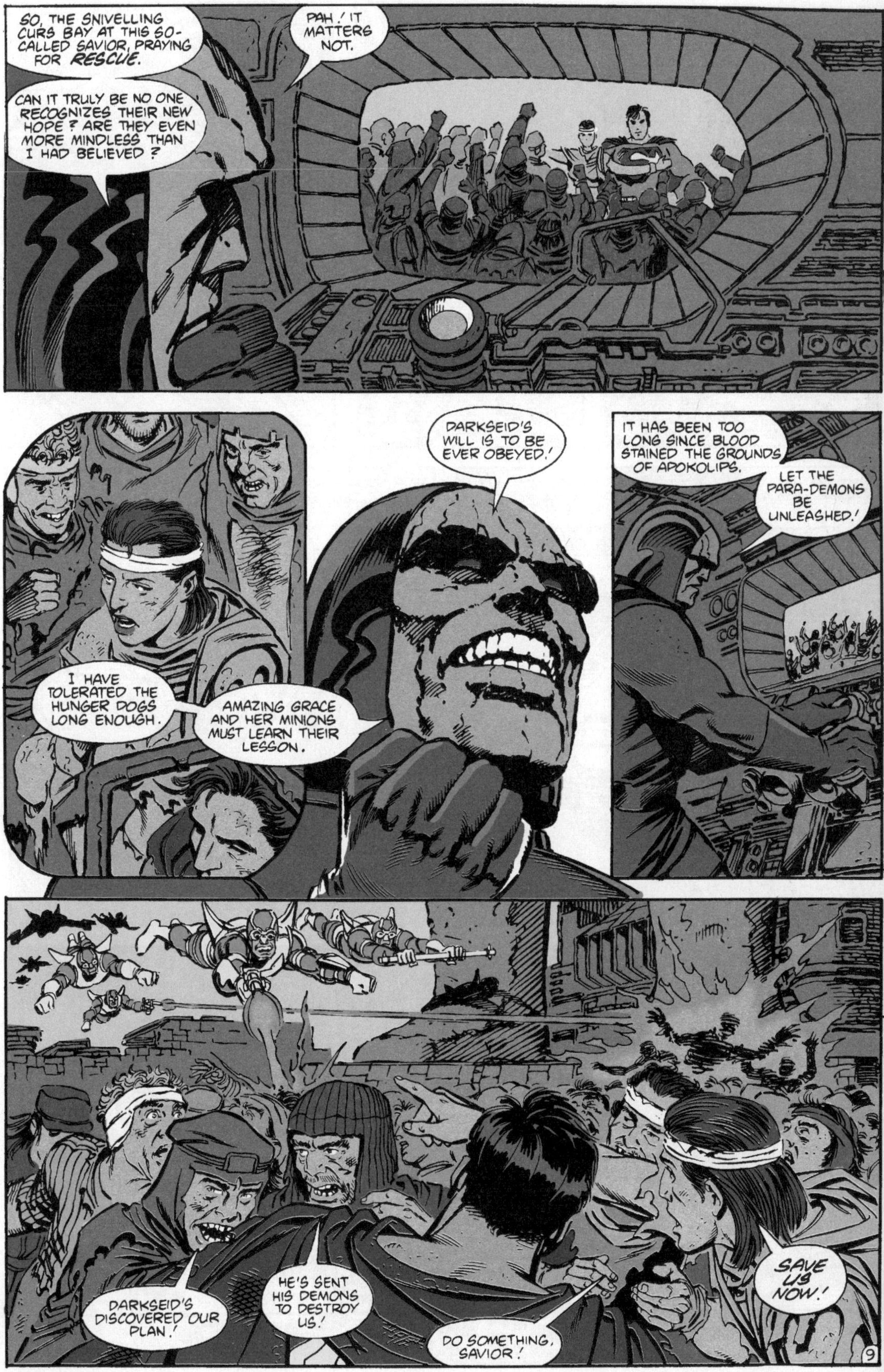

SO, THE SNIVELLING CURS BAY AT THIS SO-CALLED SAVIOR, PRAYING FOR RESCUE.
PAH! IT MATTERS NOT.
CAN IT TRULY BE NO ONE RECOGNIZES THEIR NEW HOPE? ARE THEY EVEN MORE MINDLESS THAN I HAD BELIEVED?
DARKSEID'S WILL IS TO BE EVER OBEYED!
I HAVE TOLERATED THE HUNGER DOGS LONG ENOUGH.
AMAZING GRACE AND HER MINIONS MUST LEARN THEIR LESSON.
IT HAS BEEN TOO LONG SINCE BLOOD STAINED THE GROUNDS OF APOKOLIPS.
LET THE PARA-DEMONS BE UNLEASHED!
DARKSEID'S DISCOVERED OUR PLAN!
HE'S SENT HIS DEMONS TO DESTROY US!
DO SOMETHING, SAVIOR!
SAVE US NOW!
9

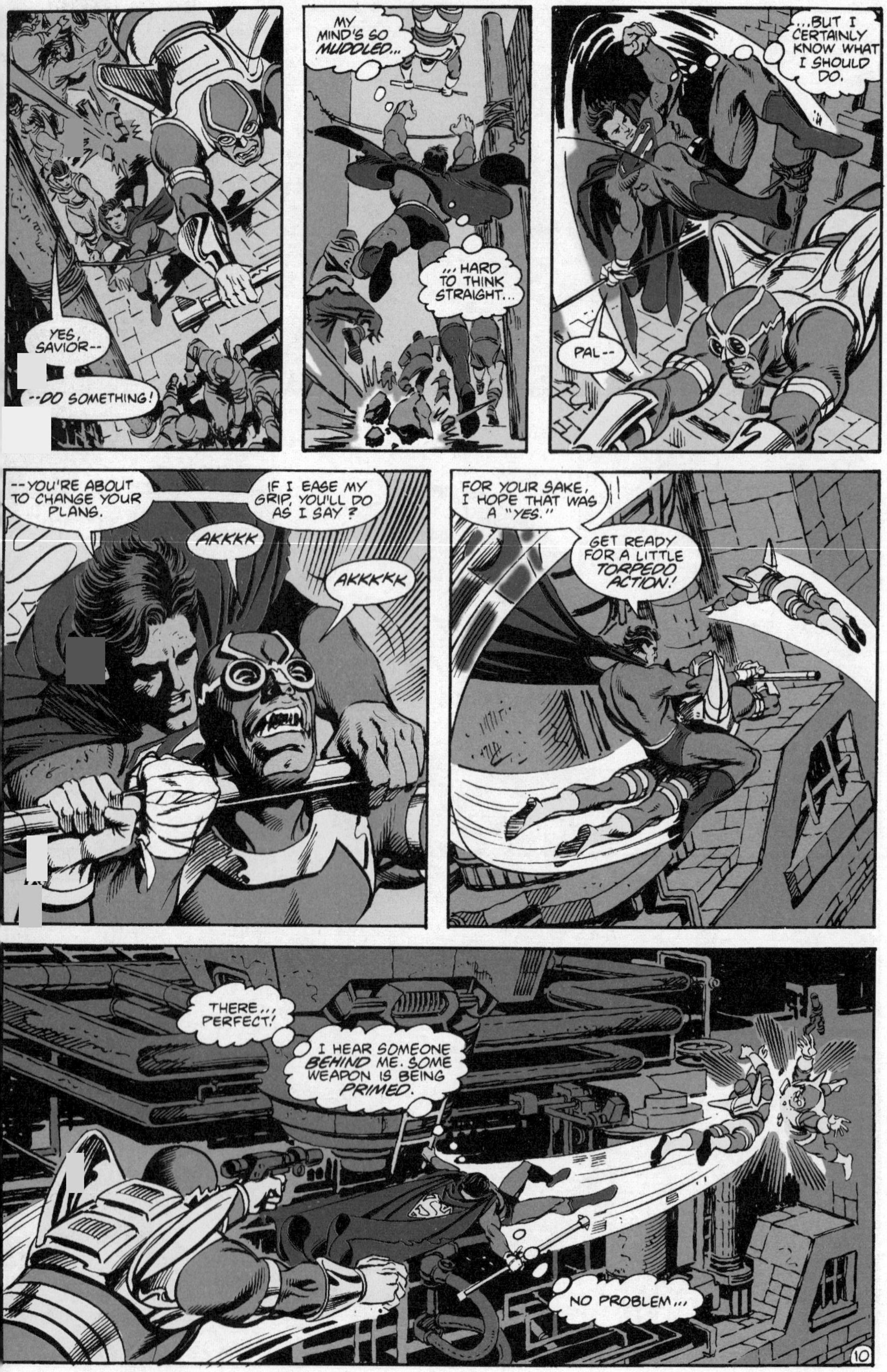
YES, SAVIOR--
--DO SOMETHING!
MY MIND'S SO MUDDLED...
...HARD TO THINK STRAIGHT...
...BUT I CERTAINLY KNOW WHAT I SHOULD DO.
PAL--
--YOU'RE ABOUT TO CHANGE YOUR PLANS.
IF I EASE MY GRIP, YOU'LL DO AS I SAY?
AKKKK
AKKKKK
FOR YOUR SAKE, I HOPE THAT WAS A "YES."
GET READY FOR A LITTLE TORPEDO ACTION!
THERE... PERFECT!
I HEAR SOMEONE BEHIND ME. SOME WEAPON IS BEING PRIMED.
NO PROBLEM...
10

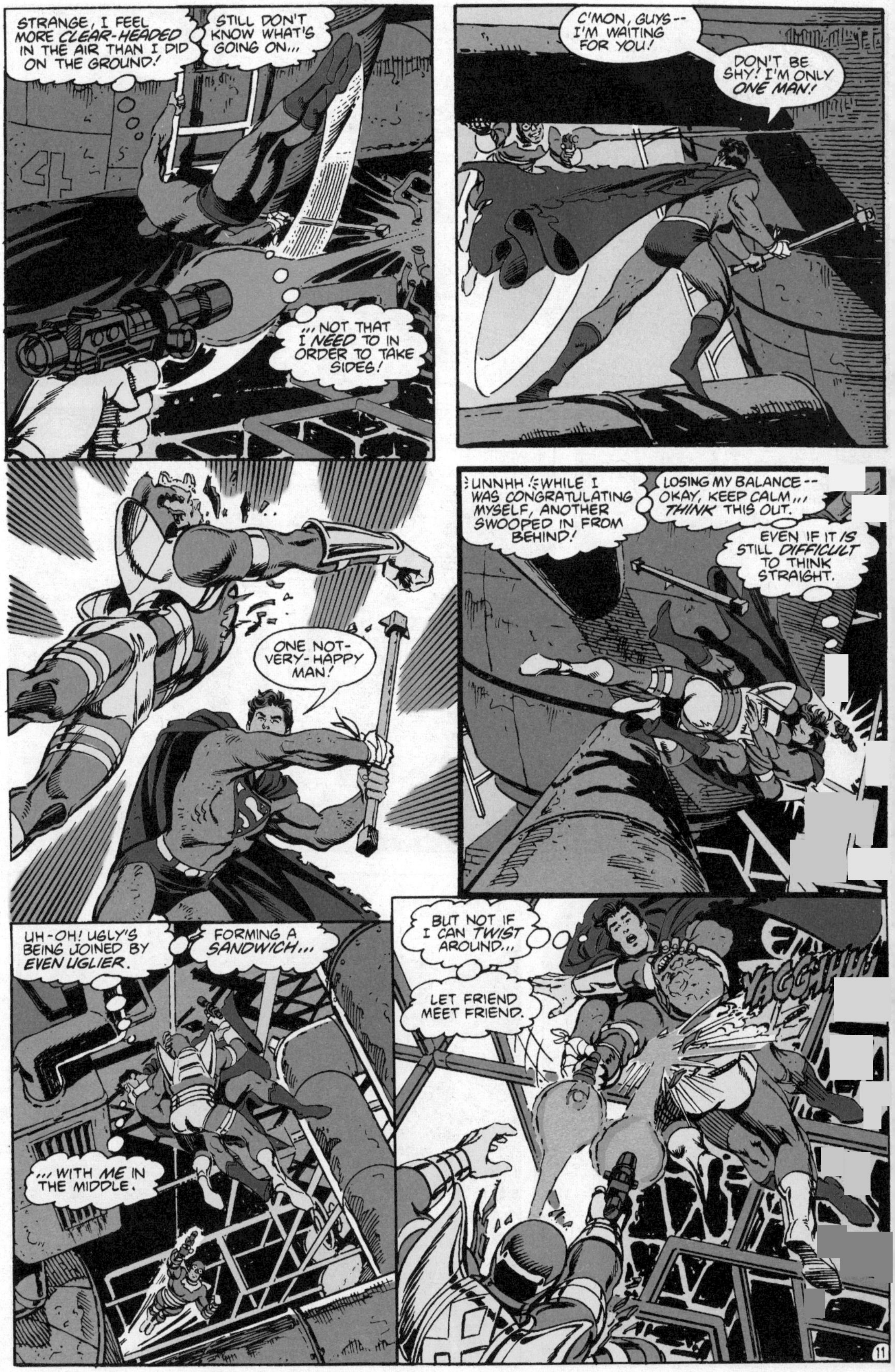

STRANGE, I FEEL MORE CLEAR-HEADED IN THE AIR THAN I DID ON THE GROUND!
STILL DON'T KNOW WHAT'S GOING ON...
...NOT THAT I NEED TO IN ORDER TO TAKE SIDES!
C'MON, GUYS-- I'M WAITING FOR YOU!
DON'T BE SHY! I'M ONLY ONE MAN!
ONE NOT-VERY-HAPPY MAN!
UNNHH! WHILE I WAS CONGRATULATING MYSELF, ANOTHER SWOOPED IN FROM BEHIND!
LOSING MY BALANCE-- OKAY, KEEP CALM... THINK THIS OUT.
EVEN IF IT IS STILL DIFFICULT TO THINK STRAIGHT.
UH-OH! UGLY'S BEING JOINED BY EVEN UGLIER.
FORMING A SANDWICH...
...WITH ME IN THE MIDDLE.
BUT NOT IF I CAN TWIST AROUND...
LET FRIEND MEET FRIEND.
YAGGHH!
11

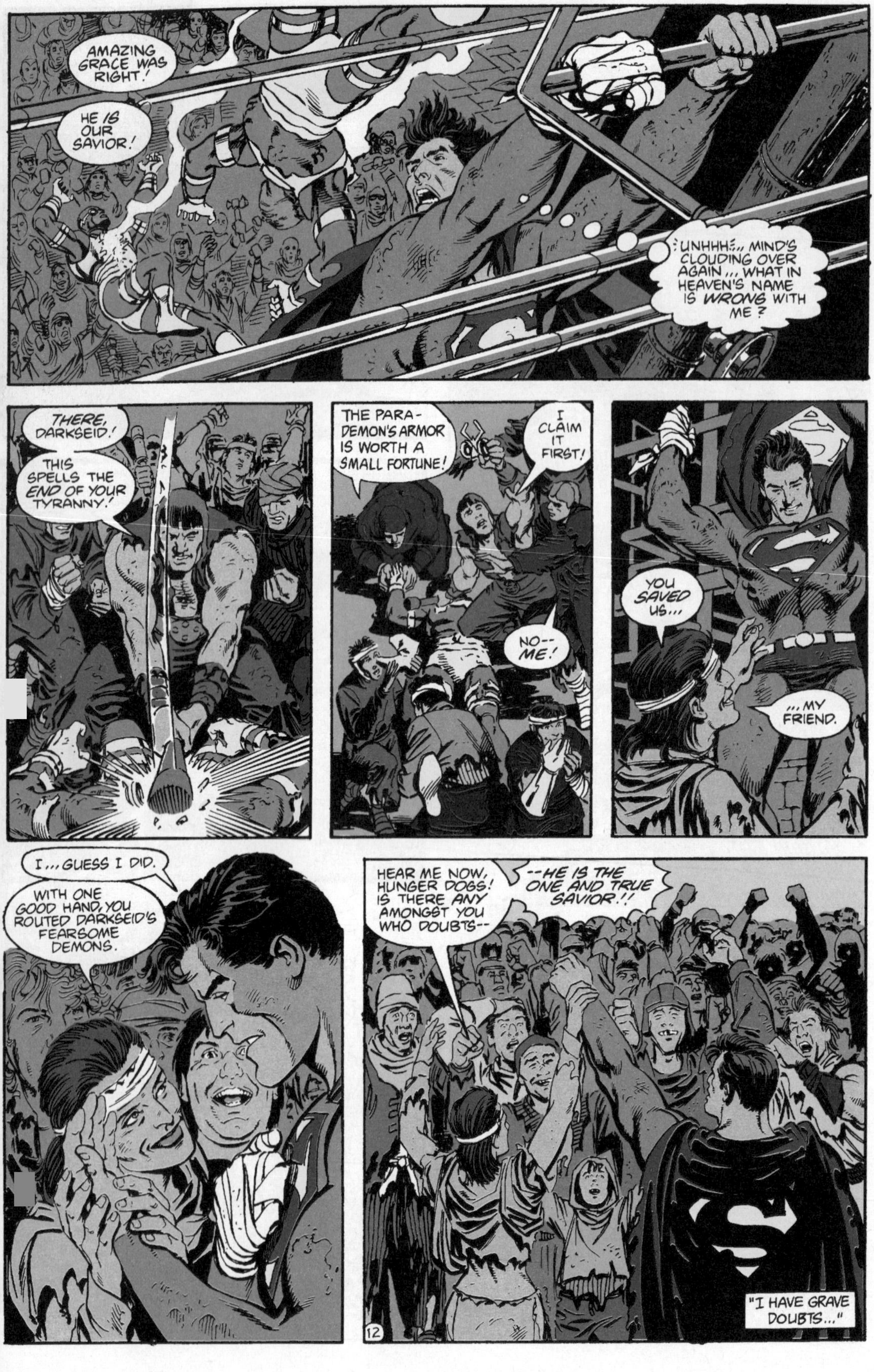
AMAZING GRACE WAS RIGHT!
HE IS OUR SAVIOR!
UNHHH... MIND'S CLOUDING OVER AGAIN... WHAT IN HEAVEN'S NAME IS WRONG WITH ME?
THERE, DARKSEID!
THIS SPELLS THE END OF YOUR TYRANNY!
THE PARA-DEMON'S ARMOR IS WORTH A SMALL FORTUNE!
I CLAIM IT FIRST!
NO-- ME!
YOU SAVED US...
...MY FRIEND.
I... GUESS I DID.
WITH ONE GOOD HAND, YOU ROUTED DARKSEID'S FEARSOME DEMONS.
HEAR ME NOW, HUNGER DOGS! IS THERE ANY AMONGST YOU WHO DOUBTS--
--HE IS THE ONE AND TRUE SAVIOR!!
"I HAVE GRAVE DOUBTS..."
12

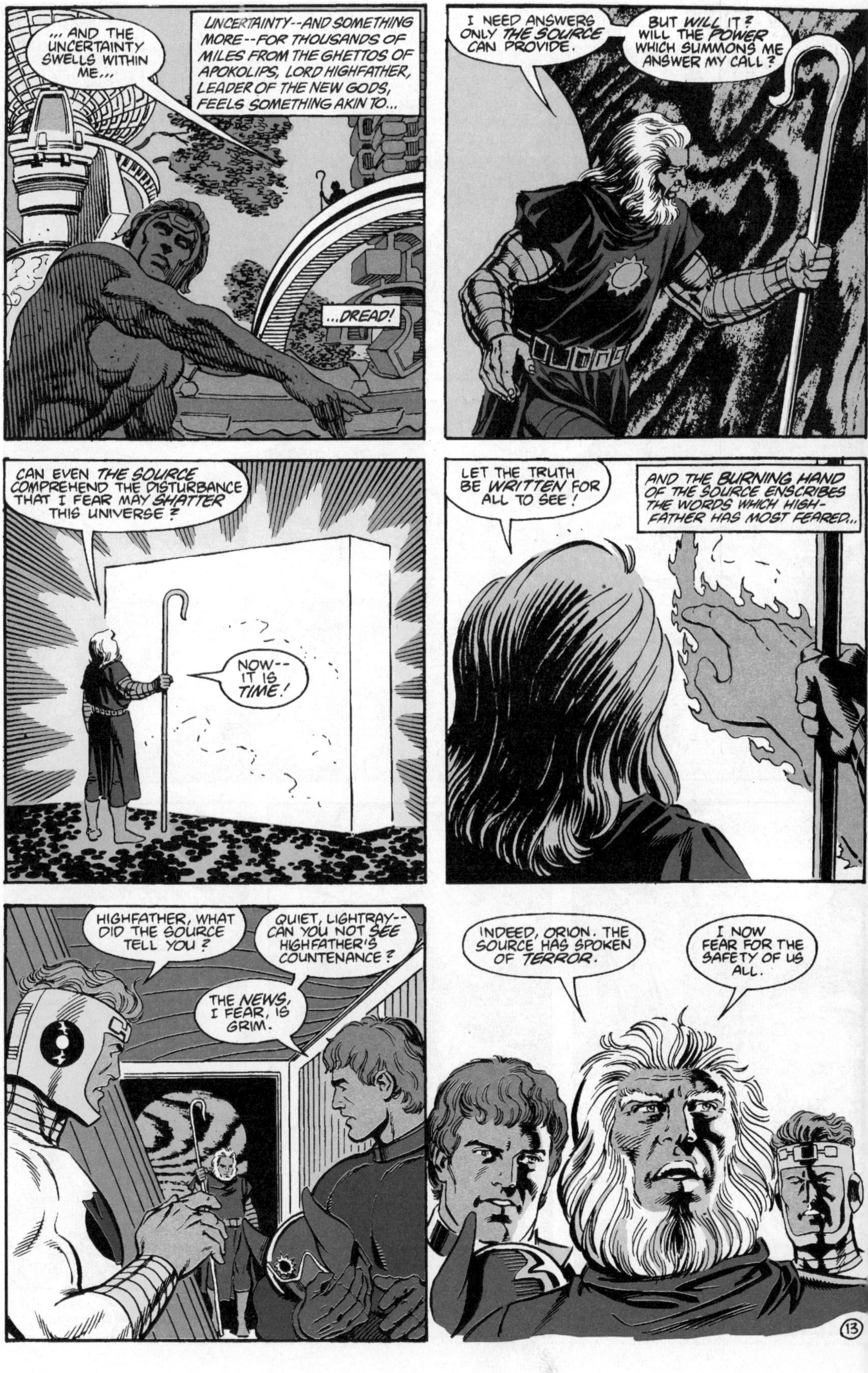
UNCERTAINTY--AND SOMETHING MORE--FOR THOUSANDS OF MILES FROM THE GHETTOS OF APOKOLIPS, LORD HIGHFATHER, LEADER OF THE NEW GODS, FEELS SOMETHING AKIN TO...
... AND THE UNCERTAINTY SWELLS WITHIN ME...
...DREAD!
I NEED ANSWERS ONLY THE SOURCE CAN PROVIDE.
BUT WILL IT? WILL THE POWER WHICH SUMMONS ME ANSWER MY CALL?
CAN EVEN THE SOURCE COMPREHEND THE DISTURBANCE THAT I FEAR MAY SHATTER THIS UNIVERSE?
NOW-- IT IS TIME!
LET THE TRUTH BE WRITTEN FOR ALL TO SEE!
AND THE BURNING HAND OF THE SOURCE ENSCRIBES THE WORDS WHICH HIGH-FATHER HAS MOST FEARED...
HIGHFATHER, WHAT DID THE SOURCE TELL YOU?
QUIET, LIGHTRAY-- CAN YOU NOT SEE HIGHFATHER'S COUNTENANCE?
THE NEWS, I FEAR, IS GRIM.
INDEED, ORION. THE SOURCE HAS SPOKEN OF TERROR.
I NOW FEAR FOR THE SAFETY OF US ALL.
13

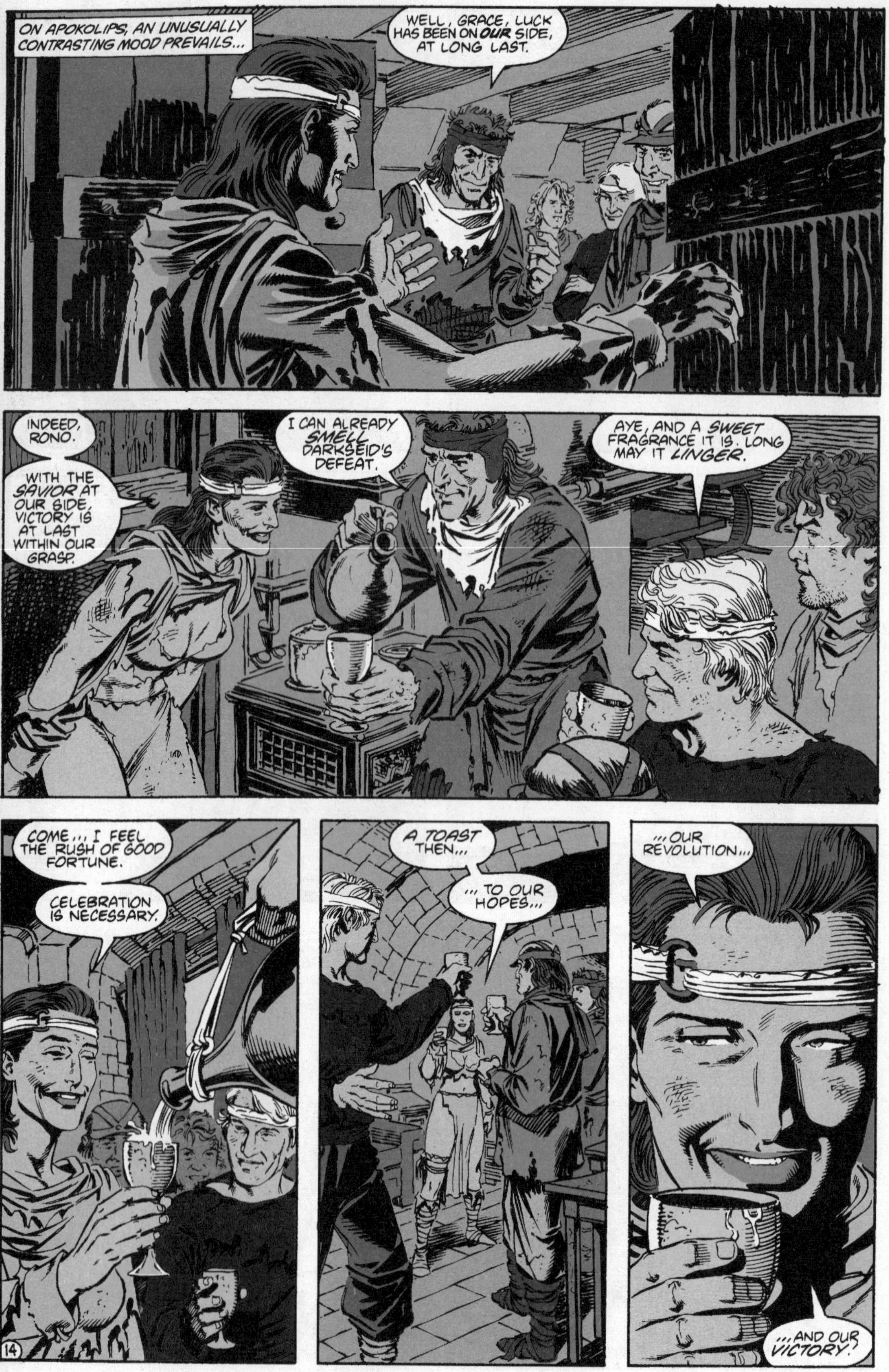

ON APOKOLIPS, AN UNUSUALLY CONTRASTING MOOD PREVAILS...
WELL, GRACE, LUCK HAS BEEN ON OUR SIDE, AT LONG LAST.
INDEED, RONO.
WITH THE SAVIOR AT OUR SIDE, VICTORY IS AT LAST WITHIN OUR GRASP.
I CAN ALREADY SMELL DARKSEID'S DEFEAT.
AYE, AND A SWEET FRAGRANCE IT IS. LONG MAY IT LINGER.
COME... I FEEL THE RUSH OF GOOD FORTUNE.
CELEBRATION IS NECESSARY.
14
A TOAST THEN...
...TO OUR HOPES...
...OUR REVOLUTION...
...AND OUR VICTORY.

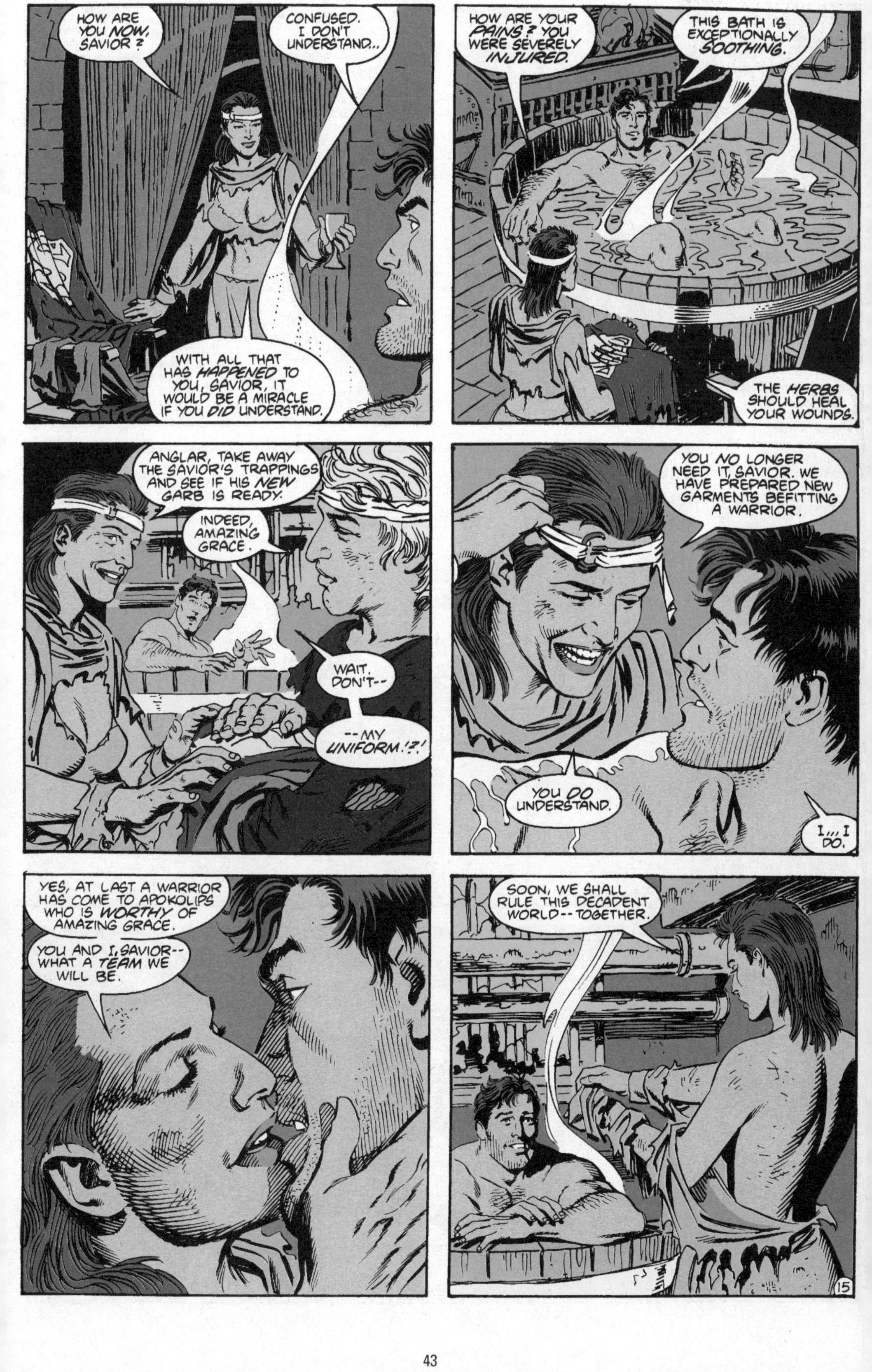
HOW ARE YOU NOW, SAVIOR ?
CONFUSED. I DON'T UNDERSTAND...
WITH ALL THAT HAS HAPPENED TO YOU, SAVIOR, IT WOULD BE A MIRACLE IF YOU DID UNDERSTAND.
HOW ARE YOUR PAINS? YOU WERE SEVERELY INJURED.
THIS BATH IS EXCEPTIONALLY SOOTHING.
THE HERBS SHOULD HEAL YOUR WOUNDS.
ANGLAR, TAKE AWAY THE SAVIOR'S TRAPPINGS AND SEE IF HIS NEW GARB IS READY.
INDEED, AMAZING GRACE.
WAIT. DON'T--
--MY UNIFORM.!?!
YOU NO LONGER NEED IT, SAVIOR. WE HAVE PREPARED NEW GARMENTS BEFITTING A WARRIOR.
YOU DO UNDERSTAND.
I... I DO.
YES, AT LAST A WARRIOR HAS COME TO APOKOLIPS WHO IS WORTHY OF AMAZING GRACE.
YOU AND I, SAVIOR-- WHAT A TEAM WE WILL BE.
SOON, WE SHALL RULE THIS DECADENT WORLD--TOGETHER.
15

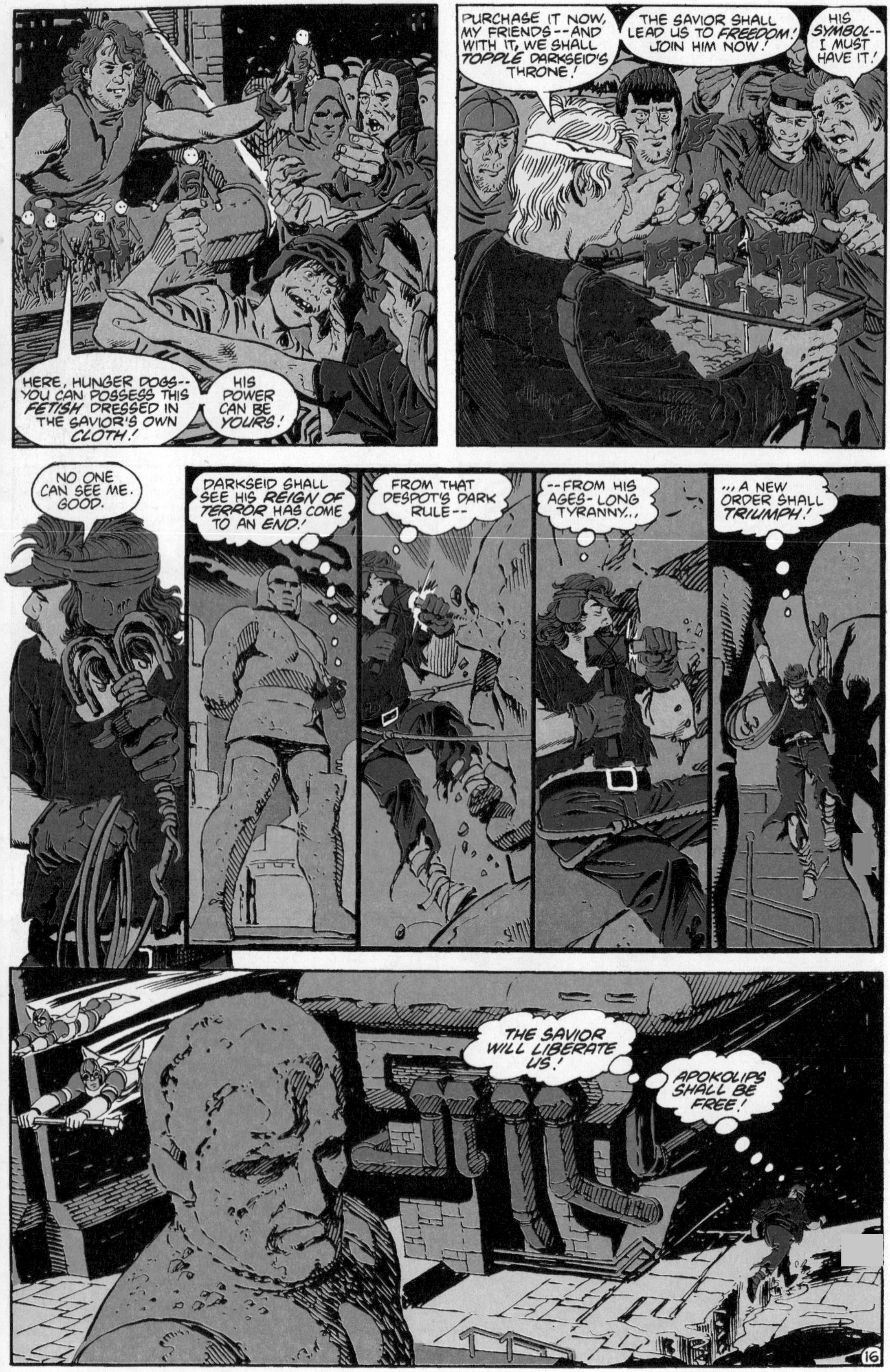
HERE, HUNGER DOGS-- YOU CAN POSSESS THIS FETISH DRESSED IN THE SAVIOR'S OWN CLOTH!
HIS POWER CAN BE YOURS!
PURCHASE IT NOW, MY FRIENDS--AND WITH IT, WE SHALL TOPPLE DARKSEID'S THRONE!
THE SAVIOR SHALL LEAD US TO FREEDOM! JOIN HIM NOW!
HIS SYMBOL-- I MUST HAVE IT!
NO ONE CAN SEE ME. GOOD.
DARKSEID SHALL SEE HIS REIGN OF TERROR HAS COME TO AN END!
FROM THAT DESPOT'S DARK RULE--
--FROM HIS AGES-LONG TYRANNY...
...A NEW ORDER SHALL TRIUMPH!
THE SAVIOR WILL LIBERATE US!
APOKOLIPS SHALL BE FREE!
16

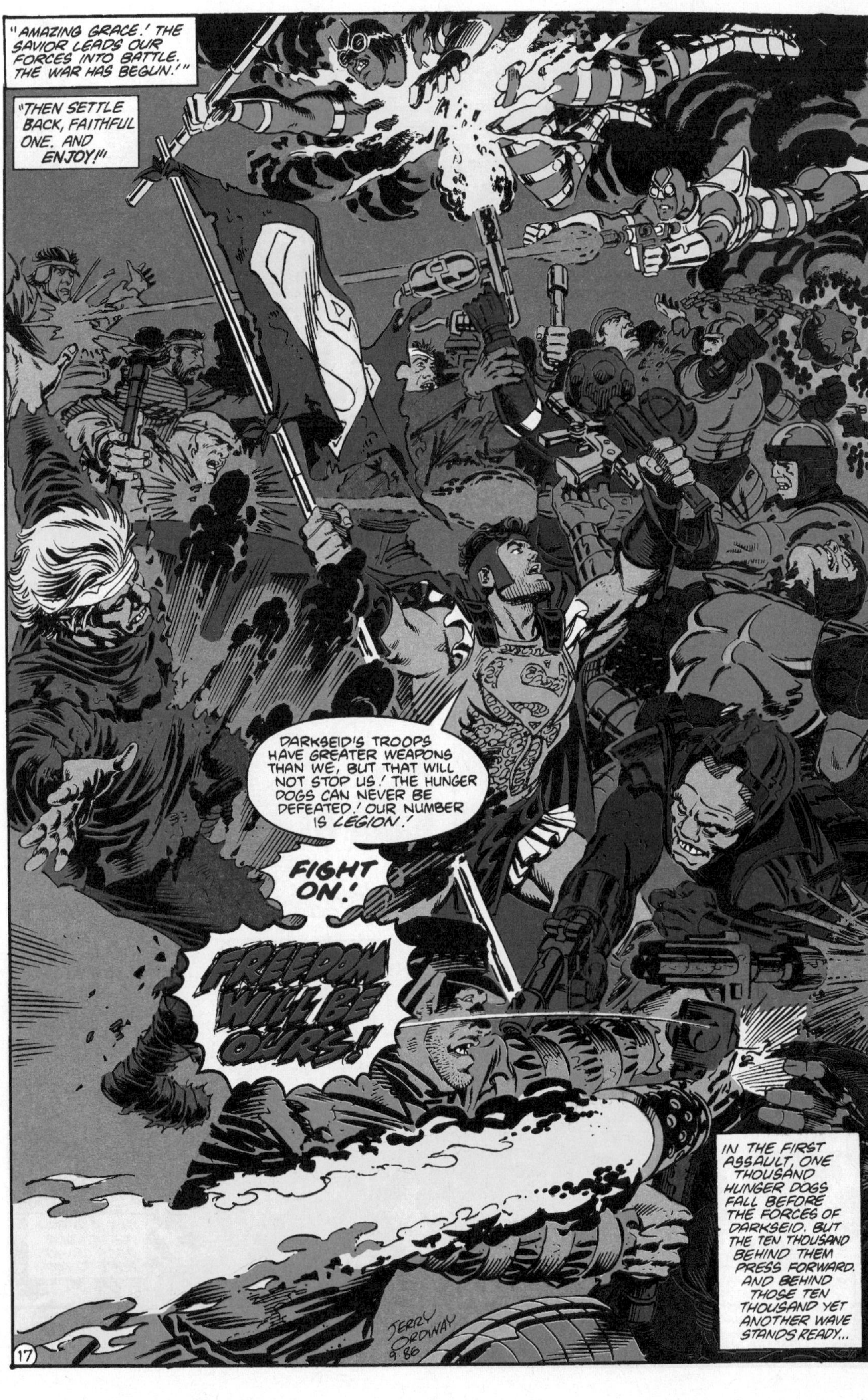
"AMAZING GRACE! THE SAVIOR LEADS OUR FORCES INTO BATTLE. THE WAR HAS BEGUN!"
"THEN SETTLE BACK, FAITHFUL ONE. AND ENJOY!"
DARKSEID'S TROOPS HAVE GREATER WEAPONS THAN WE, BUT THAT WILL NOT STOP US! THE HUNGER DOGS CAN NEVER BE DEFEATED! OUR NUMBER IS LEGION!
FIGHT ON!
FREEDOM WILL BE OURS!
IN THE FIRST ASSAULT, ONE THOUSAND HUNGER DOGS FALL BEFORE THE FORCES OF DARKSEID. BUT THE TEN THOUSAND BEHIND THEM PRESS FORWARD. AND BEHIND THOSE TEN THOUSAND YET ANOTHER WAVE STANDS READY...
JERRY ORDWAY 9-86
17

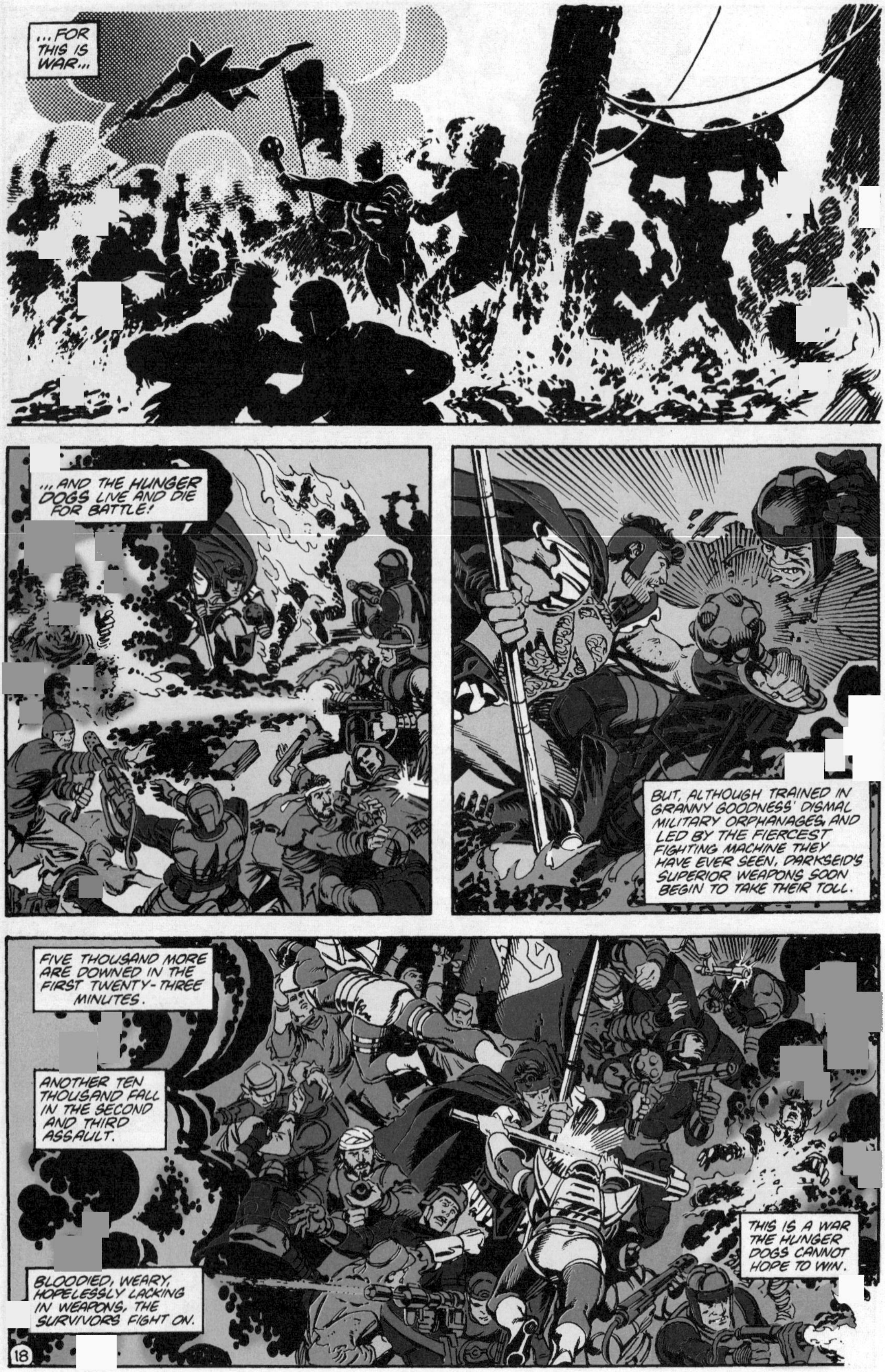
...FOR THIS IS WAR...
...AND THE HUNGER DOGS LIVE AND DIE FOR BATTLE!
BUT, ALTHOUGH TRAINED IN GRANNY GOODNESS' DISMAL MILITARY ORPHANAGES, AND LED BY THE FIERCEST FIGHTING MACHINE THEY HAVE EVER SEEN, DARKSEID'S SUPERIOR WEAPONS SOON BEGIN TO TAKE THEIR TOLL.
FIVE THOUSAND MORE ARE DOWNED IN THE FIRST TWENTY-THREE MINUTES.
ANOTHER TEN THOUSAND FALL IN THE SECOND AND THIRD ASSAULT.
THIS IS A WAR THE HUNGER DOGS CANNOT HOPE TO WIN.
BLOODIED, WEARY, HOPELESSLY LACKING IN WEAPONS, THE SURVIVORS FIGHT ON.
18

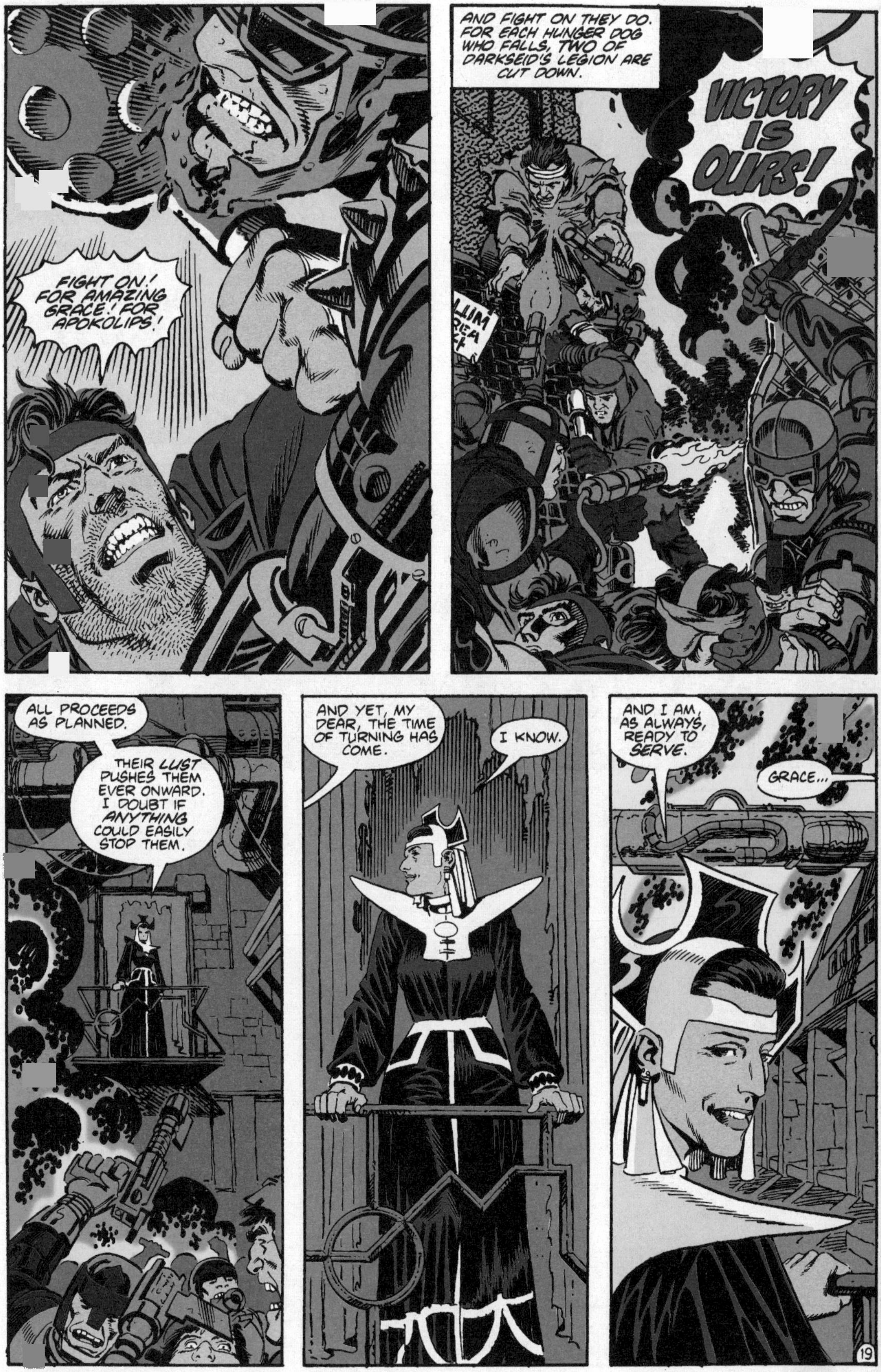

FIGHT ON! FOR AMAZING GRACE! FOR APOKOLIPS!
AND FIGHT ON THEY DO. FOR EACH HUNGER DOG WHO FALLS, TWO OF DARKSEID'S LEGION ARE CUT DOWN.
VICTORY IS OURS!
ALL PROCEEDS AS PLANNED.
THEIR LUST PUSHES THEM EVER ONWARD. I DOUBT IF ANYTHING COULD EASILY STOP THEM.
AND YET, MY DEAR, THE TIME OF TURNING HAS COME.
I KNOW.
AND I AM, AS ALWAYS, READY TO SERVE.
GRACE...
19

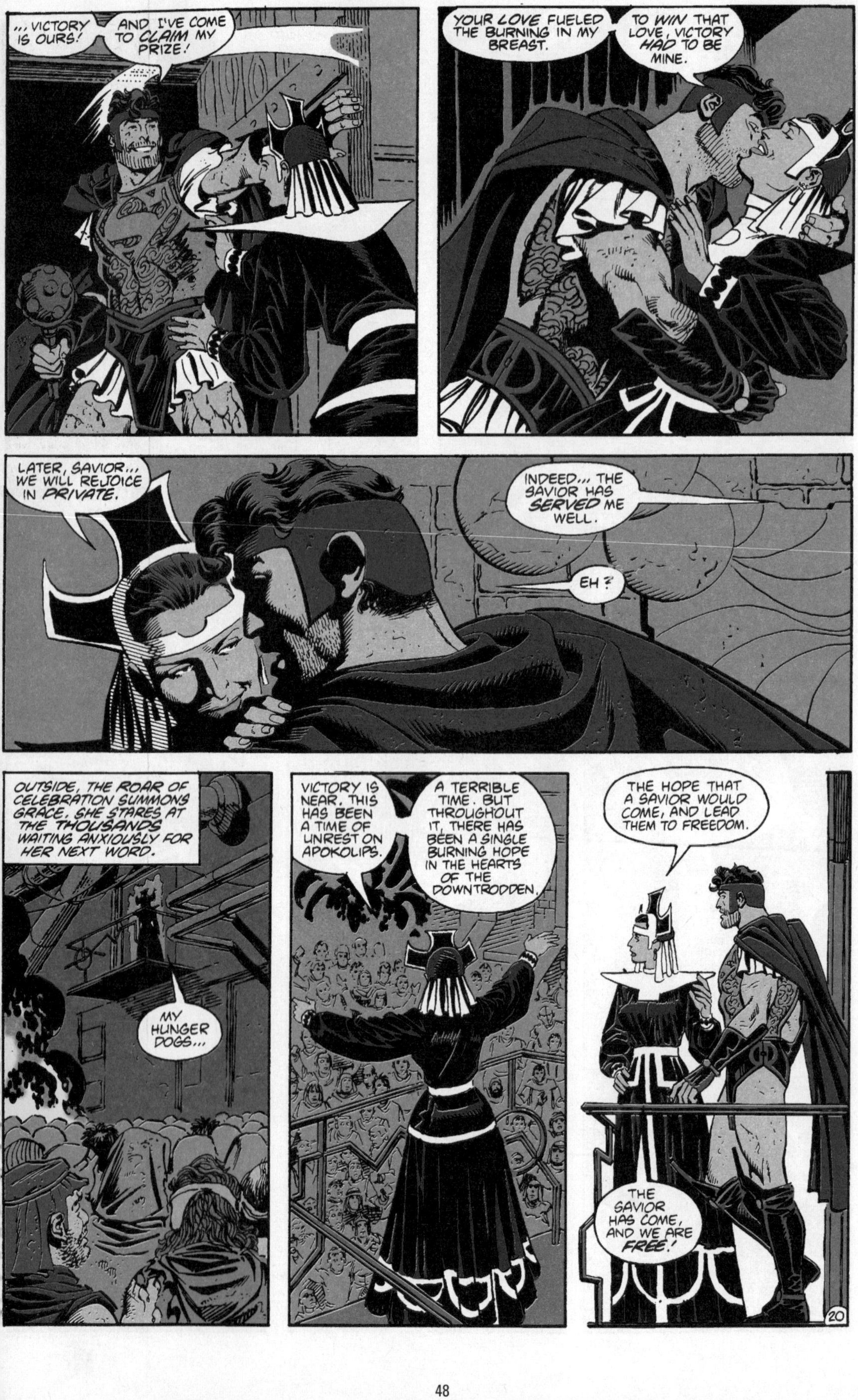
...VICTORY IS OURS!
AND I'VE COME TO CLAIM MY PRIZE!
YOUR LOVE FUELED THE BURNING IN MY BREAST.
TO WIN THAT LOVE, VICTORY HAD TO BE MINE.
LATER, SAVIOR... WE WILL REJOICE IN PRIVATE.
INDEED... THE SAVIOR HAS SERVED ME WELL.
EH?
OUTSIDE, THE ROAR OF CELEBRATION SUMMONS GRACE. SHE STARES AT THE THOUSANDS WAITING ANXIOUSLY FOR HER NEXT WORD.
MY HUNGER DOGS...
VICTORY IS NEAR. THIS HAS BEEN A TIME OF UNREST ON APOKOLIPS.
A TERRIBLE TIME. BUT THROUGHOUT IT, THERE HAS BEEN A SINGLE BURNING HOPE IN THE HEARTS OF THE DOWNTRODDEN.
THE HOPE THAT A SAVIOR WOULD COME, AND LEAD THEM TO FREEDOM.
THE SAVIOR HAS COME, AND WE ARE FREE!
20

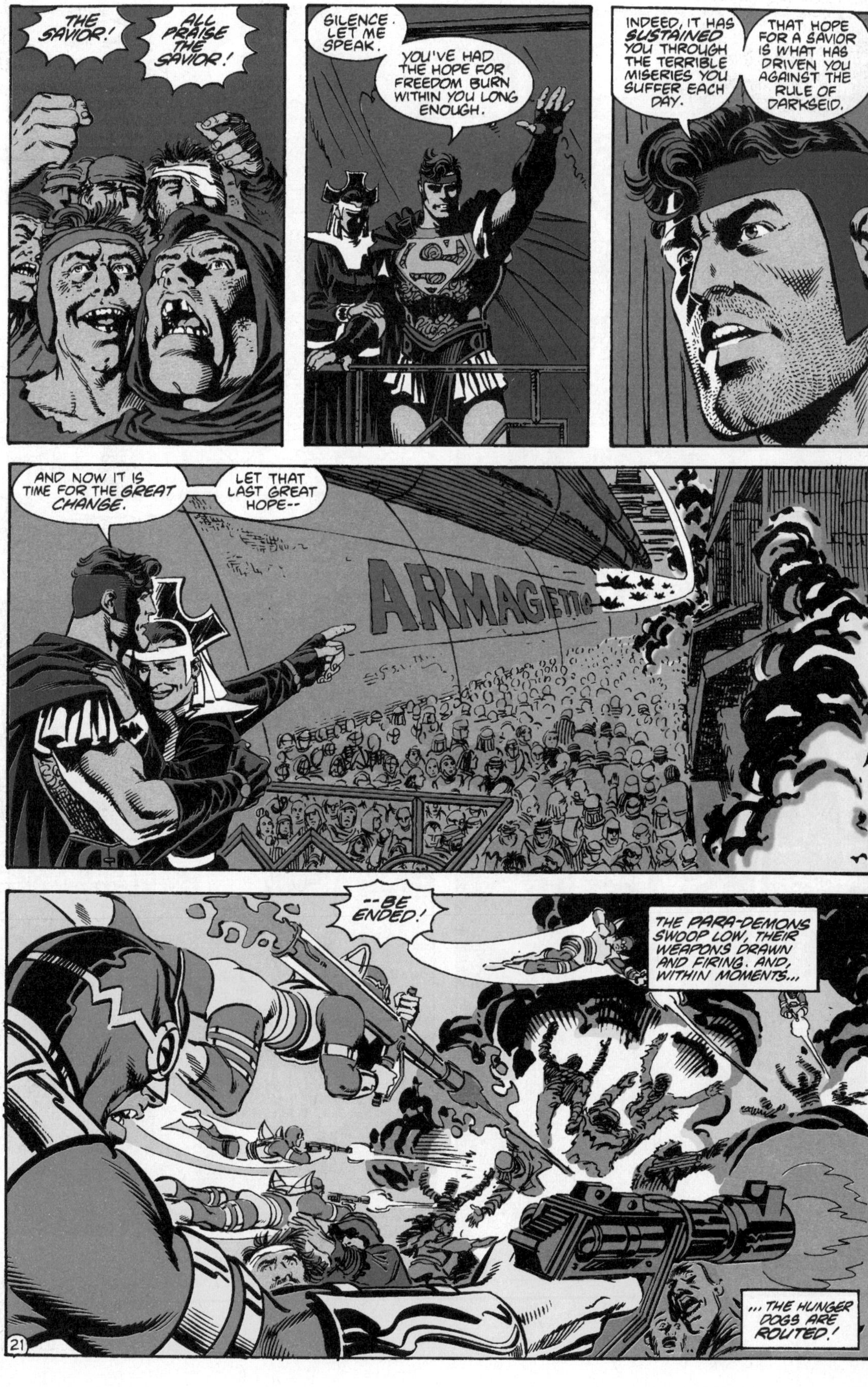
THE SAVIOR!
ALL PRAISE THE SAVIOR!
SILENCE. LET ME SPEAK.
YOU'VE HAD THE HOPE FOR FREEDOM BURN WITHIN YOU LONG ENOUGH.
INDEED, IT HAS SUSTAINED YOU THROUGH THE TERRIBLE MISERIES YOU SUFFER EACH DAY.
THAT HOPE FOR A SAVIOR IS WHAT HAS DRIVEN YOU AGAINST THE RULE OF DARKSEID.
AND NOW IT IS TIME FOR THE GREAT CHANGE.
LET THAT LAST GREAT HOPE--
ARMAGETTO
--BE ENDED!
THE PARA-DEMONS SWOOP LOW, THEIR WEAPONS DRAWN AND FIRING. AND, WITHIN MOMENTS...
...THE HUNGER DOGS ARE ROUTED!
21

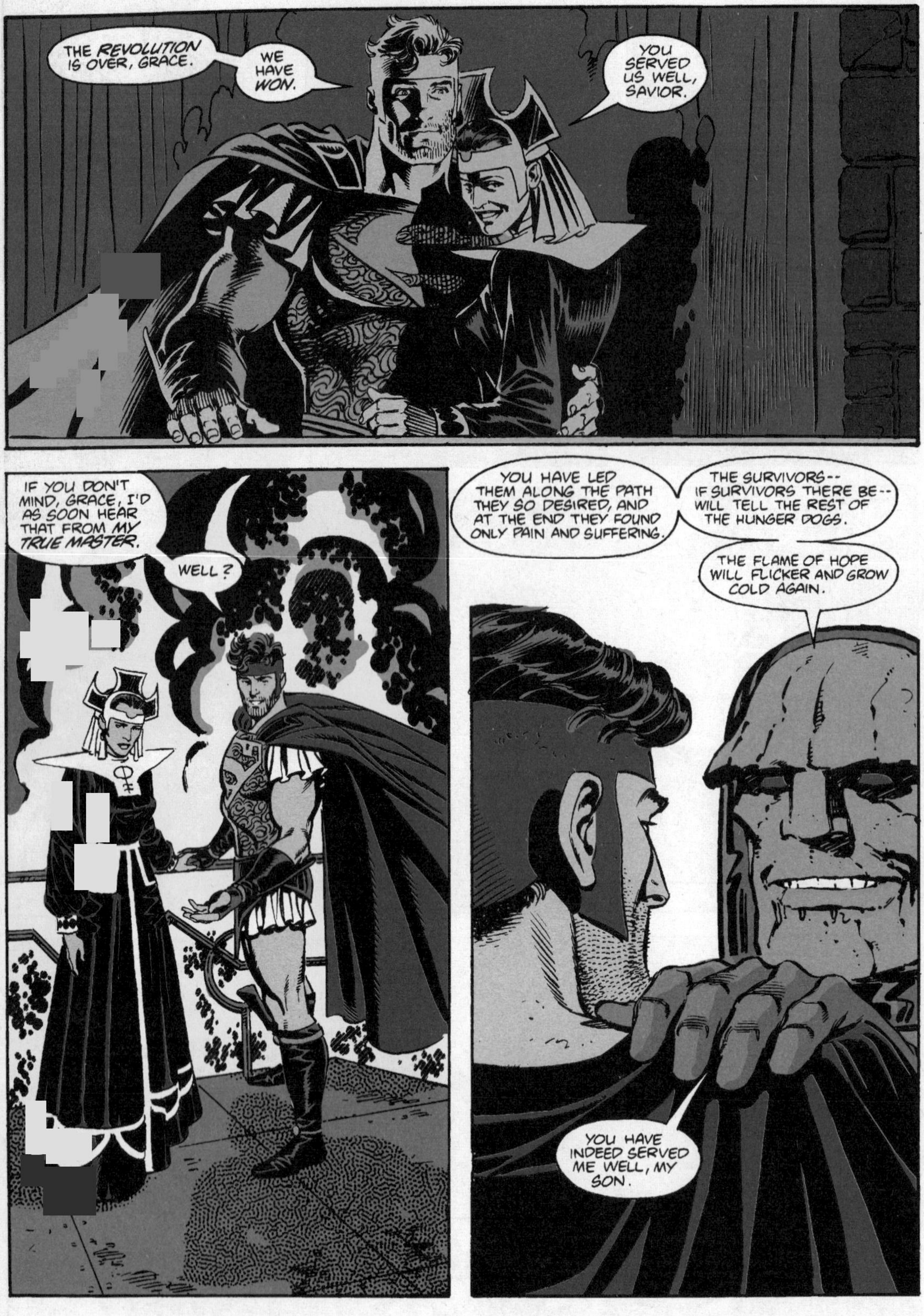

THE *REVOLUTION* IS OVER, GRACE.
WE HAVE *WON*.
YOU SERVED US WELL, SAVIOR.
IF YOU DON'T MIND, GRACE, I'D AS SOON HEAR THAT FROM *MY TRUE MASTER*.
WELL?
YOU HAVE LED THEM ALONG THE PATH THEY SO DESIRED, AND AT THE END THEY FOUND ONLY PAIN AND SUFFERING.
THE SURVIVORS-- IF SURVIVORS THERE BE-- WILL TELL THE REST OF THE HUNGER DOGS.
THE FLAME OF HOPE WILL FLICKER AND GROW COLD AGAIN.
YOU HAVE INDEED SERVED ME WELL, MY SON.

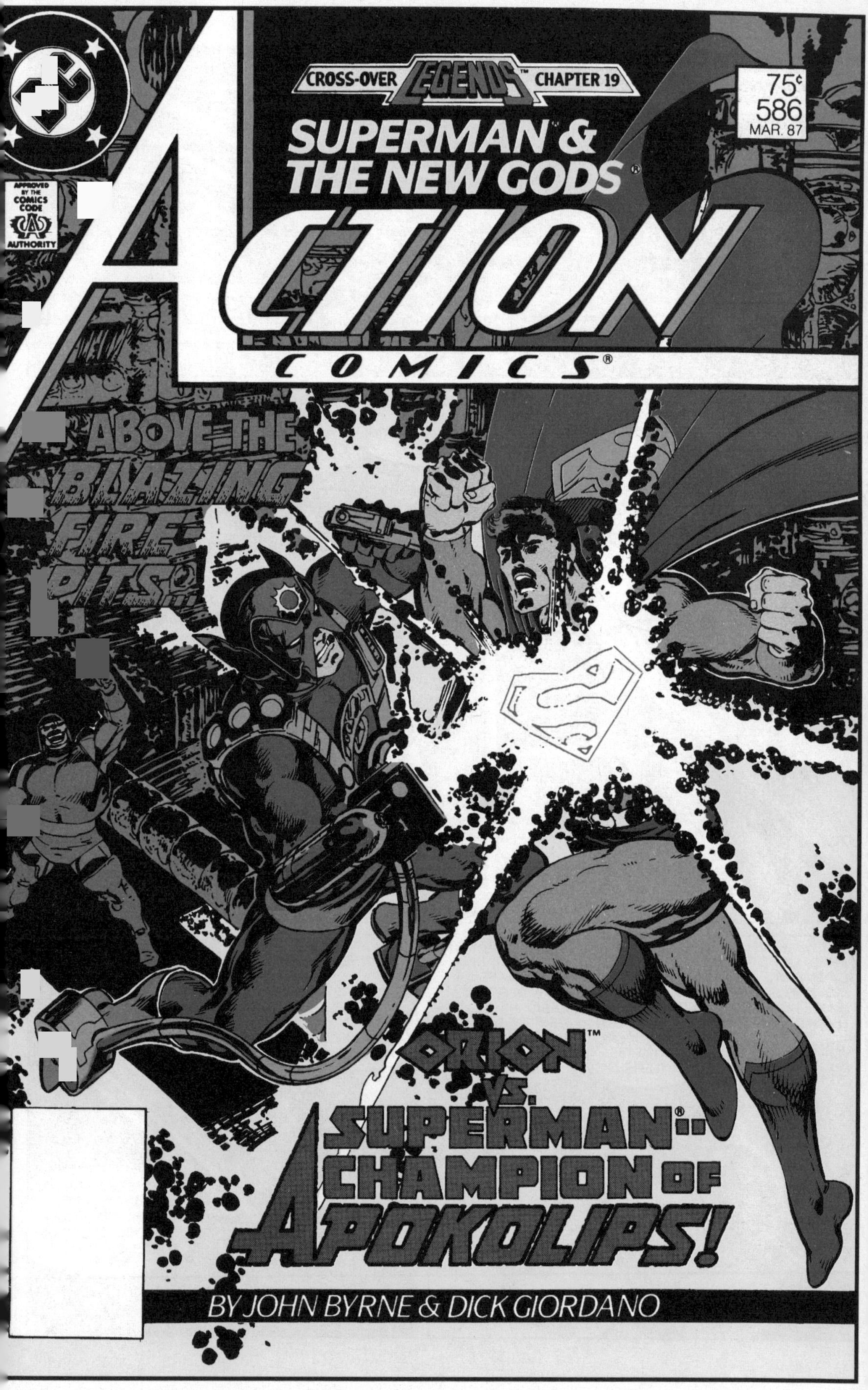

CROSS-OVER LEGENDS CHAPTER 19
75¢
586
MAR. 87
SUPERMAN & THE NEW GODS
ACTION COMICS
ABOVE THE BLAZING FIRE-PITS...
ORION VS. SUPERMAN.. CHAMPION OF APOKOLIPS!
BY JOHN BYRNE & DICK GIORDANO
APPROVED BY THE COMICS CODE AUTHORITY

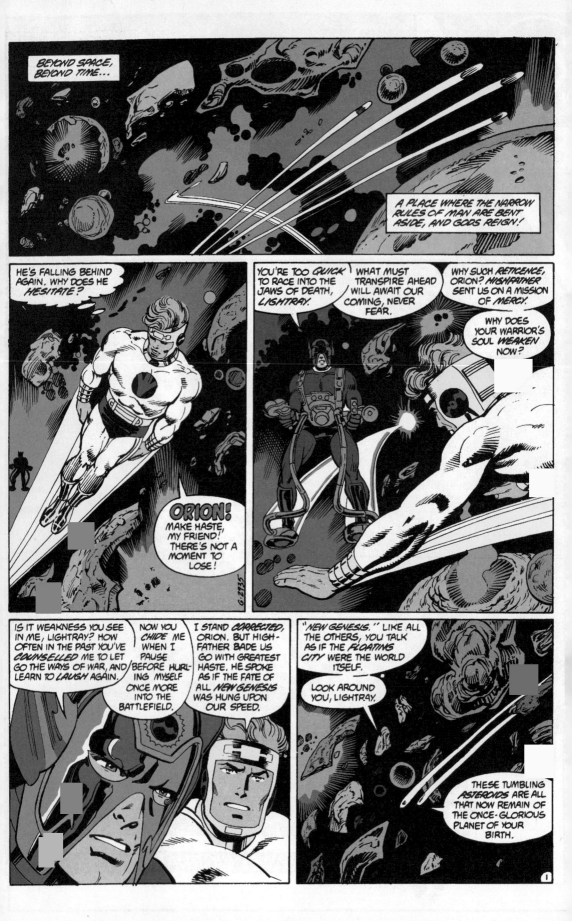

BEYOND SPACE, BEYOND TIME...

A PLACE WHERE THE NARROW RULES OF MAN ARE BENT ASIDE, AND GODS REIGN!

HE'S FALLING BEHIND AGAIN. WHY DOES HE HESITATE?

ORION! MAKE HASTE, MY FRIEND! THERE'S NOT A MOMENT TO LOSE!

YOU'RE TOO QUICK TO RACE INTO THE JAWS OF DEATH, LIGHTRAY.

WHAT MUST TRANSPIRE AHEAD WILL AWAIT OUR COMING, NEVER FEAR.

WHY SUCH RETICENCE, ORION? HIGHFATHER SENT US ON A MISSION OF MERCY.

WHY DOES YOUR WARRIOR'S SOUL WEAKEN NOW?

IS IT WEAKNESS YOU SEE IN ME, LIGHTRAY? HOW OFTEN IN THE PAST YOU'VE COUNSELLED ME TO LET GO THE WAYS OF WAR, AND LEARN TO LAUGH AGAIN.

NOW YOU CHIDE ME WHEN I PAUSE BEFORE HURLING MYSELF ONCE MORE INTO THE BATTLEFIELD.

I STAND CORRECTED, ORION, BUT HIGH-FATHER BADE US GO WITH GREATEST HASTE. HE SPOKE AS IF THE FATE OF ALL NEW GENESIS WAS HUNG UPON OUR SPEED.

"NEW GENESIS," LIKE ALL THE OTHERS, YOU TALK AS IF THE FLOATING CITY WERE THE WORLD ITSELF.

LOOK AROUND YOU, LIGHTRAY.

THESE TUMBLING ASTEROIDS ARE ALL THAT NOW REMAIN OF THE ONCE-GLORIOUS PLANET OF YOUR BIRTH.

1

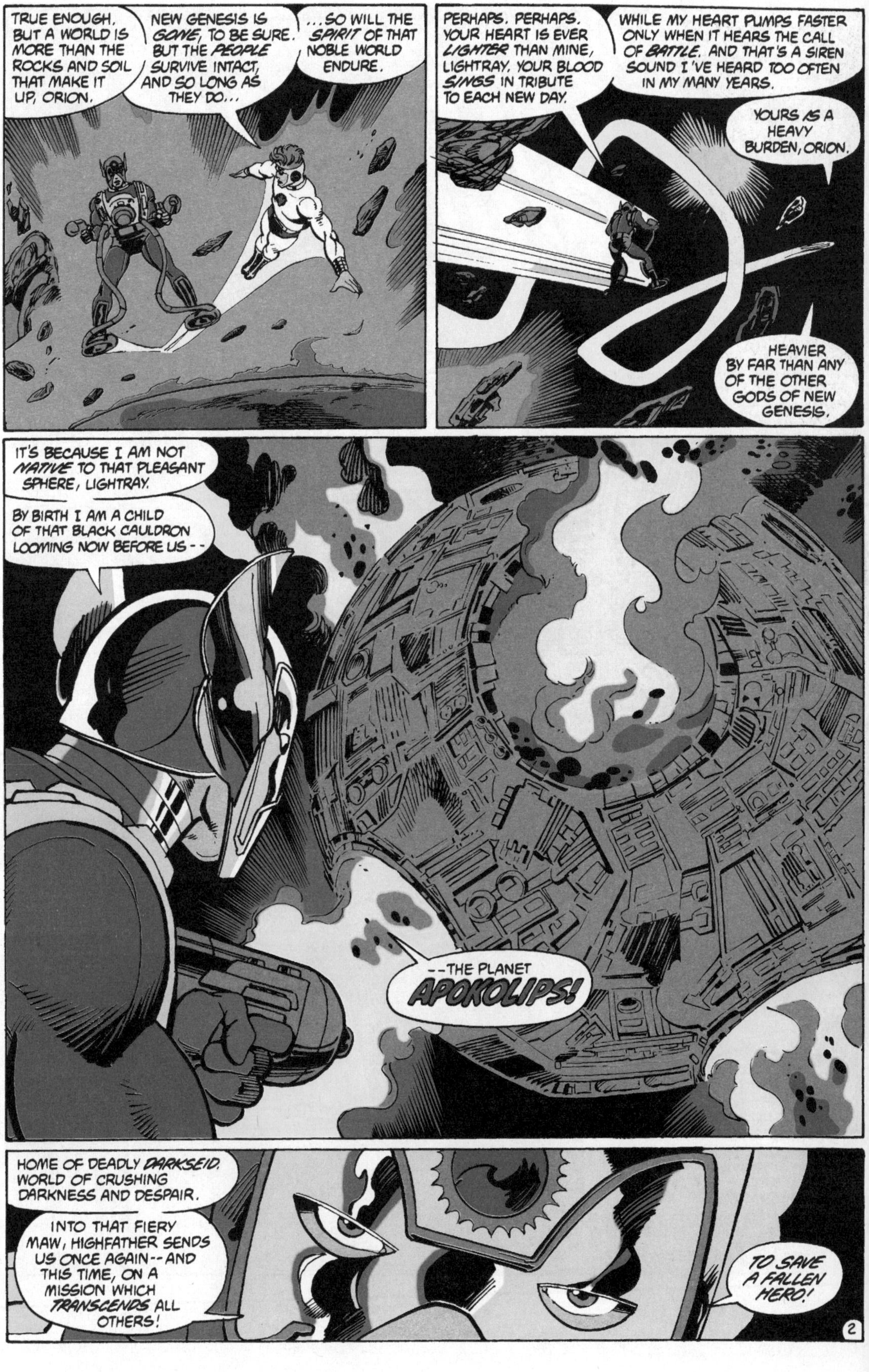
TRUE ENOUGH. BUT A WORLD IS MORE THAN THE ROCKS AND SOIL THAT MAKE IT UP, ORION.
NEW GENESIS IS GONE, TO BE SURE. BUT THE PEOPLE SURVIVE INTACT, AND SO LONG AS THEY DO...
...SO WILL THE SPIRIT OF THAT NOBLE WORLD ENDURE.
PERHAPS. PERHAPS. YOUR HEART IS EVER LIGHTER THAN MINE, LIGHTRAY. YOUR BLOOD SINGS IN TRIBUTE TO EACH NEW DAY.
WHILE MY HEART PUMPS FASTER ONLY WHEN IT HEARS THE CALL OF BATTLE. AND THAT'S A SIREN SOUND I'VE HEARD TOO OFTEN IN MY MANY YEARS.
YOURS IS A HEAVY BURDEN, ORION.
HEAVIER BY FAR THAN ANY OF THE OTHER GODS OF NEW GENESIS.
IT'S BECAUSE I AM NOT NATIVE TO THAT PLEASANT SPHERE, LIGHTRAY.
BY BIRTH I AM A CHILD OF THAT BLACK CAULDRON LOOMING NOW BEFORE US--
--THE PLANET APOKOLIPS!
HOME OF DEADLY DARKSEID. WORLD OF CRUSHING DARKNESS AND DESPAIR.
INTO THAT FIERY MAW, HIGHFATHER SENDS US ONCE AGAIN--AND THIS TIME, ON A MISSION WHICH TRANSCENDS ALL OTHERS!
TO SAVE A FALLEN HERO!
2

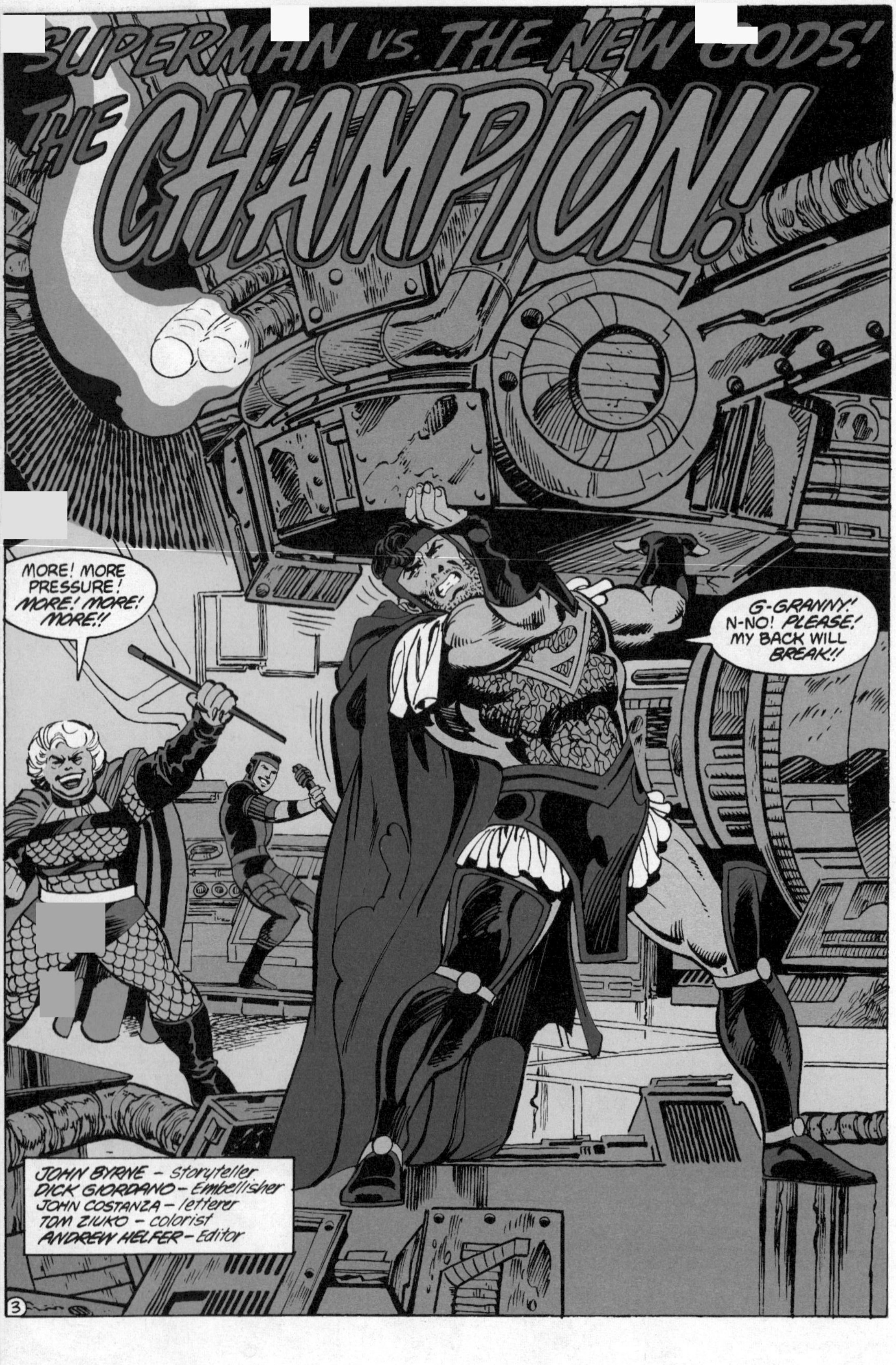
SUPERMAN VS. THE NEW GODS!
THE CHAMPION!
MORE! MORE PRESSURE! MORE! MORE! MORE!!
G-GRANNY! N-NO! PLEASE! MY BACK WILL BREAK!!
JOHN BYRNE - Storyteller
DICK GIORDANO - Embellisher
JOHN COSTANZA - letterer
TOM ZIUKO - colorist
ANDREW HELFER - Editor
3

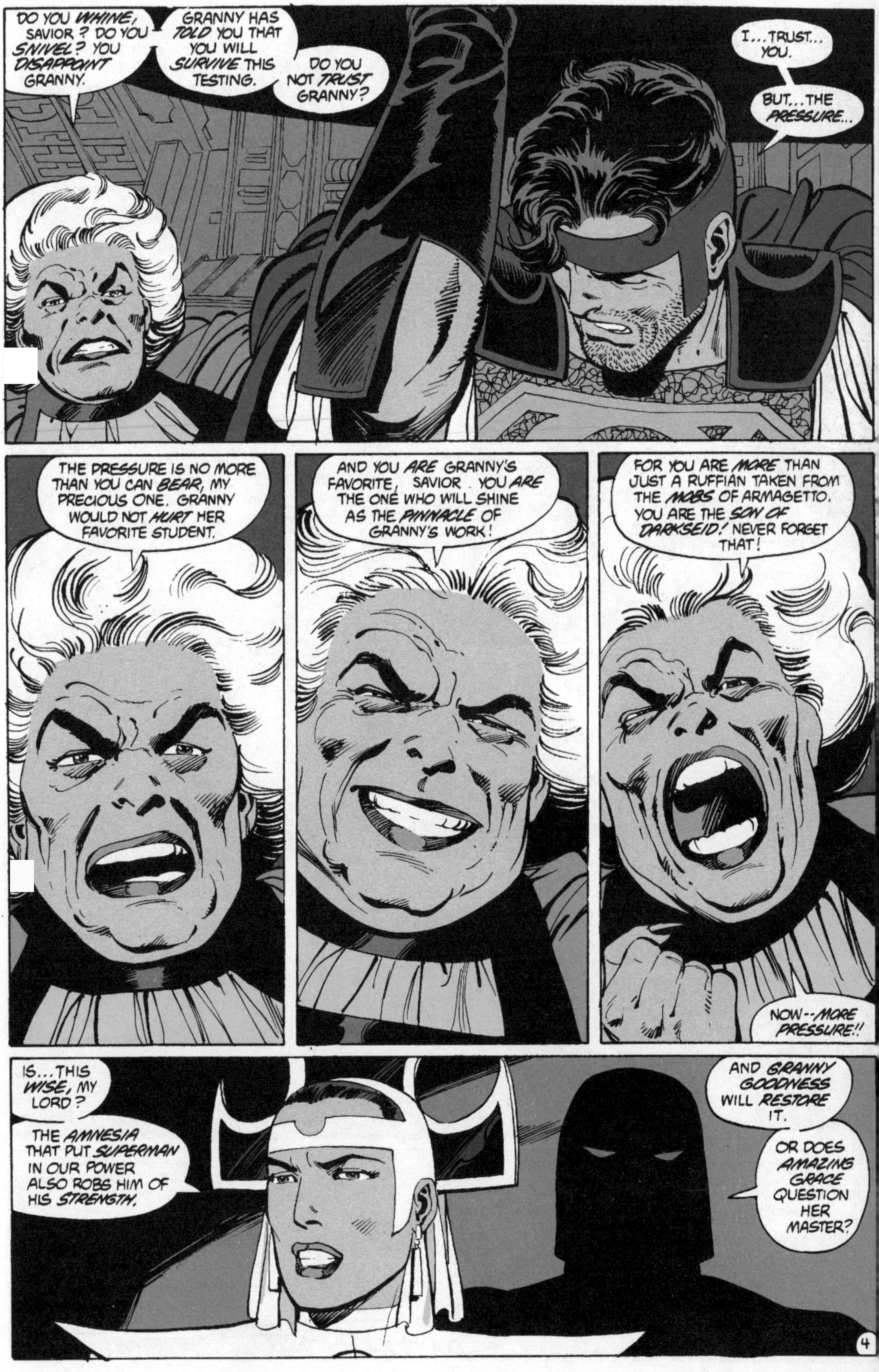
DO YOU WHINE, SAVIOR? DO YOU SNIVEL? YOU DISAPPOINT GRANNY.
GRANNY HAS TOLD YOU THAT YOU WILL SURVIVE THIS TESTING.
DO YOU NOT TRUST GRANNY?
I...TRUST... YOU.
BUT...THE PRESSURE...
THE PRESSURE IS NO MORE THAN YOU CAN BEAR, MY PRECIOUS ONE. GRANNY WOULD NOT HURT HER FAVORITE STUDENT.
AND YOU ARE GRANNY'S FAVORITE, SAVIOR. YOU ARE THE ONE WHO WILL SHINE AS THE PINNACLE OF GRANNY'S WORK!
FOR YOU ARE MORE THAN JUST A RUFFIAN TAKEN FROM THE MOBS OF ARMAGETTO. YOU ARE THE SON OF DARKSEID! NEVER FORGET THAT!
NOW--MORE PRESSURE!!
IS...THIS WISE, MY LORD?
THE AMNESIA THAT PUT SUPERMAN IN OUR POWER ALSO ROBS HIM OF HIS STRENGTH.
AND GRANNY GOODNESS WILL RESTORE IT.
OR DOES AMAZING GRACE QUESTION HER MASTER?
4

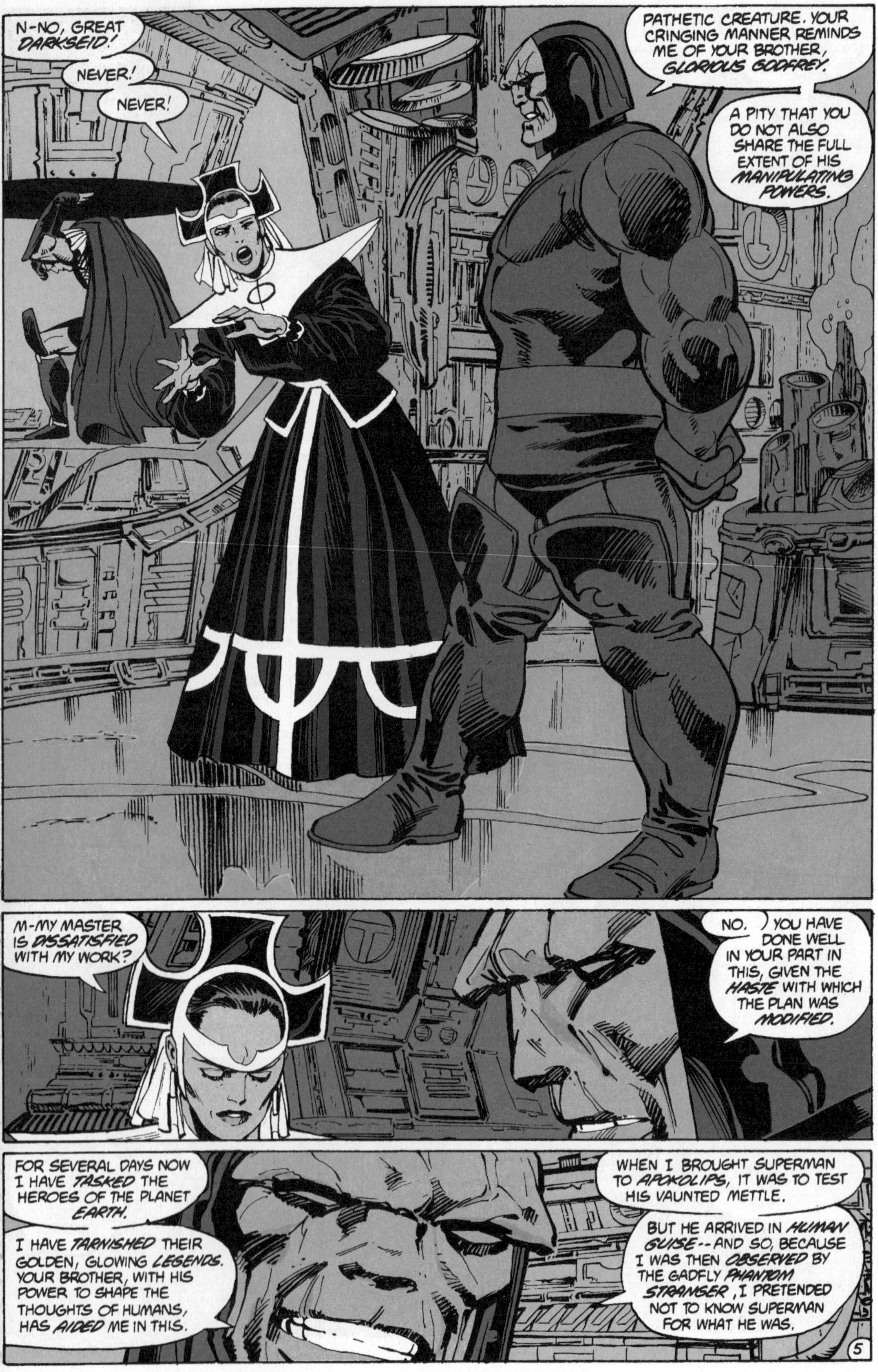
N-NO, GREAT DARKSEID!
NEVER!
NEVER!
PATHETIC CREATURE. YOUR CRINGING MANNER REMINDS ME OF YOUR BROTHER, GLORIOUS GODFREY.
A PITY THAT YOU DO NOT ALSO SHARE THE FULL EXTENT OF HIS MANIPULATING POWERS.
M-MY MASTER IS DISSATISFIED WITH MY WORK?
NO.
YOU HAVE DONE WELL IN YOUR PART IN THIS, GIVEN THE HASTE WITH WHICH THE PLAN WAS MODIFIED.
FOR SEVERAL DAYS NOW I HAVE TASKED THE HEROES OF THE PLANET EARTH.
I HAVE TARNISHED THEIR GOLDEN, GLOWING LEGENDS. YOUR BROTHER, WITH HIS POWER TO SHAPE THE THOUGHTS OF HUMANS, HAS AIDED ME IN THIS.
WHEN I BROUGHT SUPERMAN TO APOKOLIPS, IT WAS TO TEST HIS VAUNTED METTLE.
BUT HE ARRIVED IN HUMAN GUISE--AND SO, BECAUSE I WAS THEN OBSERVED BY THE GADFLY PHANTOM STRANGER, I PRETENDED NOT TO KNOW SUPERMAN FOR WHAT HE WAS.
5

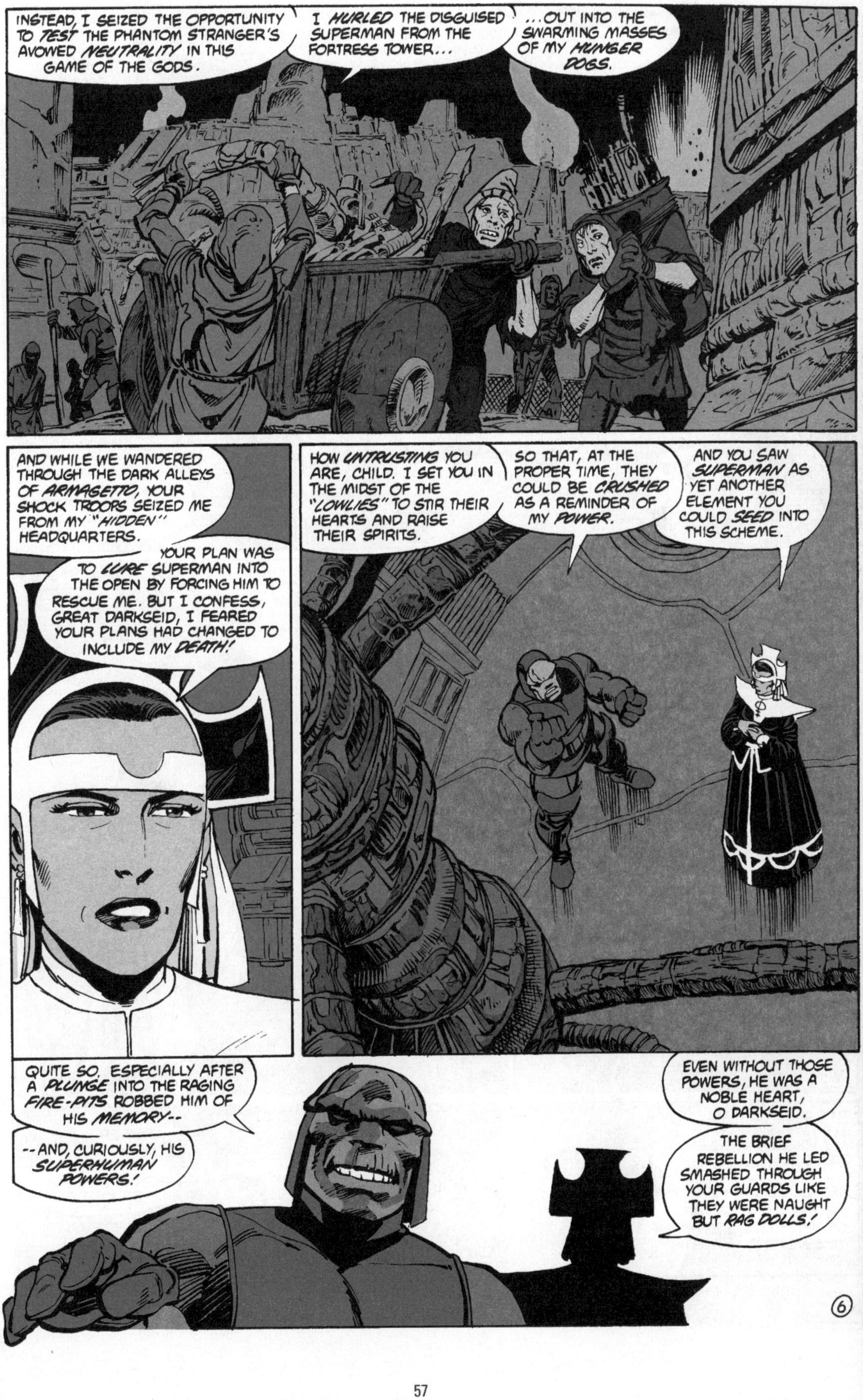

INSTEAD, I SEIZED THE OPPORTUNITY TO TEST THE PHANTOM STRANGER'S AVOWED NEUTRALITY IN THIS GAME OF THE GODS.
I HURLED THE DISGUISED SUPERMAN FROM THE FORTRESS TOWER...
...OUT INTO THE SWARMING MASSES OF MY HUNGER DOGS.
AND WHILE WE WANDERED THROUGH THE DARK ALLEYS OF ARMAGETTO, YOUR SHOCK TROOPS SEIZED ME FROM MY "HIDDEN" HEADQUARTERS.
YOUR PLAN WAS TO LURE SUPERMAN INTO THE OPEN BY FORCING HIM TO RESCUE ME. BUT I CONFESS, GREAT DARKSEID, I FEARED YOUR PLANS HAD CHANGED TO INCLUDE MY DEATH!
HOW UNTRUSTING YOU ARE, CHILD. I SET YOU IN THE MIDST OF THE "LOWLIES" TO STIR THEIR HEARTS AND RAISE THEIR SPIRITS.
SO THAT, AT THE PROPER TIME, THEY COULD BE CRUSHED AS A REMINDER OF MY POWER.
AND YOU SAW SUPERMAN AS YET ANOTHER ELEMENT YOU COULD SEED INTO THIS SCHEME.
QUITE SO. ESPECIALLY AFTER A PLUNGE INTO THE RAGING FIRE-PITS ROBBED HIM OF HIS MEMORY--
--AND, CURIOUSLY, HIS SUPERHUMAN POWERS!
EVEN WITHOUT THOSE POWERS, HE WAS A NOBLE HEART, O DARKSEID.
THE BRIEF REBELLION HE LED SMASHED THROUGH YOUR GUARDS LIKE THEY WERE NAUGHT BUT RAG DOLLS!
6

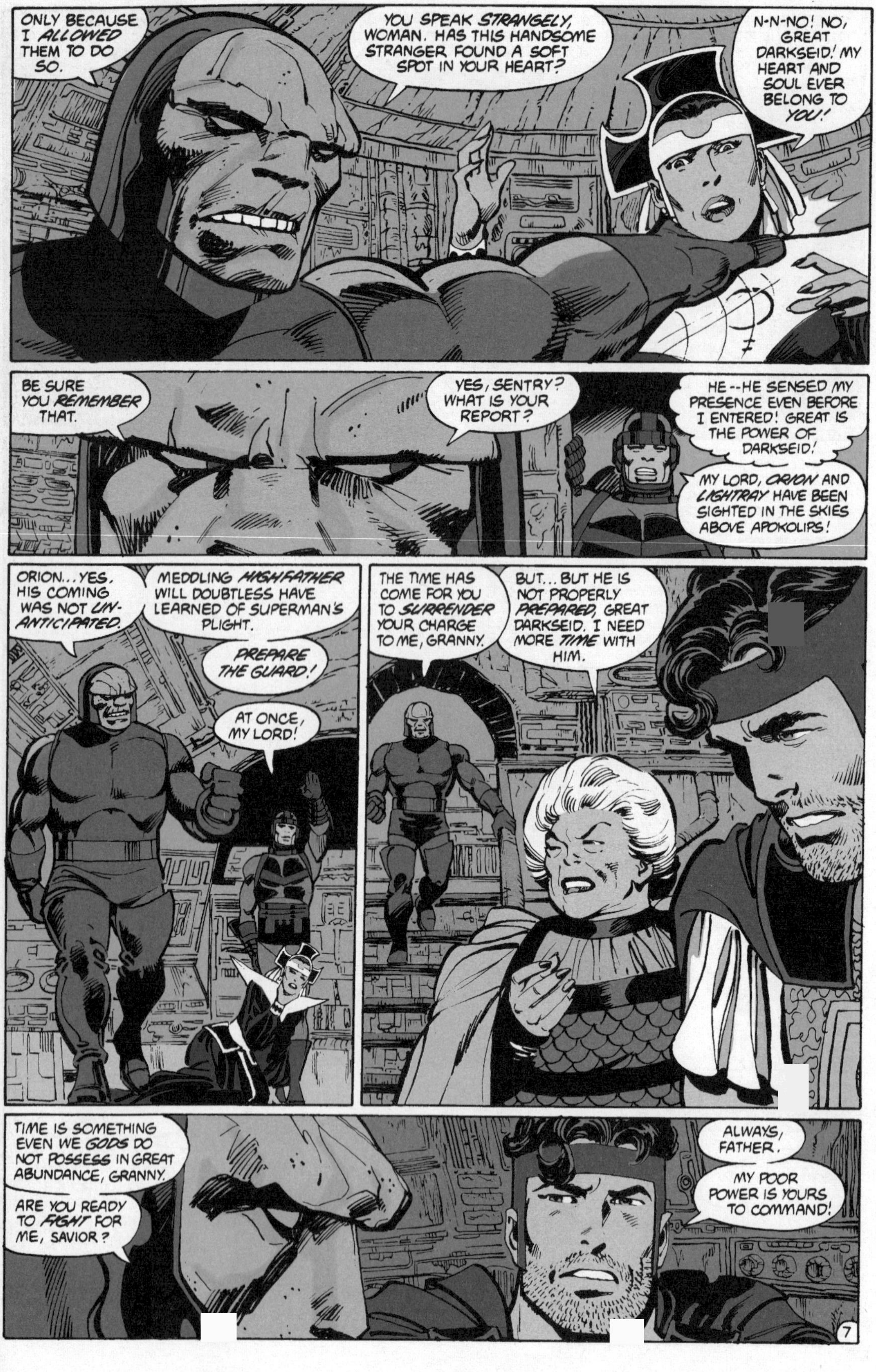
ONLY BECAUSE I ALLOWED THEM TO DO SO.
YOU SPEAK STRANGELY, WOMAN. HAS THIS HANDSOME STRANGER FOUND A SOFT SPOT IN YOUR HEART?
N-N-NO! NO, GREAT DARKSEID! MY HEART AND SOUL EVER BELONG TO YOU!
BE SURE YOU REMEMBER THAT.
YES, SENTRY? WHAT IS YOUR REPORT?
HE--HE SENSED MY PRESENCE EVEN BEFORE I ENTERED! GREAT IS THE POWER OF DARKSEID!
MY LORD, ORION AND LIGHTRAY HAVE BEEN SIGHTED IN THE SKIES ABOVE APOKOLIPS!
ORION... YES. HIS COMING WAS NOT UN-ANTICIPATED.
MEDDLING HIGHFATHER WILL DOUBTLESS HAVE LEARNED OF SUPERMAN'S PLIGHT.
PREPARE THE GUARD!
AT ONCE, MY LORD!
THE TIME HAS COME FOR YOU TO SURRENDER YOUR CHARGE TO ME, GRANNY.
BUT... BUT HE IS NOT PROPERLY PREPARED, GREAT DARKSEID. I NEED MORE TIME WITH HIM.
TIME IS SOMETHING EVEN WE GODS DO NOT POSSESS IN GREAT ABUNDANCE, GRANNY.
ARE YOU READY TO FIGHT FOR ME, SAVIOR?
ALWAYS, FATHER.
MY POOR POWER IS YOURS TO COMMAND!
7

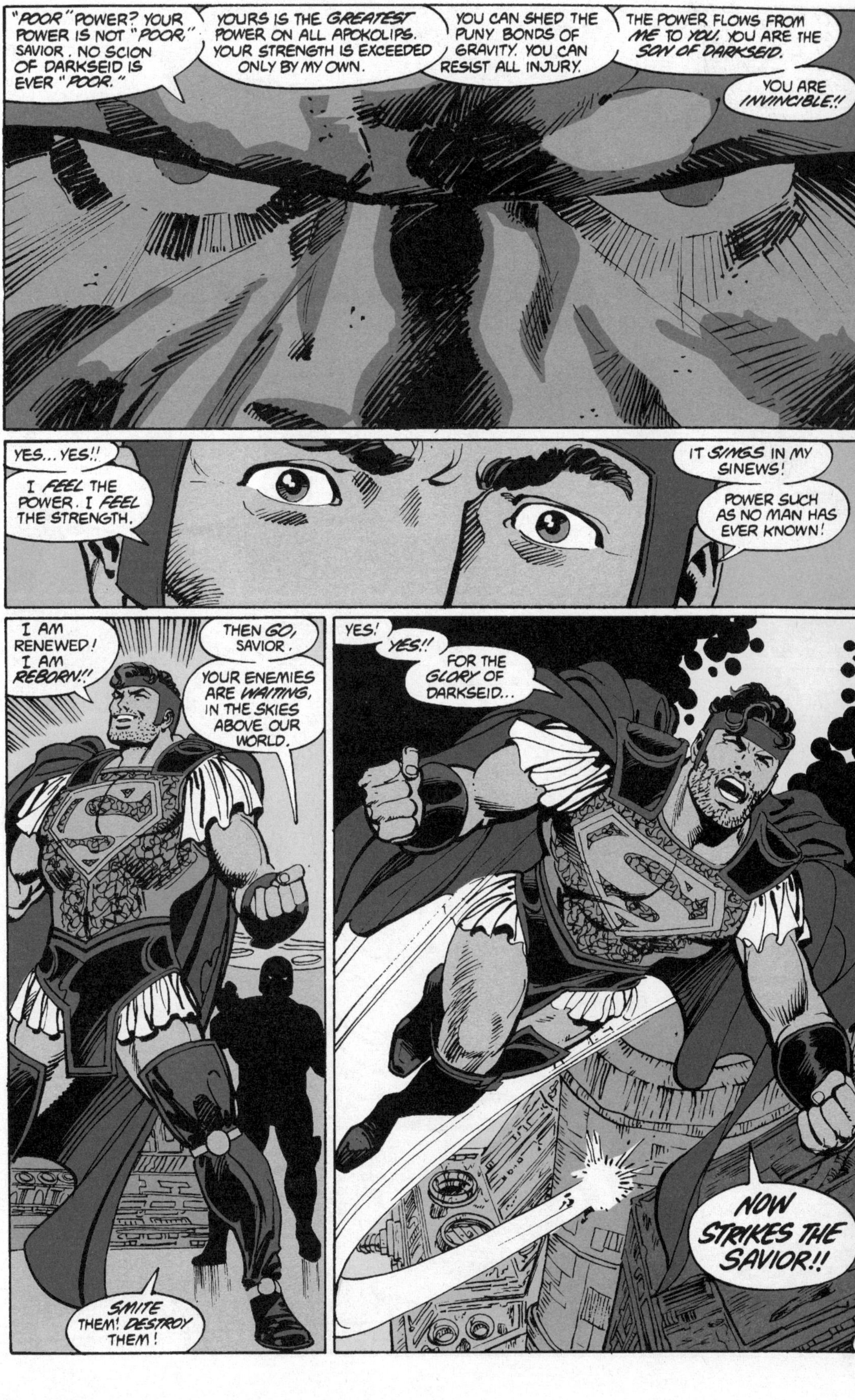
"POOR" POWER? YOUR POWER IS NOT "POOR," SAVIOR. NO SCION OF DARKSEID IS EVER "POOR."
YOURS IS THE GREATEST POWER ON ALL APOKOLIPS. YOUR STRENGTH IS EXCEEDED ONLY BY MY OWN.
YOU CAN SHED THE PUNY BONDS OF GRAVITY. YOU CAN RESIST ALL INJURY.
THE POWER FLOWS FROM ME TO YOU. YOU ARE THE SON OF DARKSEID.
YOU ARE INVINCIBLE!!
YES... YES!!
I FEEL THE POWER. I FEEL THE STRENGTH.
IT SINGS IN MY SINEWS!
POWER SUCH AS NO MAN HAS EVER KNOWN!
I AM RENEWED! I AM REBORN!!
THEN GO, SAVIOR.
YOUR ENEMIES ARE WAITING, IN THE SKIES ABOVE OUR WORLD.
SMITE THEM! DESTROY THEM!
YES!
YES!!
FOR THE GLORY OF DARKSEID...
NOW STRIKES THE SAVIOR!!
8

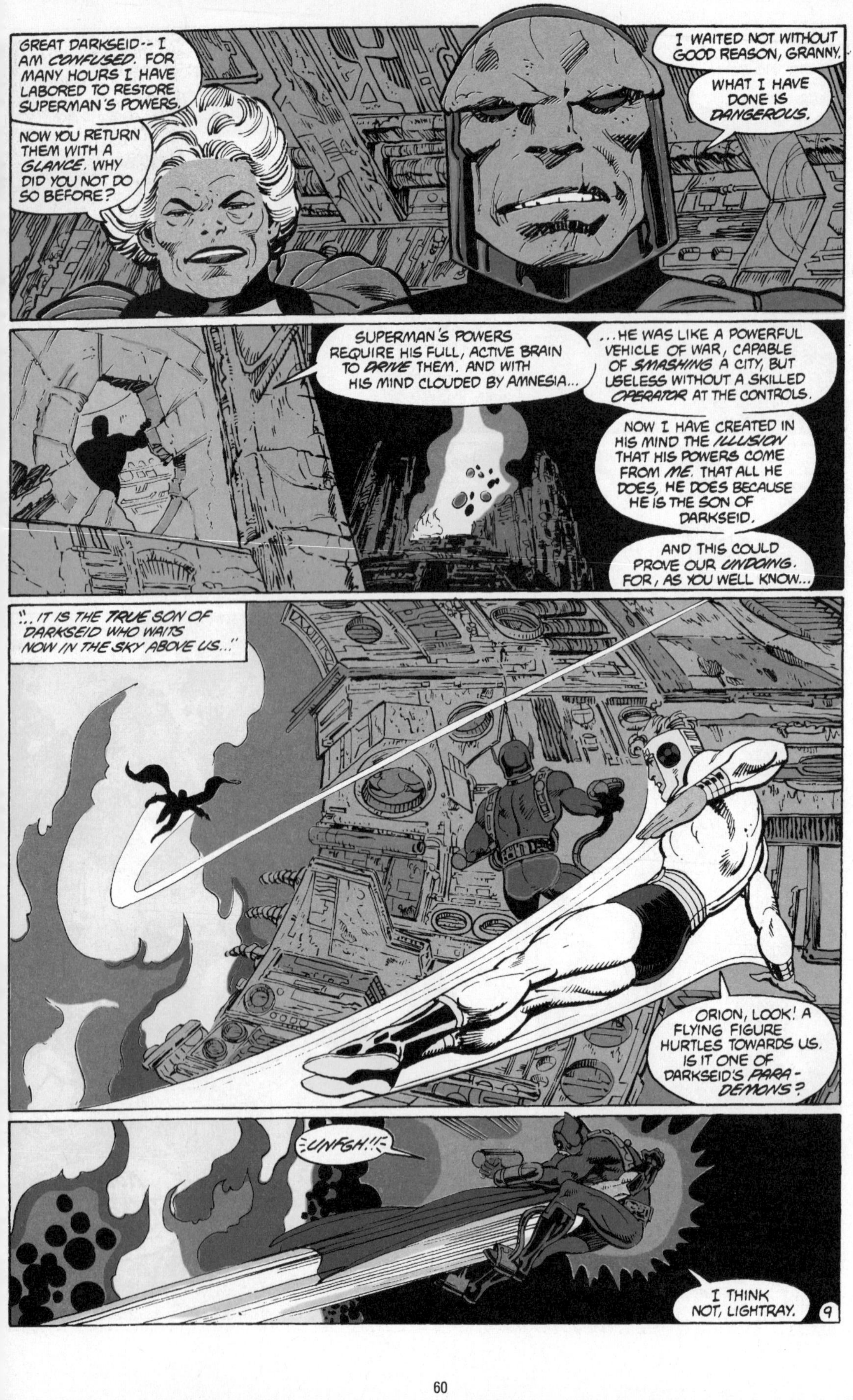
GREAT DARKSEID-- I AM CONFUSED. FOR MANY HOURS I HAVE LABORED TO RESTORE SUPERMAN'S POWERS.
NOW YOU RETURN THEM WITH A GLANCE. WHY DID YOU NOT DO SO BEFORE?
I WAITED NOT WITHOUT GOOD REASON, GRANNY.
WHAT I HAVE DONE IS DANGEROUS.
SUPERMAN'S POWERS REQUIRE HIS FULL, ACTIVE BRAIN TO DRIVE THEM. AND WITH HIS MIND CLOUDED BY AMNESIA...
...HE WAS LIKE A POWERFUL VEHICLE OF WAR, CAPABLE OF SMASHING A CITY, BUT USELESS WITHOUT A SKILLED OPERATOR AT THE CONTROLS.
NOW I HAVE CREATED IN HIS MIND THE ILLUSION THAT HIS POWERS COME FROM ME. THAT ALL HE DOES, HE DOES BECAUSE HE IS THE SON OF DARKSEID.
AND THIS COULD PROVE OUR UNDOING. FOR, AS YOU WELL KNOW...
"...IT IS THE TRUE SON OF DARKSEID WHO WAITS NOW IN THE SKY ABOVE US..."
ORION, LOOK! A FLYING FIGURE HURTLES TOWARDS US. IS IT ONE OF DARKSEID'S PARA-DEMONS?
UNFGH!!
I THINK NOT, LIGHTRAY.
9

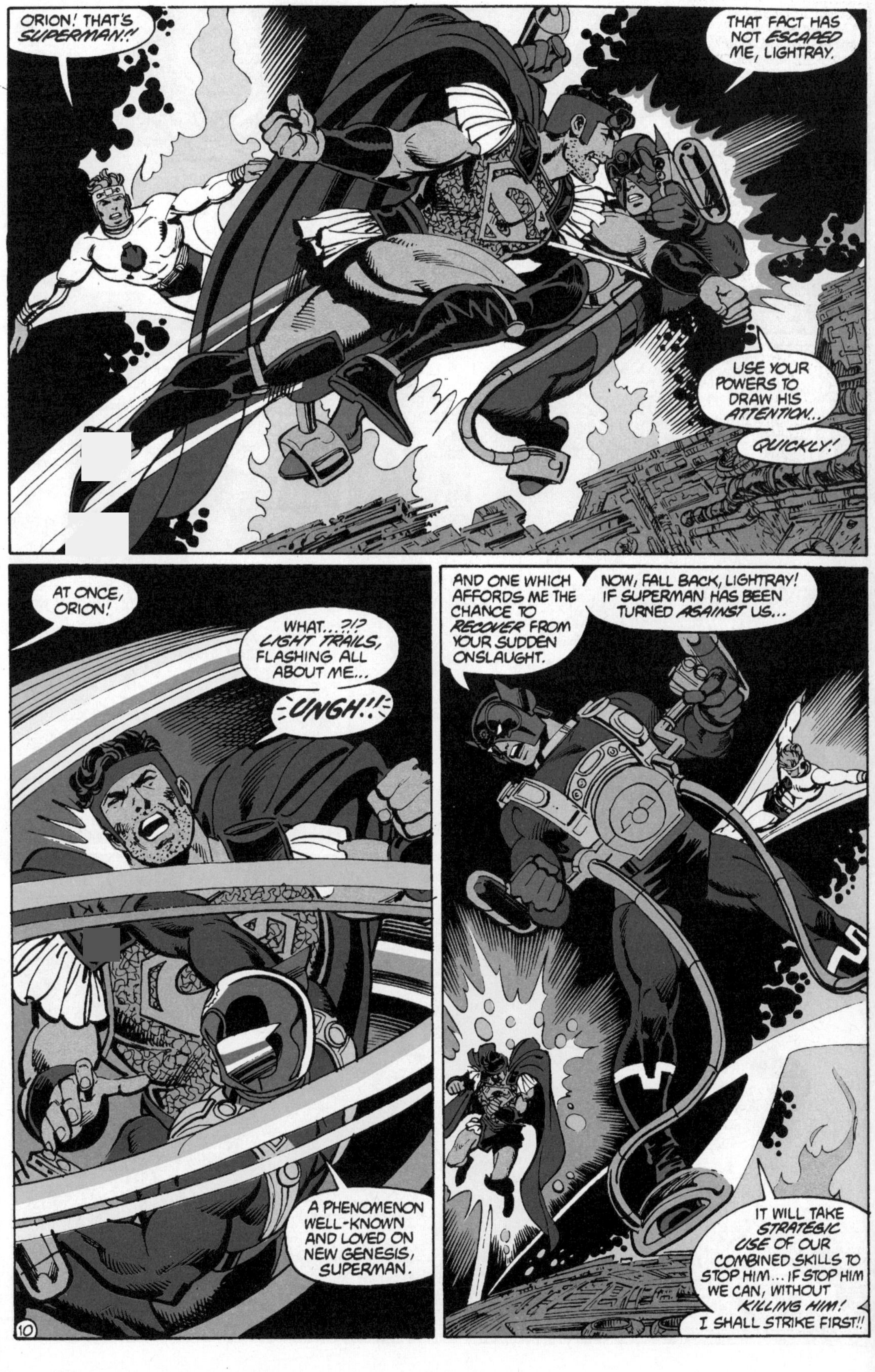

ORION! THAT'S SUPERMAN!!
THAT FACT HAS NOT ESCAPED ME, LIGHTRAY.
USE YOUR POWERS TO DRAW HIS ATTENTION...
QUICKLY!
AT ONCE, ORION!
WHAT...?!? LIGHT TRAILS, FLASHING ALL ABOUT ME...
UNGH!!
A PHENOMENON WELL-KNOWN AND LOVED ON NEW GENESIS, SUPERMAN.
10
AND ONE WHICH AFFORDS ME THE CHANCE TO RECOVER FROM YOUR SUDDEN ONSLAUGHT.
NOW, FALL BACK, LIGHTRAY! IF SUPERMAN HAS BEEN TURNED AGAINST US...
IT WILL TAKE STRATEGIC USE OF OUR COMBINED SKILLS TO STOP HIM... IF STOP HIM WE CAN, WITHOUT KILLING HIM!
I SHALL STRIKE FIRST!!

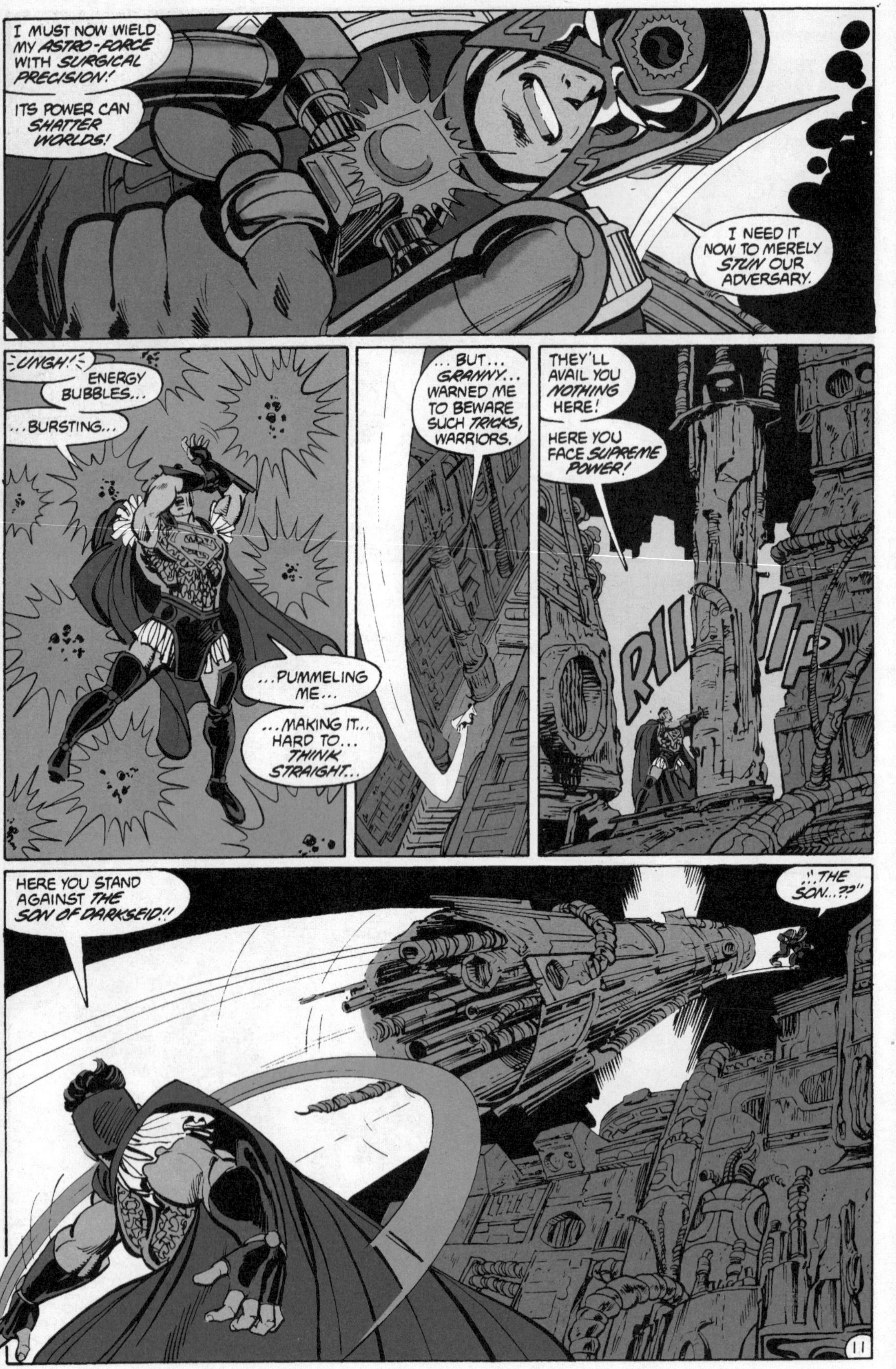
I MUST NOW WIELD MY ASTRO-FORCE WITH SURGICAL PRECISION!
ITS POWER CAN SHATTER WORLDS!
I NEED IT NOW TO MERELY STUN OUR ADVERSARY.
UNGH!
ENERGY BUBBLES...
...BURSTING...
...PUMMELING ME...
...MAKING IT... HARD TO... THINK STRAIGHT...
... BUT... GRANNY... WARNED ME TO BEWARE SUCH TRICKS, WARRIORS.
THEY'LL AVAIL YOU NOTHING HERE!
HERE YOU FACE SUPREME POWER!
RIIIIIIP
HERE YOU STAND AGAINST THE SON OF DARKSEID!!
"...THE SON...??"
11

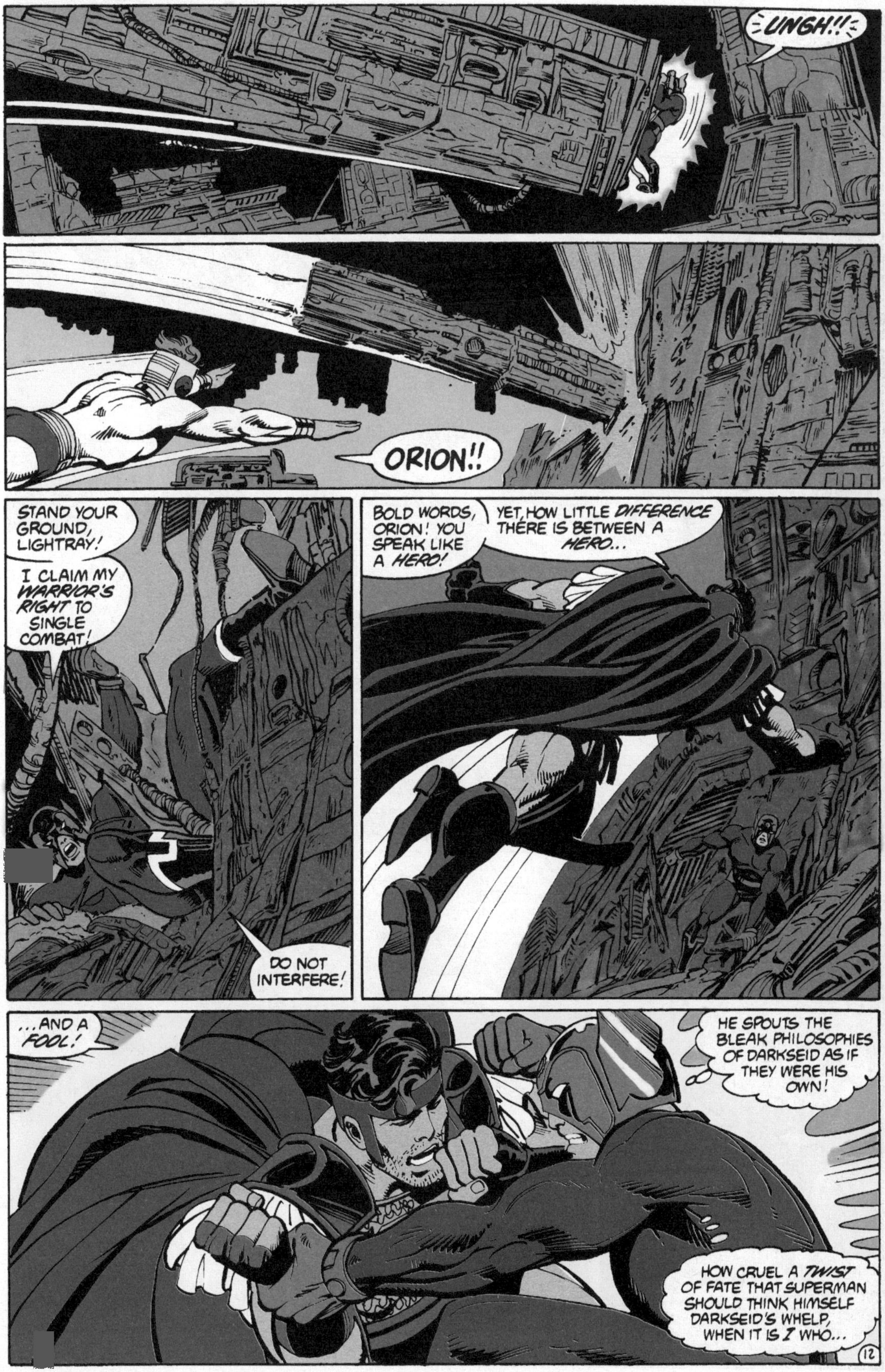
UNGH!!
ORION!!
STAND YOUR GROUND, LIGHTRAY!
I CLAIM MY WARRIOR'S RIGHT TO SINGLE COMBAT!
DO NOT INTERFERE!
BOLD WORDS, ORION! YOU SPEAK LIKE A HERO!
YET, HOW LITTLE DIFFERENCE THERE IS BETWEEN A HERO...
...AND A FOOL!
HE SPOUTS THE BLEAK PHILOSOPHIES OF DARKSEID AS IF THEY WERE HIS OWN!
HOW CRUEL A TWIST OF FATE THAT SUPERMAN SHOULD THINK HIMSELF DARKSEID'S WHELP, WHEN IT IS I WHO...
12

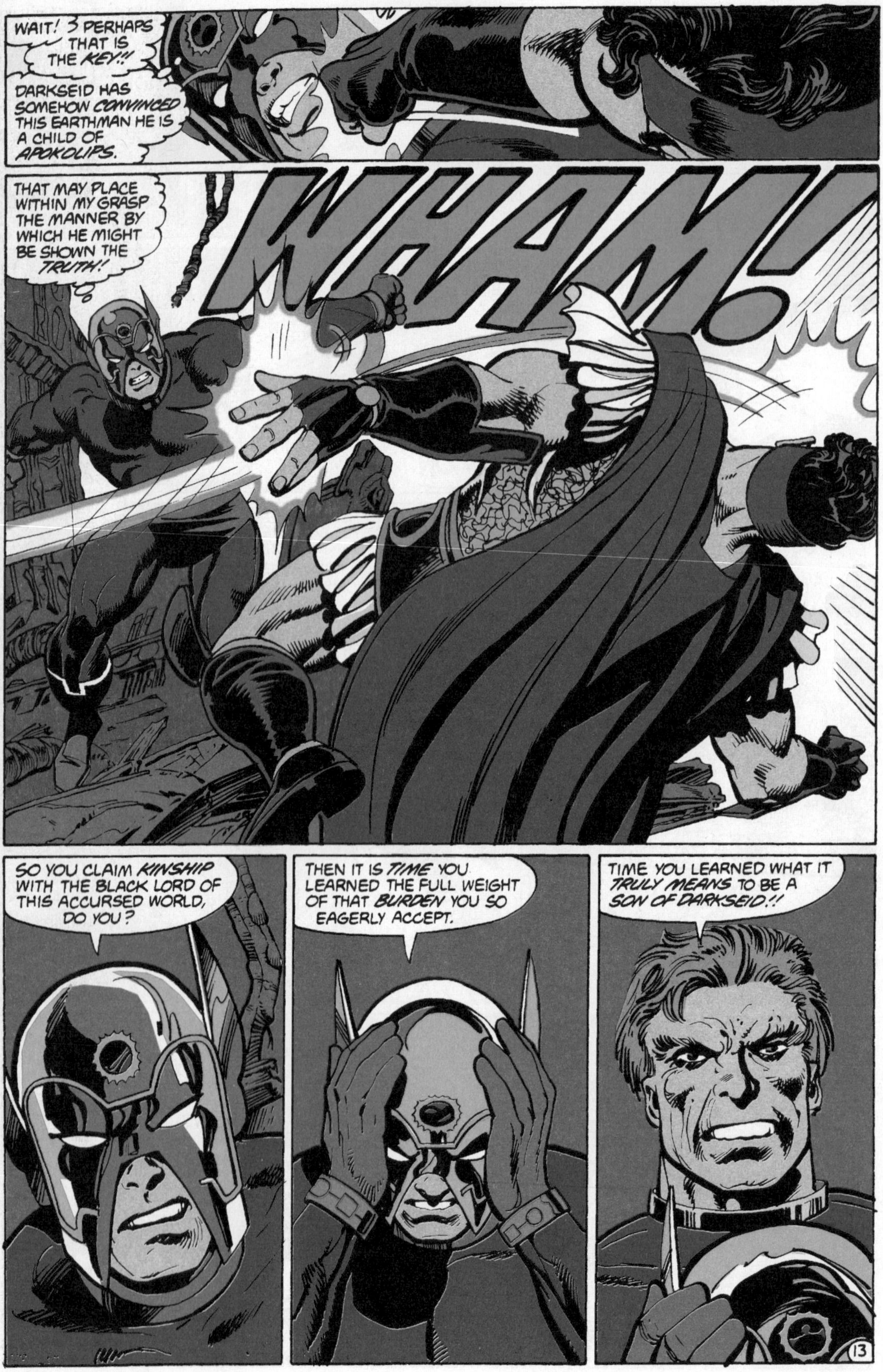
WAIT! PERHAPS THAT IS THE KEY!!
DARKSEID HAS SOMEHOW CONVINCED THIS EARTHMAN HE IS A CHILD OF APOKOLIPS.
THAT MAY PLACE WITHIN MY GRASP THE MANNER BY WHICH HE MIGHT BE SHOWN THE TRUTH!
WHAM!
SO YOU CLAIM KINSHIP WITH THE BLACK LORD OF THIS ACCURSED WORLD, DO YOU?
THEN IT IS TIME YOU LEARNED THE FULL WEIGHT OF THAT BURDEN YOU SO EAGERLY ACCEPT.
TIME YOU LEARNED WHAT IT TRULY MEANS TO BE A SON OF DARKSEID!!
13

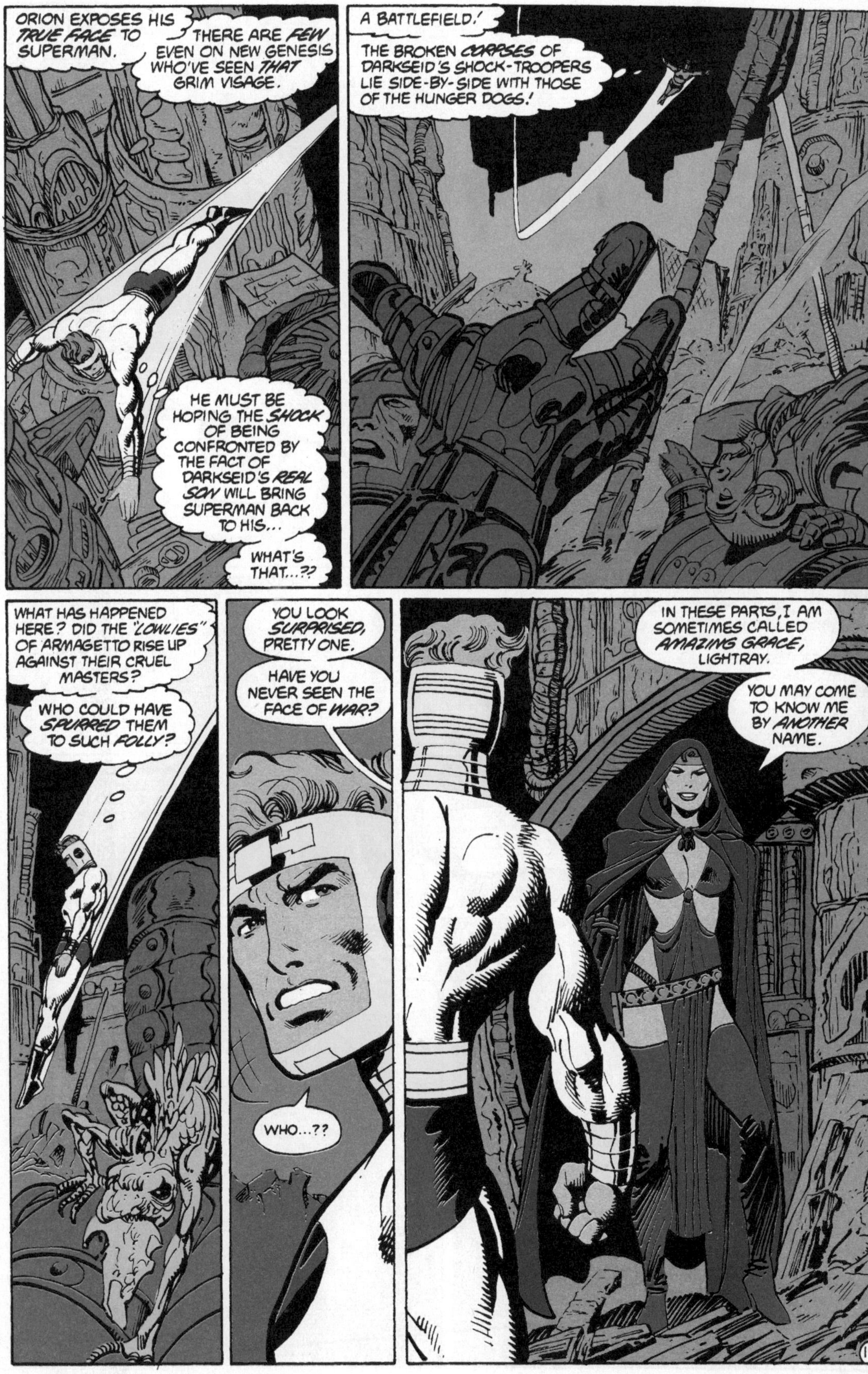
ORION EXPOSES HIS TRUE FACE TO SUPERMAN.
THERE ARE FEW EVEN ON NEW GENESIS WHO'VE SEEN THAT GRIM VISAGE.
HE MUST BE HOPING THE SHOCK OF BEING CONFRONTED BY THE FACT OF DARKSEID'S REAL SON WILL BRING SUPERMAN BACK TO HIS...
WHAT'S THAT...??
A BATTLEFIELD.!
THE BROKEN CORPSES OF DARKSEID'S SHOCK-TROOPERS LIE SIDE-BY-SIDE WITH THOSE OF THE HUNGER DOGS.!
WHAT HAS HAPPENED HERE? DID THE "LOWLIES" OF ARMAGETTO RISE UP AGAINST THEIR CRUEL MASTERS?
WHO COULD HAVE SPURRED THEM TO SUCH FOLLY?
YOU LOOK SURPRISED, PRETTY ONE.
HAVE YOU NEVER SEEN THE FACE OF WAR?
WHO...??
IN THESE PARTS, I AM SOMETIMES CALLED AMAZING GRACE, LIGHTRAY.
YOU MAY COME TO KNOW ME BY ANOTHER NAME.
14

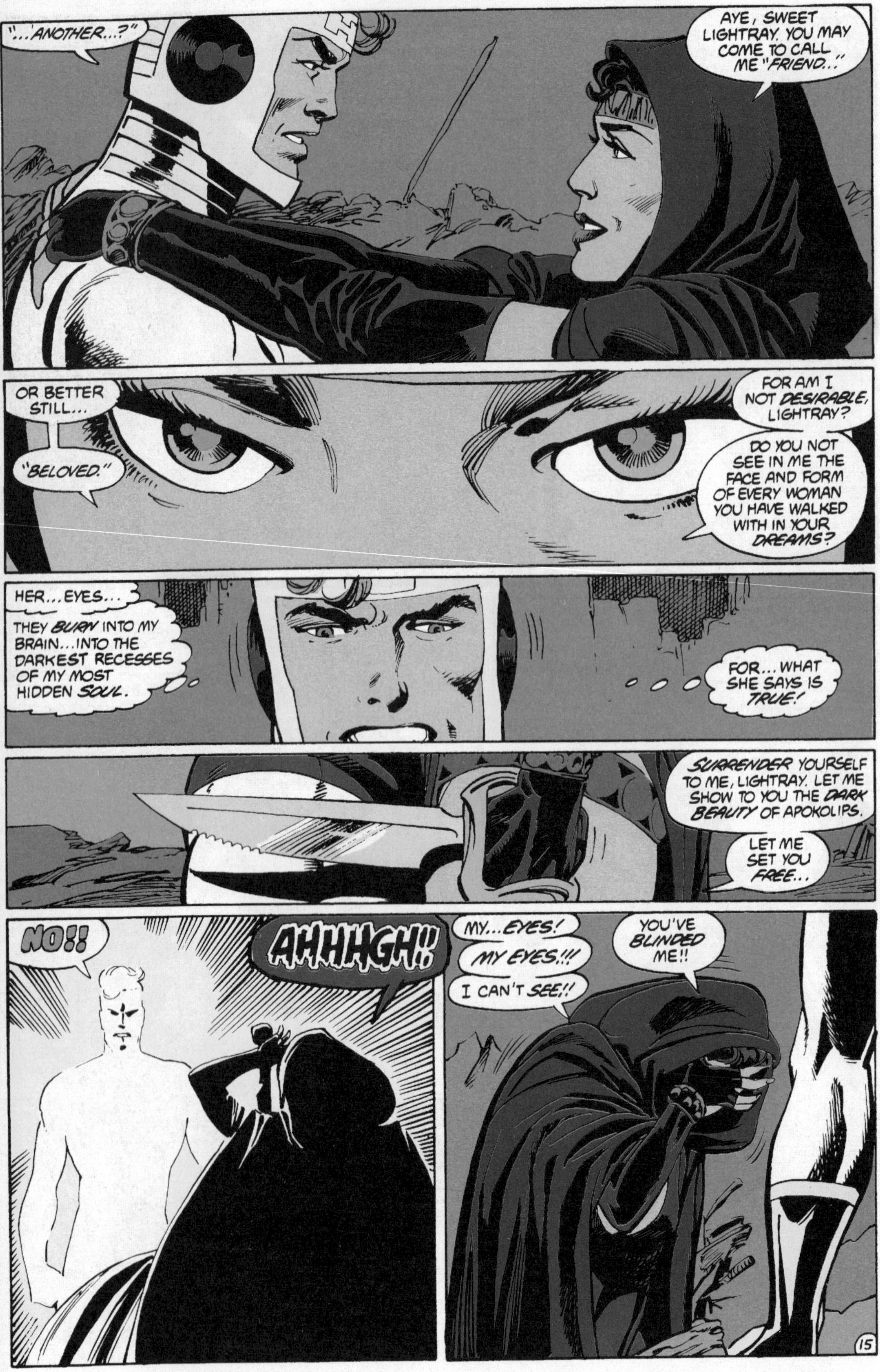
"...ANOTHER...?"
AYE, SWEET LIGHTRAY. YOU MAY COME TO CALL ME "FRIEND..."
OR BETTER STILL...
"BELOVED."
FOR AM I NOT DESIRABLE, LIGHTRAY?
DO YOU NOT SEE IN ME THE FACE AND FORM OF EVERY WOMAN YOU HAVE WALKED WITH IN YOUR DREAMS?
HER... EYES...
THEY BURN INTO MY BRAIN...INTO THE DARKEST RECESSES OF MY MOST HIDDEN SOUL.
FOR... WHAT SHE SAYS IS TRUE!
SURRENDER YOURSELF TO ME, LIGHTRAY. LET ME SHOW TO YOU THE DARK BEAUTY OF APOKOLIPS.
LET ME SET YOU FREE...
NO!!
AHHHGH!!
MY... EYES!
MY EYES!!!
I CAN'T SEE!!
YOU'VE BLINDED ME!!
15

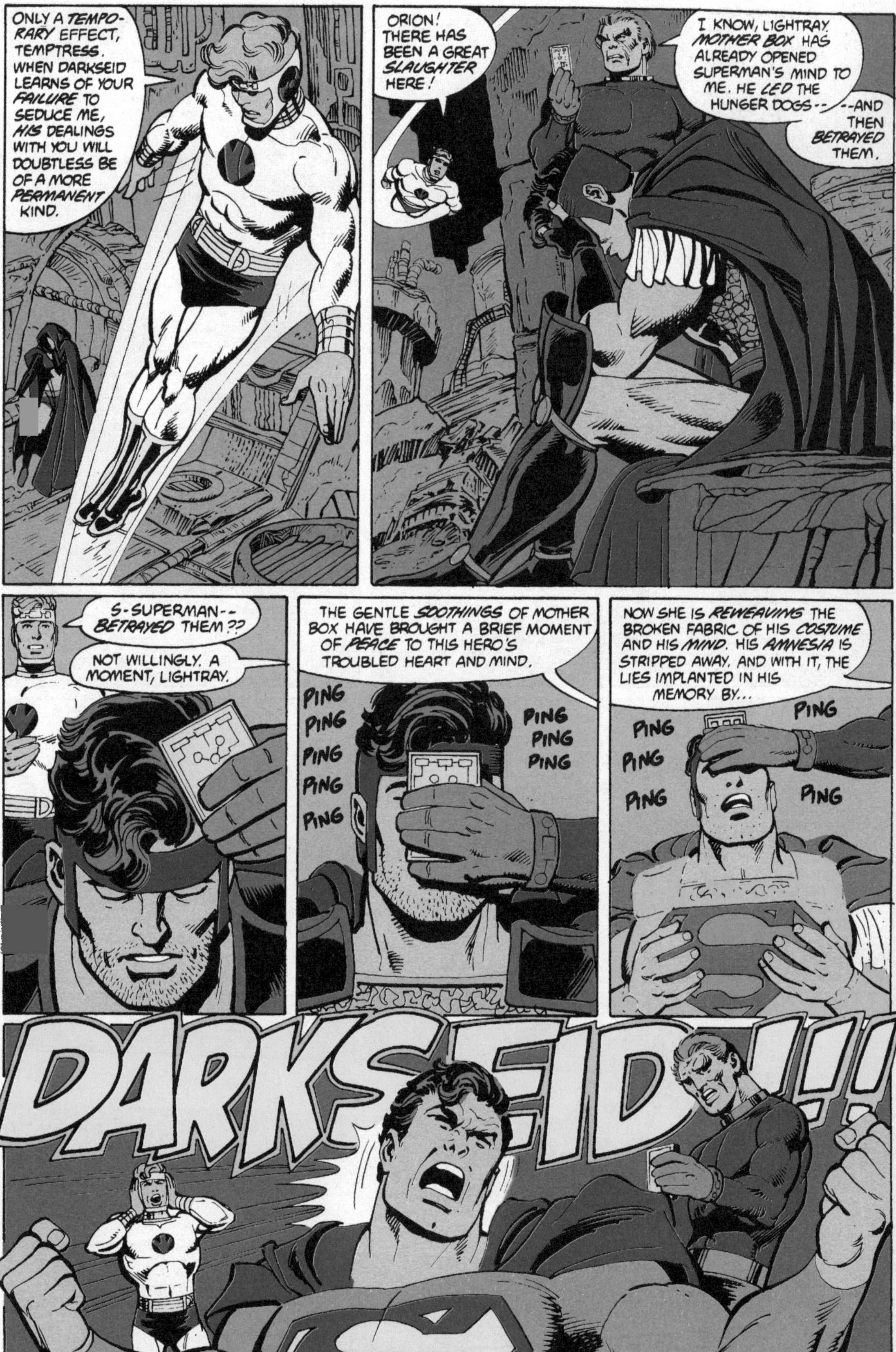

ONLY A TEMPORARY EFFECT, TEMPTRESS. WHEN DARKSEID LEARNS OF YOUR FAILURE TO SEDUCE ME, HIS DEALINGS WITH YOU WILL DOUBTLESS BE OF A MORE PERMANENT KIND.
ORION! THERE HAS BEEN A GREAT SLAUGHTER HERE!
I KNOW, LIGHTRAY. MOTHER BOX HAS ALREADY OPENED SUPERMAN'S MIND TO ME. HE LED THE HUNGER DOGS--
--AND THEN BETRAYED THEM.
S-SUPERMAN--BETRAYED THEM??
NOT WILLINGLY. A MOMENT, LIGHTRAY.
THE GENTLE SOOTHINGS OF MOTHER BOX HAVE BROUGHT A BRIEF MOMENT OF PEACE TO THIS HERO'S TROUBLED HEART AND MIND.
PING PING PING PING PING
PING PING PING
NOW SHE IS REWEAVING THE BROKEN FABRIC OF HIS COSTUME AND HIS MIND. HIS AMNESIA IS STRIPPED AWAY. AND WITH IT, THE LIES IMPLANTED IN HIS MEMORY BY...
PING PING PING PING PING
DARKSEID!!!
16

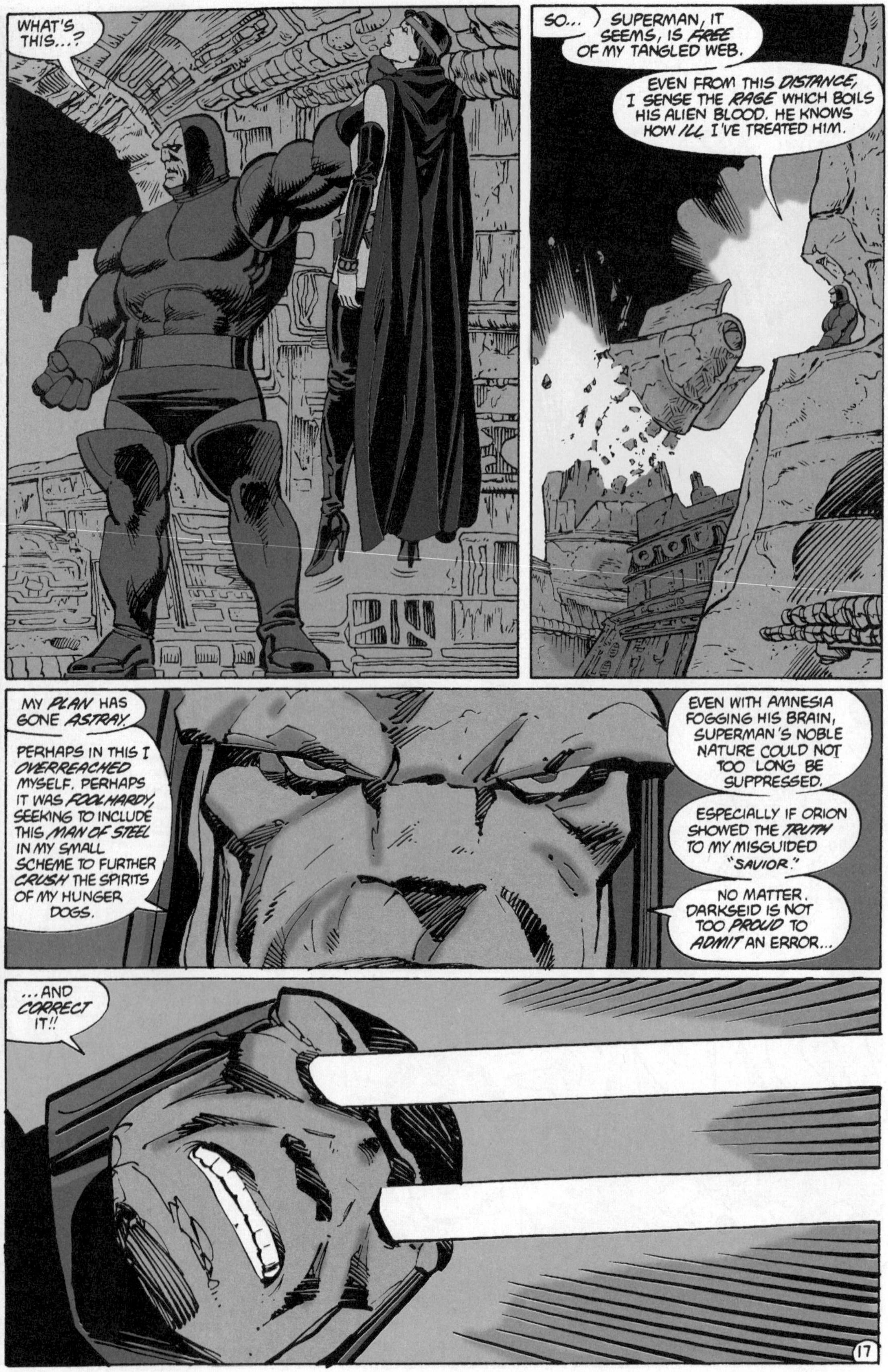
WHAT'S THIS...?
SO...
SUPERMAN, IT SEEMS, IS FREE OF MY TANGLED WEB.
EVEN FROM THIS DISTANCE, I SENSE THE RAGE WHICH BOILS HIS ALIEN BLOOD. HE KNOWS HOW ILL I'VE TREATED HIM.
MY PLAN HAS GONE ASTRAY.
PERHAPS IN THIS I OVERREACHED MYSELF. PERHAPS IT WAS FOOLHARDY, SEEKING TO INCLUDE THIS MAN OF STEEL IN MY SMALL SCHEME TO FURTHER CRUSH THE SPIRITS OF MY HUNGER DOGS.
EVEN WITH AMNESIA FOGGING HIS BRAIN, SUPERMAN'S NOBLE NATURE COULD NOT TOO LONG BE SUPPRESSED.
ESPECIALLY IF ORION SHOWED THE TRUTH TO MY MISGUIDED "SAVIOR."
NO MATTER. DARKSEID IS NOT TOO PROUD TO ADMIT AN ERROR...
...AND CORRECT IT!!
17

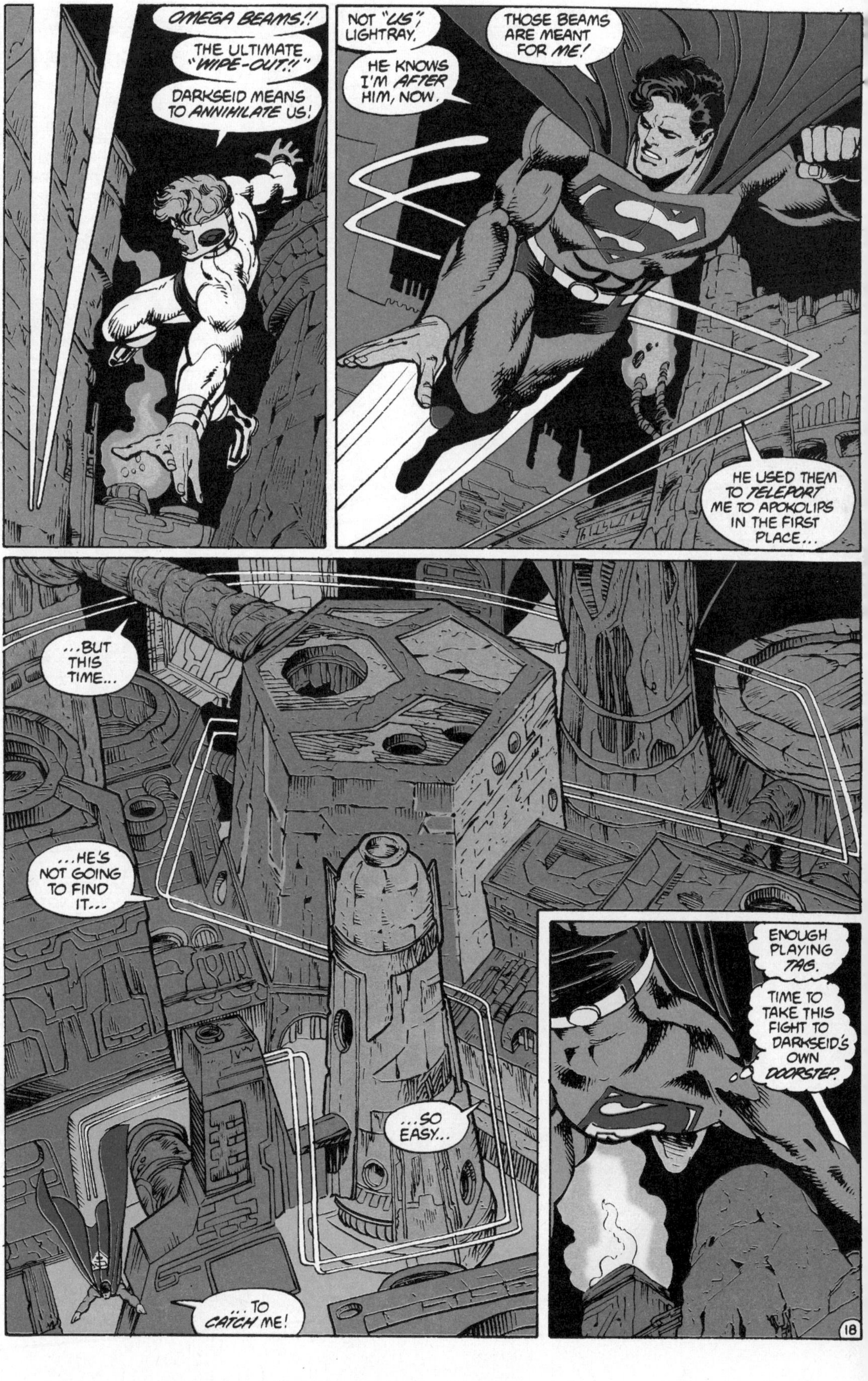
OMEGA BEAMS!!
THE ULTIMATE "WIPE-OUT!!"
DARKSEID MEANS TO ANNIHILATE US!
NOT "US", LIGHTRAY.
HE KNOWS I'M AFTER HIM, NOW.
THOSE BEAMS ARE MEANT FOR ME!
HE USED THEM TO TELEPORT ME TO APOKOLIPS IN THE FIRST PLACE...
...BUT THIS TIME...
...HE'S NOT GOING TO FIND IT...
...SO EASY...
...TO CATCH ME!
ENOUGH PLAYING TAG.
TIME TO TAKE THIS FIGHT TO DARKSEID'S OWN DOORSTEP.
18

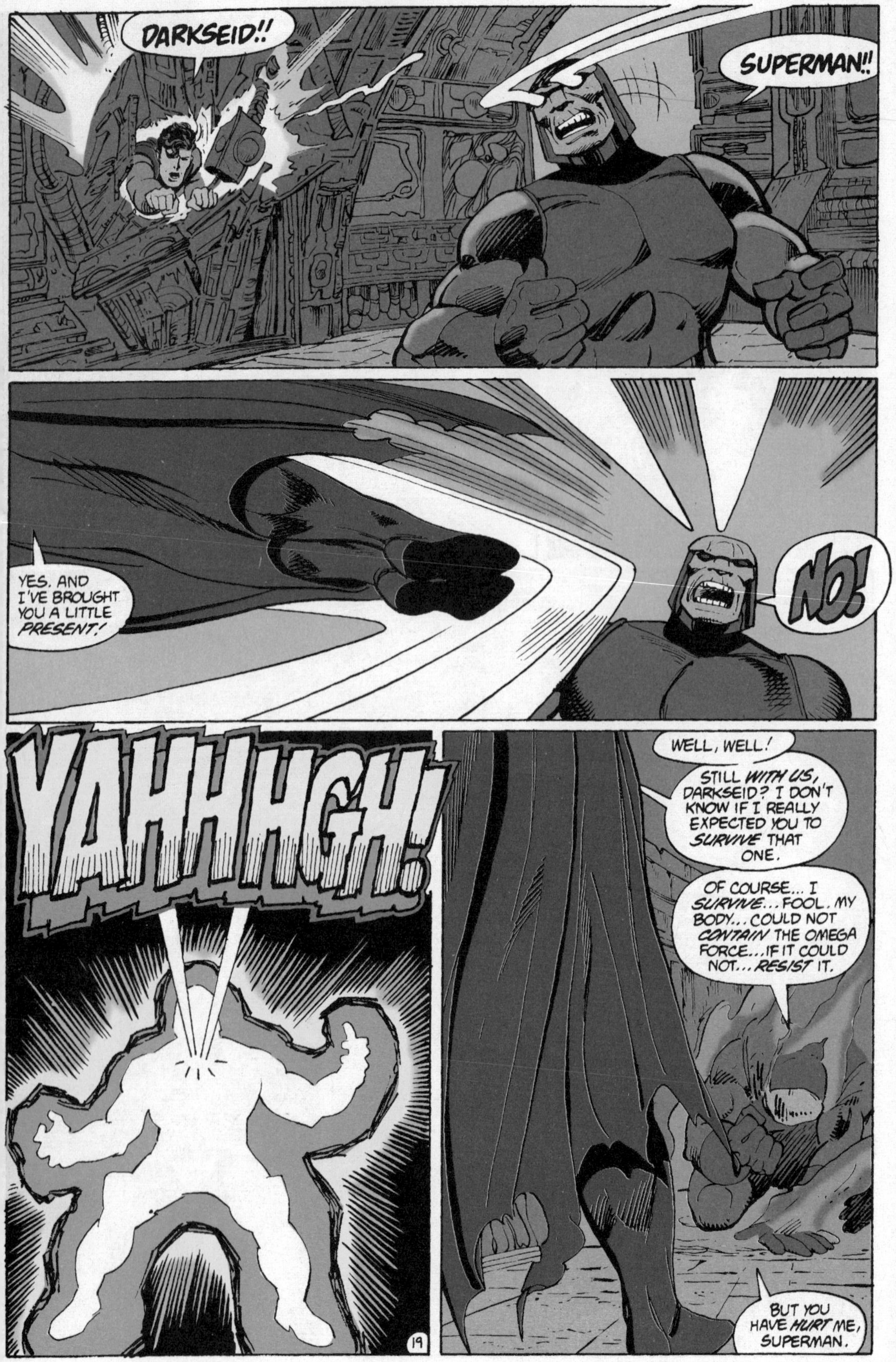
DARKSEID!!
SUPERMAN!!
YES. AND I'VE BROUGHT YOU A LITTLE PRESENT!
NO!
YAHHHGH!
19
WELL, WELL!
STILL WITH US, DARKSEID? I DON'T KNOW IF I REALLY EXPECTED YOU TO SURVIVE THAT ONE.
OF COURSE... I SURVIVE... FOOL. MY BODY... COULD NOT CONTAIN THE OMEGA FORCE... IF IT COULD NOT... RESIST IT.
BUT YOU HAVE HURT ME, SUPERMAN.

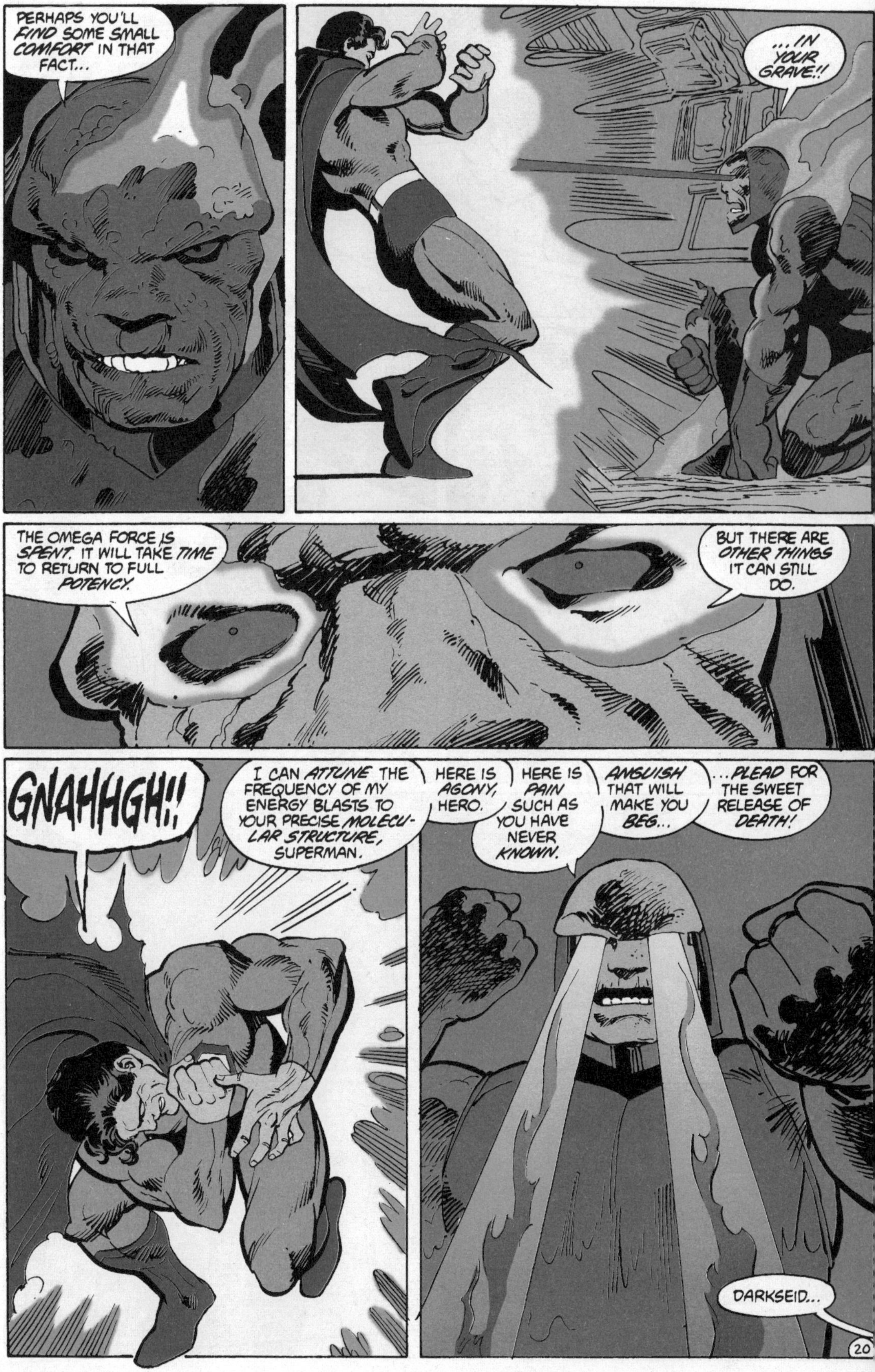
PERHAPS YOU'LL FIND SOME SMALL COMFORT IN THAT FACT...
...IN YOUR GRAVE!!
THE OMEGA FORCE IS SPENT. IT WILL TAKE TIME TO RETURN TO FULL POTENCY.
BUT THERE ARE OTHER THINGS IT CAN STILL DO.
GNAHHGH!!
I CAN ATTUNE THE FREQUENCY OF MY ENERGY BLASTS TO YOUR PRECISE MOLECULAR STRUCTURE, SUPERMAN.
HERE IS AGONY, HERO.
HERE IS PAIN SUCH AS YOU HAVE NEVER KNOWN.
ANGUISH THAT WILL MAKE YOU BEG...
...PLEAD FOR THE SWEET RELEASE OF DEATH!
DARKSEID...
20

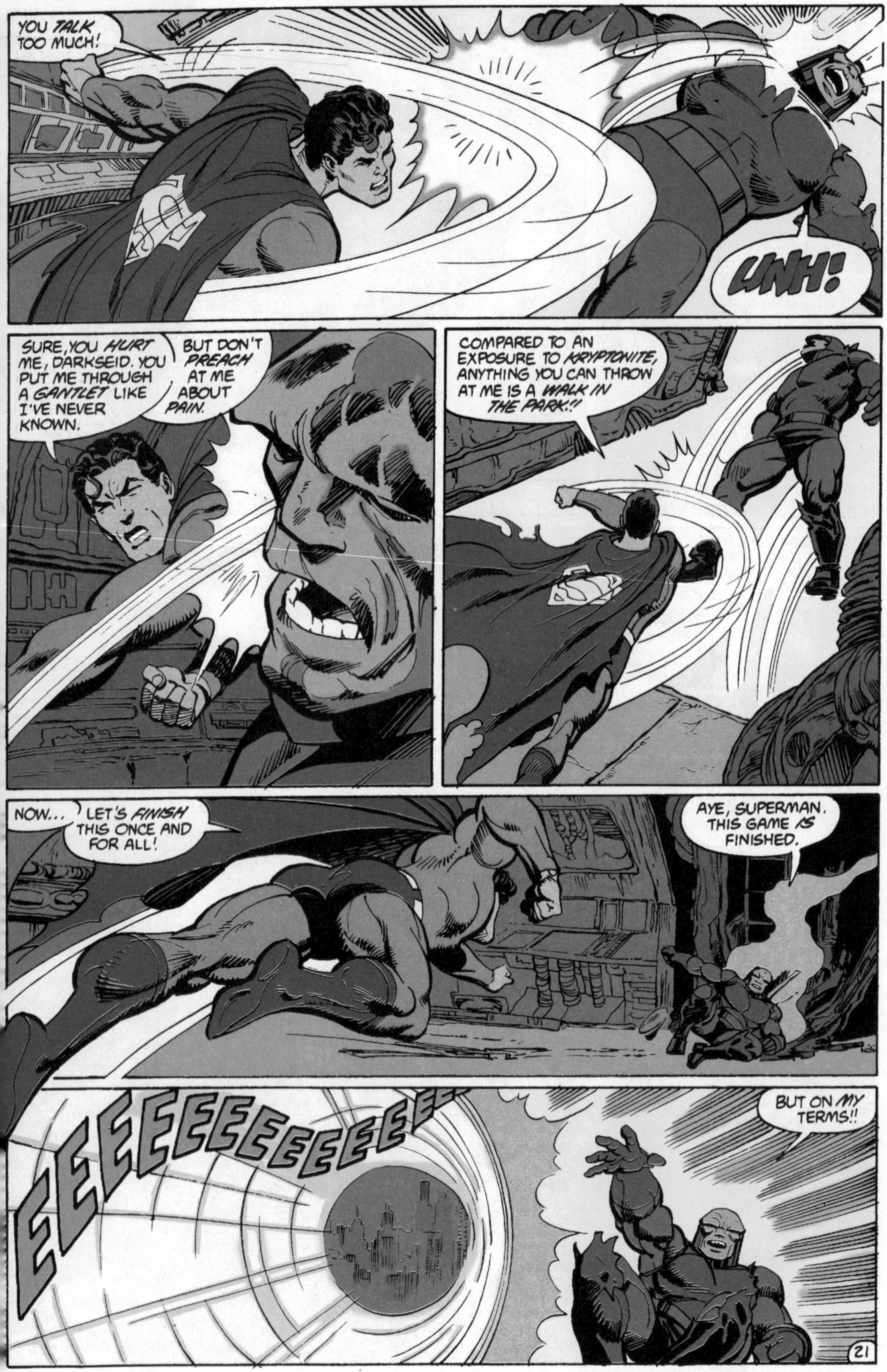
YOU TALK TOO MUCH!
UNH!
SURE, YOU HURT ME, DARKSEID. YOU PUT ME THROUGH A GANTLET LIKE I'VE NEVER KNOWN.
BUT DON'T PREACH AT ME ABOUT PAIN.
COMPARED TO AN EXPOSURE TO KRYPTONITE, ANYTHING YOU CAN THROW AT ME IS A WALK IN THE PARK!!
NOW...
LET'S FINISH THIS ONCE AND FOR ALL!
AYE, SUPERMAN. THIS GAME IS FINISHED.
EEEEEEEEEEEEE
BUT ON MY TERMS!!
21

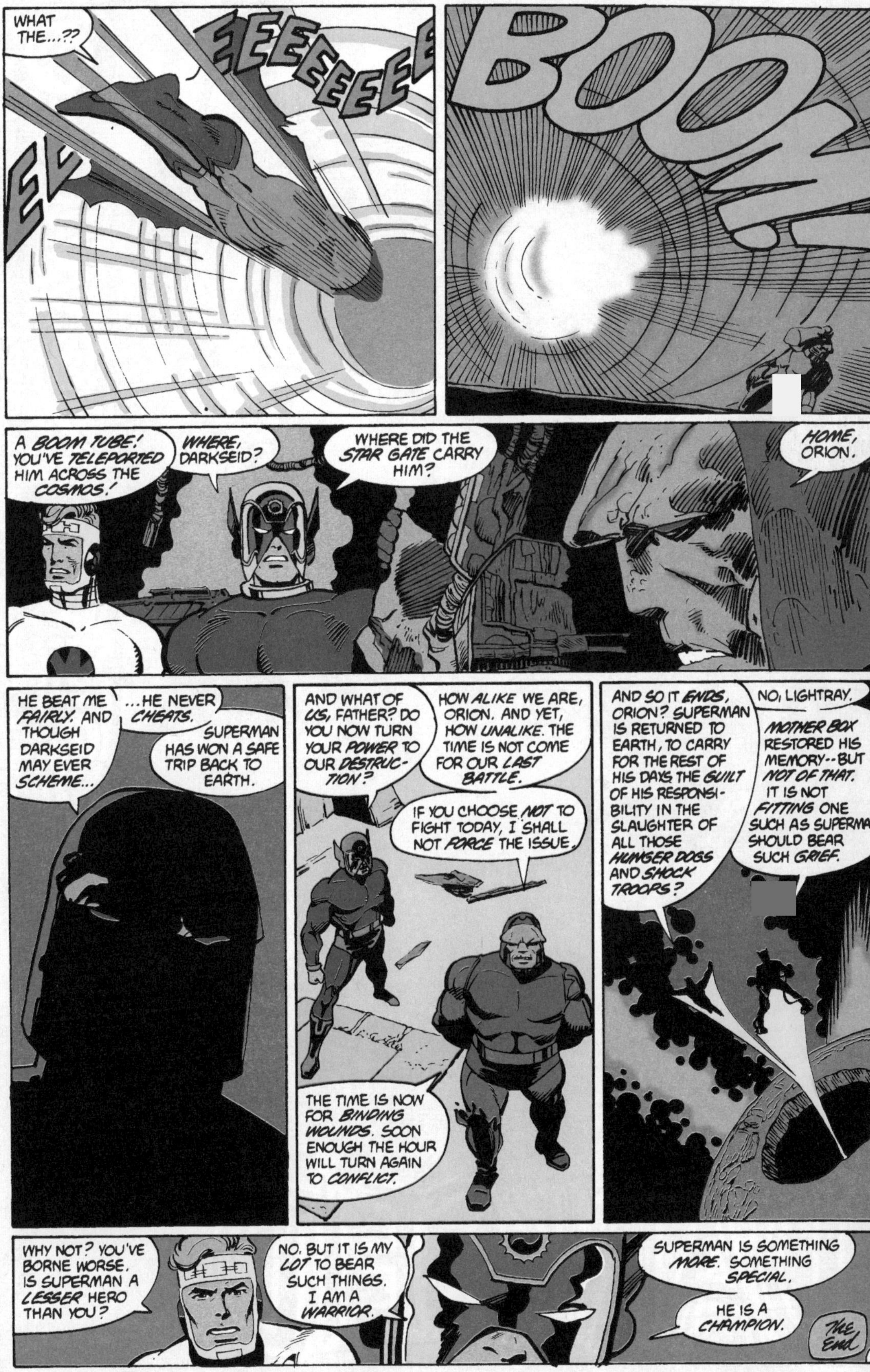
WHAT THE...??
EEEEEEEEEE
BOOM
A BOOM TUBE! YOU'VE TELEPORTED HIM ACROSS THE COSMOS!
WHERE, DARKSEID?
WHERE DID THE STAR GATE CARRY HIM?
HOME, ORION.
HE BEAT ME FAIRLY. AND THOUGH DARKSEID MAY EVER SCHEME...
...HE NEVER CHEATS.
SUPERMAN HAS WON A SAFE TRIP BACK TO EARTH.
AND WHAT OF US, FATHER? DO YOU NOW TURN YOUR POWER TO OUR DESTRUCTION?
HOW ALIKE WE ARE, ORION. AND YET, HOW UNALIKE. THE TIME IS NOT COME FOR OUR LAST BATTLE.
IF YOU CHOOSE NOT TO FIGHT TODAY, I SHALL NOT FORCE THE ISSUE.
THE TIME IS NOW FOR BINDING WOUNDS. SOON ENOUGH THE HOUR WILL TURN AGAIN TO CONFLICT.
AND SO IT ENDS, ORION? SUPERMAN IS RETURNED TO EARTH, TO CARRY FOR THE REST OF HIS DAYS THE GUILT OF HIS RESPONSIBILITY IN THE SLAUGHTER OF ALL THOSE HUNGER DOGS AND SHOCK TROOPS?
NO, LIGHTRAY.
MOTHER BOX RESTORED HIS MEMORY--BUT NOT OF THAT. IT IS NOT FITTING ONE SUCH AS SUPERMAN SHOULD BEAR SUCH GRIEF.
WHY NOT? YOU'VE BORNE WORSE. IS SUPERMAN A LESSER HERO THAN YOU?
NO. BUT IT IS MY LOT TO BEAR SUCH THINGS. I AM A WARRIOR.
SUPERMAN IS SOMETHING MORE. SOMETHING SPECIAL.
HE IS A CHAMPION.
THE END
22

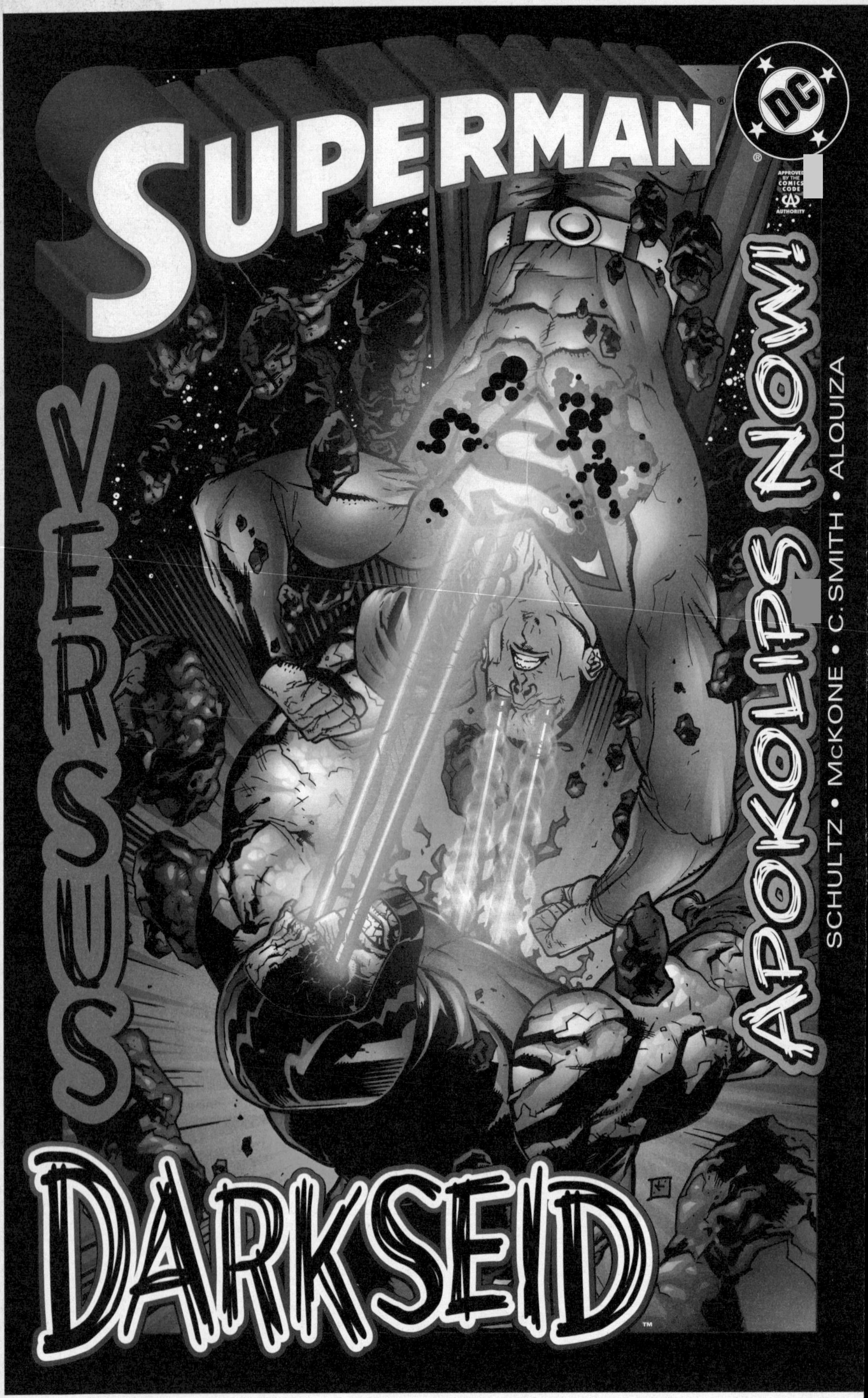
SUPERMAN®
DC
APPROVED BY THE COMICS CODE AUTHORITY
VERSUS
APOKOLIPS NOW!
SCHULTZ • McKONE • C.SMITH • ALQUIZA
DARKSEID™

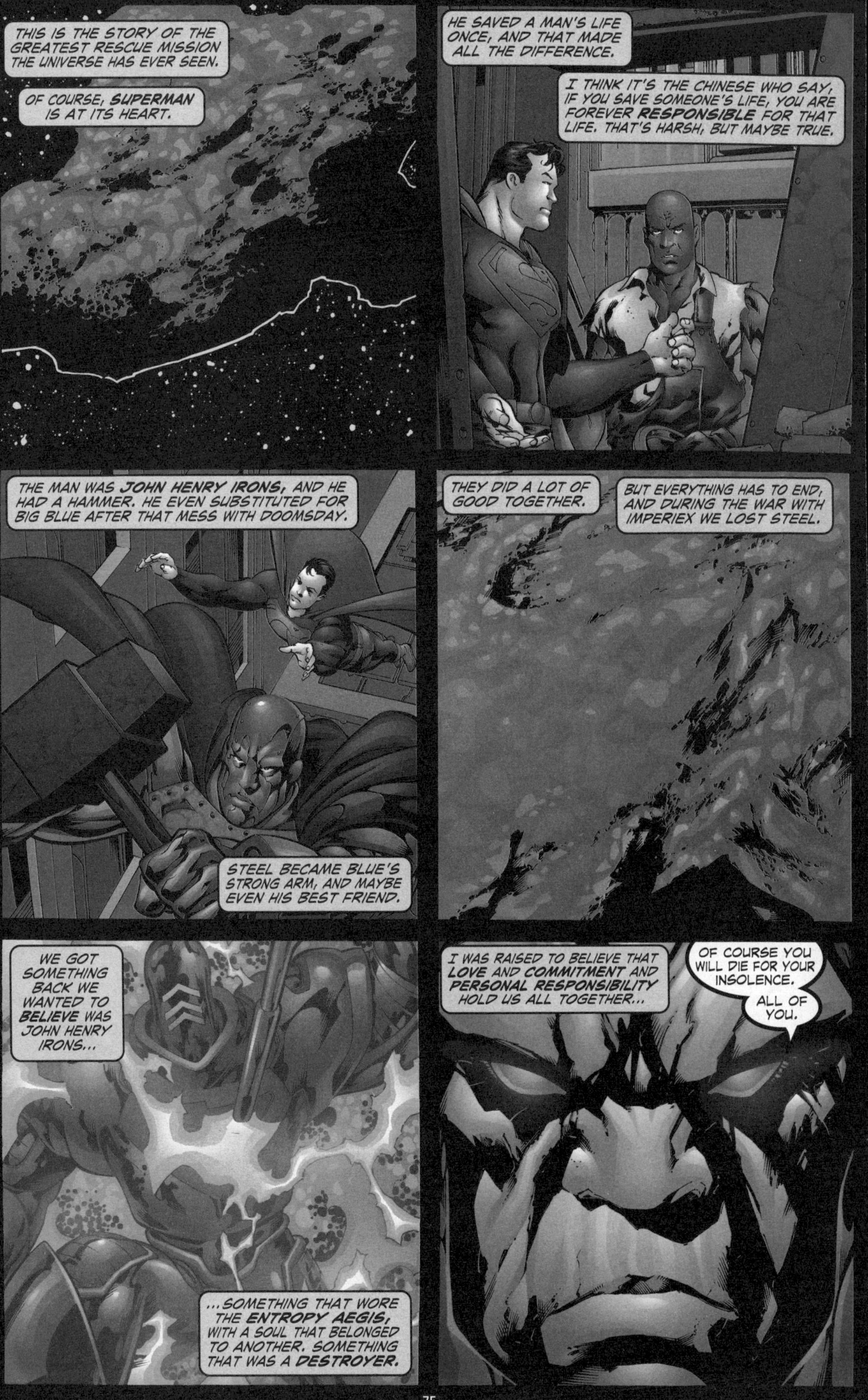

THIS IS THE STORY OF THE GREATEST RESCUE MISSION THE UNIVERSE HAS EVER SEEN.
OF COURSE, SUPERMAN IS AT ITS HEART.
HE SAVED A MAN'S LIFE ONCE, AND THAT MADE ALL THE DIFFERENCE.
I THINK IT'S THE CHINESE WHO SAY, IF YOU SAVE SOMEONE'S LIFE, YOU ARE FOREVER RESPONSIBLE FOR THAT LIFE. THAT'S HARSH, BUT MAYBE TRUE.
THE MAN WAS JOHN HENRY IRONS, AND HE HAD A HAMMER. HE EVEN SUBSTITUTED FOR BIG BLUE AFTER THAT MESS WITH DOOMSDAY.
STEEL BECAME BLUE'S STRONG ARM, AND MAYBE EVEN HIS BEST FRIEND.
THEY DID A LOT OF GOOD TOGETHER.
BUT EVERYTHING HAS TO END, AND DURING THE WAR WITH IMPERIEX WE LOST STEEL.
WE GOT SOMETHING BACK WE WANTED TO BELIEVE WAS JOHN HENRY IRONS...
...SOMETHING THAT WORE THE ENTROPY AEGIS, WITH A SOUL THAT BELONGED TO ANOTHER. SOMETHING THAT WAS A DESTROYER.
I WAS RAISED TO BELIEVE THAT LOVE AND COMMITMENT AND PERSONAL RESPONSIBILITY HOLD US ALL TOGETHER...
OF COURSE YOU WILL DIE FOR YOUR INSOLENCE.
ALL OF YOU.

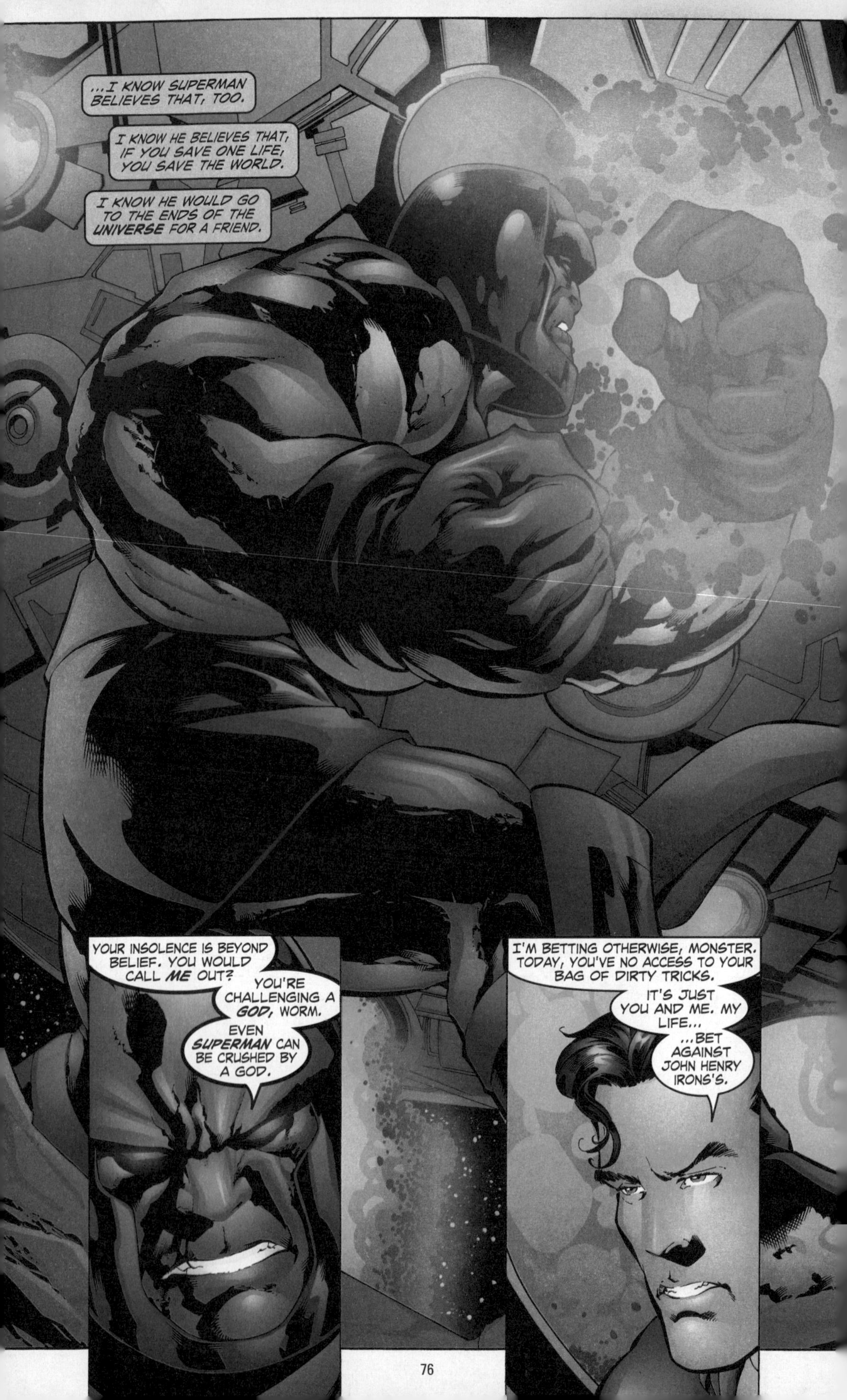
...I KNOW SUPERMAN BELIEVES THAT, TOO.
I KNOW HE BELIEVES THAT, IF YOU SAVE ONE LIFE, YOU SAVE THE WORLD.
I KNOW HE WOULD GO TO THE ENDS OF THE UNIVERSE FOR A FRIEND.
YOUR INSOLENCE IS BEYOND BELIEF. YOU WOULD CALL ME OUT?
YOU'RE CHALLENGING A GOD, WORM.
EVEN SUPERMAN CAN BE CRUSHED BY A GOD.
I'M BETTING OTHERWISE, MONSTER. TODAY, YOU'VE NO ACCESS TO YOUR BAG OF DIRTY TRICKS.
IT'S JUST YOU AND ME. MY LIFE...
...BET AGAINST JOHN HENRY IRONS'S.

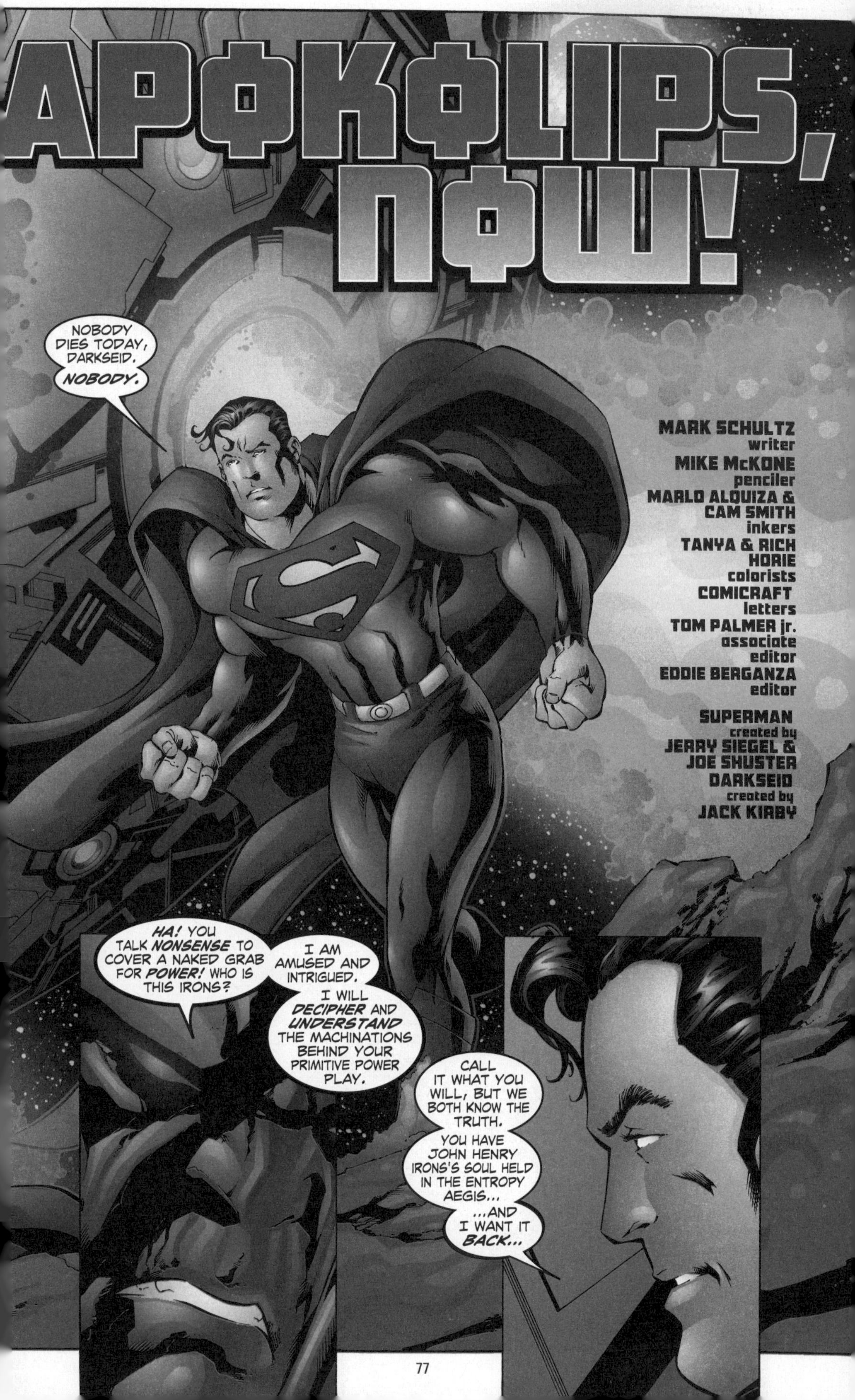

APOKOLIPS, NOW!
NOBODY DIES TODAY, DARKSEID. NOBODY.
MARK SCHULTZ writer
MIKE McKONE penciler
MARLO ALQUIZA & CAM SMITH inkers
TANYA & RICH HORIE colorists
COMICRAFT letters
TOM PALMER jr. associate editor
EDDIE BERGANZA editor
SUPERMAN created by JERRY SIEGEL & JOE SHUSTER
DARKSEID created by JACK KIRBY
HA! YOU TALK NONSENSE TO COVER A NAKED GRAB FOR POWER! WHO IS THIS IRONS?
I AM AMUSED AND INTRIGUED.
I WILL DECIPHER AND UNDERSTAND THE MACHINATIONS BEHIND YOUR PRIMITIVE POWER PLAY.
CALL IT WHAT YOU WILL, BUT WE BOTH KNOW THE TRUTH.
YOU HAVE JOHN HENRY IRONS'S SOUL HELD IN THE ENTROPY AEGIS...
...AND I WANT IT BACK...

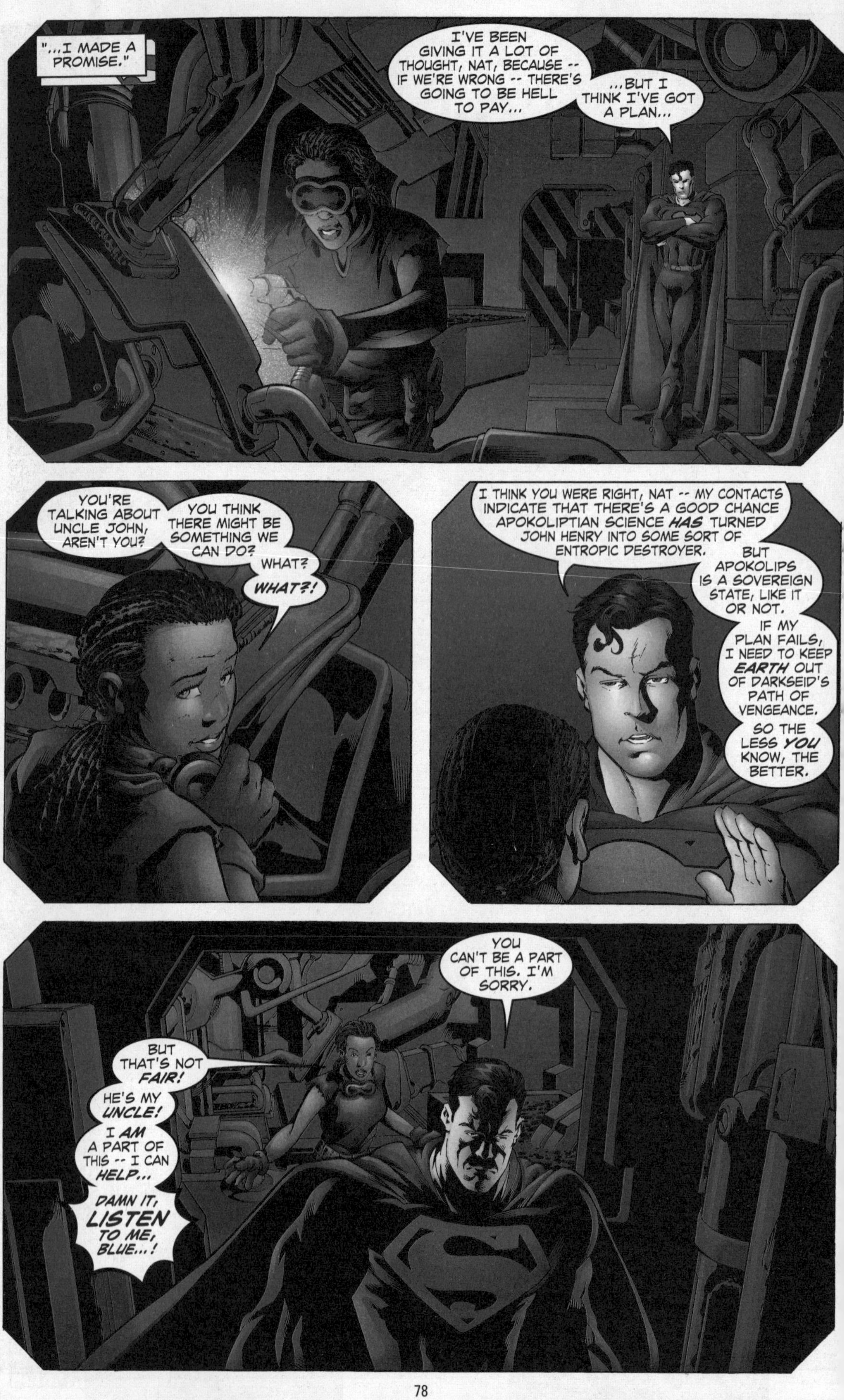
"...I MADE A PROMISE."
I'VE BEEN GIVING IT A LOT OF THOUGHT, NAT, BECAUSE -- IF WE'RE WRONG -- THERE'S GOING TO BE HELL TO PAY...
...BUT I THINK I'VE GOT A PLAN...
YOU'RE TALKING ABOUT UNCLE JOHN, AREN'T YOU?
YOU THINK THERE MIGHT BE SOMETHING WE CAN DO?
WHAT?
WHAT?!
I THINK YOU WERE RIGHT, NAT -- MY CONTACTS INDICATE THAT THERE'S A GOOD CHANCE APOKOLIPTIAN SCIENCE HAS TURNED JOHN HENRY INTO SOME SORT OF ENTROPIC DESTROYER.
BUT APOKOLIPS IS A SOVEREIGN STATE, LIKE IT OR NOT.
IF MY PLAN FAILS, I NEED TO KEEP EARTH OUT OF DARKSEID'S PATH OF VENGEANCE.
SO THE LESS YOU KNOW, THE BETTER.
YOU CAN'T BE A PART OF THIS. I'M SORRY.
BUT THAT'S NOT FAIR!
HE'S MY UNCLE!
I AM A PART OF THIS -- I CAN HELP...
DAMN IT, LISTEN TO ME, BLUE...!

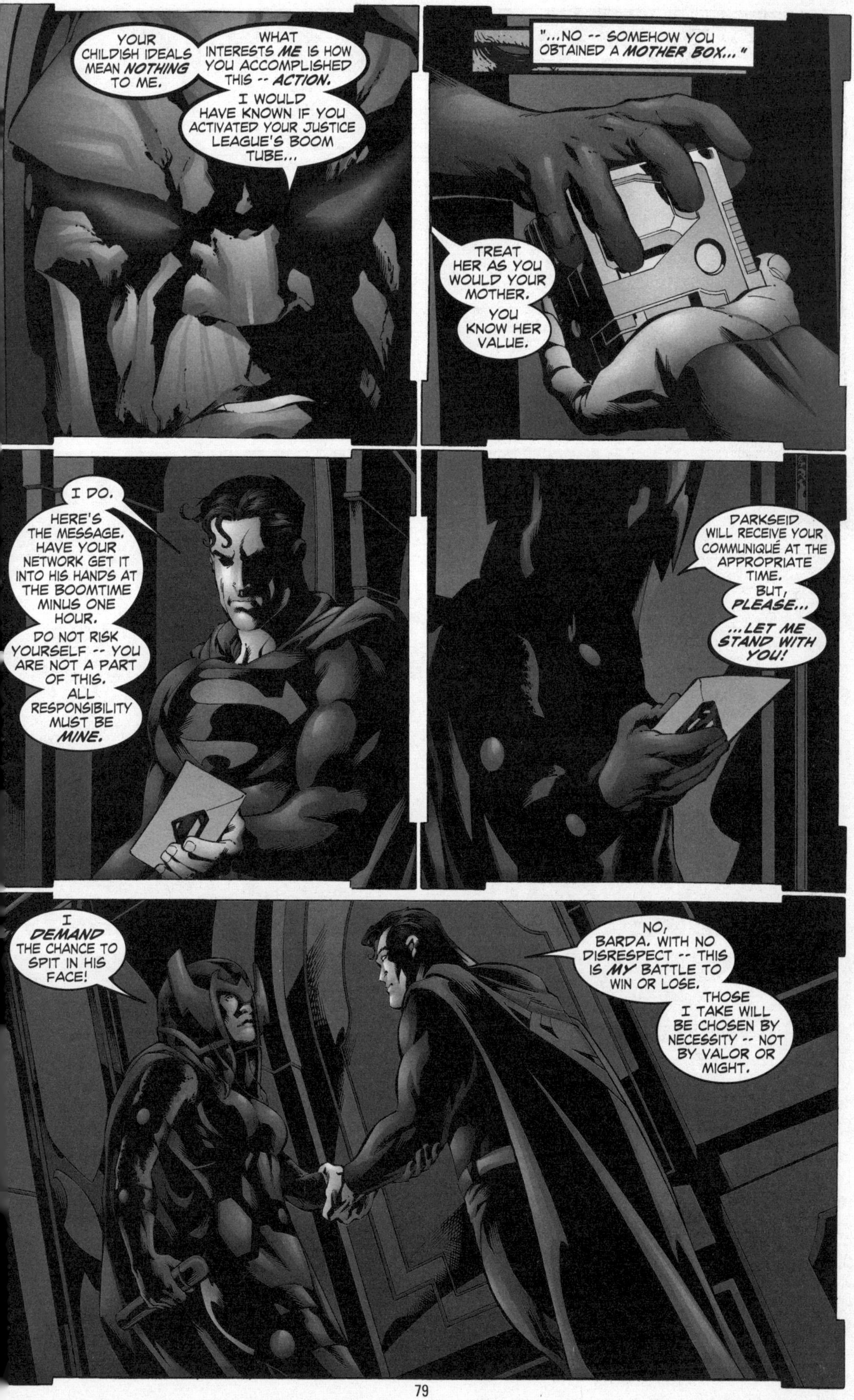

YOUR CHILDISH IDEALS MEAN *NOTHING* TO ME.
WHAT INTERESTS *ME* IS HOW YOU ACCOMPLISHED THIS -- *ACTION.*
I WOULD HAVE KNOWN IF YOU ACTIVATED YOUR JUSTICE LEAGUE'S BOOM TUBE...
"...NO -- SOMEHOW YOU OBTAINED A *MOTHER BOX...*"
TREAT HER AS YOU WOULD YOUR MOTHER.
YOU KNOW HER VALUE.
I DO.
HERE'S THE MESSAGE. HAVE YOUR NETWORK GET IT INTO HIS HANDS AT THE BOOMTIME MINUS ONE HOUR.
DO NOT RISK YOURSELF -- YOU ARE NOT A PART OF THIS.
ALL RESPONSIBILITY MUST BE *MINE.*
DARKSEID WILL RECEIVE YOUR COMMUNIQUÉ AT THE APPROPRIATE TIME.
BUT, *PLEASE...*
...LET ME STAND WITH YOU!
I *DEMAND* THE CHANCE TO SPIT IN HIS FACE!
NO, BARDA. WITH NO DISRESPECT -- THIS IS *MY* BATTLE TO WIN OR LOSE.
THOSE I TAKE WILL BE CHOSEN BY NECESSITY -- NOT BY VALOR OR MIGHT.

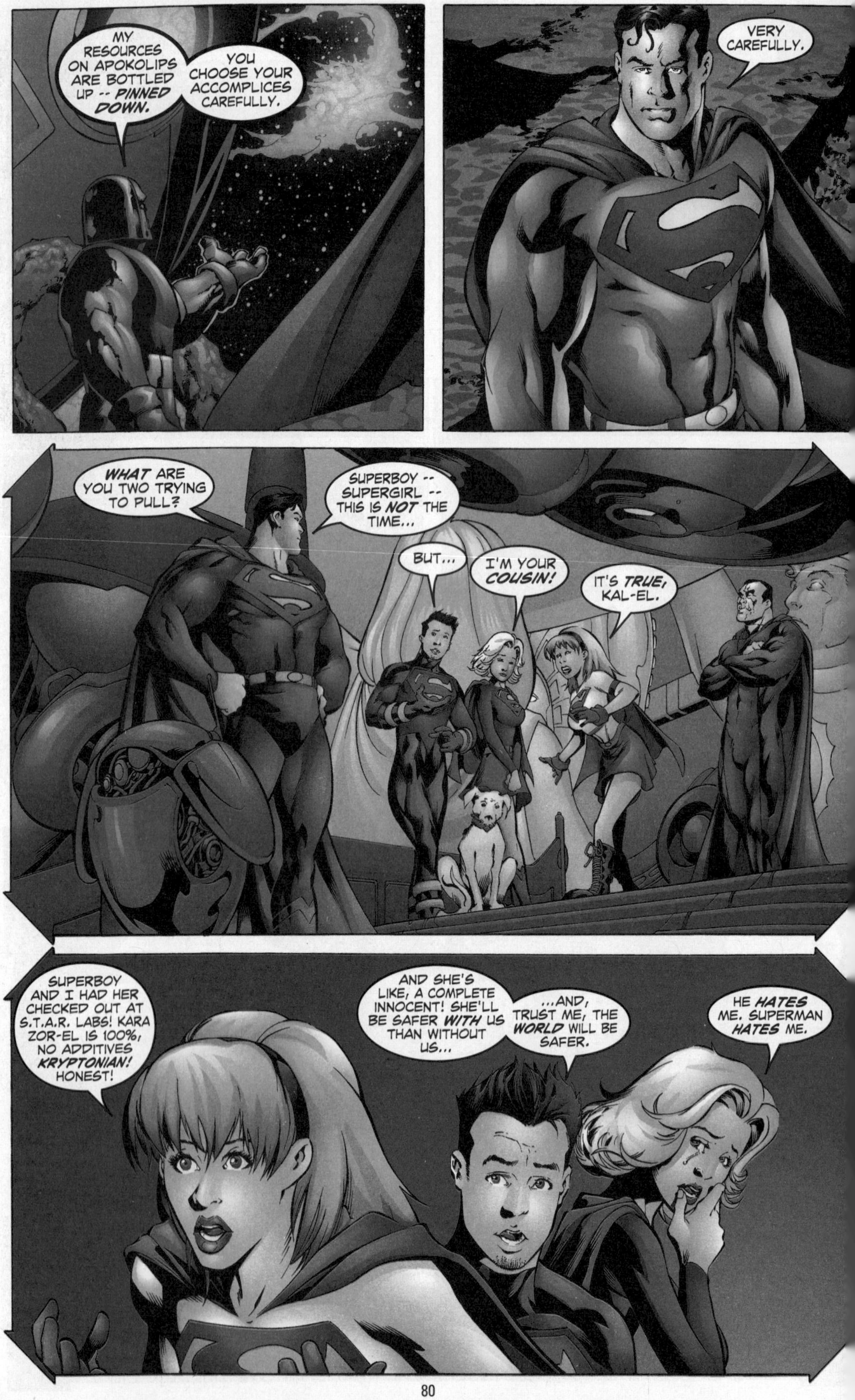

MY RESOURCES ON APOKOLIPS ARE BOTTLED UP -- PINNED DOWN.
YOU CHOOSE YOUR ACCOMPLICES CAREFULLY.
VERY CAREFULLY.
WHAT ARE YOU TWO TRYING TO PULL?
SUPERBOY -- SUPERGIRL -- THIS IS NOT THE TIME...
BUT...
I'M YOUR COUSIN!
IT'S TRUE, KAL-EL.
SUPERBOY AND I HAD HER CHECKED OUT AT S.T.A.R. LABS! KARA ZOR-EL IS 100%, NO ADDITIVES KRYPTONIAN! HONEST!
AND SHE'S LIKE, A COMPLETE INNOCENT! SHE'LL BE SAFER WITH US THAN WITHOUT US...
...AND, TRUST ME, THE WORLD WILL BE SAFER.
HE HATES ME. SUPERMAN HATES ME.

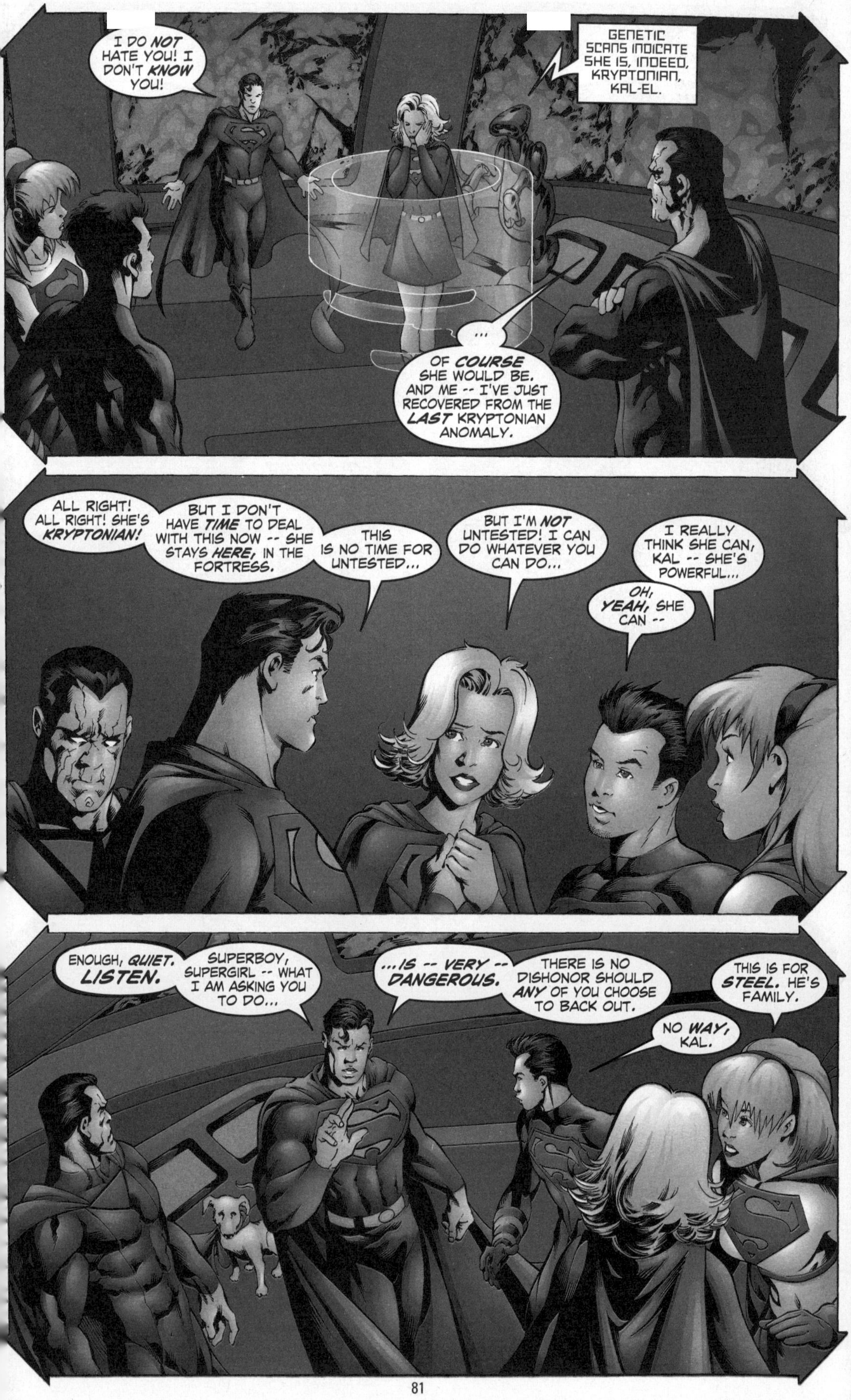
I DO NOT HATE YOU! I DON'T KNOW YOU!
GENETIC SCANS INDICATE SHE IS, INDEED, KRYPTONIAN, KAL-EL.
...
OF COURSE SHE WOULD BE. AND ME -- I'VE JUST RECOVERED FROM THE LAST KRYPTONIAN ANOMALY.
ALL RIGHT! ALL RIGHT! SHE'S KRYPTONIAN!
BUT I DON'T HAVE TIME TO DEAL WITH THIS NOW -- SHE STAYS HERE, IN THE FORTRESS.
THIS IS NO TIME FOR UNTESTED...
BUT I'M NOT UNTESTED! I CAN DO WHATEVER YOU CAN DO...
I REALLY THINK SHE CAN, KAL -- SHE'S POWERFUL...
OH, YEAH, SHE CAN --
ENOUGH, QUIET. LISTEN.
SUPERBOY, SUPERGIRL -- WHAT I AM ASKING YOU TO DO...
...IS -- VERY -- DANGEROUS.
THERE IS NO DISHONOR SHOULD ANY OF YOU CHOOSE TO BACK OUT.
THIS IS FOR STEEL. HE'S FAMILY.
NO WAY, KAL.

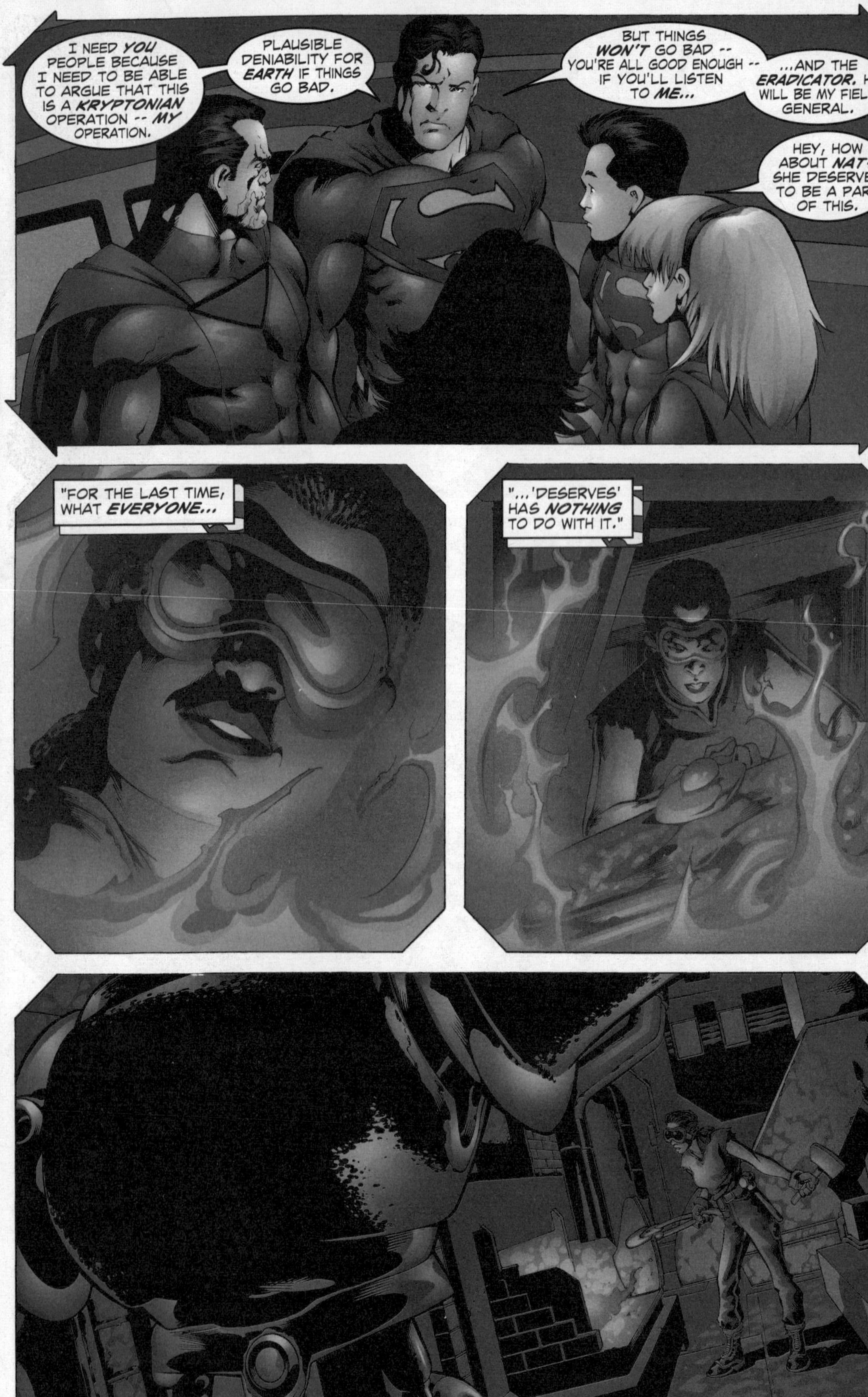
I NEED YOU PEOPLE BECAUSE I NEED TO BE ABLE TO ARGUE THAT THIS IS A KRYPTONIAN OPERATION -- MY OPERATION.
PLAUSIBLE DENIABILITY FOR EARTH IF THINGS GO BAD.
BUT THINGS WON'T GO BAD -- YOU'RE ALL GOOD ENOUGH -- IF YOU'LL LISTEN TO ME...
...AND THE ERADICATOR. HE WILL BE MY FIELD GENERAL.
HEY, HOW ABOUT NAT? SHE DESERVES TO BE A PART OF THIS.
"FOR THE LAST TIME, WHAT EVERYONE...
"...'DESERVES' HAS NOTHING TO DO WITH IT."

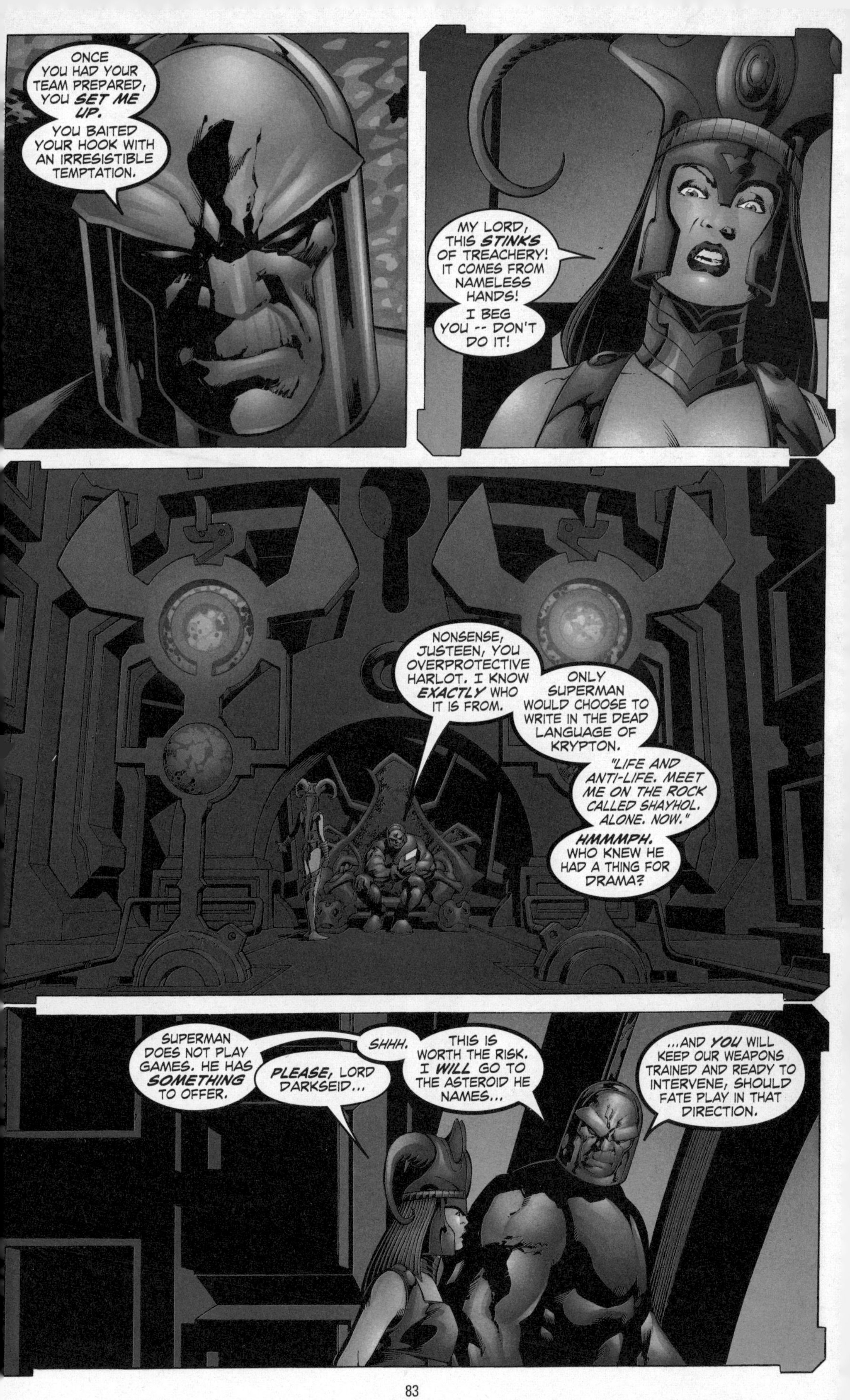

ONCE YOU HAD YOUR TEAM PREPARED, YOU SET ME UP.
YOU BAITED YOUR HOOK WITH AN IRRESISTIBLE TEMPTATION.
MY LORD, THIS STINKS OF TREACHERY! IT COMES FROM NAMELESS HANDS!
I BEG YOU -- DON'T DO IT!
NONSENSE, JUSTEEN, YOU OVERPROTECTIVE HARLOT. I KNOW EXACTLY WHO IT IS FROM.
ONLY SUPERMAN WOULD CHOOSE TO WRITE IN THE DEAD LANGUAGE OF KRYPTON.
"LIFE AND ANTI-LIFE. MEET ME ON THE ROCK CALLED SHAYHOL. ALONE. NOW."
HMMMPH. WHO KNEW HE HAD A THING FOR DRAMA?
SUPERMAN DOES NOT PLAY GAMES. HE HAS SOMETHING TO OFFER.
SHHH.
PLEASE, LORD DARKSEID...
THIS IS WORTH THE RISK. I WILL GO TO THE ASTEROID HE NAMES...
...AND YOU WILL KEEP OUR WEAPONS TRAINED AND READY TO INTERVENE, SHOULD FATE PLAY IN THAT DIRECTION.

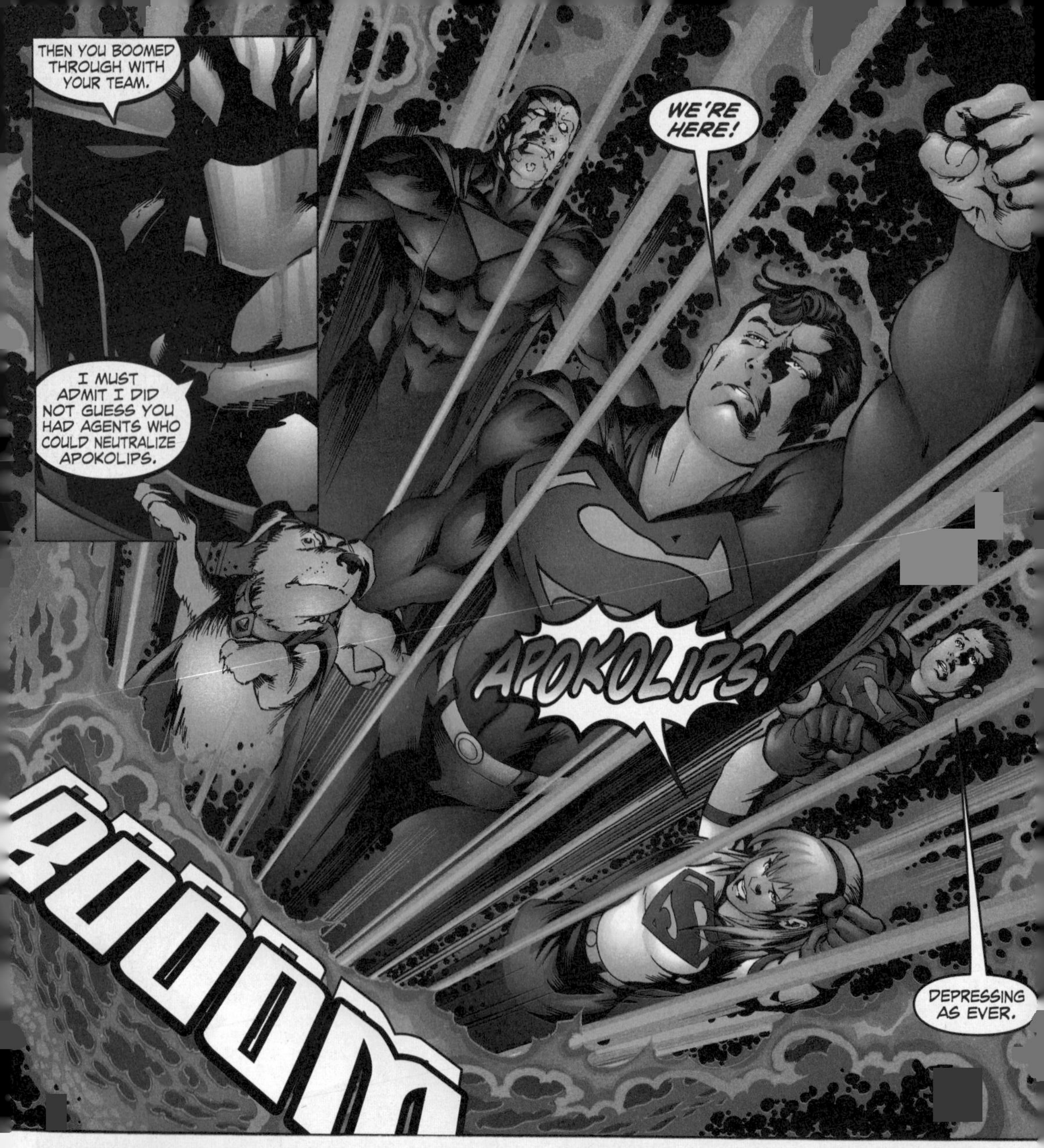
THEN YOU BOOMED THROUGH WITH YOUR TEAM.
WE'RE HERE!
I MUST ADMIT I DID NOT GUESS YOU HAD AGENTS WHO COULD NEUTRALIZE APOKOLIPS.
APOKOLIPS!
BOOOM
DEPRESSING AS EVER.

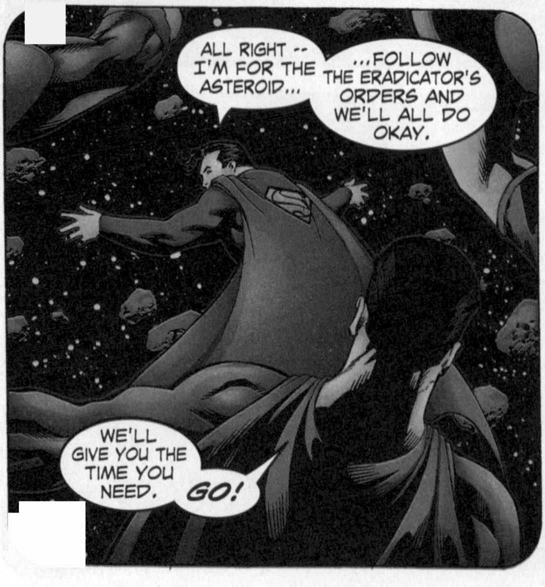
ALL RIGHT -- I'M FOR THE ASTEROID...
...FOLLOW THE ERADICATOR'S ORDERS AND WE'LL ALL DO OKAY.
WE'LL GIVE YOU THE TIME YOU NEED.
GO!

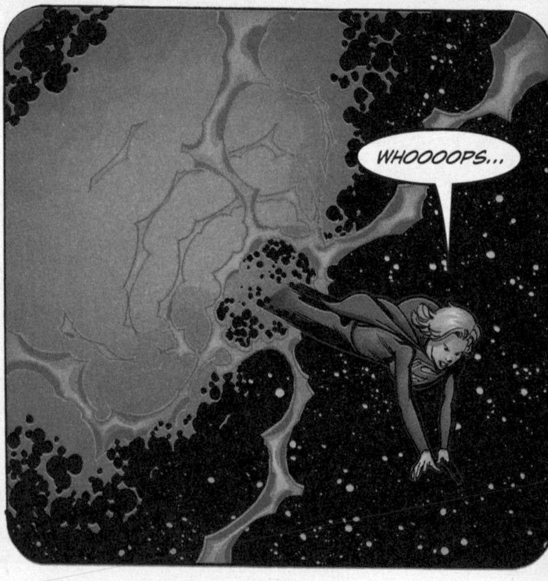
WHOOOOPS...

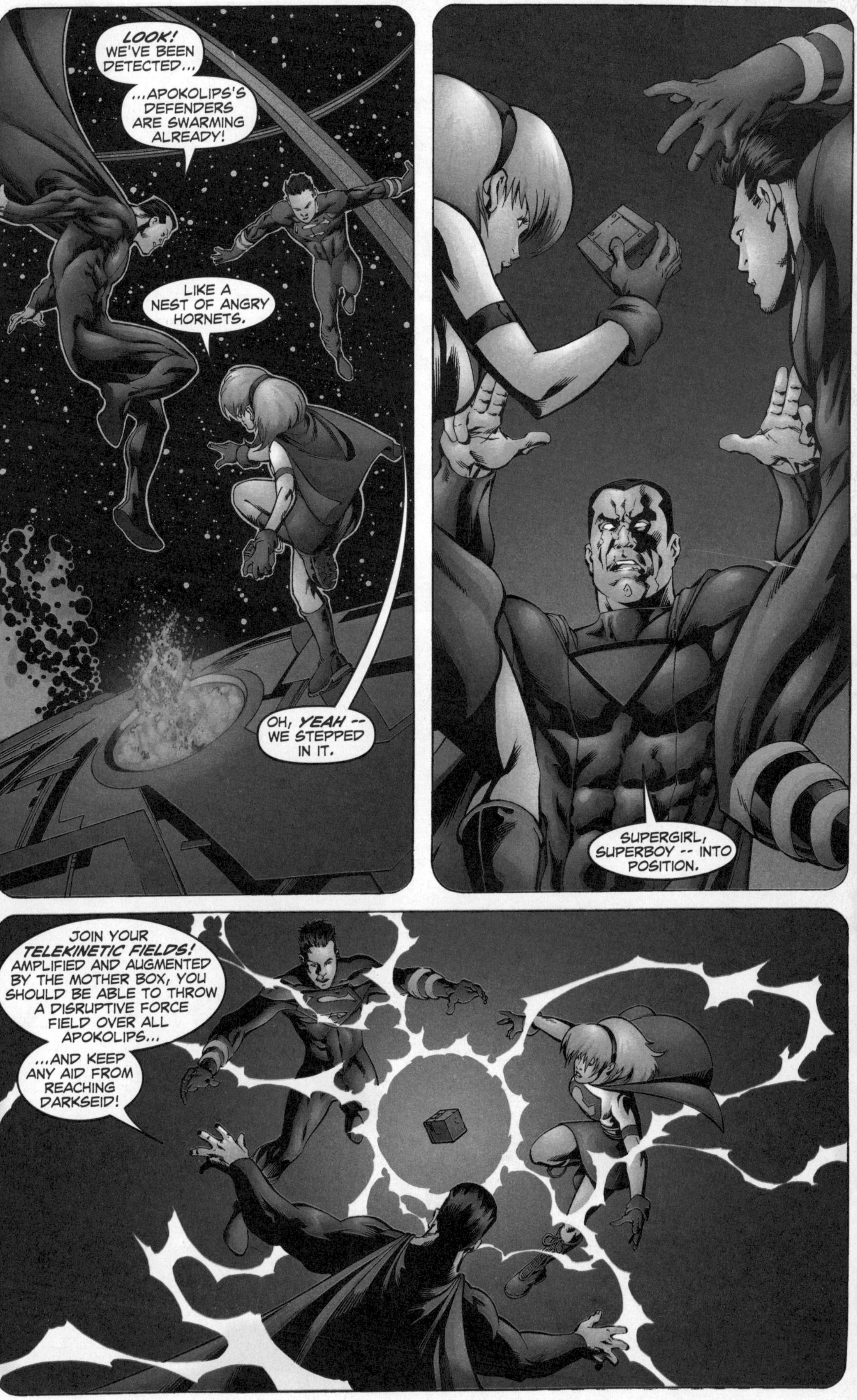

LOOK! WE'VE BEEN DETECTED...
...APOKOLIPS'S DEFENDERS ARE SWARMING ALREADY!
LIKE A NEST OF ANGRY HORNETS.
OH, YEAH -- WE STEPPED IN IT.
SUPERGIRL, SUPERBOY -- INTO POSITION.
JOIN YOUR TELEKINETIC FIELDS! AMPLIFIED AND AUGMENTED BY THE MOTHER BOX, YOU SHOULD BE ABLE TO THROW A DISRUPTIVE FORCE FIELD OVER ALL APOKOLIPS...
...AND KEEP ANY AID FROM REACHING DARKSEID!

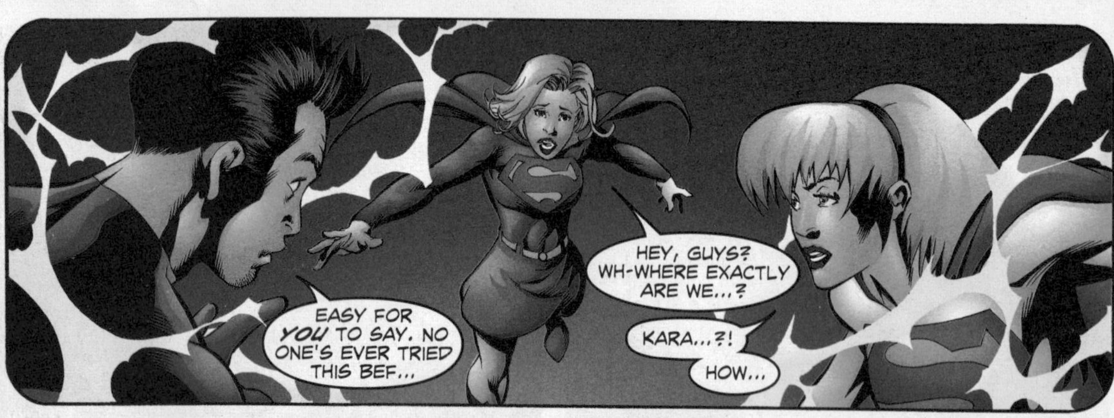
HEY, GUYS? WH-WHERE EXACTLY ARE WE...?
EASY FOR YOU TO SAY. NO ONE'S EVER TRIED THIS BEF...
KARA...?!
HOW...

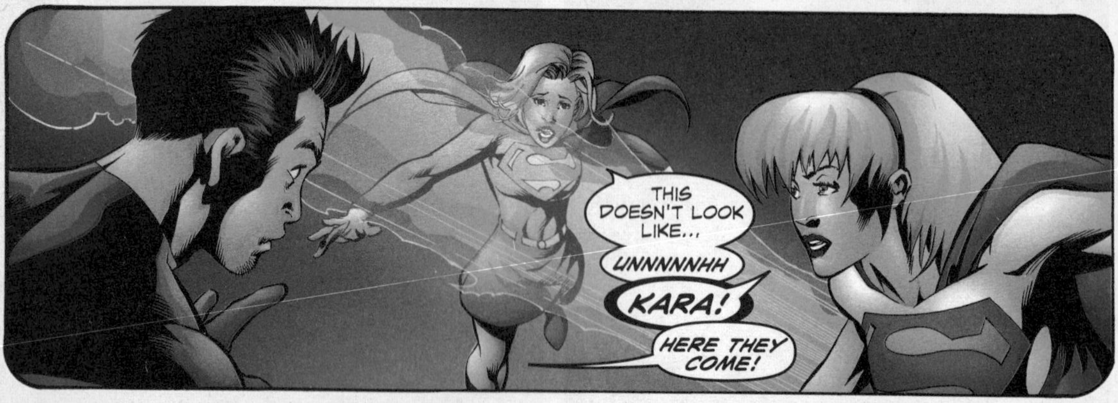
THIS DOESN'T LOOK LIKE...
UNNNNNHH
KARA!
HERE THEY COME!

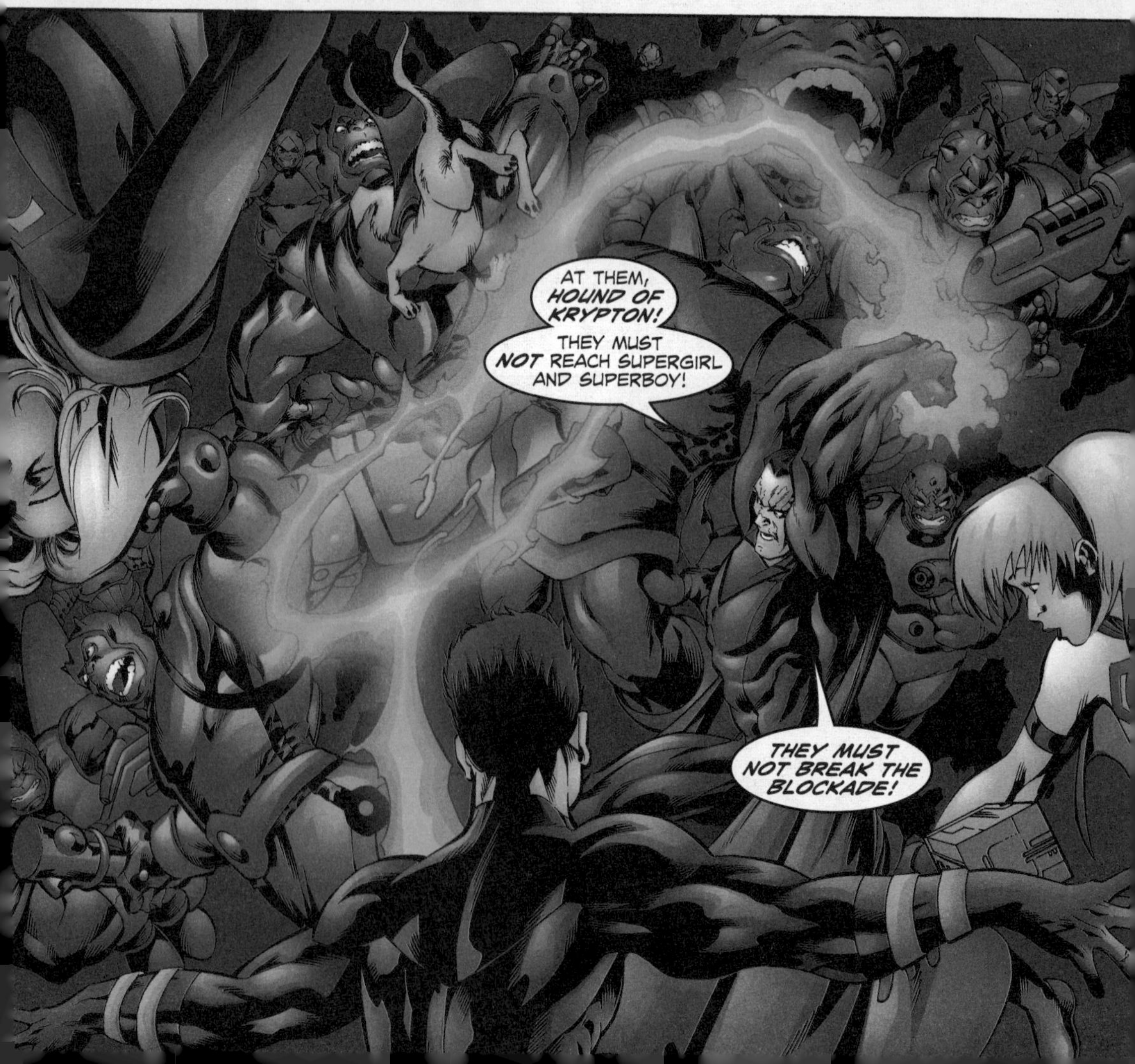
AT THEM, HOUND OF KRYPTON!
THEY MUST NOT REACH SUPERGIRL AND SUPERBOY!
THEY MUST NOT BREAK THE BLOCKADE!

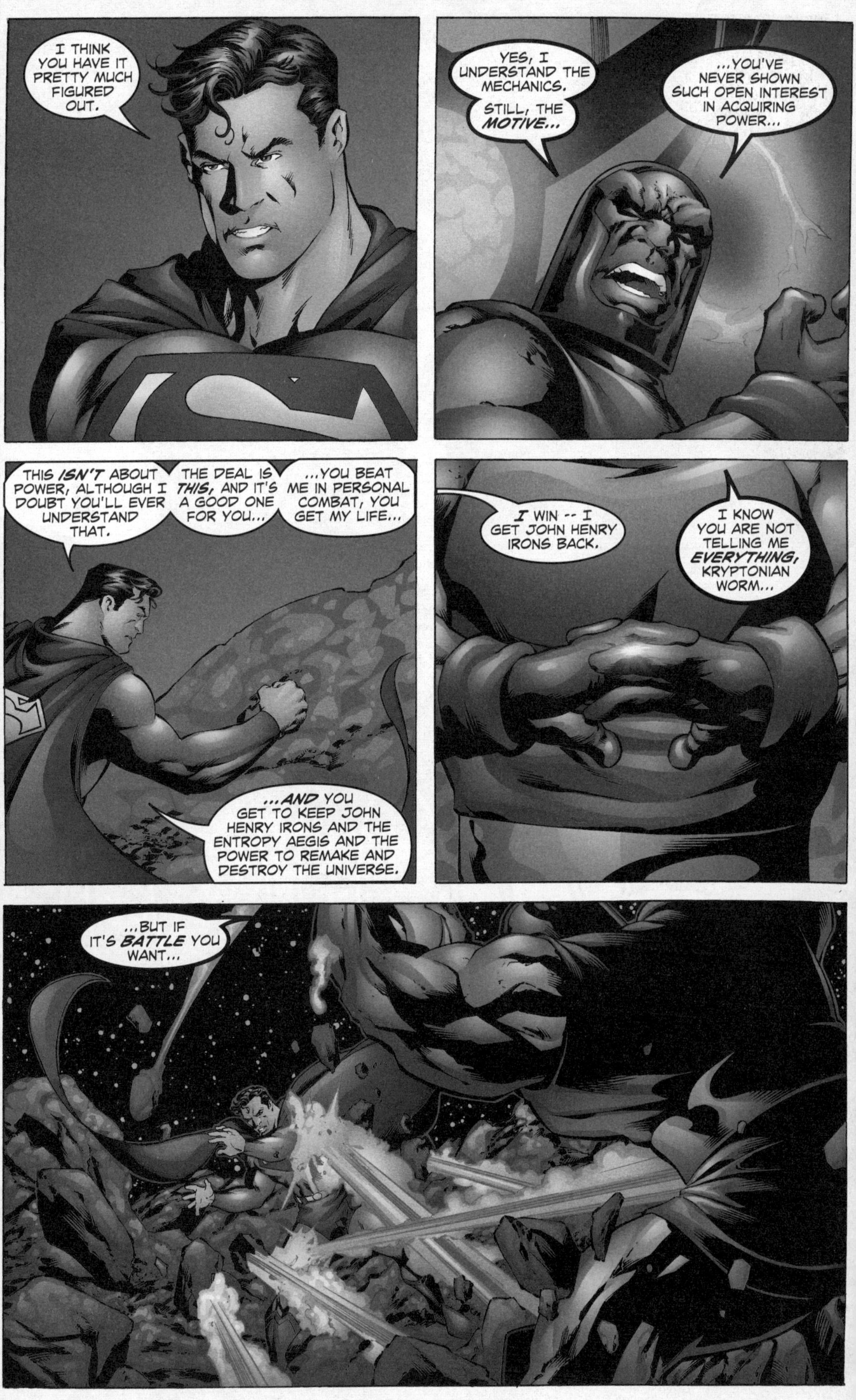

I THINK YOU HAVE IT PRETTY MUCH FIGURED OUT.
YES, I UNDERSTAND THE MECHANICS.
STILL, THE MOTIVE...
...YOU'VE NEVER SHOWN SUCH OPEN INTEREST IN ACQUIRING POWER...
THIS ISN'T ABOUT POWER, ALTHOUGH I DOUBT YOU'LL EVER UNDERSTAND THAT.
THE DEAL IS THIS, AND IT'S A GOOD ONE FOR YOU...
...YOU BEAT ME IN PERSONAL COMBAT, YOU GET MY LIFE...
...AND YOU GET TO KEEP JOHN HENRY IRONS AND THE ENTROPY AEGIS AND THE POWER TO REMAKE AND DESTROY THE UNIVERSE.
I WIN -- I GET JOHN HENRY IRONS BACK.
I KNOW YOU ARE NOT TELLING ME EVERYTHING, KRYPTONIAN WORM...
...BUT IF IT'S BATTLE YOU WANT...

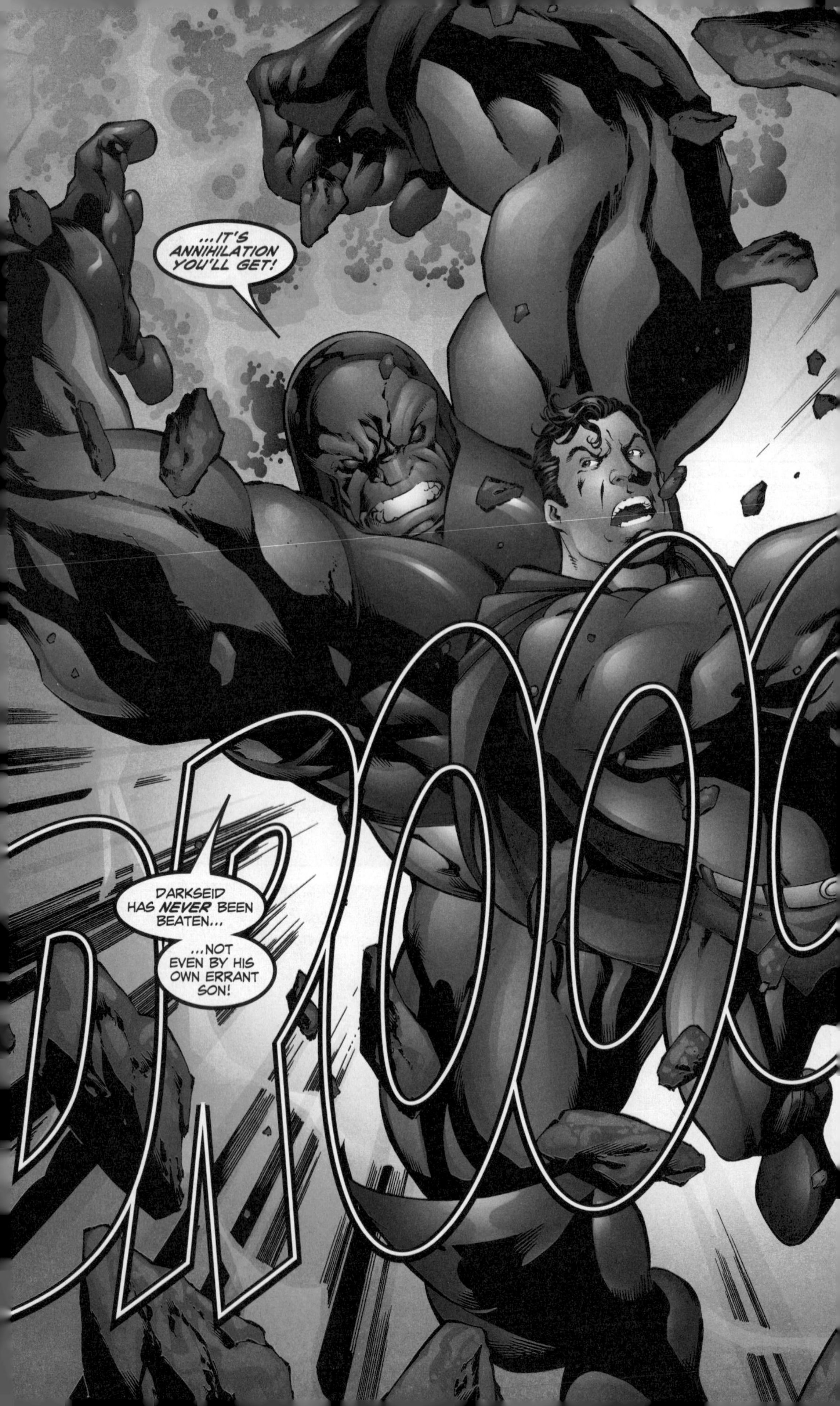
...IT'S ANNIHILATION YOU'LL GET!
DARKSEID HAS **NEVER** BEEN BEATEN...
...NOT EVEN BY HIS OWN ERRANT SON!

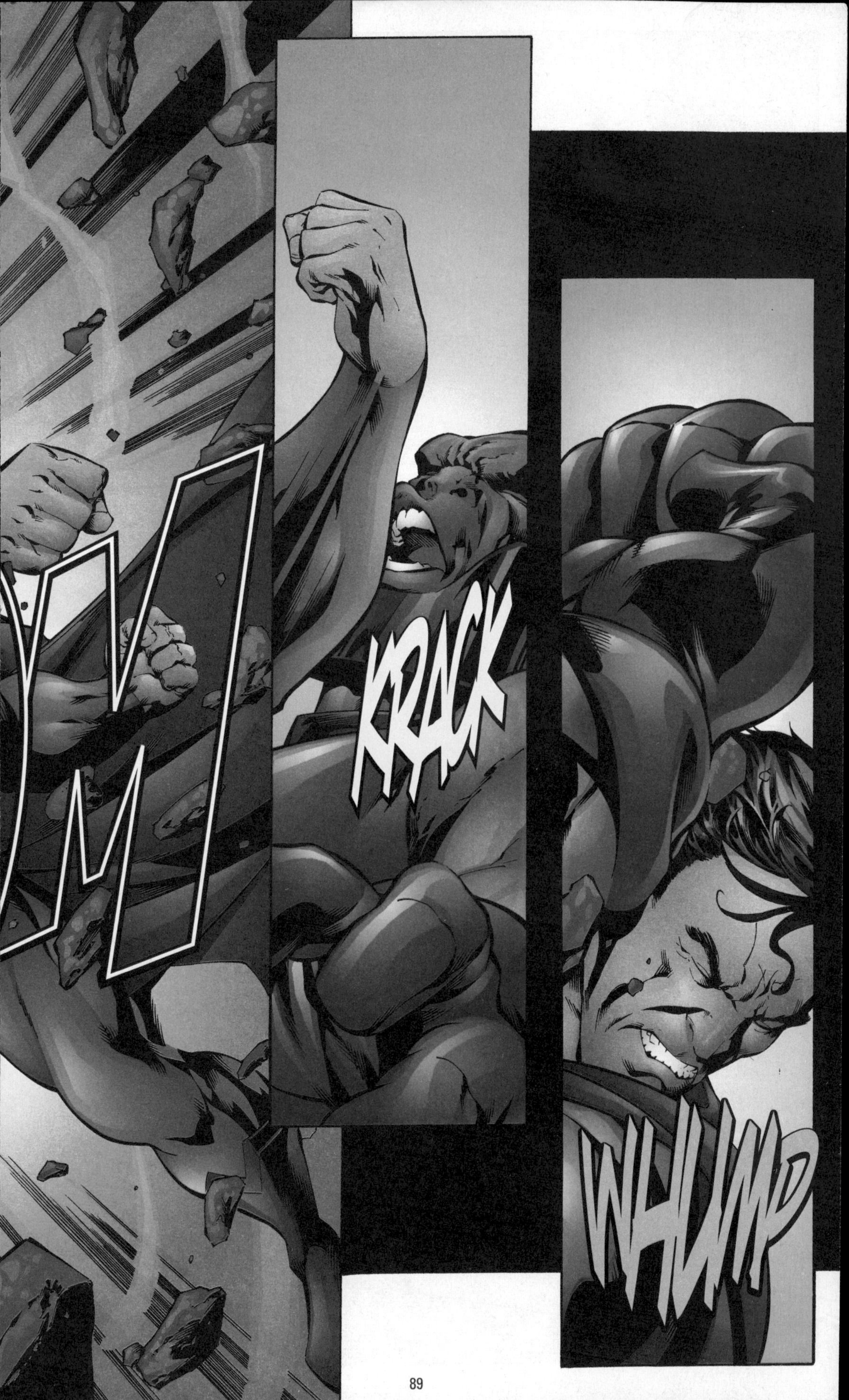

KRACK
WHUMP

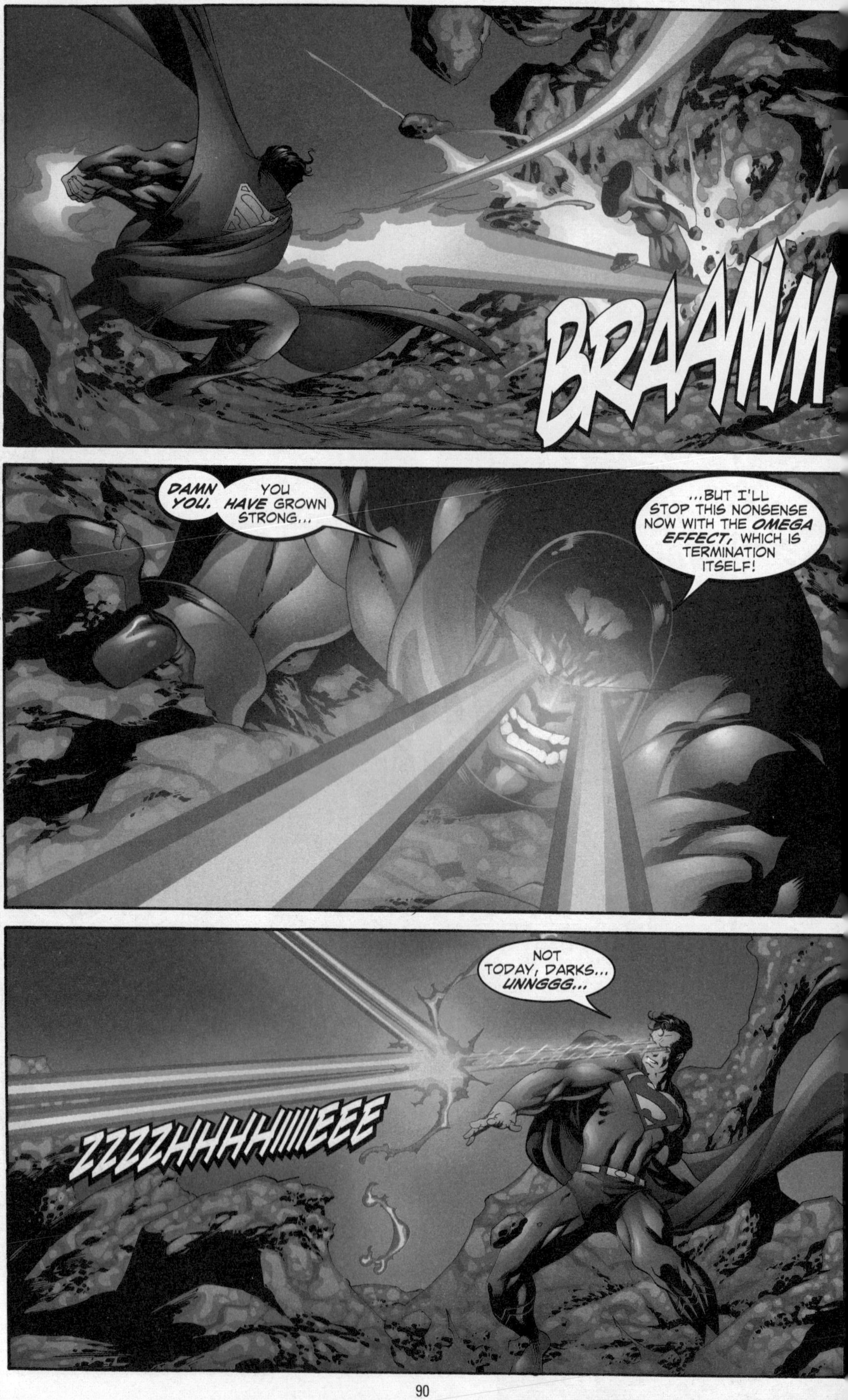
BRAAMM
DAMN YOU.
YOU HAVE GROWN STRONG...
...BUT I'LL STOP THIS NONSENSE NOW WITH THE OMEGA EFFECT, WHICH IS TERMINATION ITSELF!
NOT TODAY, DARKS... UNNGGG...
ZZZZHHHHIIIIIEEE

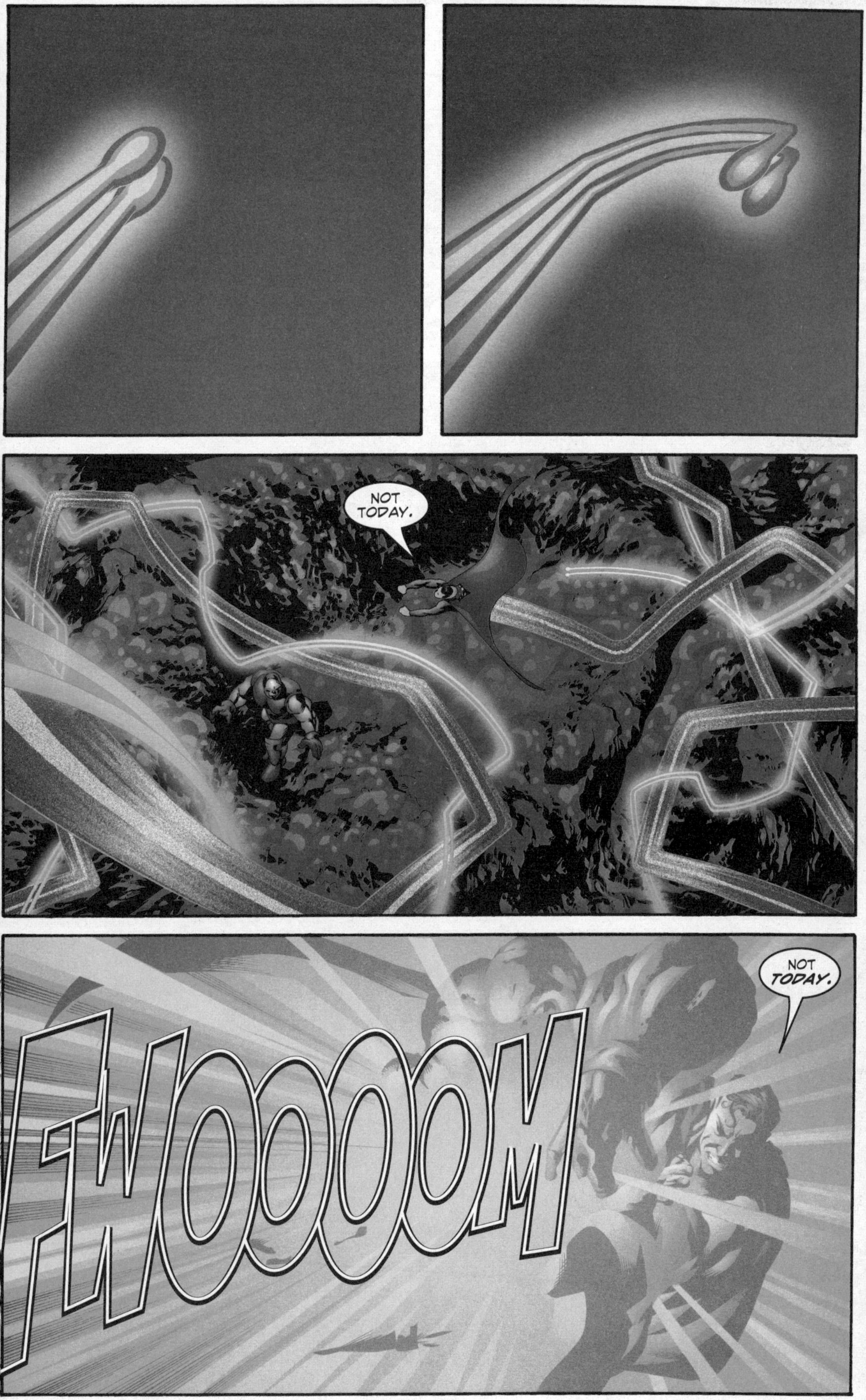
NOT TODAY.
NOT TODAY.
FWOOOOOM

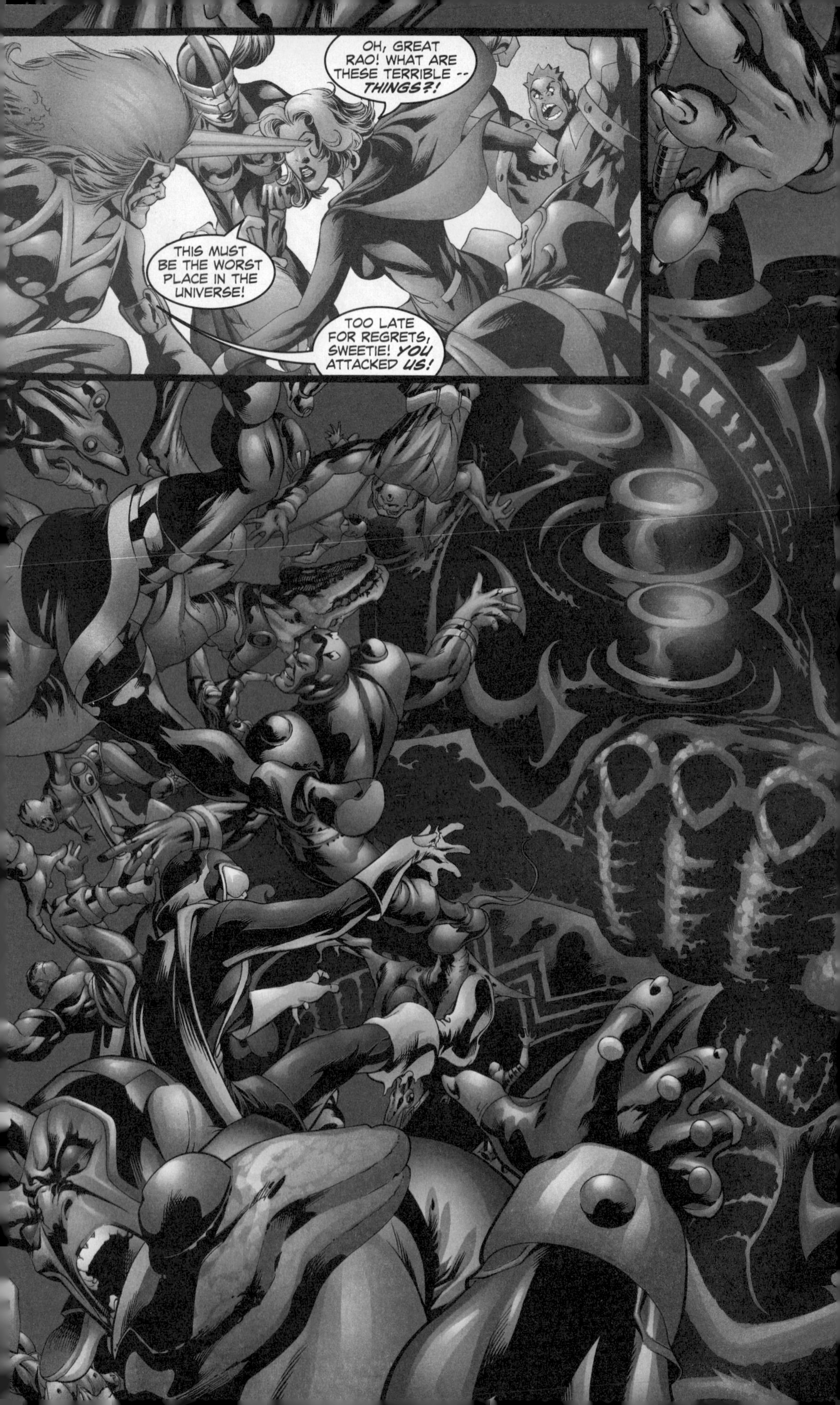
OH, GREAT RAO! WHAT ARE THESE TERRIBLE -- *THINGS?!*
THIS MUST BE THE WORST PLACE IN THE UNIVERSE!
TOO LATE FOR REGRETS, SWEETIE! *YOU* ATTACKED *US!*

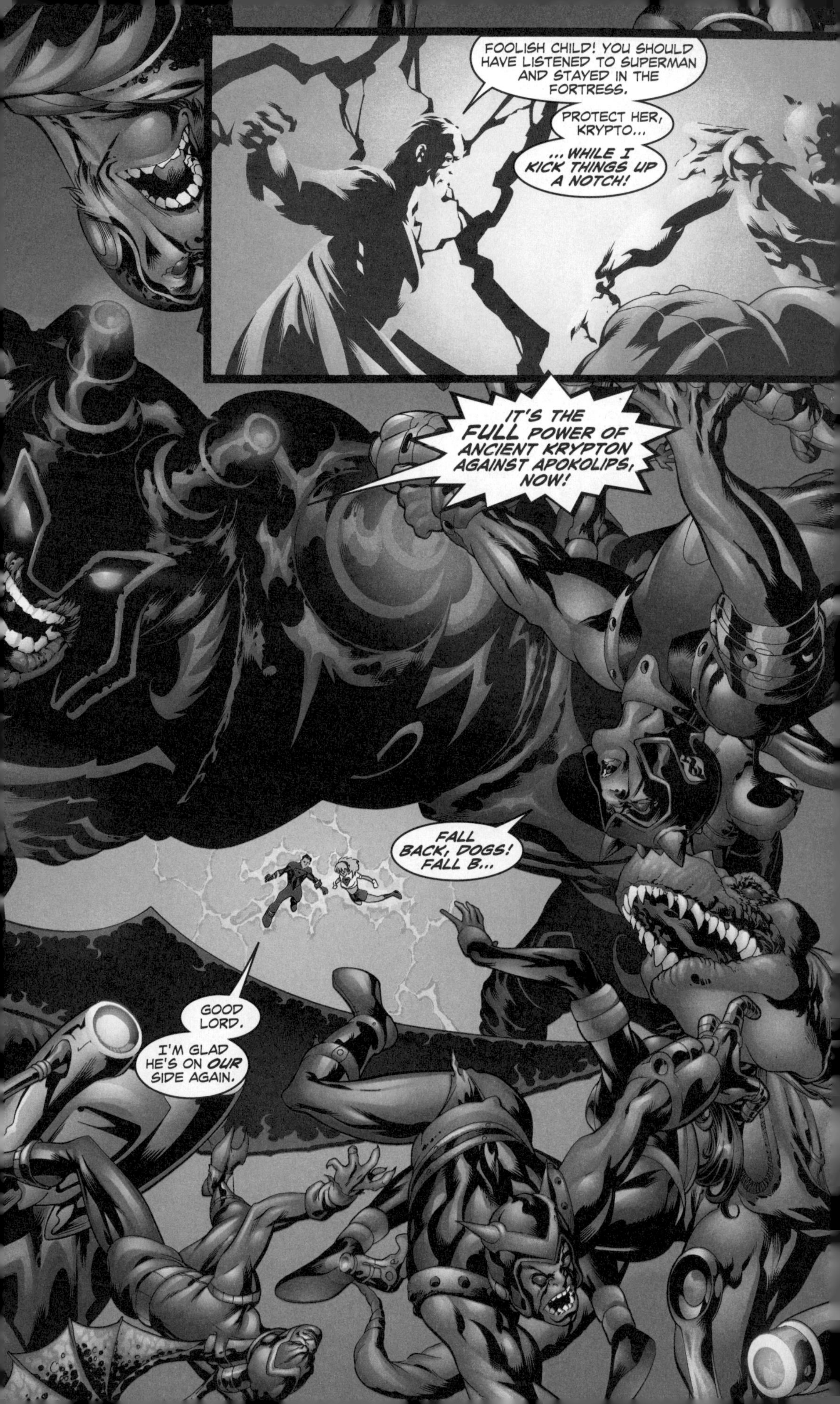
FOOLISH CHILD! YOU SHOULD HAVE LISTENED TO SUPERMAN AND STAYED IN THE FORTRESS.
PROTECT HER, KRYPTO...
...WHILE I KICK THINGS UP A NOTCH!
IT'S THE FULL POWER OF ANCIENT KRYPTON AGAINST APOKOLIPS, NOW!
FALL BACK, DOGS! FALL B...
GOOD LORD.
I'M GLAD HE'S ON OUR SIDE AGAIN.

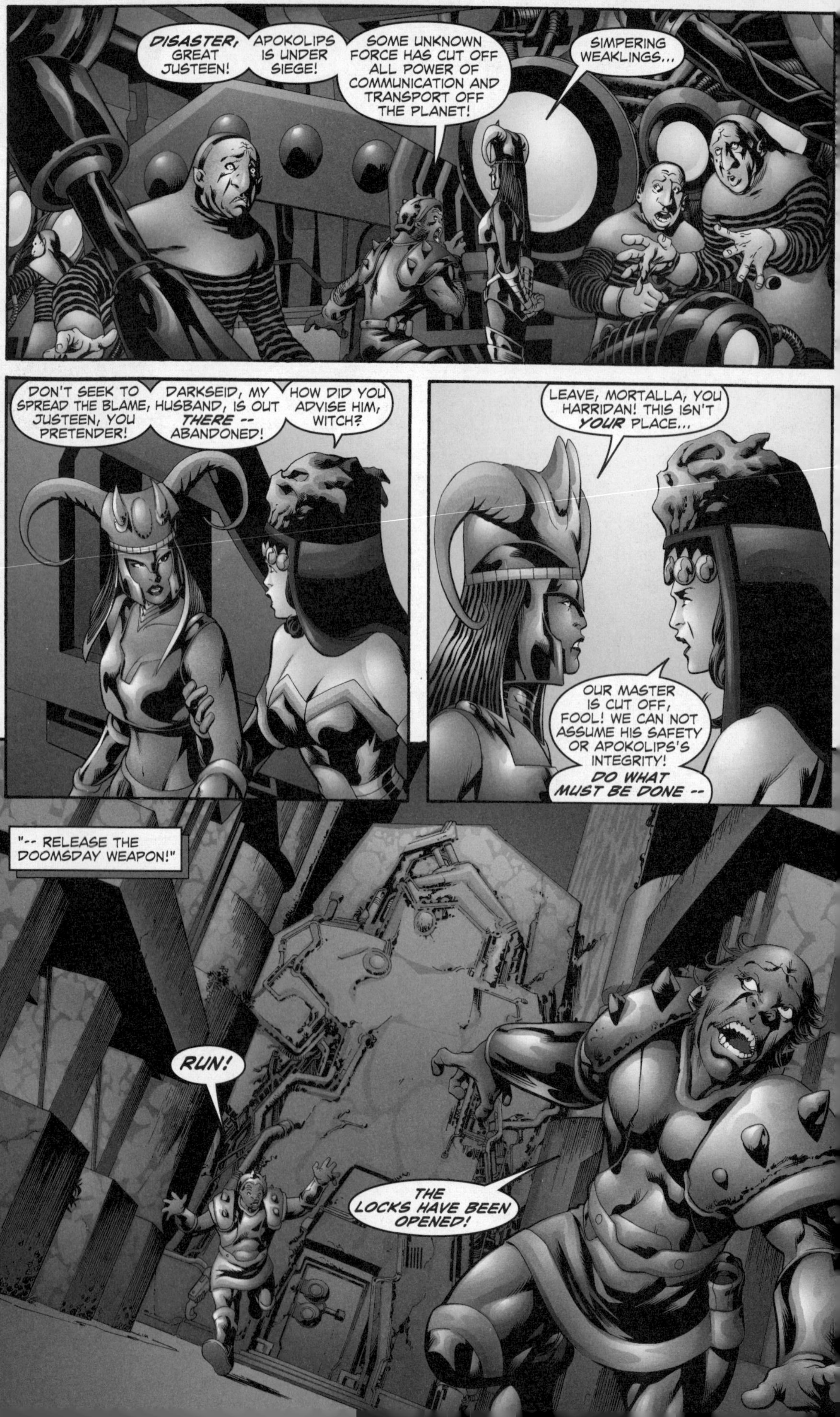
DISASTER, GREAT JUSTEEN!
APOKOLIPS IS UNDER SIEGE!
SOME UNKNOWN FORCE HAS CUT OFF ALL POWER OF COMMUNICATION AND TRANSPORT OFF THE PLANET!
SIMPERING WEAKLINGS...
DON'T SEEK TO SPREAD THE BLAME, JUSTEEN, YOU PRETENDER!
DARKSEID, MY HUSBAND, IS OUT THERE -- ABANDONED!
HOW DID YOU ADVISE HIM, WITCH?
LEAVE, MORTALLA, YOU HARRIDAN! THIS ISN'T YOUR PLACE...
OUR MASTER IS CUT OFF, FOOL! WE CAN NOT ASSUME HIS SAFETY OR APOKOLIPS'S INTEGRITY!
DO WHAT MUST BE DONE --
"-- RELEASE THE DOOMSDAY WEAPON!"
RUN!
THE LOCKS HAVE BEEN OPENED!

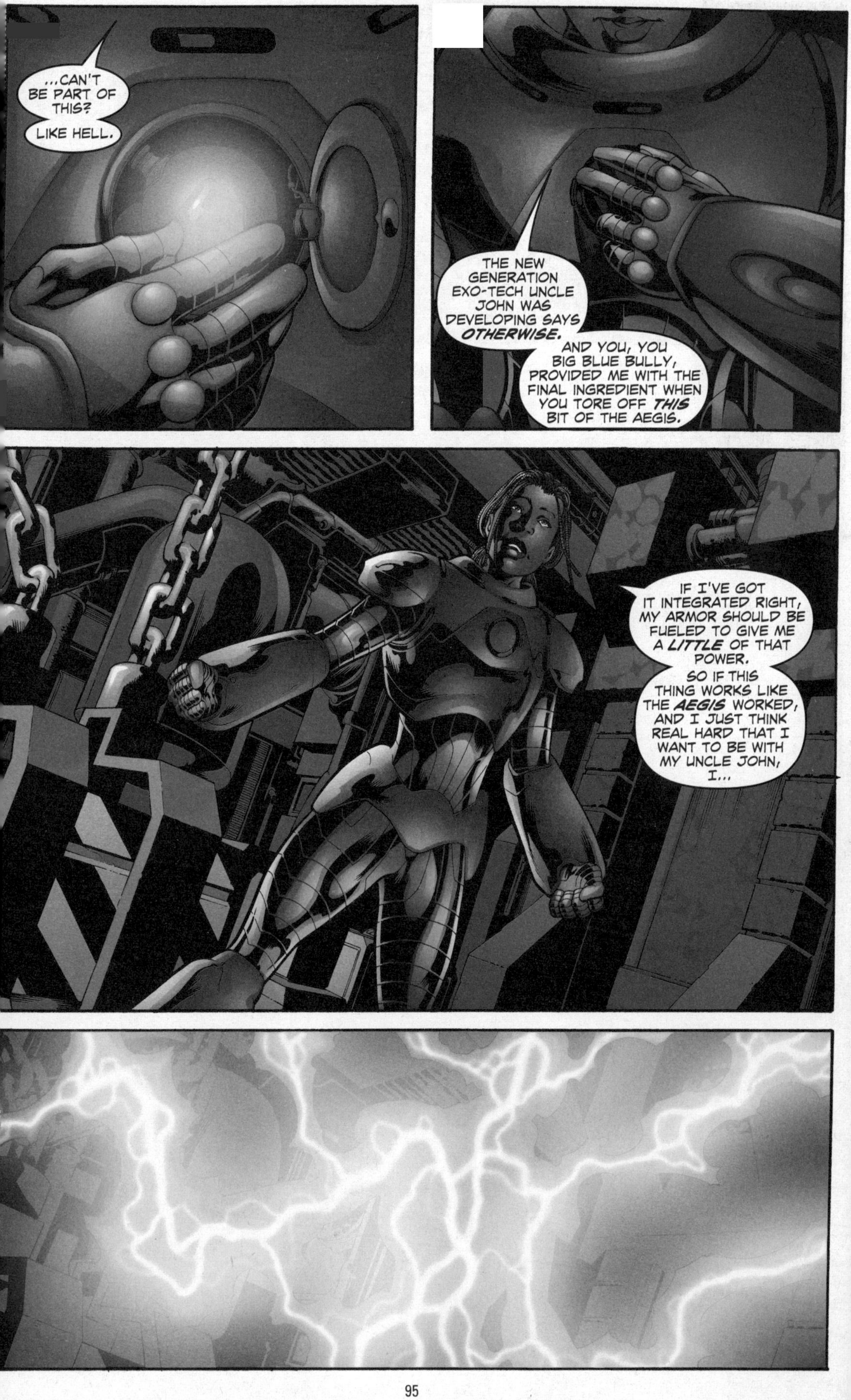
...CAN'T BE PART OF THIS?
LIKE HELL.
THE NEW GENERATION EXO-TECH UNCLE JOHN WAS DEVELOPING SAYS OTHERWISE.
AND YOU, YOU BIG BLUE BULLY, PROVIDED ME WITH THE FINAL INGREDIENT WHEN YOU TORE OFF THIS BIT OF THE AEGIS.
IF I'VE GOT IT INTEGRATED RIGHT, MY ARMOR SHOULD BE FUELED TO GIVE ME A LITTLE OF THAT POWER.
SO IF THIS THING WORKS LIKE THE AEGIS WORKED, AND I JUST THINK REAL HARD THAT I WANT TO BE WITH MY UNCLE JOHN, I...

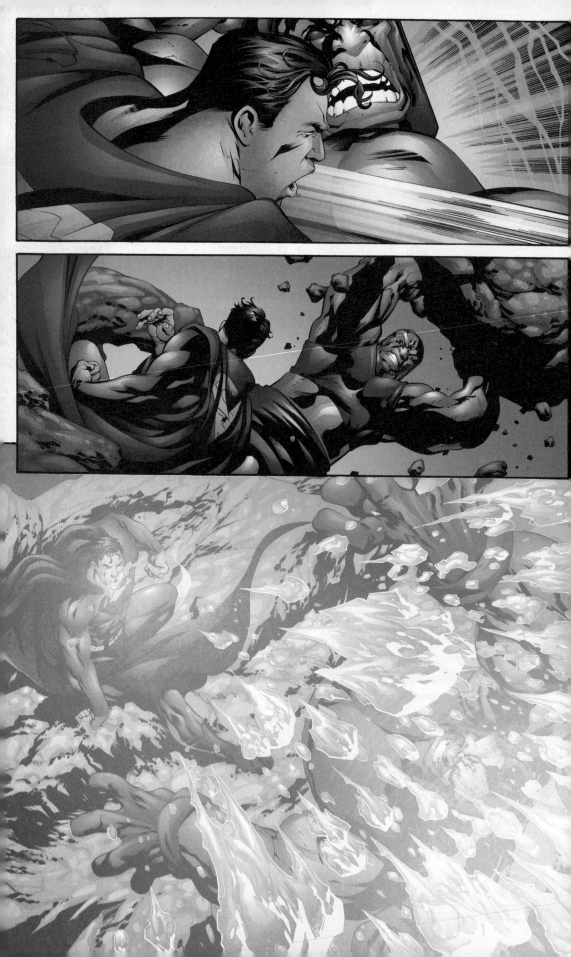

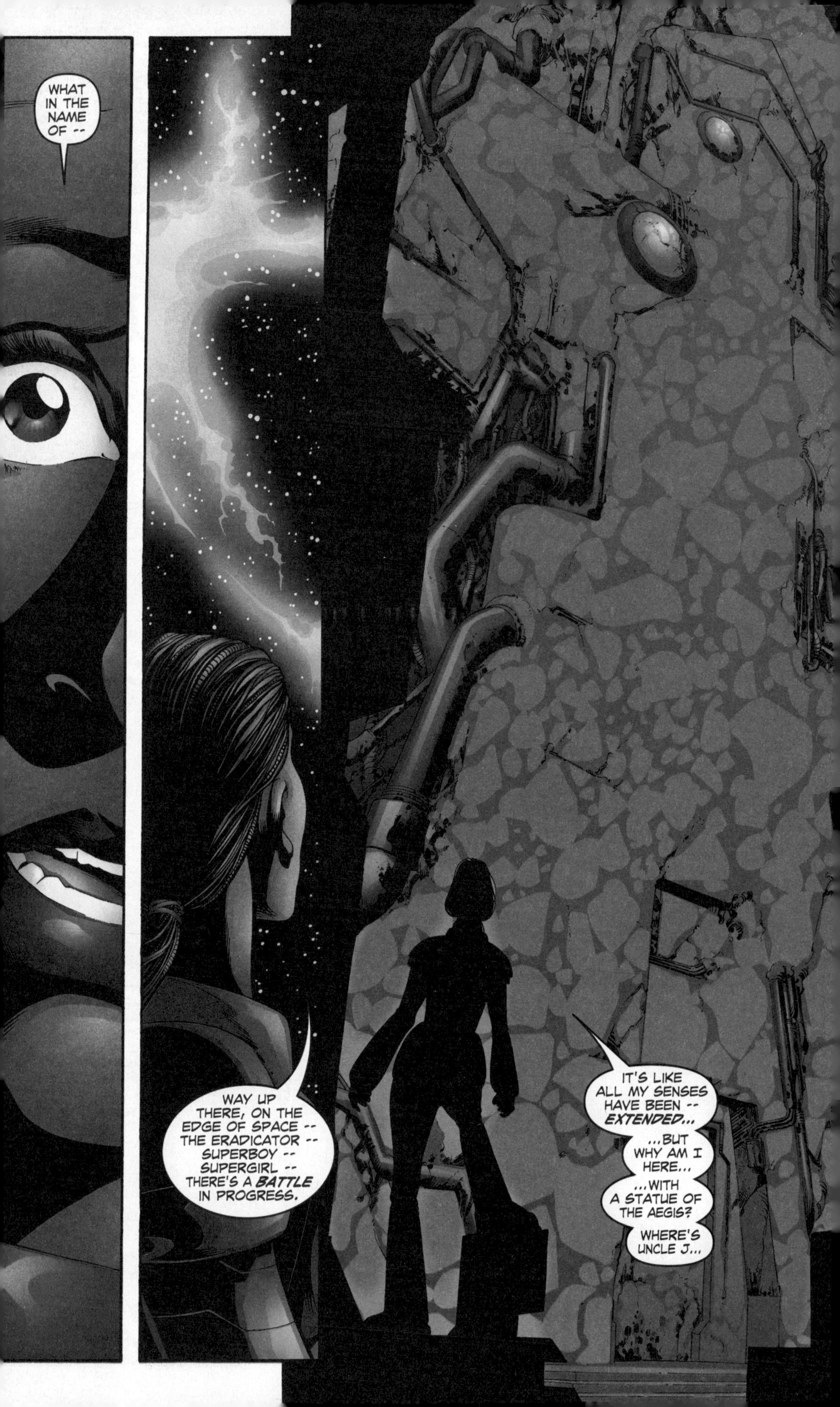
WHAT IN THE NAME OF --
WAY UP THERE, ON THE EDGE OF SPACE -- THE ERADICATOR -- SUPERBOY -- SUPERGIRL -- THERE'S A *BATTLE* IN PROGRESS.
IT'S LIKE ALL MY SENSES HAVE BEEN -- *EXTENDED...*
...BUT WHY AM I HERE...
...WITH A STATUE OF THE AEGIS?
WHERE'S UNCLE J...

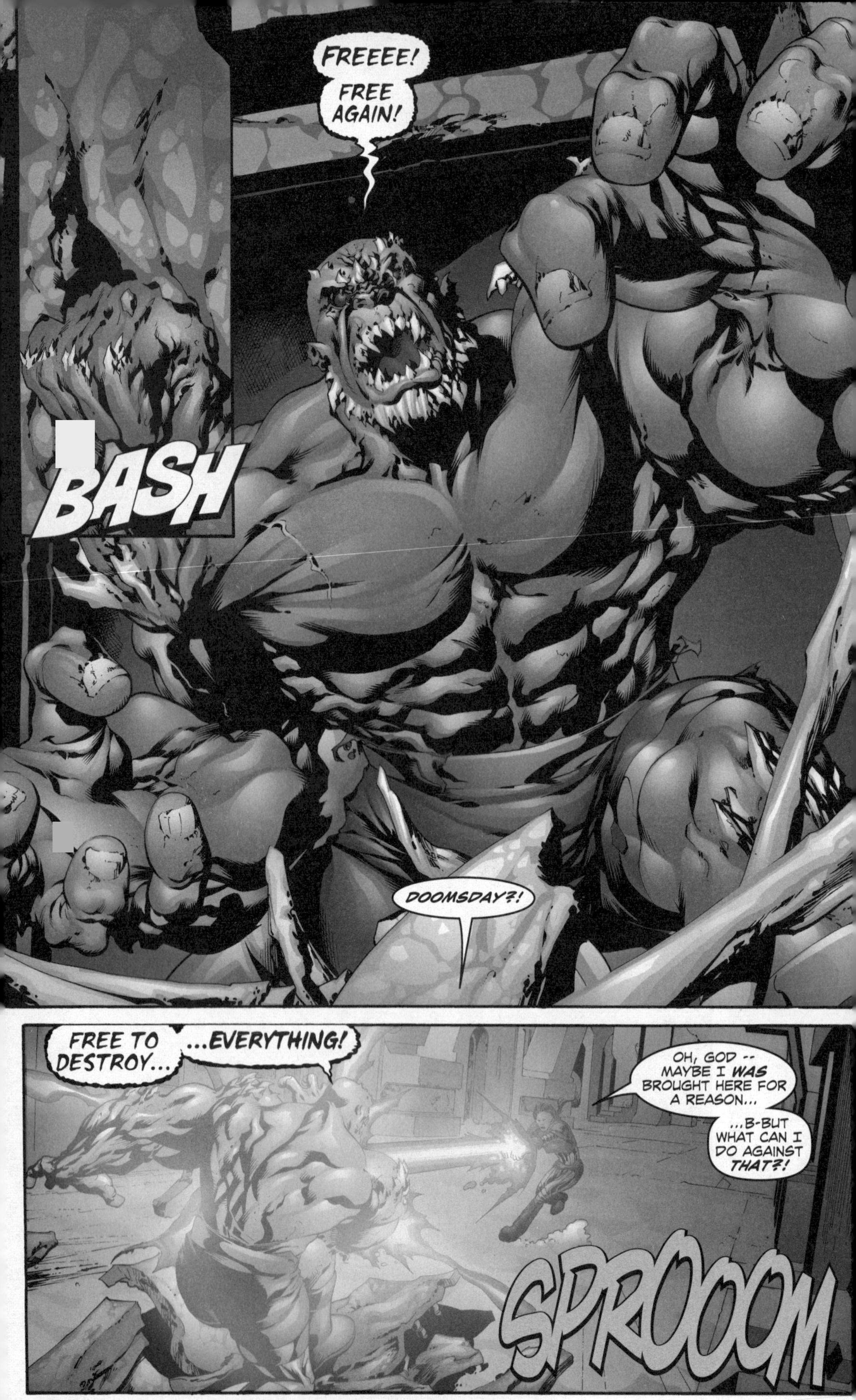
FREEEE!
FREE AGAIN!
BASH
DOOMSDAY?!
FREE TO DESTROY...
...EVERYTHING!
OH, GOD -- MAYBE I *WAS* BROUGHT HERE FOR A REASON...
...B-BUT WHAT CAN I DO AGAINST *THAT*?!
SPROOOM

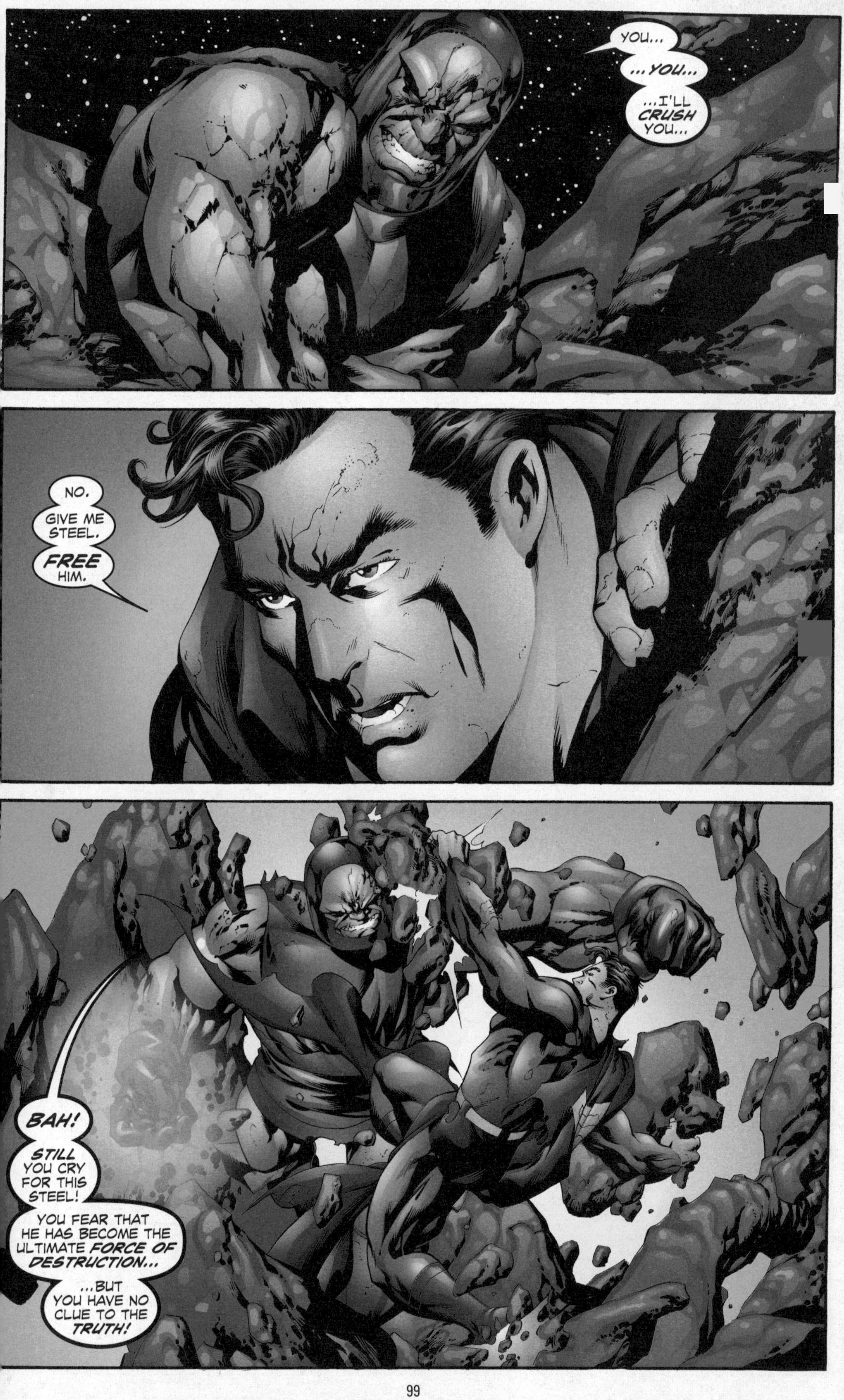

YOU...
...YOU...
...I'LL CRUSH YOU...
NO.
GIVE ME STEEL.
FREE HIM.
BAH!
STILL YOU CRY FOR THIS STEEL!
YOU FEAR THAT HE HAS BECOME THE ULTIMATE FORCE OF DESTRUCTION...
...BUT YOU HAVE NO CLUE TO THE TRUTH!

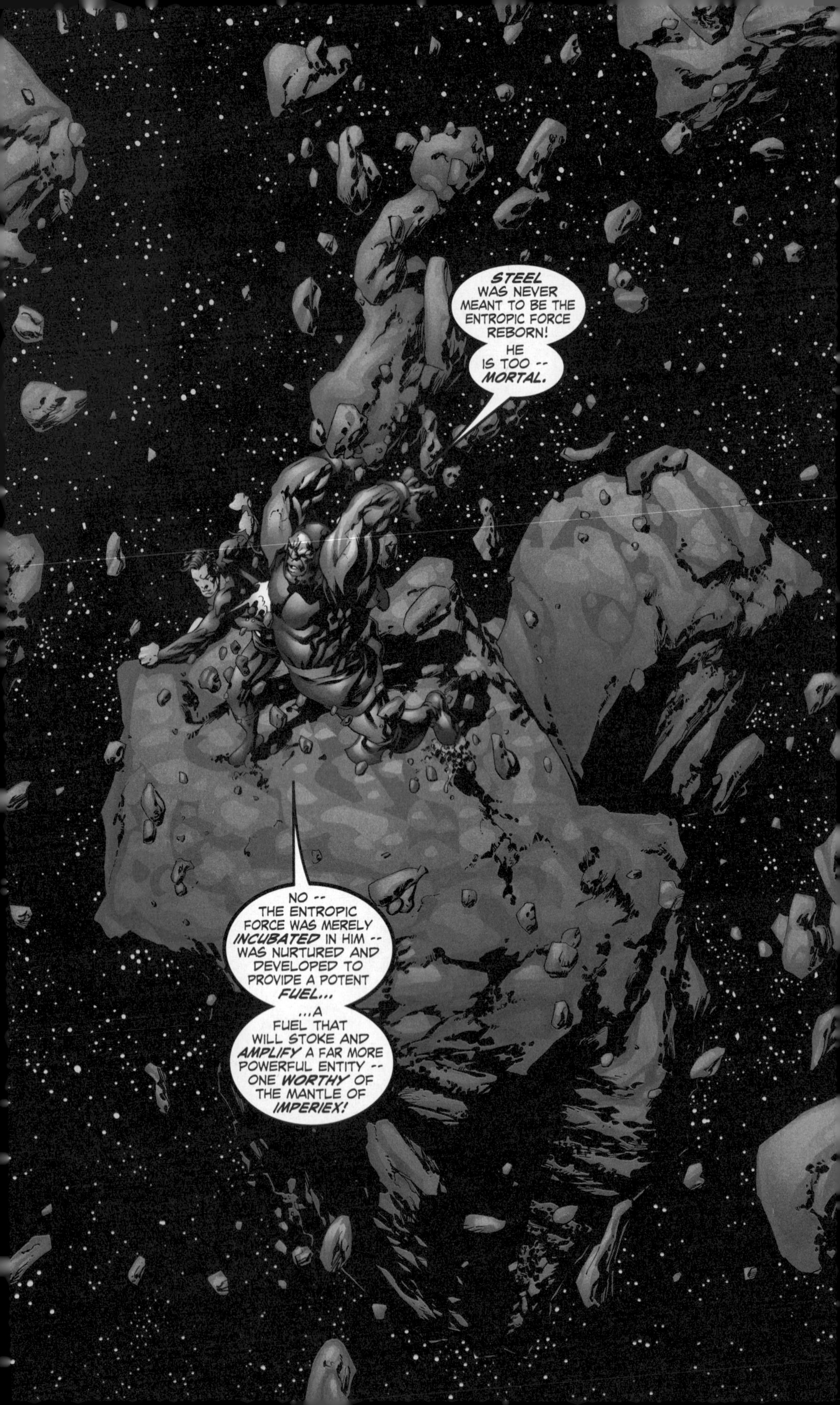

STEEL WAS NEVER MEANT TO BE THE ENTROPIC FORCE REBORN! HE IS TOO -- MORTAL.
NO -- THE ENTROPIC FORCE WAS MERELY INCUBATED IN HIM -- WAS NURTURED AND DEVELOPED TO PROVIDE A POTENT FUEL...
...A FUEL THAT WILL STOKE AND AMPLIFY A FAR MORE POWERFUL ENTITY -- ONE WORTHY OF THE MANTLE OF IMPERIEX!

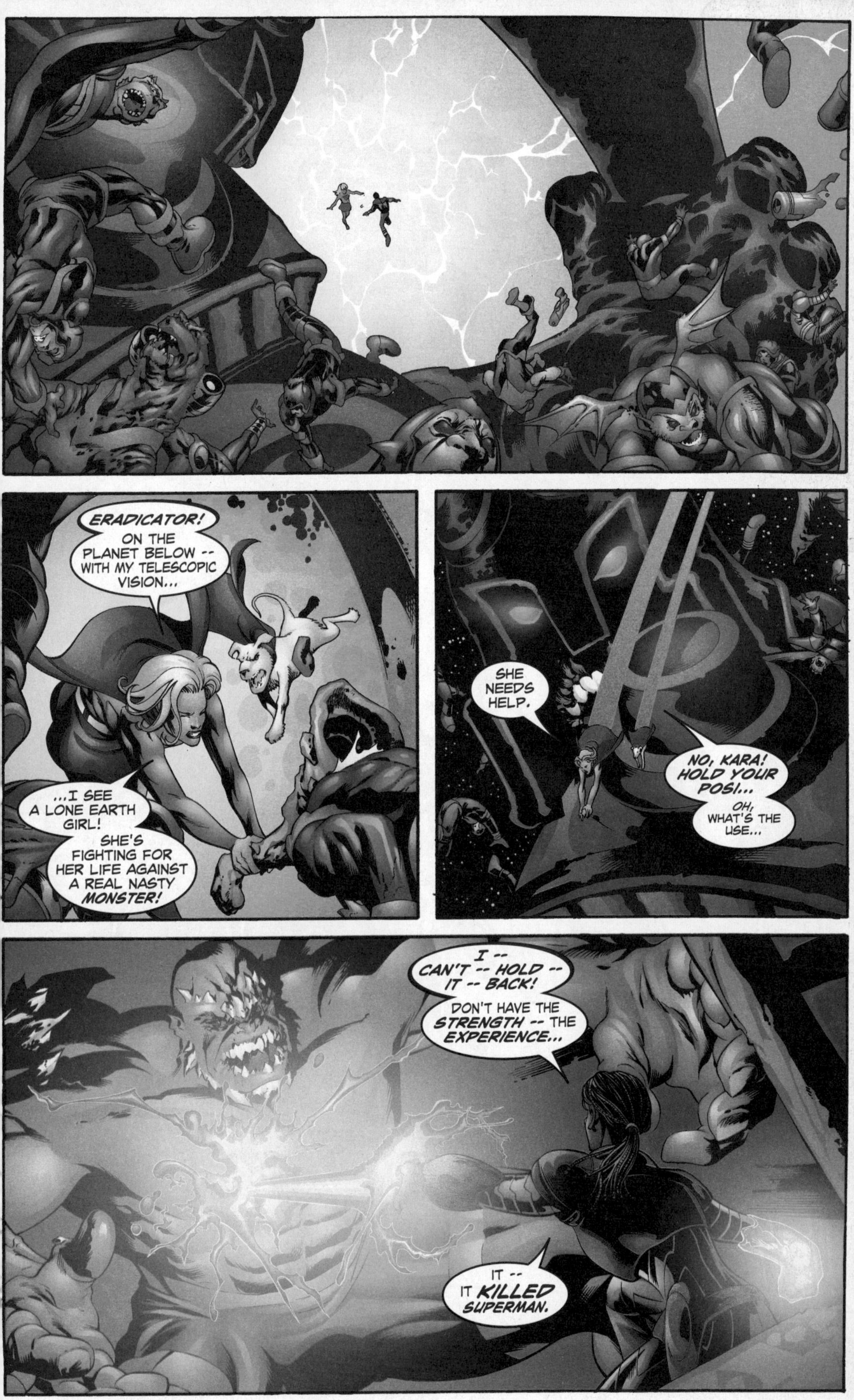
ERADICATOR! ON THE PLANET BELOW -- WITH MY TELESCOPIC VISION...
...I SEE A LONE EARTH GIRL! SHE'S FIGHTING FOR HER LIFE AGAINST A REAL NASTY MONSTER!
SHE NEEDS HELP.
NO, KARA! HOLD YOUR POSI... OH, WHAT'S THE USE...
I -- CAN'T -- HOLD -- IT -- BACK! DON'T HAVE THE STRENGTH -- THE EXPERIENCE...
IT -- IT KILLED SUPERMAN.

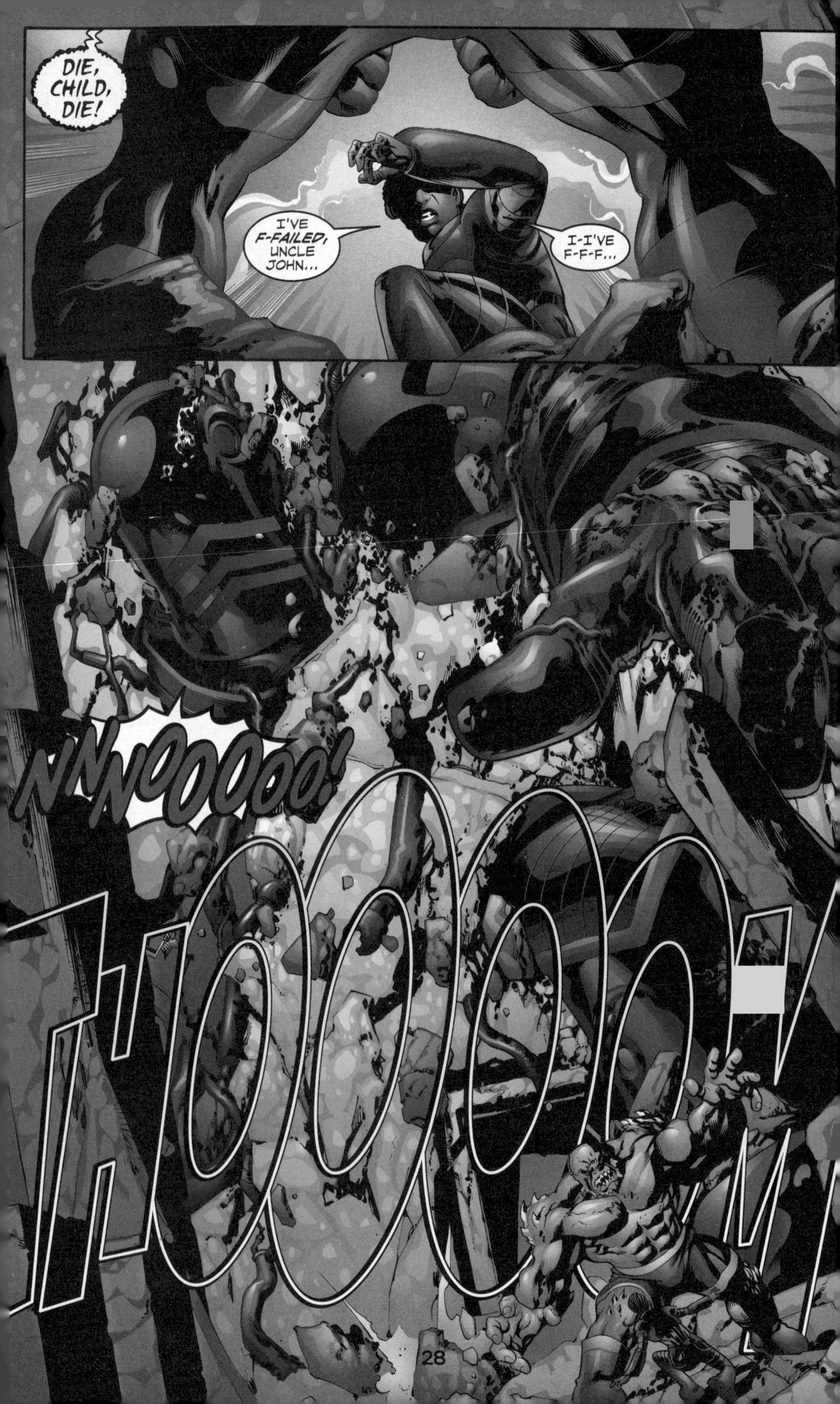
DIE, CHILD, DIE!
I'VE F-FAILED, UNCLE JOHN...
I-I'VE F-F-F...
NNNOOOOOO!
THOOOOOM

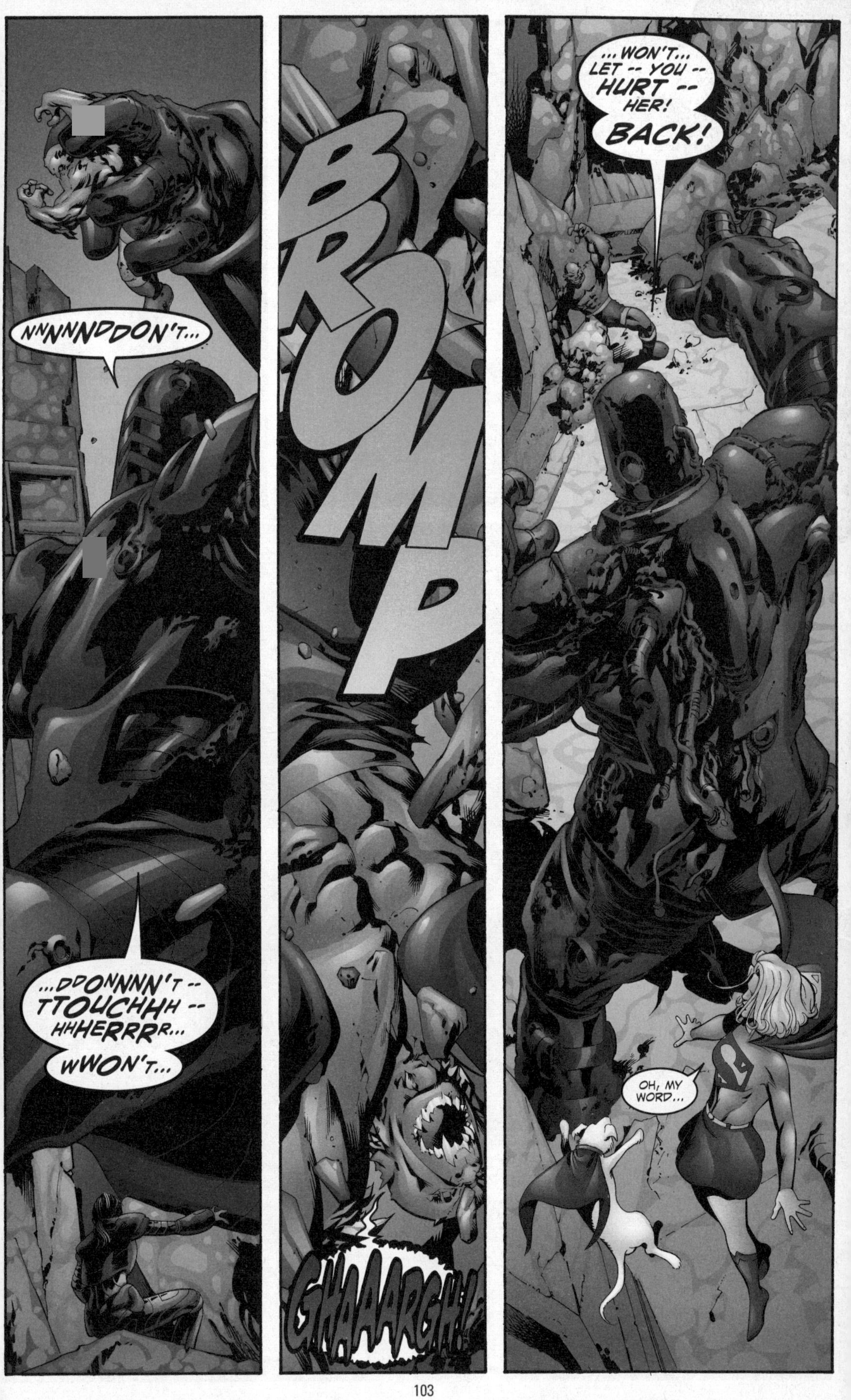
NNNNDDON'T...
...DDONNNN'T -- TTOUCHHH -- HHHERRRR...
WWON'T...
BROMP
GHAAARGH!!
...WON'T... LET -- YOU -- HURT -- HER! BACK!
OH, MY WORD...

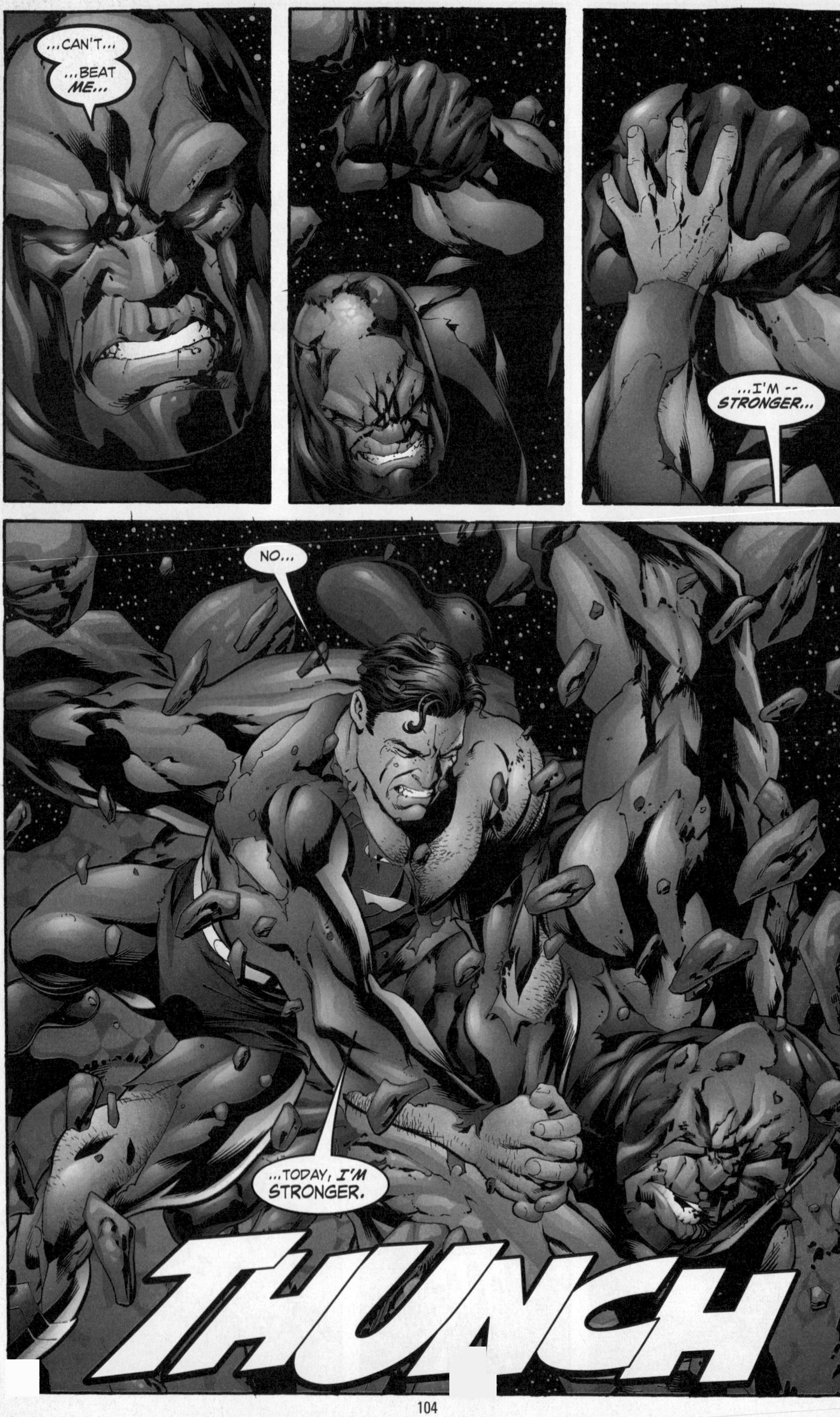
...CAN'T...
...BEAT ME...
...I'M -- STRONGER...
NO...
...TODAY, I'M STRONGER.
THUNCH

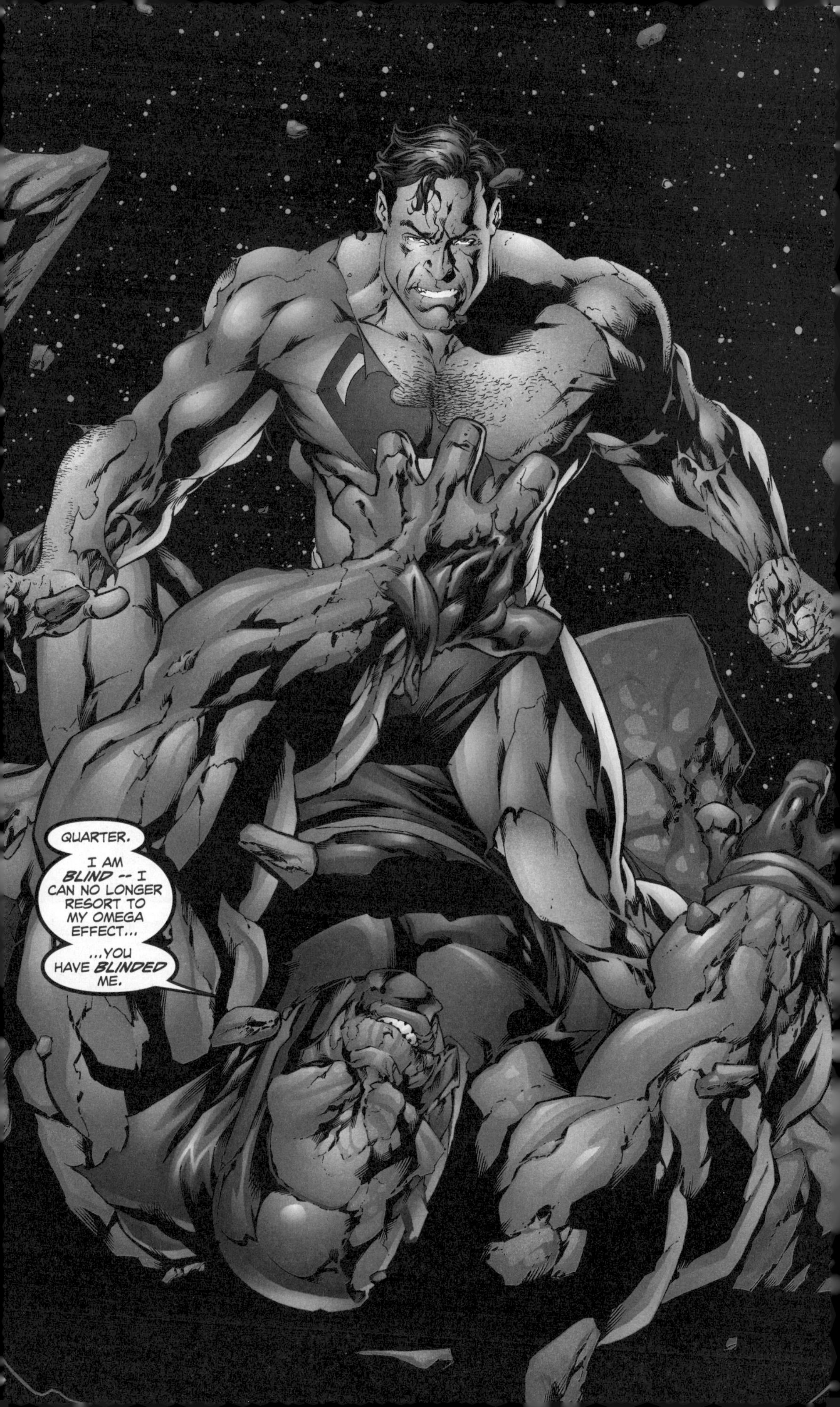
QUARTER.
I AM *BLIND* -- I CAN NO LONGER RESORT TO MY OMEGA EFFECT...
...YOU HAVE *BLINDED* ME.

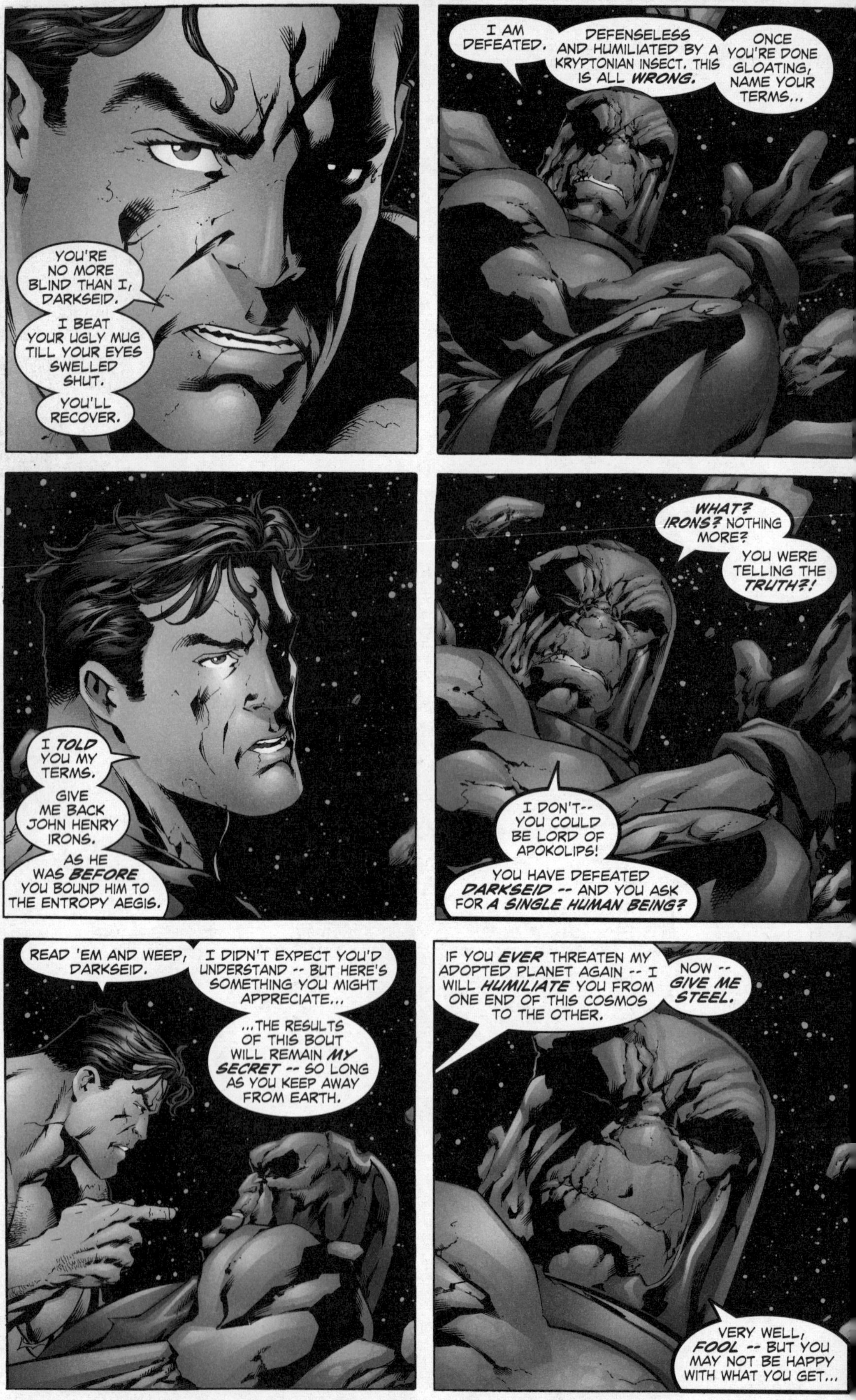

YOU'RE NO MORE BLIND THAN I, DARKSEID.
I BEAT YOUR UGLY MUG TILL YOUR EYES SWELLED SHUT.
YOU'LL RECOVER.
I AM DEFEATED.
DEFENSELESS AND HUMILIATED BY A KRYPTONIAN INSECT. THIS IS ALL WRONG.
ONCE YOU'RE DONE GLOATING, NAME YOUR TERMS...
I TOLD YOU MY TERMS.
GIVE ME BACK JOHN HENRY IRONS.
AS HE WAS BEFORE YOU BOUND HIM TO THE ENTROPY AEGIS.
WHAT? IRONS? NOTHING MORE?
YOU WERE TELLING THE TRUTH?!
I DON'T-- YOU COULD BE LORD OF APOKOLIPS!
YOU HAVE DEFEATED DARKSEID -- AND YOU ASK FOR A SINGLE HUMAN BEING?
READ 'EM AND WEEP, DARKSEID.
I DIDN'T EXPECT YOU'D UNDERSTAND -- BUT HERE'S SOMETHING YOU MIGHT APPRECIATE...
...THE RESULTS OF THIS BOUT WILL REMAIN MY SECRET -- SO LONG AS YOU KEEP AWAY FROM EARTH.
IF YOU EVER THREATEN MY ADOPTED PLANET AGAIN -- I WILL HUMILIATE YOU FROM ONE END OF THIS COSMOS TO THE OTHER.
NOW -- GIVE ME STEEL.
VERY WELL, FOOL -- BUT YOU MAY NOT BE HAPPY WITH WHAT YOU GET...

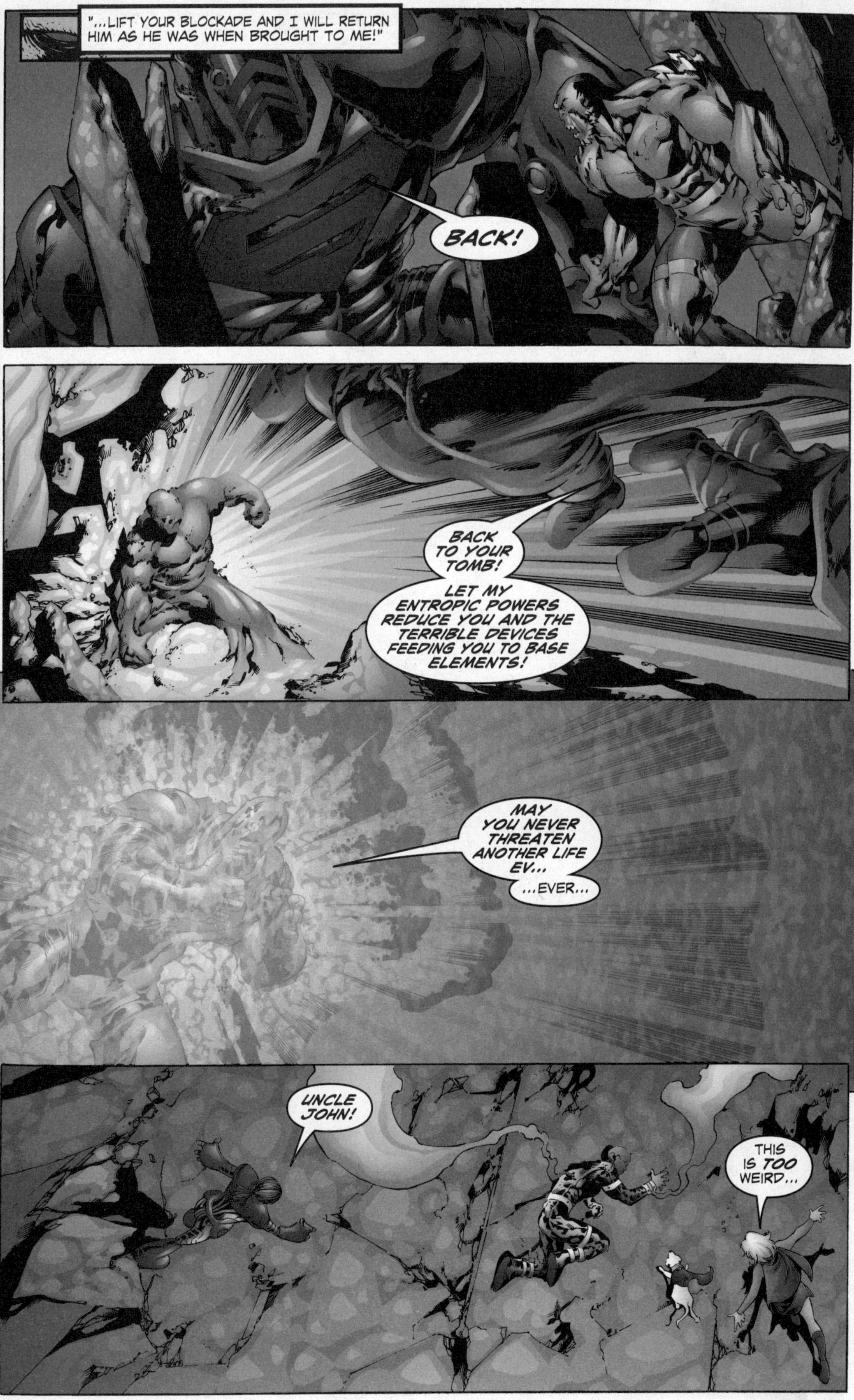
"...LIFT YOUR BLOCKADE AND I WILL RETURN HIM AS HE WAS WHEN BROUGHT TO ME!"
BACK!
BACK TO YOUR TOMB!
LET MY ENTROPIC POWERS REDUCE YOU AND THE TERRIBLE DEVICES FEEDING YOU TO BASE ELEMENTS!
MAY YOU NEVER THREATEN ANOTHER LIFE EV...
...EVER...
UNCLE JOHN!
THIS IS TOO WEIRD...

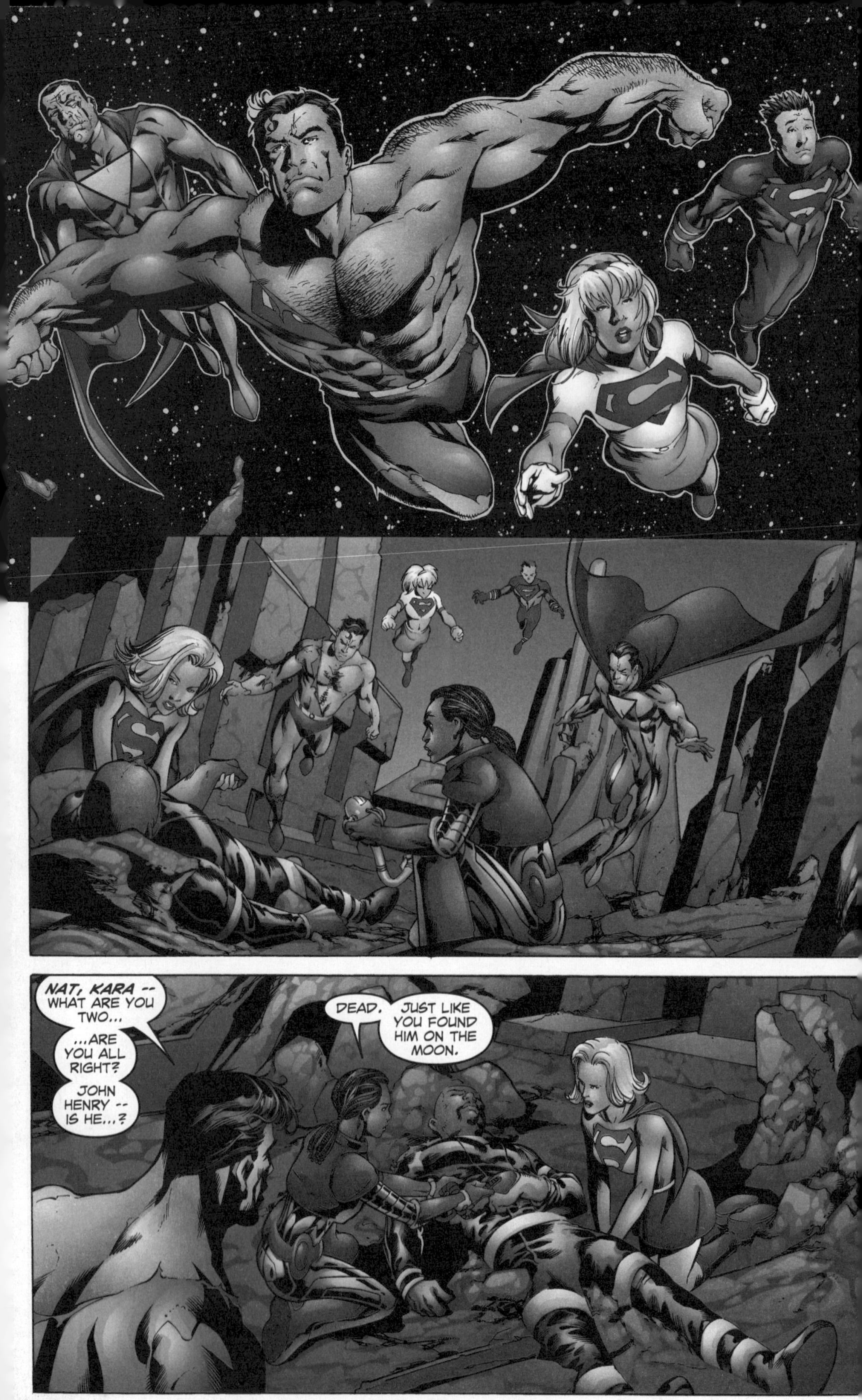
NAT, KARA -- WHAT ARE YOU TWO...
...ARE YOU ALL RIGHT?
JOHN HENRY -- IS HE...?
DEAD.
JUST LIKE YOU FOUND HIM ON THE MOON.

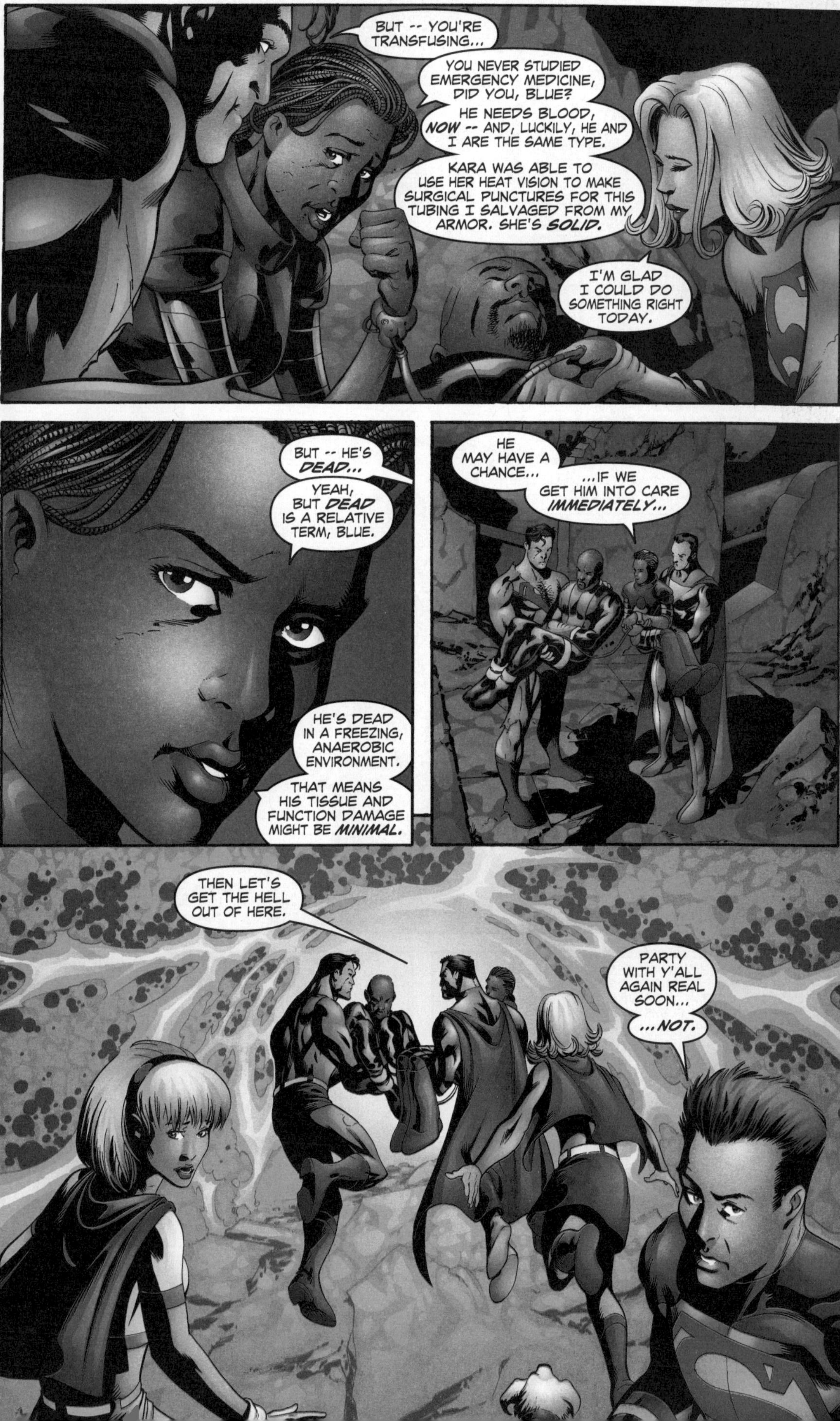
BUT -- YOU'RE TRANSFUSING...
YOU NEVER STUDIED EMERGENCY MEDICINE, DID YOU, BLUE?
HE NEEDS BLOOD, NOW -- AND, LUCKILY, HE AND I ARE THE SAME TYPE.
KARA WAS ABLE TO USE HER HEAT VISION TO MAKE SURGICAL PUNCTURES FOR THIS TUBING I SALVAGED FROM MY ARMOR. SHE'S SOLID.
I'M GLAD I COULD DO SOMETHING RIGHT TODAY.
BUT -- HE'S DEAD...
YEAH, BUT DEAD IS A RELATIVE TERM, BLUE.
HE'S DEAD IN A FREEZING, ANAEROBIC ENVIRONMENT.
THAT MEANS HIS TISSUE AND FUNCTION DAMAGE MIGHT BE MINIMAL.
HE MAY HAVE A CHANCE...
...IF WE GET HIM INTO CARE IMMEDIATELY...
THEN LET'S GET THE HELL OUT OF HERE.
PARTY WITH Y'ALL AGAIN REAL SOON...
...NOT.

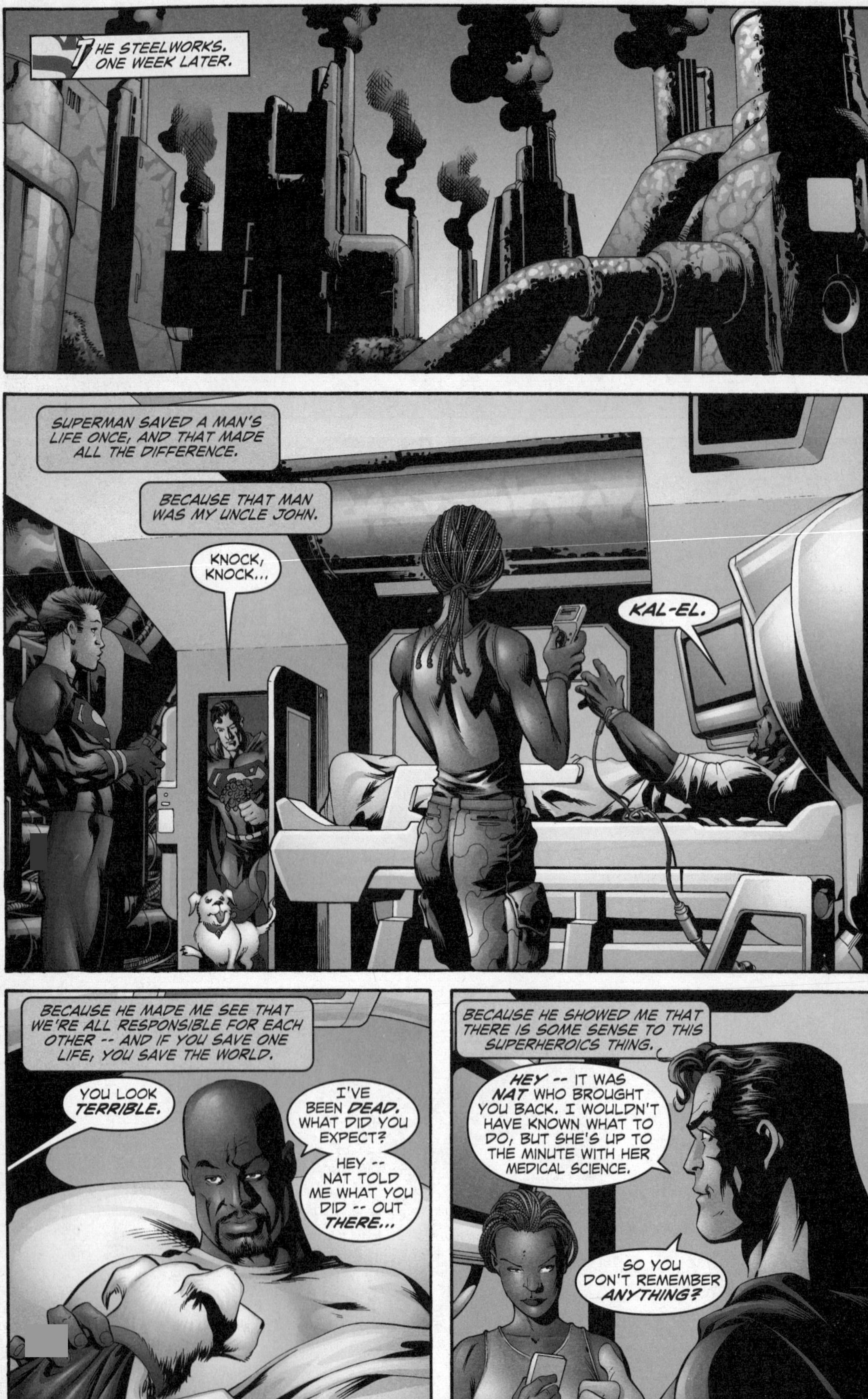
THE STEELWORKS. ONE WEEK LATER.
SUPERMAN SAVED A MAN'S LIFE ONCE, AND THAT MADE ALL THE DIFFERENCE.
BECAUSE THAT MAN WAS MY UNCLE JOHN.
KNOCK, KNOCK...
KAL-EL.
BECAUSE HE MADE ME SEE THAT WE'RE ALL RESPONSIBLE FOR EACH OTHER -- AND IF YOU SAVE ONE LIFE, YOU SAVE THE WORLD.
YOU LOOK TERRIBLE.
I'VE BEEN DEAD. WHAT DID YOU EXPECT?
HEY -- NAT TOLD ME WHAT YOU DID -- OUT THERE...
BECAUSE HE SHOWED ME THAT THERE IS SOME SENSE TO THIS SUPERHEROICS THING.
HEY -- IT WAS NAT WHO BROUGHT YOU BACK. I WOULDN'T HAVE KNOWN WHAT TO DO, BUT SHE'S UP TO THE MINUTE WITH HER MEDICAL SCIENCE.
SO YOU DON'T REMEMBER ANYTHING?

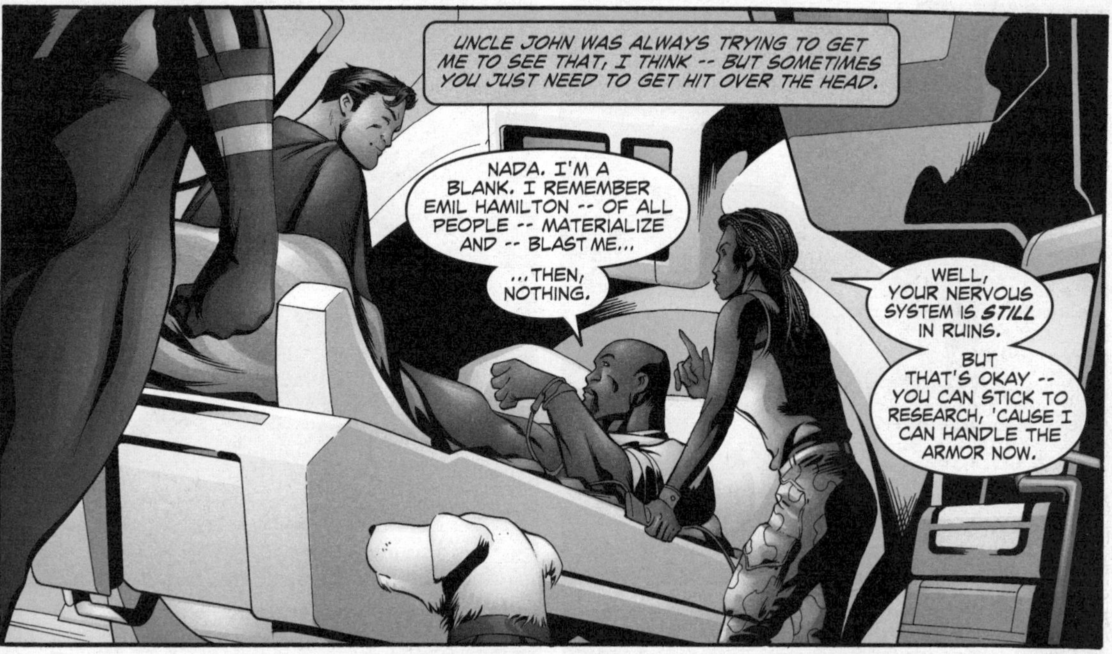
UNCLE JOHN WAS ALWAYS TRYING TO GET ME TO SEE THAT, I THINK -- BUT SOMETIMES YOU JUST NEED TO GET HIT OVER THE HEAD.
NADA. I'M A BLANK. I REMEMBER EMIL HAMILTON -- OF ALL PEOPLE -- MATERIALIZE AND -- BLAST ME...
...THEN, NOTHING.
WELL, YOUR NERVOUS SYSTEM IS STILL IN RUINS.
BUT THAT'S OKAY -- YOU CAN STICK TO RESEARCH, 'CAUSE I CAN HANDLE THE ARMOR NOW.

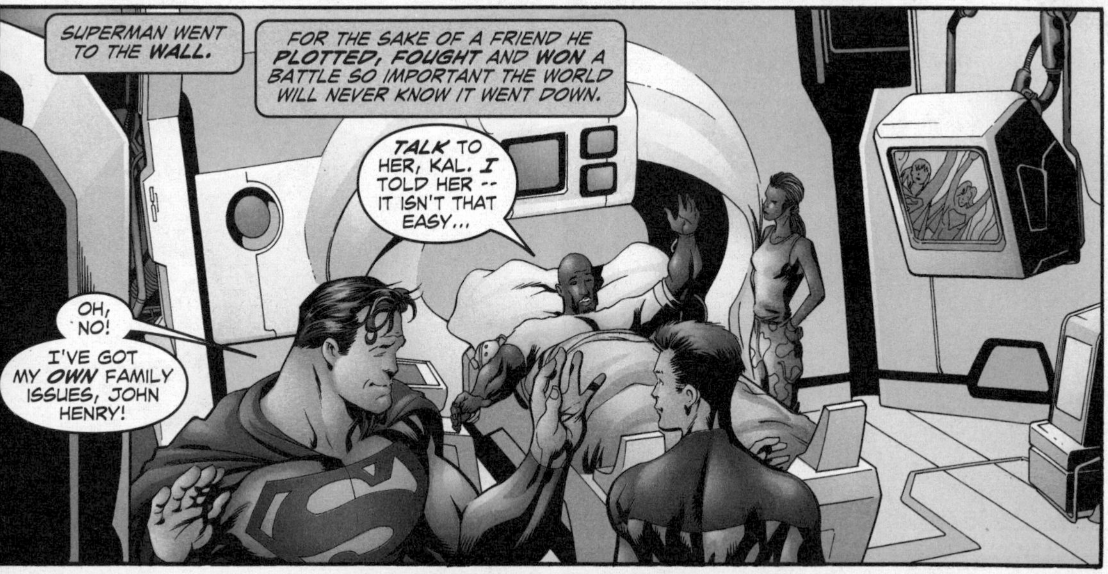
SUPERMAN WENT TO THE WALL.
FOR THE SAKE OF A FRIEND HE PLOTTED, FOUGHT AND WON A BATTLE SO IMPORTANT THE WORLD WILL NEVER KNOW IT WENT DOWN.
TALK TO HER, KAL. I TOLD HER -- IT ISN'T THAT EASY...
OH, NO! I'VE GOT MY OWN FAMILY ISSUES, JOHN HENRY!

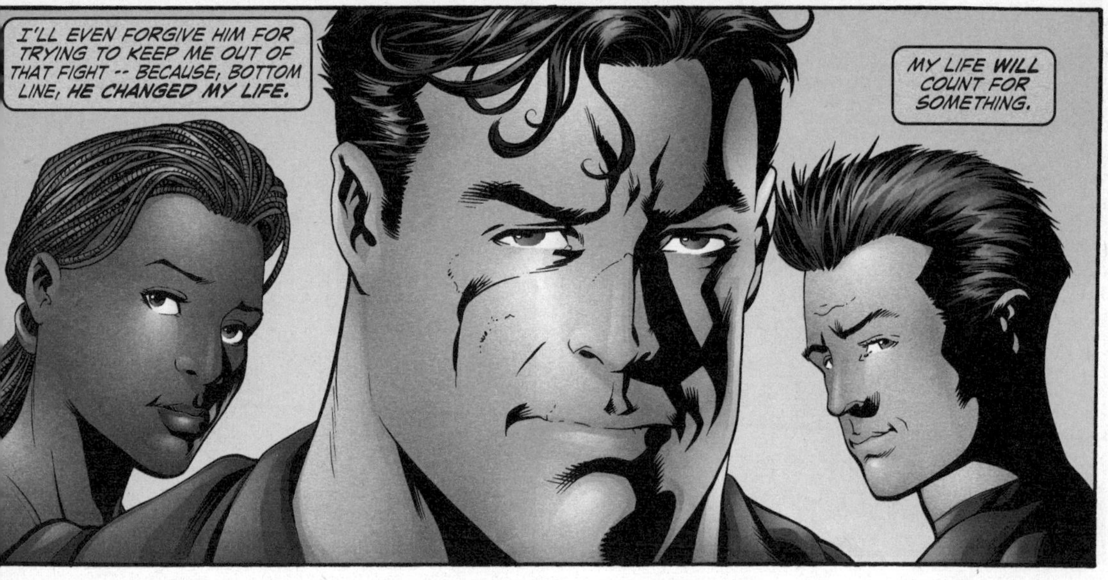
I'LL EVEN FORGIVE HIM FOR TRYING TO KEEP ME OUT OF THAT FIGHT -- BECAUSE, BOTTOM LINE, HE CHANGED MY LIFE.
MY LIFE WILL COUNT FOR SOMETHING.

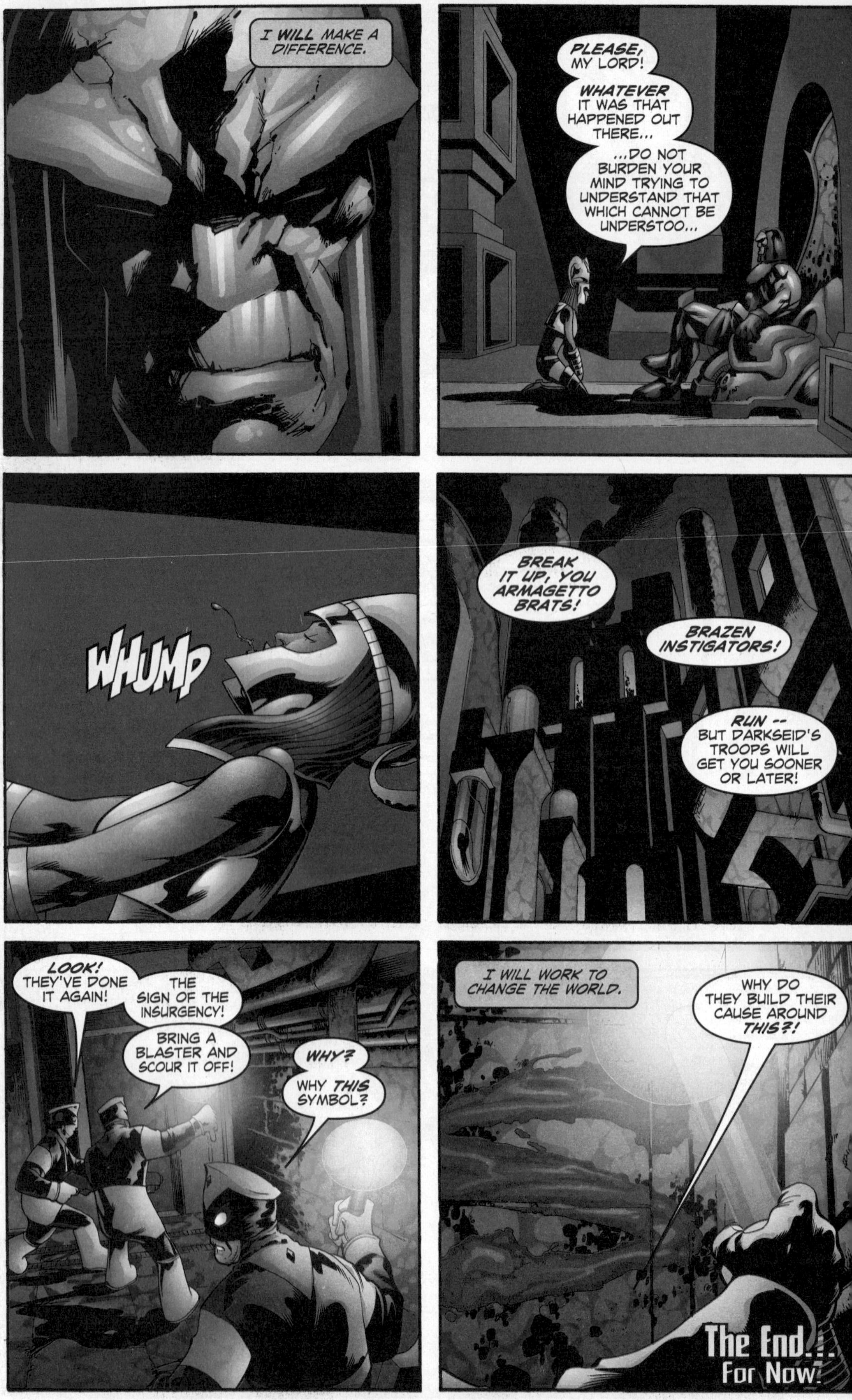
I WILL MAKE A DIFFERENCE.
PLEASE, MY LORD!
WHATEVER IT WAS THAT HAPPENED OUT THERE...
...DO NOT BURDEN YOUR MIND TRYING TO UNDERSTAND THAT WHICH CANNOT BE UNDERSTOO...
WHUMP
BREAK IT UP, YOU ARMAGETTO BRATS!
BRAZEN INSTIGATORS!
RUN -- BUT DARKSEID'S TROOPS WILL GET YOU SOONER OR LATER!
LOOK! THEY'VE DONE IT AGAIN!
THE SIGN OF THE INSURGENCY!
BRING A BLASTER AND SCOUR IT OFF!
WHY?
WHY THIS SYMBOL?
I WILL WORK TO CHANGE THE WORLD.
WHY DO THEY BUILD THEIR CAUSE AROUND THIS?!
The End...
For Now!

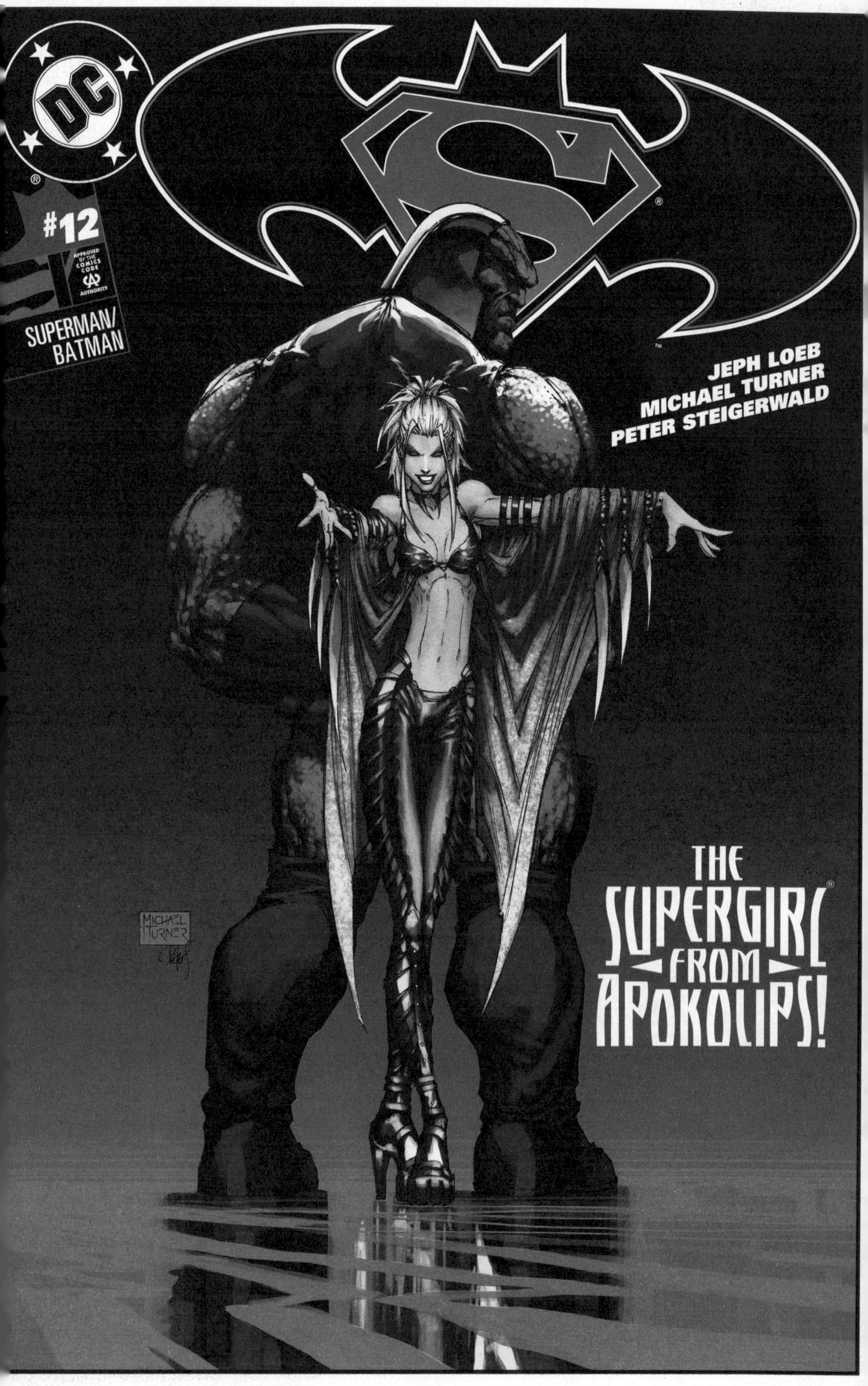
DC
#12
APPROVED BY THE COMICS CODE AUTHORITY
SUPERMAN/ BATMAN
JEPH LOEB
MICHAEL TURNER
PETER STEIGERWALD
MICHAEL TURNER
THE SUPERGIRL FROM APOKOLIPS!

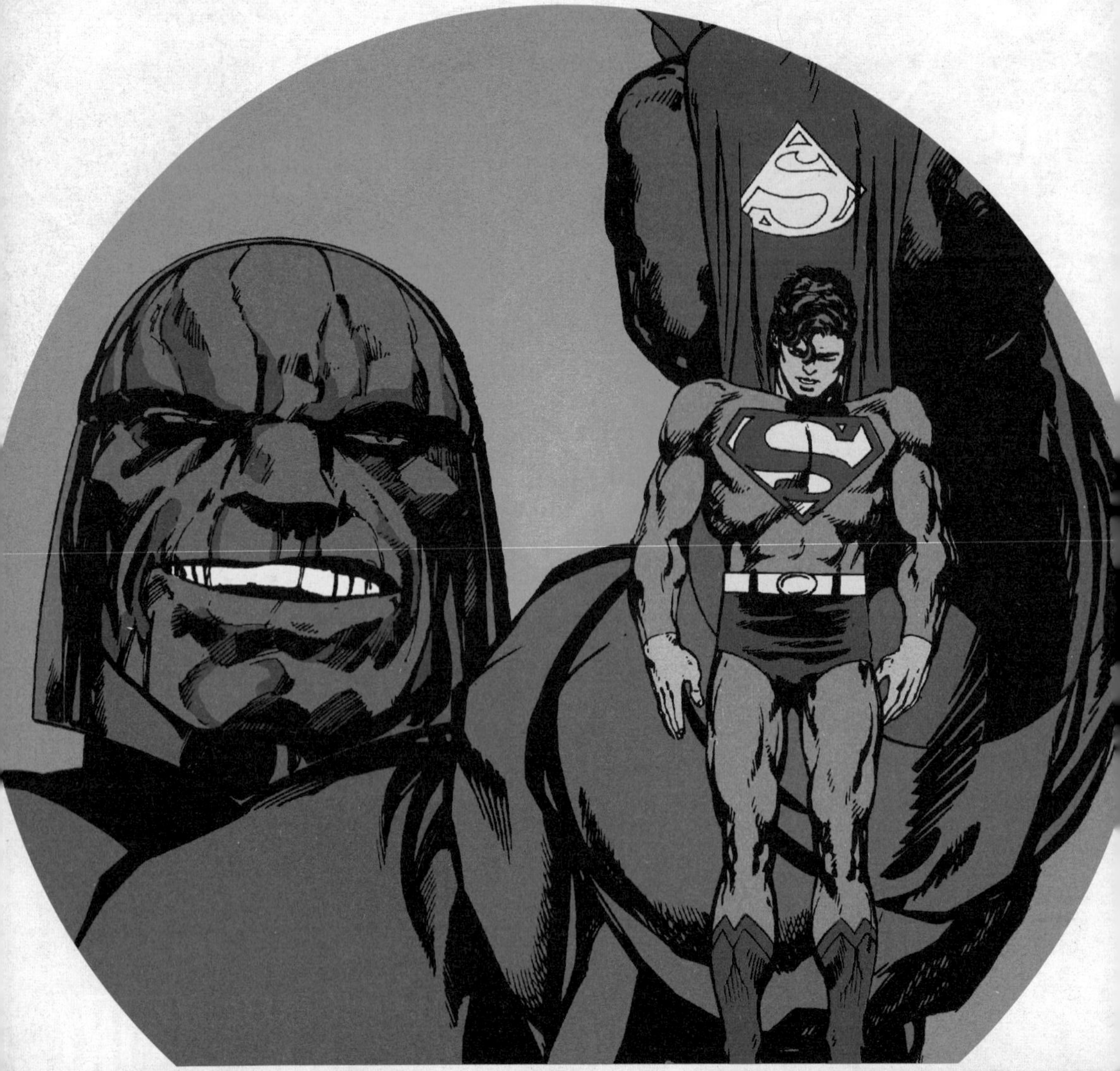

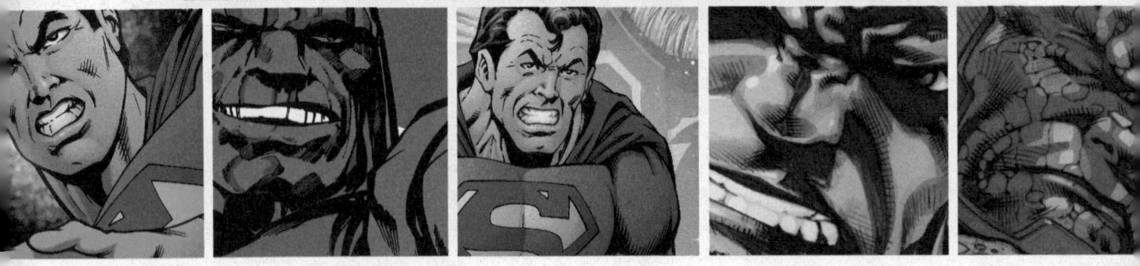

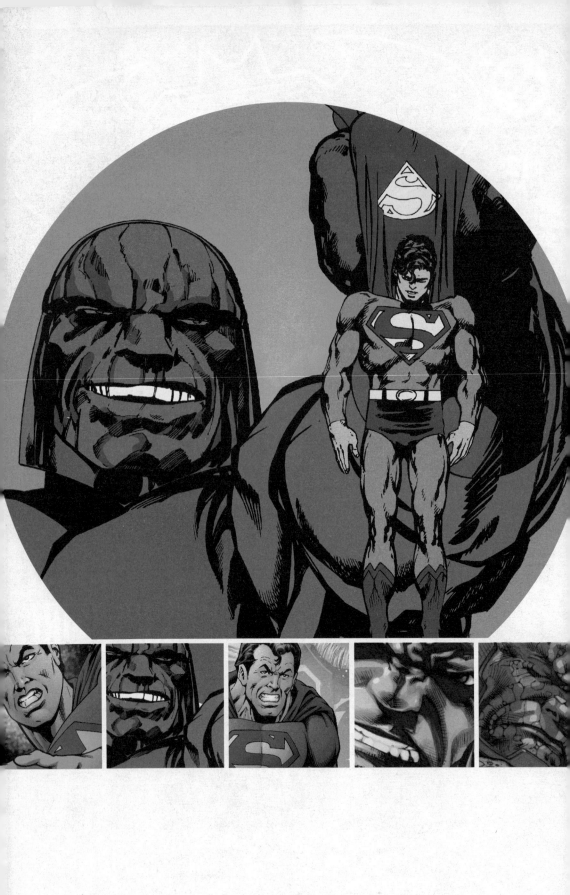

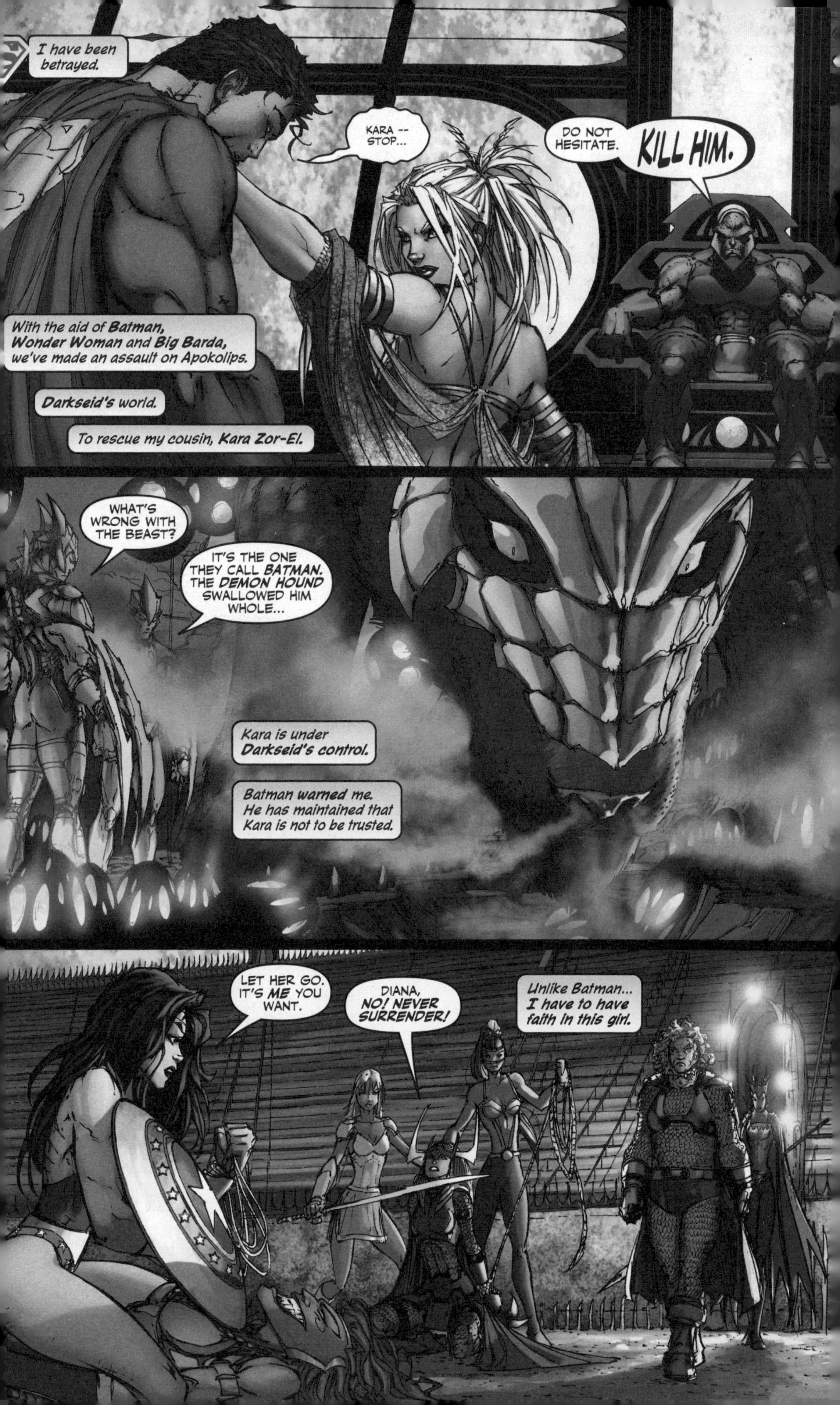
I have been betrayed.
KARA -- STOP...
DO NOT HESITATE.
KILL HIM.
With the aid of Batman, Wonder Woman and Big Barda, we've made an assault on Apokolips.
Darkseid's world.
To rescue my cousin, Kara Zor-El.
WHAT'S WRONG WITH THE BEAST?
IT'S THE ONE THEY CALL BATMAN. THE DEMON HOUND SWALLOWED HIM WHOLE...
Kara is under Darkseid's control.
Batman warned me. He has maintained that Kara is not to be trusted.
LET HER GO. IT'S ME YOU WANT.
DIANA, NO! NEVER SURRENDER!
Unlike Batman... I have to have faith in this girl.

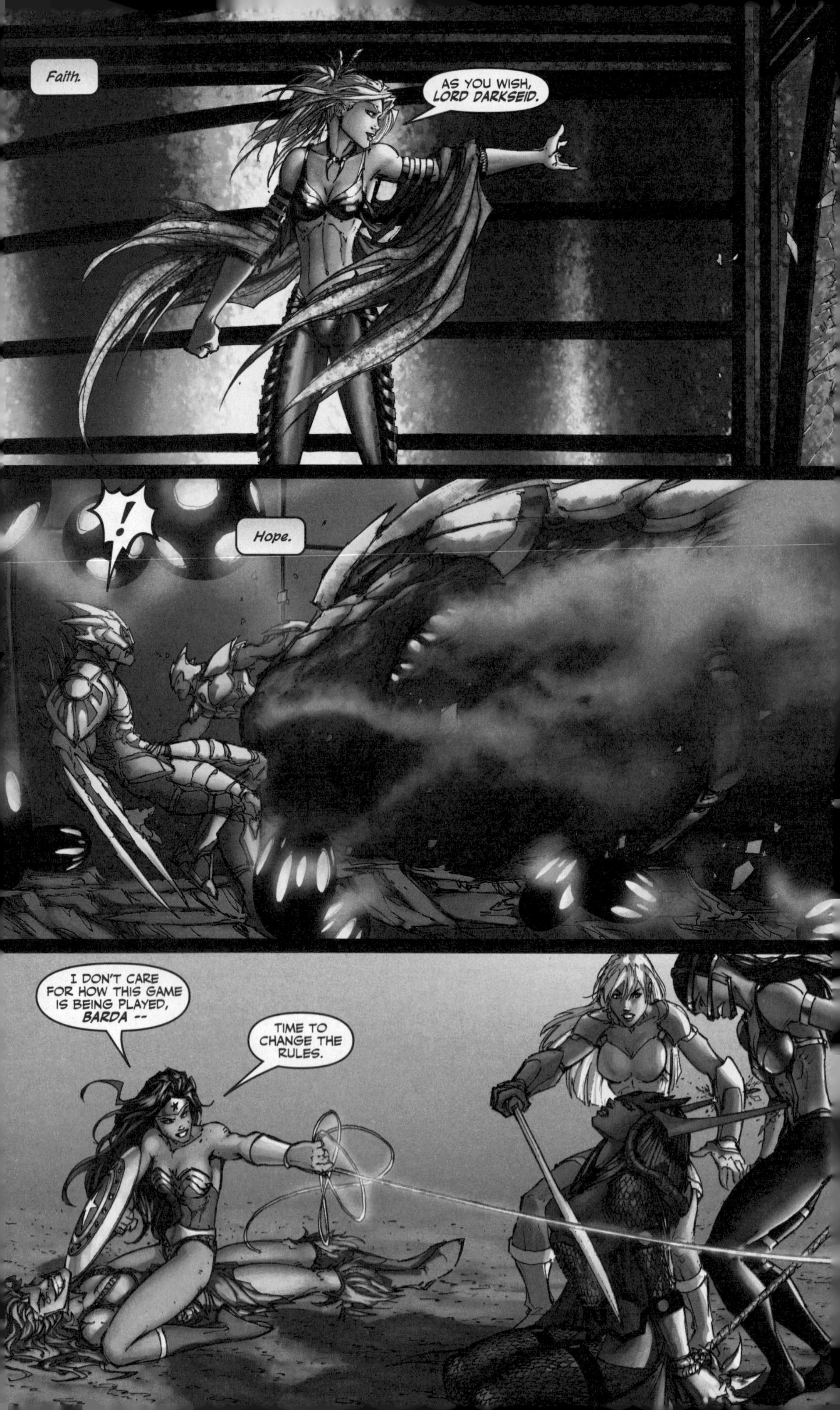

Faith.
AS YOU WISH, LORD DARKSEID.
!
Hope.
I DON'T CARE FOR HOW THIS GAME IS BEING PLAYED, BARDA --
TIME TO CHANGE THE RULES.

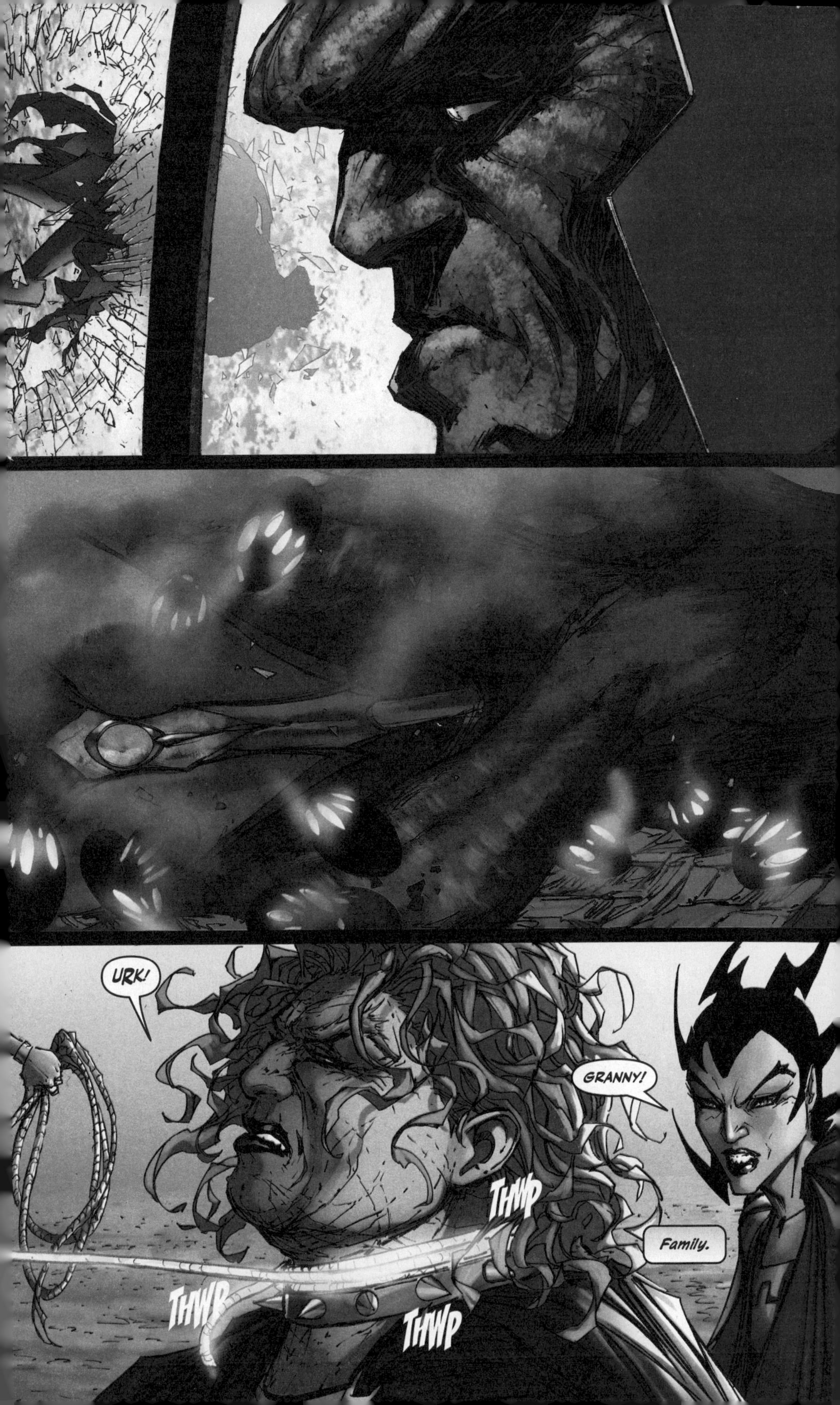
URK!
GRANNY!
THWP
THWP
THWP
Family.

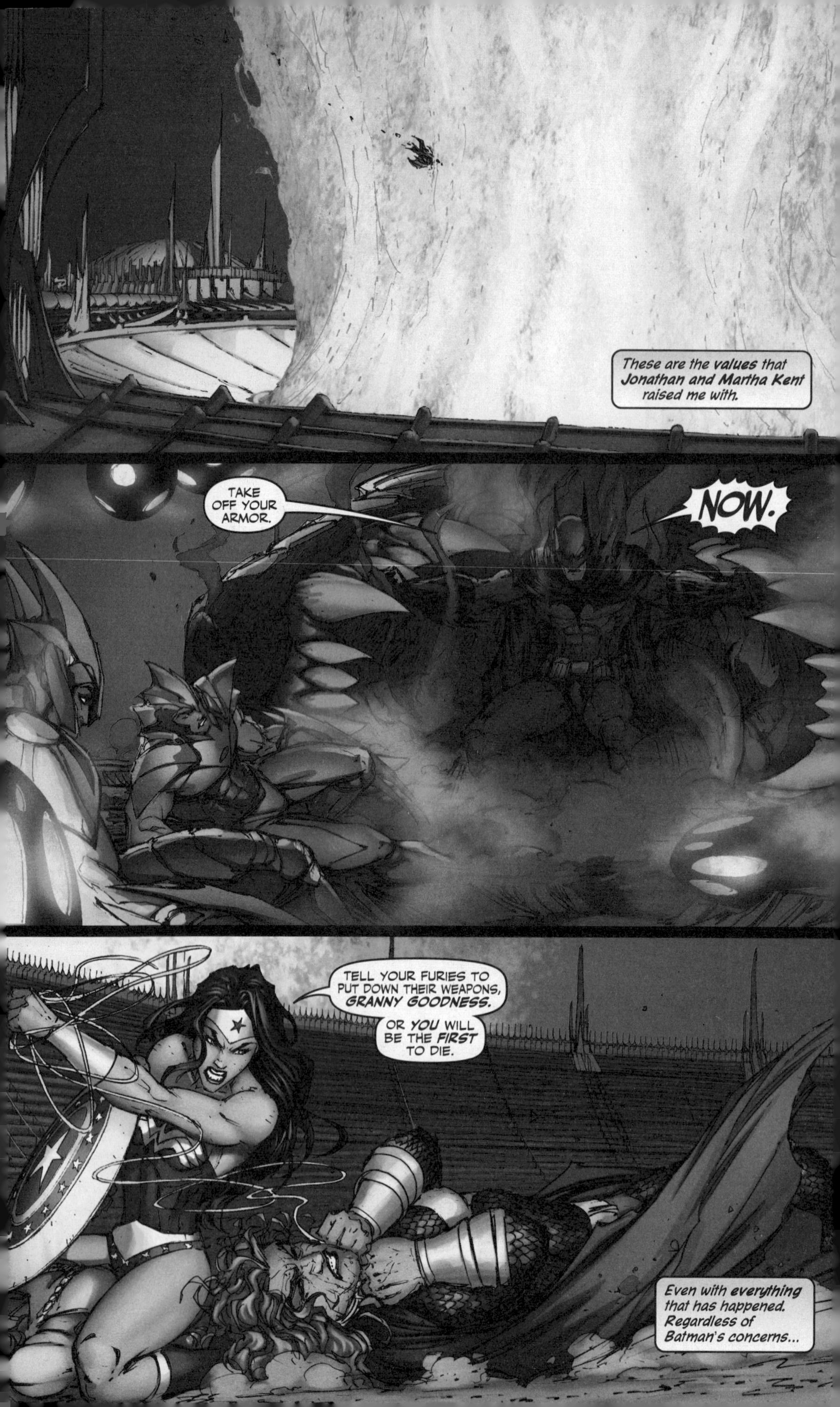
These are the values that Jonathan and Martha Kent raised me with.
TAKE OFF YOUR ARMOR.
NOW.
TELL YOUR FURIES TO PUT DOWN THEIR WEAPONS, GRANNY GOODNESS.
OR YOU WILL BE THE FIRST TO DIE.
Even with everything that has happened. Regardless of Batman's concerns...

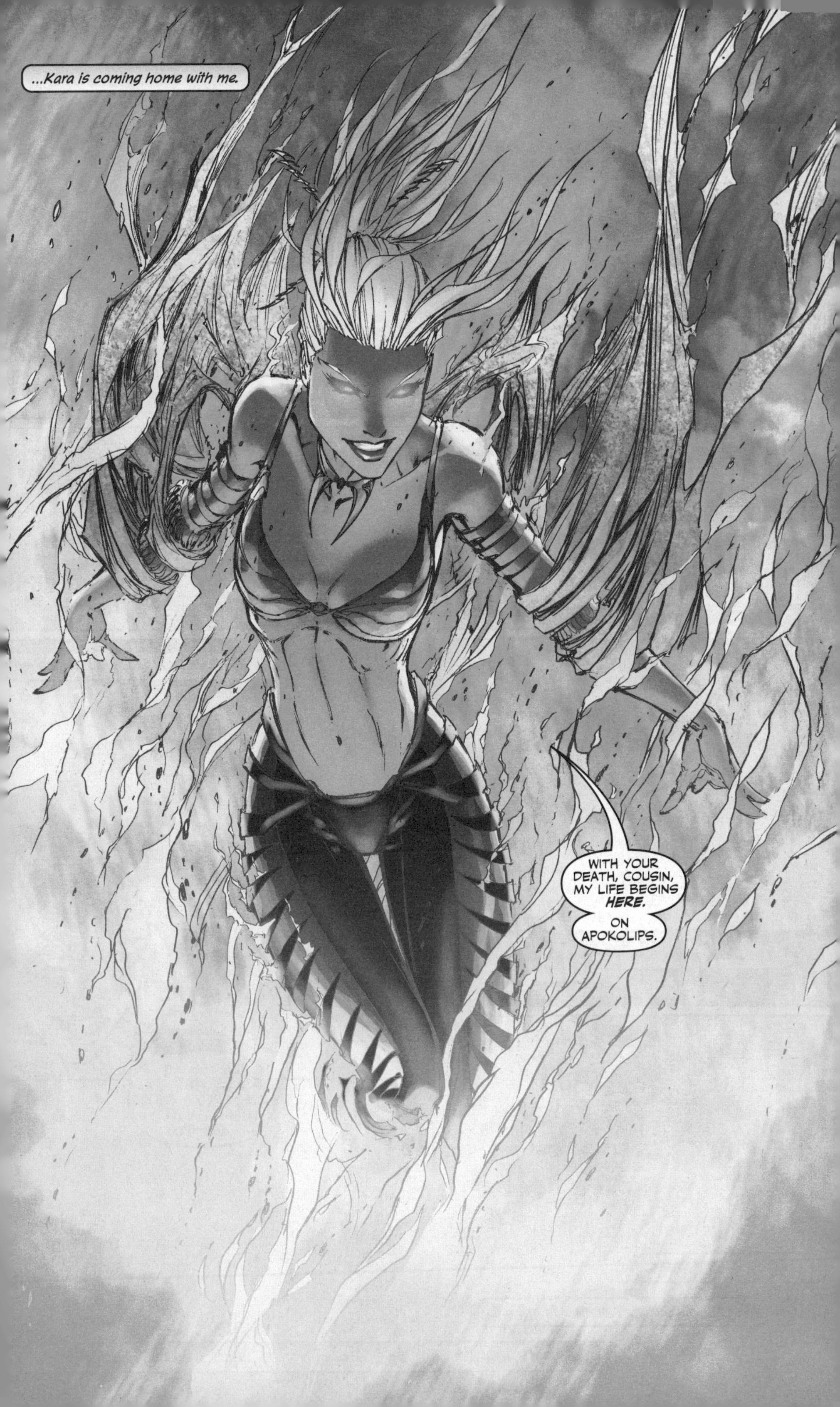

...Kara is coming home with me.
WITH YOUR DEATH, COUSIN, MY LIFE BEGINS HERE.
ON APOKOLIPS.

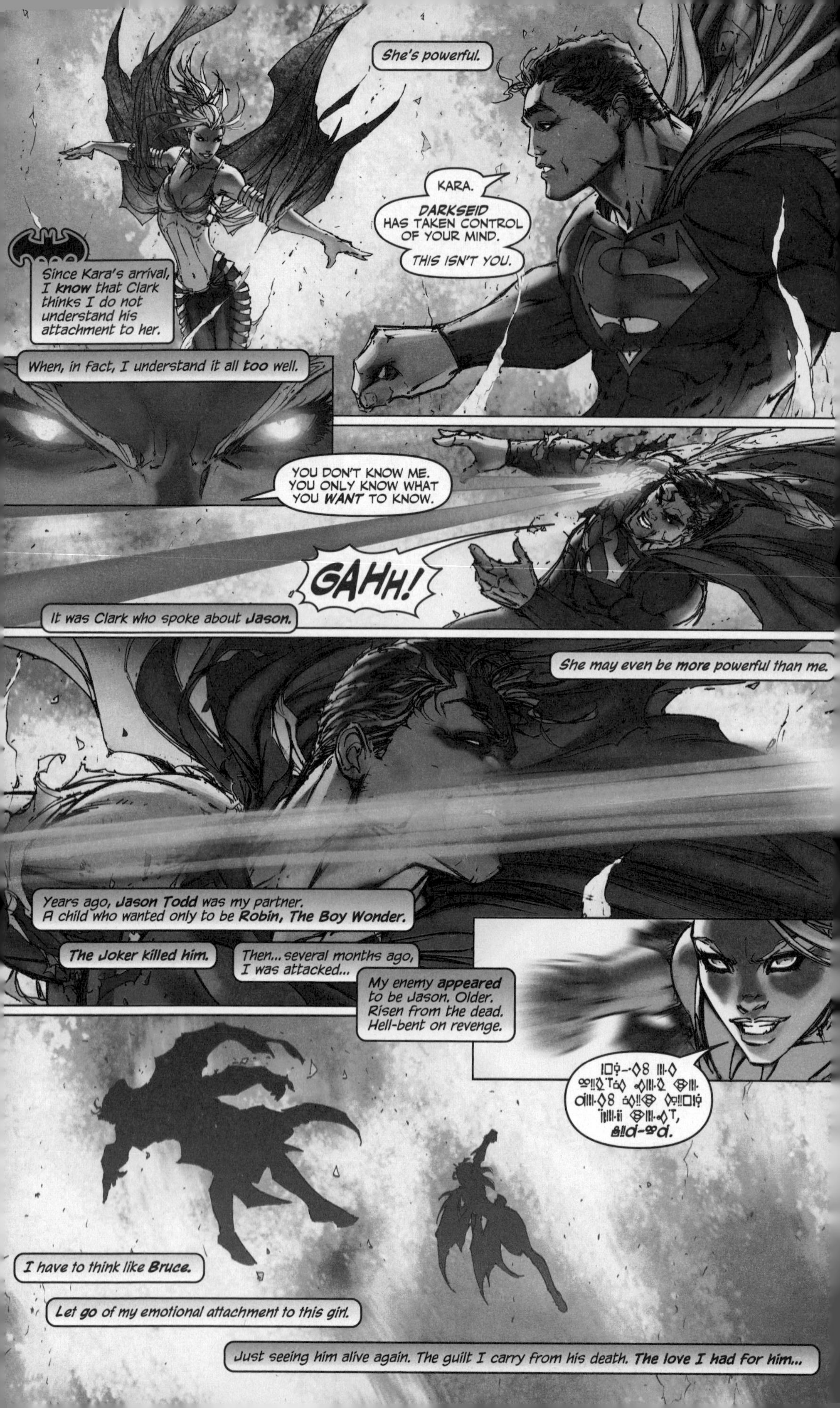
She's powerful.
KARA. DARKSEID HAS TAKEN CONTROL OF YOUR MIND.
THIS ISN'T YOU.
Since Kara's arrival, I know that Clark thinks I do not understand his attachment to her.
When, in fact, I understand it all too well.
YOU DON'T KNOW ME. YOU ONLY KNOW WHAT YOU WANT TO KNOW.
GAHH!
It was Clark who spoke about Jason.
She may even be more powerful than me.
Years ago, Jason Todd was my partner. A child who wanted only to be Robin, The Boy Wonder.
The Joker killed him.
Then... several months ago, I was attacked...
My enemy appeared to be Jason. Older. Risen from the dead. Hell-bent on revenge.
I have to think like Bruce.
Let go of my emotional attachment to this girl.
Just seeing him alive again. The guilt I carry from his death. The love I had for him...

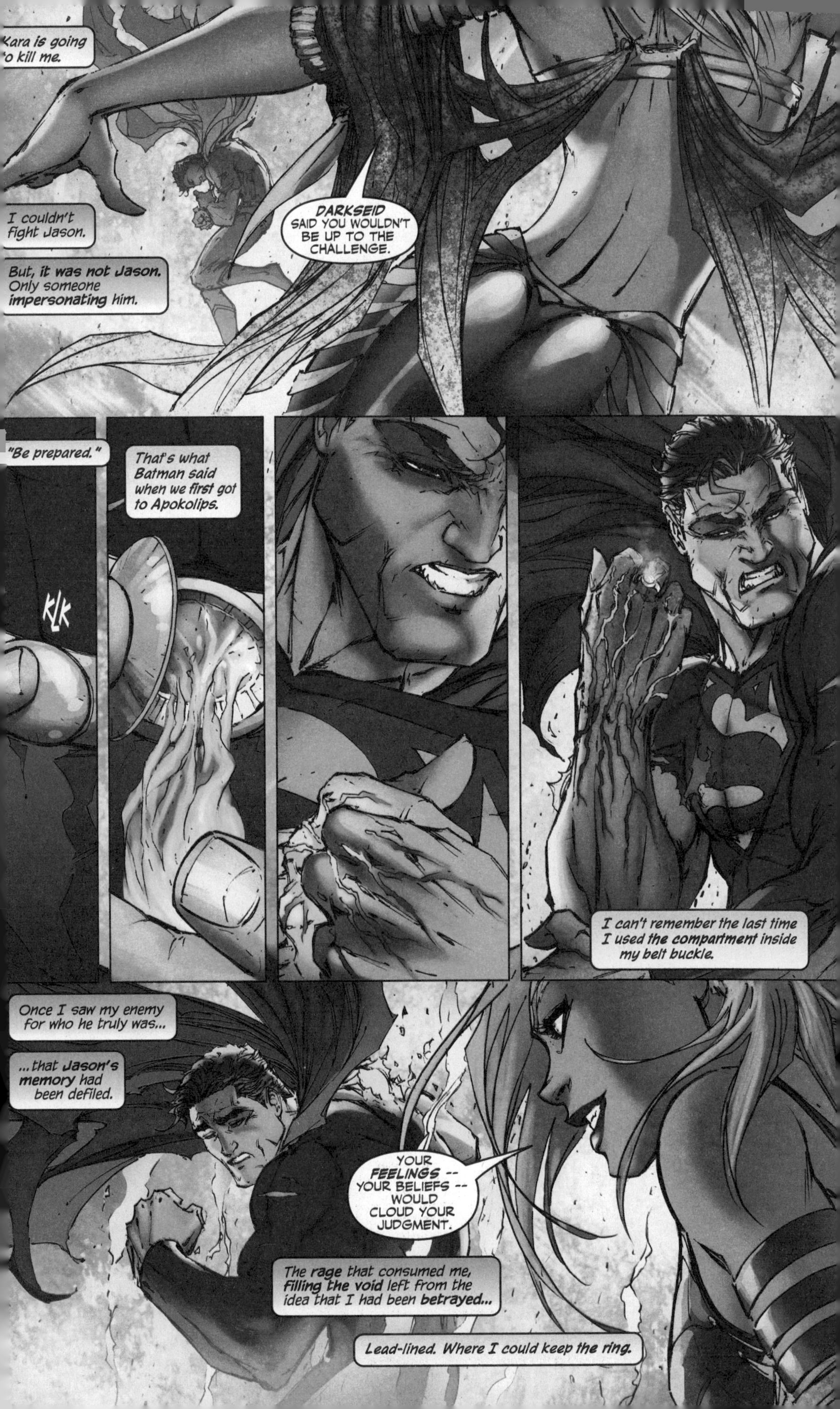
Kara is going to kill me.
I couldn't fight Jason.
But, it was not Jason. Only someone impersonating him.
DARKSEID SAID YOU WOULDN'T BE UP TO THE CHALLENGE.
"Be prepared."
That's what Batman said when we first got to Apokolips.
KLIK
I can't remember the last time I used the compartment inside my belt buckle.
Once I saw my enemy for who he truly was...
...that Jason's memory had been defiled.
YOUR FEELINGS -- YOUR BELIEFS -- WOULD CLOUD YOUR JUDGMENT.
The rage that consumed me, filling the void left from the idea that I had been betrayed...
Lead-lined. Where I could keep the ring.

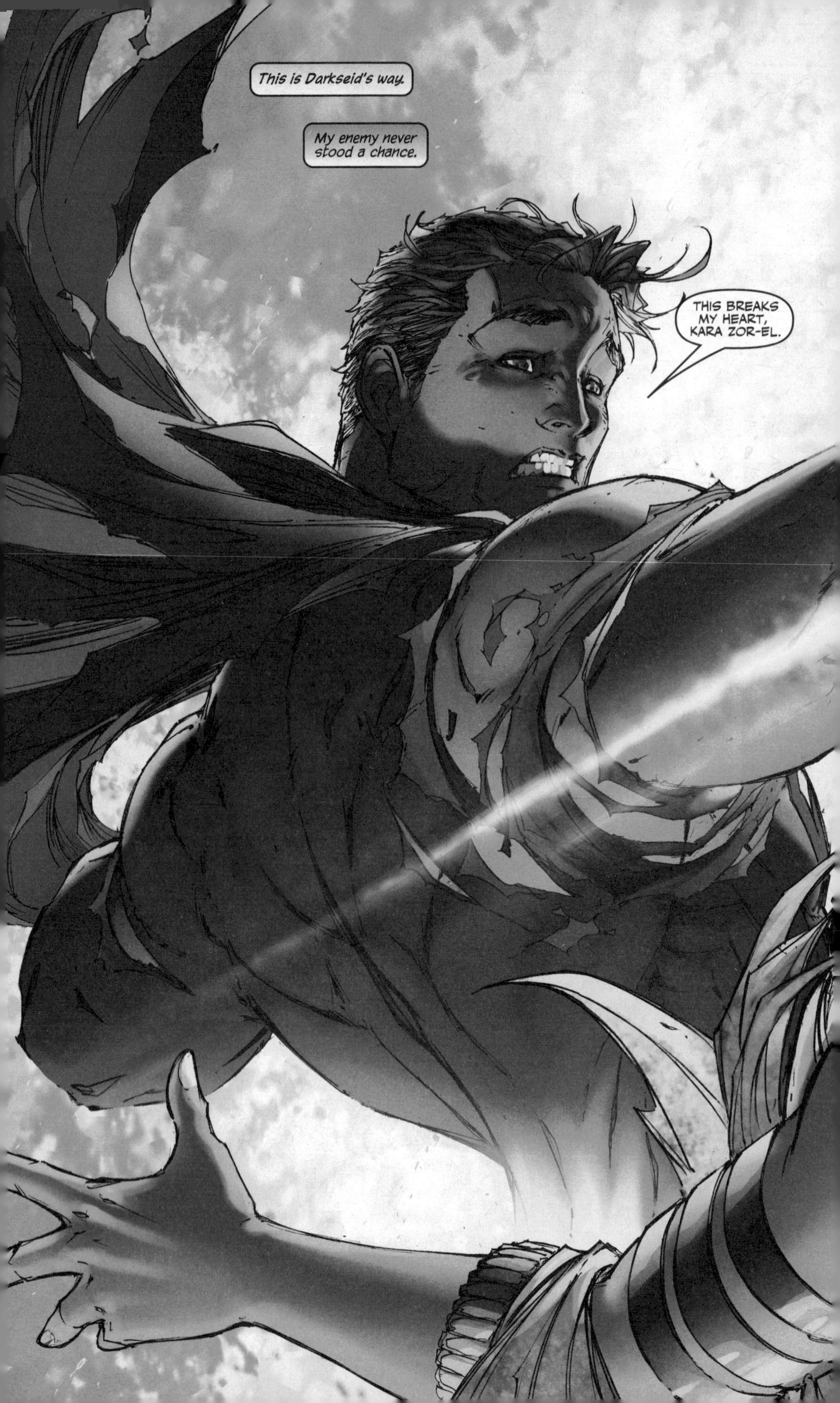

This is Darkseid's way.
My enemy never stood a chance.
THIS BREAKS MY HEART, KARA ZOR-EL.

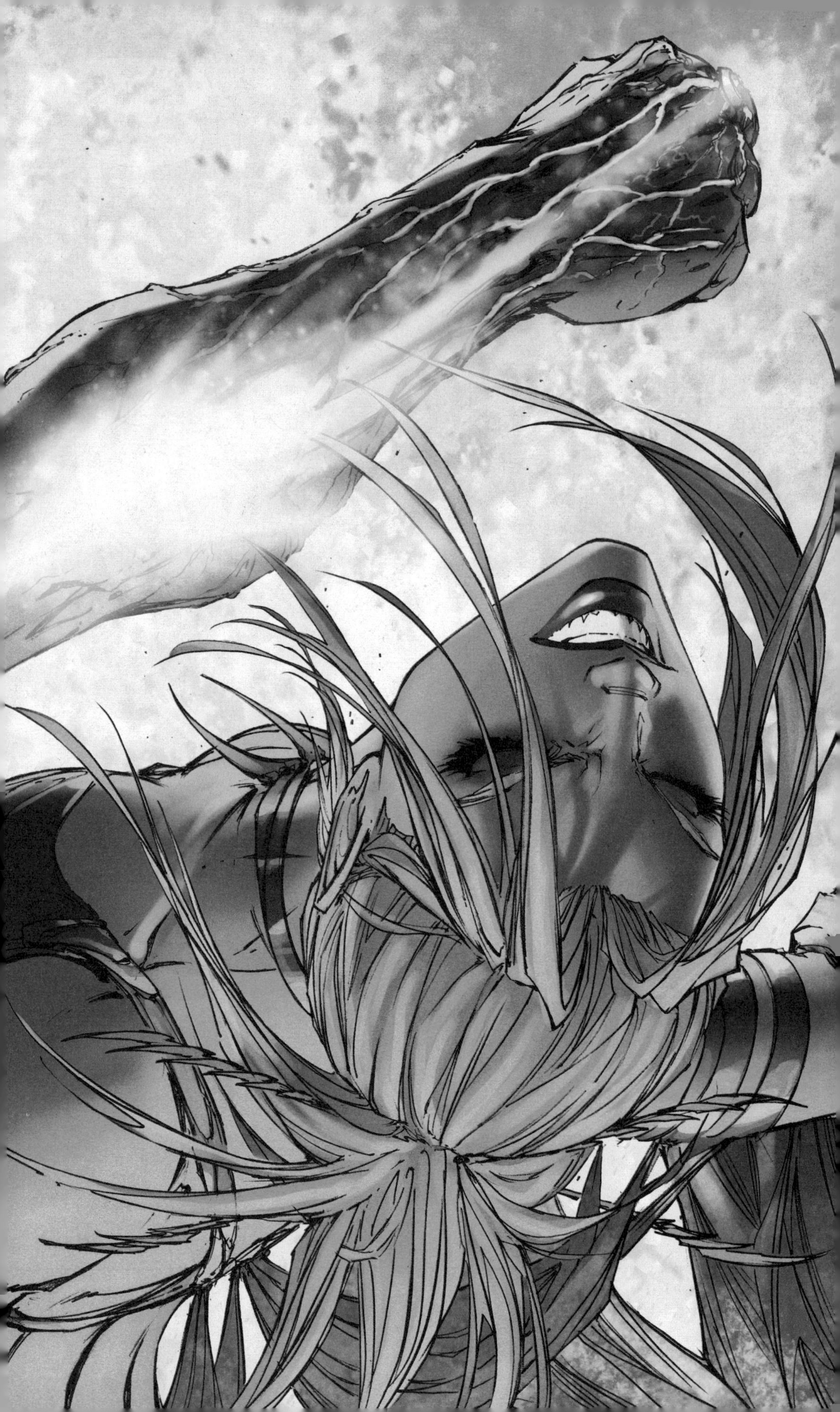

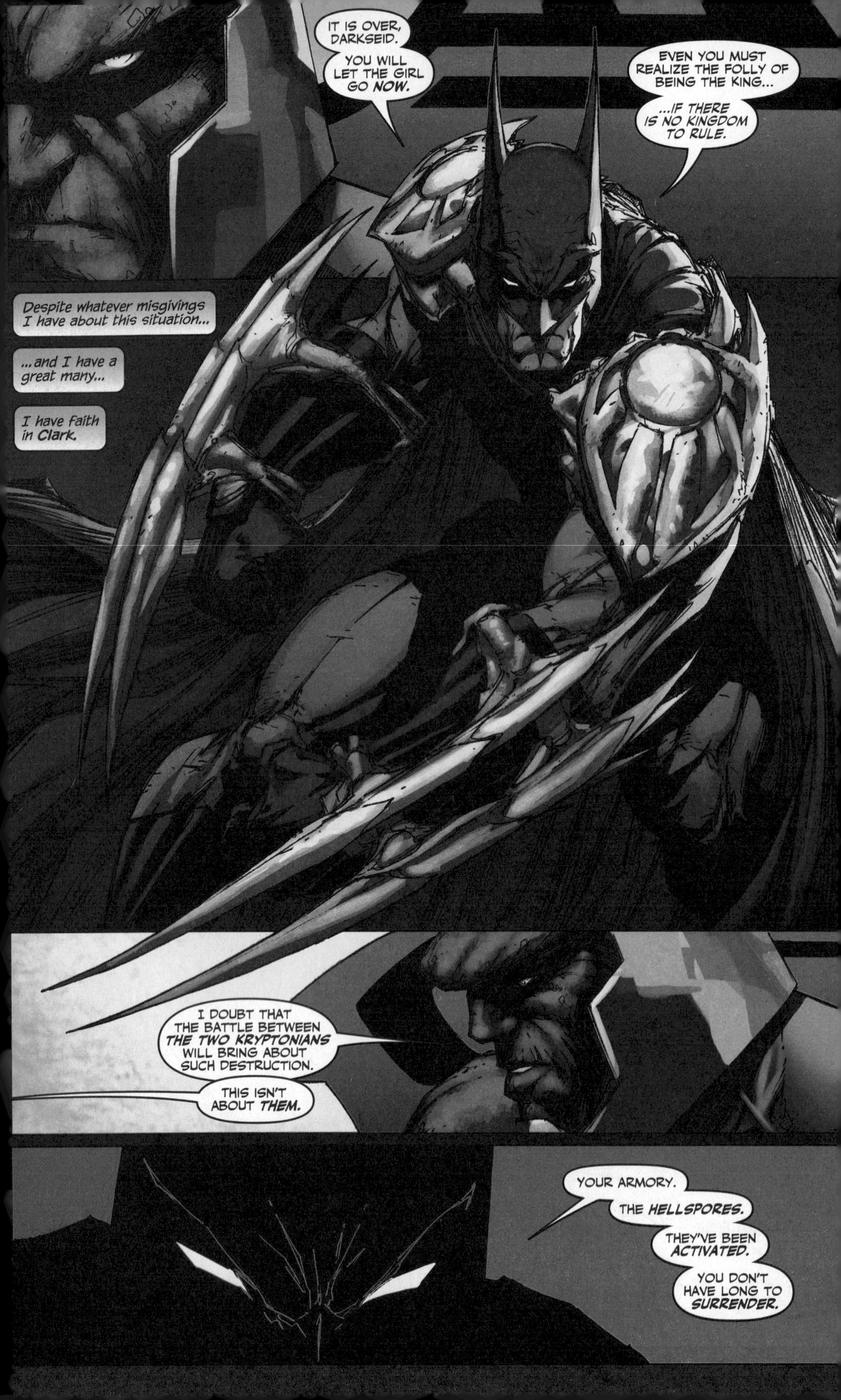
IT IS OVER, DARKSEID.
YOU WILL LET THE GIRL GO NOW.
EVEN YOU MUST REALIZE THE FOLLY OF BEING THE KING...
...IF THERE IS NO KINGDOM TO RULE.
Despite whatever misgivings I have about this situation...
...and I have a great many...
I have faith in Clark.
I DOUBT THAT THE BATTLE BETWEEN THE TWO KRYPTONIANS WILL BRING ABOUT SUCH DESTRUCTION.
THIS ISN'T ABOUT THEM.
YOUR ARMORY.
THE HELLSPORES.
THEY'VE BEEN ACTIVATED.
YOU DON'T HAVE LONG TO SURRENDER.

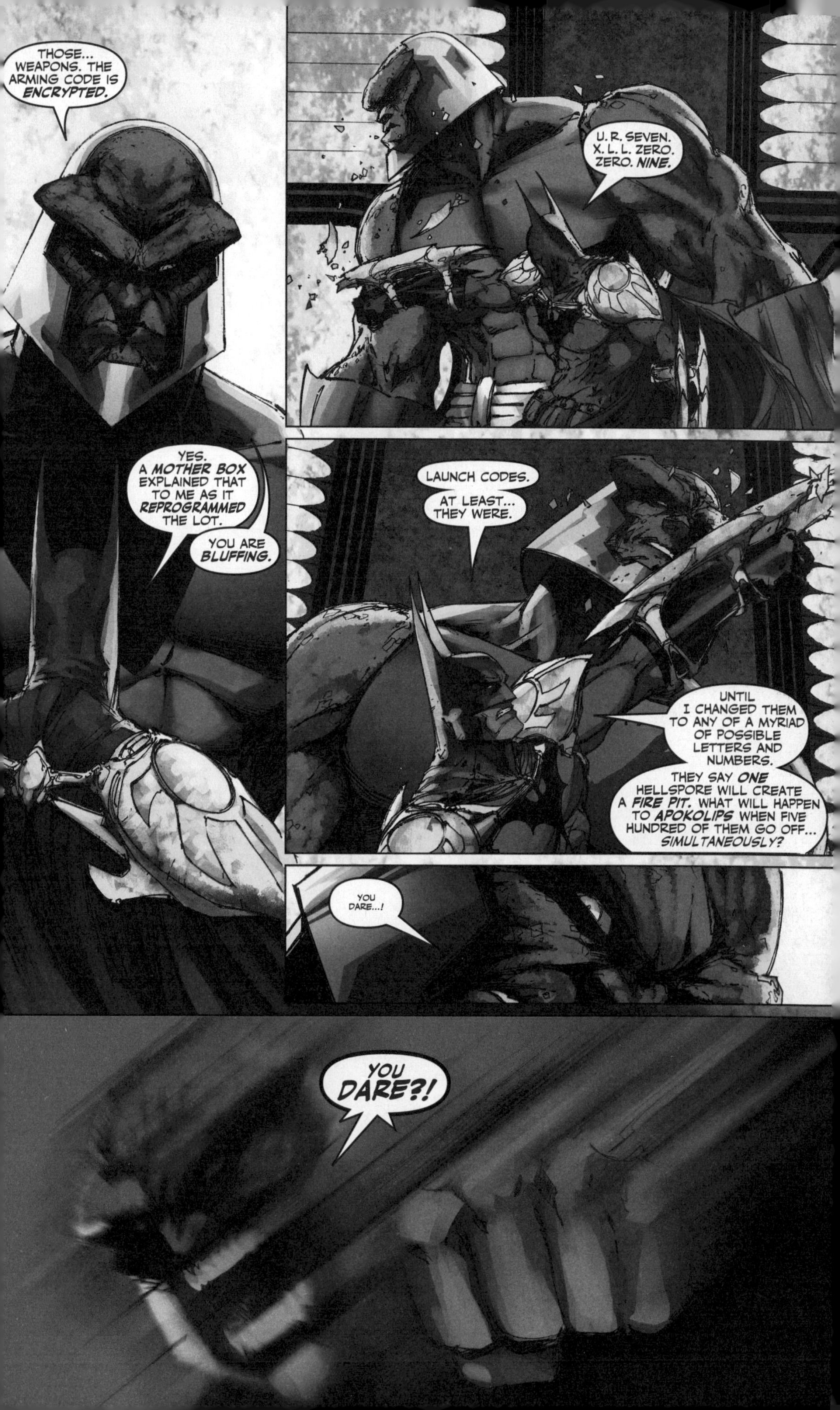
THOSE... WEAPONS. THE ARMING CODE IS *ENCRYPTED.*
U. R. SEVEN. X. L. L. ZERO. ZERO. *NINE.*
YES. A *MOTHER BOX* EXPLAINED THAT TO ME AS IT *REPROGRAMMED* THE LOT.
YOU ARE *BLUFFING.*
LAUNCH CODES.
AT LEAST... THEY WERE.
UNTIL I CHANGED THEM TO ANY OF A MYRIAD OF POSSIBLE LETTERS AND NUMBERS.
THEY SAY *ONE* HELLSPORE WILL CREATE A *FIRE PIT.* WHAT WILL HAPPEN TO *APOKOLIPS* WHEN FIVE HUNDRED OF THEM GO OFF... *SIMULTANEOUSLY?*
YOU DARE...!
YOU DARE?!

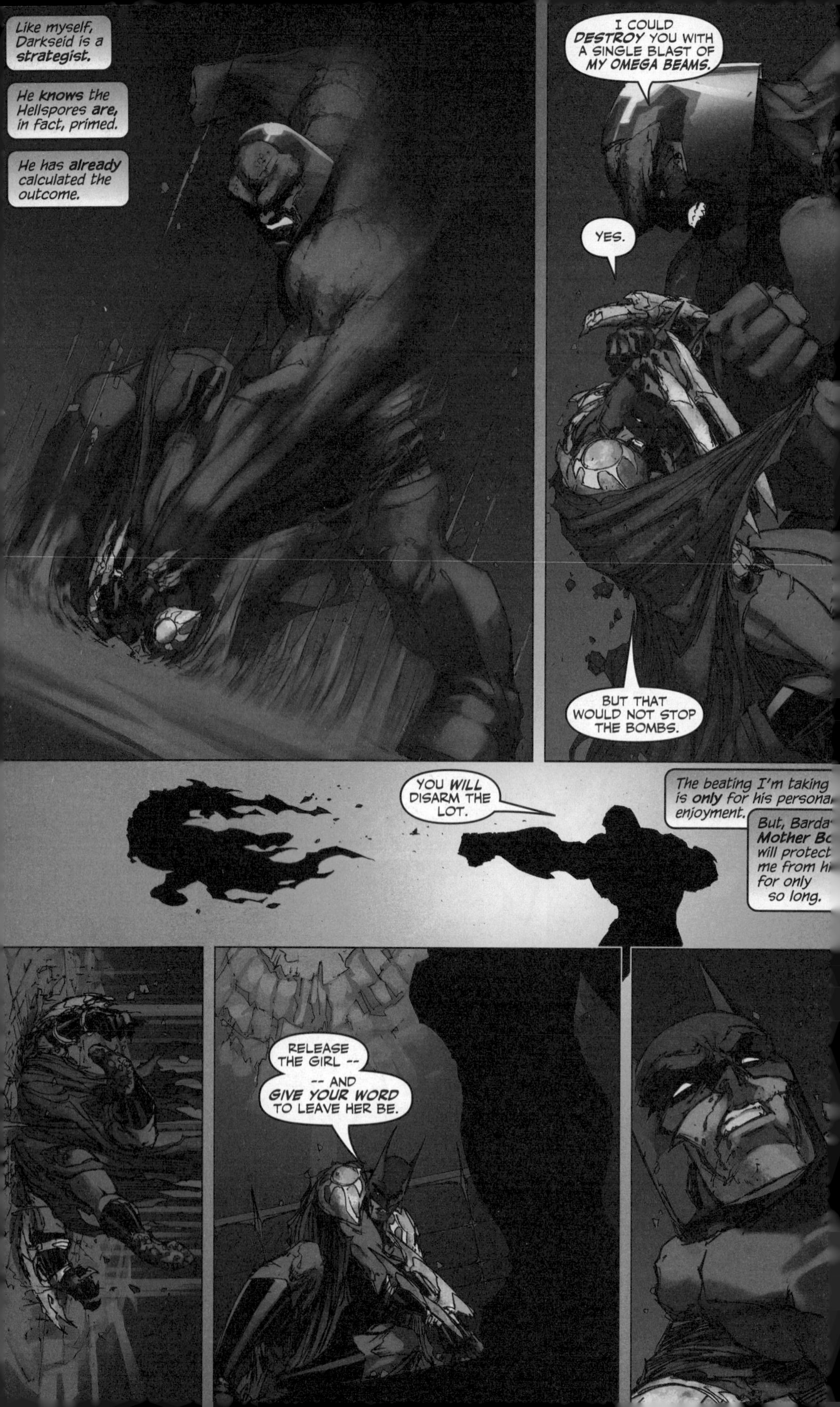

Like myself, Darkseid is a strategist.
He knows the Hellspores are, in fact, primed.
He has already calculated the outcome.
I COULD DESTROY YOU WITH A SINGLE BLAST OF MY OMEGA BEAMS.
YES.
BUT THAT WOULD NOT STOP THE BOMBS.
YOU WILL DISARM THE LOT.
The beating I'm taking is only for his persona
enjoyment.
But, Barda
Mother Bo
will protect
me from hi
for only
so long.
RELEASE THE GIRL --
-- AND GIVE YOUR WORD TO LEAVE HER BE.

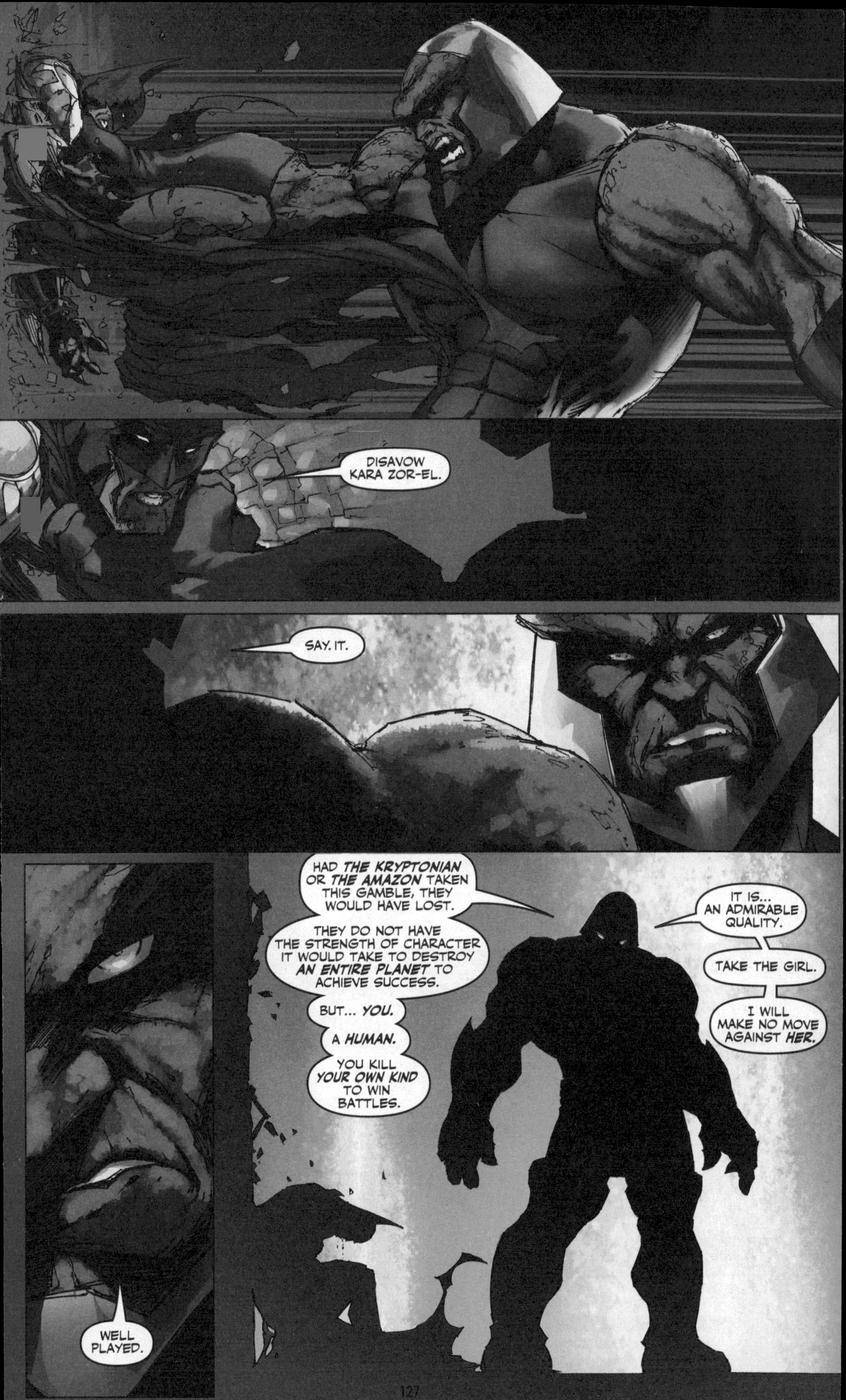
DISAVOW KARA ZOR-EL.
SAY. IT.
WELL PLAYED.
HAD THE KRYPTONIAN OR THE AMAZON TAKEN THIS GAMBLE, THEY WOULD HAVE LOST.
THEY DO NOT HAVE THE STRENGTH OF CHARACTER IT WOULD TAKE TO DESTROY AN ENTIRE PLANET TO ACHIEVE SUCCESS.
BUT... YOU.
A HUMAN.
YOU KILL YOUR OWN KIND TO WIN BATTLES.
IT IS... AN ADMIRABLE QUALITY.
TAKE THE GIRL.
I WILL MAKE NO MOVE AGAINST HER.

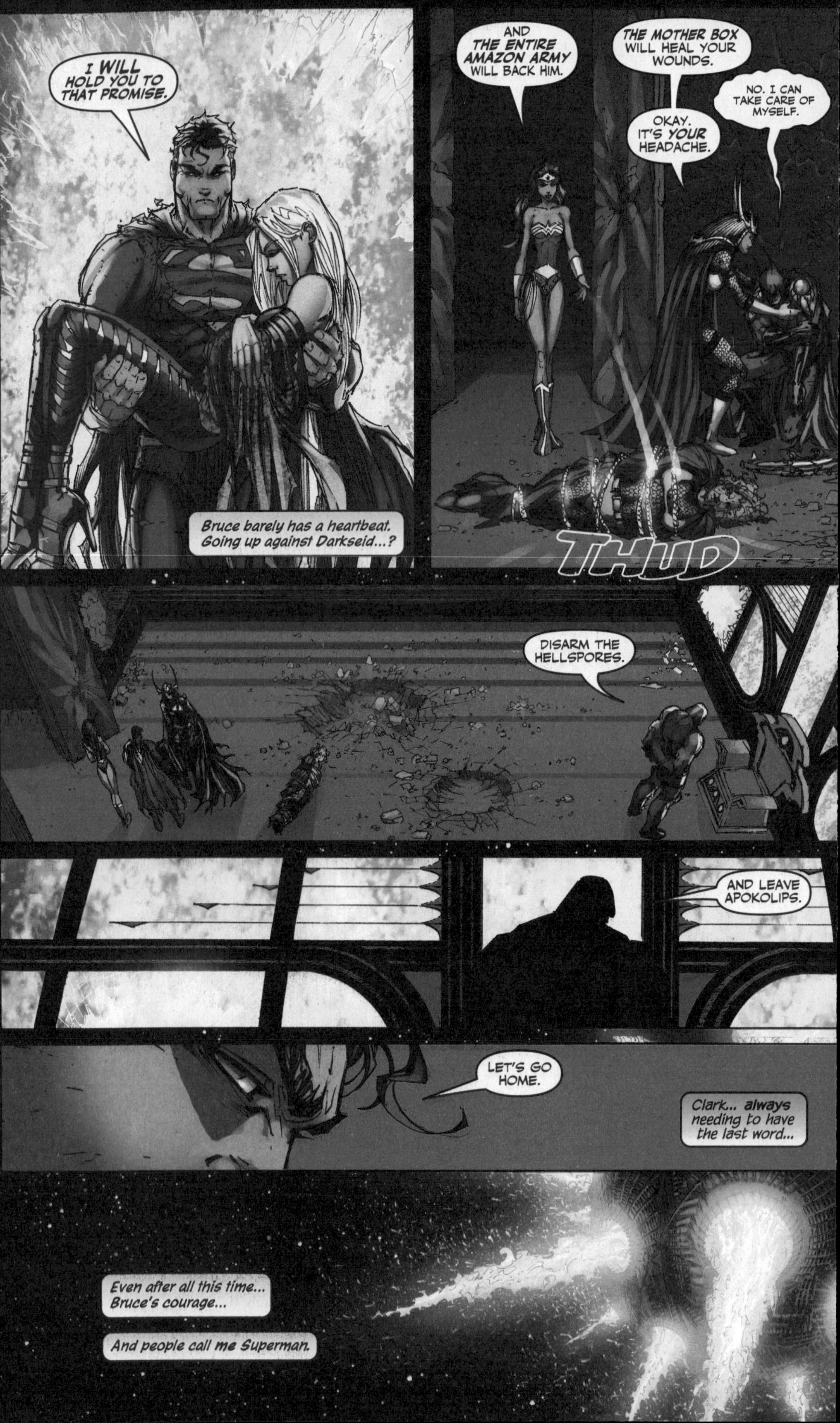

I WILL HOLD YOU TO THAT PROMISE.
Bruce barely has a heartbeat. Going up against Darkseid...?
AND THE ENTIRE AMAZON ARMY WILL BACK HIM.
THE MOTHER BOX WILL HEAL YOUR WOUNDS.
NO. I CAN TAKE CARE OF MYSELF.
OKAY. IT'S YOUR HEADACHE.
THUD
DISARM THE HELLSPORES.
AND LEAVE APOKOLIPS.
LET'S GO HOME.
Clark... always needing to have the last word...
Even after all this time... Bruce's courage...
And people call me Superman.

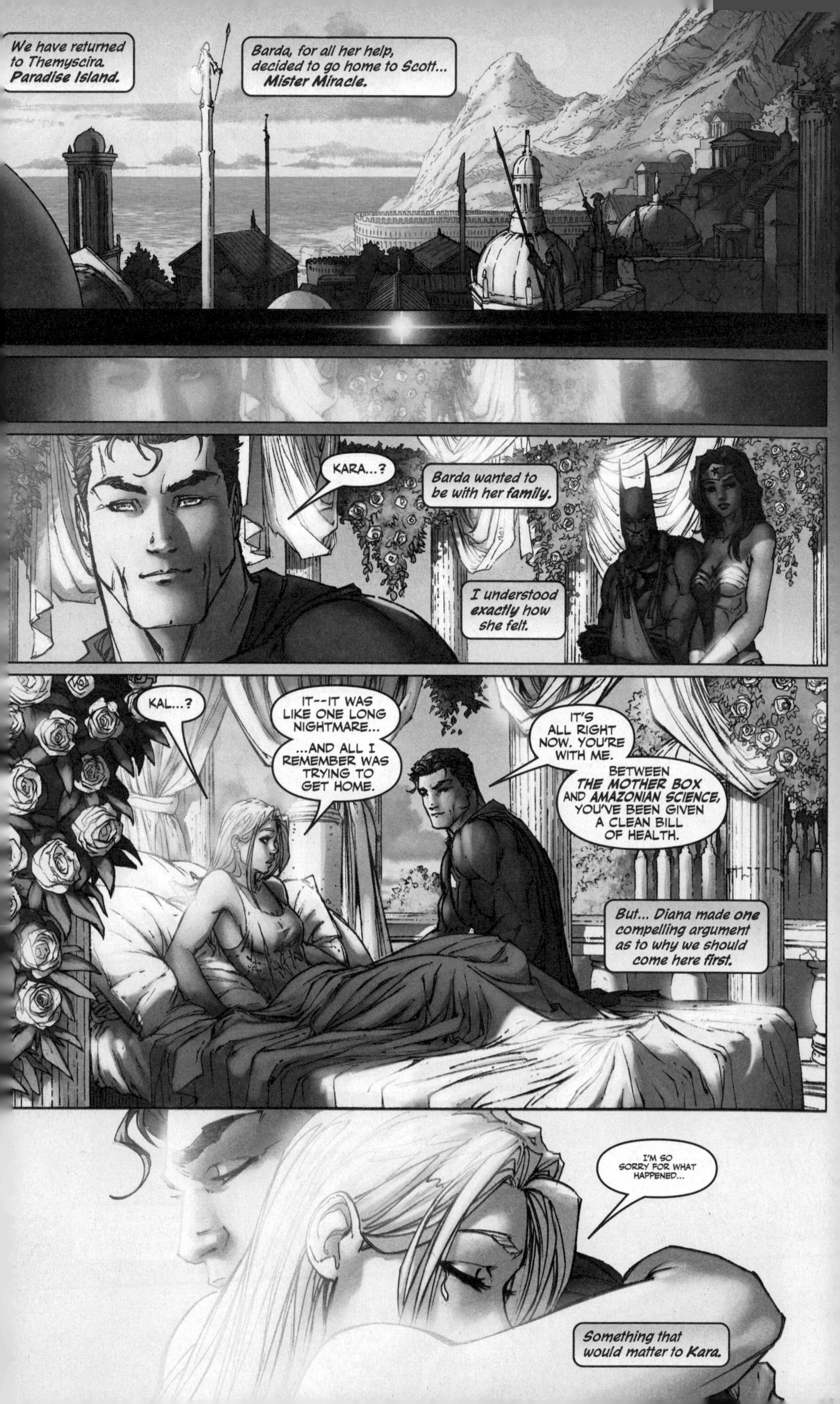

We have returned to Themyscira. Paradise Island.
Barda, for all her help, decided to go home to Scott... Mister Miracle.
KARA...?
Barda wanted to be with her family.
I understood exactly how she felt.
KAL...?
IT--IT WAS LIKE ONE LONG NIGHTMARE...
...AND ALL I REMEMBER WAS TRYING TO GET HOME.
IT'S ALL RIGHT NOW. YOU'RE WITH ME.
BETWEEN THE MOTHER BOX AND AMAZONIAN SCIENCE, YOU'VE BEEN GIVEN A CLEAN BILL OF HEALTH.
But... Diana made one compelling argument as to why we should come here first.
I'M SO SORRY FOR WHAT HAPPENED...
Something that would matter to Kara.

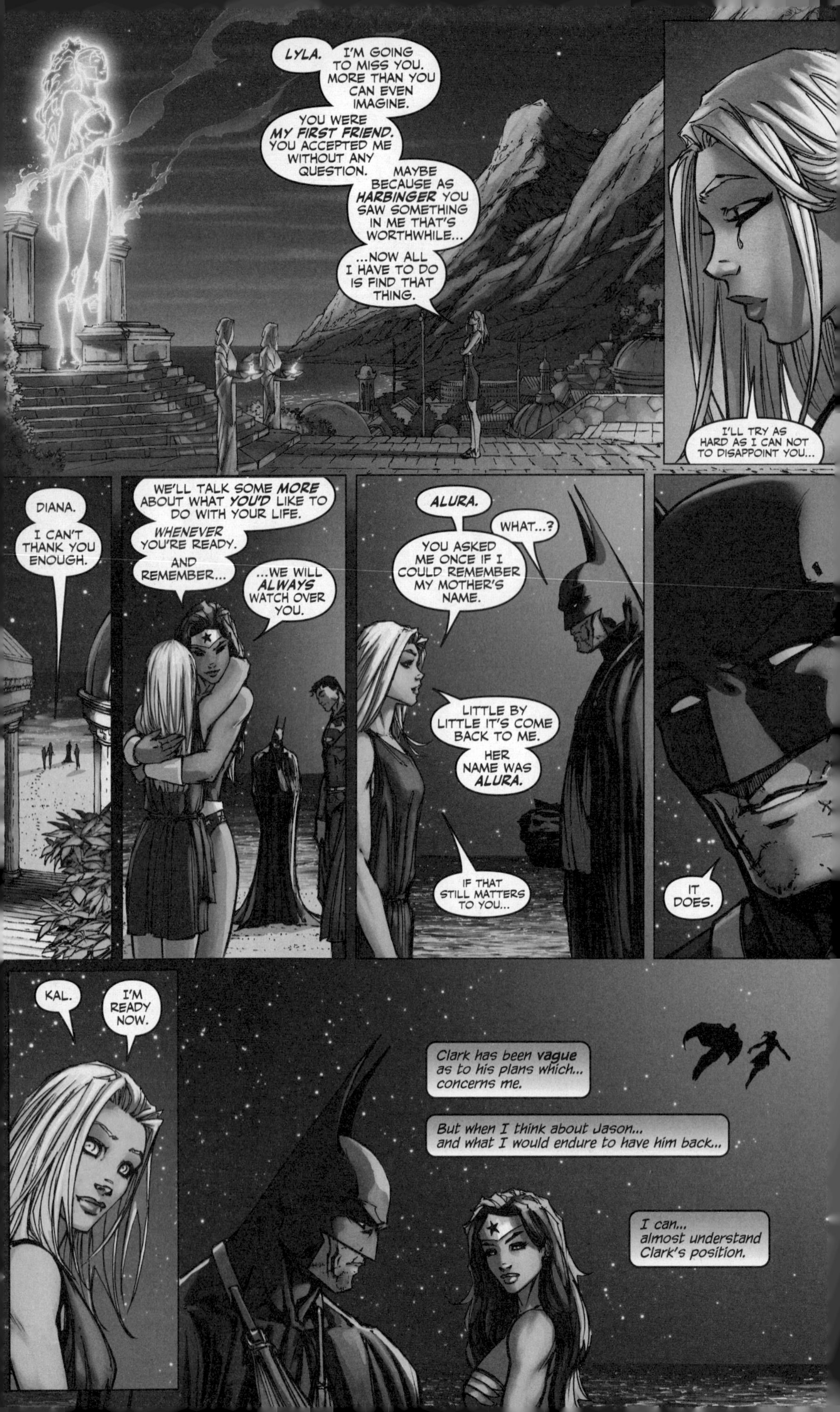
LYLA. I'M GOING TO MISS YOU. MORE THAN YOU CAN EVEN IMAGINE.
YOU WERE MY FIRST FRIEND. YOU ACCEPTED ME WITHOUT ANY QUESTION.
MAYBE BECAUSE AS HARBINGER YOU SAW SOMETHING IN ME THAT'S WORTHWHILE...
...NOW ALL I HAVE TO DO IS FIND THAT THING.
I'LL TRY AS HARD AS I CAN NOT TO DISAPPOINT YOU...
DIANA.
I CAN'T THANK YOU ENOUGH.
WE'LL TALK SOME MORE ABOUT WHAT YOU'D LIKE TO DO WITH YOUR LIFE.
WHENEVER YOU'RE READY.
AND REMEMBER...
...WE WILL ALWAYS WATCH OVER YOU.
ALURA.
WHAT...?
YOU ASKED ME ONCE IF I COULD REMEMBER MY MOTHER'S NAME.
LITTLE BY LITTLE IT'S COME BACK TO ME.
HER NAME WAS ALURA.
IF THAT STILL MATTERS TO YOU...
IT DOES.
KAL.
I'M READY NOW.
Clark has been vague as to his plans which... concerns me.
But when I think about Jason... and what I would endure to have him back...
I can... almost understand Clark's position.

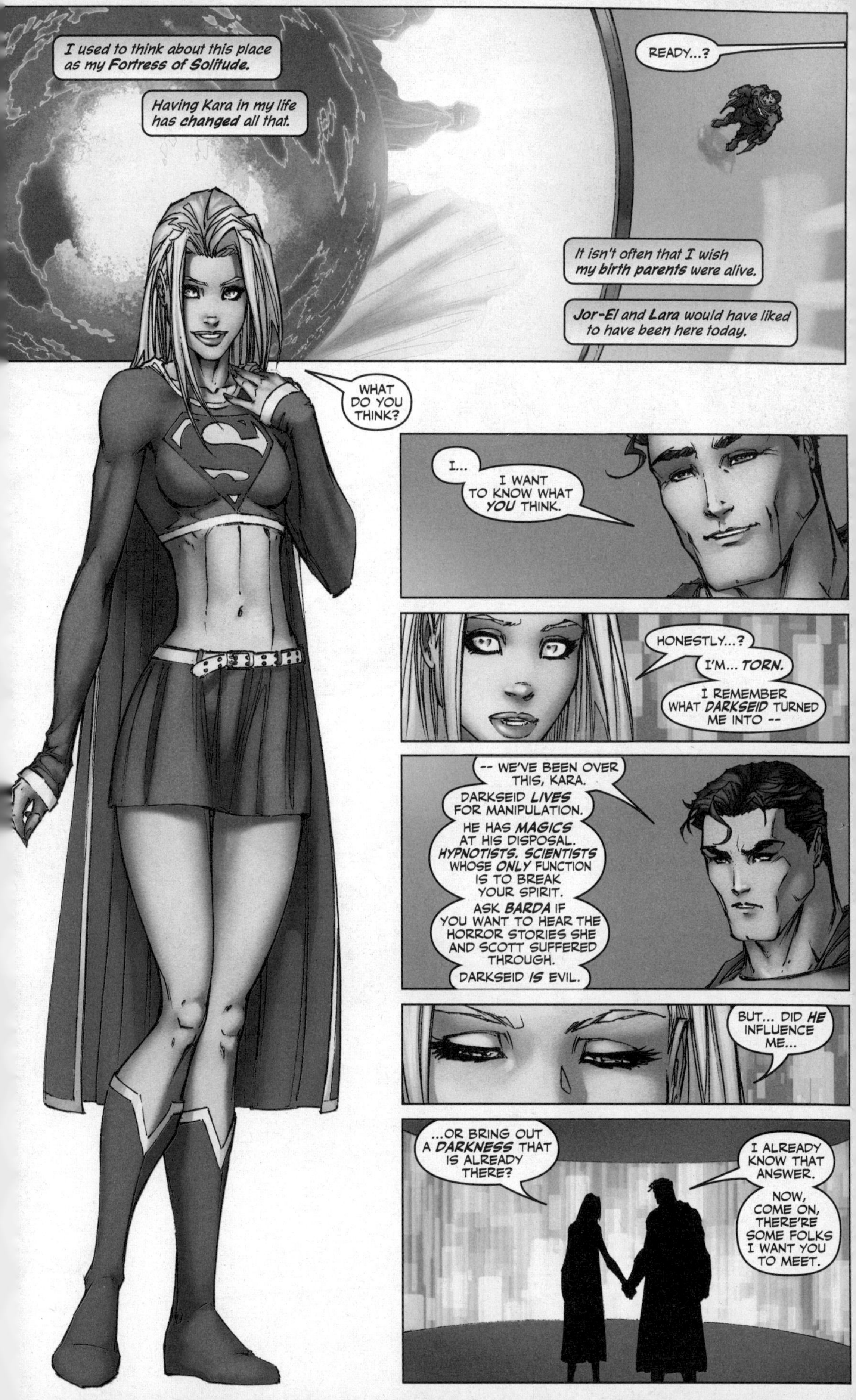
I used to think about this place as my Fortress of Solitude.
Having Kara in my life has changed all that.
READY...?
It isn't often that I wish my birth parents were alive.
Jor-El and Lara would have liked to have been here today.
WHAT DO YOU THINK?
I... I WANT TO KNOW WHAT YOU THINK.
HONESTLY...?
I'M... TORN.
I REMEMBER WHAT DARKSEID TURNED ME INTO --
-- WE'VE BEEN OVER THIS, KARA.
DARKSEID LIVES FOR MANIPULATION.
HE HAS MAGICS AT HIS DISPOSAL. HYPNOTISTS. SCIENTISTS WHOSE ONLY FUNCTION IS TO BREAK YOUR SPIRIT.
ASK BARDA IF YOU WANT TO HEAR THE HORROR STORIES SHE AND SCOTT SUFFERED THROUGH.
DARKSEID IS EVIL.
BUT... DID HE INFLUENCE ME...
...OR BRING OUT A DARKNESS THAT IS ALREADY THERE?
I ALREADY KNOW THAT ANSWER.
NOW, COME ON, THERE'RE SOME FOLKS I WANT YOU TO MEET.

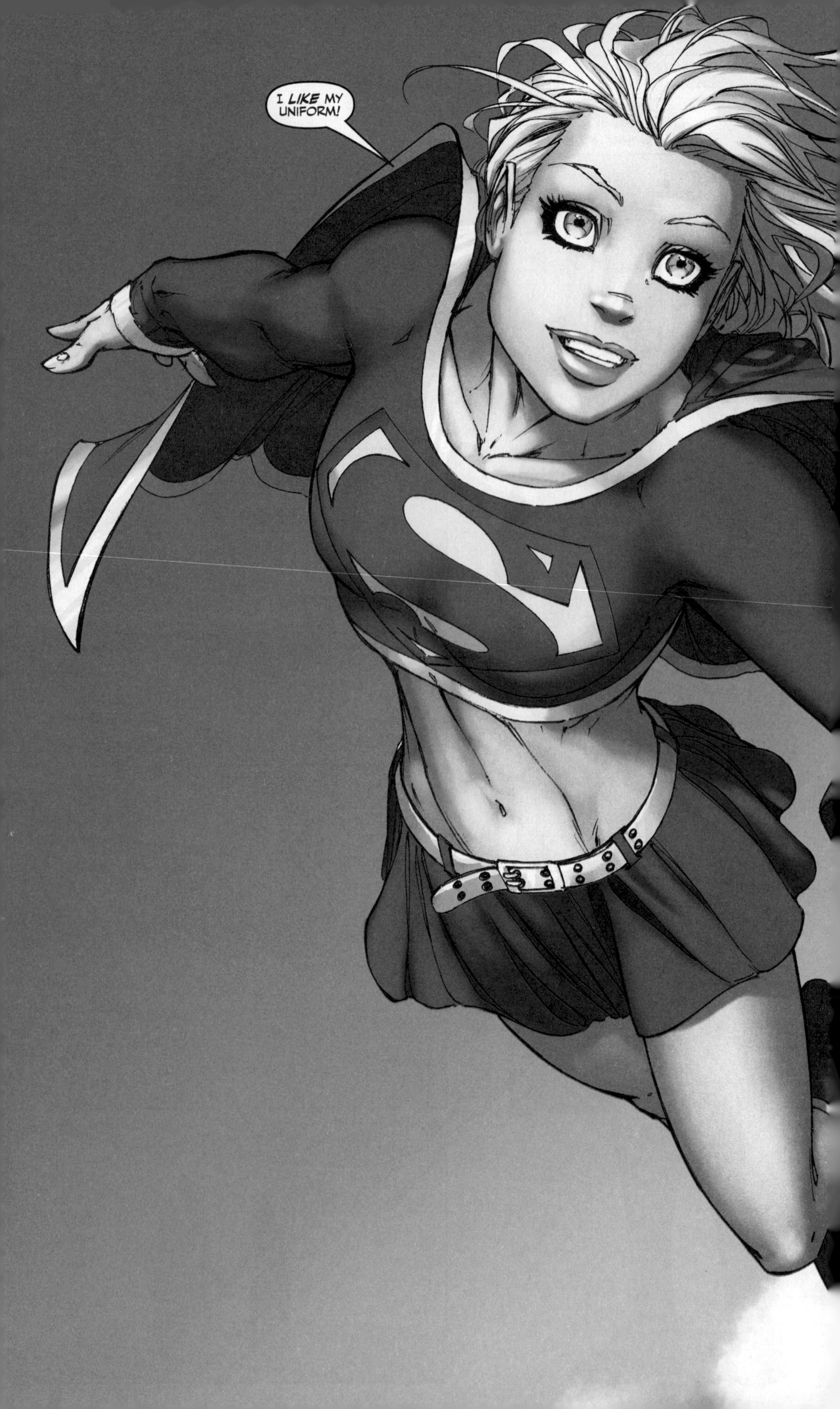
I LIKE MY UNIFORM!

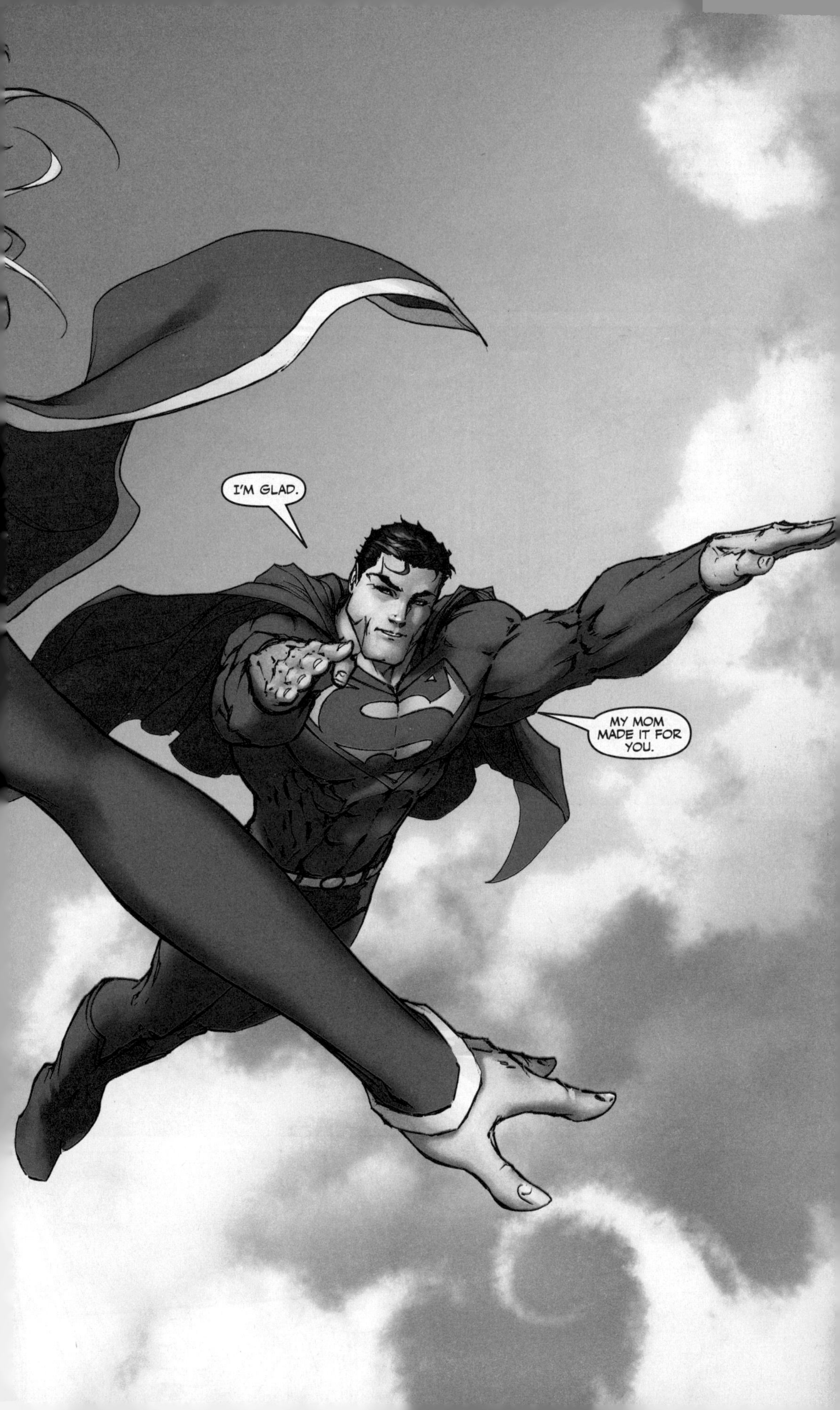
I'M GLAD.
MY MOM MADE IT FOR YOU.

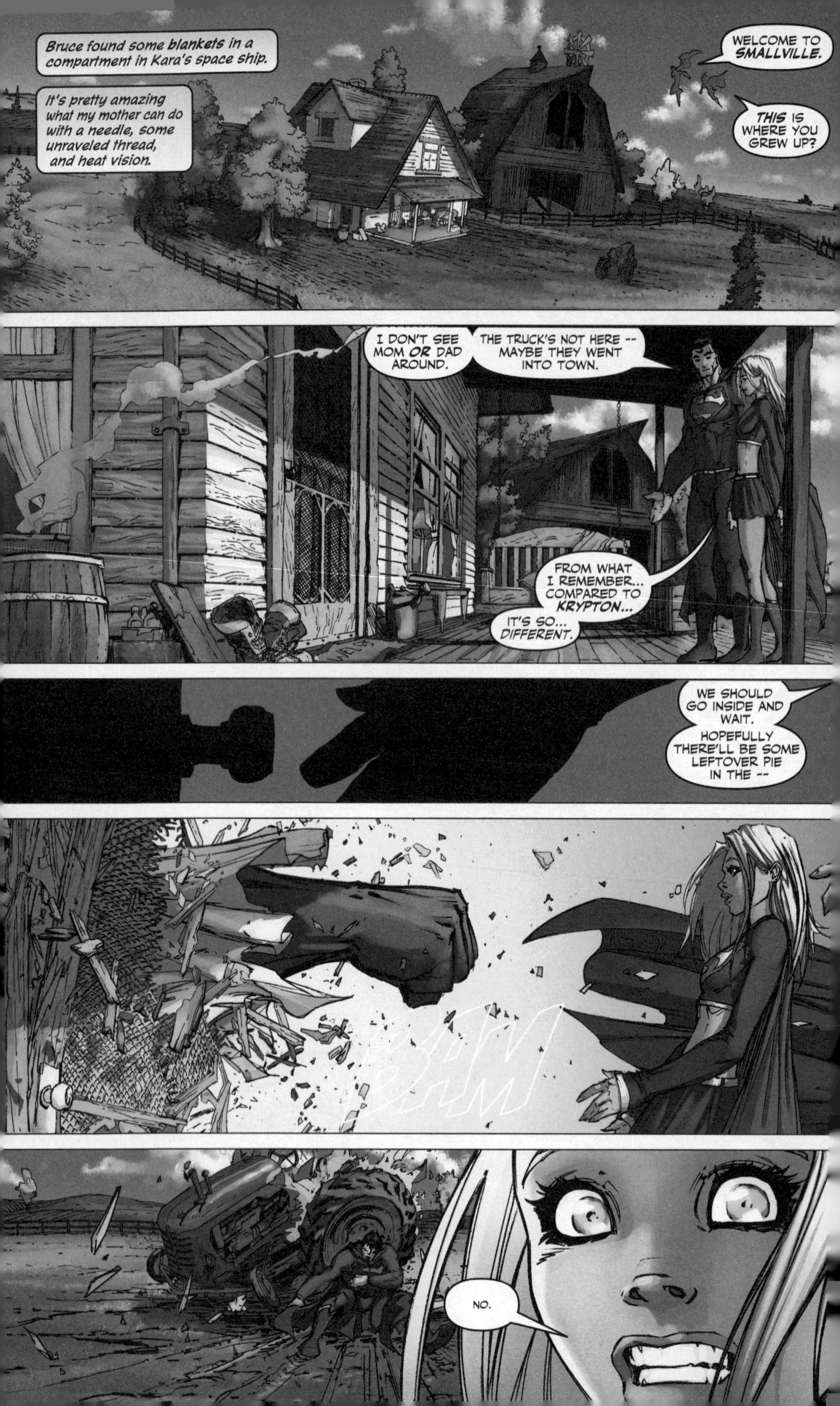
Bruce found some blankets in a compartment in Kara's space ship.
It's pretty amazing what my mother can do with a needle, some unraveled thread, and heat vision.
WELCOME TO SMALLVILLE.
THIS IS WHERE YOU GREW UP?
I DON'T SEE MOM OR DAD AROUND.
THE TRUCK'S NOT HERE -- MAYBE THEY WENT INTO TOWN.
FROM WHAT I REMEMBER... COMPARED TO KRYPTON...
IT'S SO... DIFFERENT.
WE SHOULD GO INSIDE AND WAIT.
HOPEFULLY THERE'LL BE SOME LEFTOVER PIE IN THE --
BAM
NO.

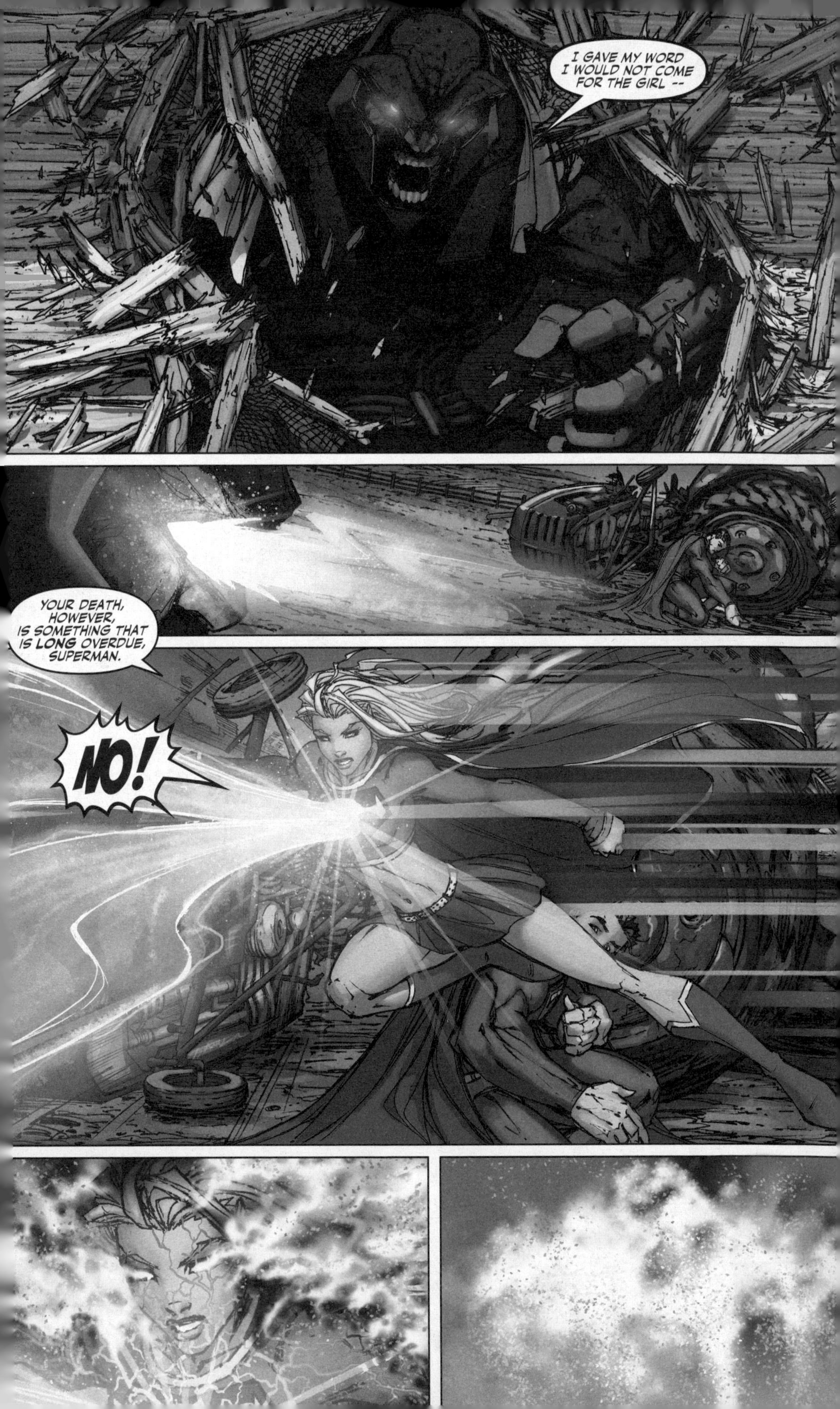
I GAVE MY WORD I WOULD NOT COME FOR THE GIRL --
YOUR DEATH, HOWEVER, IS SOMETHING THAT IS **LONG** OVERDUE, SUPERMAN.
NO!

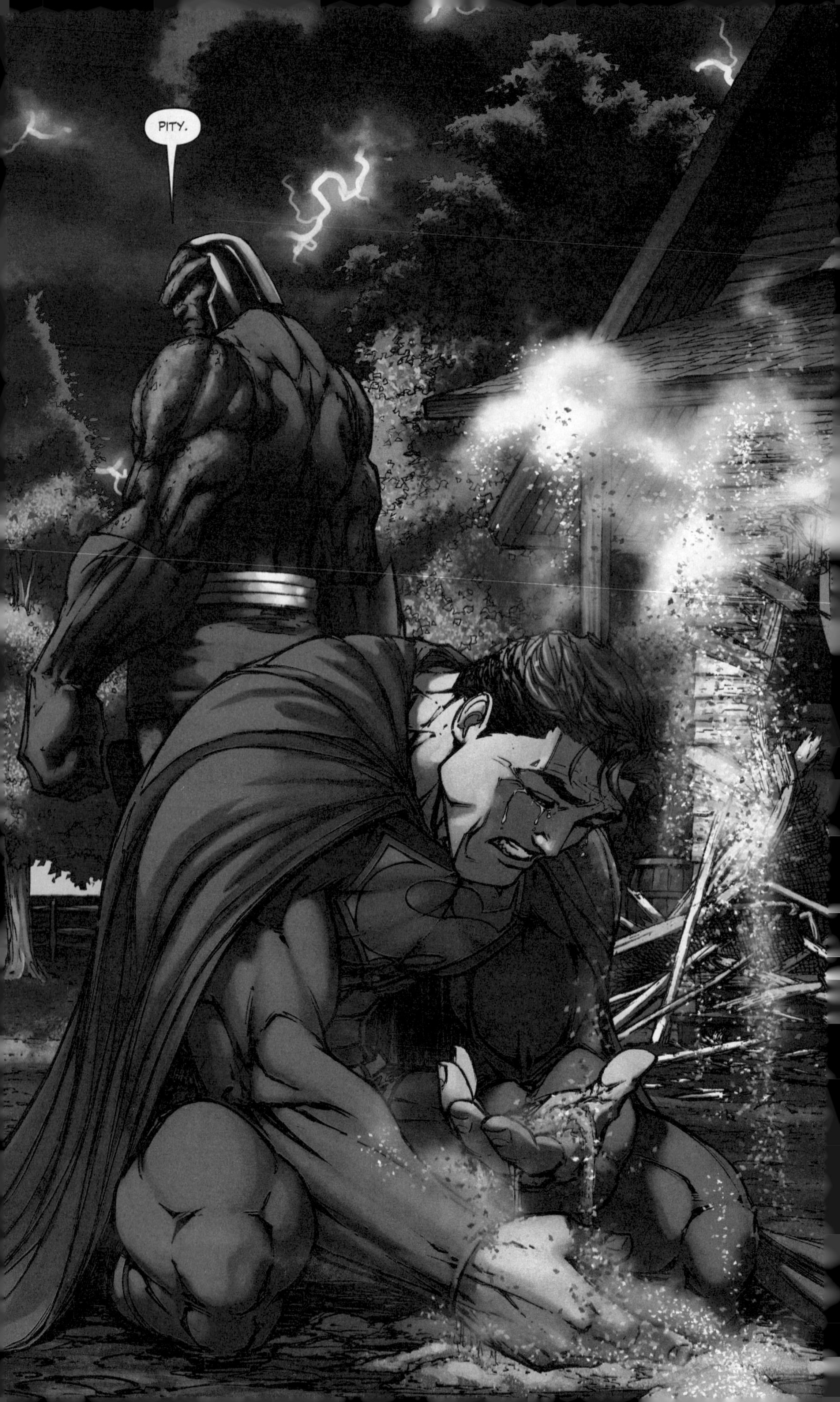
PITY.

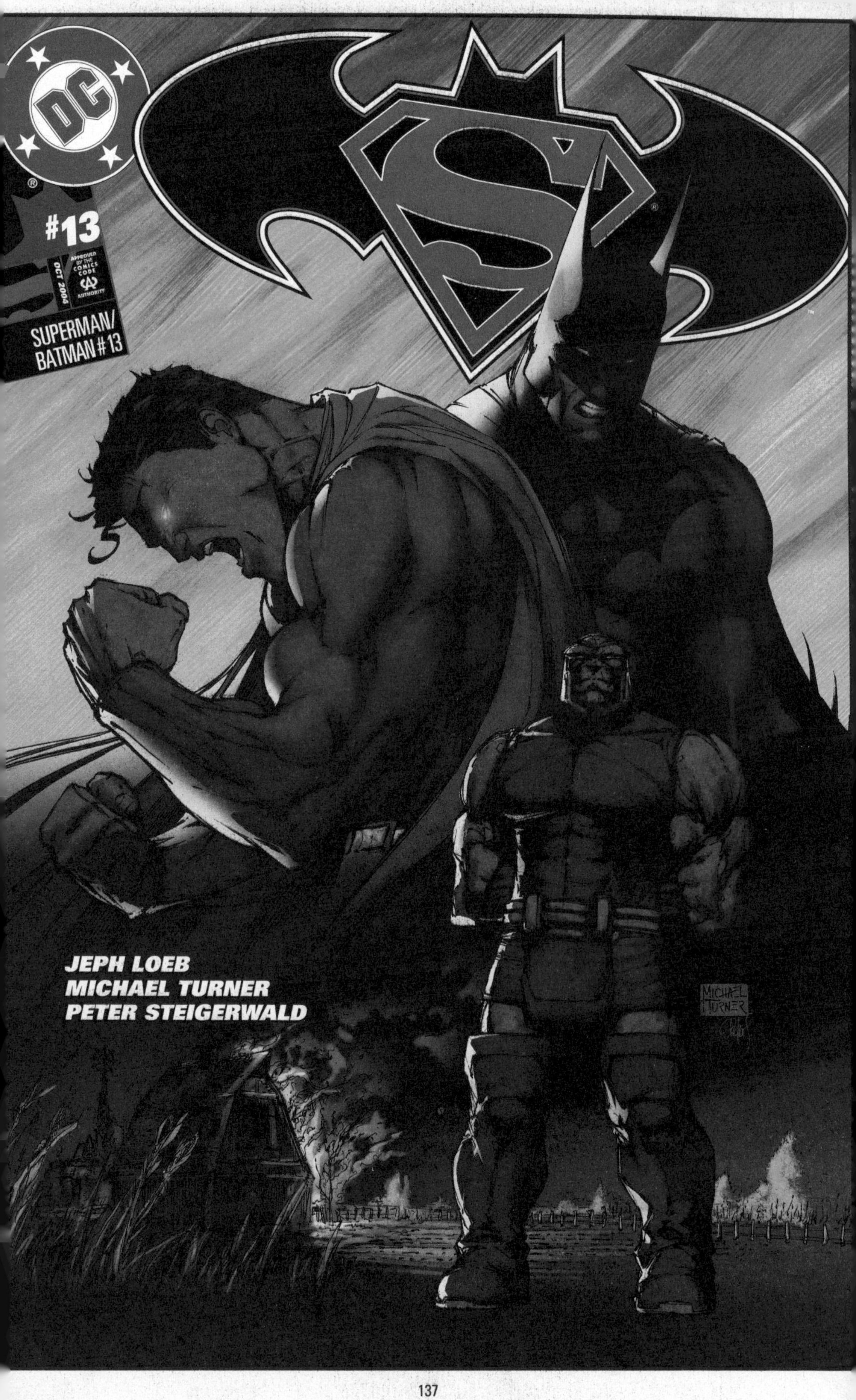
DC
#13
APPROVED BY THE COMICS CODE AUTHORITY
OCT 2004
SUPERMAN/
BATMAN #13
JEPH LOEB
MICHAEL TURNER
PETER STEIGERWALD
MICHAEL TURNER

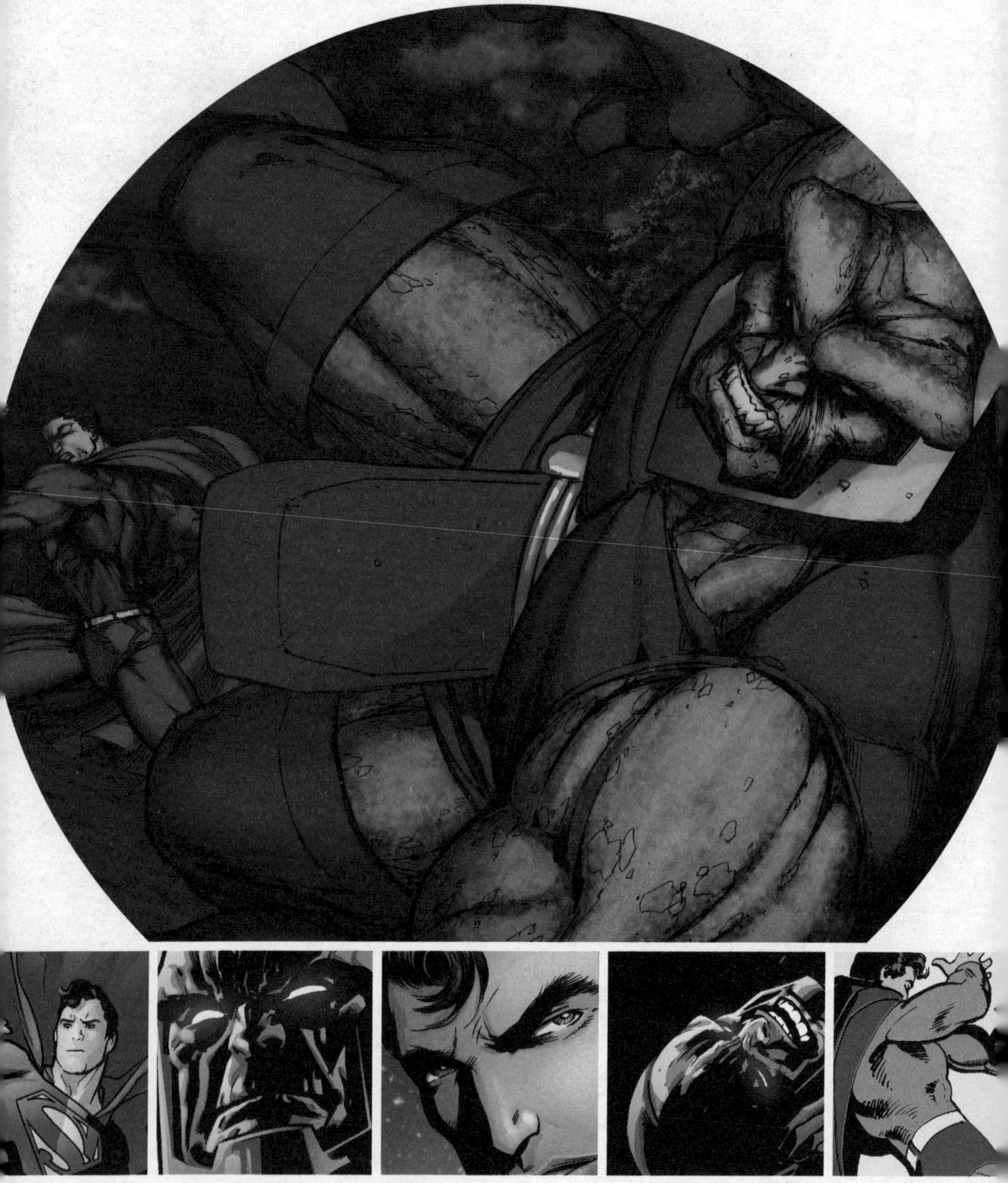

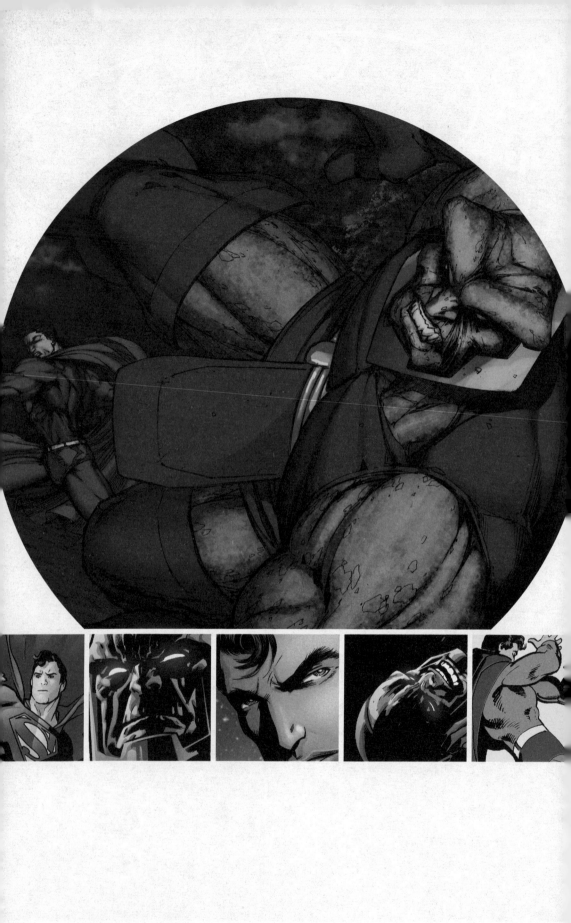

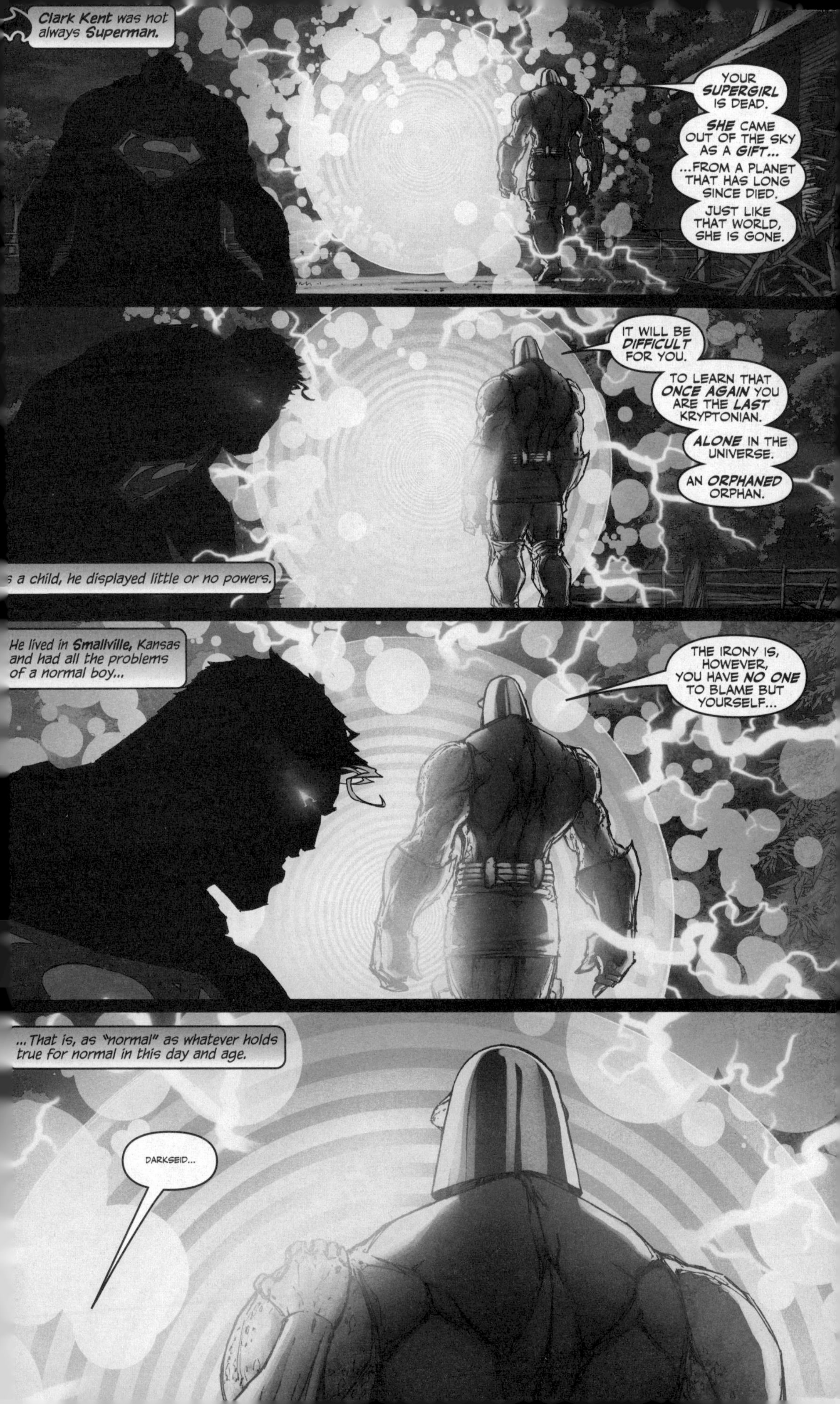
Clark Kent was not always Superman.
YOUR SUPERGIRL IS DEAD.
SHE CAME OUT OF THE SKY AS A GIFT...
...FROM A PLANET THAT HAS LONG SINCE DIED.
JUST LIKE THAT WORLD, SHE IS GONE.
IT WILL BE DIFFICULT FOR YOU.
TO LEARN THAT ONCE AGAIN YOU ARE THE LAST KRYPTONIAN.
ALONE IN THE UNIVERSE.
AN ORPHANED ORPHAN.
s a child, he displayed little or no powers.
He lived in Smallville, Kansas and had all the problems of a normal boy...
THE IRONY IS, HOWEVER, YOU HAVE NO ONE TO BLAME BUT YOURSELF...
...That is, as "normal" as whatever holds true for normal in this day and age.
DARKSEID...

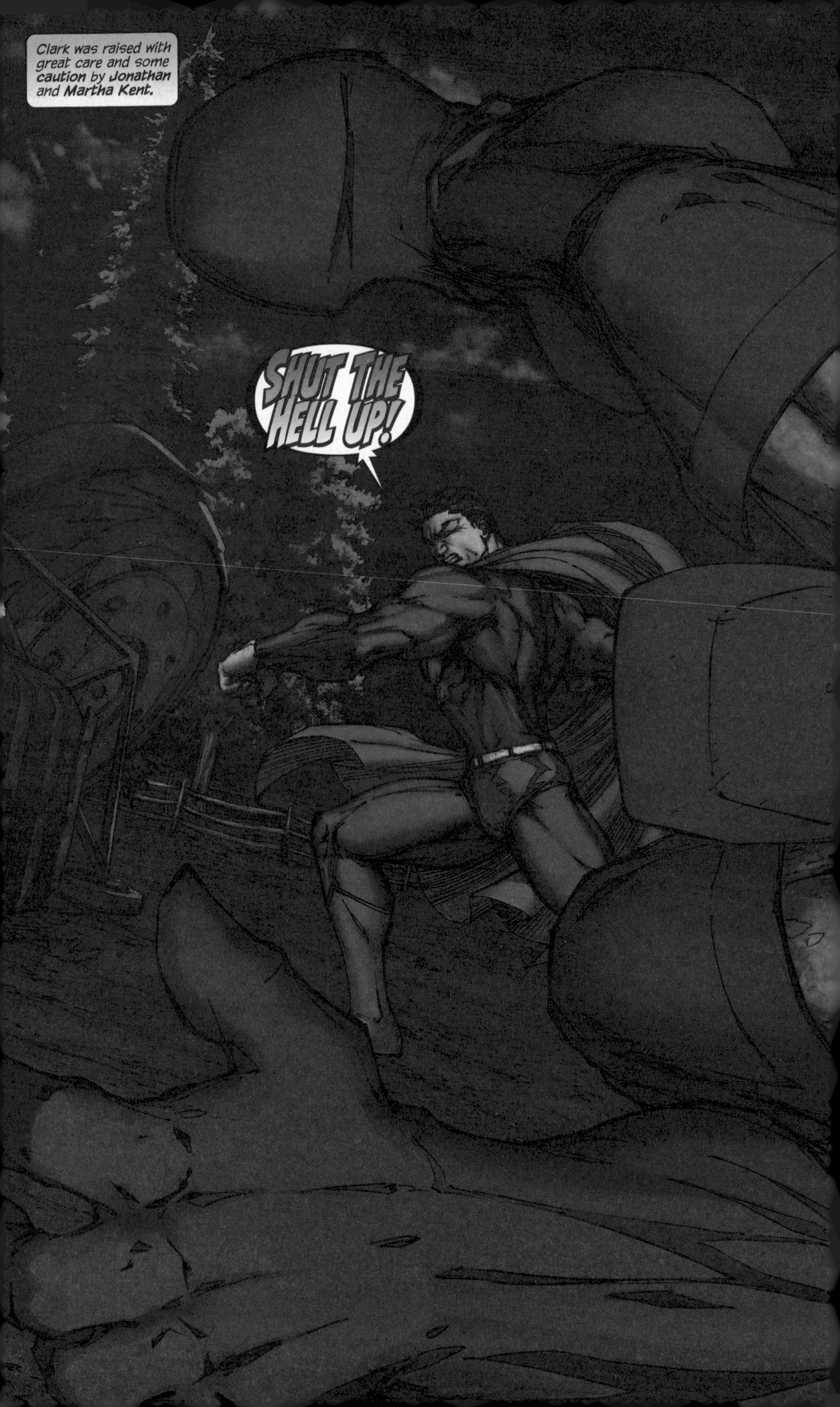
Clark was raised with great care and some caution by Jonathan and Martha Kent.
SHUT THE HELL UP!

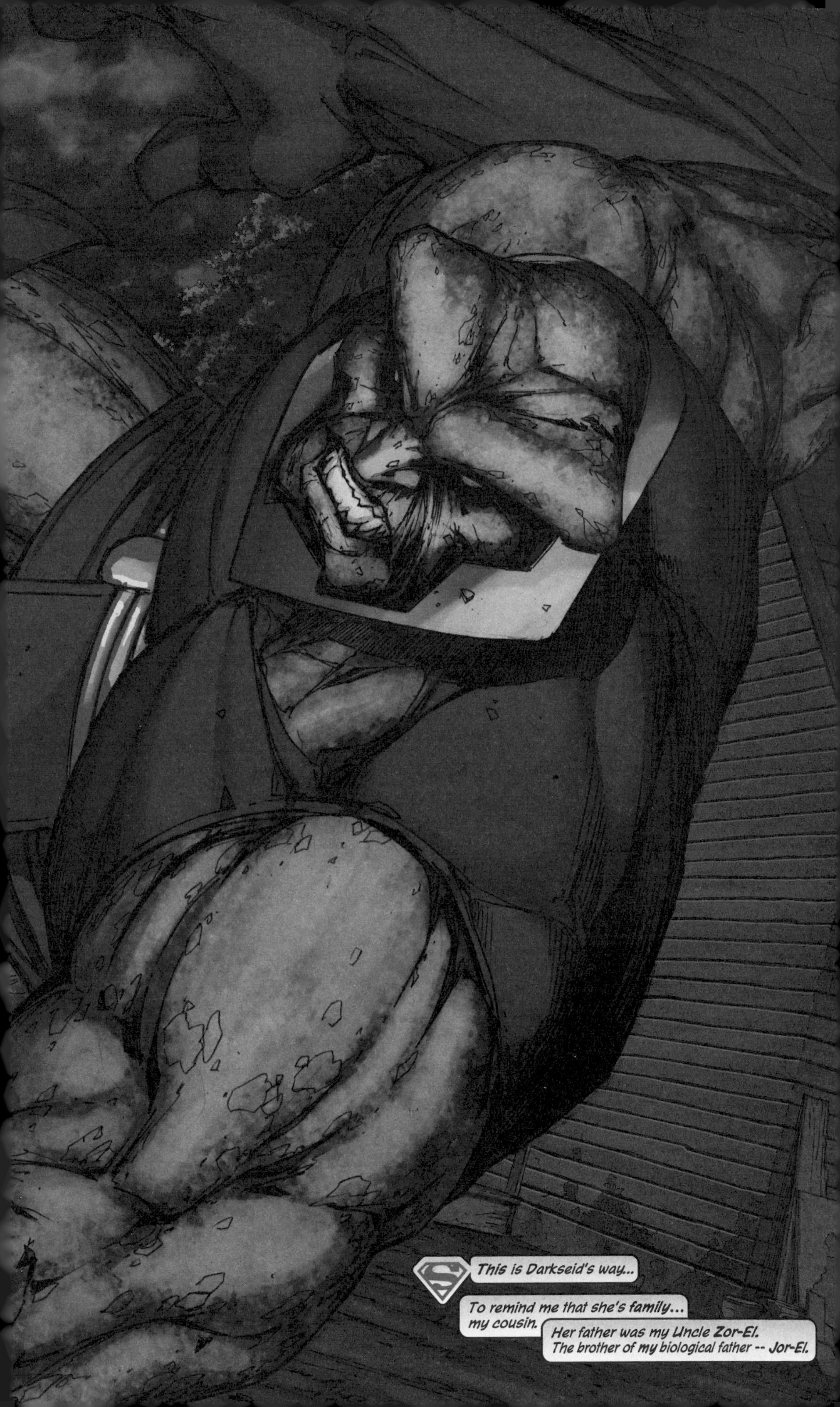

This is Darkseid's way...
To remind me that she's family... my cousin.
Her father was my Uncle Zor-El. The brother of my biological father -- Jor-El.

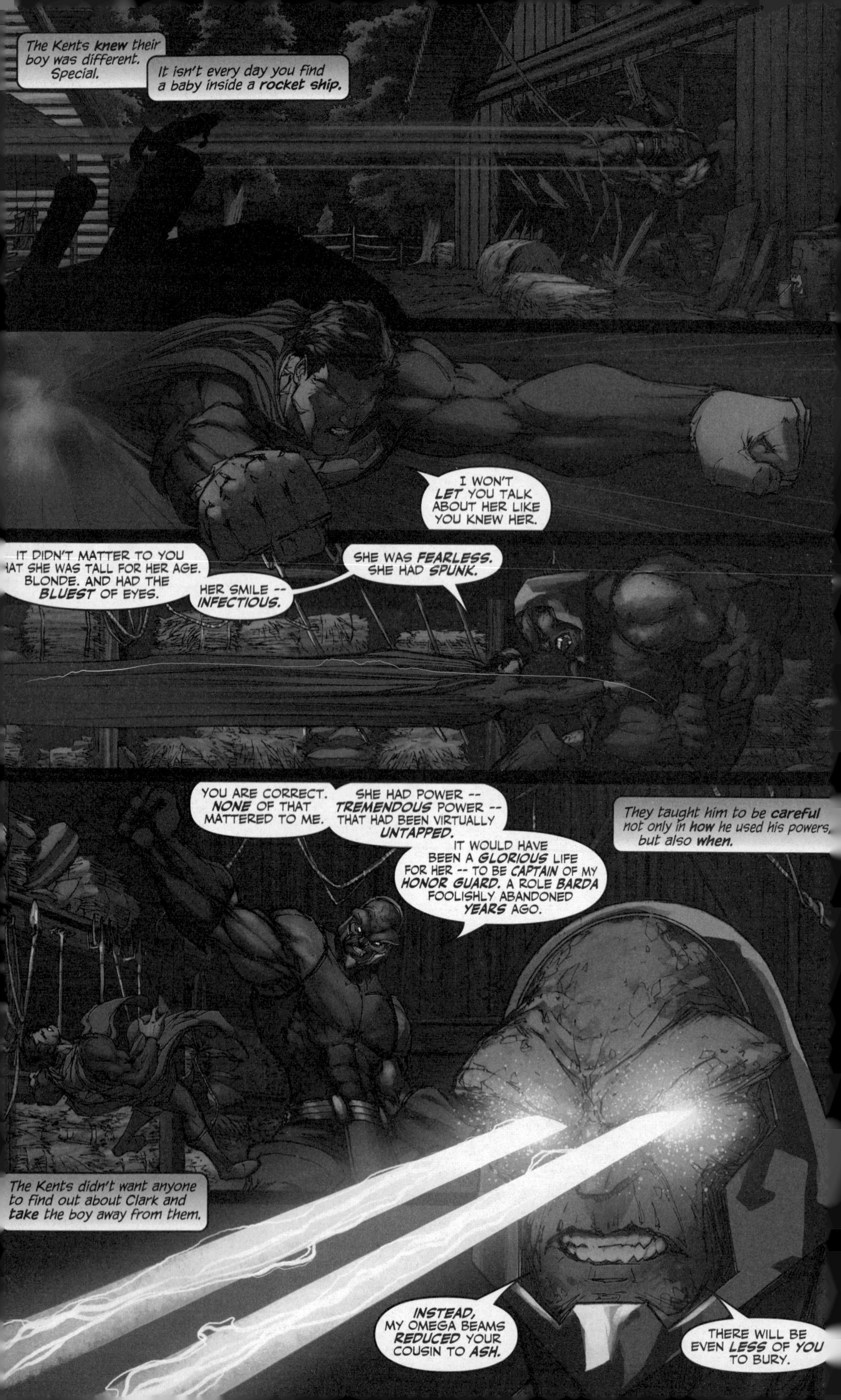

The Kents knew their boy was different. Special.
It isn't every day you find a baby inside a rocket ship.
I WON'T LET YOU TALK ABOUT HER LIKE YOU KNEW HER.
IT DIDN'T MATTER TO YOU THAT SHE WAS TALL FOR HER AGE. BLONDE. AND HAD THE BLUEST OF EYES.
HER SMILE -- INFECTIOUS.
SHE WAS FEARLESS. SHE HAD SPUNK.
YOU ARE CORRECT. NONE OF THAT MATTERED TO ME.
SHE HAD POWER -- TREMENDOUS POWER -- THAT HAD BEEN VIRTUALLY UNTAPPED.
IT WOULD HAVE BEEN A GLORIOUS LIFE FOR HER -- TO BE CAPTAIN OF MY HONOR GUARD. A ROLE BARDA FOOLISHLY ABANDONED YEARS AGO.
They taught him to be careful not only in how he used his powers, but also when.
The Kents didn't want anyone to find out about Clark and take the boy away from them.
INSTEAD, MY OMEGA BEAMS REDUCED YOUR COUSIN TO ASH.
THERE WILL BE EVEN LESS OF YOU TO BURY.

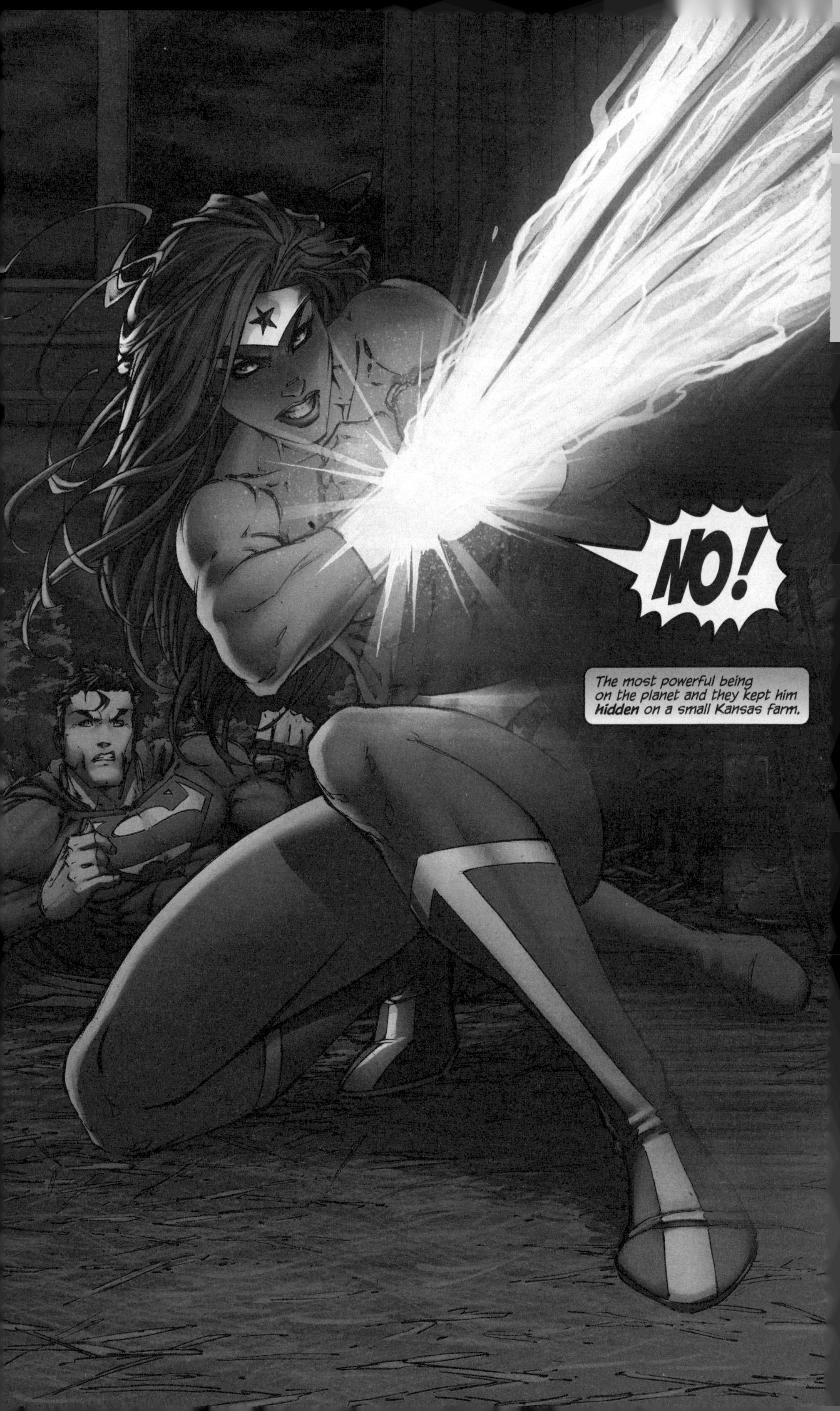

NO!
The most powerful being on the planet and they kept him **hidden** on a small Kansas farm.

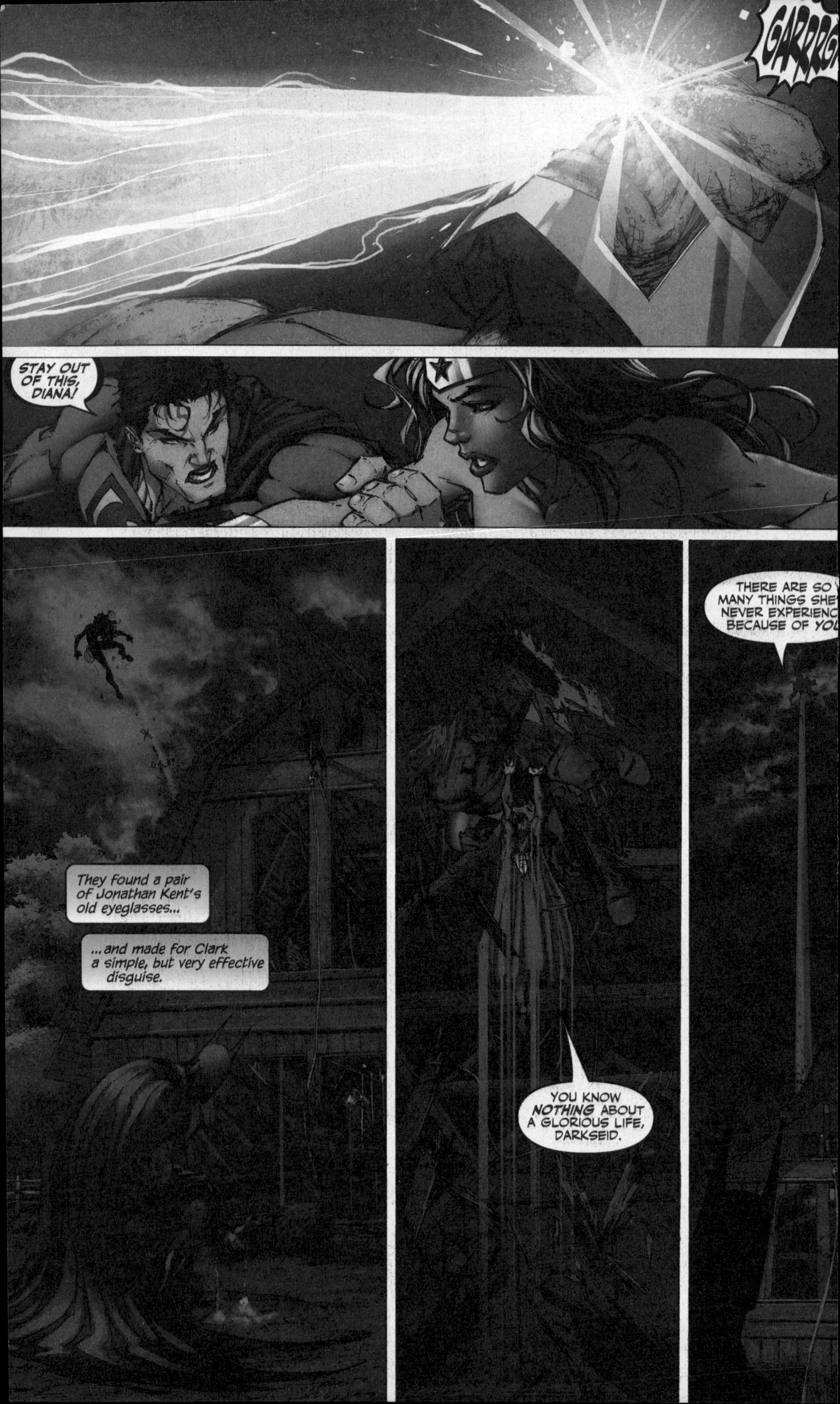
GARRRG
STAY OUT OF THIS, DIANA!
They found a pair of Jonathan Kent's old eyeglasses...
...and made for Clark a simple, but very effective disguise.
YOU KNOW *NOTHING* ABOUT A GLORIOUS LIFE, DARKSEID.
THERE ARE SO MANY THINGS SHE NEVER EXPERIENC BECAUSE OF YO

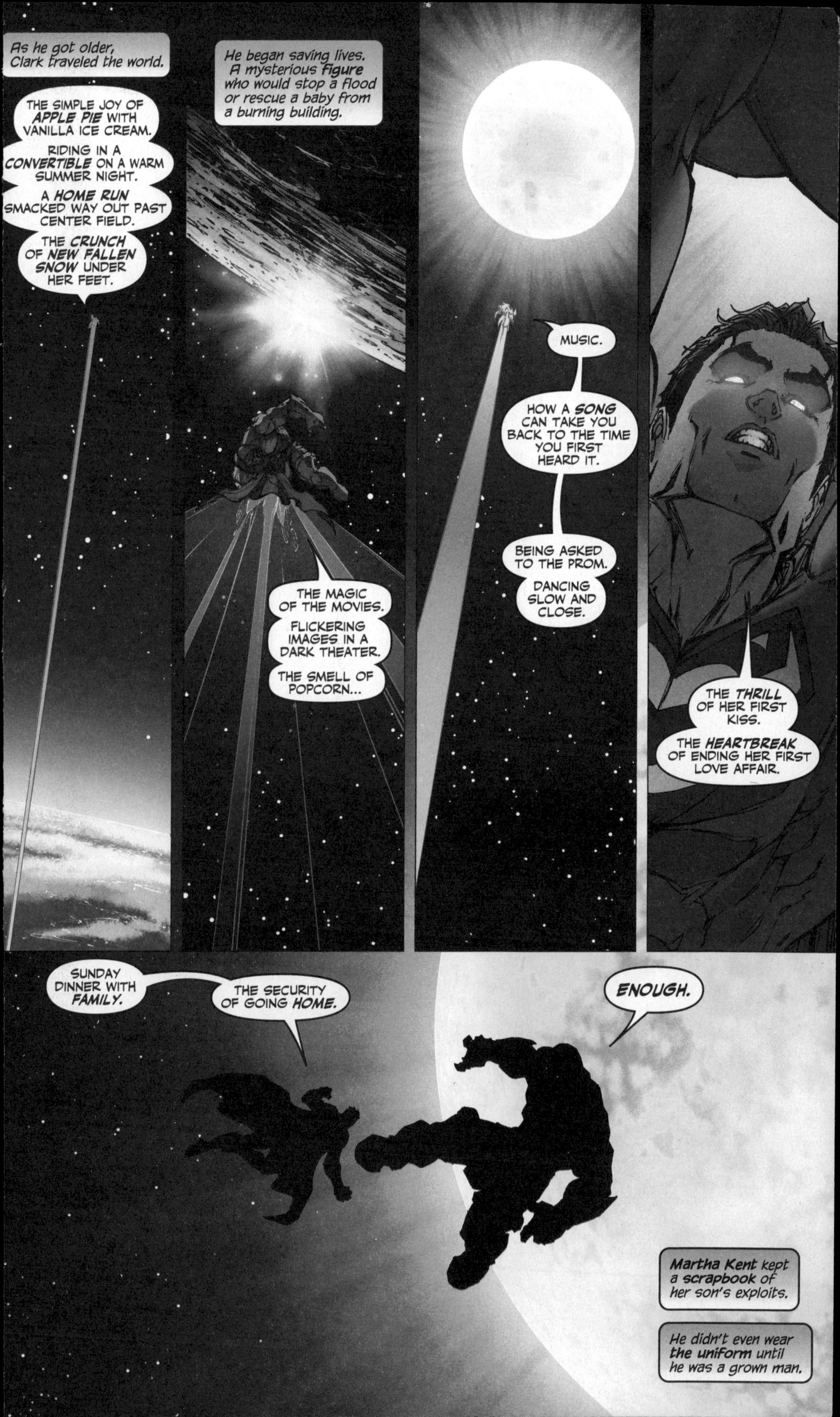

As he got older, Clark traveled the world.
THE SIMPLE JOY OF APPLE PIE WITH VANILLA ICE CREAM.
RIDING IN A CONVERTIBLE ON A WARM SUMMER NIGHT.
A HOME RUN SMACKED WAY OUT PAST CENTER FIELD.
THE CRUNCH OF NEW FALLEN SNOW UNDER HER FEET.
He began saving lives. A mysterious figure who would stop a flood or rescue a baby from a burning building.
THE MAGIC OF THE MOVIES.
FLICKERING IMAGES IN A DARK THEATER.
THE SMELL OF POPCORN...
MUSIC.
HOW A SONG CAN TAKE YOU BACK TO THE TIME YOU FIRST HEARD IT.
BEING ASKED TO THE PROM.
DANCING SLOW AND CLOSE.
THE THRILL OF HER FIRST KISS.
THE HEARTBREAK OF ENDING HER FIRST LOVE AFFAIR.
SUNDAY DINNER WITH FAMILY.
THE SECURITY OF GOING HOME.
ENOUGH.
Martha Kent kept a scrapbook of her son's exploits.
He didn't even wear the uniform until he was a grown man.

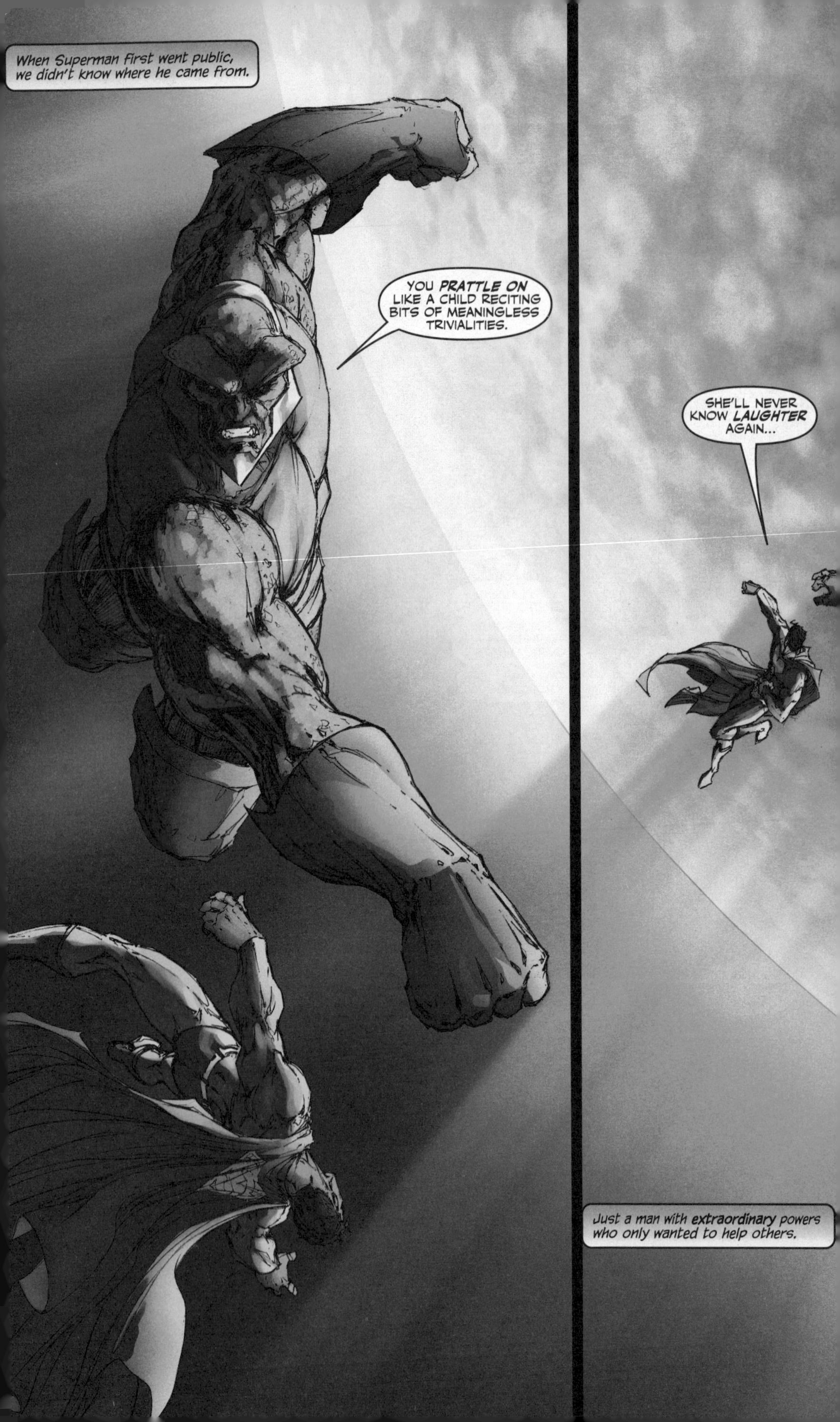
When Superman first went public, we didn't know where he came from.
YOU PRATTLE ON LIKE A CHILD RECITING BITS OF MEANINGLESS TRIVIALITIES.
SHE'LL NEVER KNOW LAUGHTER AGAIN...
Just a man with extraordinary powers who only wanted to help others.

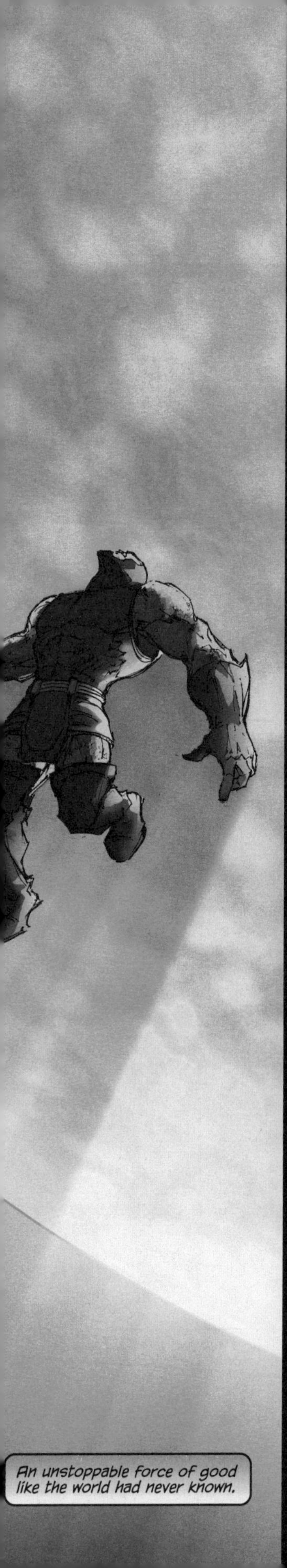
An unstoppable force of good like the world had never known.

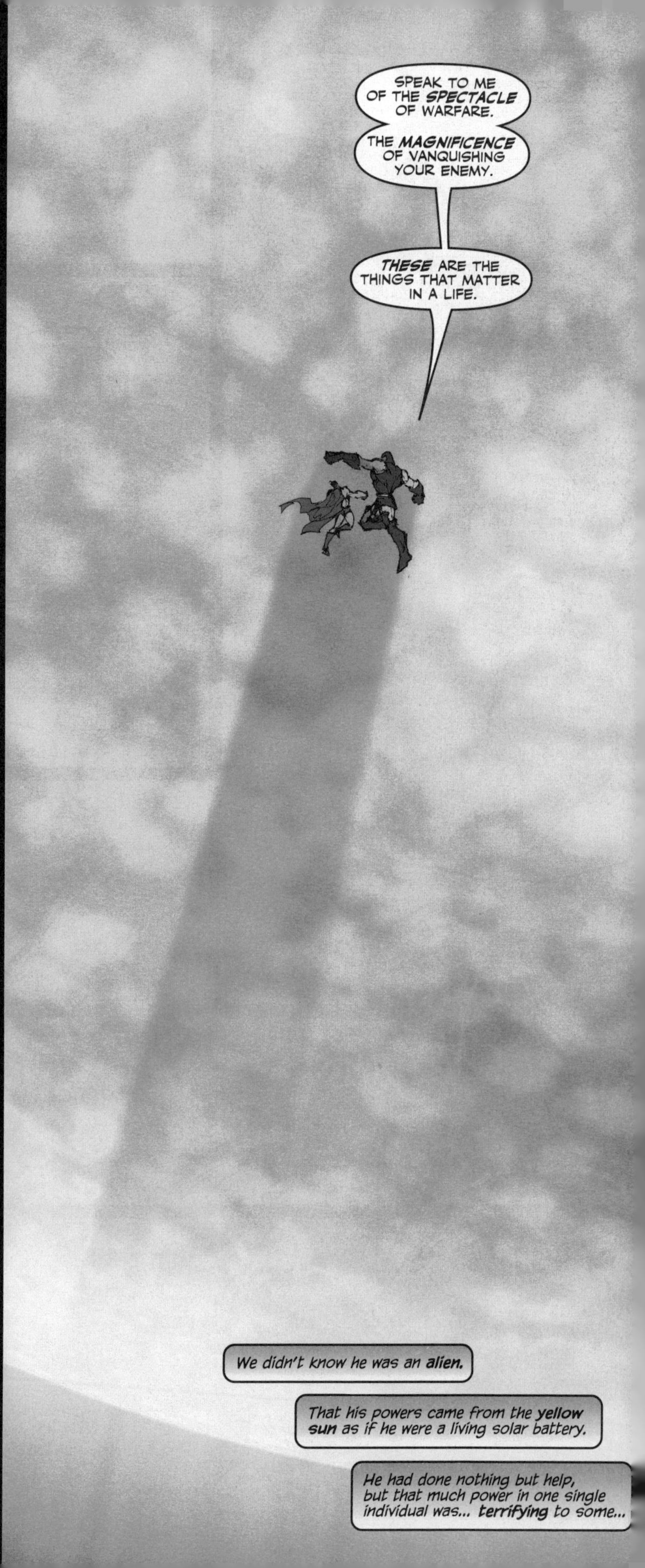
SPEAK TO ME OF THE SPECTACLE OF WARFARE.
THE MAGNIFICENCE OF VANQUISHING YOUR ENEMY.
THESE ARE THE THINGS THAT MATTER IN A LIFE.
We didn't know he was an alien.
That his powers came from the yellow sun as if he were a living solar battery.
He had done nothing but help, but that much power in one single individual was... terrifying to some...

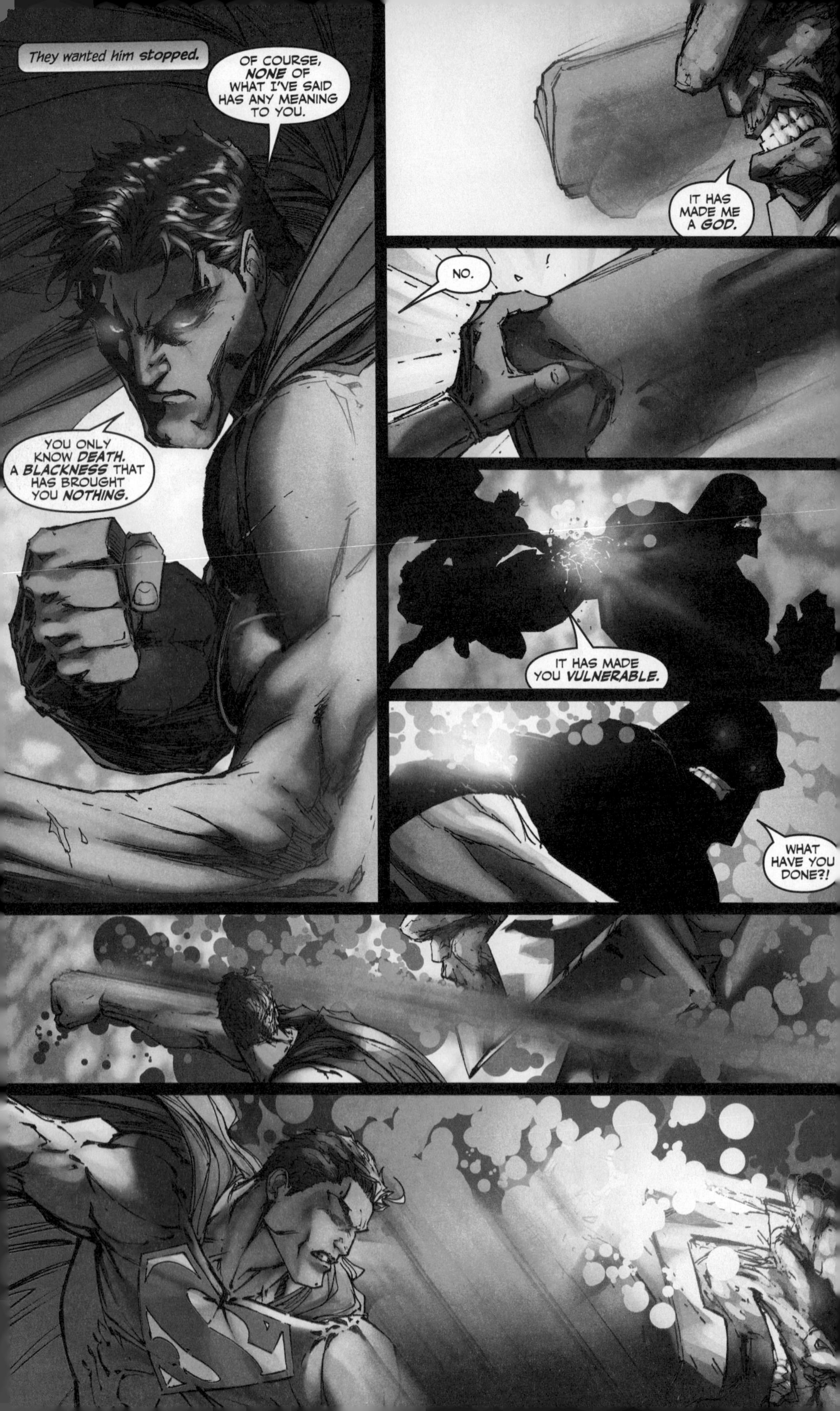

They wanted him stopped.
OF COURSE, NONE OF WHAT I'VE SAID HAS ANY MEANING TO YOU.
YOU ONLY KNOW DEATH. A BLACKNESS THAT HAS BROUGHT YOU NOTHING.
IT HAS MADE ME A GOD.
NO.
IT HAS MADE YOU VULNERABLE.
WHAT HAVE YOU DONE?!

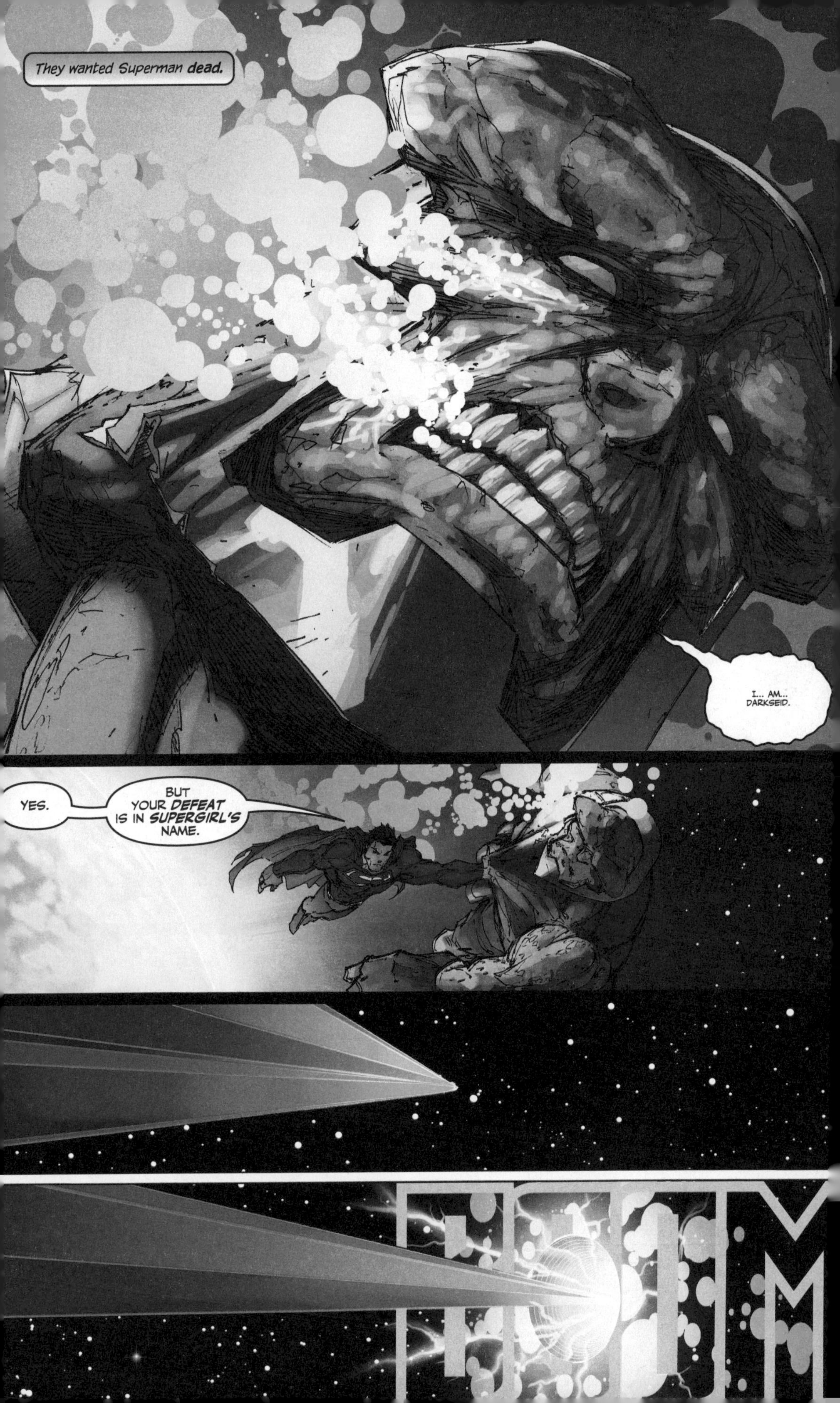
They wanted Superman dead.
I... AM... DARKSEID.
YES.
BUT YOUR DEFEAT IS IN SUPERGIRL'S NAME.

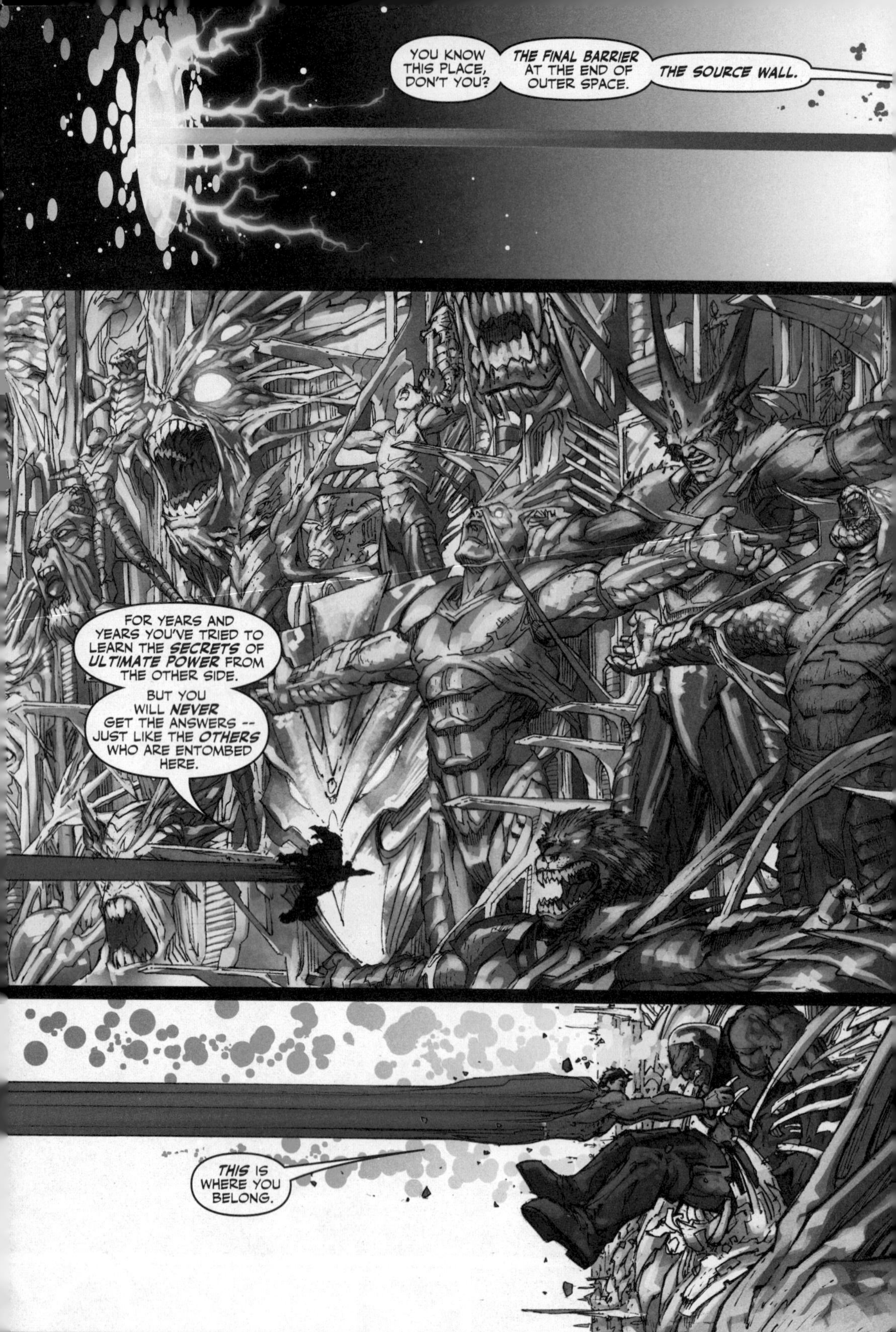

YOU KNOW THIS PLACE, DON'T YOU?
THE FINAL BARRIER AT THE END OF OUTER SPACE.
THE SOURCE WALL.
FOR YEARS AND YEARS YOU'VE TRIED TO LEARN THE SECRETS OF ULTIMATE POWER FROM THE OTHER SIDE.
BUT YOU WILL NEVER GET THE ANSWERS -- JUST LIKE THE OTHERS WHO ARE ENTOMBED HERE.
THIS IS WHERE YOU BELONG.

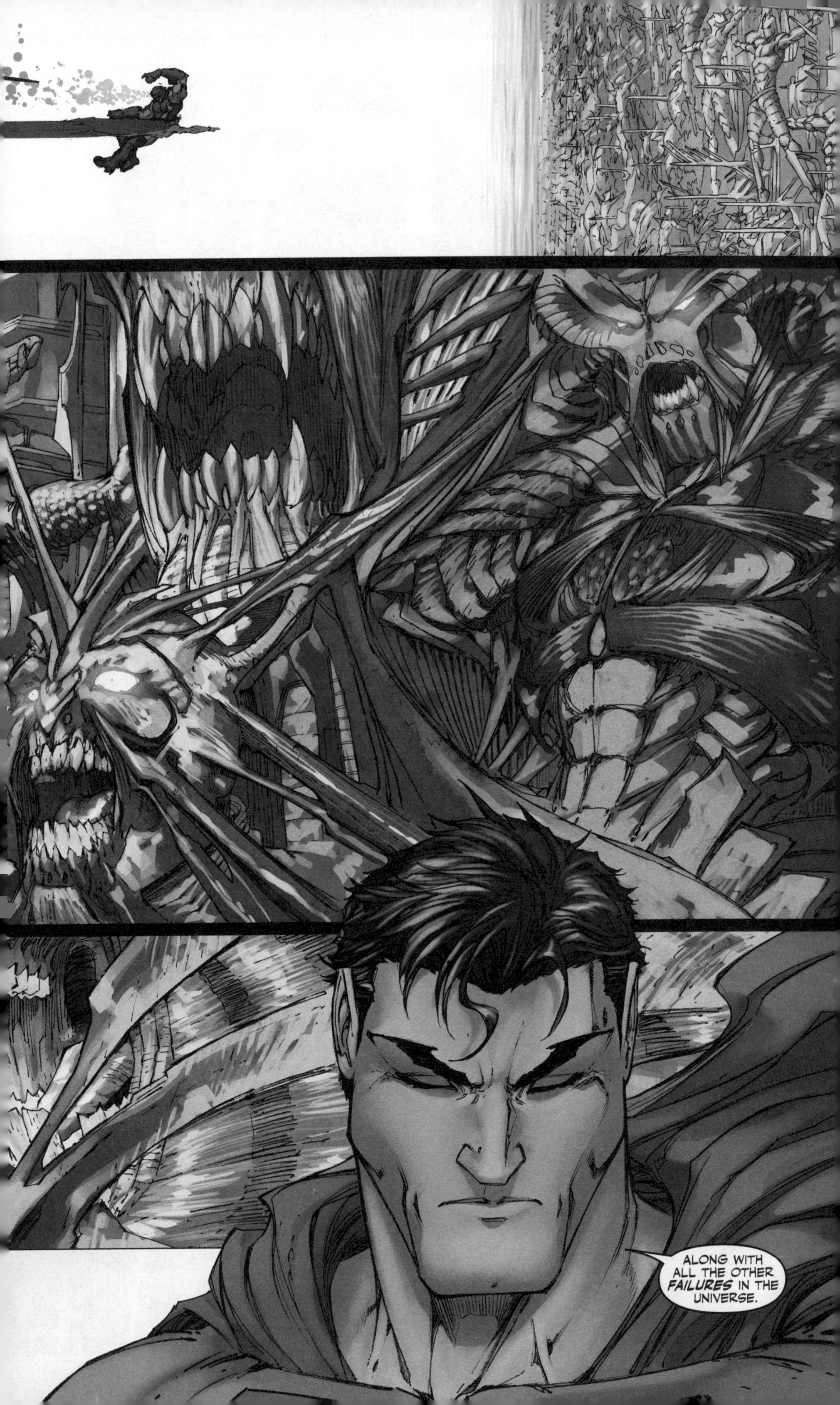
ALONG WITH ALL THE OTHER FAILURES IN THE UNIVERSE.

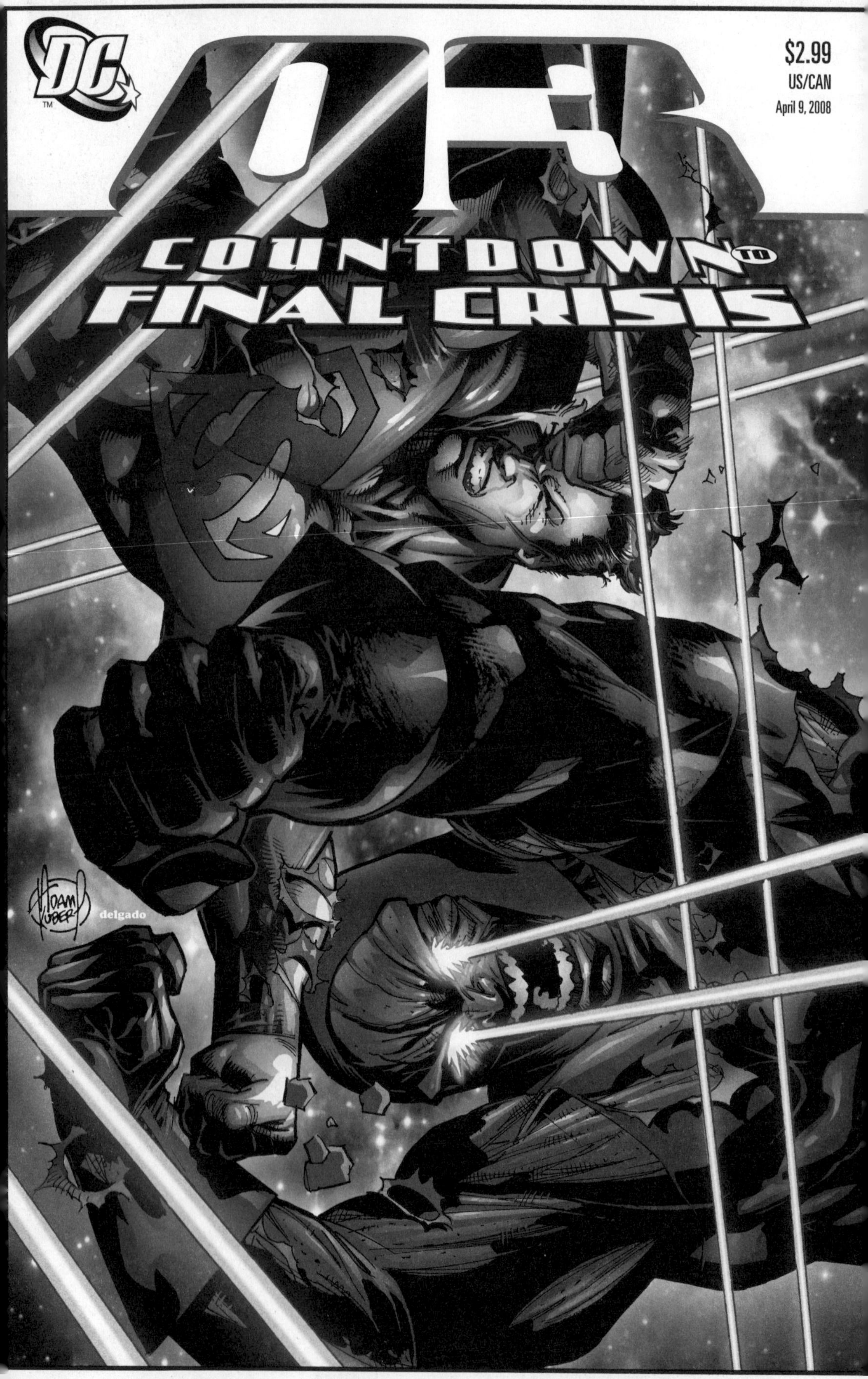

03
$2.99
US/CAN
April 9, 2008
COUNTDOWN TO
FINAL CRISIS
delgado

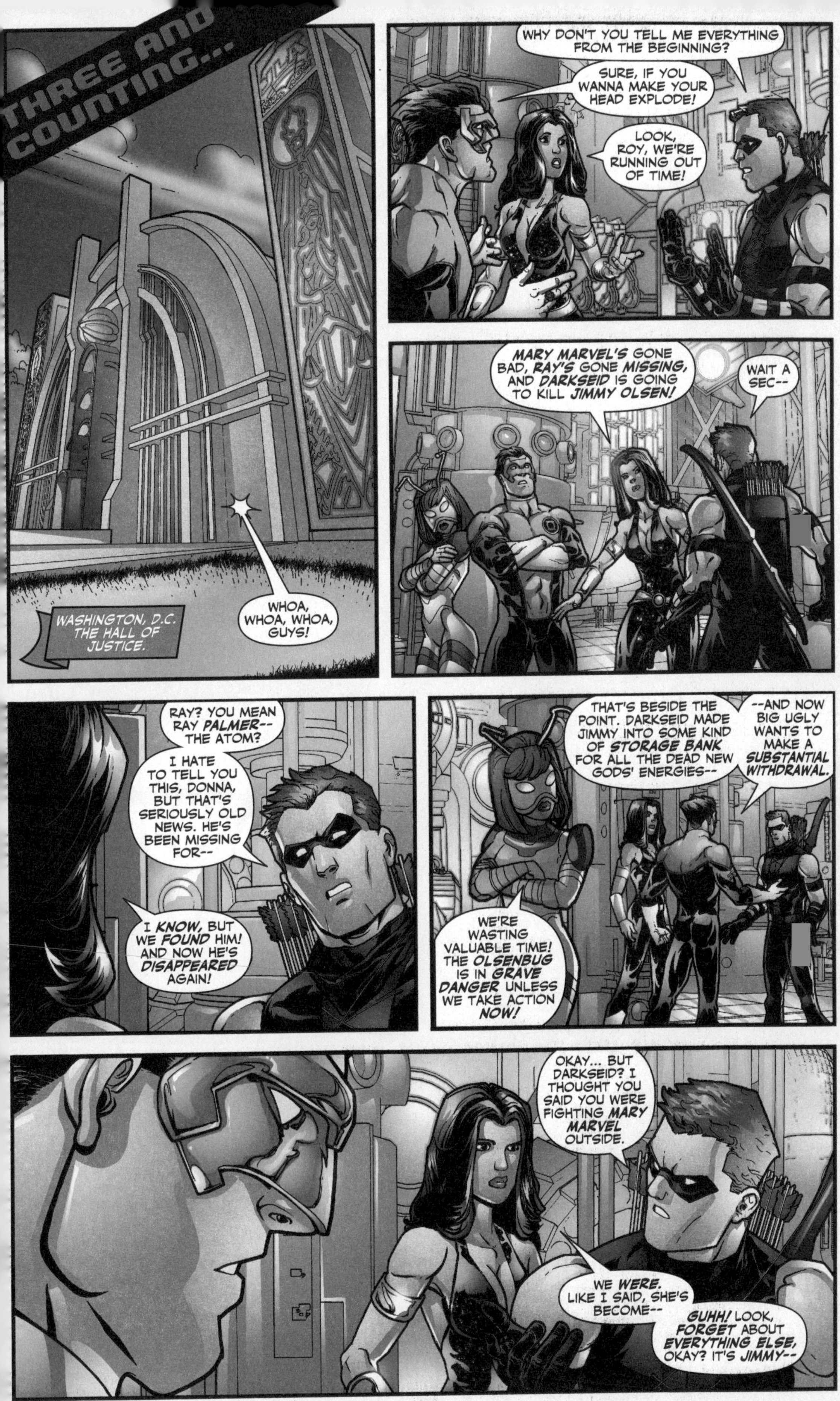
THREE AND COUNTING...
WASHINGTON, D.C. THE HALL OF JUSTICE.
WHOA, WHOA, WHOA, GUYS!
WHY DON'T YOU TELL ME EVERYTHING FROM THE BEGINNING?
SURE, IF YOU WANNA MAKE YOUR HEAD EXPLODE!
LOOK, ROY, WE'RE RUNNING OUT OF TIME!
MARY MARVEL'S GONE BAD, RAY'S GONE MISSING, AND DARKSEID IS GOING TO KILL JIMMY OLSEN!
WAIT A SEC--
RAY? YOU MEAN RAY PALMER-- THE ATOM?
I HATE TO TELL YOU THIS, DONNA, BUT THAT'S SERIOUSLY OLD NEWS. HE'S BEEN MISSING FOR--
I KNOW, BUT WE FOUND HIM! AND NOW HE'S DISAPPEARED AGAIN!
THAT'S BESIDE THE POINT. DARKSEID MADE JIMMY INTO SOME KIND OF STORAGE BANK FOR ALL THE DEAD NEW GODS' ENERGIES--
--AND NOW BIG UGLY WANTS TO MAKE A SUBSTANTIAL WITHDRAWAL.
WE'RE WASTING VALUABLE TIME! THE OLSENBUG IS IN GRAVE DANGER UNLESS WE TAKE ACTION NOW!
OKAY... BUT DARKSEID? I THOUGHT YOU SAID YOU WERE FIGHTING MARY MARVEL OUTSIDE.
WE WERE. LIKE I SAID, SHE'S BECOME--
GUHH! LOOK, FORGET ABOUT EVERYTHING ELSE, OKAY? IT'S JIMMY--

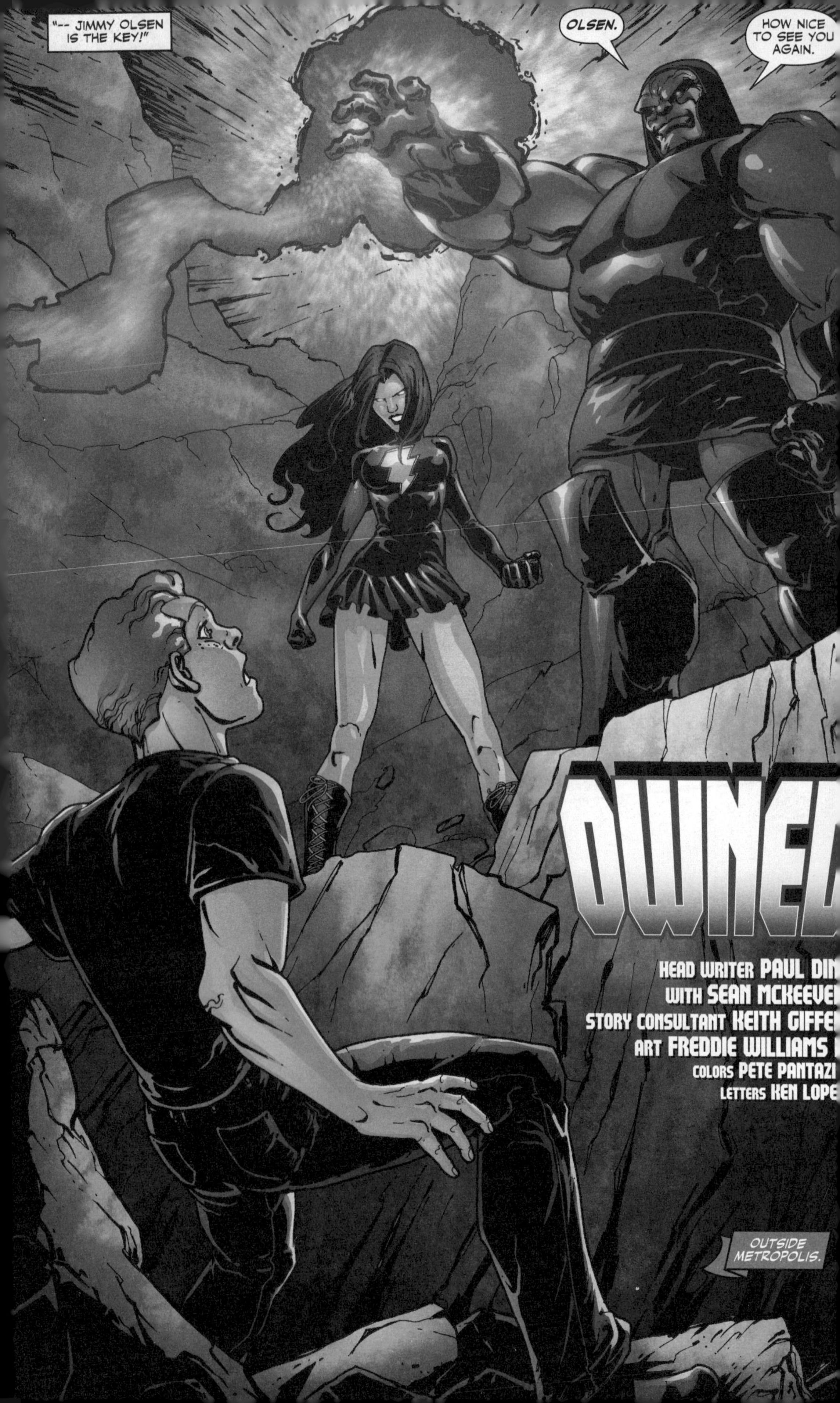

"-- JIMMY OLSEN IS THE KEY!"
OLSEN.
HOW NICE TO SEE YOU AGAIN.
OWNED
HEAD WRITER PAUL DIN
WITH SEAN MCKEEVE
STORY CONSULTANT KEITH GIFFE
ART FREDDIE WILLIAMS
COLORS PETE PANTAZI
LETTERS KEN LOPE
OUTSIDE METROPOLIS.

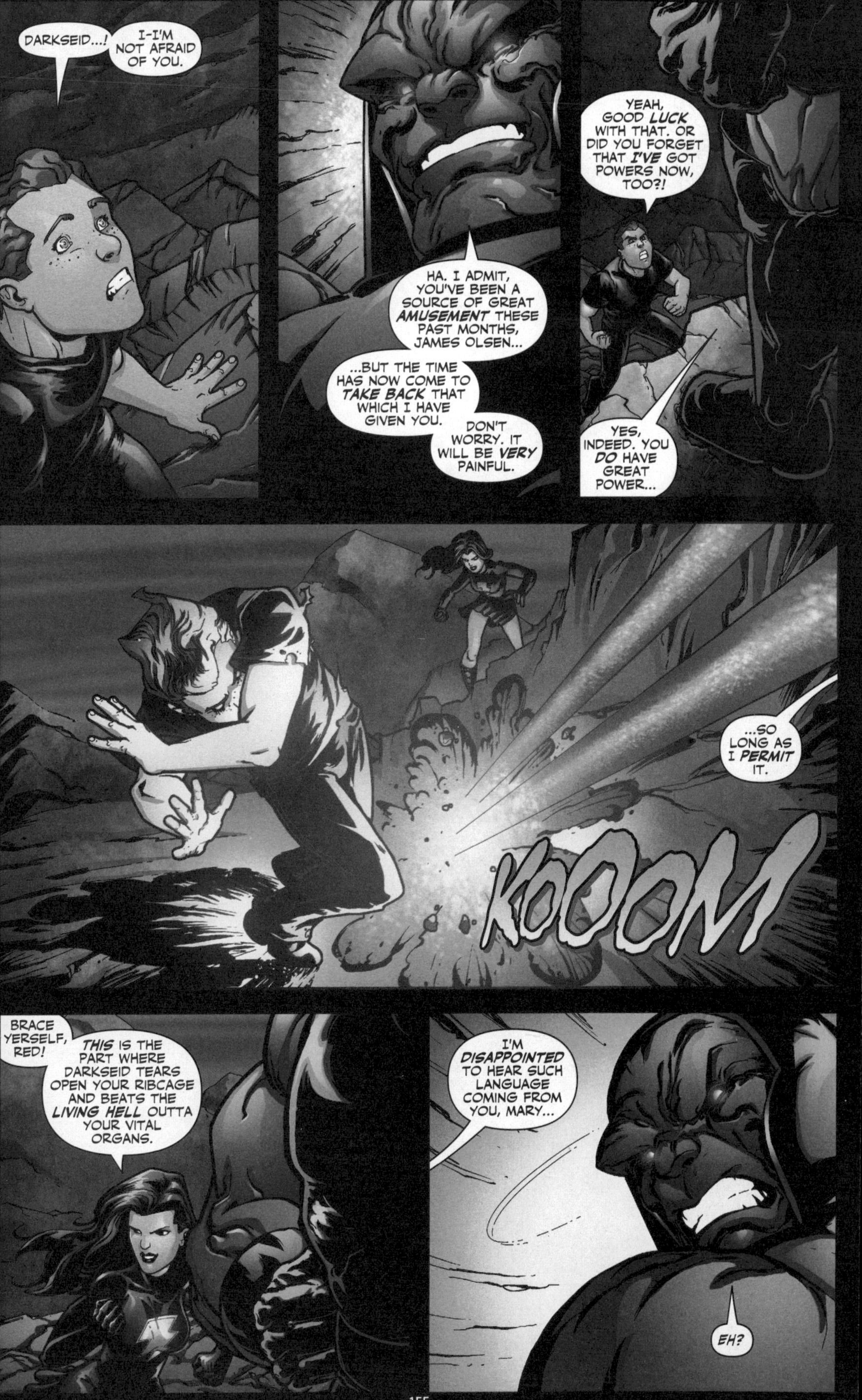
DARKSEID...!
I-I'M NOT AFRAID OF YOU.
HA. I ADMIT, YOU'VE BEEN A SOURCE OF GREAT AMUSEMENT THESE PAST MONTHS, JAMES OLSEN...
...BUT THE TIME HAS NOW COME TO TAKE BACK THAT WHICH I HAVE GIVEN YOU.
DON'T WORRY. IT WILL BE VERY PAINFUL.
YEAH, GOOD LUCK WITH THAT. OR DID YOU FORGET THAT I'VE GOT POWERS NOW, TOO?!
YES, INDEED. YOU DO HAVE GREAT POWER...
...SO LONG AS I PERMIT IT.
KOOOM
BRACE YERSELF, RED!
THIS IS THE PART WHERE DARKSEID TEARS OPEN YOUR RIBCAGE AND BEATS THE LIVING HELL OUTTA YOUR VITAL ORGANS.
I'M DISAPPOINTED TO HEAR SUCH LANGUAGE COMING FROM YOU, MARY...
EH?

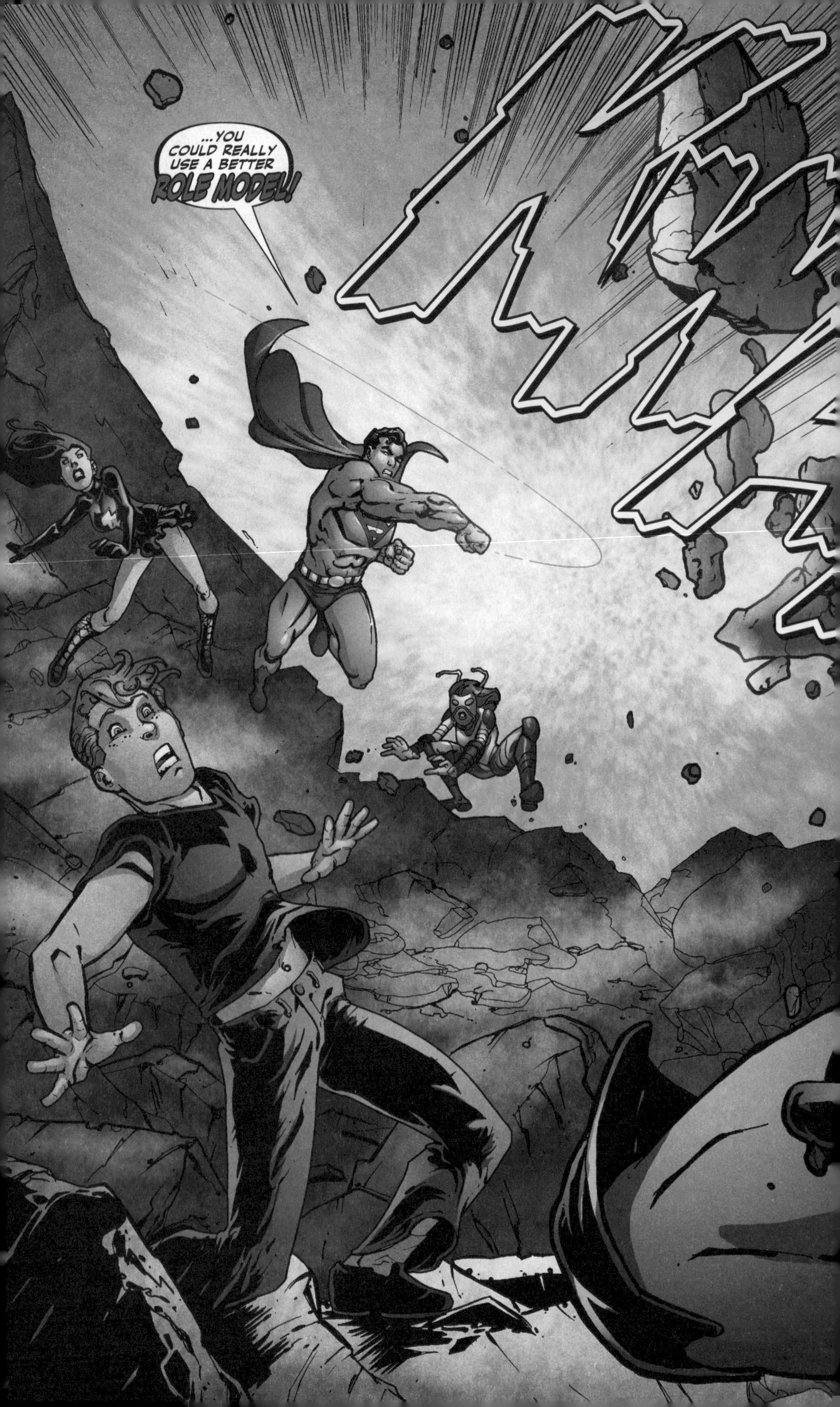
...YOU COULD REALLY USE A BETTER ROLE MODEL!

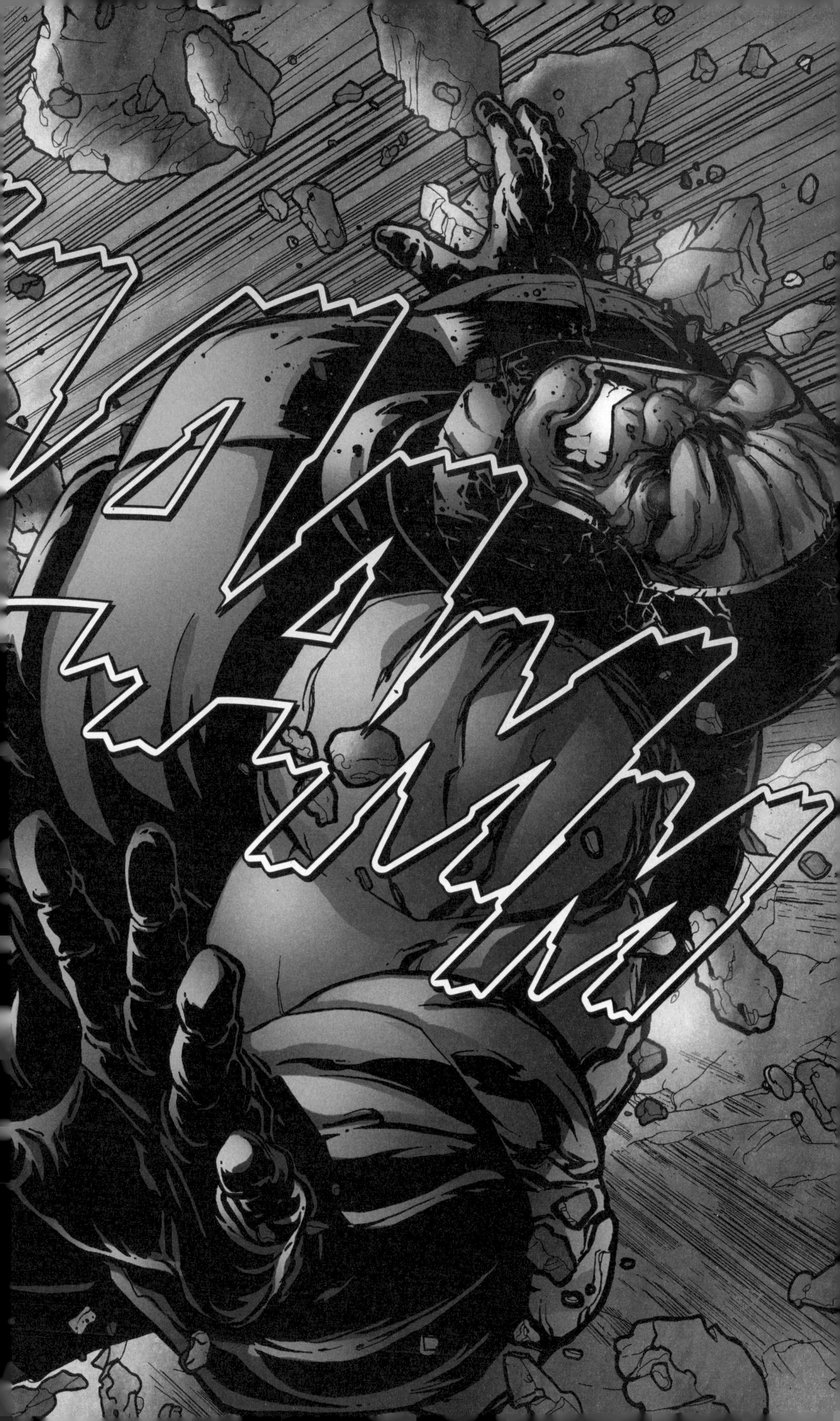

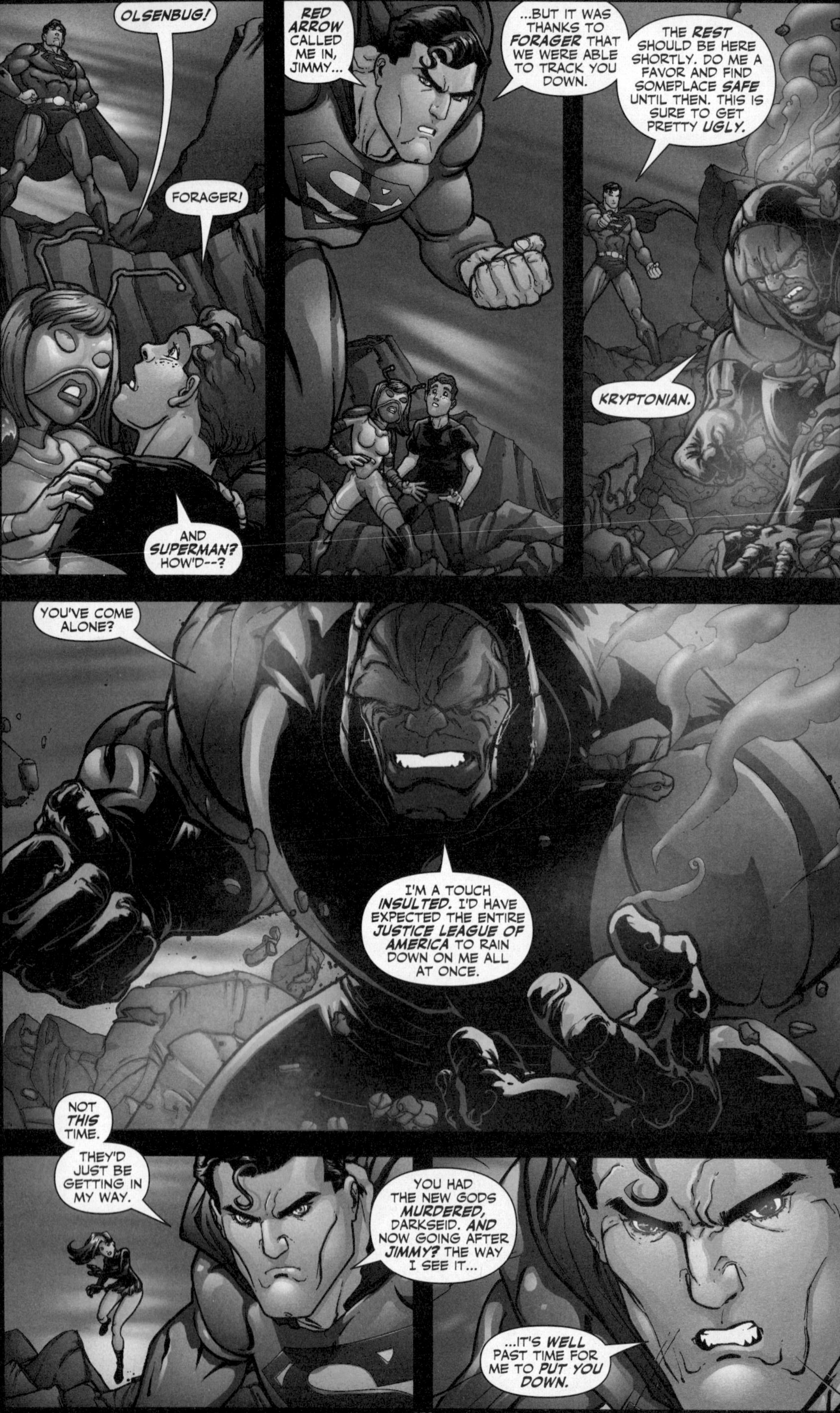
OLSENBUG!
FORAGER!
AND SUPERMAN? HOW'D--?
RED ARROW CALLED ME IN, JIMMY...
...BUT IT WAS THANKS TO FORAGER THAT WE WERE ABLE TO TRACK YOU DOWN.
THE REST SHOULD BE HERE SHORTLY. DO ME A FAVOR AND FIND SOMEPLACE SAFE UNTIL THEN. THIS IS SURE TO GET PRETTY UGLY.
KRYPTONIAN.
YOU'VE COME ALONE?
I'M A TOUCH INSULTED. I'D HAVE EXPECTED THE ENTIRE JUSTICE LEAGUE OF AMERICA TO RAIN DOWN ON ME ALL AT ONCE.
NOT THIS TIME.
THEY'D JUST BE GETTING IN MY WAY.
YOU HAD THE NEW GODS MURDERED, DARKSEID. AND NOW GOING AFTER JIMMY? THE WAY I SEE IT...
...IT'S WELL PAST TIME FOR ME TO PUT YOU DOWN.

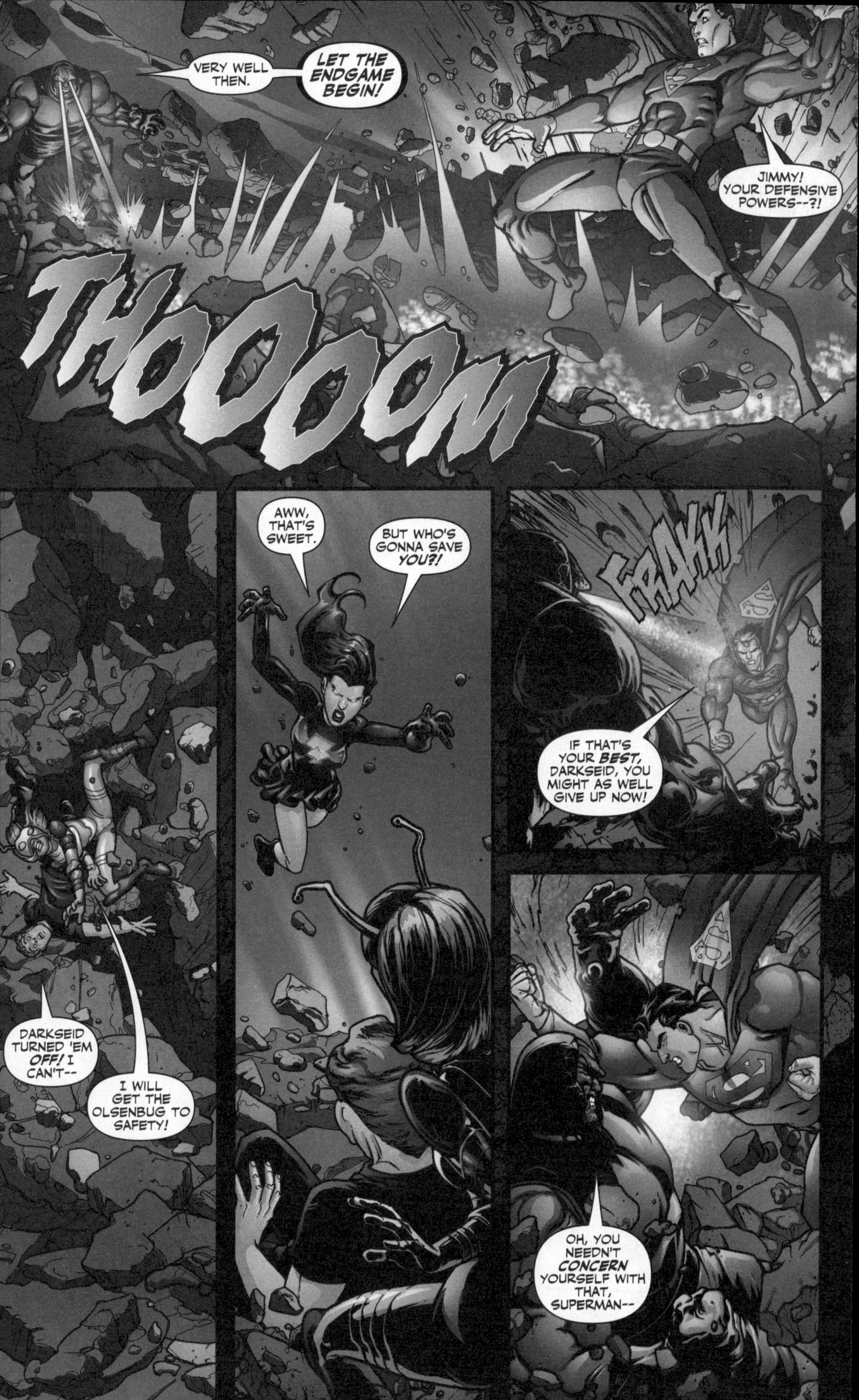
VERY WELL THEN.
LET THE ENDGAME BEGIN!
JIMMY! YOUR DEFENSIVE POWERS--?!
THOOOOM
DARKSEID TURNED 'EM OFF! I CAN'T--
I WILL GET THE OLSENBUG TO SAFETY!
AWW, THAT'S SWEET.
BUT WHO'S GONNA SAVE YOU?!
FRAKK
IF THAT'S YOUR BEST, DARKSEID, YOU MIGHT AS WELL GIVE UP NOW!
OH, YOU NEEDN'T CONCERN YOURSELF WITH THAT, SUPERMAN--

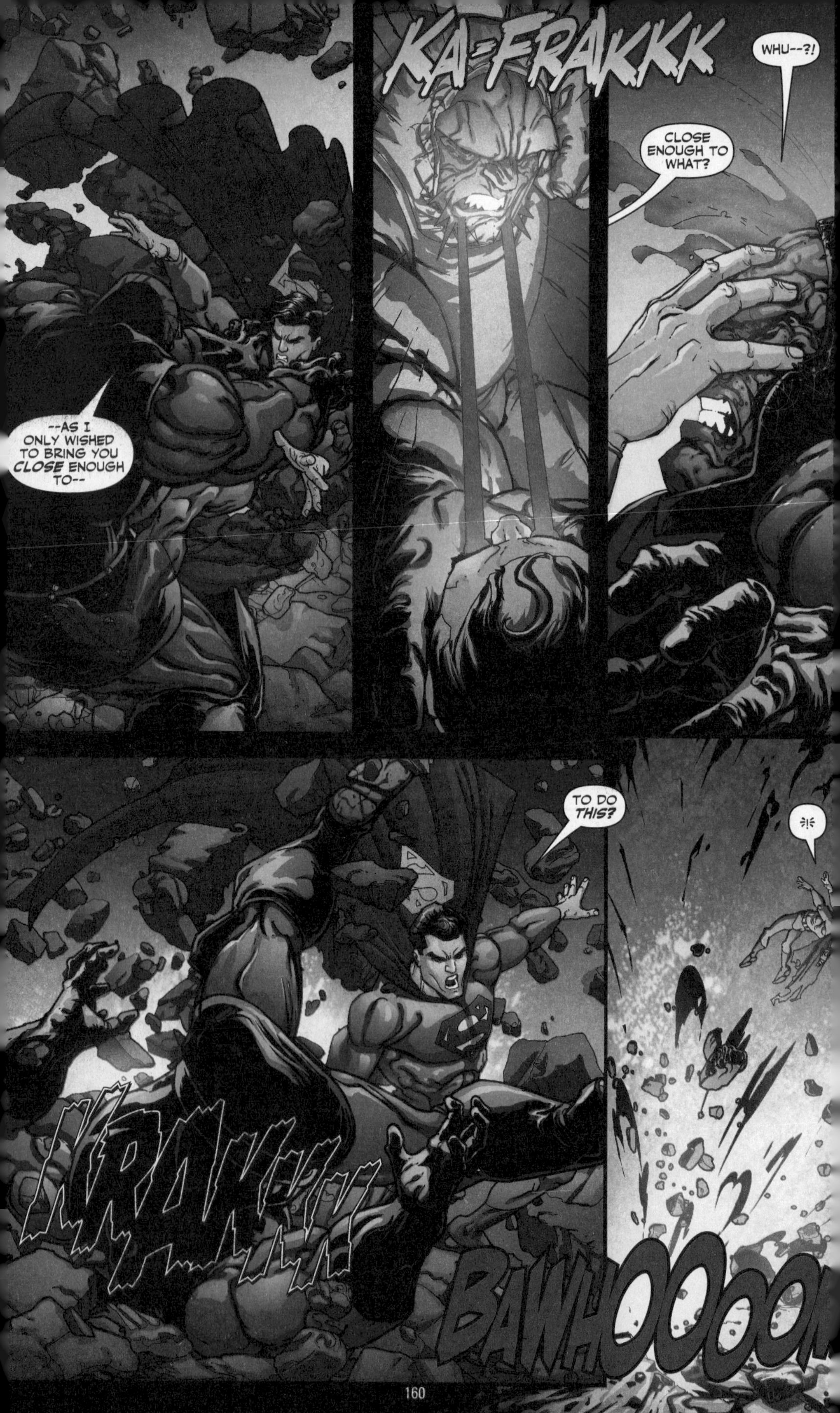
--AS I ONLY WISHED TO BRING YOU CLOSE ENOUGH TO--
KA-FRAKKK
WHU--?!
CLOSE ENOUGH TO WHAT?
TO DO THIS?
?!
BAWHOOOOOM

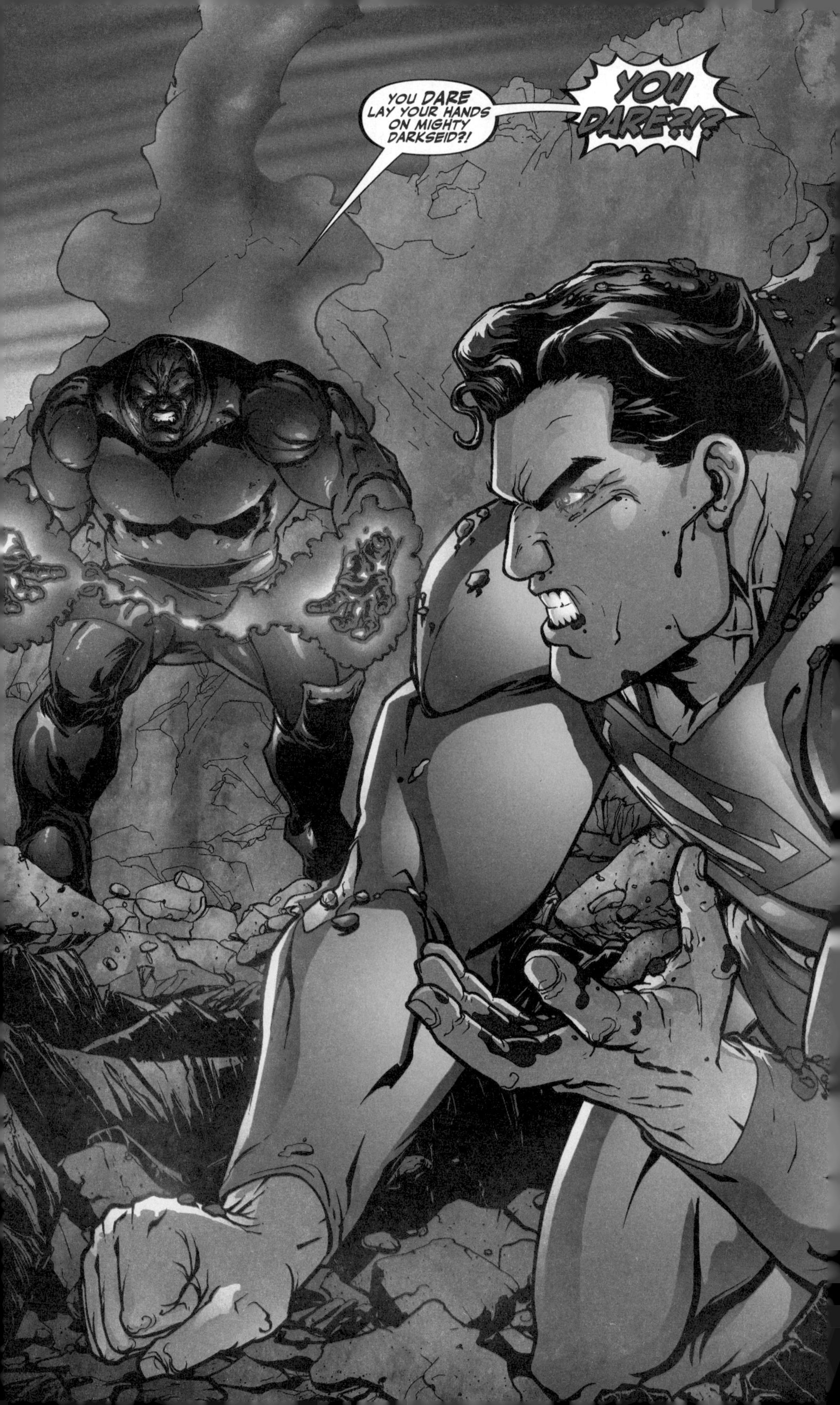
YOU DARE LAY YOUR HANDS ON MIGHTY DARKSEID?!
YOU DARE?!?

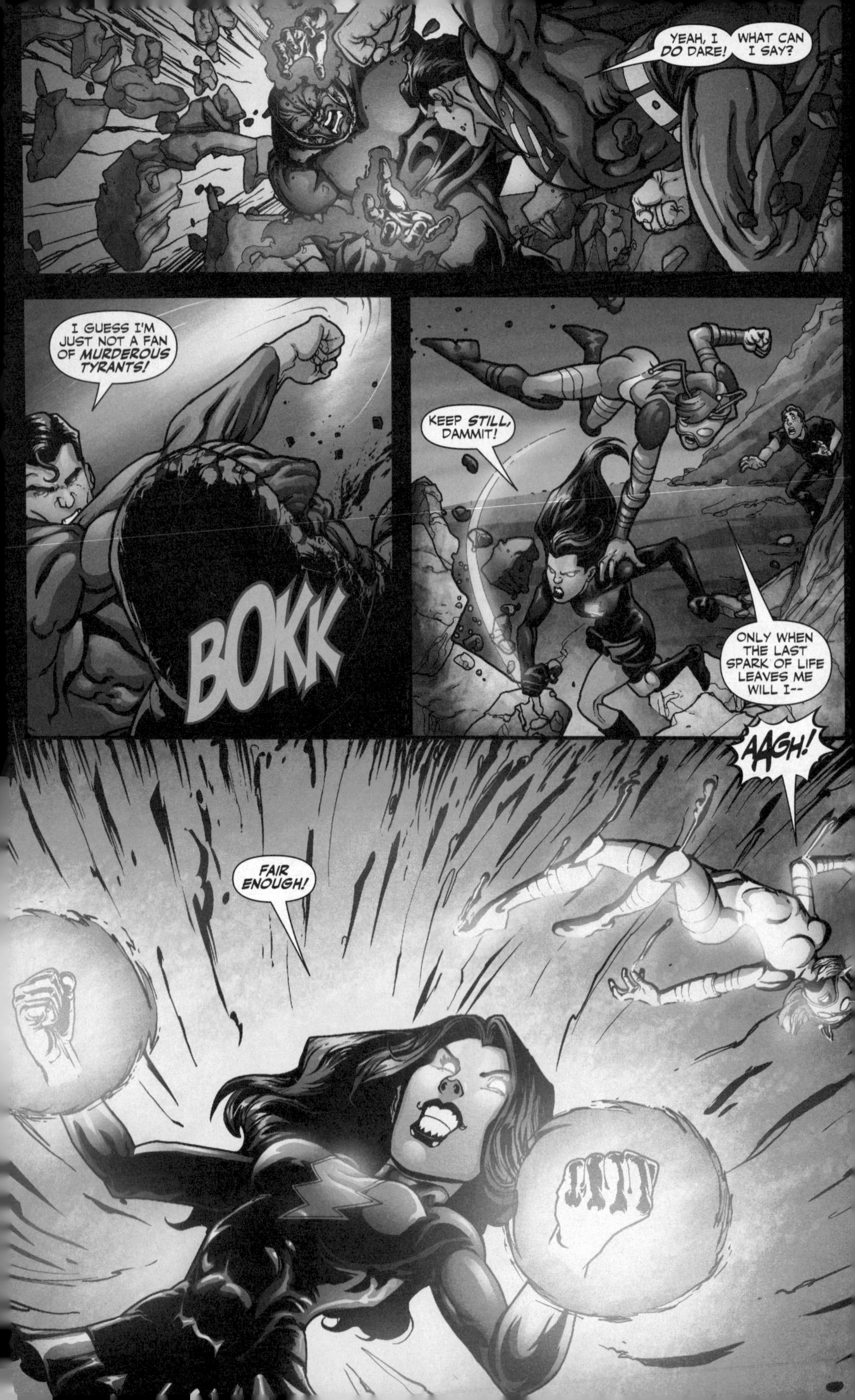

YEAH, I DO DARE!
WHAT CAN I SAY?
I GUESS I'M JUST NOT A FAN OF MURDEROUS TYRANTS!
BOKK
KEEP STILL, DAMMIT!
ONLY WHEN THE LAST SPARK OF LIFE LEAVES ME WILL I--
AAGH!
FAIR ENOUGH!

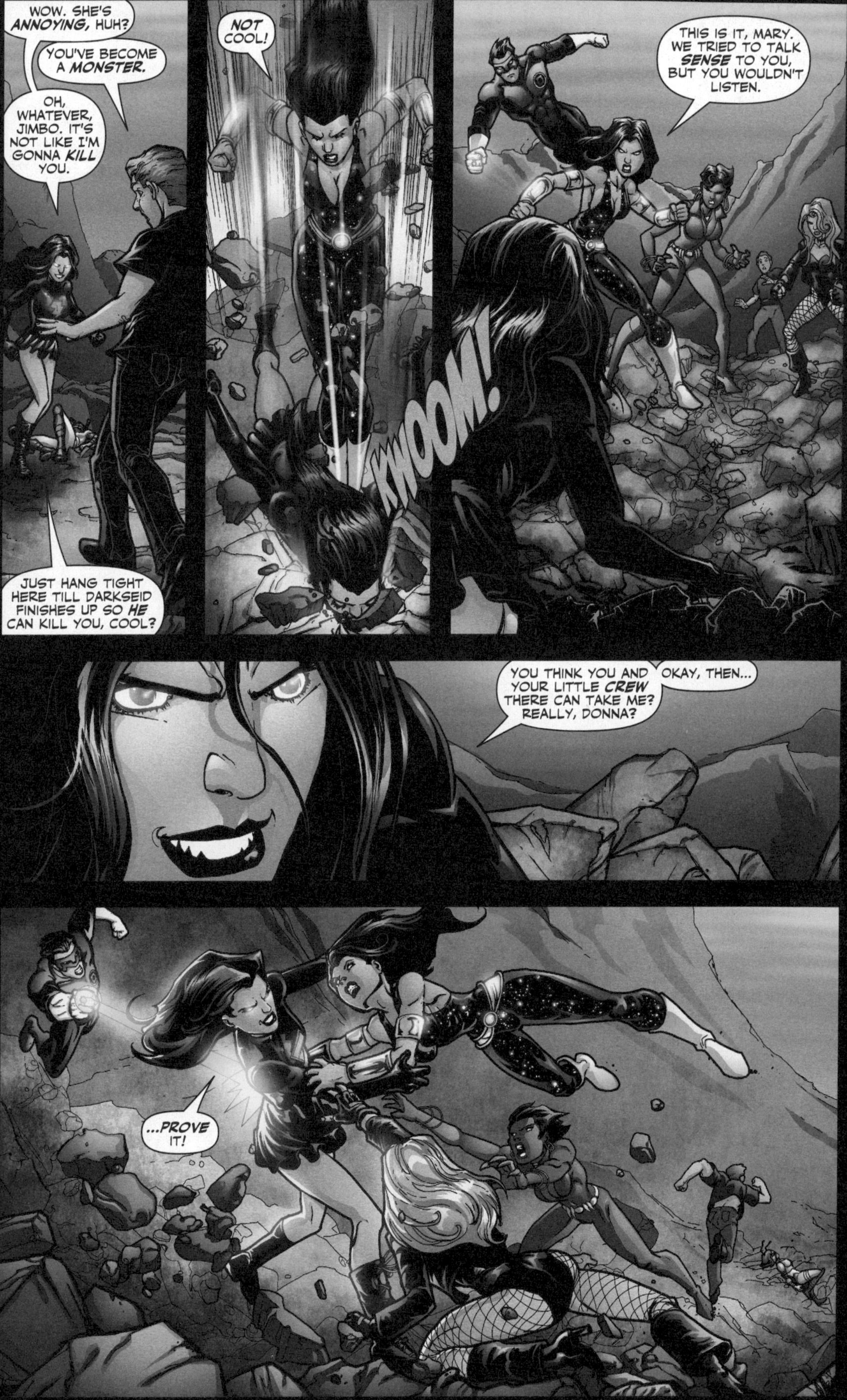

WOW. SHE'S ANNOYING, HUH?
YOU'VE BECOME A MONSTER.
OH, WHATEVER, JIMBO. IT'S NOT LIKE I'M GONNA KILL YOU.
JUST HANG TIGHT HERE TILL DARKSEID FINISHES UP SO HE CAN KILL YOU, COOL?
NOT COOL!
KWOOM!
THIS IS IT, MARY. WE TRIED TO TALK SENSE TO YOU, BUT YOU WOULDN'T LISTEN.
YOU THINK YOU AND YOUR LITTLE CREW THERE CAN TAKE ME? REALLY, DONNA?
OKAY, THEN...
...PROVE IT!

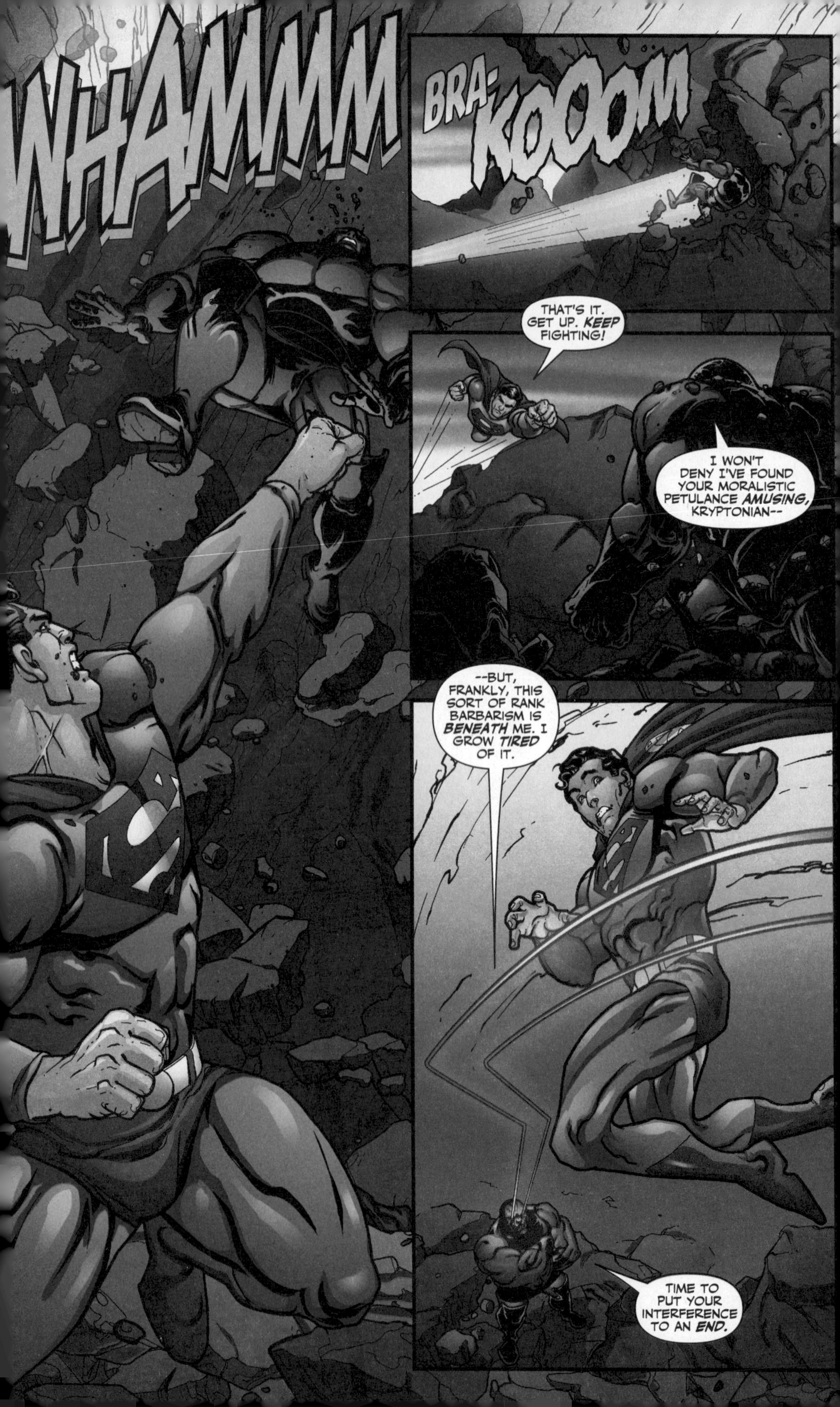
WHAMMM
BRA-KOOOM
THAT'S IT. GET UP. KEEP FIGHTING!
I WON'T DENY I'VE FOUND YOUR MORALISTIC PETULANCE AMUSING, KRYPTONIAN--
--BUT, FRANKLY, THIS SORT OF RANK BARBARISM IS BENEATH ME. I GROW TIRED OF IT.
TIME TO PUT YOUR INTERFERENCE TO AN END.

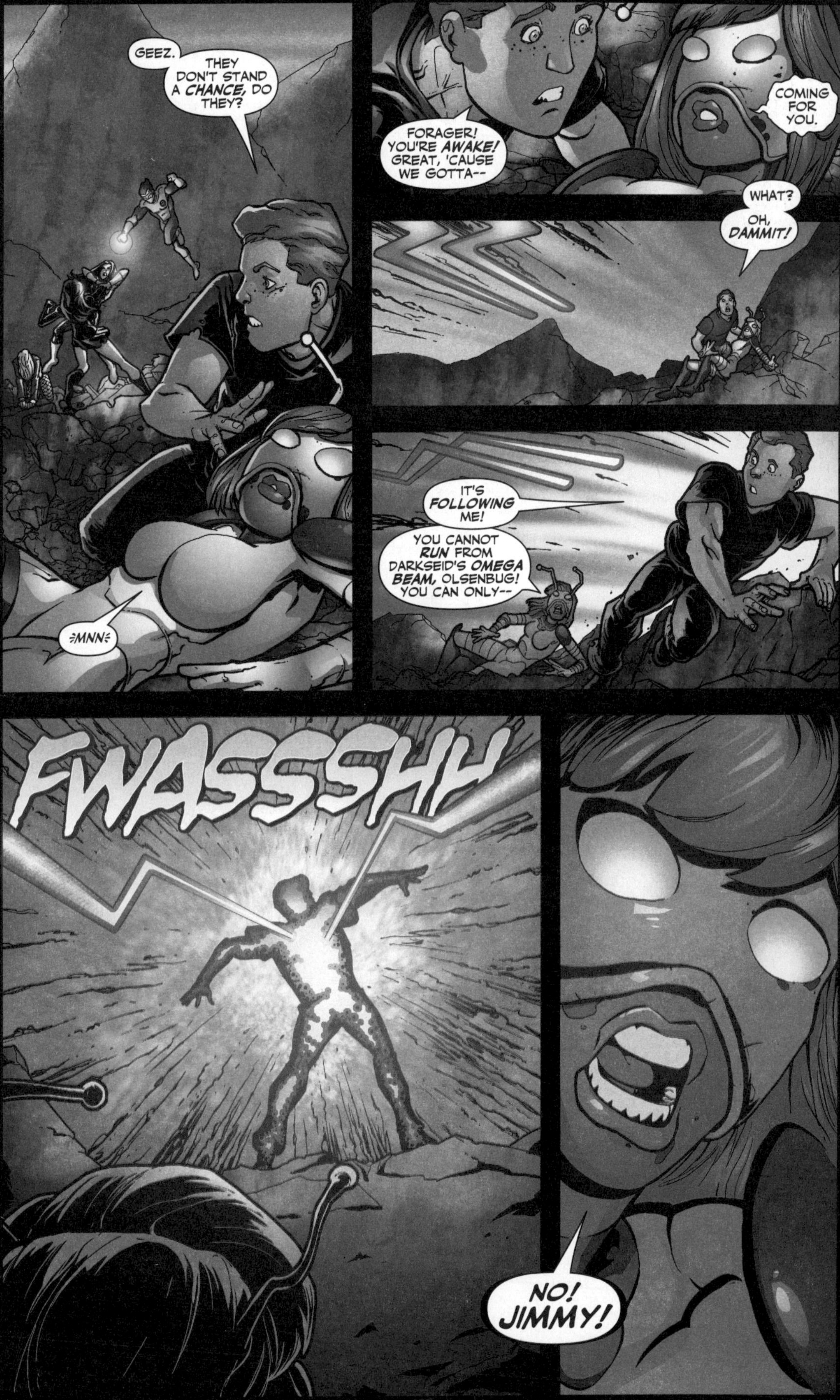
GEEZ.
THEY DON'T STAND A *CHANCE,* DO THEY?
≡MNN≡
FORAGER! YOU'RE *AWAKE!* GREAT, 'CAUSE WE GOTTA--
COMING FOR YOU.
WHAT?
OH, *DAMMIT!*
IT'S *FOLLOWING* ME!
YOU CANNOT *RUN* FROM DARKSEID'S *OMEGA BEAM,* OLSENBUG! YOU CAN ONLY--
FWASSSHH
NO! JIMMY!

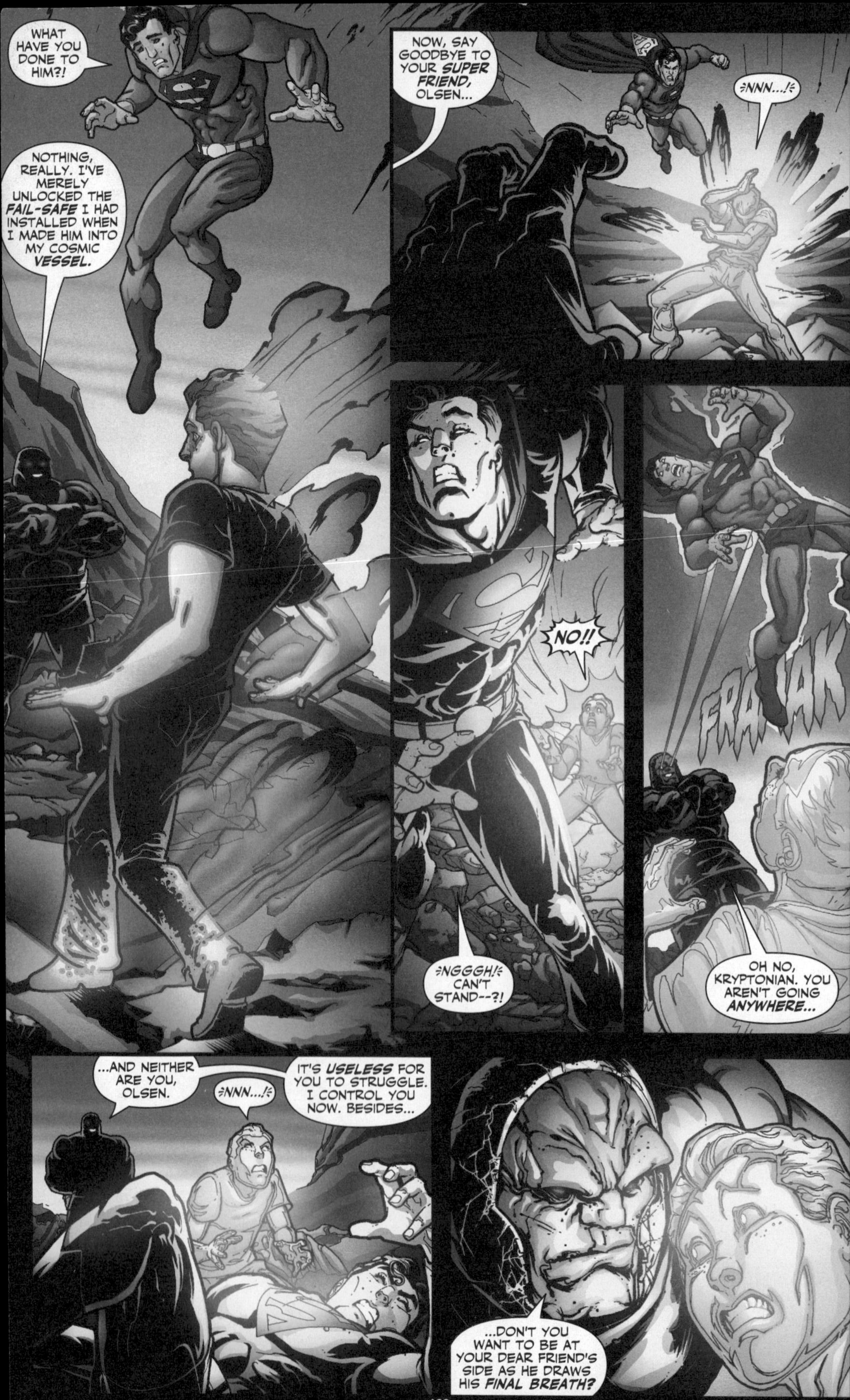
WHAT HAVE YOU DONE TO HIM?!
NOTHING, REALLY. I'VE MERELY UNLOCKED THE FAIL-SAFE I HAD INSTALLED WHEN I MADE HIM INTO MY COSMIC VESSEL.
NOW, SAY GOODBYE TO YOUR SUPER FRIEND, OLSEN...
NNN...!
NO!!
NGGGH! CAN'T STAND--?!
OH NO, KRYPTONIAN. YOU AREN'T GOING ANYWHERE...
...AND NEITHER ARE YOU, OLSEN.
NNN...!
IT'S USELESS FOR YOU TO STRUGGLE. I CONTROL YOU NOW. BESIDES...
...DON'T YOU WANT TO BE AT YOUR DEAR FRIEND'S SIDE AS HE DRAWS HIS FINAL BREATH?

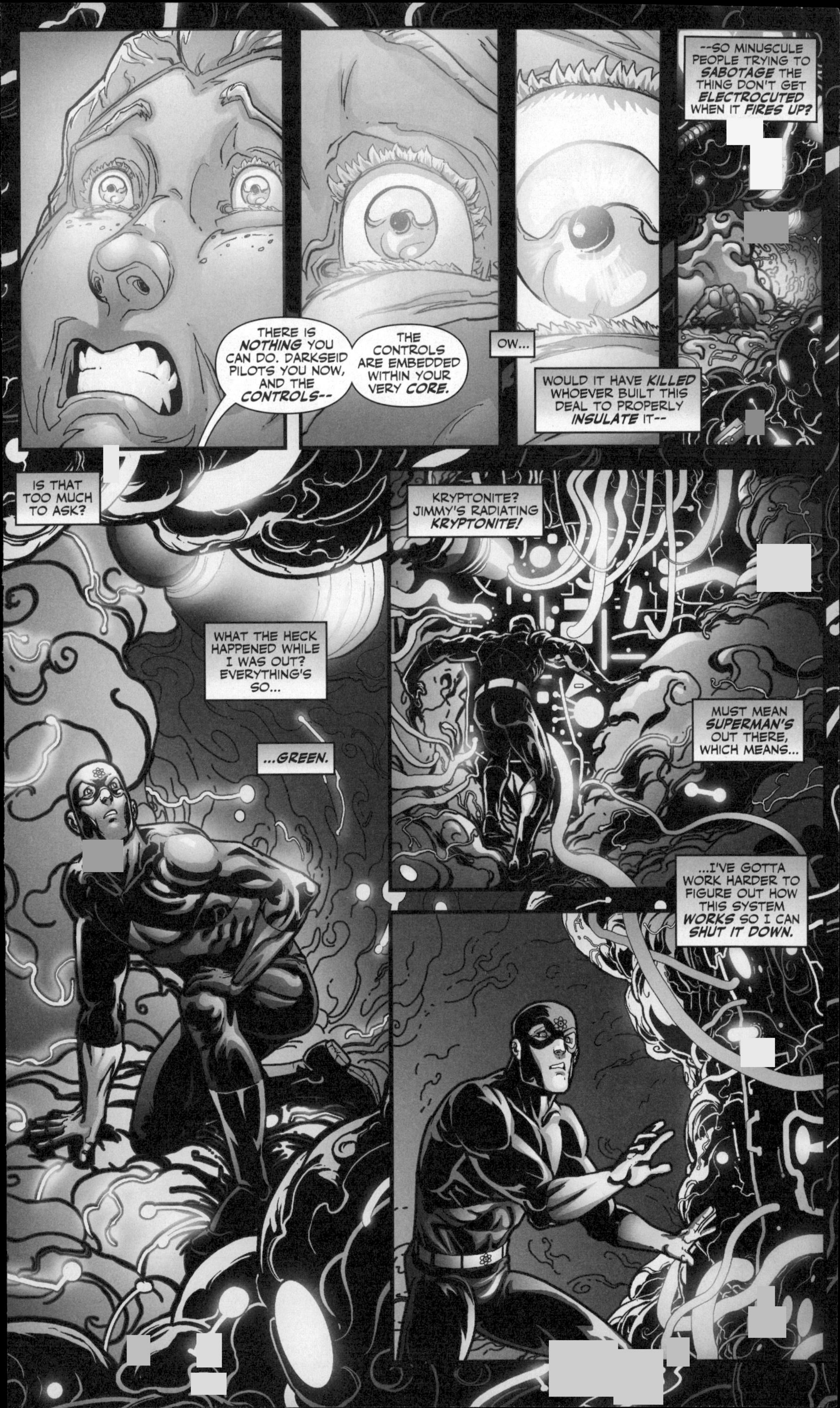
THERE IS NOTHING YOU CAN DO. DARKSEID PILOTS YOU NOW, AND THE CONTROLS--
THE CONTROLS ARE EMBEDDED WITHIN YOUR VERY CORE.
OW...
WOULD IT HAVE KILLED WHOEVER BUILT THIS DEAL TO PROPERLY INSULATE IT--
--SO MINUSCULE PEOPLE TRYING TO SABOTAGE THE THING DON'T GET ELECTROCUTED WHEN IT FIRES UP?
IS THAT TOO MUCH TO ASK?
WHAT THE HECK HAPPENED WHILE I WAS OUT? EVERYTHING'S SO...
...GREEN.
KRYPTONITE? JIMMY'S RADIATING KRYPTONITE!
MUST MEAN SUPERMAN'S OUT THERE, WHICH MEANS...
...I'VE GOTTA WORK HARDER TO FIGURE OUT HOW THIS SYSTEM WORKS SO I CAN SHUT IT DOWN.

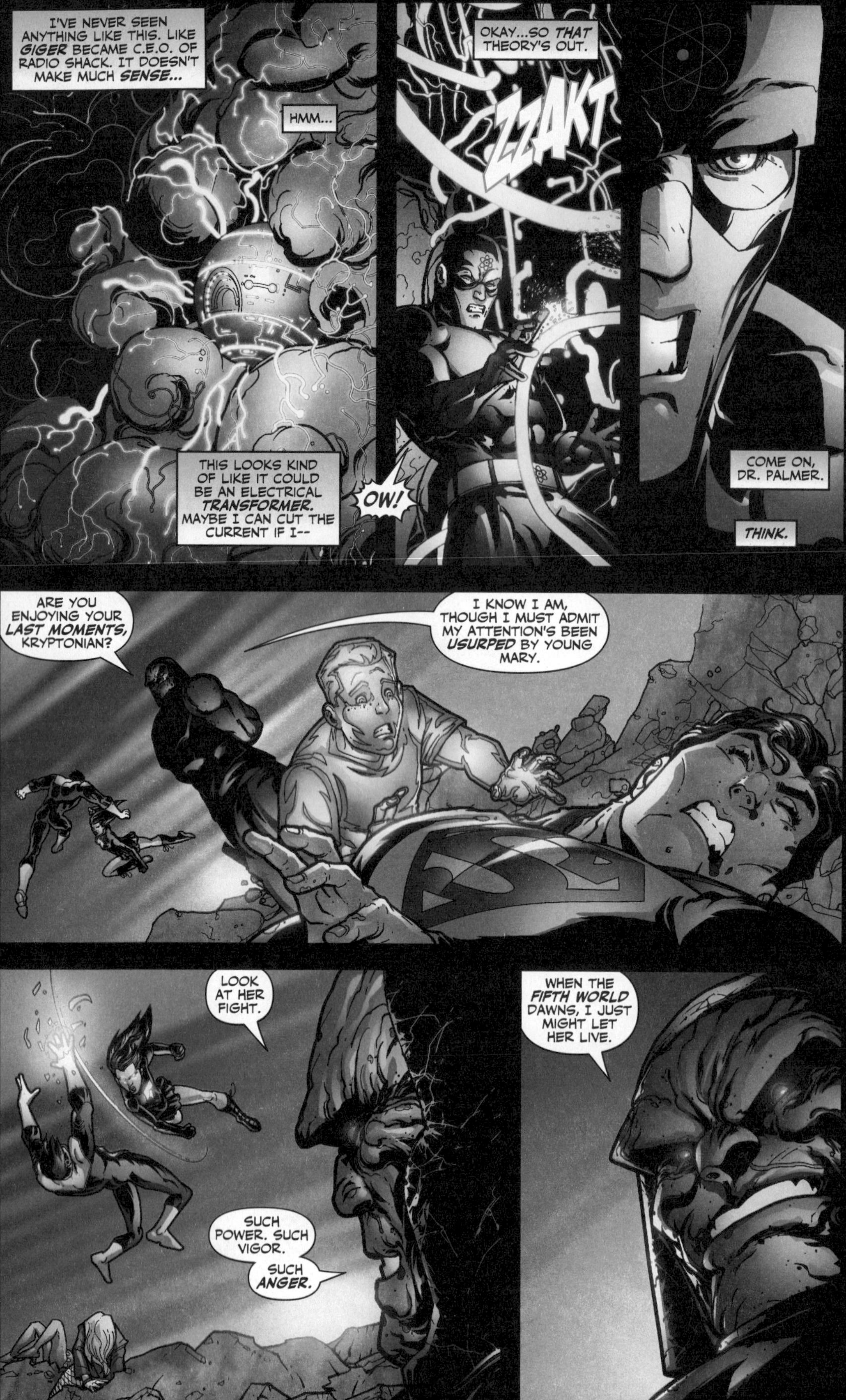
I'VE NEVER SEEN ANYTHING LIKE THIS. LIKE GIGER BECAME C.E.O. OF RADIO SHACK. IT DOESN'T MAKE MUCH SENSE...
HMM...
THIS LOOKS KIND OF LIKE IT COULD BE AN ELECTRICAL TRANSFORMER. MAYBE I CAN CUT THE CURRENT IF I--
OW!
ZZAKT
OKAY...SO THAT THEORY'S OUT.
COME ON, DR. PALMER.
THINK.
ARE YOU ENJOYING YOUR LAST MOMENTS, KRYPTONIAN?
I KNOW I AM, THOUGH I MUST ADMIT MY ATTENTION'S BEEN USURPED BY YOUNG MARY.
LOOK AT HER FIGHT.
SUCH POWER. SUCH VIGOR.
SUCH ANGER.
WHEN THE FIFTH WORLD DAWNS, I JUST MIGHT LET HER LIVE.

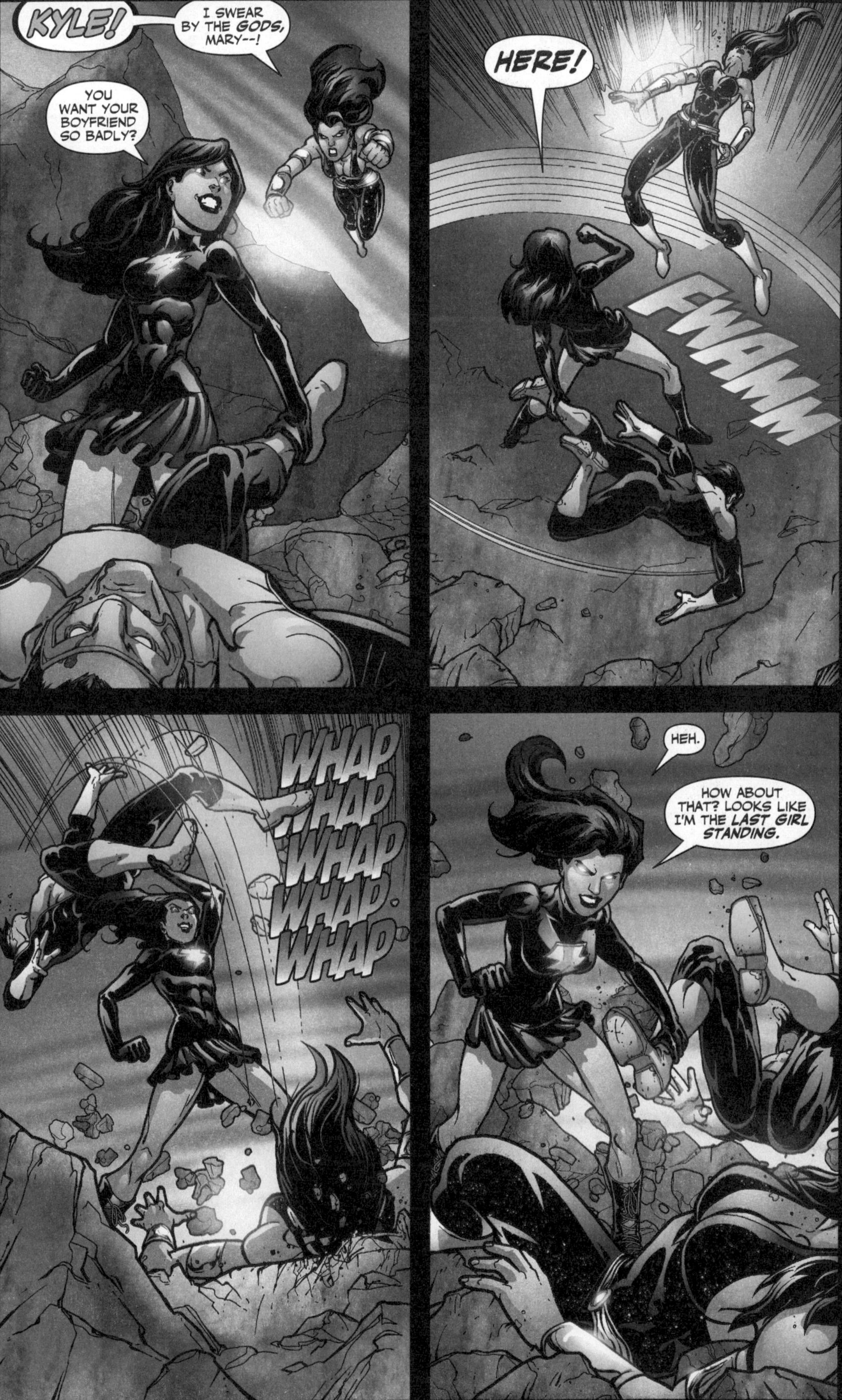
KYLE!
I SWEAR BY THE *GODS,* MARY--!
YOU WANT YOUR BOYFRIEND SO BADLY?
HERE!
FWAMM
WHAP WHAP WHAP WHAP WHAP
HEH.
HOW ABOUT THAT? LOOKS LIKE I'M THE *LAST GIRL STANDING.*

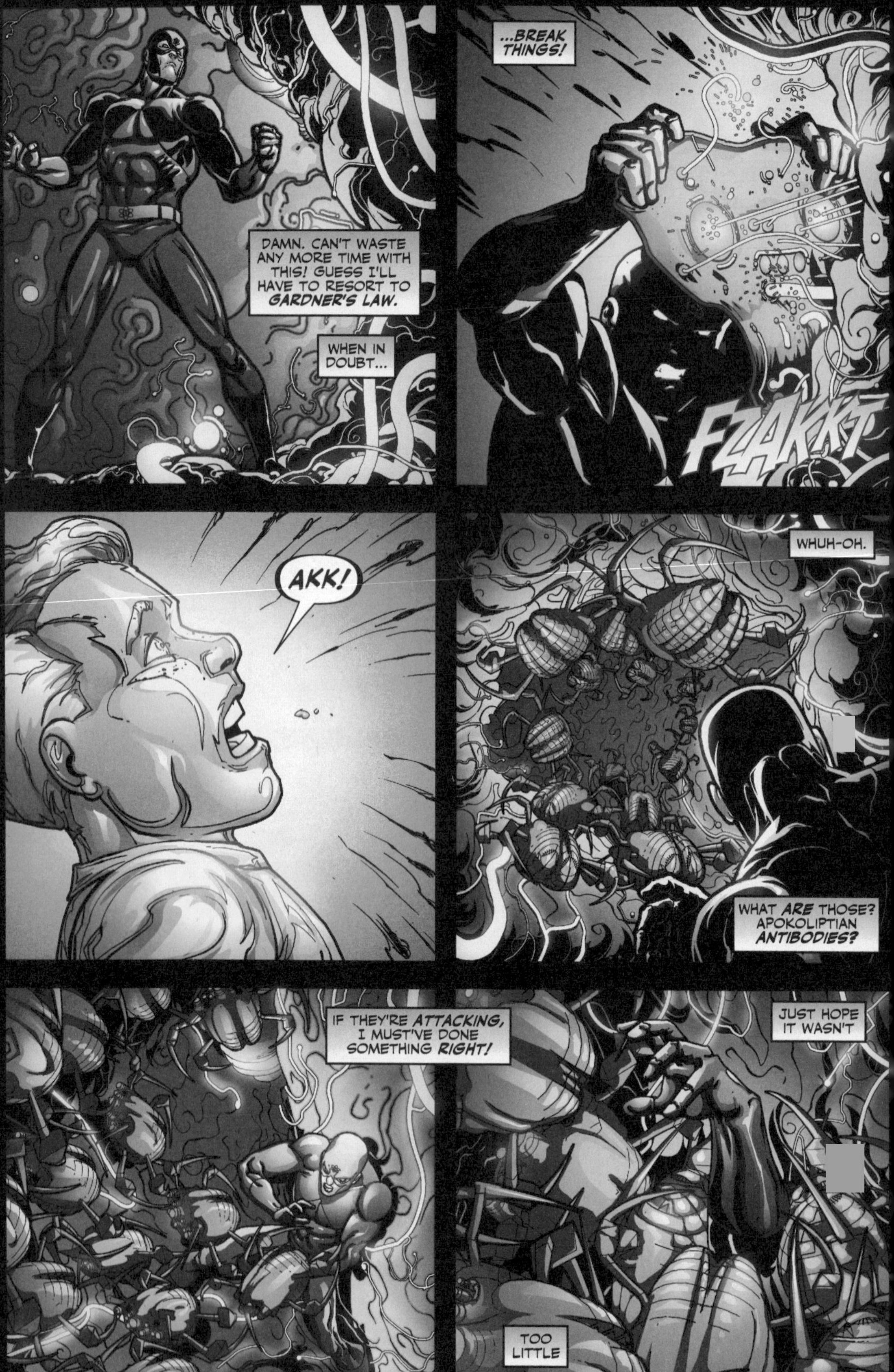

DAMN. CAN'T WASTE ANY MORE TIME WITH THIS! GUESS I'LL HAVE TO RESORT TO GARDNER'S LAW.
WHEN IN DOUBT...
...BREAK THINGS!
FZAKKT
AKK!
WHUH-OH.
WHAT ARE THOSE? APOKOLIPTIAN ANTIBODIES?
IF THEY'RE ATTACKING, I MUST'VE DONE SOMETHING RIGHT!
JUST HOPE IT WASN'T
TOO LITTLE
TOO

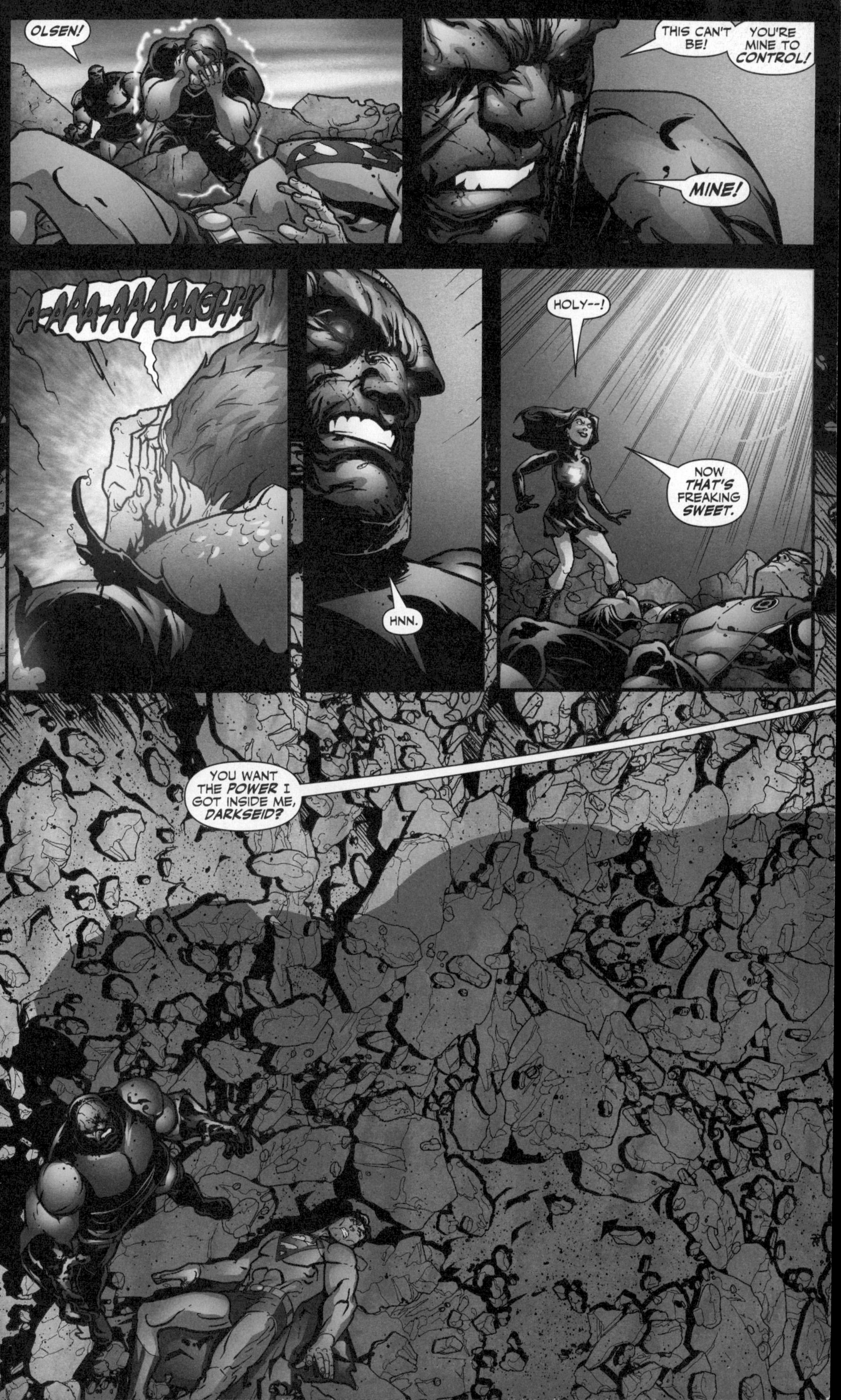
OLSEN!
THIS CAN'T BE!
YOU'RE MINE TO CONTROL!
MINE!
A-AAA-AAAAAAGHH!
HNN.
HOLY--!
NOW THAT'S FREAKING SWEET.
YOU WANT THE POWER I GOT INSIDE ME, DARKSEID?

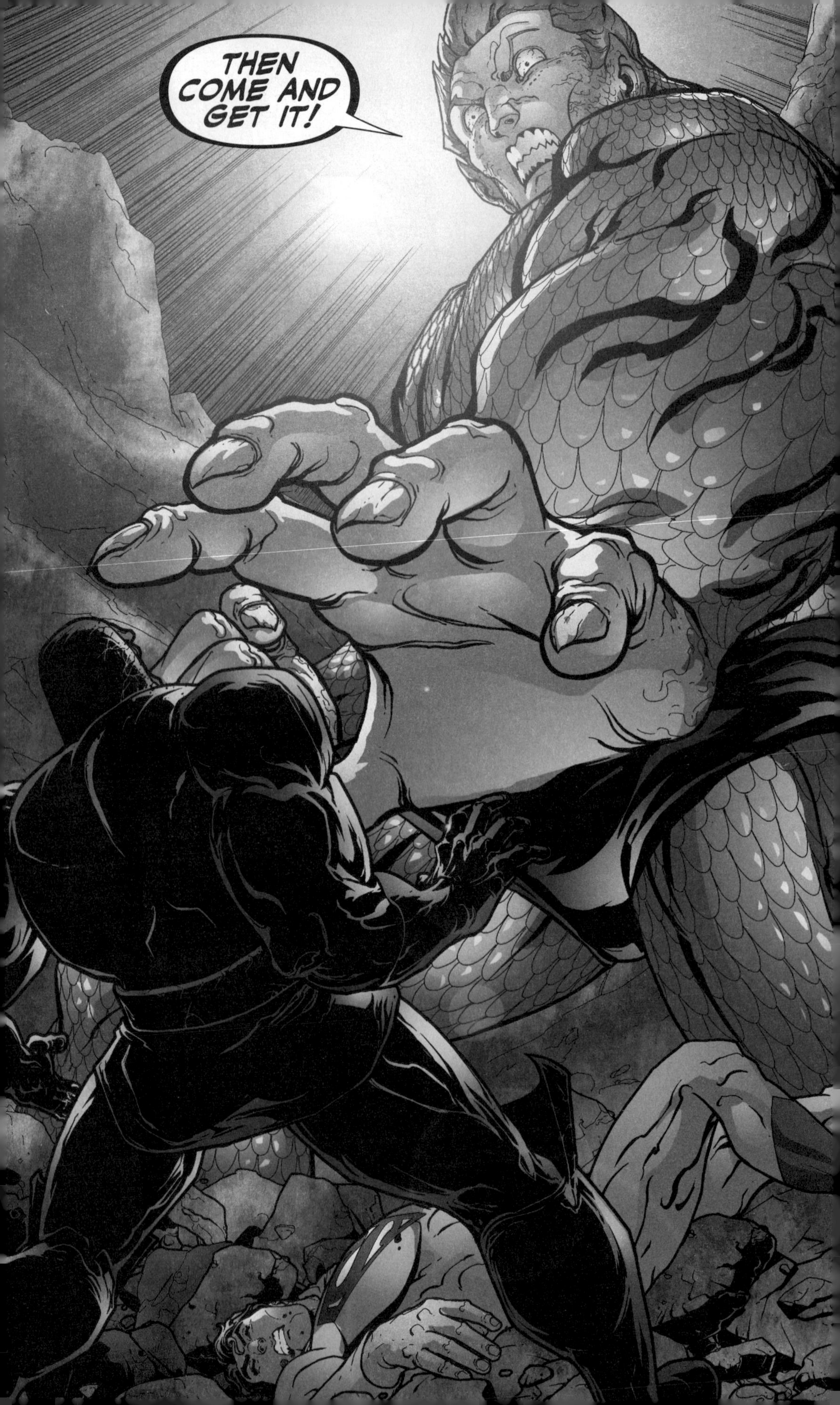
THEN COME AND GET IT!

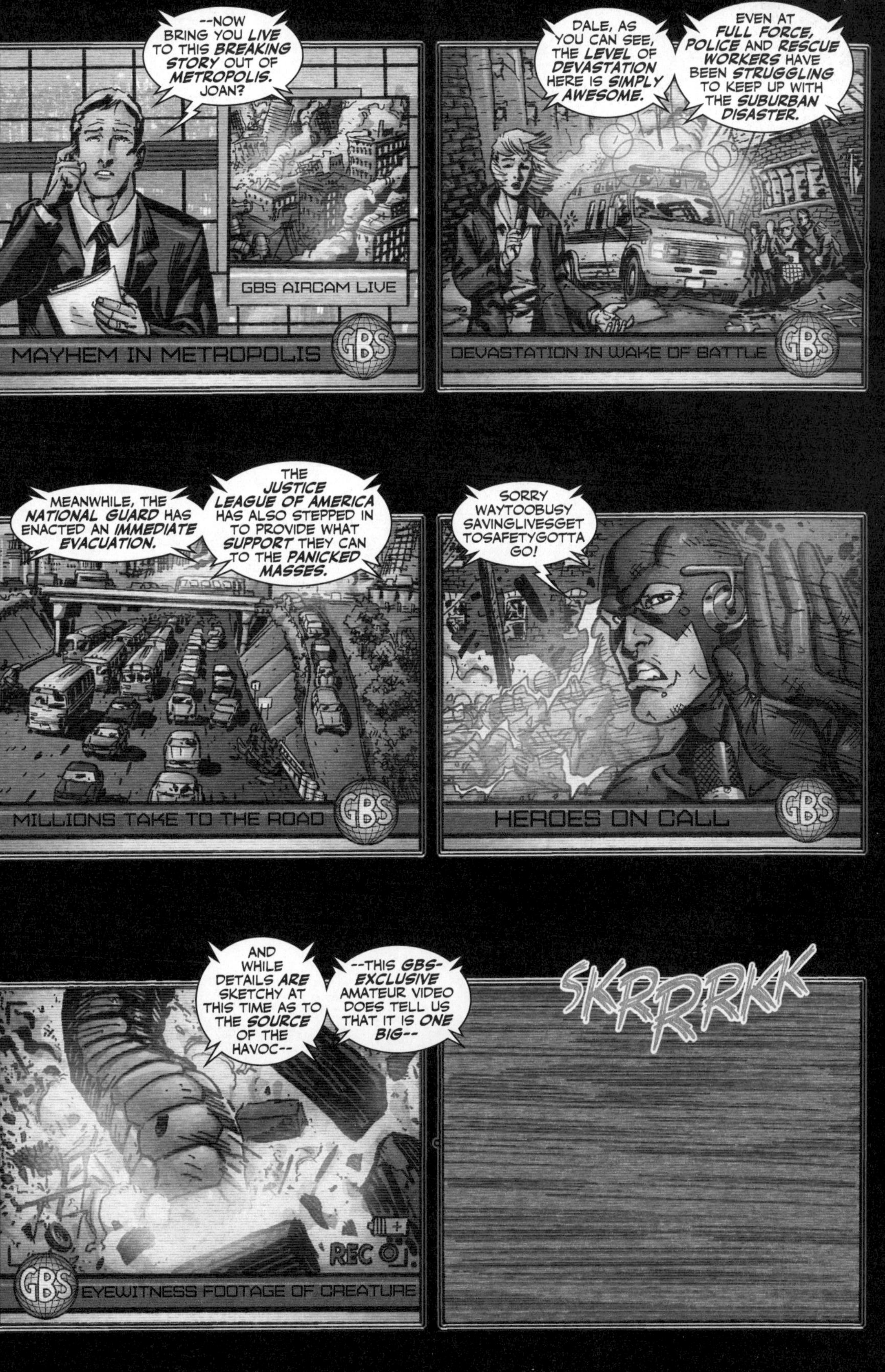
--NOW BRING YOU LIVE TO THIS BREAKING STORY OUT OF METROPOLIS. JOAN?
GBS AIRCAM LIVE
MAYHEM IN METROPOLIS
GBS
DALE, AS YOU CAN SEE, THE LEVEL OF DEVASTATION HERE IS SIMPLY AWESOME.
EVEN AT FULL FORCE, POLICE AND RESCUE WORKERS HAVE BEEN STRUGGLING TO KEEP UP WITH THE SUBURBAN DISASTER.
DEVASTATION IN WAKE OF BATTLE
GBS
MEANWHILE, THE NATIONAL GUARD HAS ENACTED AN IMMEDIATE EVACUATION.
THE JUSTICE LEAGUE OF AMERICA HAS ALSO STEPPED IN TO PROVIDE WHAT SUPPORT THEY CAN TO THE PANICKED MASSES.
MILLIONS TAKE TO THE ROAD
GBS
SORRY WAYTOOBUSY SAVINGLIVESGET TOSAFETYGOTTA GO!
HEROES ON CALL
GBS
AND WHILE DETAILS ARE SKETCHY AT THIS TIME AS TO THE SOURCE OF THE HAVOC--
--THIS GBS-EXCLUSIVE AMATEUR VIDEO DOES TELL US THAT IT IS ONE BIG--
REC
GBS
EYEWITNESS FOOTAGE OF CREATURE
SKRRRKK

TWO AND COUNTING...

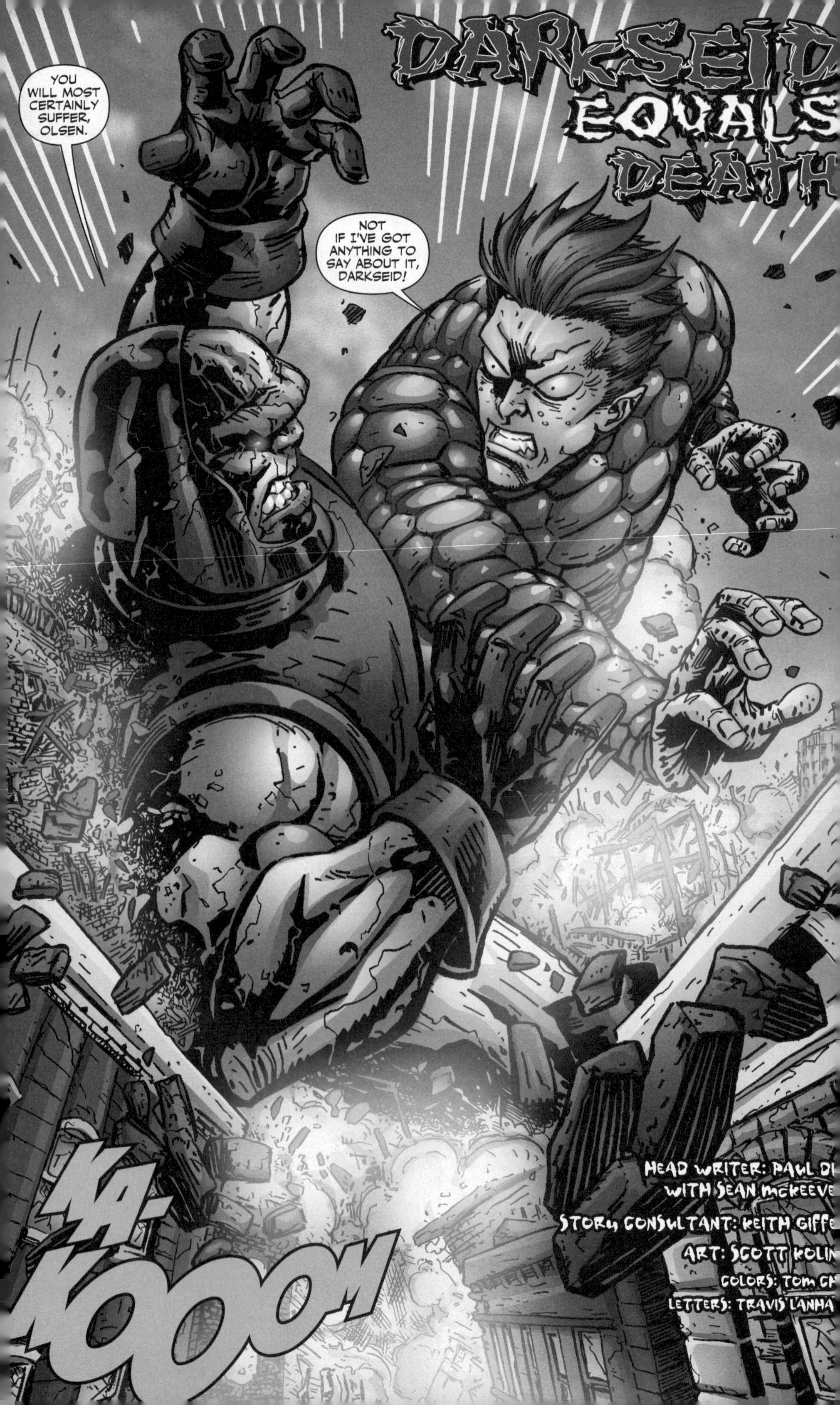
DARKSEID EQUALS DEATH
YOU WILL MOST CERTAINLY SUFFER, OLSEN.
NOT IF I'VE GOT ANYTHING TO SAY ABOUT IT, DARKSEID!
KA-KOOOM
HEAD WRITER: PAUL DI
WITH SEAN MCKEEVE
STORY CONSULTANT: KEITH GIFFE
ART: SCOTT KOLIN
COLORS: TOM
LETTERS: TRAVIS LANHA

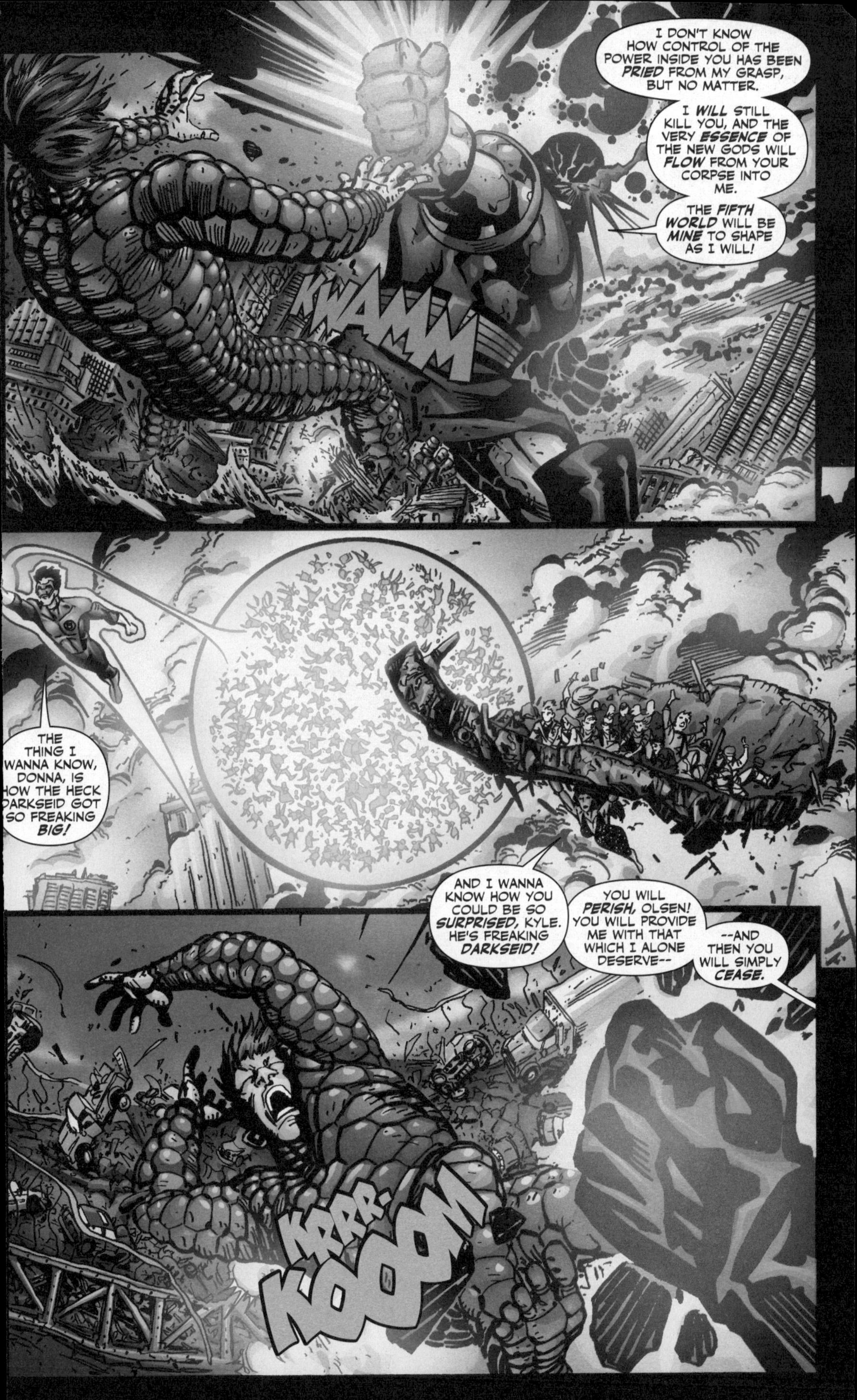

I DON'T KNOW HOW CONTROL OF THE POWER INSIDE YOU HAS BEEN PRIED FROM MY GRASP, BUT NO MATTER.
I WILL STILL KILL YOU, AND THE VERY ESSENCE OF THE NEW GODS WILL FLOW FROM YOUR CORPSE INTO ME.
THE FIFTH WORLD WILL BE MINE TO SHAPE AS I WILL!
KWAMM
THE THING I WANNA KNOW, DONNA, IS HOW THE HECK DARKSEID GOT SO FREAKING BIG!
AND I WANNA KNOW HOW YOU COULD BE SO SURPRISED, KYLE. HE'S FREAKING DARKSEID!
YOU WILL PERISH, OLSEN! YOU WILL PROVIDE ME WITH THAT WHICH I ALONE DESERVE--
--AND THEN YOU WILL SIMPLY CEASE.
KRRR-KOOOM

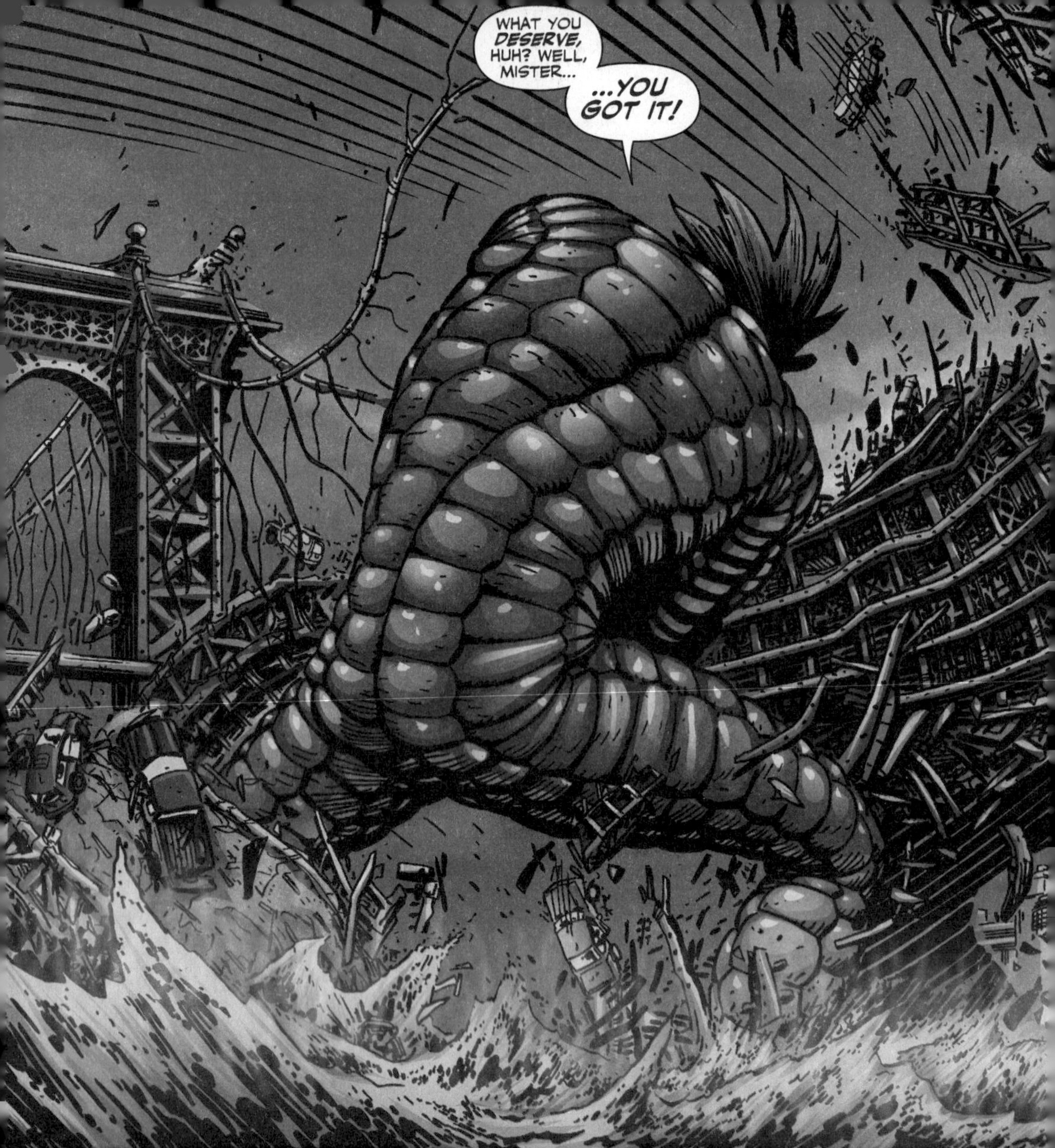
WHAT YOU DESERVE, HUH? WELL, MISTER...
...YOU GOT IT!

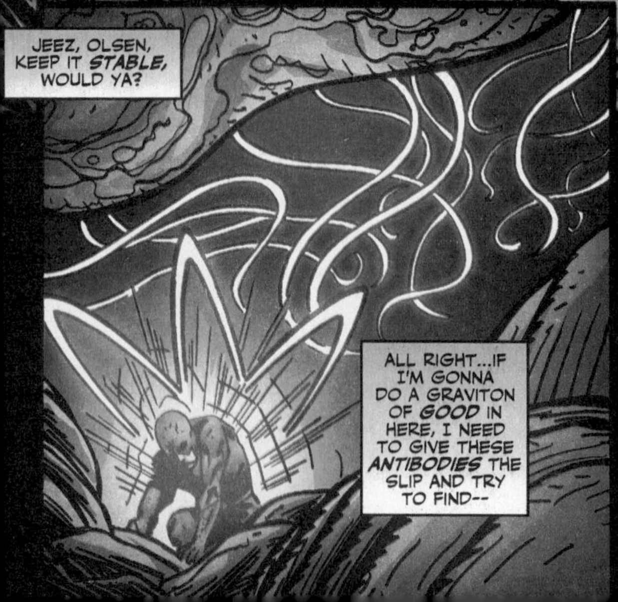
JEEZ, OLSEN, KEEP IT STABLE, WOULD YA?
ALL RIGHT...IF I'M GONNA DO A GRAVITON OF GOOD IN HERE, I NEED TO GIVE THESE ANTIBODIES THE SLIP AND TRY TO FIND--

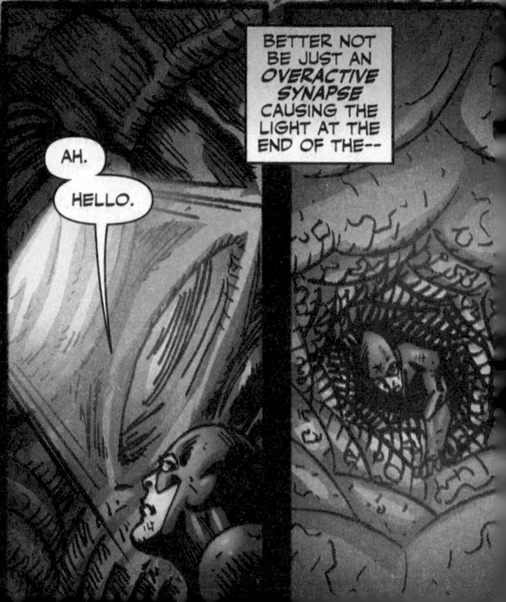
BETTER NOT BE JUST AN OVERACTIVE SYNAPSE CAUSING THE LIGHT AT THE END OF THE--
AH.
HELLO.

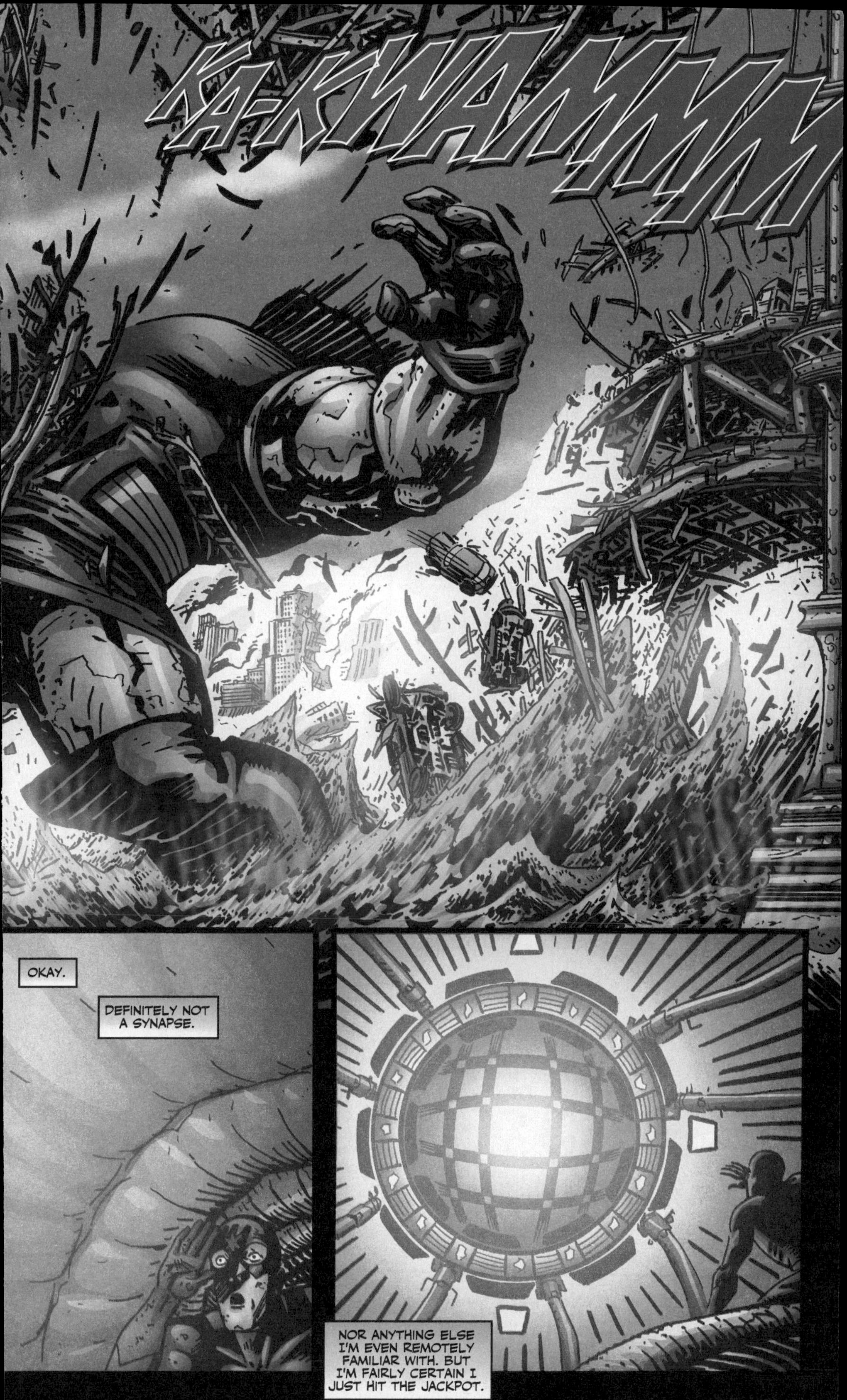
KA-KWAMMM
OKAY.
DEFINITELY NOT A SYNAPSE.
NOR ANYTHING ELSE I'M EVEN REMOTELY FAMILIAR WITH. BUT I'M FAIRLY CERTAIN I JUST HIT THE JACKPOT.

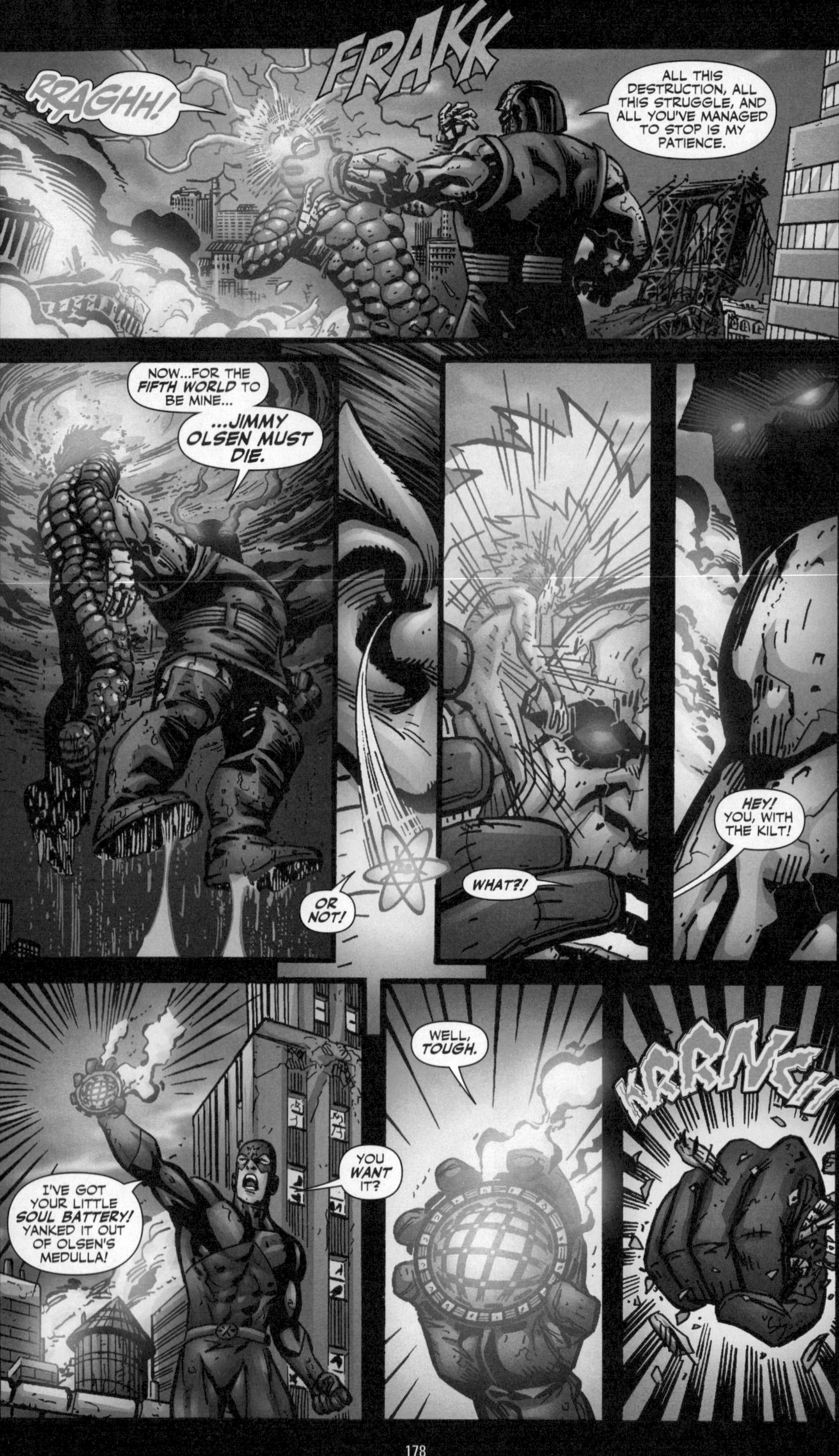
FRAKK
RRAGHH!
ALL THIS DESTRUCTION, ALL THIS STRUGGLE, AND ALL YOU'VE MANAGED TO STOP IS MY PATIENCE.
NOW...FOR THE FIFTH WORLD TO BE MINE...
...JIMMY OLSEN MUST DIE.
OR NOT!
WHAT?!
HEY! YOU, WITH THE KILT!
I'VE GOT YOUR LITTLE SOUL BATTERY! YANKED IT OUT OF OLSEN'S MEDULLA!
YOU WANT IT?
WELL, TOUGH.
KRRNCH

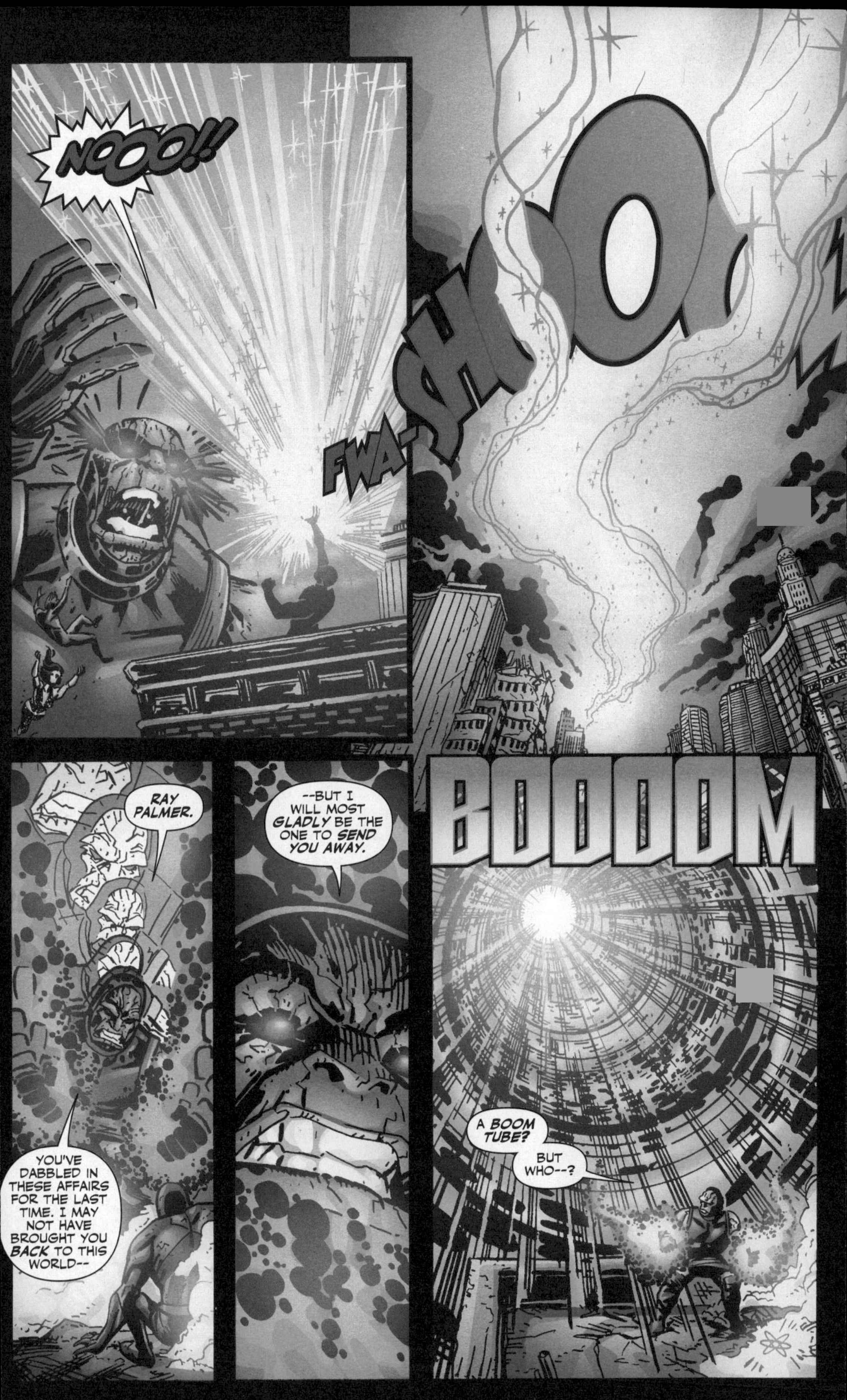
NOOOO!!
FWA-SHOOO
RAY PALMER.
YOU'VE DABBLED IN THESE AFFAIRS FOR THE LAST TIME. I MAY NOT HAVE BROUGHT YOU BACK TO THIS WORLD--
--BUT I WILL MOST GLADLY BE THE ONE TO SEND YOU AWAY.
BOOOOM
A BOOM TUBE?
BUT WHO--?

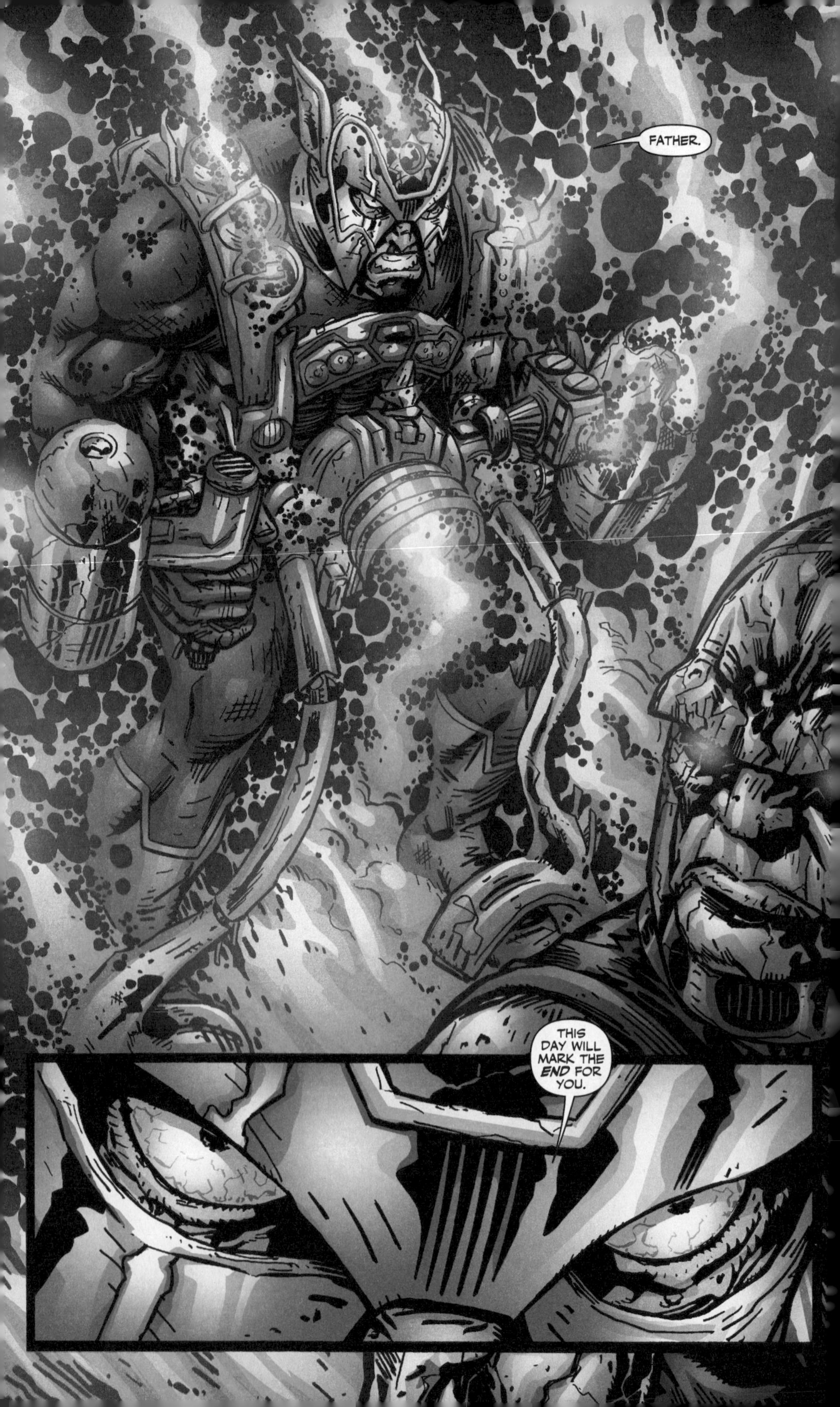
FATHER.
THIS DAY WILL MARK THE *END* FOR YOU.

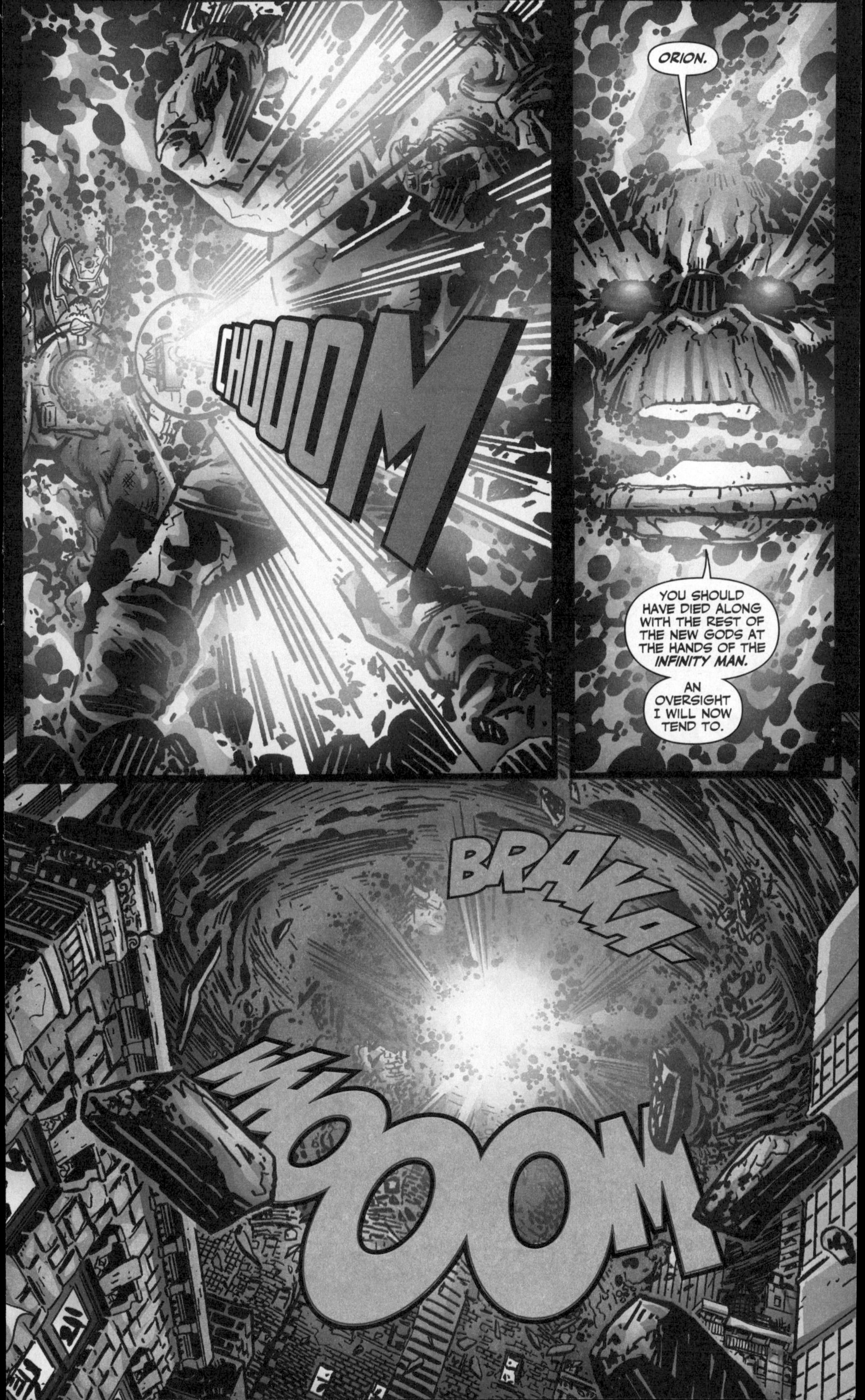
CHOOOM
ORION.
YOU SHOULD HAVE DIED ALONG WITH THE REST OF THE NEW GODS AT THE HANDS OF THE *INFINITY MAN.*
AN OVERSIGHT I WILL NOW TEND TO.
BRAKA-
WHOOOM

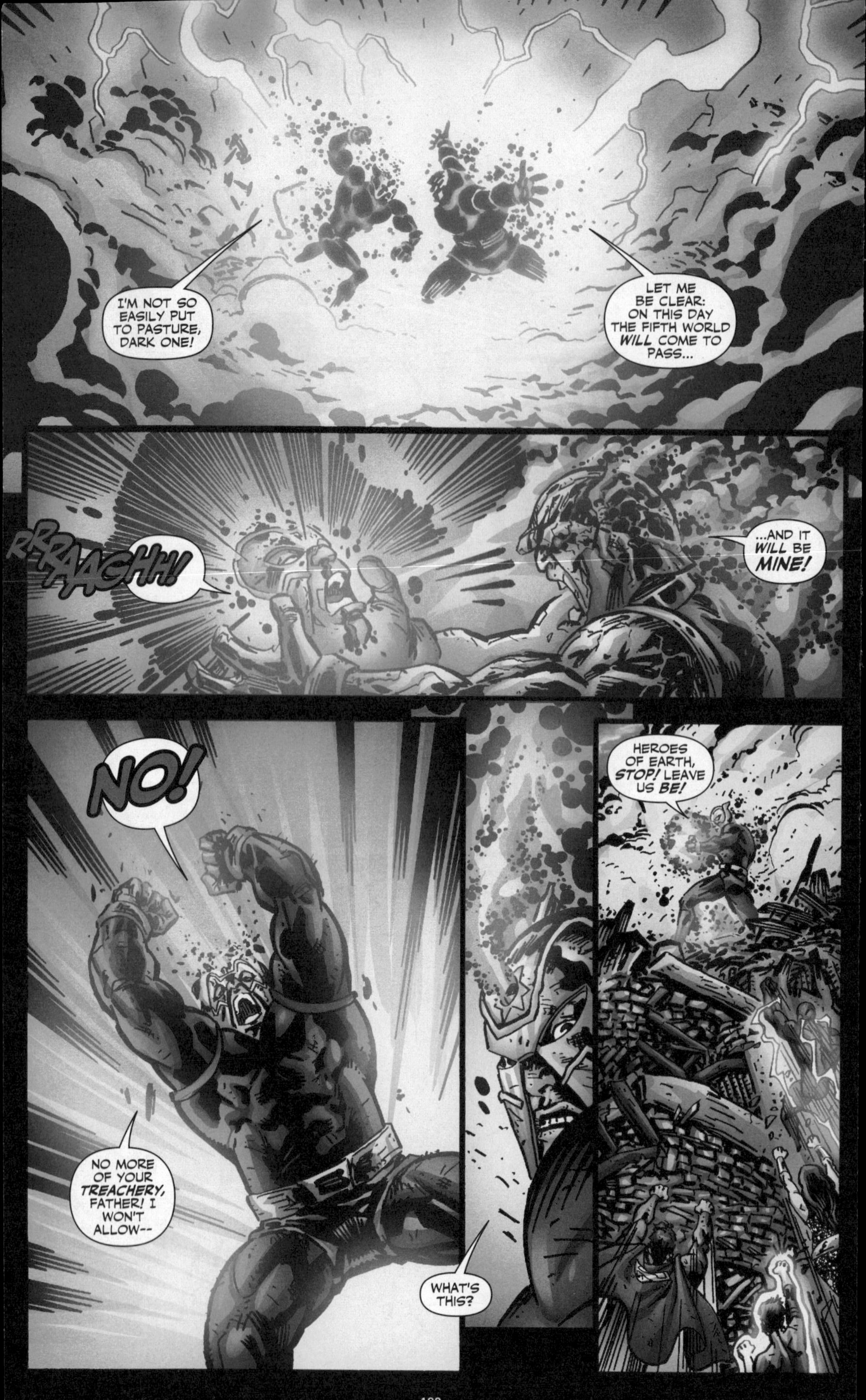
I'M NOT SO EASILY PUT TO PASTURE, DARK ONE!
LET ME BE CLEAR: ON THIS DAY THE FIFTH WORLD WILL COME TO PASS...
RRRAACHH!
...AND IT WILL BE MINE!
NO!
NO MORE OF YOUR TREACHERY, FATHER! I WON'T ALLOW--
WHAT'S THIS?
HEROES OF EARTH, STOP! LEAVE US BE!

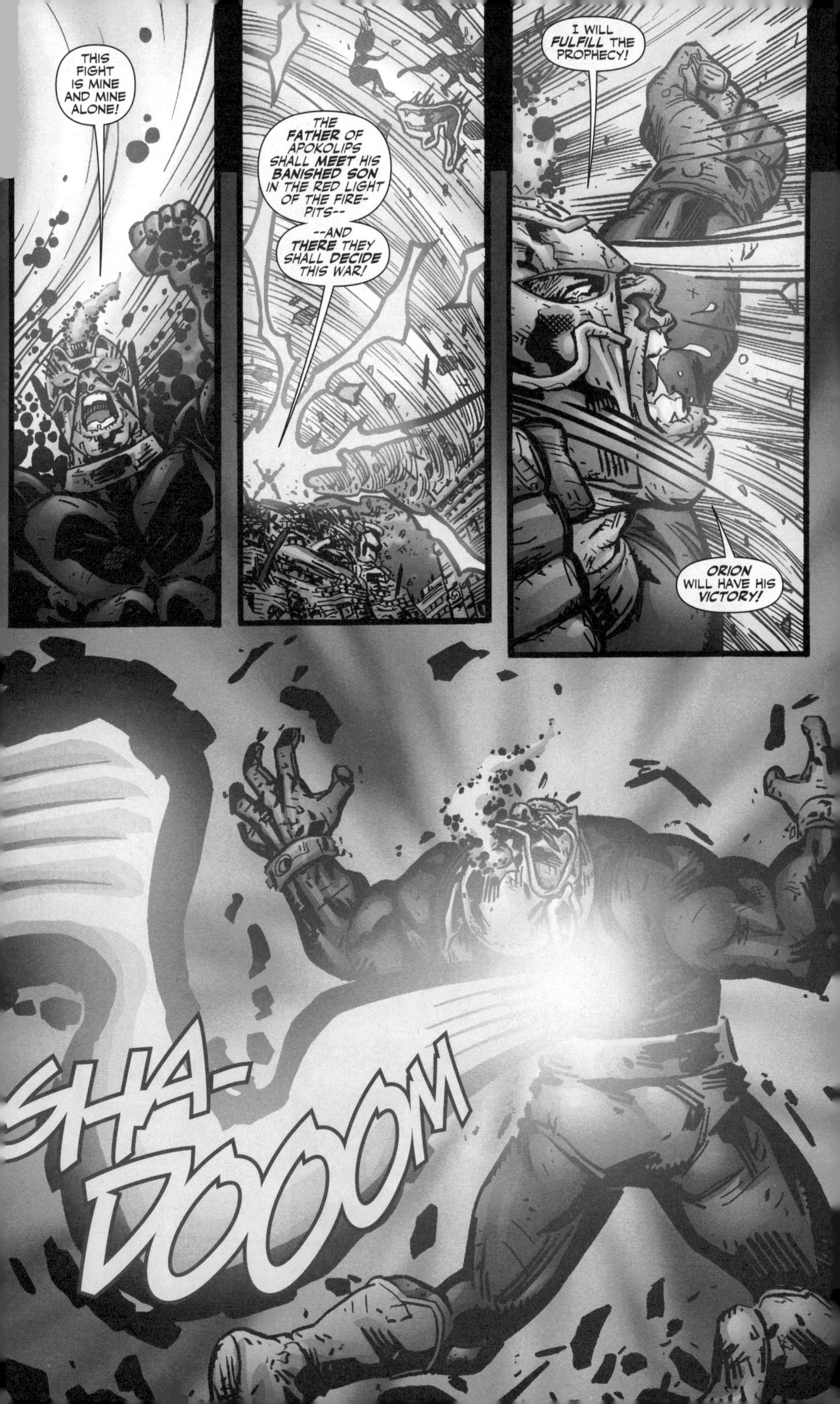
THIS FIGHT IS MINE AND MINE ALONE!
THE FATHER OF APOKOLIPS SHALL MEET HIS BANISHED SON IN THE RED LIGHT OF THE FIRE-PITS--
--AND THERE THEY SHALL DECIDE THIS WAR!
I WILL FULFILL THE PROPHECY!
ORION WILL HAVE HIS VICTORY!
SHA-DOOOM

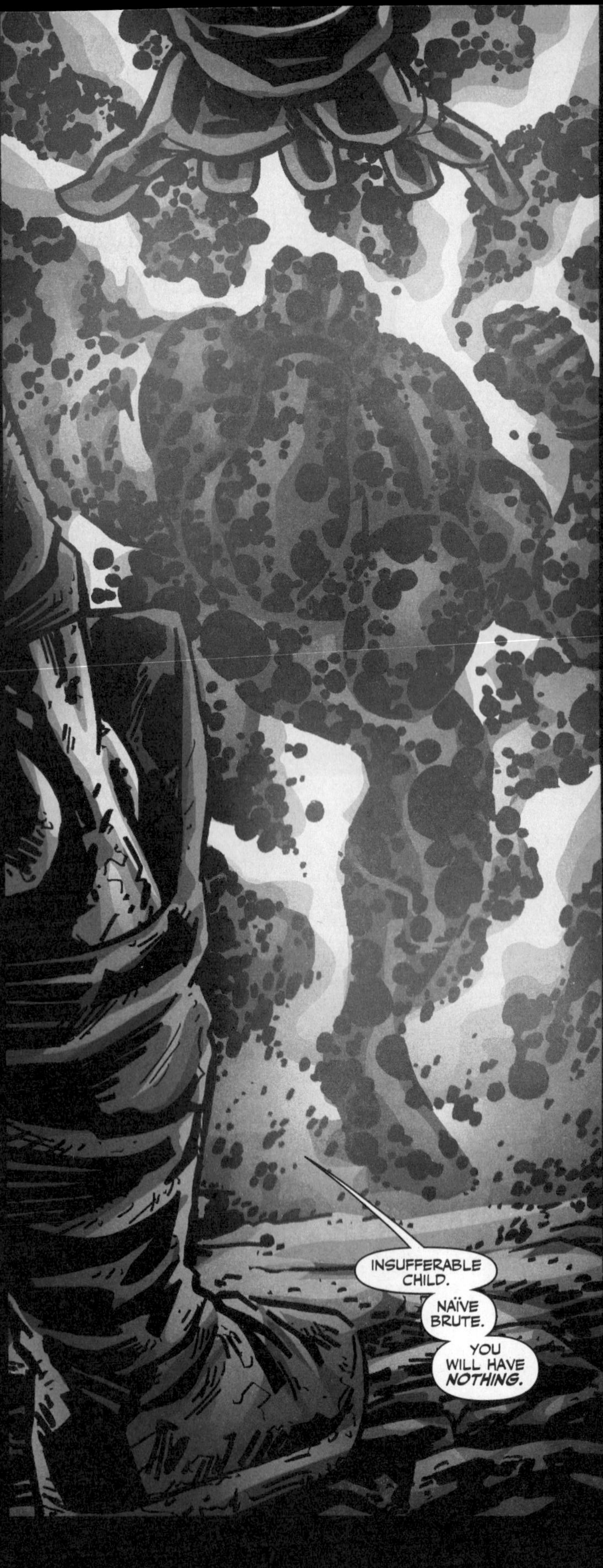
INSUFFERABLE CHILD.
NAÏVE BRUTE.
YOU WILL HAVE *NOTHING*.

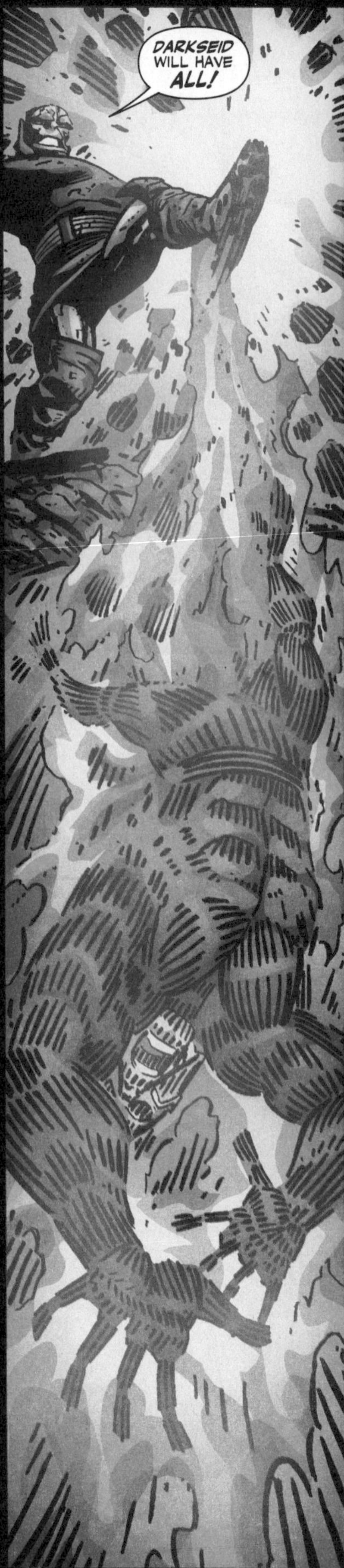
DARKSEID WILL HAVE *ALL!*

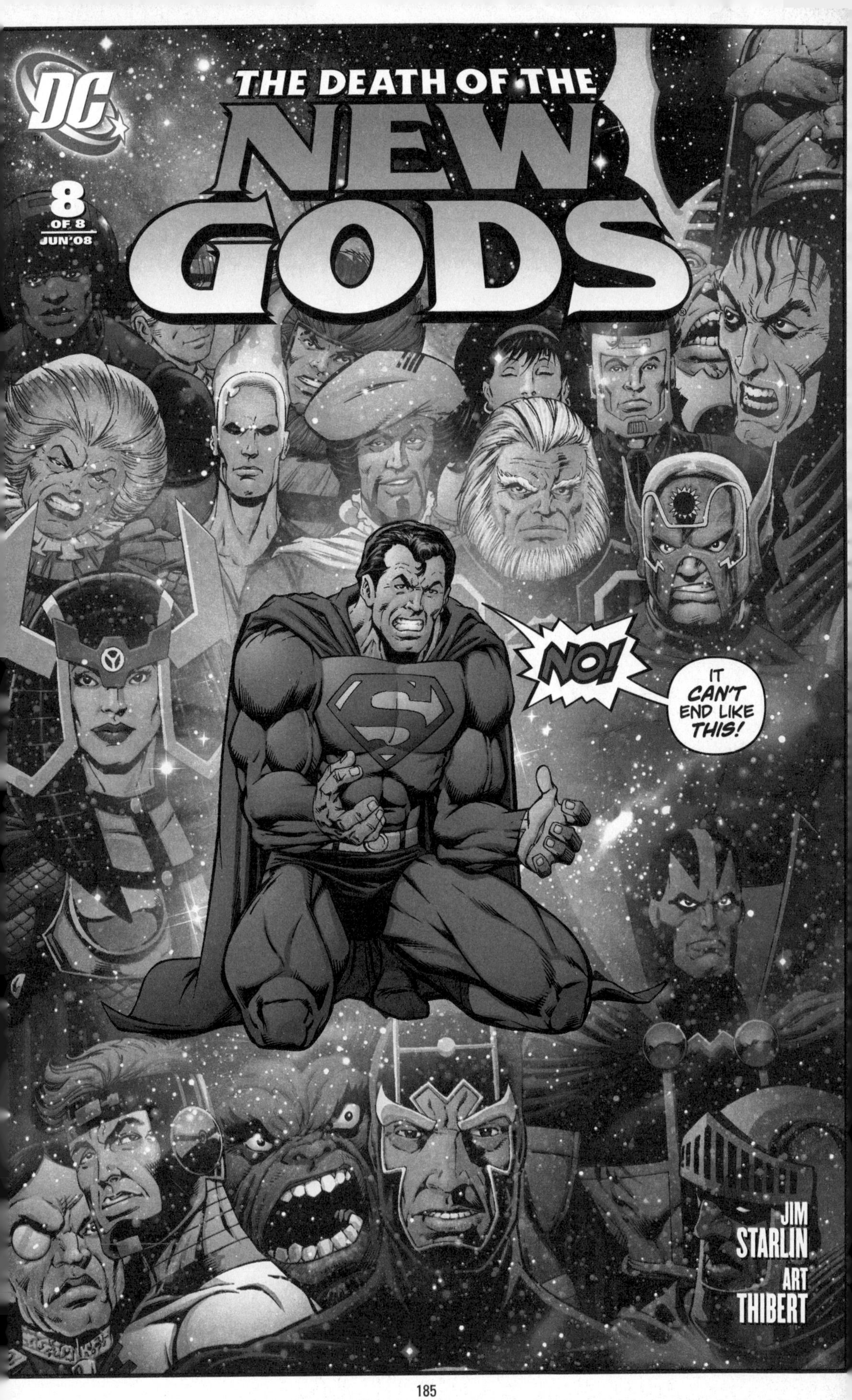
DC
THE DEATH OF THE
NEW GODS
8
OF 8
JUN'08
NO!
IT CAN'T END LIKE THIS!
JIM STARLIN
ART THIBERT

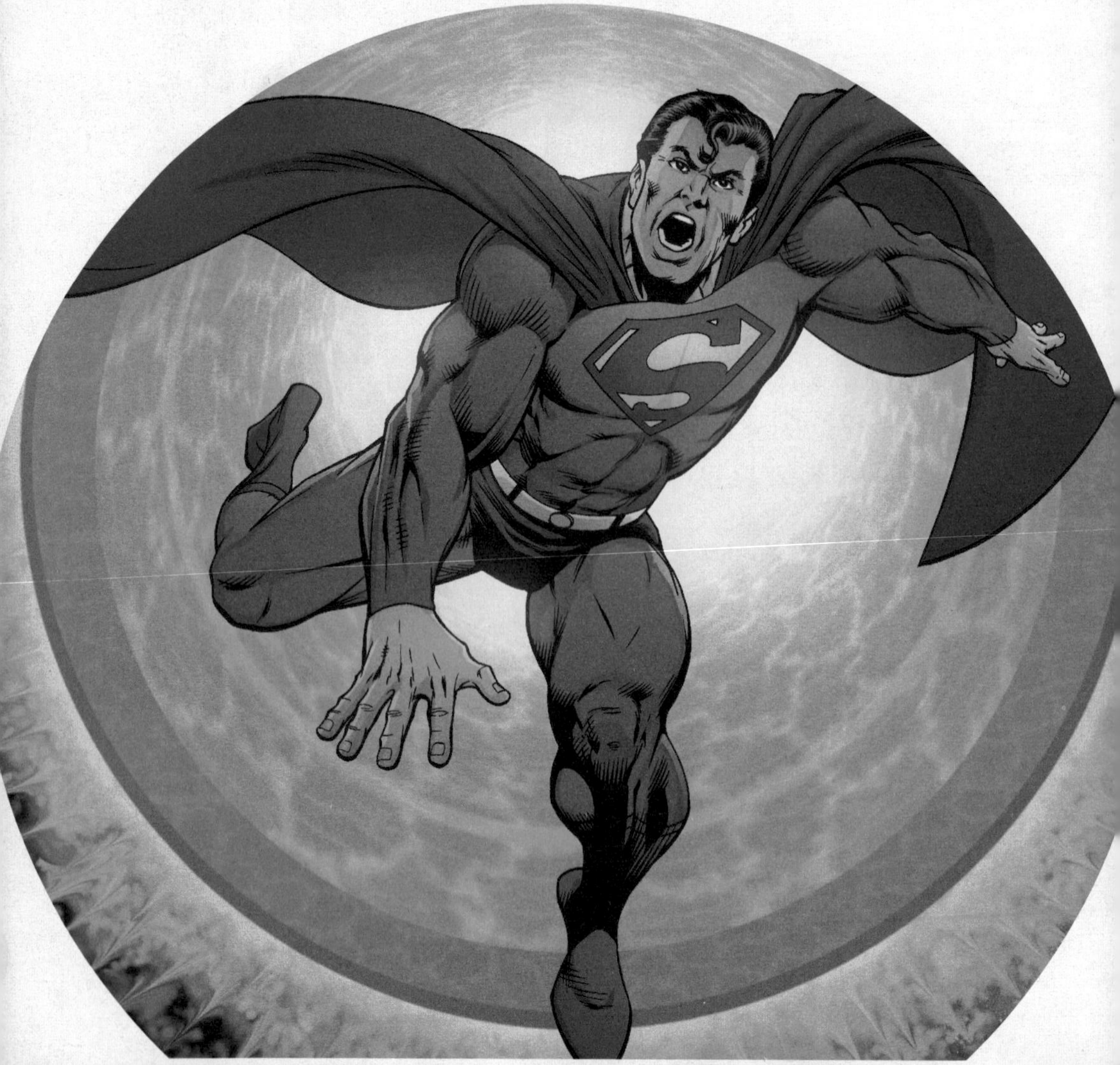

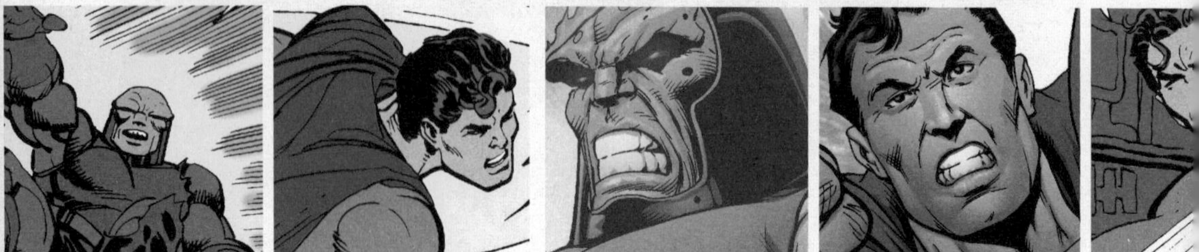

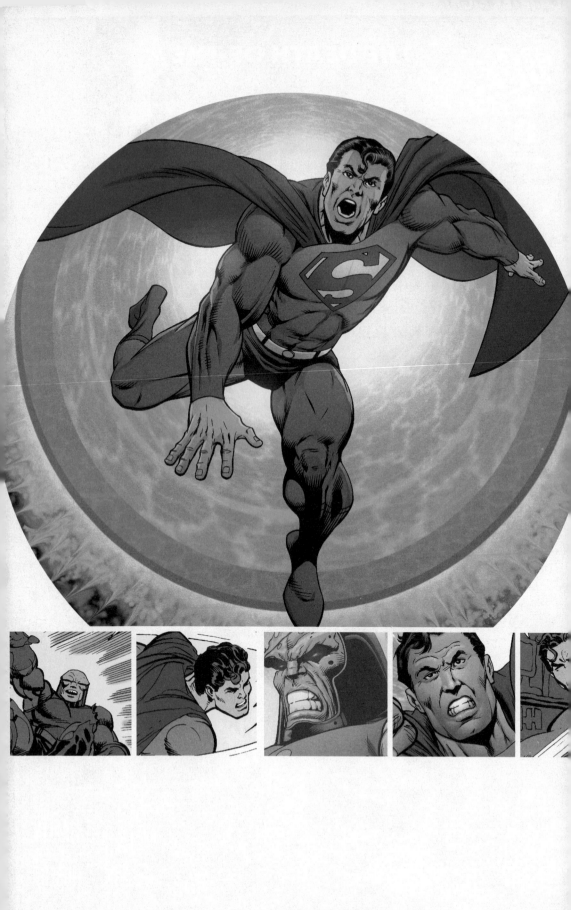

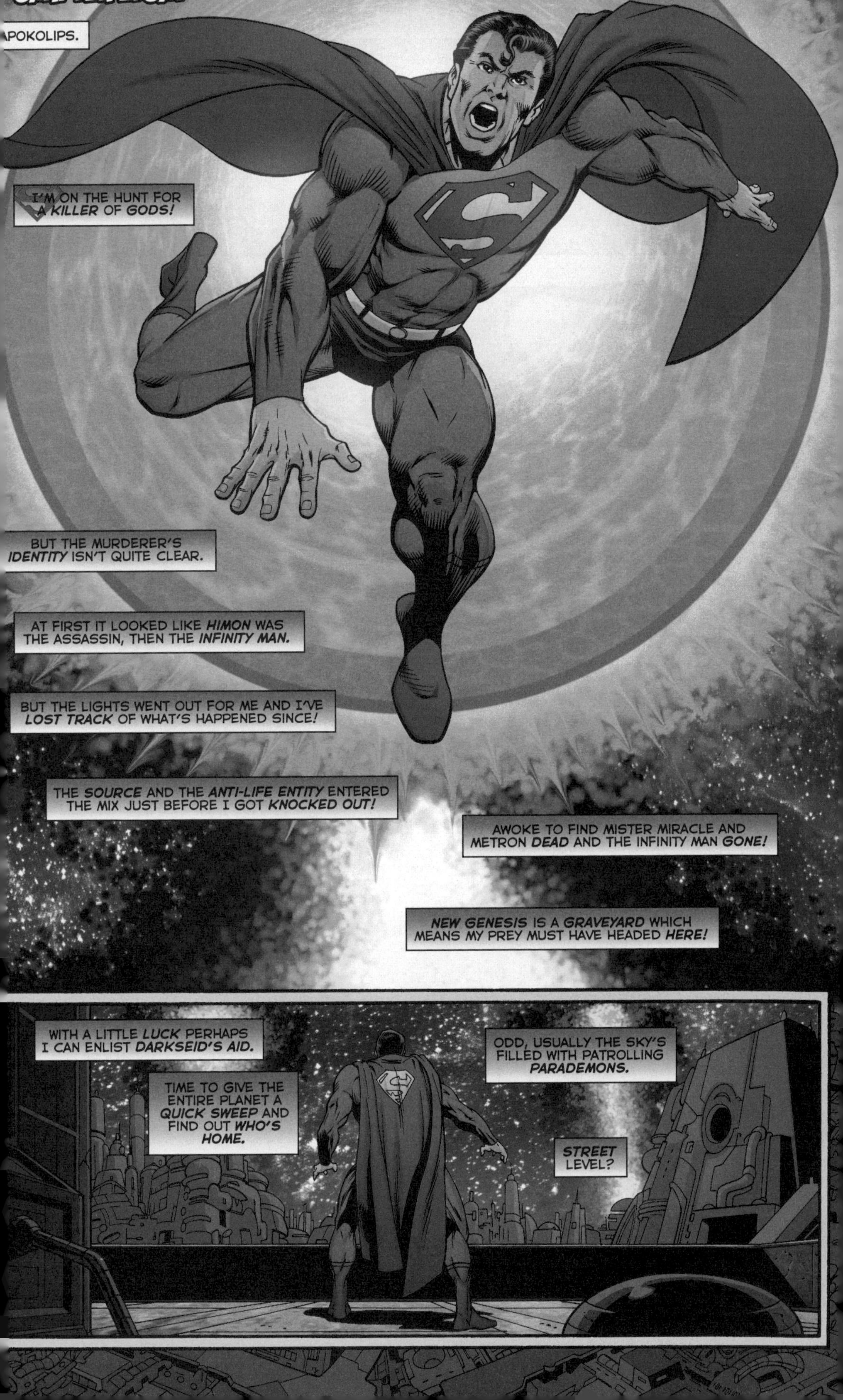
APOKOLIPS.
I'M ON THE HUNT FOR A KILLER OF GODS!
BUT THE MURDERER'S IDENTITY ISN'T QUITE CLEAR.
AT FIRST IT LOOKED LIKE HIMON WAS THE ASSASSIN, THEN THE INFINITY MAN.
BUT THE LIGHTS WENT OUT FOR ME AND I'VE LOST TRACK OF WHAT'S HAPPENED SINCE!
THE SOURCE AND THE ANTI-LIFE ENTITY ENTERED THE MIX JUST BEFORE I GOT KNOCKED OUT!
AWOKE TO FIND MISTER MIRACLE AND METRON DEAD AND THE INFINITY MAN GONE!
NEW GENESIS IS A GRAVEYARD WHICH MEANS MY PREY MUST HAVE HEADED HERE!
WITH A LITTLE LUCK PERHAPS I CAN ENLIST DARKSEID'S AID.
TIME TO GIVE THE ENTIRE PLANET A QUICK SWEEP AND FIND OUT WHO'S HOME.
ODD, USUALLY THE SKY'S FILLED WITH PATROLLING PARADEMONS.
STREET LEVEL?

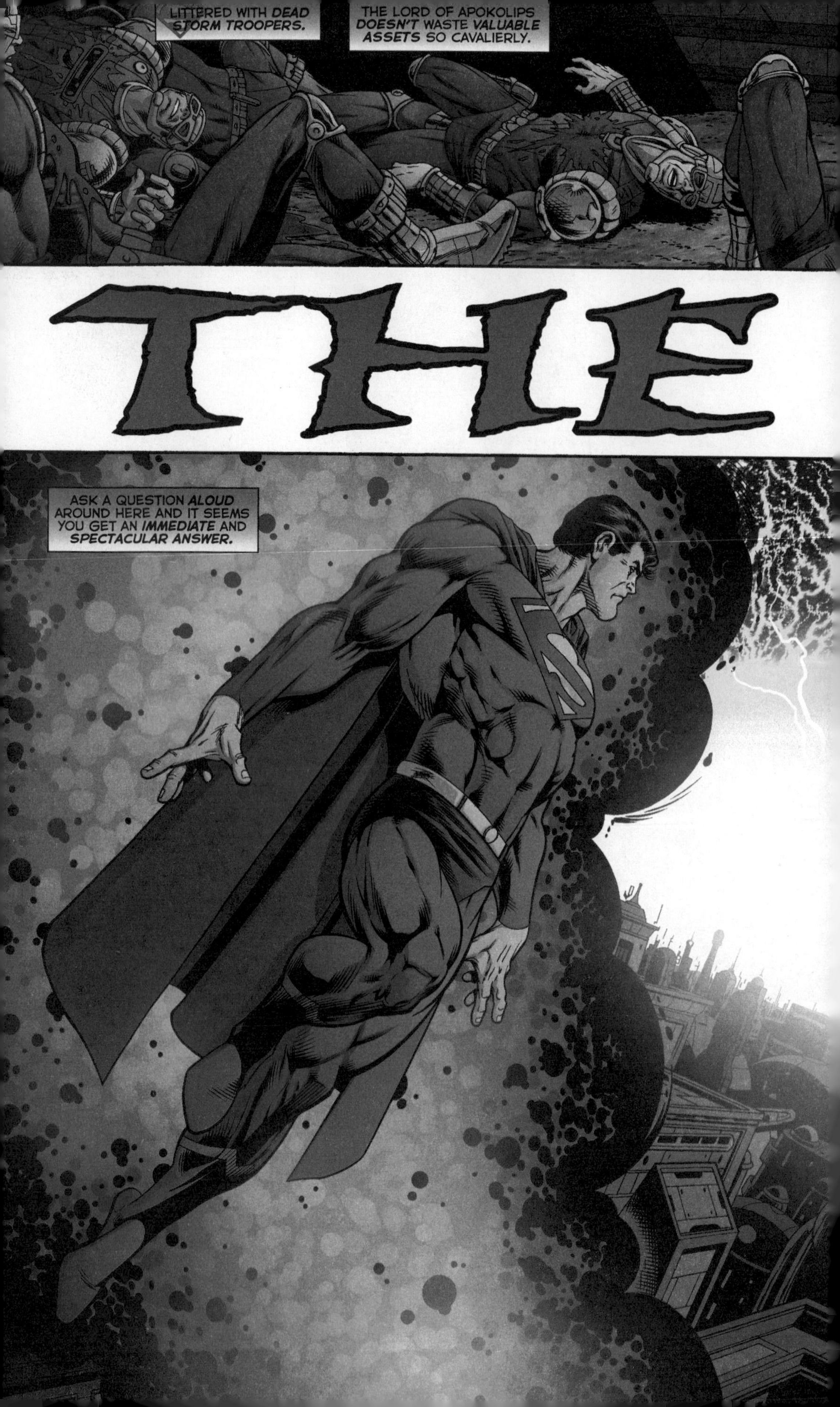

LITTERED WITH *DEAD STORM TROOPERS.*
THE LORD OF APOKOLIPS *DOESN'T* WASTE *VALUABLE ASSETS* SO CAVALIERLY.
THE
ASK A QUESTION *ALOUD* AROUND HERE AND IT SEEMS YOU GET AN *IMMEDIATE* AND *SPECTACULAR ANSWER.*

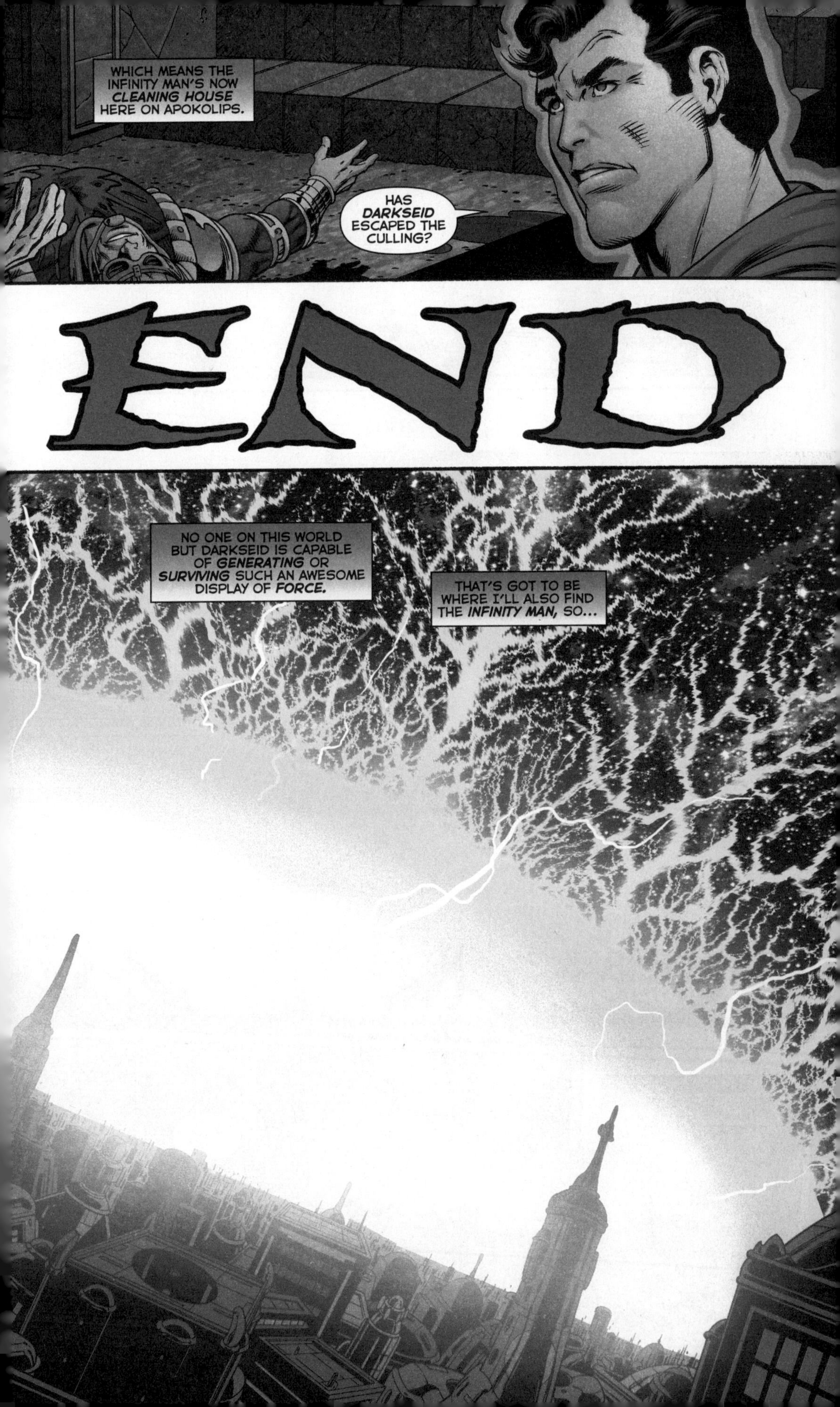

WHICH MEANS THE INFINITY MAN'S NOW *CLEANING HOUSE* HERE ON APOKOLIPS.
HAS *DARKSEID* ESCAPED THE CULLING?
END
NO ONE ON THIS WORLD BUT DARKSEID IS CAPABLE OF *GENERATING* OR *SURVIVING* SUCH AN AWESOME DISPLAY OF *FORCE.*
THAT'S GOT TO BE WHERE I'LL ALSO FIND THE *INFINITY MAN,* SO...

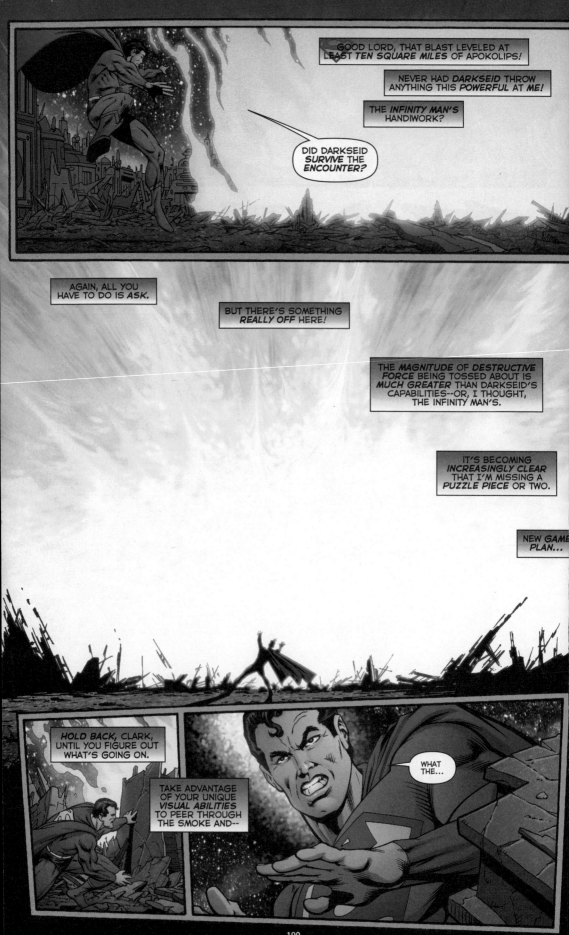

GOOD LORD, THAT BLAST LEVELED AT LEAST *TEN SQUARE MILES* OF APOKOLIPS!

NEVER HAD *DARKSEID* THROW ANYTHING THIS *POWERFUL* AT *ME!*

THE *INFINITY MAN'S* HANDIWORK?

DID DARKSEID *SURVIVE* THE *ENCOUNTER?*

AGAIN, ALL YOU HAVE TO DO IS *ASK.*

BUT THERE'S SOMETHING *REALLY OFF* HERE!

THE *MAGNITUDE* OF *DESTRUCTIVE FORCE* BEING TOSSED ABOUT IS *MUCH GREATER* THAN DARKSEID'S CAPABILITIES--OR, I THOUGHT, THE INFINITY MAN'S.

IT'S BECOMING *INCREASINGLY CLEAR* THAT I'M MISSING A *PUZZLE PIECE* OR TWO.

NEW GAME PLAN...

HOLD BACK, CLARK, UNTIL YOU FIGURE OUT WHAT'S GOING ON.

TAKE ADVANTAGE OF YOUR UNIQUE *VISUAL ABILITIES* TO PEER THROUGH THE SMOKE AND--

WHAT THE...

190

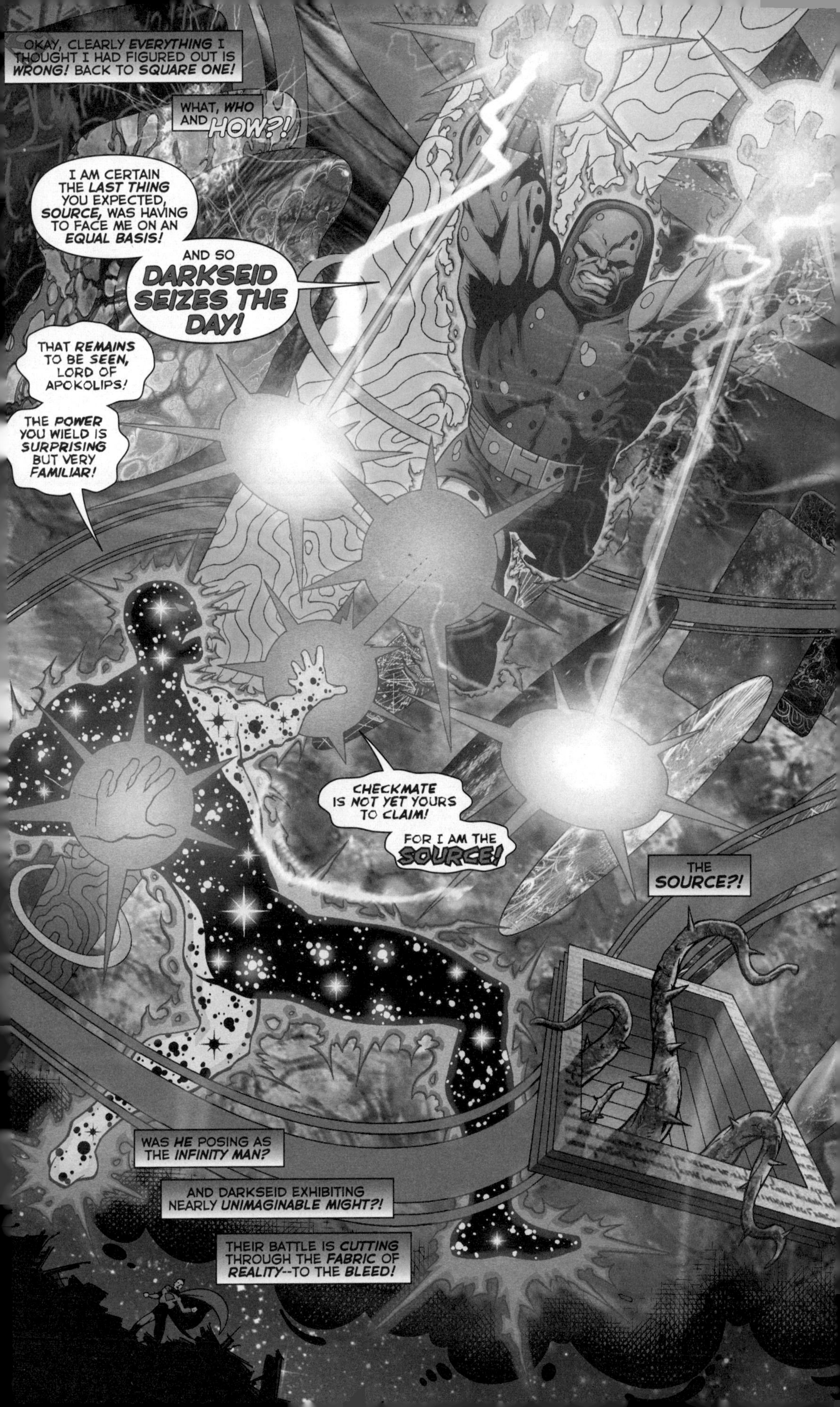
OKAY, CLEARLY EVERYTHING I THOUGHT I HAD FIGURED OUT IS WRONG! BACK TO SQUARE ONE!
WHAT, WHO AND HOW?!
I AM CERTAIN THE LAST THING YOU EXPECTED, SOURCE, WAS HAVING TO FACE ME ON AN EQUAL BASIS!
AND SO DARKSEID SEIZES THE DAY!
THAT REMAINS TO BE SEEN, LORD OF APOKOLIPS!
THE POWER YOU WIELD IS SURPRISING BUT VERY FAMILIAR!
CHECKMATE IS NOT YET YOURS TO CLAIM!
FOR I AM THE SOURCE!
THE SOURCE?!
WAS HE POSING AS THE INFINITY MAN?
AND DARKSEID EXHIBITING NEARLY UNIMAGINABLE MIGHT?!
THEIR BATTLE IS CUTTING THROUGH THE FABRIC OF REALITY--TO THE BLEED!

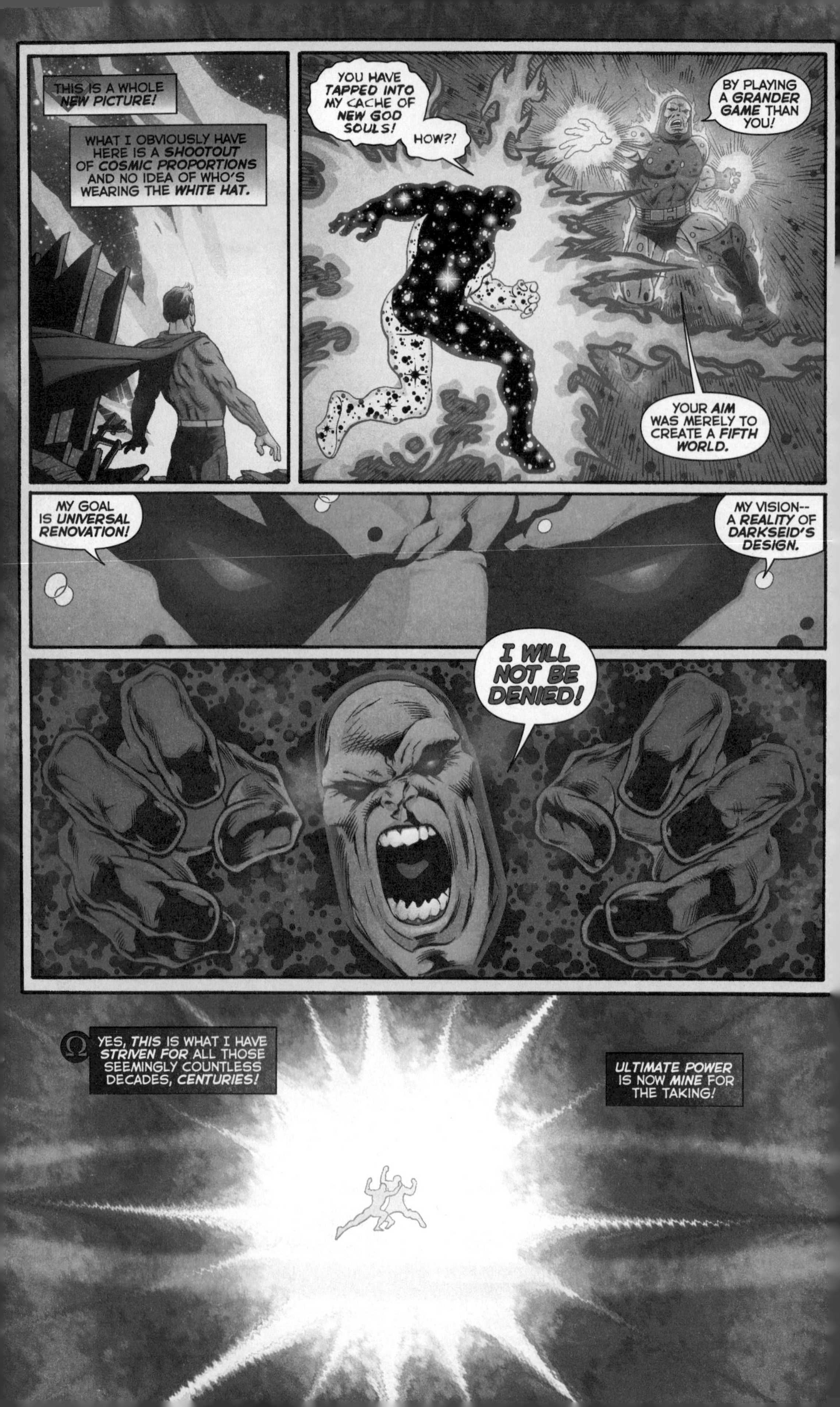

THIS IS A WHOLE NEW PICTURE!
WHAT I OBVIOUSLY HAVE HERE IS A SHOOTOUT OF COSMIC PROPORTIONS AND NO IDEA OF WHO'S WEARING THE WHITE HAT.
YOU HAVE TAPPED INTO MY CACHE OF NEW GOD SOULS!
HOW?!
BY PLAYING A GRANDER GAME THAN YOU!
YOUR AIM WAS MERELY TO CREATE A FIFTH WORLD.
MY GOAL IS UNIVERSAL RENOVATION!
MY VISION-- A REALITY OF DARKSEID'S DESIGN.
I WILL NOT BE DENIED!
YES, THIS IS WHAT I HAVE STRIVEN FOR ALL THOSE SEEMINGLY COUNTLESS DECADES, CENTURIES!
ULTIMATE POWER IS NOW MINE FOR THE TAKING!

Ω THERE WILL BE ORDER!

OPPOSITION TO MY WILL SHALL BECOME INCONCEIVABLE!

FOR NOW *THOUGHT* IS BUT A MERE *DECISION AWAY* FROM *ACTUALITY* FOR ME.

THE *POWER* OF THE *ANTI-LIFE EQUATION* IS UTTERLY *INSIGNIFICANT* COMPARED TO THE *MIGHT* I NOW FLOURISH.

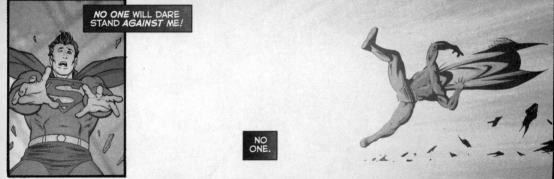

NO ONE WILL DARE STAND *AGAINST* ME!

NO ONE.

DARKSEID IS SUPREME!

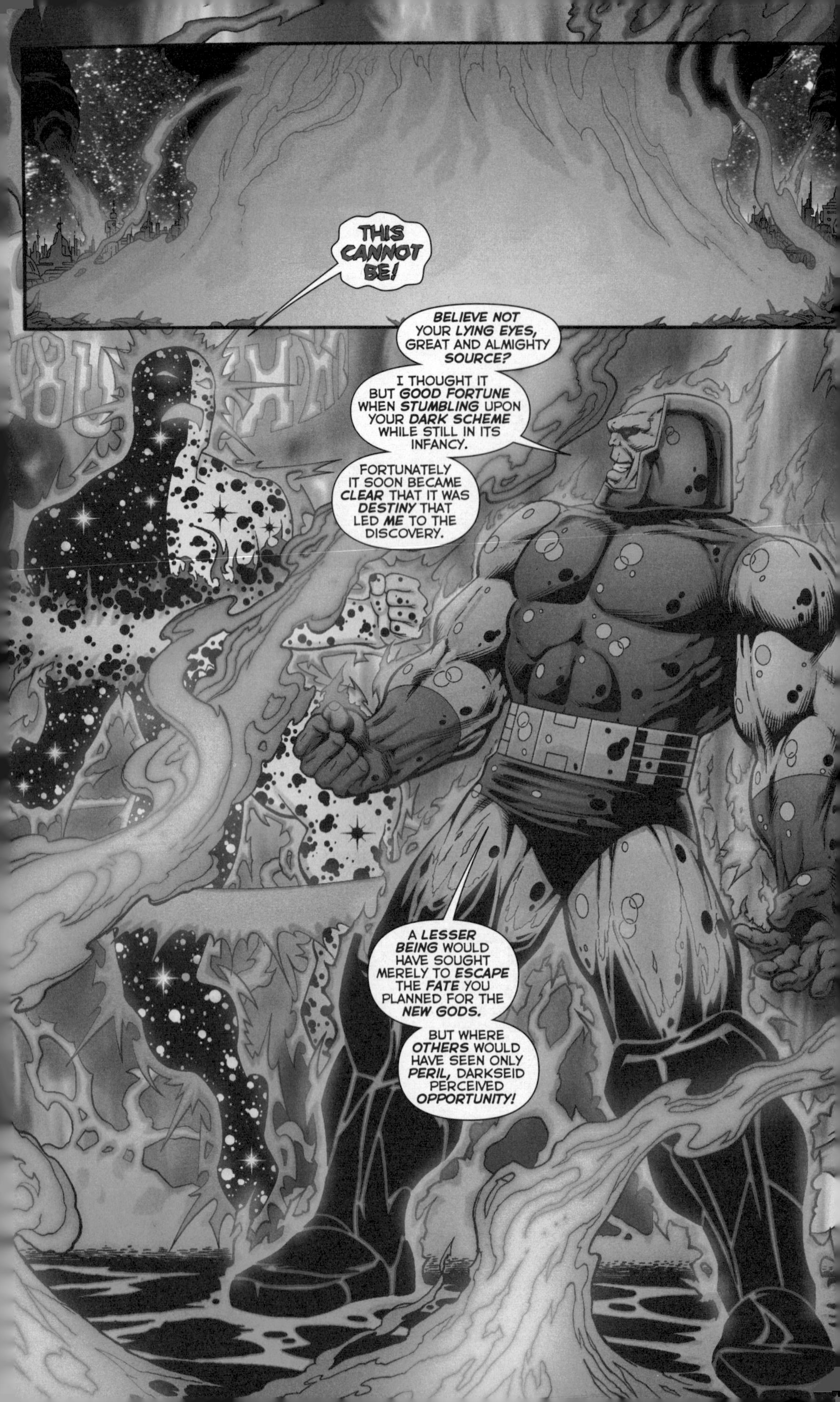
THIS CANNOT BE!
BELIEVE NOT YOUR LYING EYES, GREAT AND ALMIGHTY SOURCE?
I THOUGHT IT BUT GOOD FORTUNE WHEN STUMBLING UPON YOUR DARK SCHEME WHILE STILL IN ITS INFANCY.
FORTUNATELY IT SOON BECAME CLEAR THAT IT WAS DESTINY THAT LED ME TO THE DISCOVERY.
A LESSER BEING WOULD HAVE SOUGHT MERELY TO ESCAPE THE FATE YOU PLANNED FOR THE NEW GODS.
BUT WHERE OTHERS WOULD HAVE SEEN ONLY PERIL, DARKSEID PERCEIVED OPPORTUNITY!

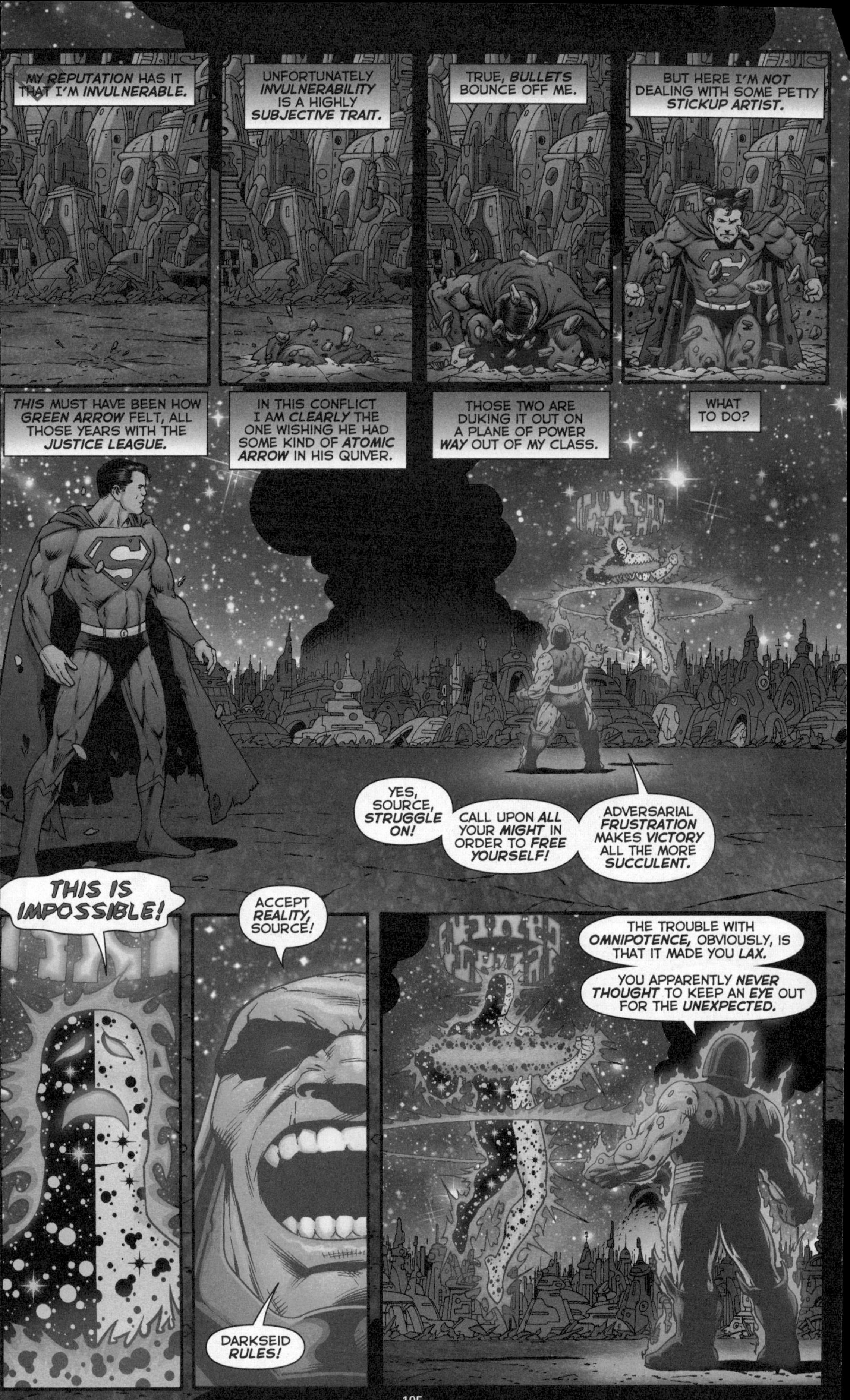

MY REPUTATION HAS IT THAT I'M INVULNERABLE.
UNFORTUNATELY INVULNERABILITY IS A HIGHLY SUBJECTIVE TRAIT.
TRUE, BULLETS BOUNCE OFF ME.
BUT HERE I'M NOT DEALING WITH SOME PETTY STICKUP ARTIST.
THIS MUST HAVE BEEN HOW GREEN ARROW FELT, ALL THOSE YEARS WITH THE JUSTICE LEAGUE.
IN THIS CONFLICT I AM CLEARLY THE ONE WISHING HE HAD SOME KIND OF ATOMIC ARROW IN HIS QUIVER.
THOSE TWO ARE DUKING IT OUT ON A PLANE OF POWER WAY OUT OF MY CLASS.
WHAT TO DO?
YES, SOURCE, STRUGGLE ON!
CALL UPON ALL YOUR MIGHT IN ORDER TO FREE YOURSELF!
ADVERSARIAL FRUSTRATION MAKES VICTORY ALL THE MORE SUCCULENT.
THIS IS IMPOSSIBLE!
ACCEPT REALITY, SOURCE!
DARKSEID RULES!
THE TROUBLE WITH OMNIPOTENCE, OBVIOUSLY, IS THAT IT MADE YOU LAX.
YOU APPARENTLY NEVER THOUGHT TO KEEP AN EYE OUT FOR THE UNEXPECTED.

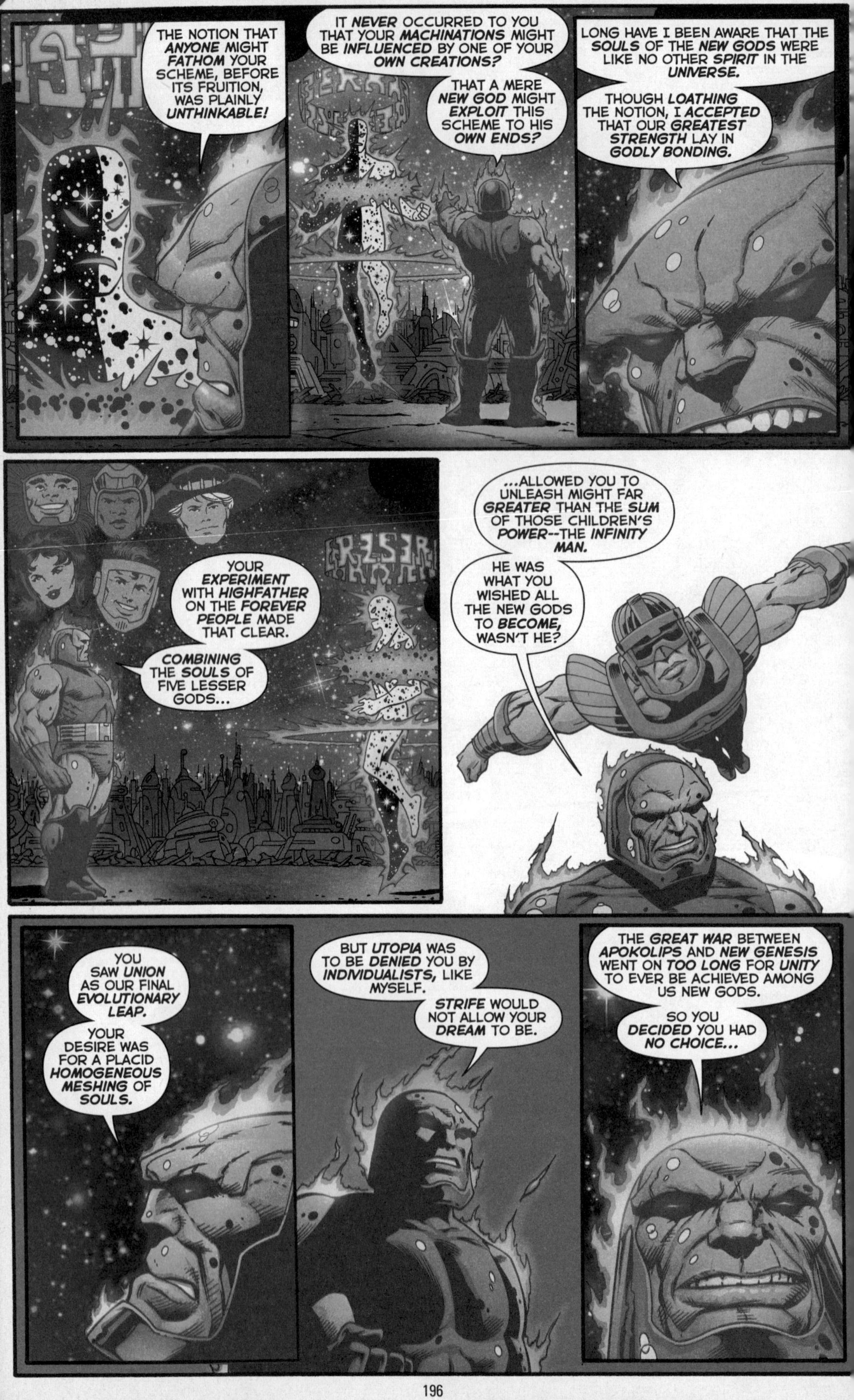
THE NOTION THAT ANYONE MIGHT FATHOM YOUR SCHEME, BEFORE ITS FRUITION, WAS PLAINLY UNTHINKABLE!
IT NEVER OCCURRED TO YOU THAT YOUR MACHINATIONS MIGHT BE INFLUENCED BY ONE OF YOUR OWN CREATIONS?
THAT A MERE NEW GOD MIGHT EXPLOIT THIS SCHEME TO HIS OWN ENDS?
LONG HAVE I BEEN AWARE THAT THE SOULS OF THE NEW GODS WERE LIKE NO OTHER SPIRIT IN THE UNIVERSE.
THOUGH LOATHING THE NOTION, I ACCEPTED THAT OUR GREATEST STRENGTH LAY IN GODLY BONDING.
YOUR EXPERIMENT WITH HIGHFATHER ON THE FOREVER PEOPLE MADE THAT CLEAR.
COMBINING THE SOULS OF FIVE LESSER GODS...
...ALLOWED YOU TO UNLEASH MIGHT FAR GREATER THAN THE SUM OF THOSE CHILDREN'S POWER--THE INFINITY MAN.
HE WAS WHAT YOU WISHED ALL THE NEW GODS TO BECOME, WASN'T HE?
YOU SAW UNION AS OUR FINAL EVOLUTIONARY LEAP.
YOUR DESIRE WAS FOR A PLACID HOMOGENEOUS MESHING OF SOULS.
BUT UTOPIA WAS TO BE DENIED YOU BY INDIVIDUALISTS, LIKE MYSELF.
STRIFE WOULD NOT ALLOW YOUR DREAM TO BE.
THE GREAT WAR BETWEEN APOKOLIPS AND NEW GENESIS WENT ON TOO LONG FOR UNITY TO EVER BE ACHIEVED AMONG US NEW GODS.
SO YOU DECIDED YOU HAD NO CHOICE...

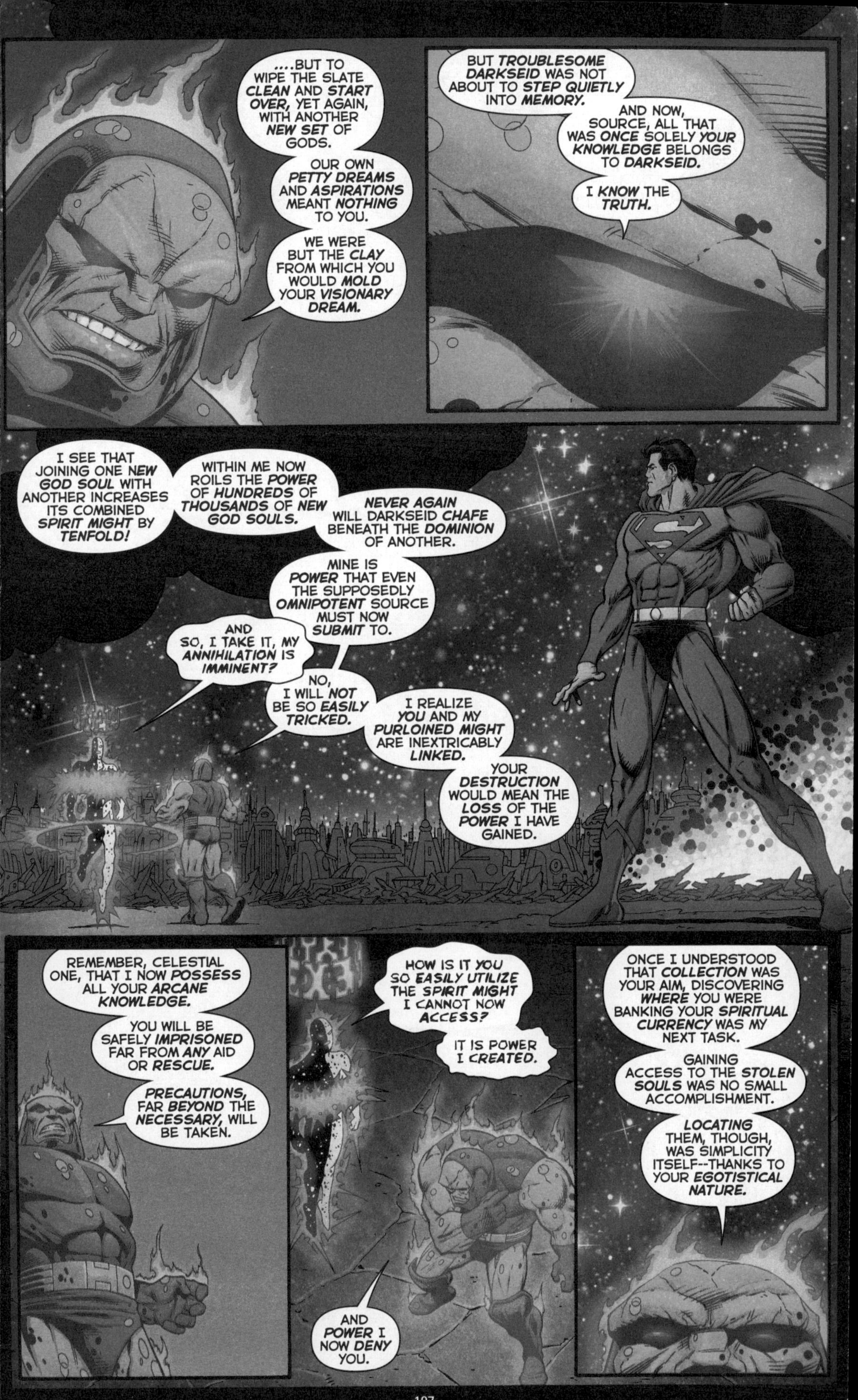
....BUT TO WIPE THE SLATE CLEAN AND START OVER, YET AGAIN, WITH ANOTHER NEW SET OF GODS.
OUR OWN PETTY DREAMS AND ASPIRATIONS MEANT NOTHING TO YOU.
WE WERE BUT THE CLAY FROM WHICH YOU WOULD MOLD YOUR VISIONARY DREAM.
BUT TROUBLESOME DARKSEID WAS NOT ABOUT TO STEP QUIETLY INTO MEMORY.
AND NOW, SOURCE, ALL THAT WAS ONCE SOLELY YOUR KNOWLEDGE BELONGS TO DARKSEID.
I KNOW THE TRUTH.
I SEE THAT JOINING ONE NEW GOD SOUL WITH ANOTHER INCREASES ITS COMBINED SPIRIT MIGHT BY TENFOLD!
WITHIN ME NOW ROILS THE POWER OF HUNDREDS OF THOUSANDS OF NEW GOD SOULS.
NEVER AGAIN WILL DARKSEID CHAFE BENEATH THE DOMINION OF ANOTHER.
MINE IS POWER THAT EVEN THE SUPPOSEDLY OMNIPOTENT SOURCE MUST NOW SUBMIT TO.
AND SO, I TAKE IT, MY ANNIHILATION IS IMMINENT?
NO, I WILL NOT BE SO EASILY TRICKED.
I REALIZE YOU AND MY PURLOINED MIGHT ARE INEXTRICABLY LINKED.
YOUR DESTRUCTION WOULD MEAN THE LOSS OF THE POWER I HAVE GAINED.
REMEMBER, CELESTIAL ONE, THAT I NOW POSSESS ALL YOUR ARCANE KNOWLEDGE.
YOU WILL BE SAFELY IMPRISONED FAR FROM ANY AID OR RESCUE.
PRECAUTIONS, FAR BEYOND THE NECESSARY, WILL BE TAKEN.
HOW IS IT YOU SO EASILY UTILIZE THE SPIRIT MIGHT I CANNOT NOW ACCESS?
IT IS POWER I CREATED.
AND POWER I NOW DENY YOU.
ONCE I UNDERSTOOD THAT COLLECTION WAS YOUR AIM, DISCOVERING WHERE YOU WERE BANKING YOUR SPIRITUAL CURRENCY WAS MY NEXT TASK.
GAINING ACCESS TO THE STOLEN SOULS WAS NO SMALL ACCOMPLISHMENT.
LOCATING THEM, THOUGH, WAS SIMPLICITY ITSELF--THANKS TO YOUR EGOTISTICAL NATURE.

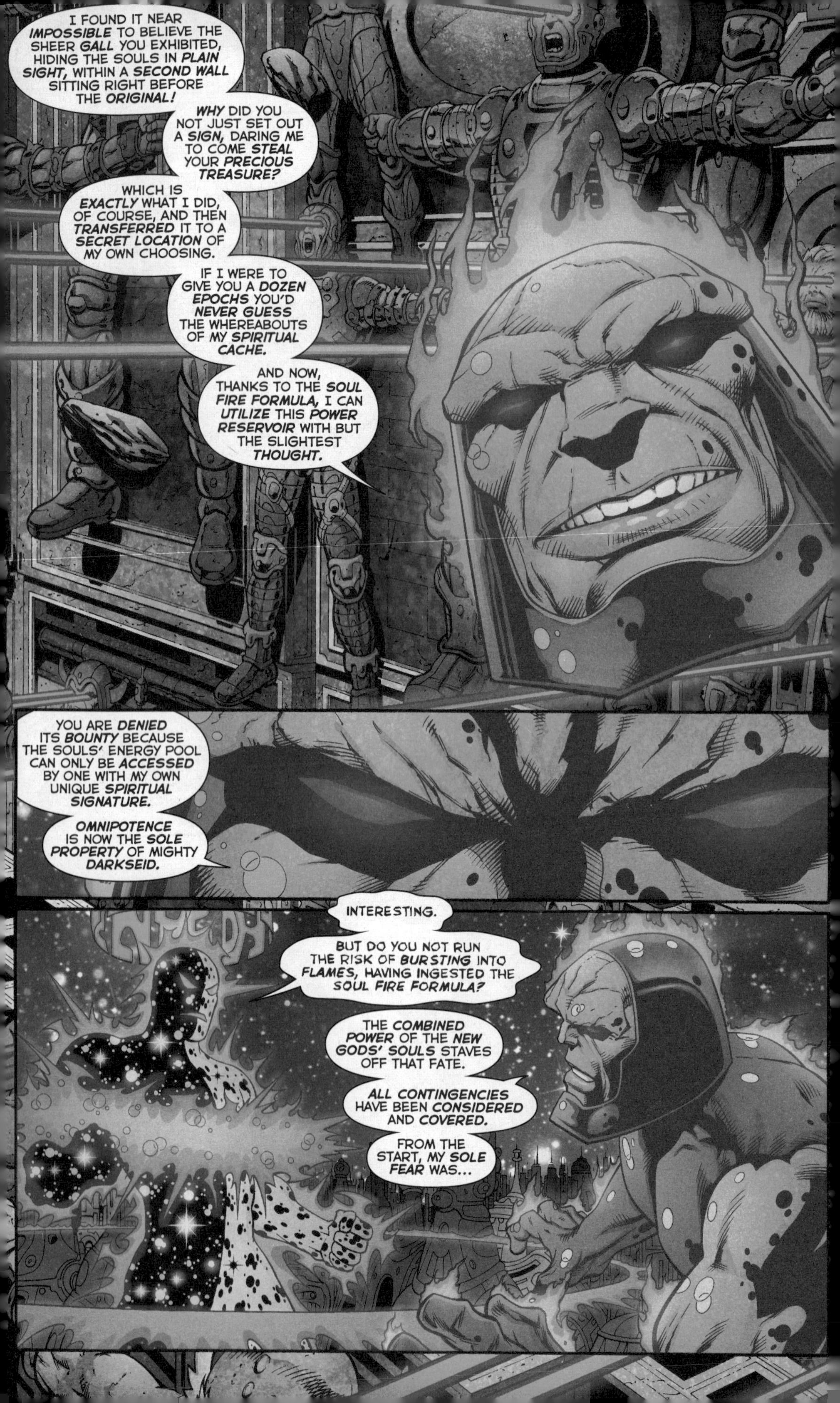
I FOUND IT NEAR IMPOSSIBLE TO BELIEVE THE SHEER GALL YOU EXHIBITED, HIDING THE SOULS IN PLAIN SIGHT, WITHIN A SECOND WALL SITTING RIGHT BEFORE THE ORIGINAL!
WHY DID YOU NOT JUST SET OUT A SIGN, DARING ME TO COME STEAL YOUR PRECIOUS TREASURE?
WHICH IS EXACTLY WHAT I DID, OF COURSE, AND THEN TRANSFERRED IT TO A SECRET LOCATION OF MY OWN CHOOSING.
IF I WERE TO GIVE YOU A DOZEN EPOCHS YOU'D NEVER GUESS THE WHEREABOUTS OF MY SPIRITUAL CACHE.
AND NOW, THANKS TO THE SOUL FIRE FORMULA, I CAN UTILIZE THIS POWER RESERVOIR WITH BUT THE SLIGHTEST THOUGHT.
YOU ARE DENIED ITS BOUNTY BECAUSE THE SOULS' ENERGY POOL CAN ONLY BE ACCESSED BY ONE WITH MY OWN UNIQUE SPIRITUAL SIGNATURE.
OMNIPOTENCE IS NOW THE SOLE PROPERTY OF MIGHTY DARKSEID.
INTERESTING.
BUT DO YOU NOT RUN THE RISK OF BURSTING INTO FLAMES, HAVING INGESTED THE SOUL FIRE FORMULA?
THE COMBINED POWER OF THE NEW GODS' SOULS STAVES OFF THAT FATE.
ALL CONTINGENCIES HAVE BEEN CONSIDERED AND COVERED.
FROM THE START, MY SOLE FEAR WAS...

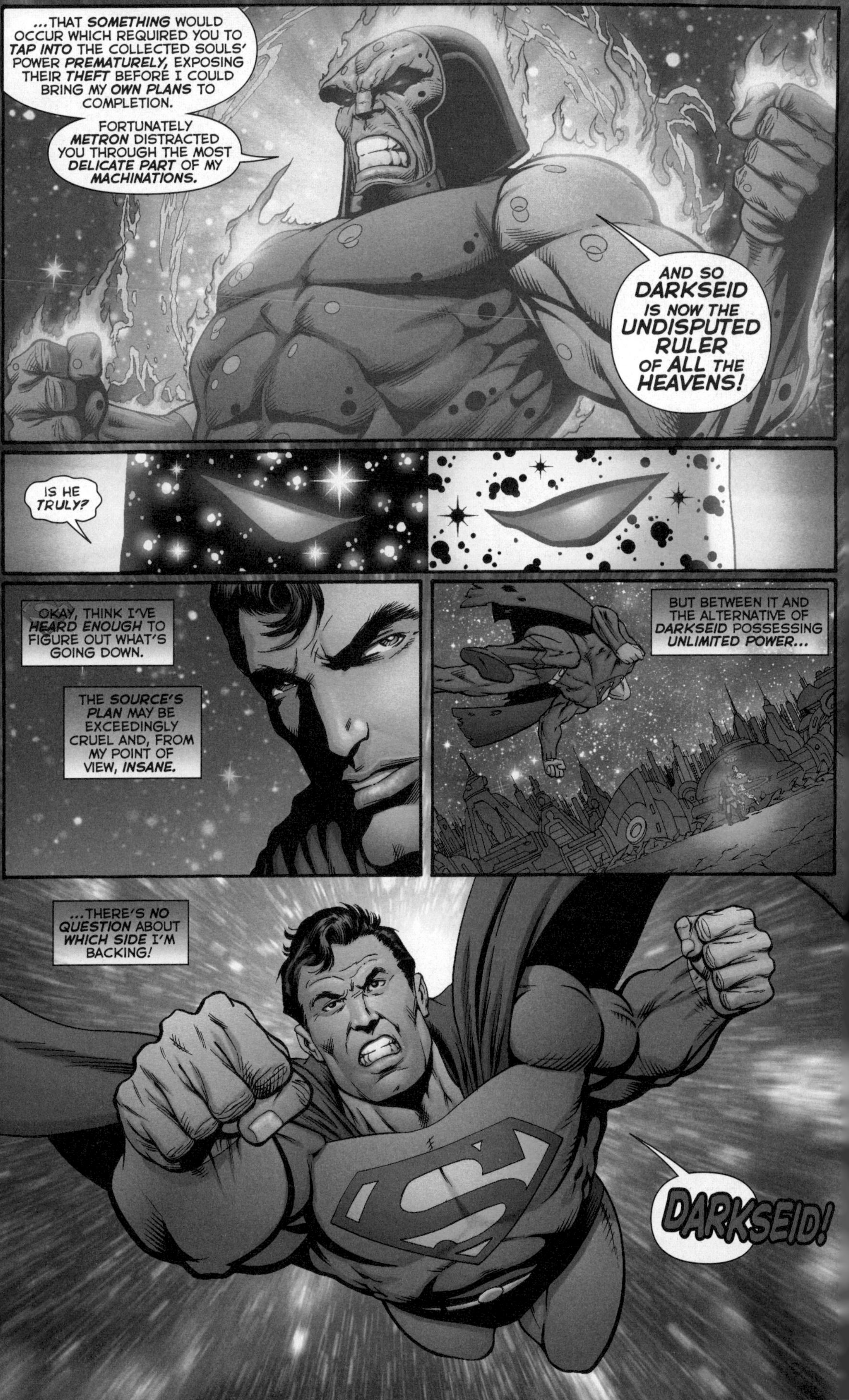
...THAT SOMETHING WOULD OCCUR WHICH REQUIRED YOU TO TAP INTO THE COLLECTED SOULS' POWER PREMATURELY, EXPOSING THEIR THEFT BEFORE I COULD BRING MY OWN PLANS TO COMPLETION.
FORTUNATELY METRON DISTRACTED YOU THROUGH THE MOST DELICATE PART OF MY MACHINATIONS.
AND SO DARKSEID IS NOW THE UNDISPUTED RULER OF ALL THE HEAVENS!
IS HE TRULY?
OKAY, THINK I'VE HEARD ENOUGH TO FIGURE OUT WHAT'S GOING DOWN.
THE SOURCE'S PLAN MAY BE EXCEEDINGLY CRUEL AND, FROM MY POINT OF VIEW, INSANE.
BUT BETWEEN IT AND THE ALTERNATIVE OF DARKSEID POSSESSING UNLIMITED POWER...
...THERE'S NO QUESTION ABOUT WHICH SIDE I'M BACKING!
DARKSEID!

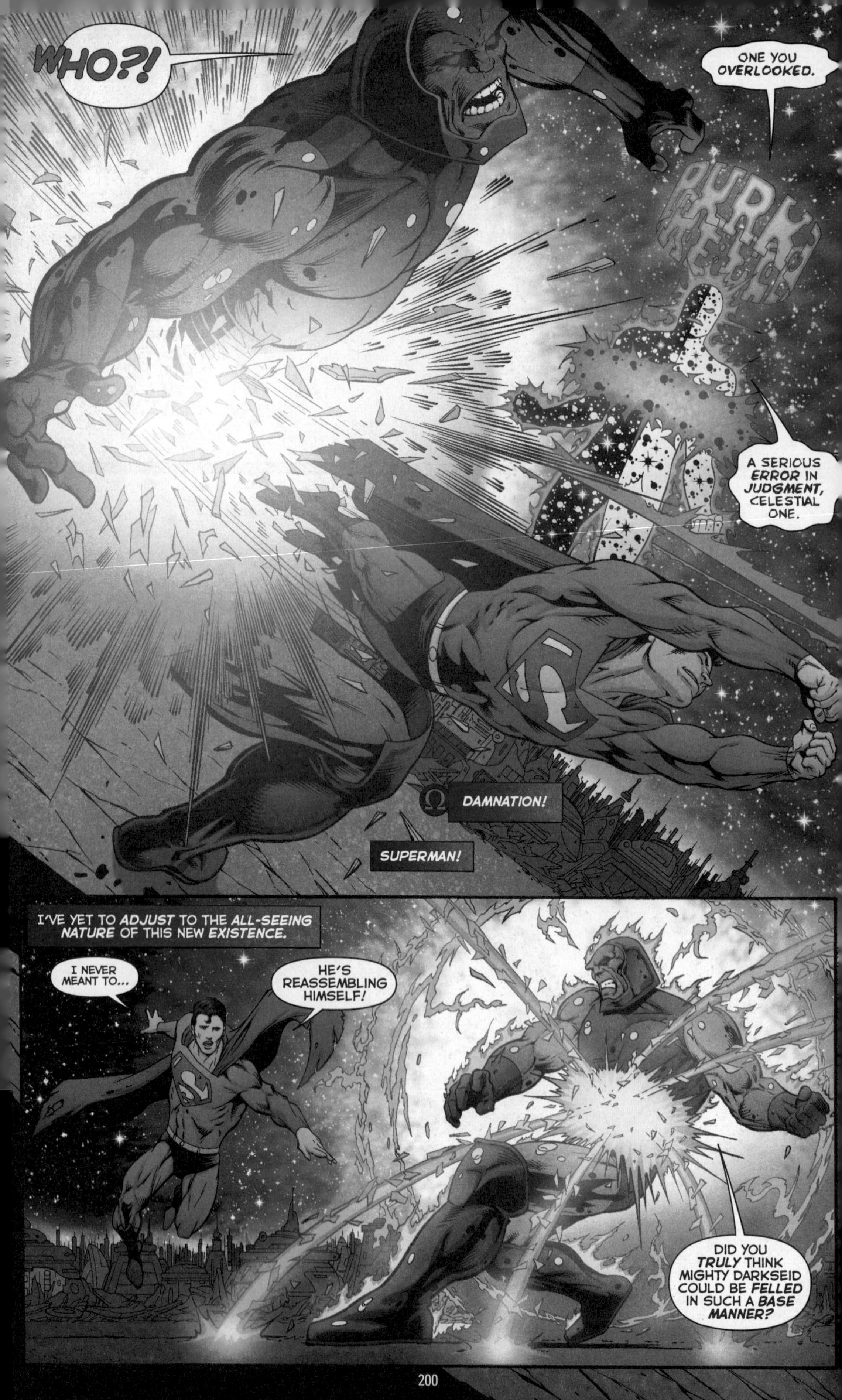
WHO?!
ONE YOU OVERLOOKED.
A SERIOUS ERROR IN JUDGMENT, CELESTIAL ONE.
DAMNATION!
SUPERMAN!
I'VE YET TO ADJUST TO THE ALL-SEEING NATURE OF THIS NEW EXISTENCE.
I NEVER MEANT TO...
HE'S REASSEMBLING HIMSELF!
DID YOU TRULY THINK MIGHTY DARKSEID COULD BE FELLED IN SUCH A BASE MANNER?

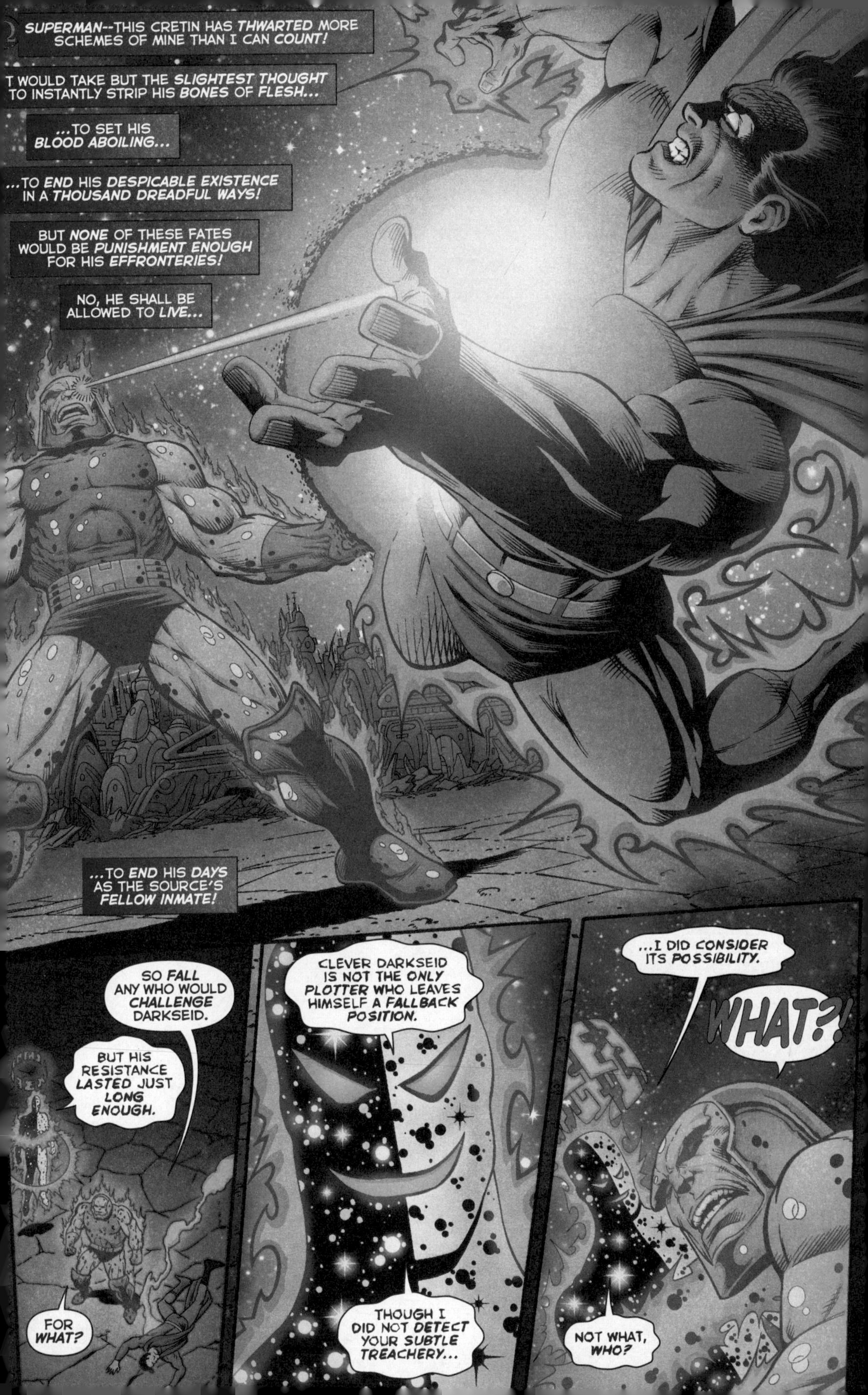
SUPERMAN--THIS CRETIN HAS THWARTED MORE SCHEMES OF MINE THAN I CAN COUNT!
T WOULD TAKE BUT THE SLIGHTEST THOUGHT TO INSTANTLY STRIP HIS BONES OF FLESH...
...TO SET HIS BLOOD ABOILING...
...TO END HIS DESPICABLE EXISTENCE IN A THOUSAND DREADFUL WAYS!
BUT NONE OF THESE FATES WOULD BE PUNISHMENT ENOUGH FOR HIS EFFRONTERIES!
NO, HE SHALL BE ALLOWED TO LIVE...
...TO END HIS DAYS AS THE SOURCE'S FELLOW INMATE!
SO FALL ANY WHO WOULD CHALLENGE DARKSEID.
BUT HIS RESISTANCE LASTED JUST LONG ENOUGH.
FOR WHAT?
CLEVER DARKSEID IS NOT THE ONLY PLOTTER WHO LEAVES HIMSELF A FALLBACK POSITION.
THOUGH I DID NOT DETECT YOUR SUBTLE TREACHERY...
...I DID CONSIDER ITS POSSIBILITY.
WHAT?!
NOT WHAT, WHO?

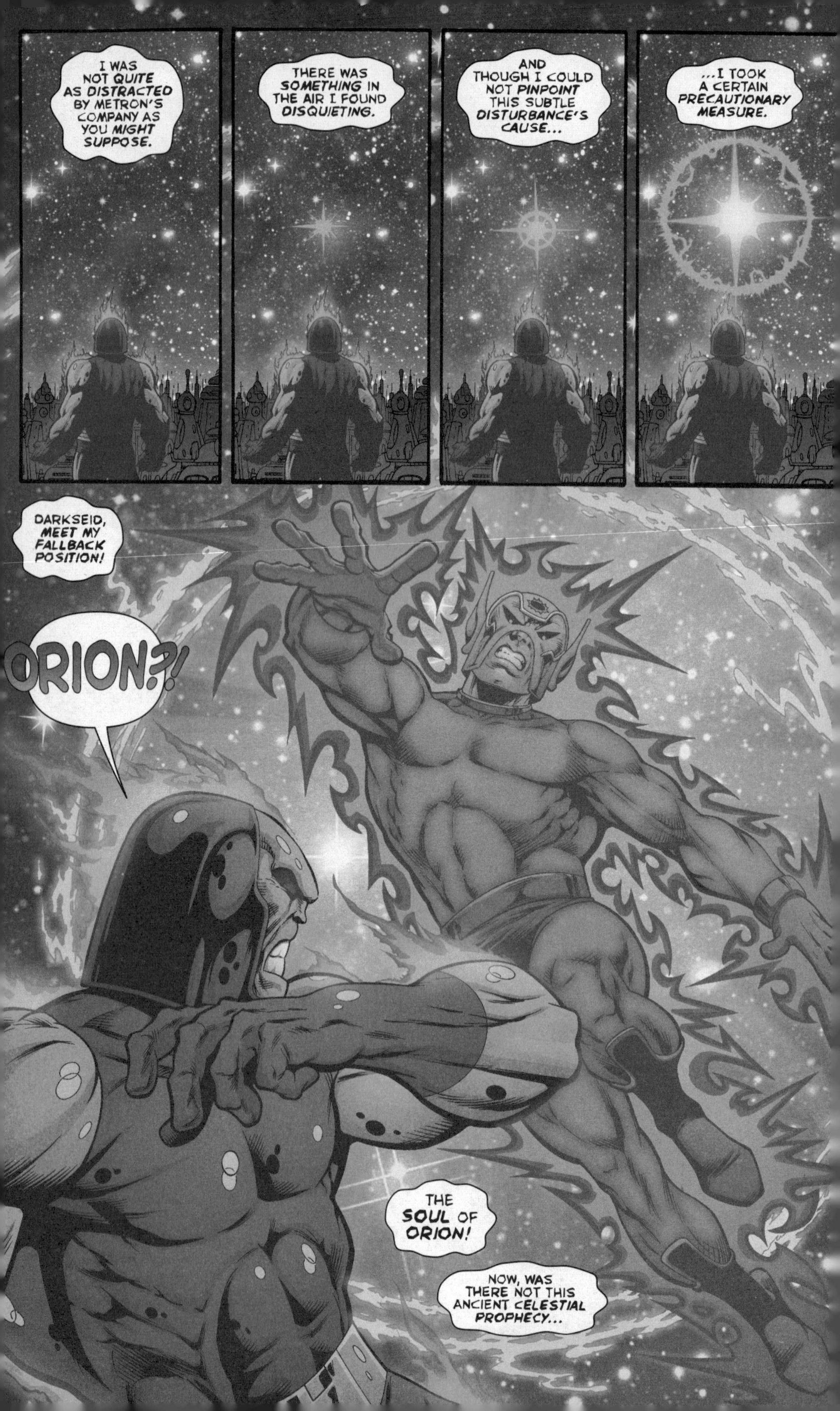
I WAS NOT QUITE AS DISTRACTED BY METRON'S COMPANY AS YOU MIGHT SUPPOSE.
THERE WAS SOMETHING IN THE AIR I FOUND DISQUIETING.
AND THOUGH I COULD NOT PINPOINT THIS SUBTLE DISTURBANCE'S CAUSE...
...I TOOK A CERTAIN PRECAUTIONARY MEASURE.
DARKSEID, MEET MY FALLBACK POSITION!
ORION?!
THE SOUL OF ORION!
NOW, WAS THERE NOT THIS ANCIENT CELESTIAL PROPHECY...

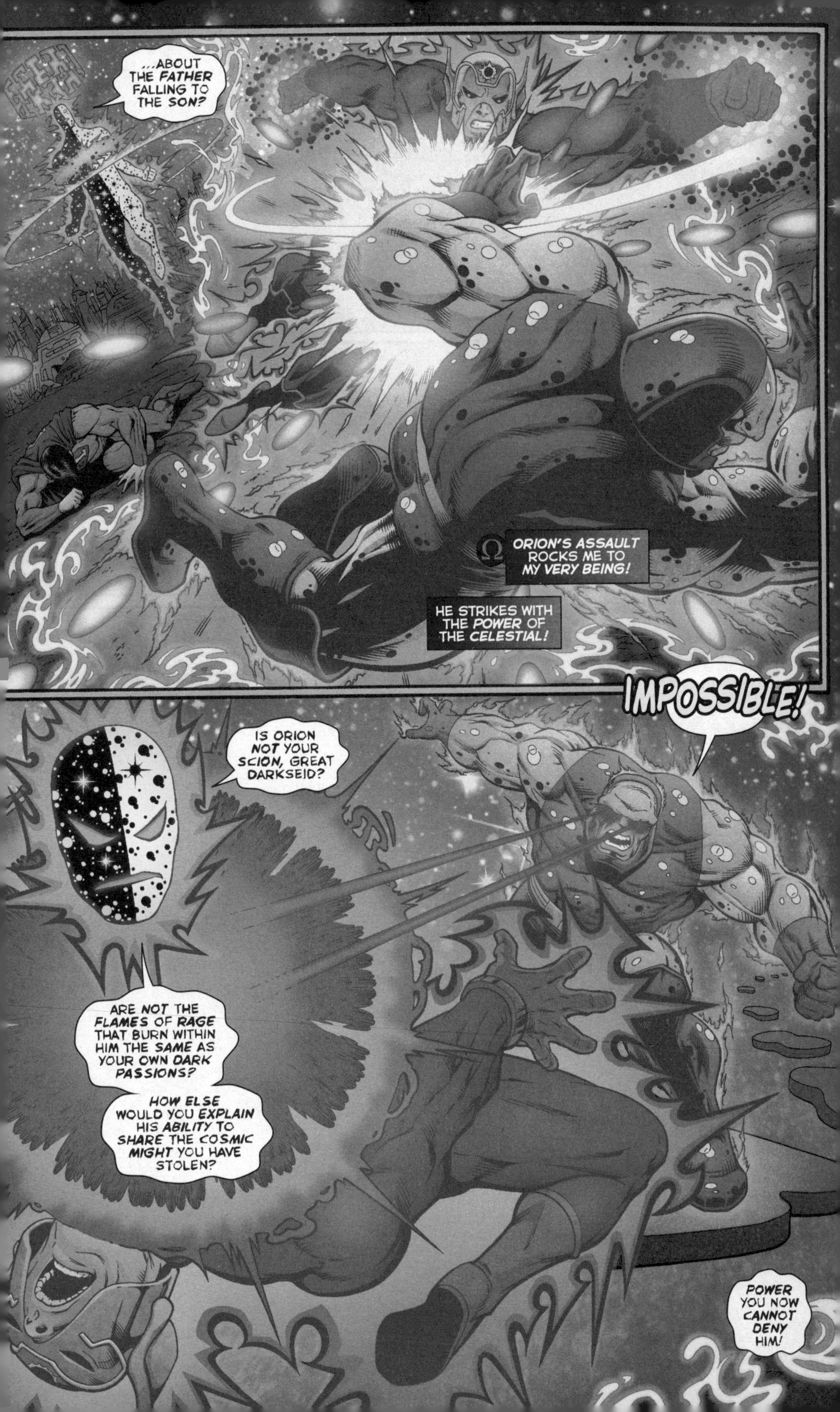
...ABOUT THE FATHER FALLING TO THE SON?
ORION'S ASSAULT ROCKS ME TO MY VERY BEING!
HE STRIKES WITH THE POWER OF THE CELESTIAL!
IMPOSSIBLE!
IS ORION NOT YOUR SCION, GREAT DARKSEID?
ARE NOT THE FLAMES OF RAGE THAT BURN WITHIN HIM THE SAME AS YOUR OWN DARK PASSIONS?
HOW ELSE WOULD YOU EXPLAIN HIS ABILITY TO SHARE THE COSMIC MIGHT YOU HAVE STOLEN?
POWER YOU NOW CANNOT DENY HIM!

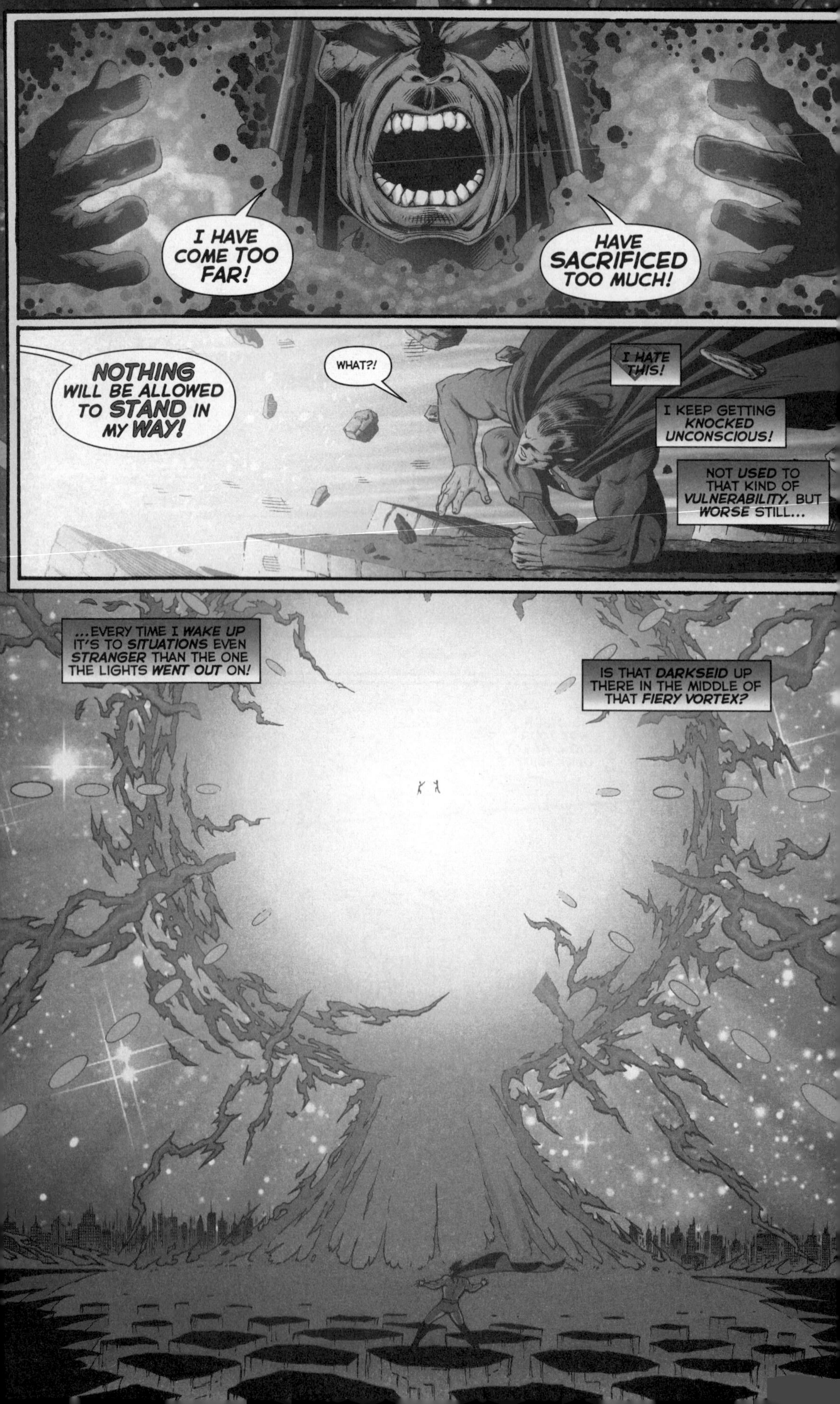
I HAVE COME TOO FAR!
HAVE SACRIFICED TOO MUCH!
NOTHING WILL BE ALLOWED TO STAND IN MY WAY!
WHAT?!
I HATE THIS!
I KEEP GETTING KNOCKED UNCONSCIOUS!
NOT USED TO THAT KIND OF VULNERABILITY. BUT WORSE STILL...
...EVERY TIME I WAKE UP IT'S TO SITUATIONS EVEN STRANGER THAN THE ONE THE LIGHTS WENT OUT ON!
IS THAT DARKSEID UP THERE IN THE MIDDLE OF THAT FIERY VORTEX?

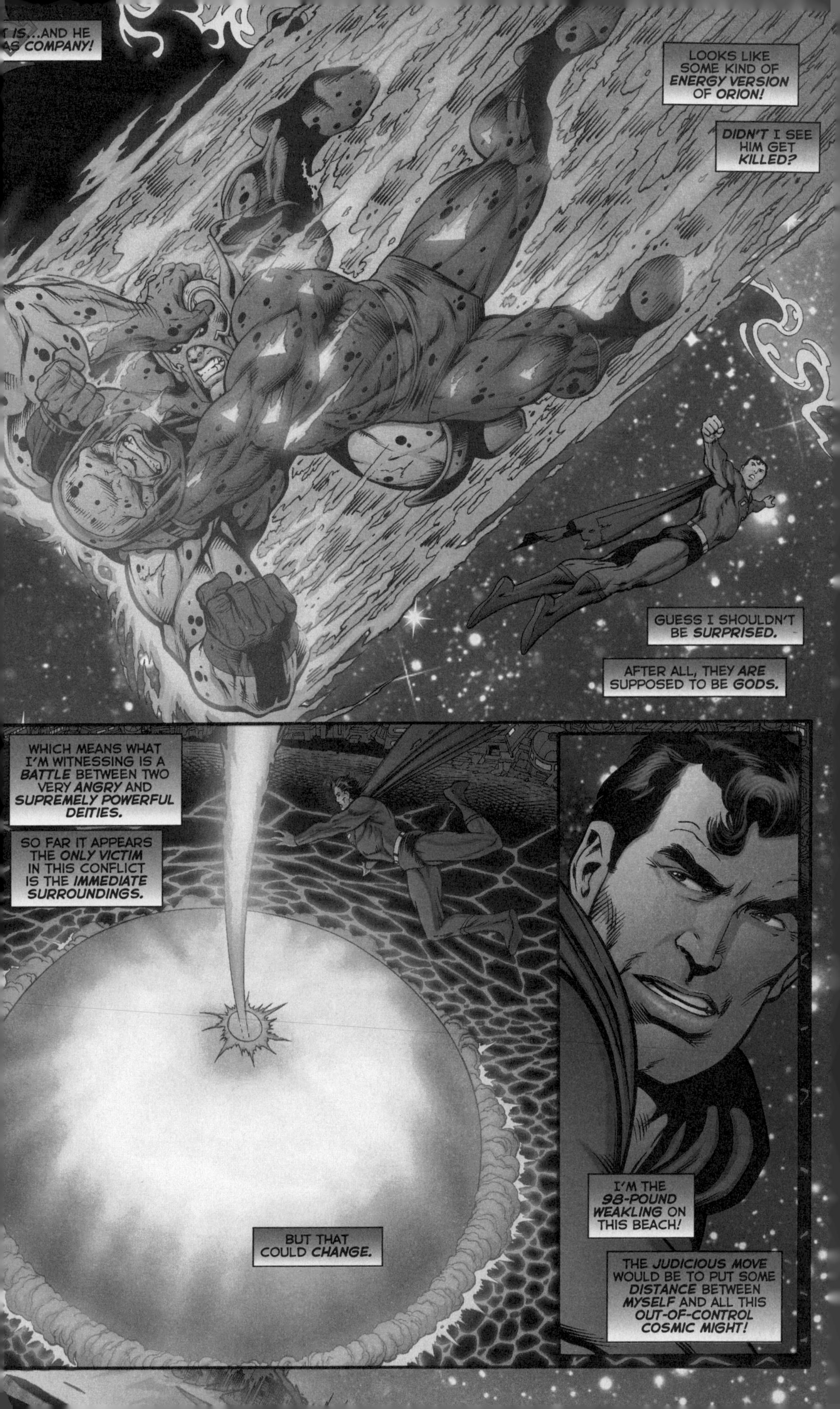

…T IS...AND HE
…AS COMPANY!
LOOKS LIKE SOME KIND OF ENERGY VERSION OF ORION!
DIDN'T I SEE HIM GET KILLED?
GUESS I SHOULDN'T BE SURPRISED.
AFTER ALL, THEY ARE SUPPOSED TO BE GODS.
WHICH MEANS WHAT I'M WITNESSING IS A BATTLE BETWEEN TWO VERY ANGRY AND SUPREMELY POWERFUL DEITIES.
SO FAR IT APPEARS THE ONLY VICTIM IN THIS CONFLICT IS THE IMMEDIATE SURROUNDINGS.
BUT THAT COULD CHANGE.
I'M THE 98-POUND WEAKLING ON THIS BEACH!
THE JUDICIOUS MOVE WOULD BE TO PUT SOME DISTANCE BETWEEN MYSELF AND ALL THIS OUT-OF-CONTROL COSMIC MIGHT!

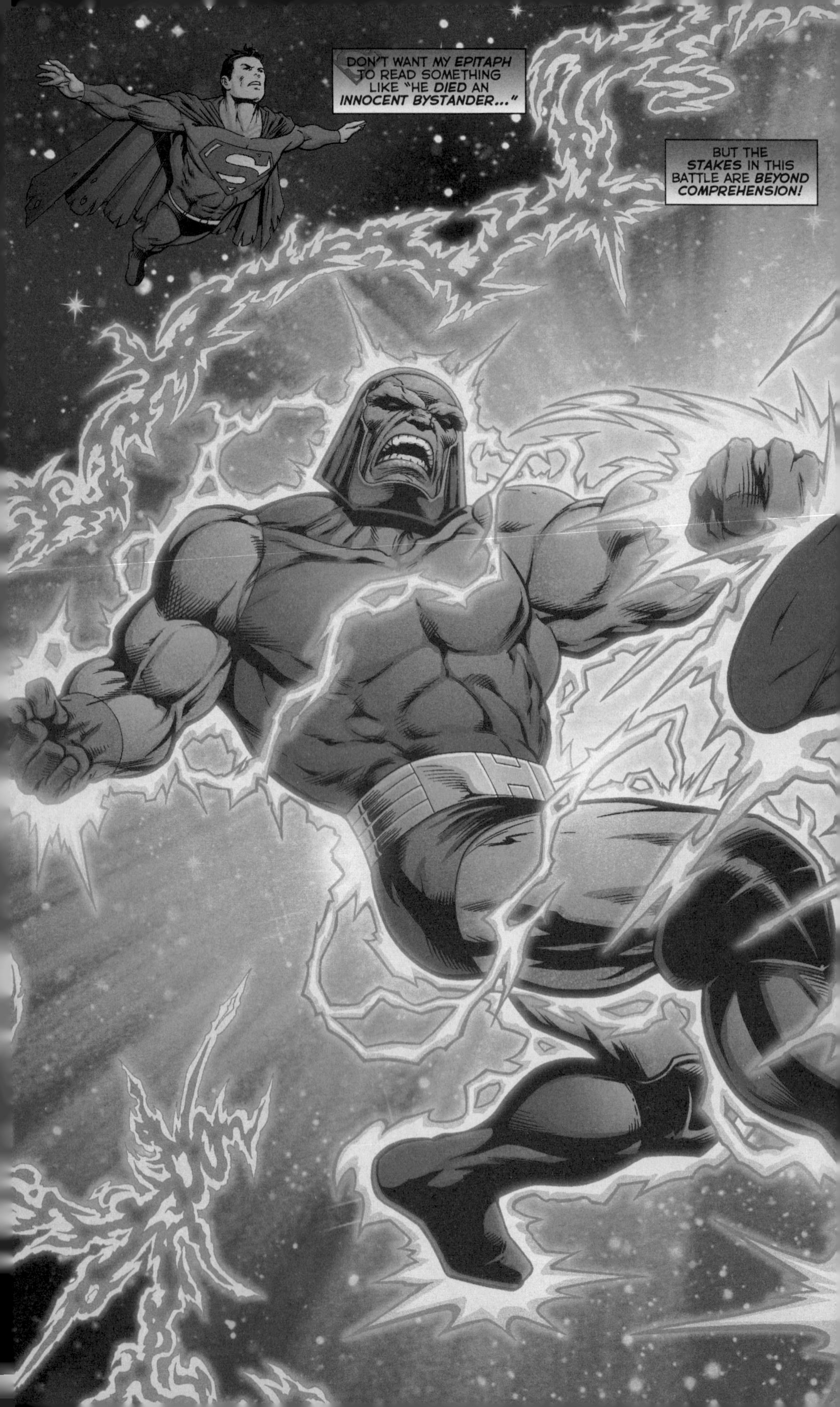

DON'T WANT MY EPITAPH TO READ SOMETHING LIKE "HE DIED AN INNOCENT BYSTANDER..."
BUT THE STAKES IN THIS BATTLE ARE BEYOND COMPREHENSION!

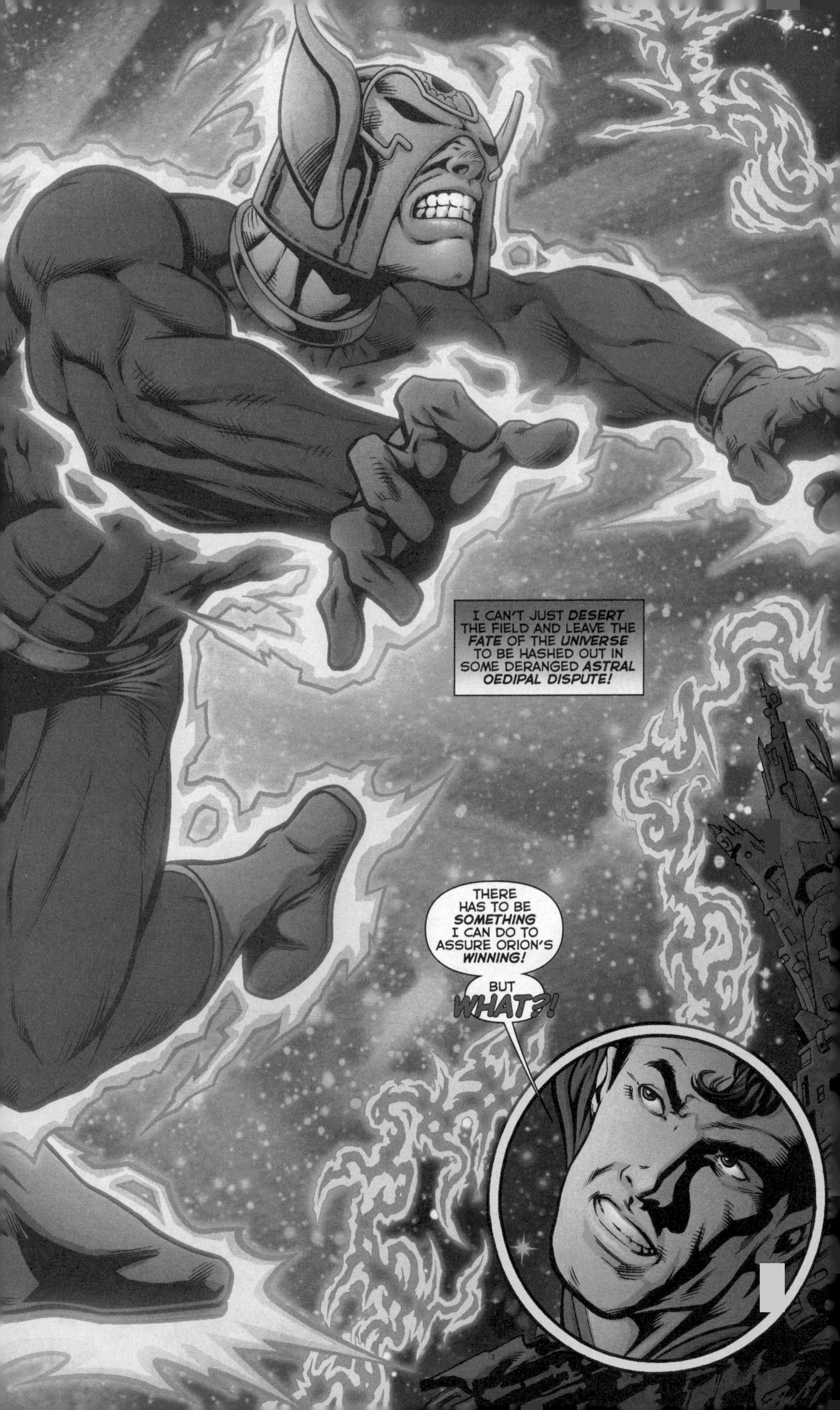
I CAN'T JUST DESERT THE FIELD AND LEAVE THE FATE OF THE UNIVERSE TO BE HASHED OUT IN SOME DERANGED ASTRAL OEDIPAL DISPUTE!
THERE HAS TO BE SOMETHING I CAN DO TO ASSURE ORION'S WINNING!
BUT WHAT?!

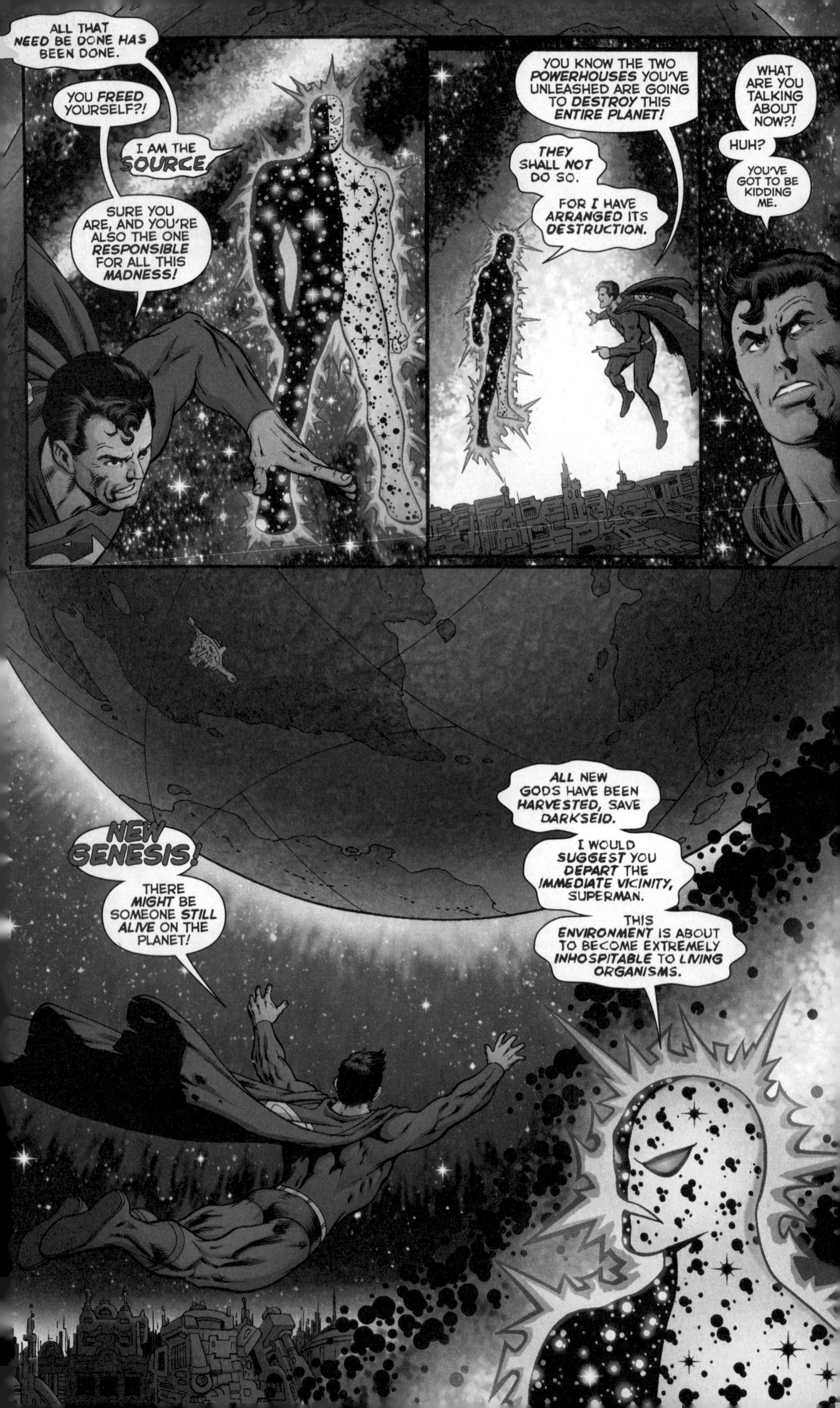
ALL THAT NEED BE DONE HAS BEEN DONE.
YOU FREED YOURSELF?!
I AM THE SOURCE.
SURE YOU ARE, AND YOU'RE ALSO THE ONE RESPONSIBLE FOR ALL THIS MADNESS!
YOU KNOW THE TWO POWERHOUSES YOU'VE UNLEASHED ARE GOING TO DESTROY THIS ENTIRE PLANET!
THEY SHALL NOT DO SO.
FOR I HAVE ARRANGED ITS DESTRUCTION.
WHAT ARE YOU TALKING ABOUT NOW?!
HUH?
YOU'VE GOT TO BE KIDDING ME.
NEW GENESIS!
THERE MIGHT BE SOMEONE STILL ALIVE ON THE PLANET!
ALL NEW GODS HAVE BEEN HARVESTED, SAVE DARKSEID.
I WOULD SUGGEST YOU DEPART THE IMMEDIATE VICINITY, SUPERMAN.
THIS ENVIRONMENT IS ABOUT TO BECOME EXTREMELY INHOSPITABLE TO LIVING ORGANISMS.

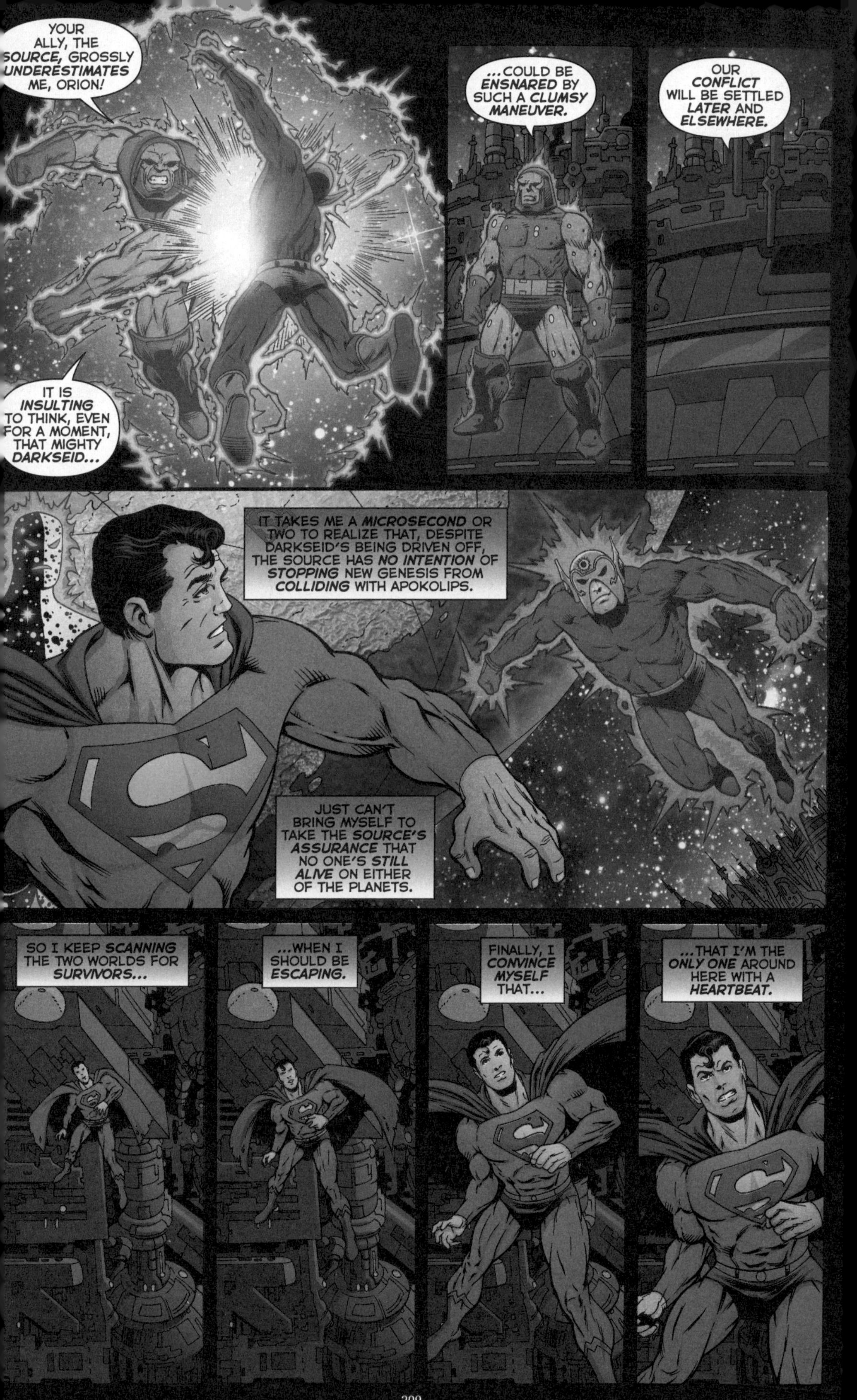
YOUR ALLY, THE SOURCE, GROSSLY UNDERESTIMATES ME, ORION!
IT IS INSULTING TO THINK, EVEN FOR A MOMENT, THAT MIGHTY DARKSEID...
...COULD BE ENSNARED BY SUCH A CLUMSY MANEUVER.
OUR CONFLICT WILL BE SETTLED LATER AND ELSEWHERE.
IT TAKES ME A MICROSECOND OR TWO TO REALIZE THAT, DESPITE DARKSEID'S BEING DRIVEN OFF, THE SOURCE HAS NO INTENTION OF STOPPING NEW GENESIS FROM COLLIDING WITH APOKOLIPS.
JUST CAN'T BRING MYSELF TO TAKE THE SOURCE'S ASSURANCE THAT NO ONE'S STILL ALIVE ON EITHER OF THE PLANETS.
SO I KEEP SCANNING THE TWO WORLDS FOR SURVIVORS...
...WHEN I SHOULD BE ESCAPING.
FINALLY, I CONVINCE MYSELF THAT...
...THAT I'M THE ONLY ONE AROUND HERE WITH A HEARTBEAT.

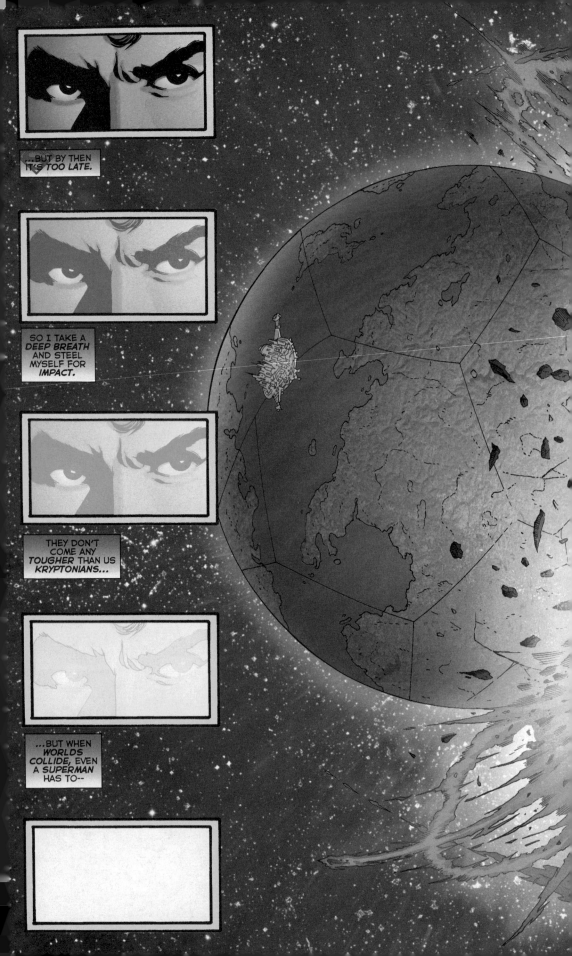

...BUT BY THEN IT'S *TOO LATE.*

SO I TAKE A *DEEP BREATH* AND STEEL MYSELF FOR *IMPACT.*

THEY DON'T COME ANY *TOUGHER* THAN US *KRYPTONIANS...*

...BUT WHEN *WORLDS COLLIDE,* EVEN A *SUPERMAN* HAS TO--

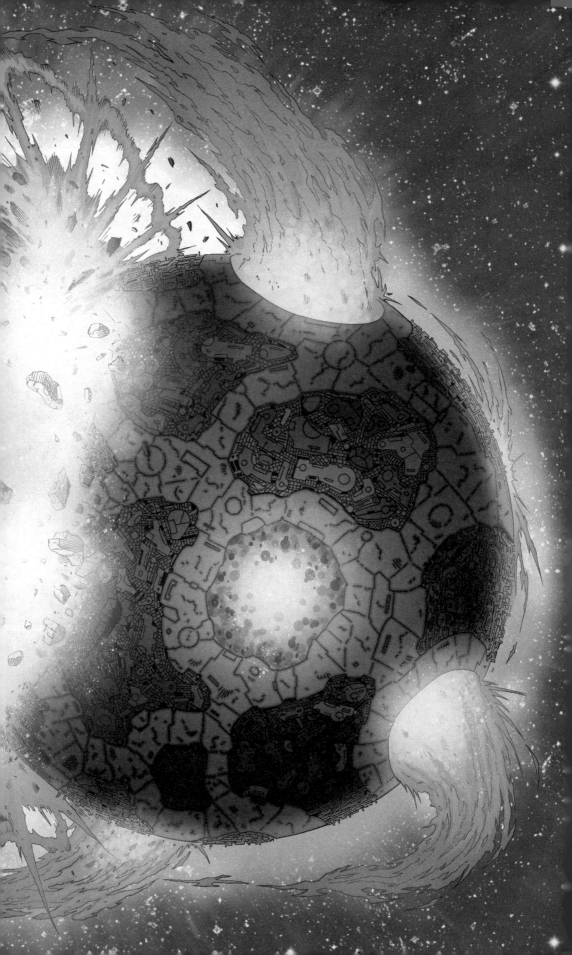

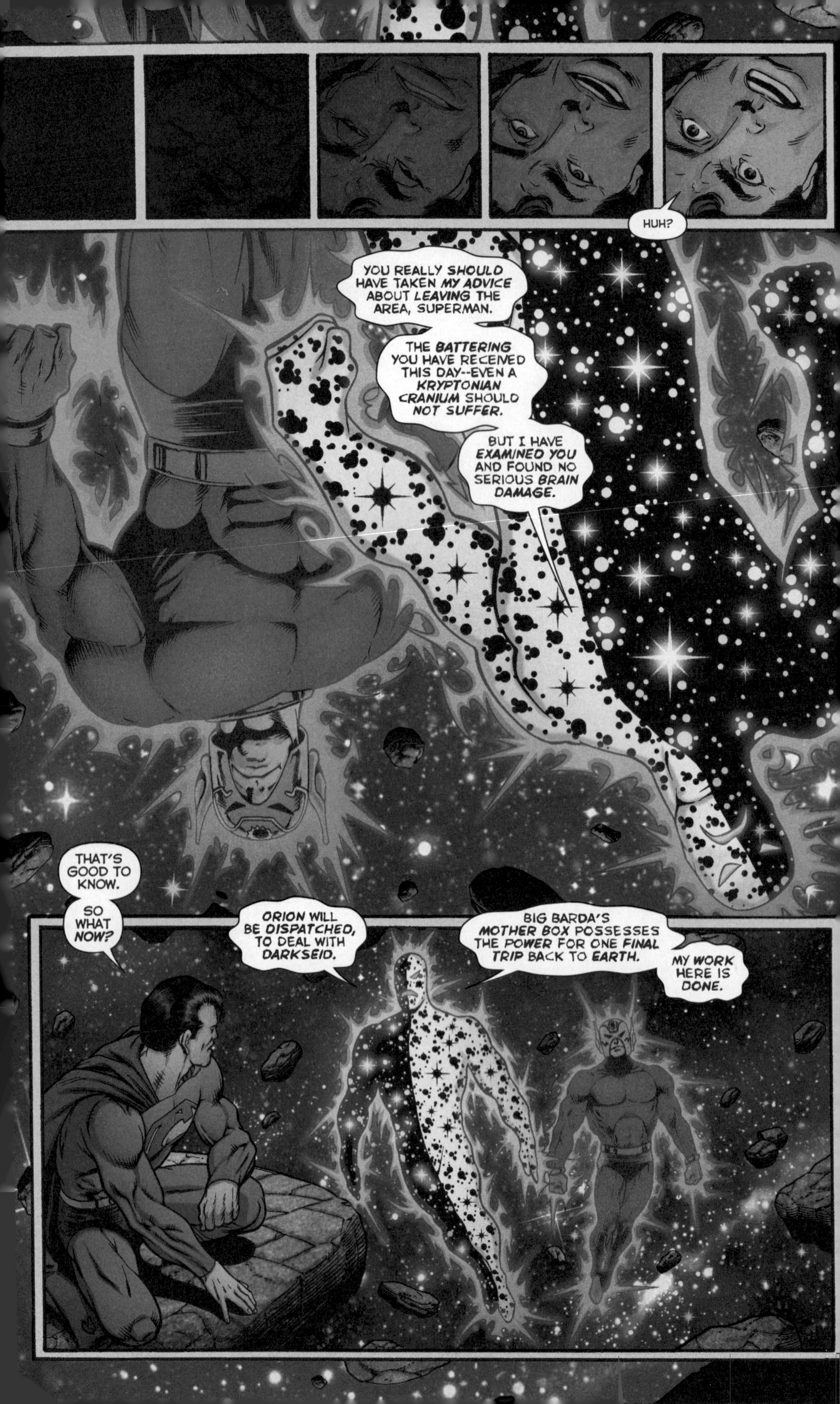

HUH?
YOU REALLY SHOULD HAVE TAKEN MY ADVICE ABOUT LEAVING THE AREA, SUPERMAN.
THE BATTERING YOU HAVE RECEIVED THIS DAY--EVEN A KRYPTONIAN CRANIUM SHOULD NOT SUFFER.
BUT I HAVE EXAMINED YOU AND FOUND NO SERIOUS BRAIN DAMAGE.
THAT'S GOOD TO KNOW.
SO WHAT NOW?
ORION WILL BE DISPATCHED, TO DEAL WITH DARKSEID.
BIG BARDA'S MOTHER BOX POSSESSES THE POWER FOR ONE FINAL TRIP BACK TO EARTH.
MY WORK HERE IS DONE.

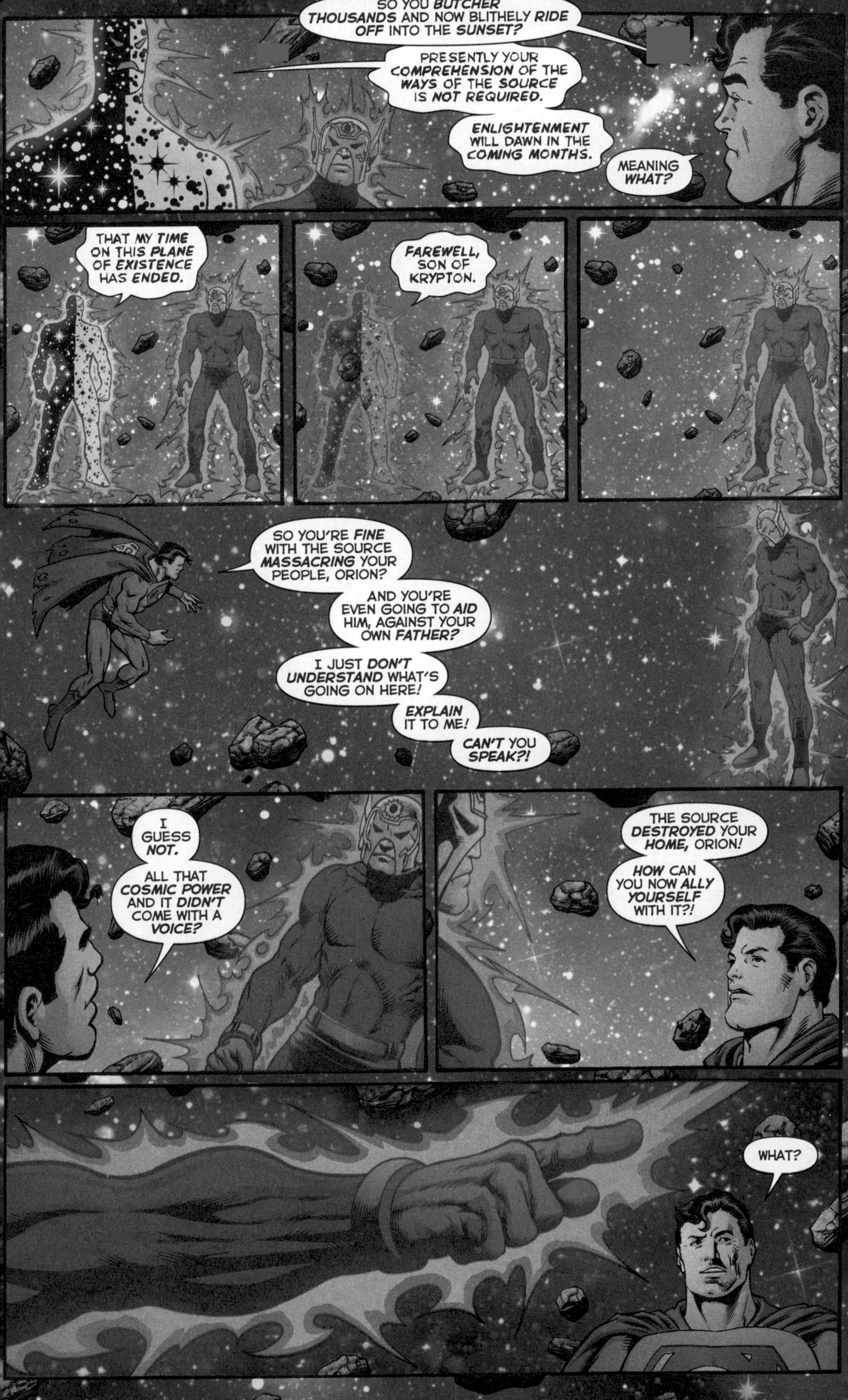
SO YOU BUTCHER THOUSANDS AND NOW BLITHELY RIDE OFF INTO THE SUNSET?
PRESENTLY YOUR COMPREHENSION OF THE WAYS OF THE SOURCE IS NOT REQUIRED.
ENLIGHTENMENT WILL DAWN IN THE COMING MONTHS.
MEANING WHAT?
THAT MY TIME ON THIS PLANE OF EXISTENCE HAS ENDED.
FAREWELL, SON OF KRYPTON.
SO YOU'RE FINE WITH THE SOURCE MASSACRING YOUR PEOPLE, ORION?
AND YOU'RE EVEN GOING TO AID HIM, AGAINST YOUR OWN FATHER?
I JUST DON'T UNDERSTAND WHAT'S GOING ON HERE!
EXPLAIN IT TO ME!
CAN'T YOU SPEAK?!
I GUESS NOT.
ALL THAT COSMIC POWER AND IT DIDN'T COME WITH A VOICE?
THE SOURCE DESTROYED YOUR HOME, ORION!
HOW CAN YOU NOW ALLY YOURSELF WITH IT?!
WHAT?

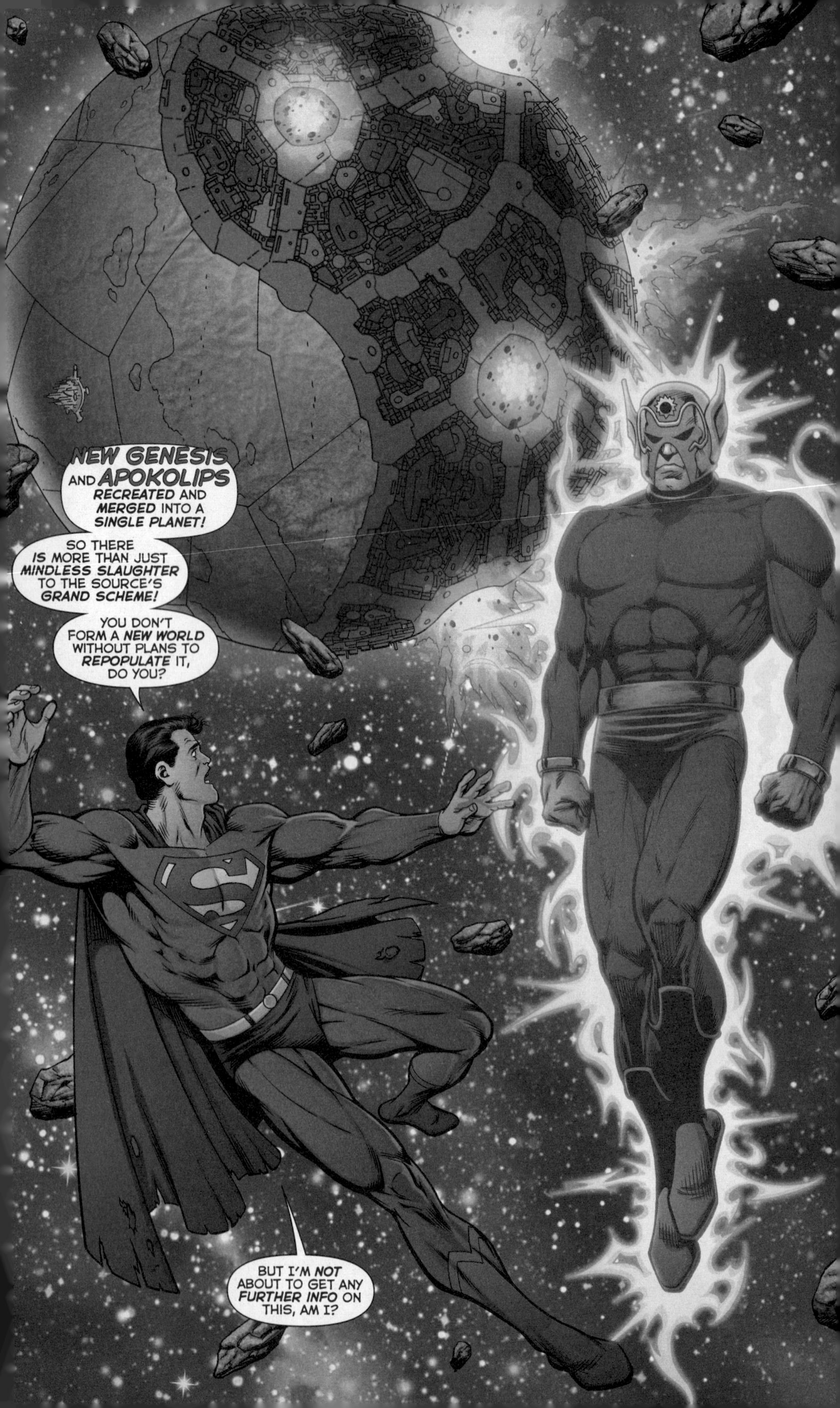
NEW GENESIS AND APOKOLIPS RECREATED AND MERGED INTO A SINGLE PLANET!
SO THERE IS MORE THAN JUST MINDLESS SLAUGHTER TO THE SOURCE'S GRAND SCHEME!
YOU DON'T FORM A NEW WORLD WITHOUT PLANS TO REPOPULATE IT, DO YOU?
BUT I'M NOT ABOUT TO GET ANY FURTHER INFO ON THIS, AM I?

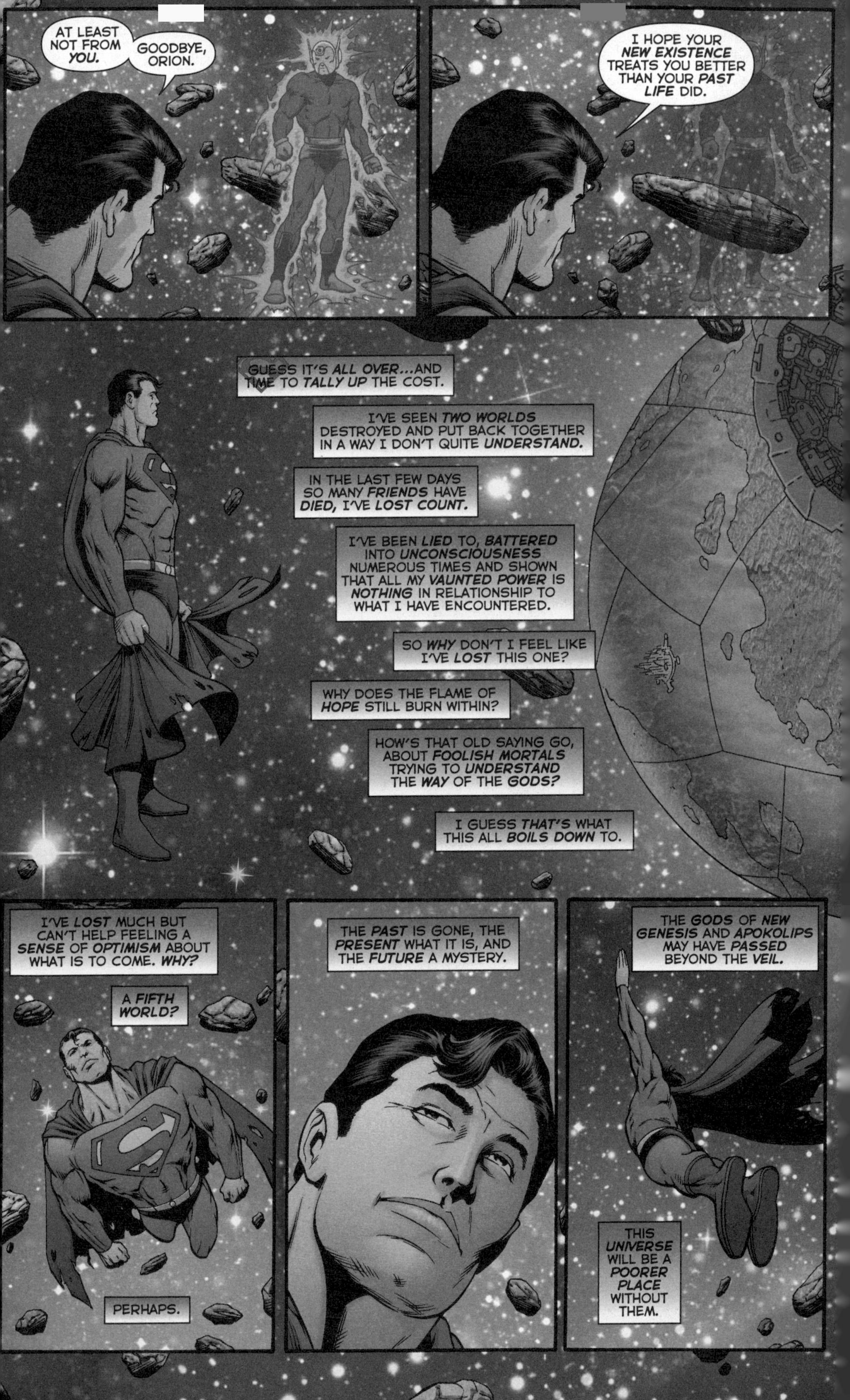
AT LEAST NOT FROM YOU.
GOODBYE, ORION.
I HOPE YOUR NEW EXISTENCE TREATS YOU BETTER THAN YOUR PAST LIFE DID.
GUESS IT'S ALL OVER...AND TIME TO TALLY UP THE COST.
I'VE SEEN TWO WORLDS DESTROYED AND PUT BACK TOGETHER IN A WAY I DON'T QUITE UNDERSTAND.
IN THE LAST FEW DAYS SO MANY FRIENDS HAVE DIED, I'VE LOST COUNT.
I'VE BEEN LIED TO, BATTERED INTO UNCONSCIOUSNESS NUMEROUS TIMES AND SHOWN THAT ALL MY VAUNTED POWER IS NOTHING IN RELATIONSHIP TO WHAT I HAVE ENCOUNTERED.
SO WHY DON'T I FEEL LIKE I'VE LOST THIS ONE?
WHY DOES THE FLAME OF HOPE STILL BURN WITHIN?
HOW'S THAT OLD SAYING GO, ABOUT FOOLISH MORTALS TRYING TO UNDERSTAND THE WAY OF THE GODS?
I GUESS THAT'S WHAT THIS ALL BOILS DOWN TO.
I'VE LOST MUCH BUT CAN'T HELP FEELING A SENSE OF OPTIMISM ABOUT WHAT IS TO COME. WHY?
A FIFTH WORLD?
PERHAPS.
THE PAST IS GONE, THE PRESENT WHAT IT IS, AND THE FUTURE A MYSTERY.
THE GODS OF NEW GENESIS AND APOKOLIPS MAY HAVE PASSED BEYOND THE VEIL.
THIS UNIVERSE WILL BE A POORER PLACE WITHOUT THEM.

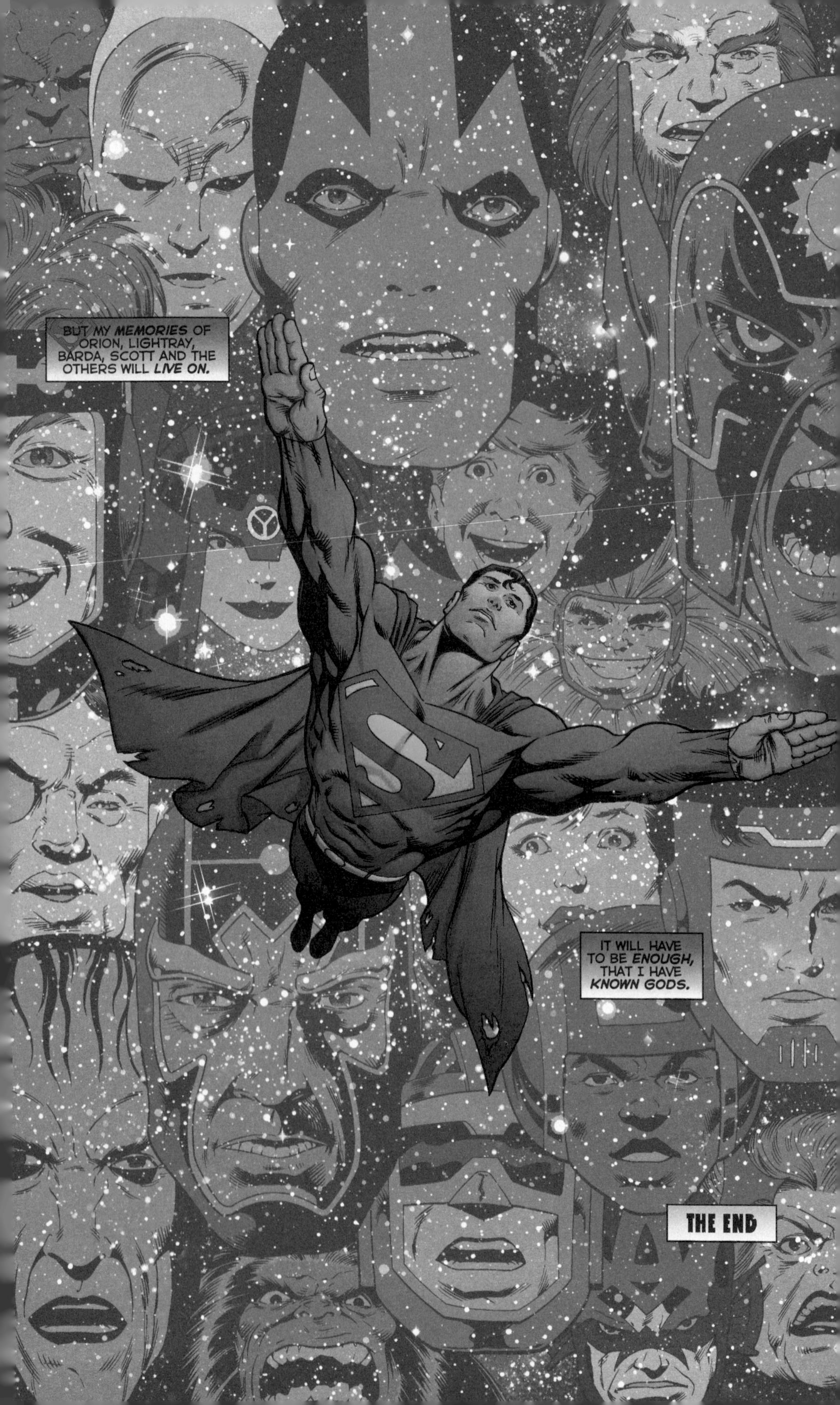
BUT MY *MEMORIES* OF ORION, LIGHTRAY, BARDA, SCOTT AND THE OTHERS WILL *LIVE ON.*
IT WILL HAVE TO BE *ENOUGH,* THAT I HAVE *KNOWN GODS.*
THE END

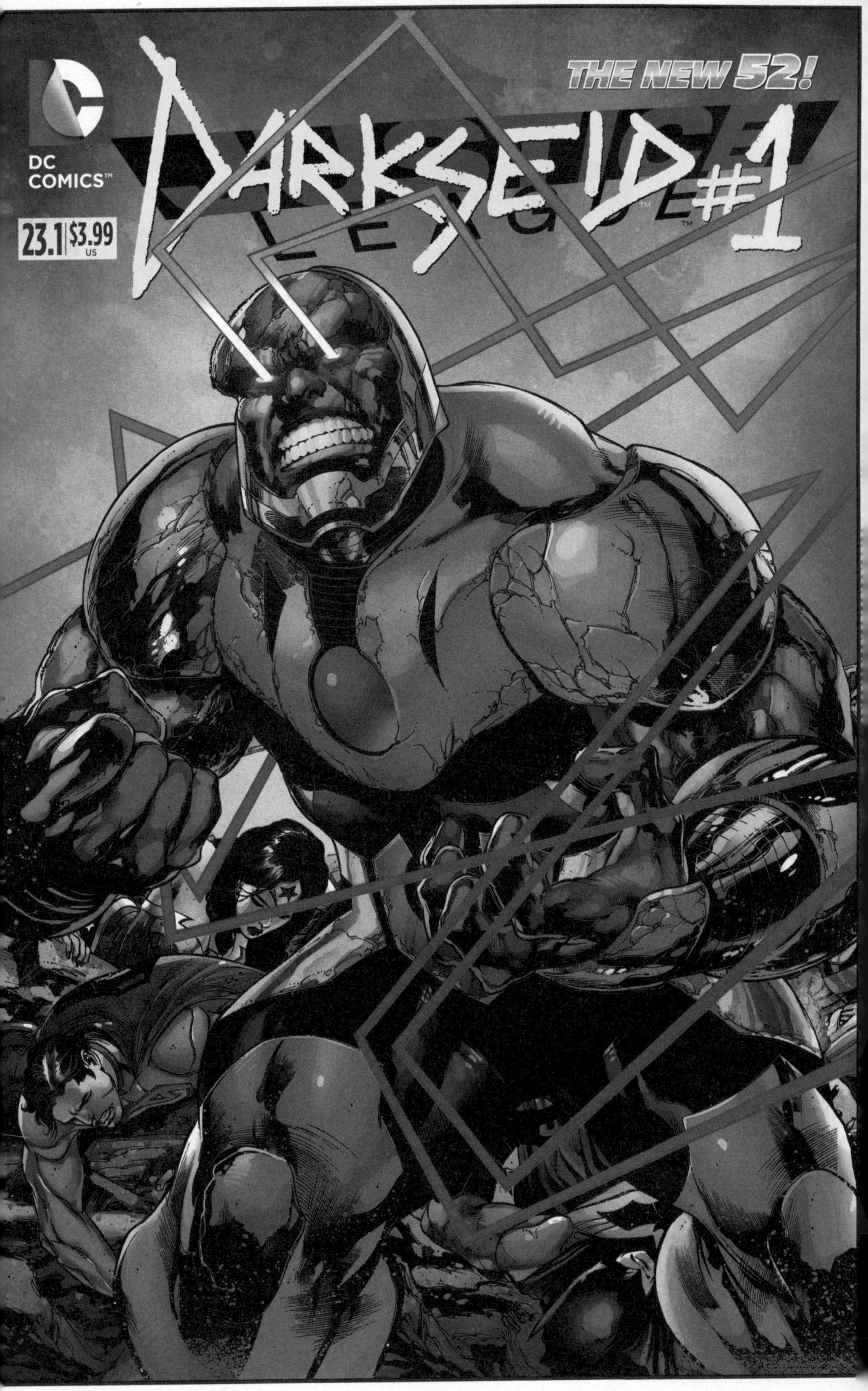

DC COMICS
THE NEW 52!
DARKSEID #1
JUSTICE LEAGUE
23.1 $3.99 US

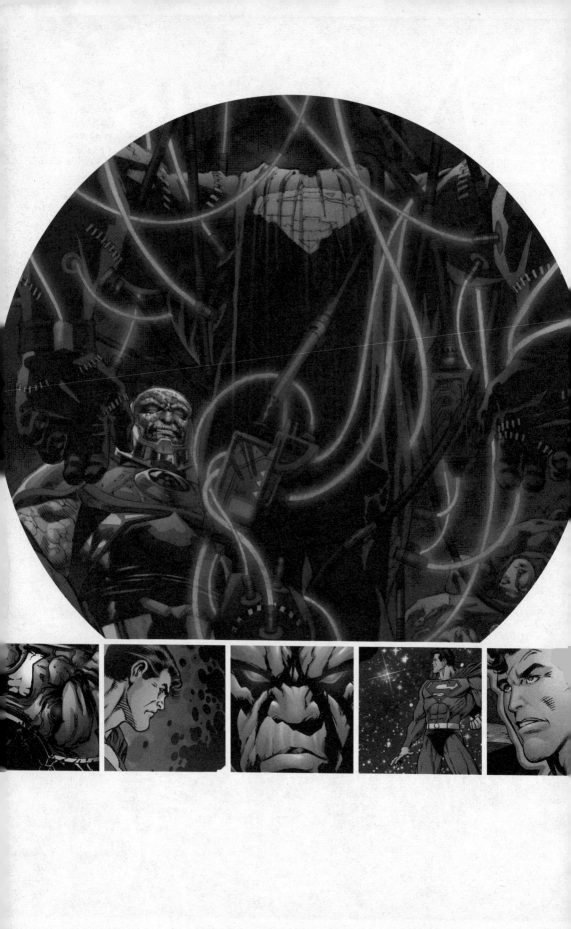

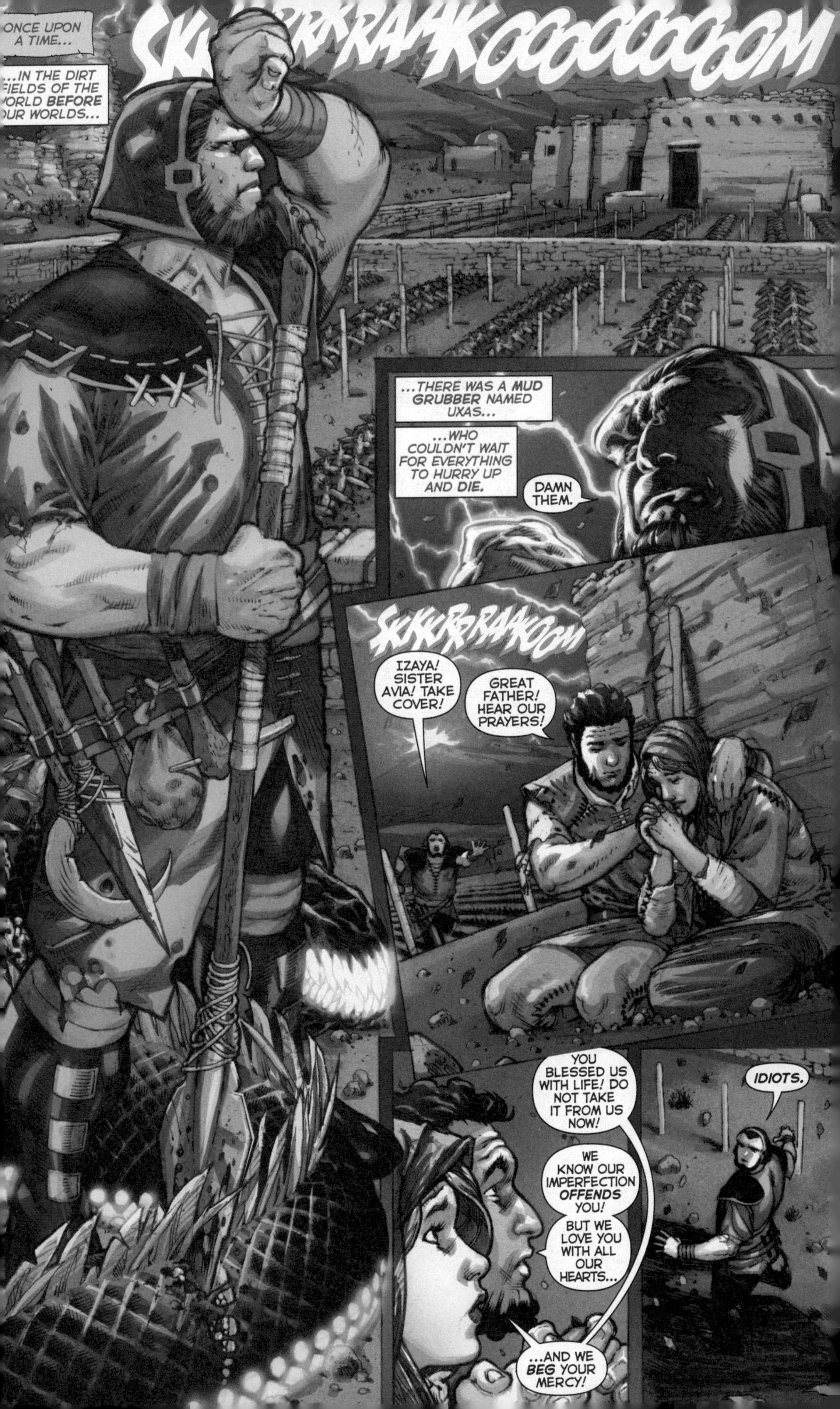

ONCE UPON A TIME...
...IN THE DIRT FIELDS OF THE WORLD BEFORE OUR WORLDS...
SKKRRKRAKKOOOOOOOOOM
...THERE WAS A MUD GRUBBER NAMED UXAS...
...WHO COULDN'T WAIT FOR EVERYTHING TO HURRY UP AND DIE.
DAMN THEM.
SKKKRRRAKKOOM
IZAYA! SISTER AVIA! TAKE COVER!
GREAT FATHER! HEAR OUR PRAYERS!
YOU BLESSED US WITH LIFE! DO NOT TAKE IT FROM US NOW!
WE KNOW OUR IMPERFECTION OFFENDS YOU!
BUT WE LOVE YOU WITH ALL OUR HEARTS...
...AND WE BEG YOUR MERCY!
IDIOTS.

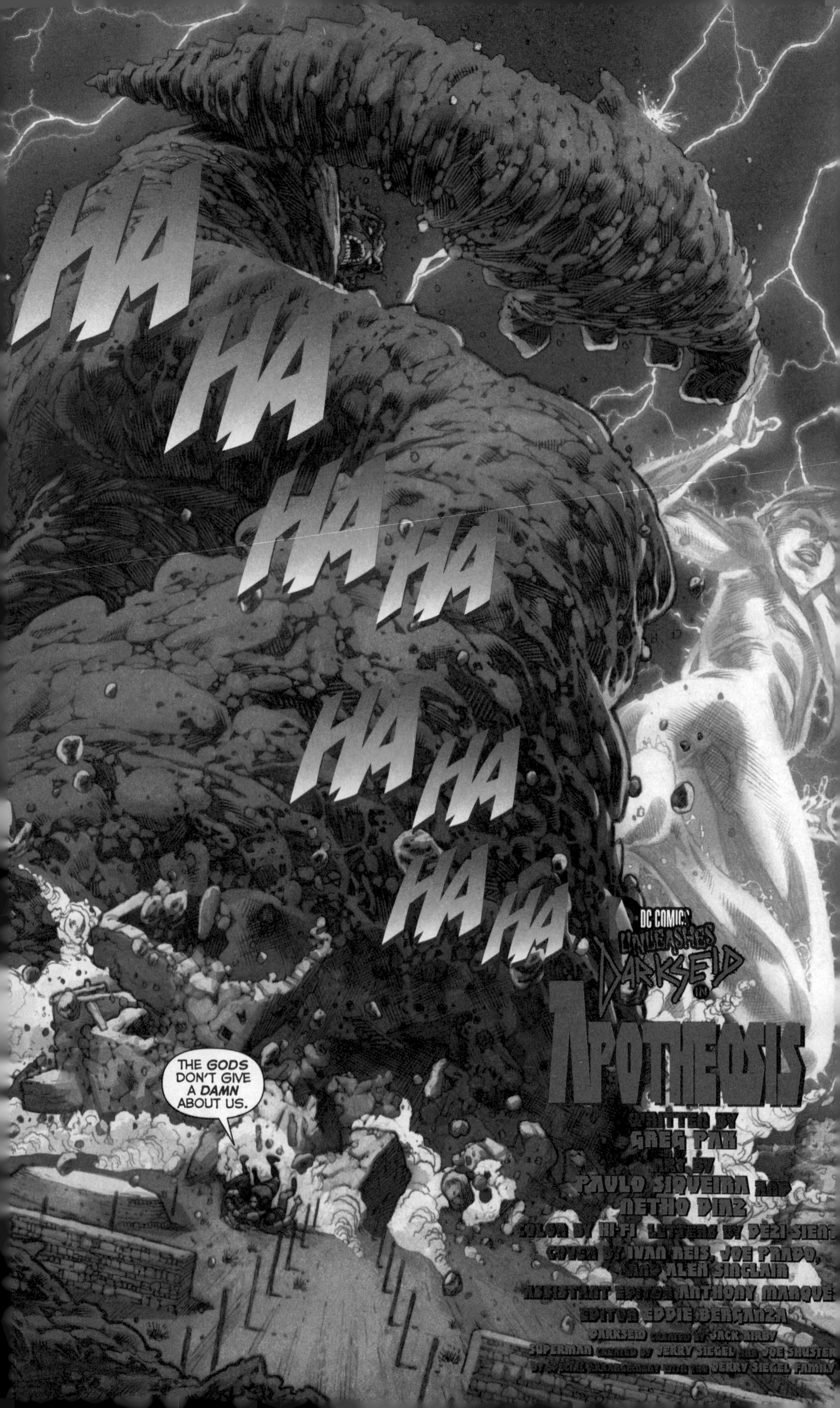
HA HA HA HA HA HA HA HA
THE GODS DON'T GIVE A DAMN ABOUT US.
DC COMICS UNLEASHES DARKSEID IN
APOTHEOSIS
WRITTEN BY GREG PAK
ART BY PAULO SIQUEIRA AND NETHO DIAZ
COLOR BY HI-FI LETTERS BY DEZI SIENT
COVER BY IVAN REIS, JOE PRADO, AND ALEX SINCLAIR
ASSISTANT EDITOR ANTHONY MARQUE
EDITOR EDDIE BERGANZA
DARKSEID CREATED BY JACK KIRBY
SUPERMAN CREATED BY JERRY SIEGEL AND JOE SHUSTER
JERRY SIEGEL FAMILY

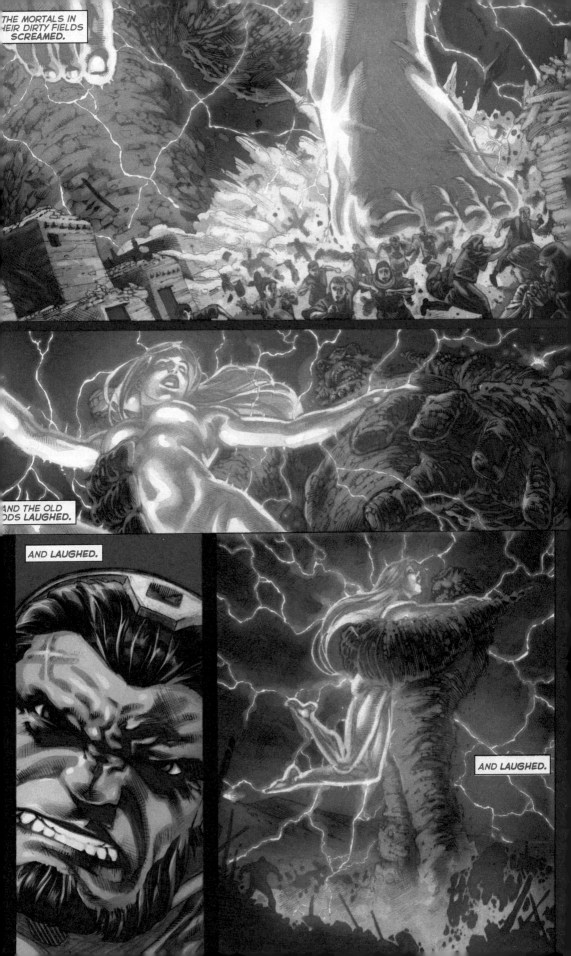

THE MORTALS IN THEIR DIRTY FIELDS SCREAMED.

AND THE OLD GODS LAUGHED.

AND LAUGHED.

AND LAUGHED.

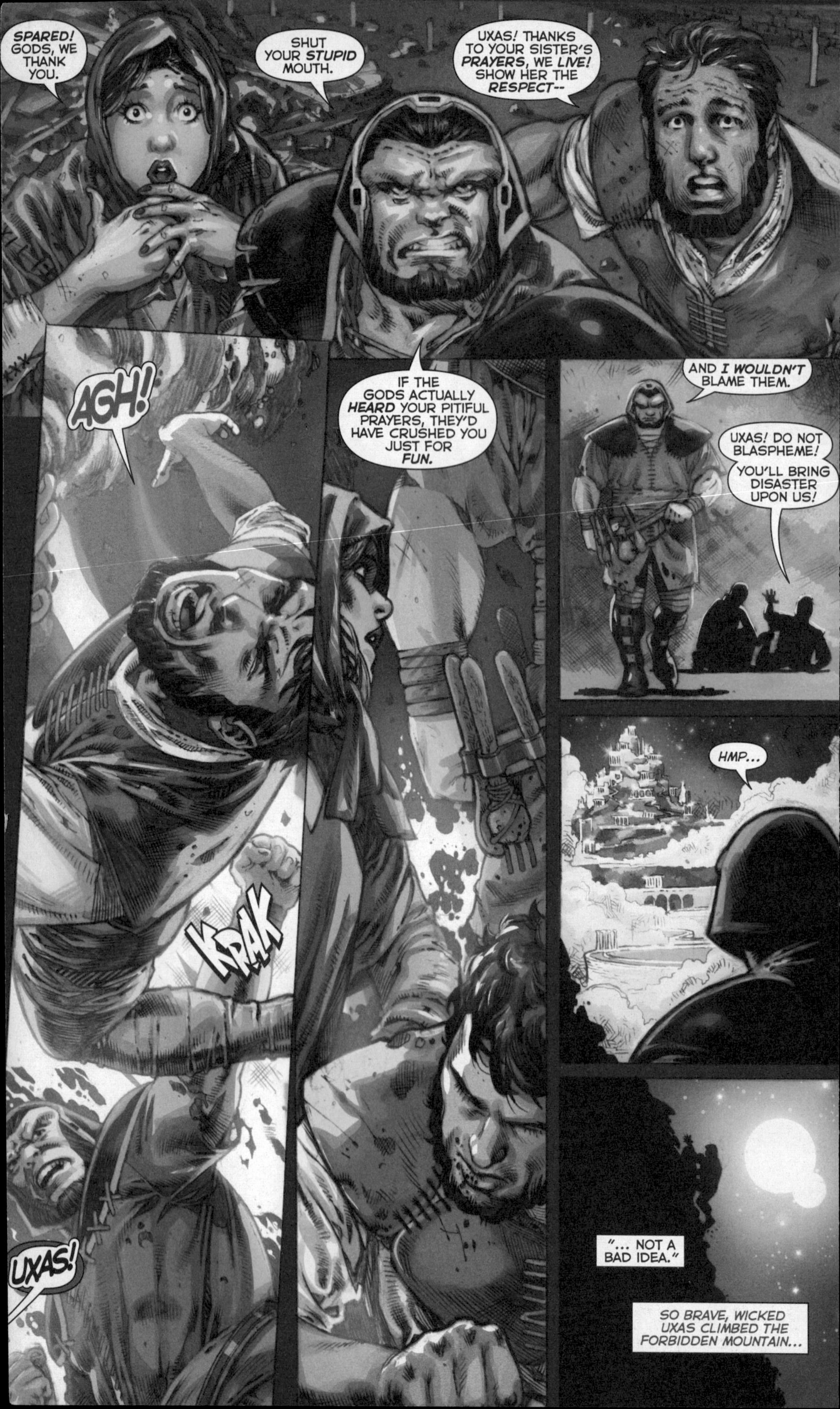
SPARED! GODS, WE THANK YOU.
SHUT YOUR STUPID MOUTH.
UXAS! THANKS TO YOUR SISTER'S PRAYERS, WE LIVE! SHOW HER THE RESPECT--
AGH!
KRAK
UXAS!
IF THE GODS ACTUALLY HEARD YOUR PITIFUL PRAYERS, THEY'D HAVE CRUSHED YOU JUST FOR FUN.
AND I WOULDN'T BLAME THEM.
UXAS! DO NOT BLASPHEME!
YOU'LL BRING DISASTER UPON US!
HMP...
"... NOT A BAD IDEA."
SO BRAVE, WICKED UXAS CLIMBED THE FORBIDDEN MOUNTAIN...

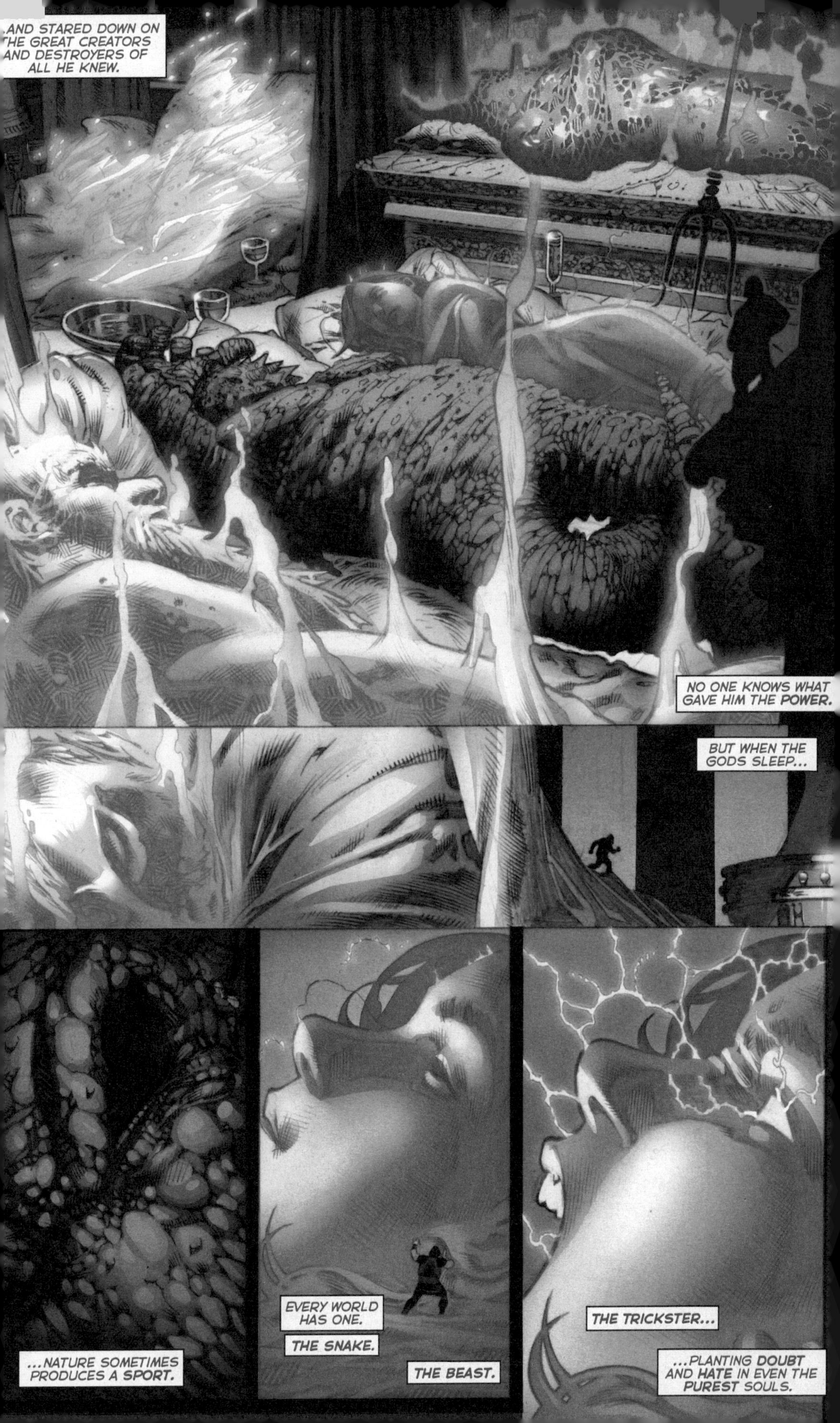
AND STARED DOWN ON THE GREAT CREATORS AND DESTROYERS OF ALL HE KNEW.
NO ONE KNOWS WHAT GAVE HIM THE POWER.
BUT WHEN THE GODS SLEEP...
...NATURE SOMETIMES PRODUCES A SPORT.
EVERY WORLD HAS ONE.
THE SNAKE.
THE BEAST.
THE TRICKSTER...
...PLANTING DOUBT AND HATE IN EVEN THE PUREST SOULS.

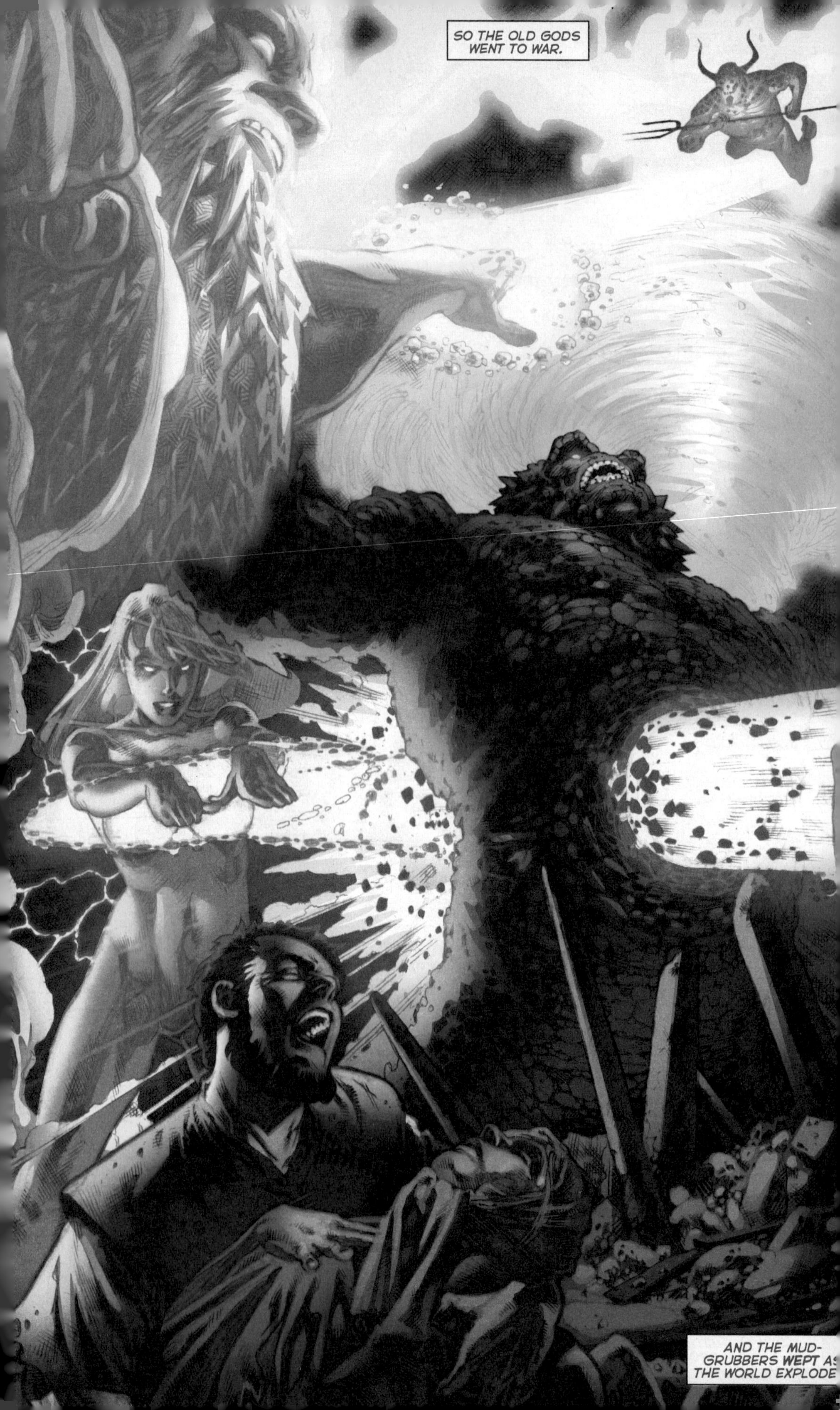
SO THE OLD GODS WENT TO WAR.
AND THE MUD-GRUBBERS WEPT AS THE WORLD EXPLODE

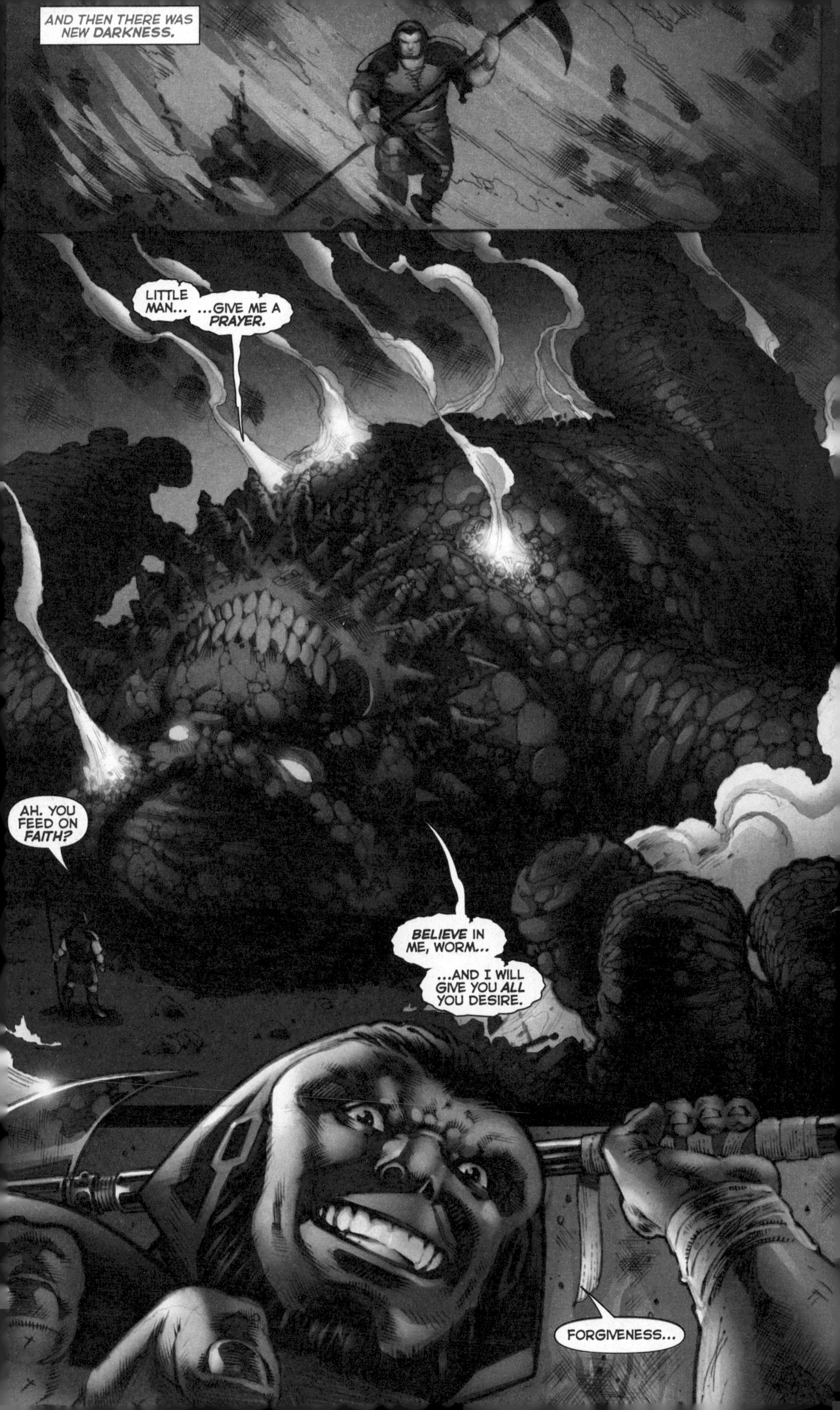
AND THEN THERE WAS NEW DARKNESS.
LITTLE MAN...
...GIVE ME A PRAYER.
AH. YOU FEED ON FAITH?
BELIEVE IN ME, WORM...
...AND I WILL GIVE YOU ALL YOU DESIRE.
FORGIVENESS...

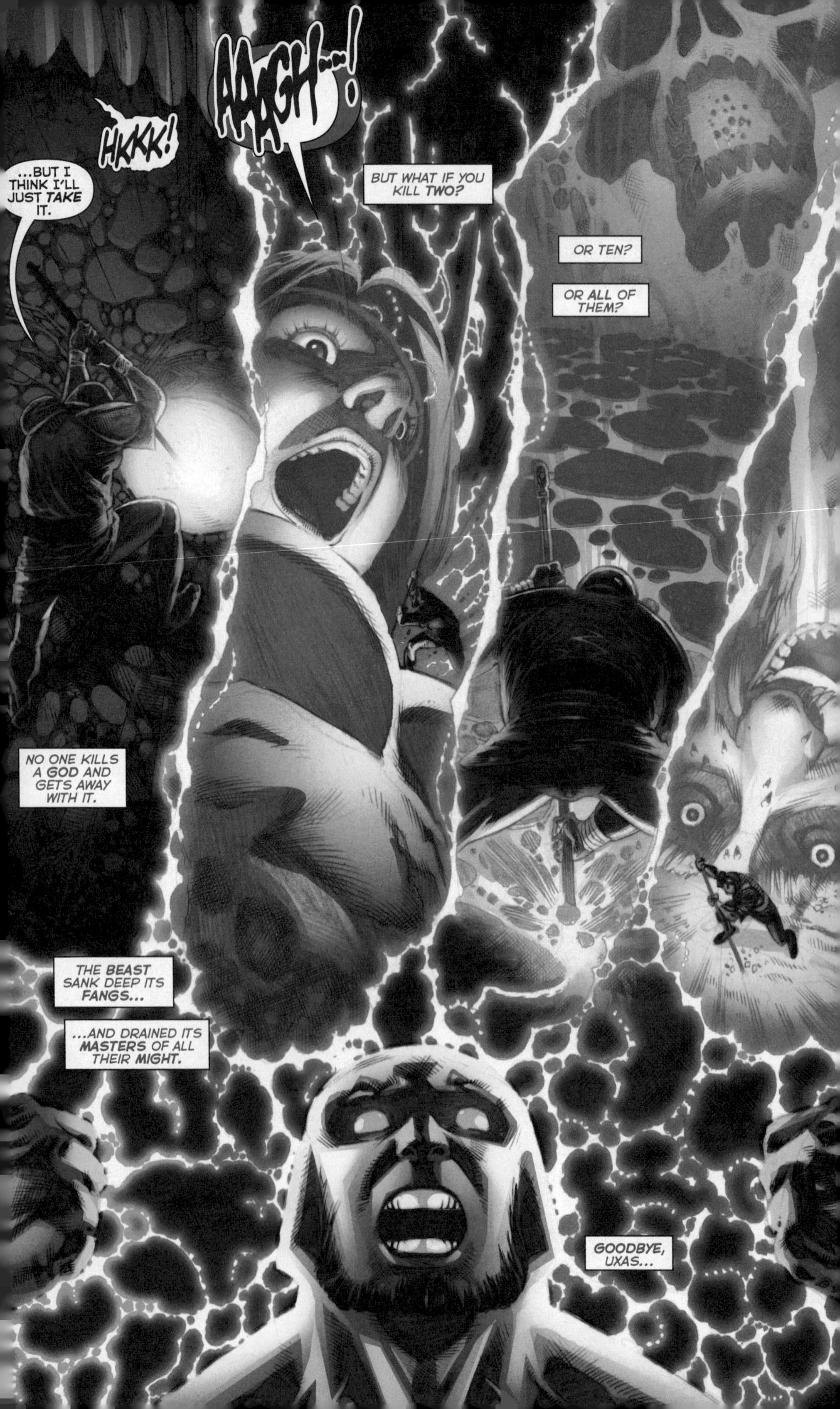
HKKK!
AAAGH...!
...BUT I THINK I'LL JUST TAKE IT.
BUT WHAT IF YOU KILL TWO?
OR TEN?
OR ALL OF THEM?
NO ONE KILLS A GOD AND GETS AWAY WITH IT.
THE BEAST SANK DEEP ITS FANGS...
...AND DRAINED ITS MASTERS OF ALL THEIR MIGHT.
GOODBYE, UXAS...

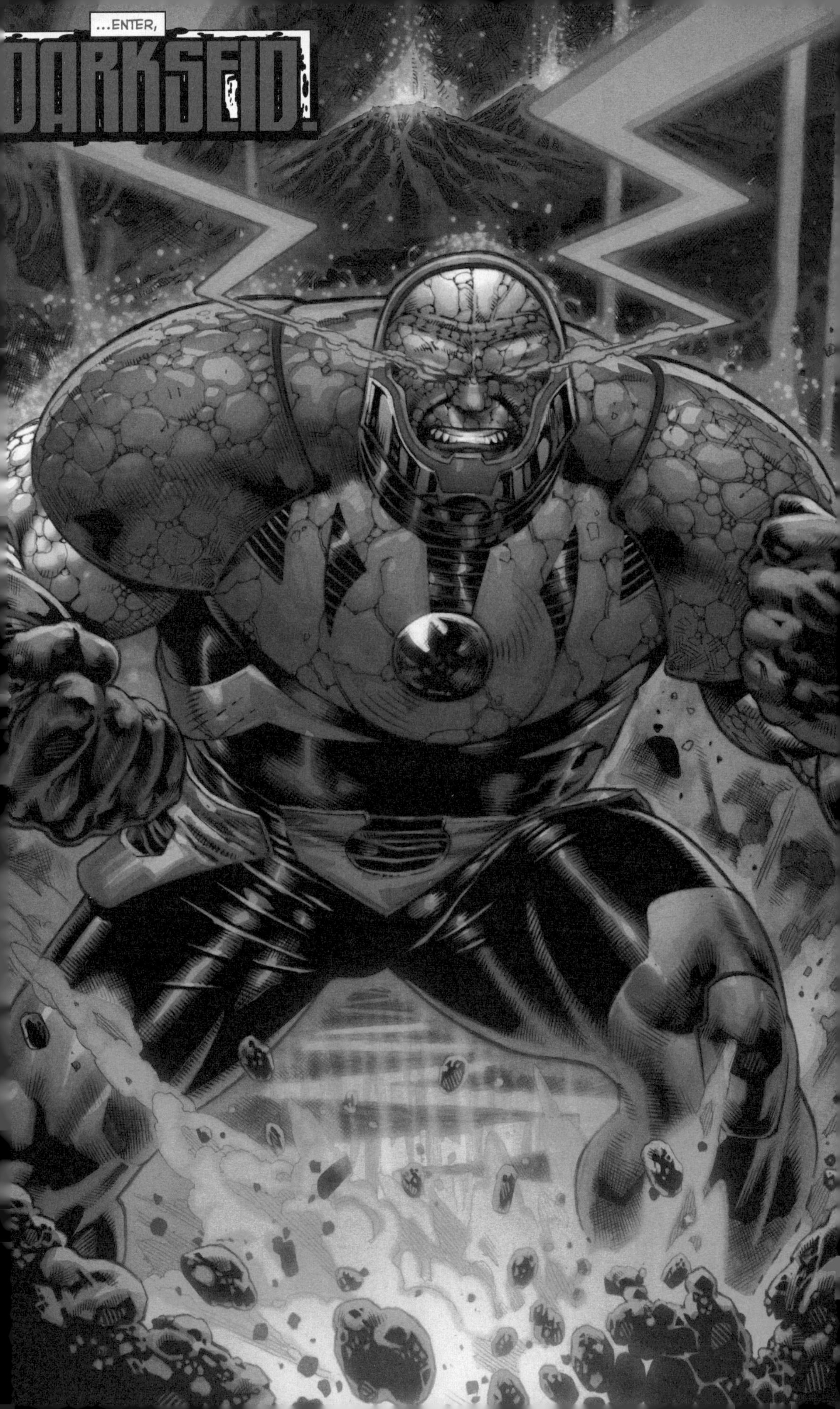

...ENTER,
DARKSEID!

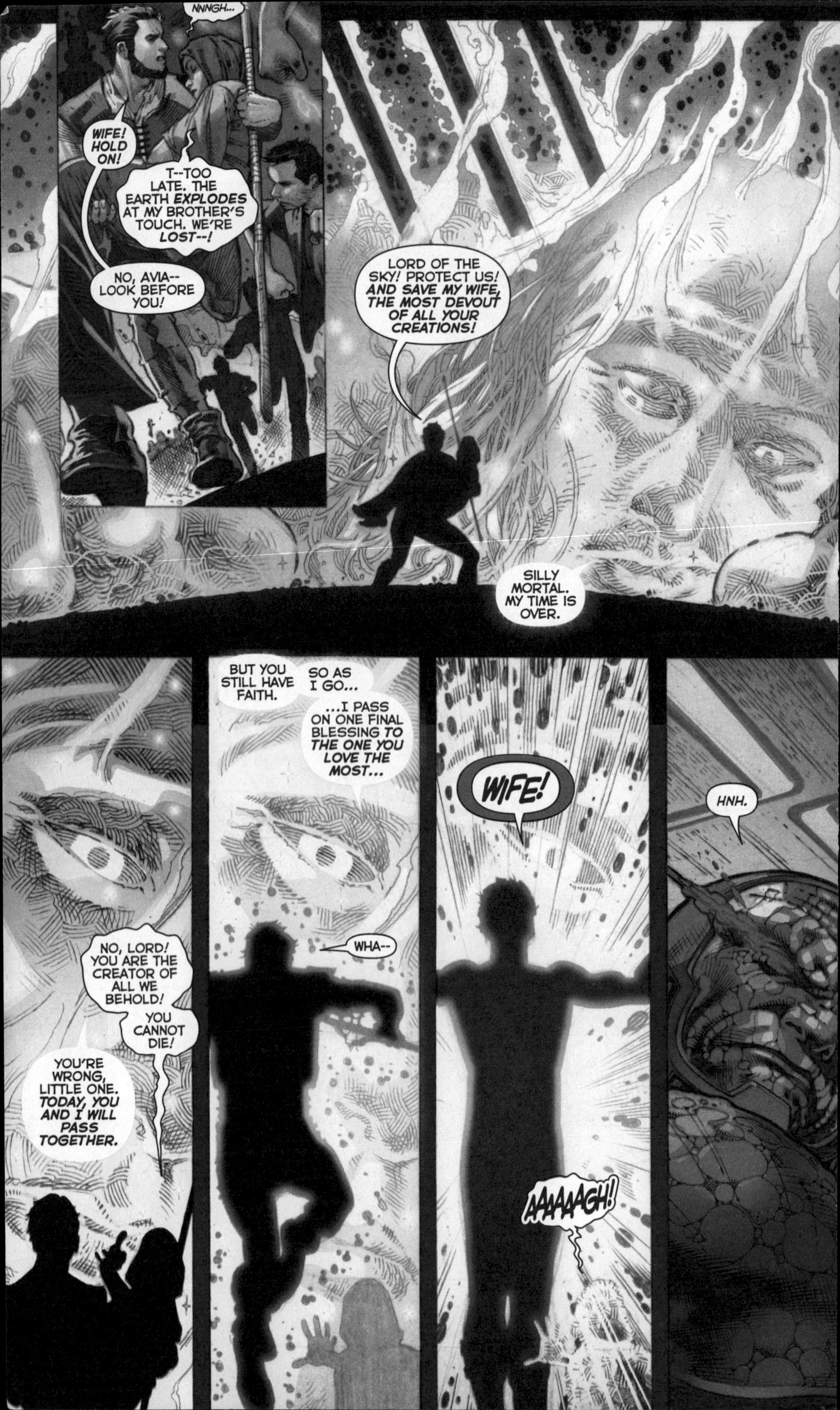
NNNGH...
WIFE! HOLD ON!
T--TOO LATE. THE EARTH EXPLODES AT MY BROTHER'S TOUCH. WE'RE LOST--!
NO, AVIA-- LOOK BEFORE YOU!
LORD OF THE SKY! PROTECT US! AND SAVE MY WIFE, THE MOST DEVOUT OF ALL YOUR CREATIONS!
SILLY MORTAL. MY TIME IS OVER.
NO, LORD! YOU ARE THE CREATOR OF ALL WE BEHOLD!
YOU CANNOT DIE!
YOU'RE WRONG, LITTLE ONE. TODAY, YOU AND I WILL PASS TOGETHER.
BUT YOU STILL HAVE FAITH.
SO AS I GO...
...I PASS ON ONE FINAL BLESSING TO THE ONE YOU LOVE THE MOST...
WHA--
WIFE!
AAAAAAGH!
HNH.

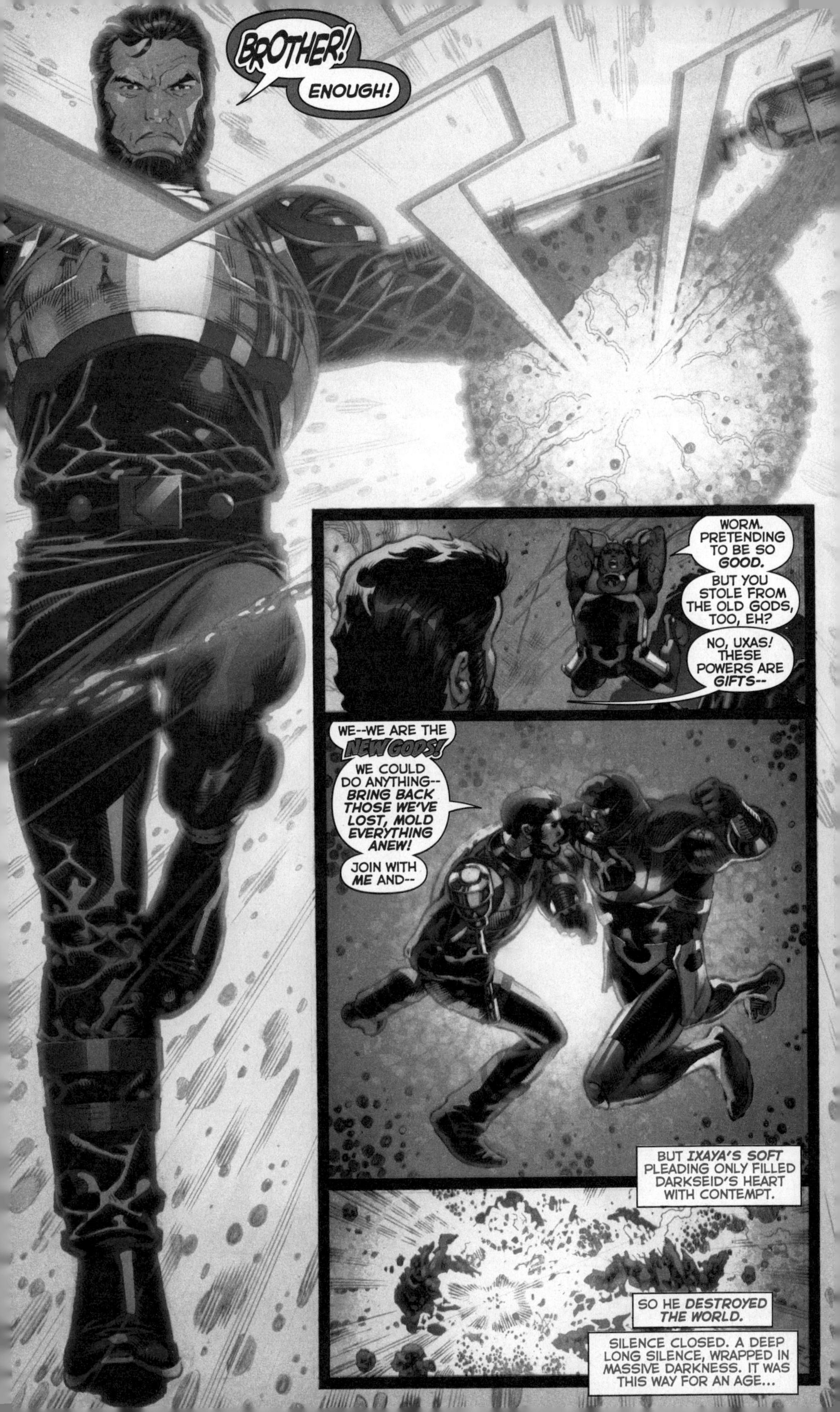
BROTHER! ENOUGH!
WORM. PRETENDING TO BE SO GOOD.
BUT YOU STOLE FROM THE OLD GODS, TOO, EH?
NO, UXAS! THESE POWERS ARE GIFTS--
WE--WE ARE THE NEW GODS!
WE COULD DO ANYTHING-- BRING BACK THOSE WE'VE LOST, MOLD EVERYTHING ANEW!
JOIN WITH ME AND--
BUT IXAYA'S SOFT PLEADING ONLY FILLED DARKSEID'S HEART WITH CONTEMPT.
SO HE DESTROYED THE WORLD.
SILENCE CLOSED. A DEEP LONG SILENCE, WRAPPED IN MASSIVE DARKNESS. IT WAS THIS WAY FOR AN AGE...

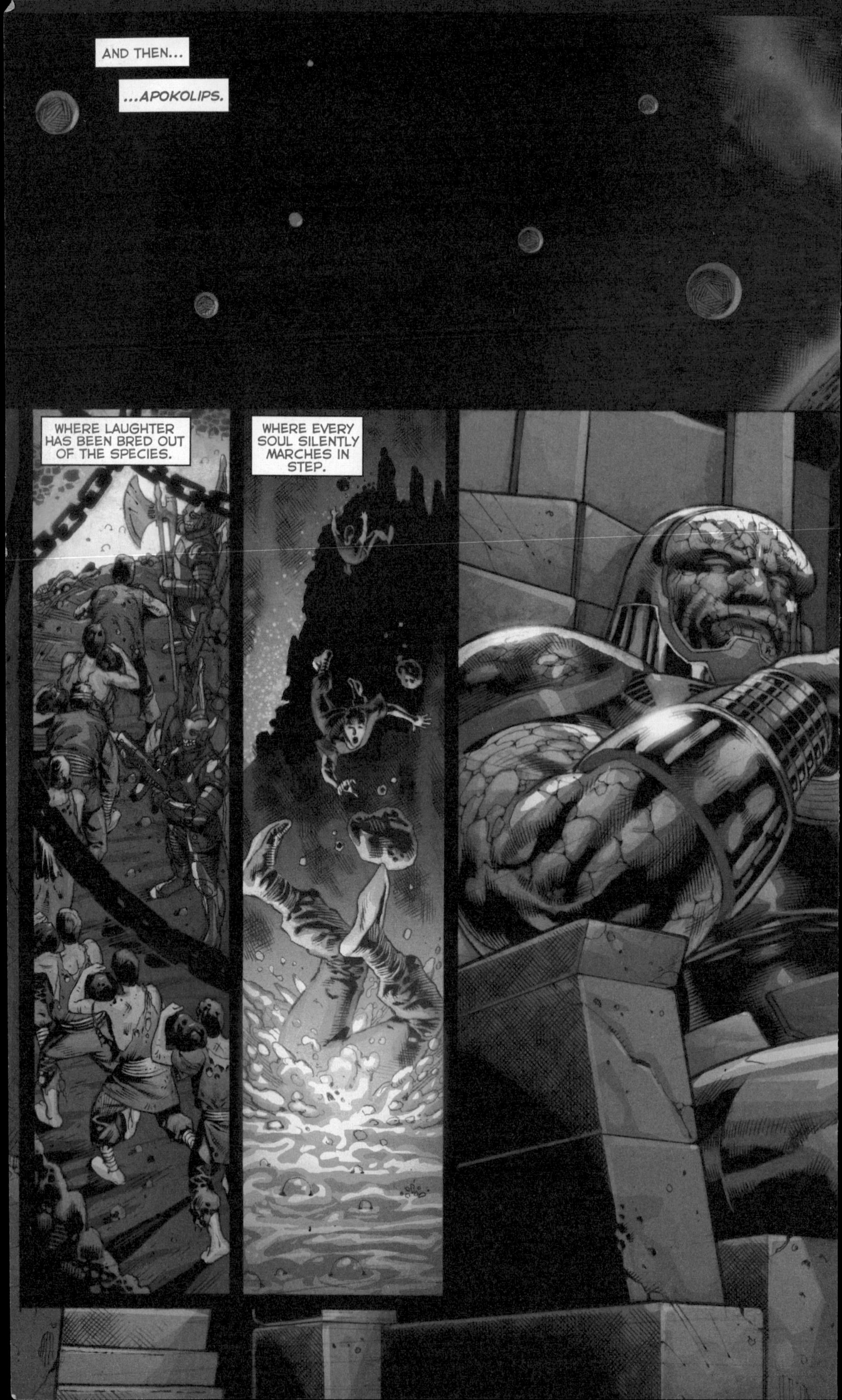
AND THEN...
...APOKOLIPS.
WHERE LAUGHTER HAS BEEN BRED OUT OF THE SPECIES.
WHERE EVERY SOUL SILENTLY MARCHES IN STEP.

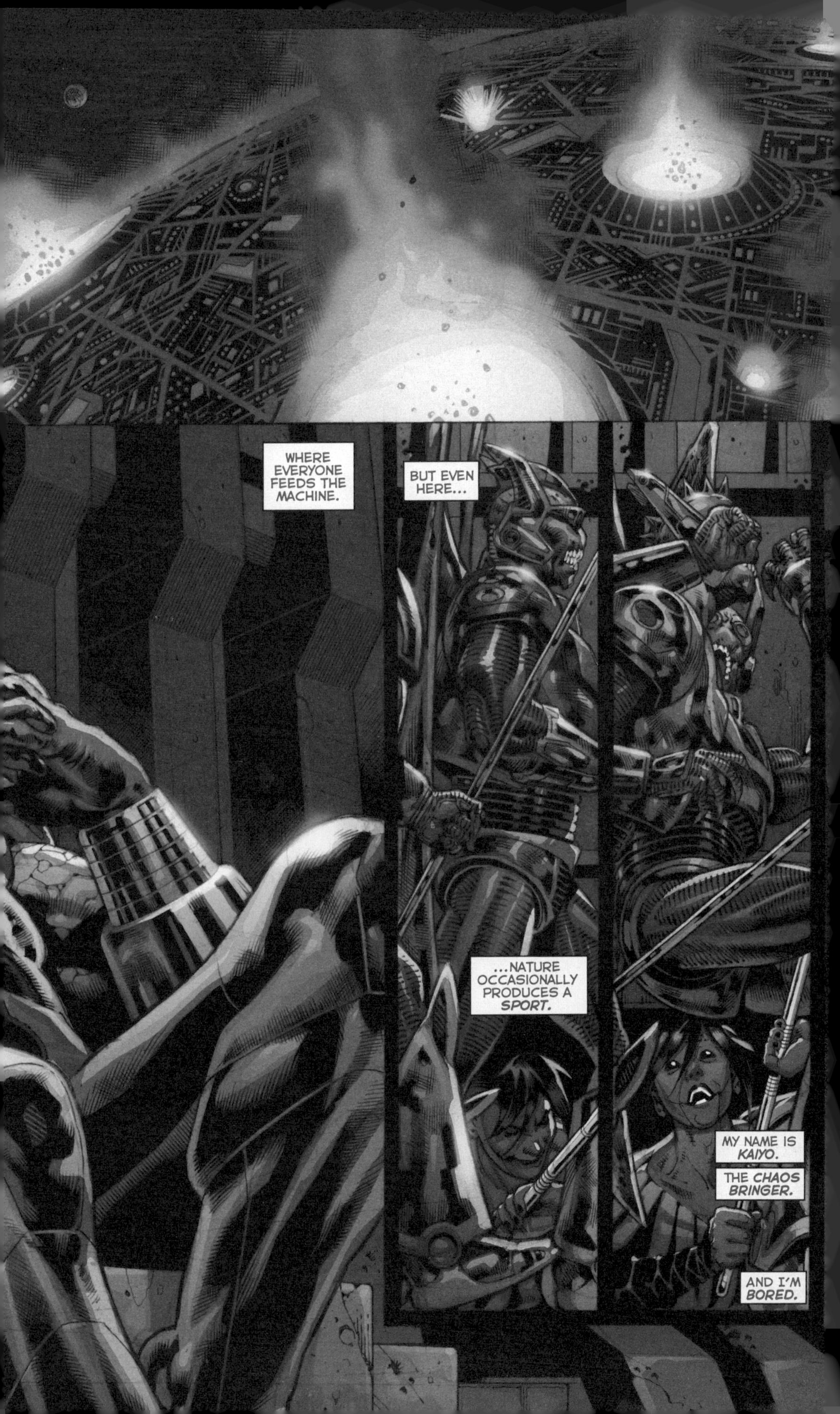
WHERE EVERYONE FEEDS THE MACHINE.
BUT EVEN HERE...
...NATURE OCCASIONALLY PRODUCES A SPORT.
MY NAME IS KAIYO.
THE CHAOS BRINGER.
AND I'M BORED.

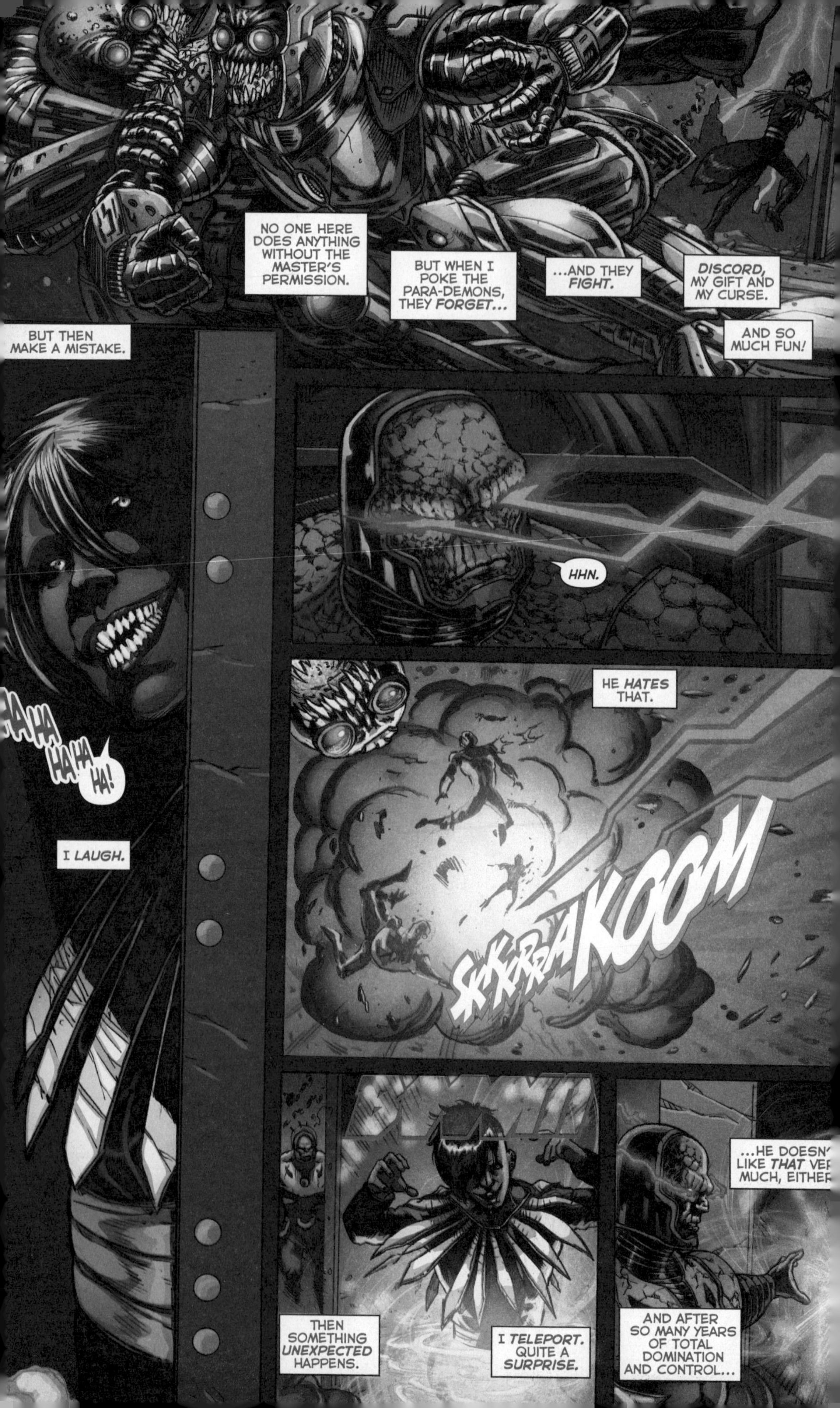
NO ONE HERE DOES ANYTHING WITHOUT THE MASTER'S PERMISSION.
BUT WHEN I POKE THE PARA-DEMONS, THEY FORGET...
...AND THEY FIGHT.
DISCORD, MY GIFT AND MY CURSE.
AND SO MUCH FUN!
BUT THEN MAKE A MISTAKE.
HHN.
HE HATES THAT.
HA HA HA HA HA!
I LAUGH.
SKKRRAKOOM
...HE DOESN' LIKE THAT VER MUCH, EITHER
THEN SOMETHING UNEXPECTED HAPPENS.
I TELEPORT. QUITE A SURPRISE.
AND AFTER SO MANY YEARS OF TOTAL DOMINATION AND CONTROL...

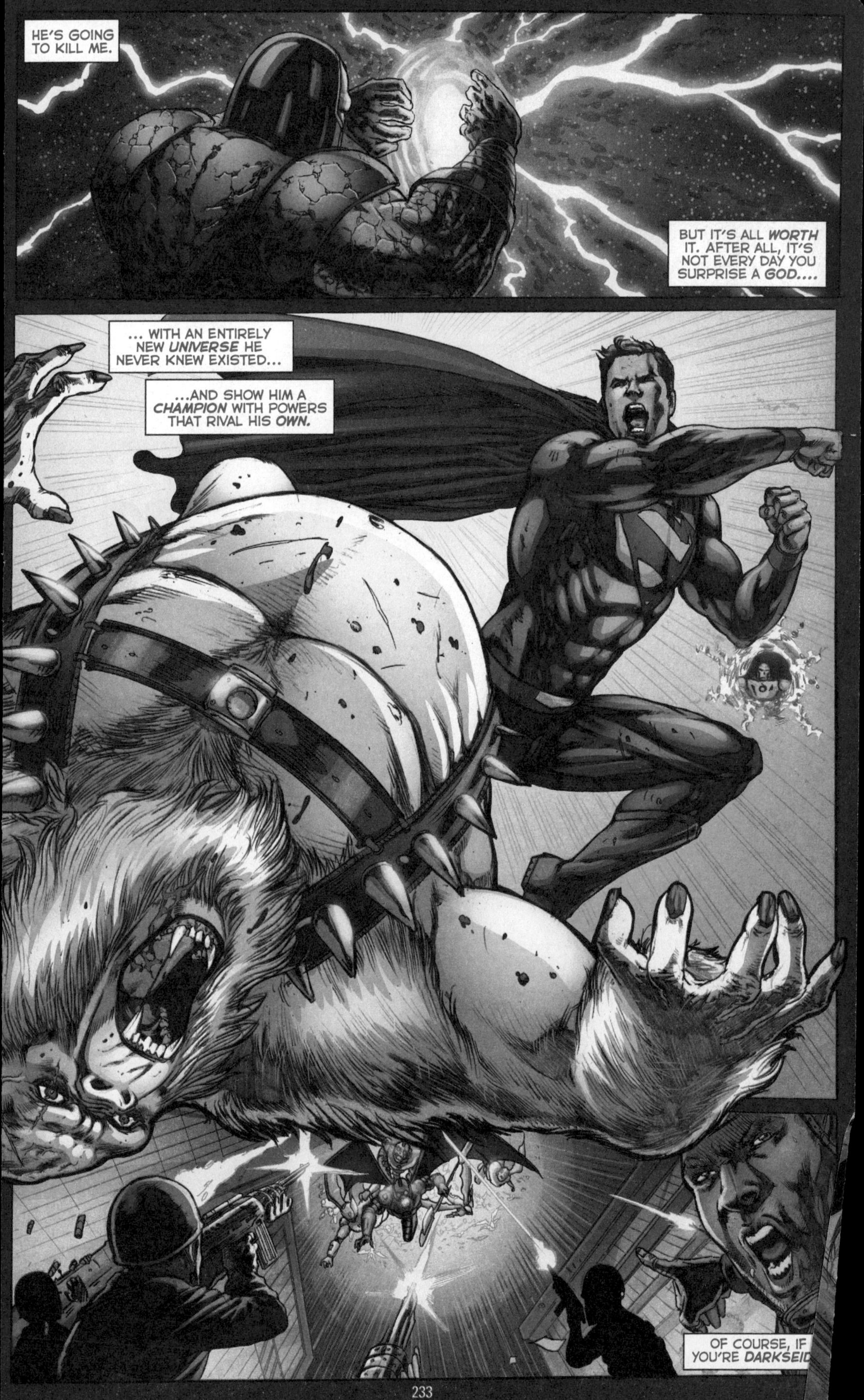
HE'S GOING TO KILL ME.
BUT IT'S ALL WORTH IT. AFTER ALL, IT'S NOT EVERY DAY YOU SURPRISE A GOD....
... WITH AN ENTIRELY NEW UNIVERSE HE NEVER KNEW EXISTED...
...AND SHOW HIM A CHAMPION WITH POWERS THAT RIVAL HIS OWN.
OF COURSE, IF YOU'RE DARKSEID

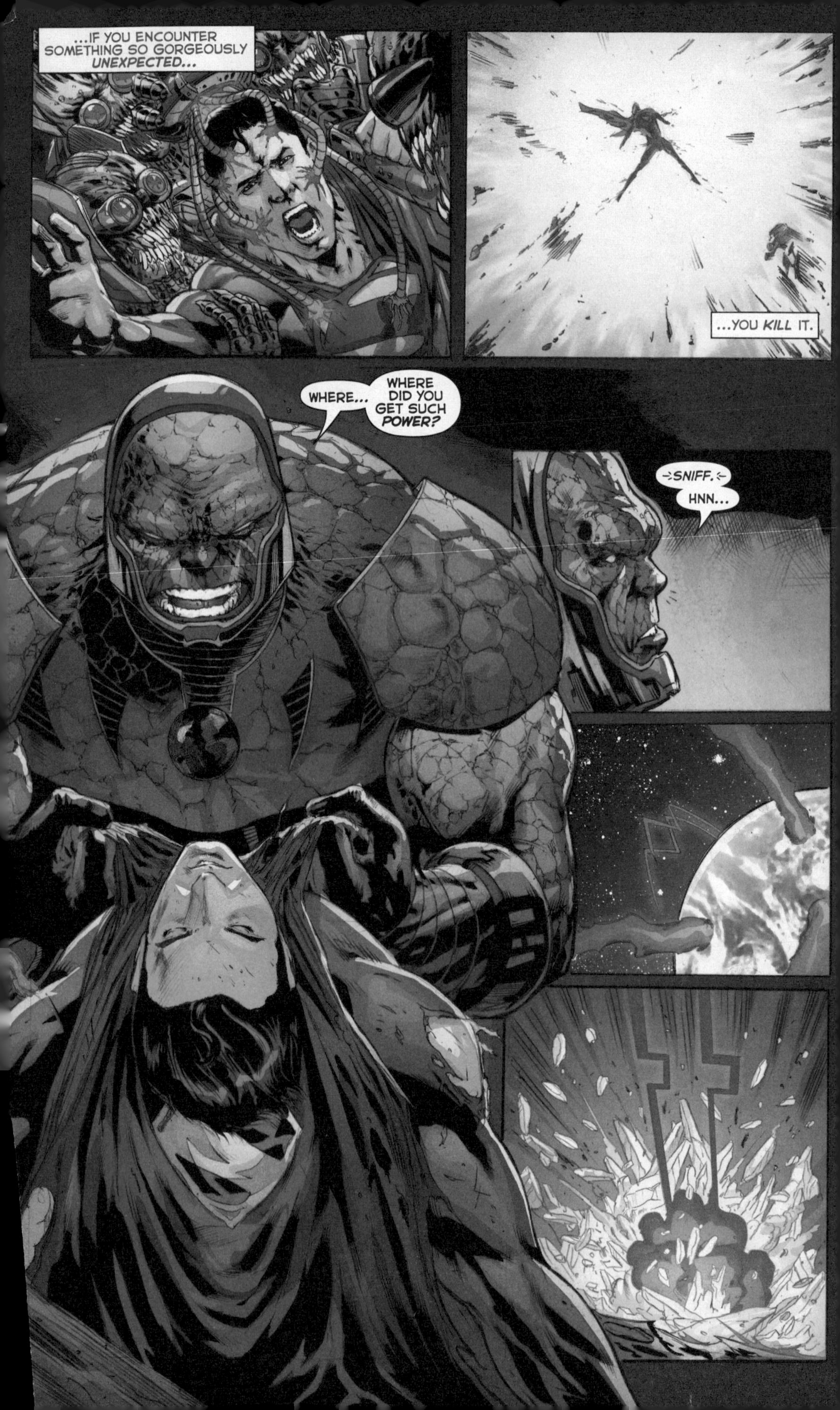
...IF YOU ENCOUNTER SOMETHING SO GORGEOUSLY UNEXPECTED...
...YOU KILL IT.
WHERE...
WHERE DID YOU GET SUCH POWER?
-SNIFF.-
HNN...

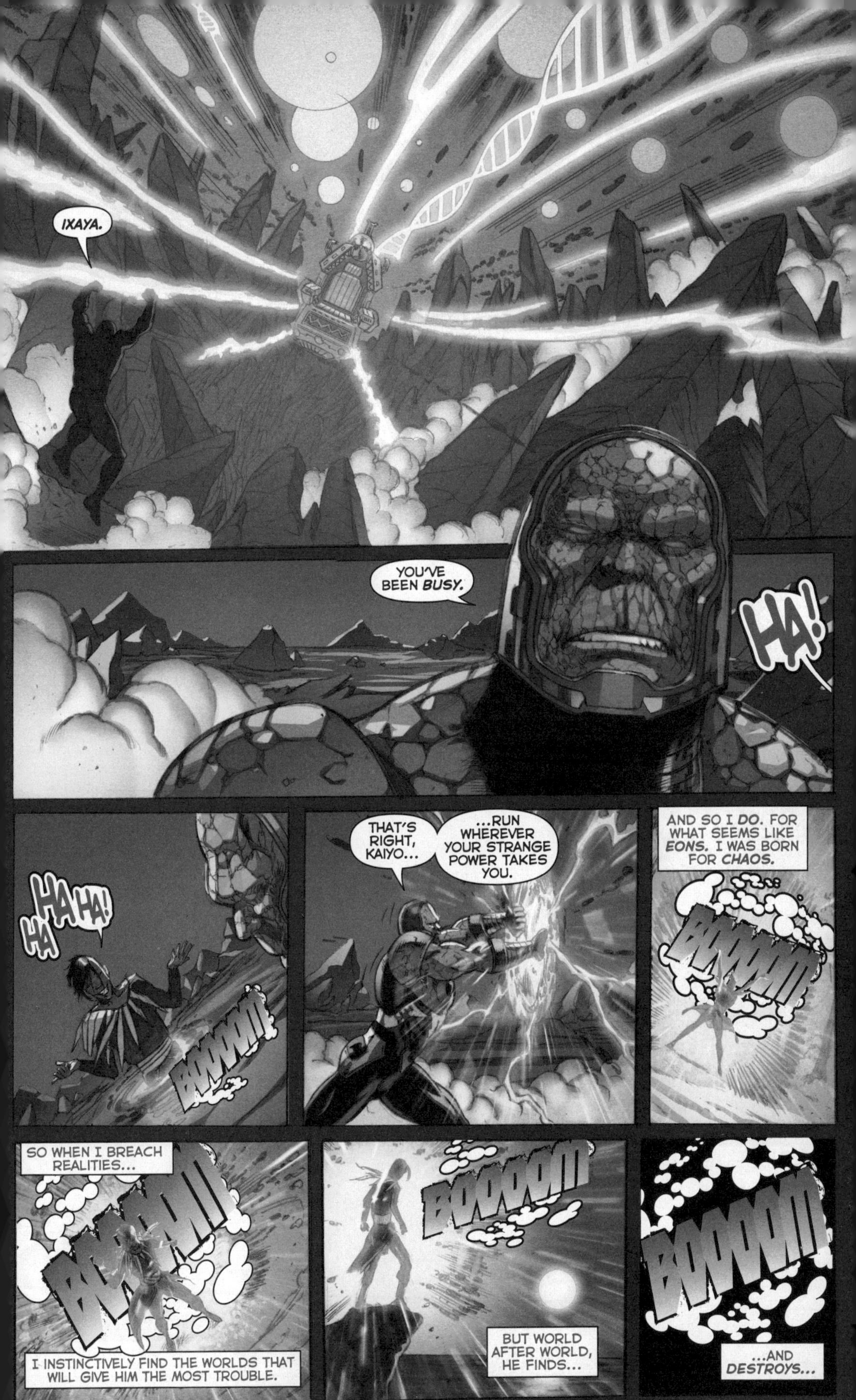
IXAYA.
YOU'VE BEEN BUSY.
HA!
HA HA HA!
BOOOM!
THAT'S RIGHT, KAIYO...
...RUN WHEREVER YOUR STRANGE POWER TAKES YOU.
AND SO I DO. FOR WHAT SEEMS LIKE EONS. I WAS BORN FOR CHAOS.
BOOOOM
SO WHEN I BREACH REALITIES...
BOOOM
I INSTINCTIVELY FIND THE WORLDS THAT WILL GIVE HIM THE MOST TROUBLE.
BOOOOM
BUT WORLD AFTER WORLD, HE FINDS...
BOOOOM
...AND DESTROYS...

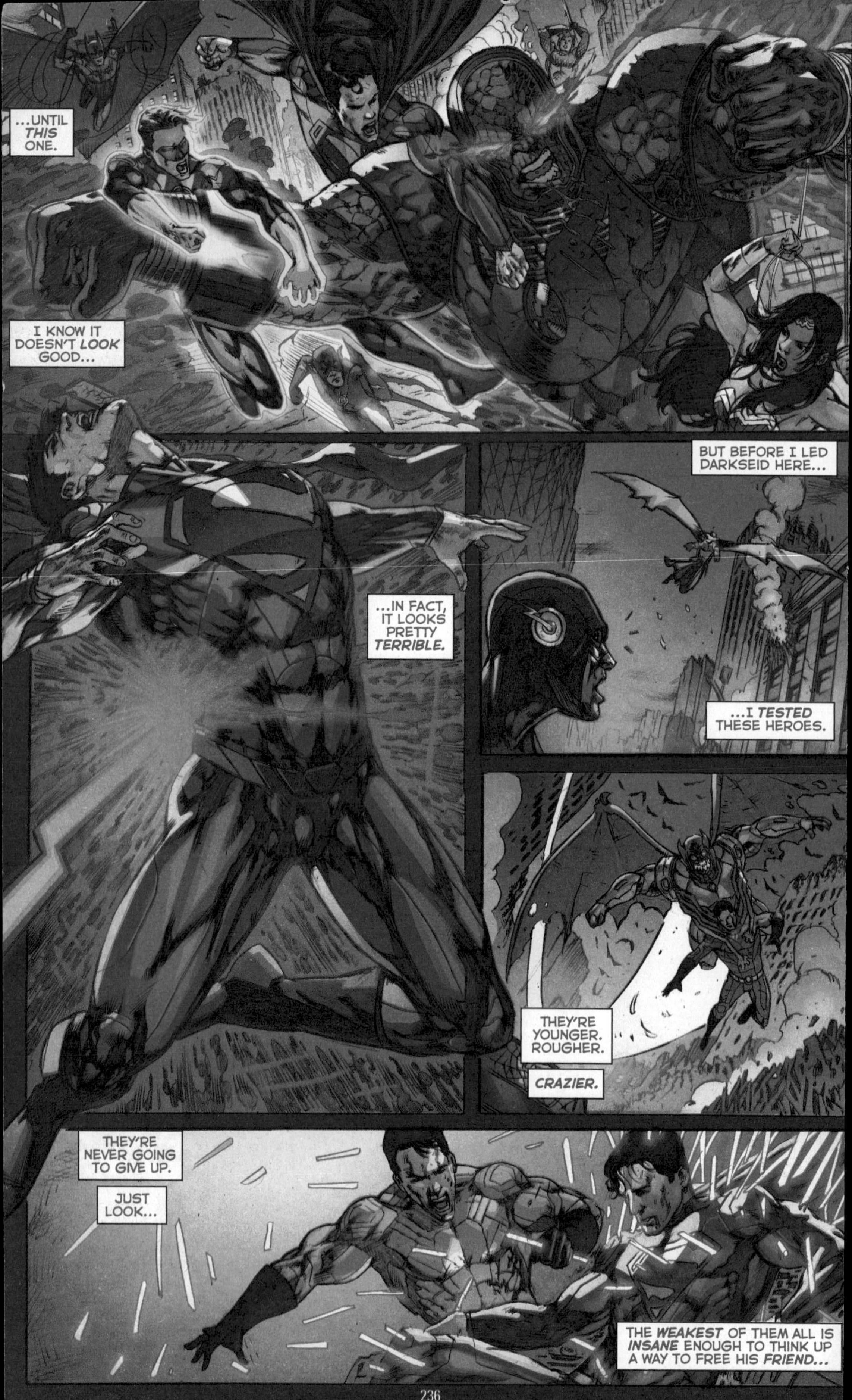

...UNTIL THIS ONE.
I KNOW IT DOESN'T LOOK GOOD...
...IN FACT, IT LOOKS PRETTY TERRIBLE.
BUT BEFORE I LED DARKSEID HERE...
...I TESTED THESE HEROES.
THEY'RE YOUNGER. ROUGHER.
CRAZIER.
THEY'RE NEVER GOING TO GIVE UP.
JUST LOOK...
THE WEAKEST OF THEM ALL IS INSANE ENOUGH TO THINK UP A WAY TO FREE HIS FRIEND...

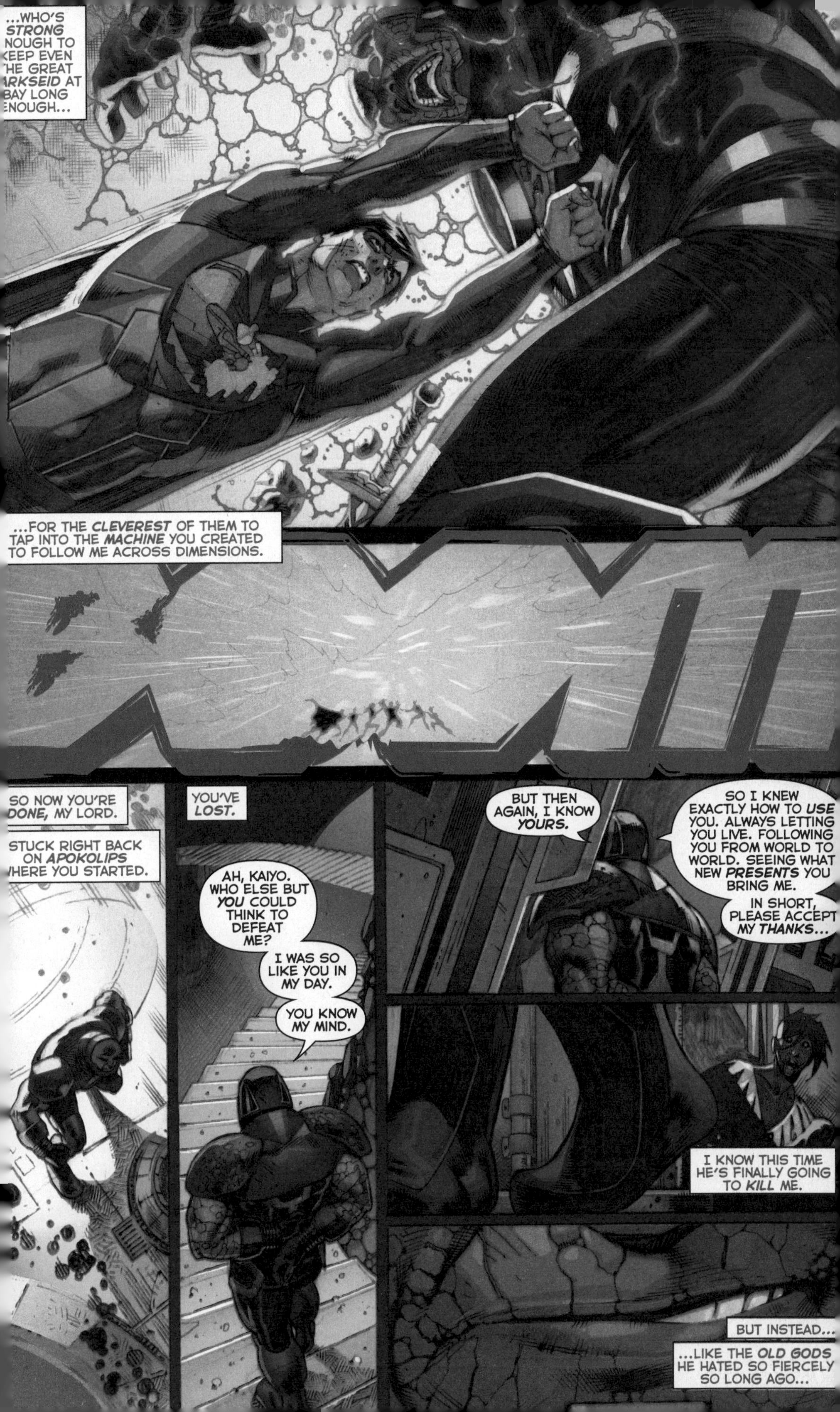
...WHO'S STRONG NOUGH TO KEEP EVEN THE GREAT ARKSEID AT BAY LONG ENOUGH...
...FOR THE CLEVEREST OF THEM TO TAP INTO THE MACHINE YOU CREATED TO FOLLOW ME ACROSS DIMENSIONS.
SO NOW YOU'RE DONE, MY LORD.
STUCK RIGHT BACK ON APOKOLIPS WHERE YOU STARTED.
YOU'VE LOST.
AH, KAIYO. WHO ELSE BUT YOU COULD THINK TO DEFEAT ME?
I WAS SO LIKE YOU IN MY DAY.
YOU KNOW MY MIND.
BUT THEN AGAIN, I KNOW YOURS.
SO I KNEW EXACTLY HOW TO USE YOU. ALWAYS LETTING YOU LIVE. FOLLOWING YOU FROM WORLD TO WORLD. SEEING WHAT NEW PRESENTS YOU BRING ME.
IN SHORT, PLEASE ACCEPT MY THANKS...
I KNOW THIS TIME HE'S FINALLY GOING TO KILL ME.
BUT INSTEAD...
...LIKE THE OLD GODS HE HATED SO FIERCELY SO LONG AGO...

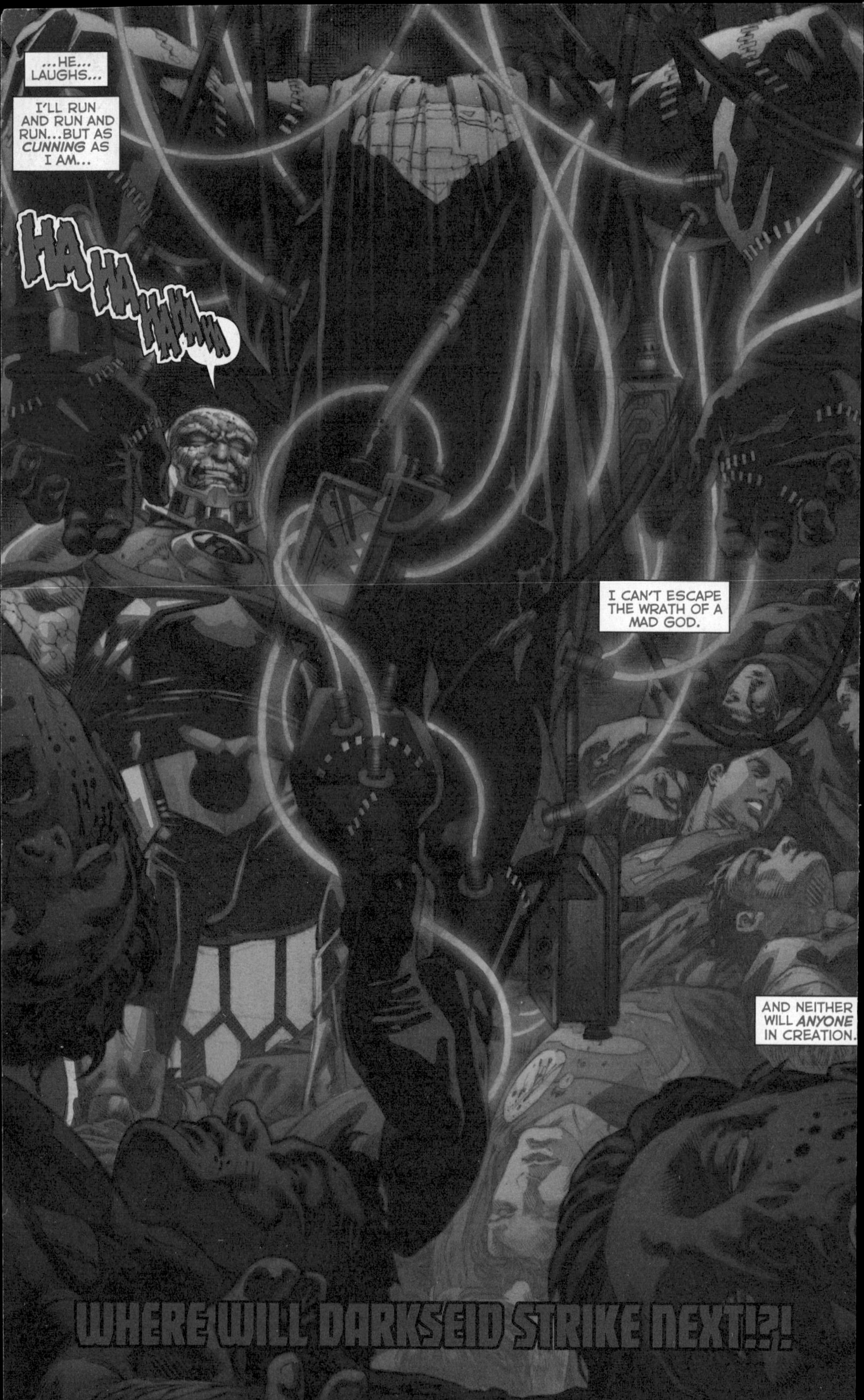
...HE... LAUGHS...
I'LL RUN AND RUN AND RUN...BUT AS CUNNING AS I AM...
HA HA HA HA HA HA HA
I CAN'T ESCAPE THE WRATH OF A MAD GOD.
AND NEITHER WILL ANYONE IN CREATION.
WHERE WILL DARKSEID STRIKE NEXT!?!

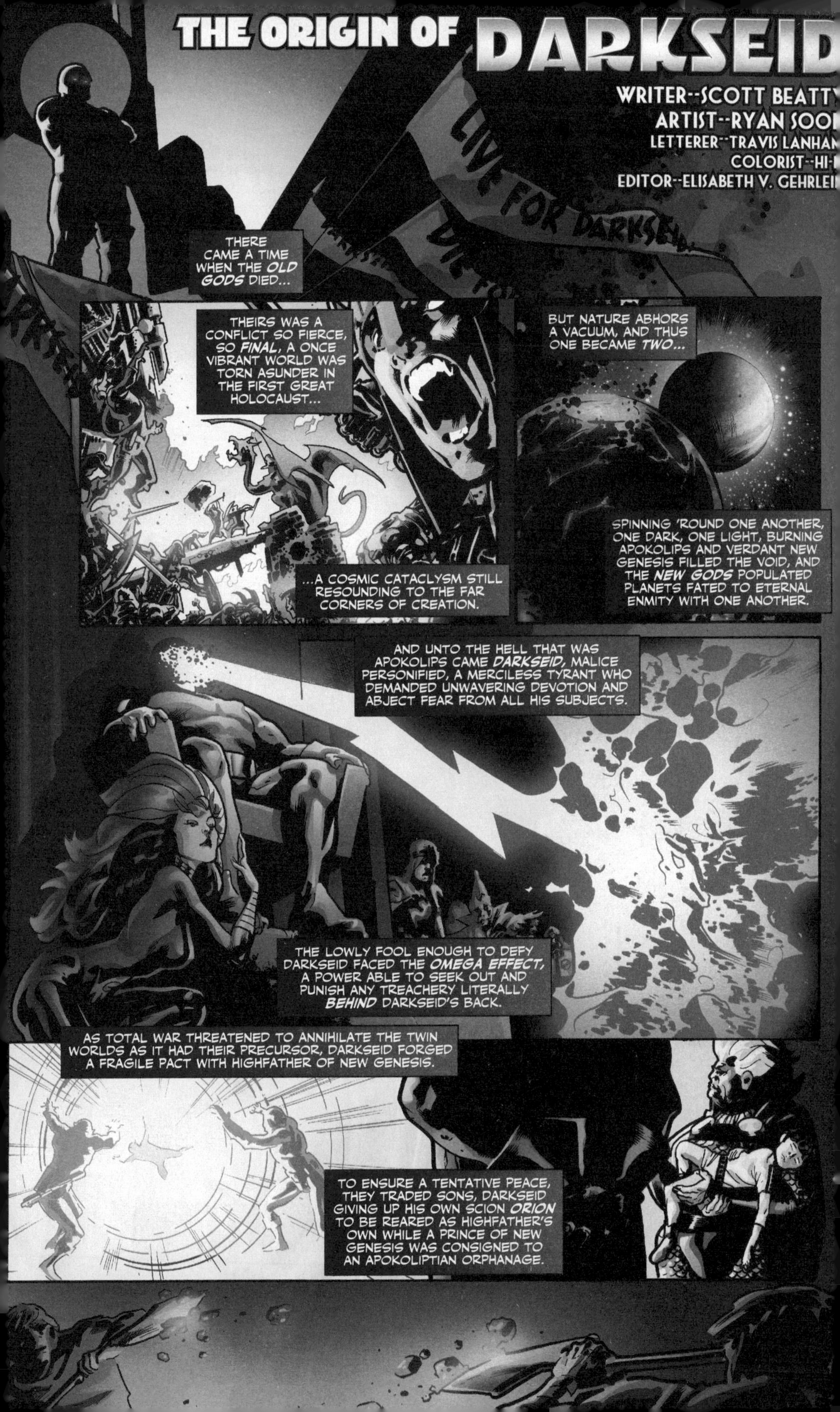

THE ORIGIN OF DARKSEID
WRITER--SCOTT BEATT
ARTIST--RYAN SOO
LETTERER--TRAVIS LANHA
COLORIST--HI-
EDITOR--ELISABETH V. GEHRLEI
THERE CAME A TIME WHEN THE OLD GODS DIED...
THEIRS WAS A CONFLICT SO FIERCE, SO FINAL, A ONCE VIBRANT WORLD WAS TORN ASUNDER IN THE FIRST GREAT HOLOCAUST...
...A COSMIC CATACLYSM STILL RESOUNDING TO THE FAR CORNERS OF CREATION.
BUT NATURE ABHORS A VACUUM, AND THUS ONE BECAME TWO...
SPINNING 'ROUND ONE ANOTHER, ONE DARK, ONE LIGHT, BURNING APOKOLIPS AND VERDANT NEW GENESIS FILLED THE VOID, AND THE NEW GODS POPULATED PLANETS FATED TO ETERNAL ENMITY WITH ONE ANOTHER.
AND UNTO THE HELL THAT WAS APOKOLIPS CAME DARKSEID, MALICE PERSONIFIED, A MERCILESS TYRANT WHO DEMANDED UNWAVERING DEVOTION AND ABJECT FEAR FROM ALL HIS SUBJECTS.
THE LOWLY FOOL ENOUGH TO DEFY DARKSEID FACED THE OMEGA EFFECT, A POWER ABLE TO SEEK OUT AND PUNISH ANY TREACHERY LITERALLY BEHIND DARKSEID'S BACK.
AS TOTAL WAR THREATENED TO ANNIHILATE THE TWIN WORLDS AS IT HAD THEIR PRECURSOR, DARKSEID FORGED A FRAGILE PACT WITH HIGHFATHER OF NEW GENESIS.
TO ENSURE A TENTATIVE PEACE, THEY TRADED SONS, DARKSEID GIVING UP HIS OWN SCION ORION TO BE REARED AS HIGHFATHER'S OWN WHILE A PRINCE OF NEW GENESIS WAS CONSIGNED TO AN APOKOLIPTIAN ORPHANAGE.

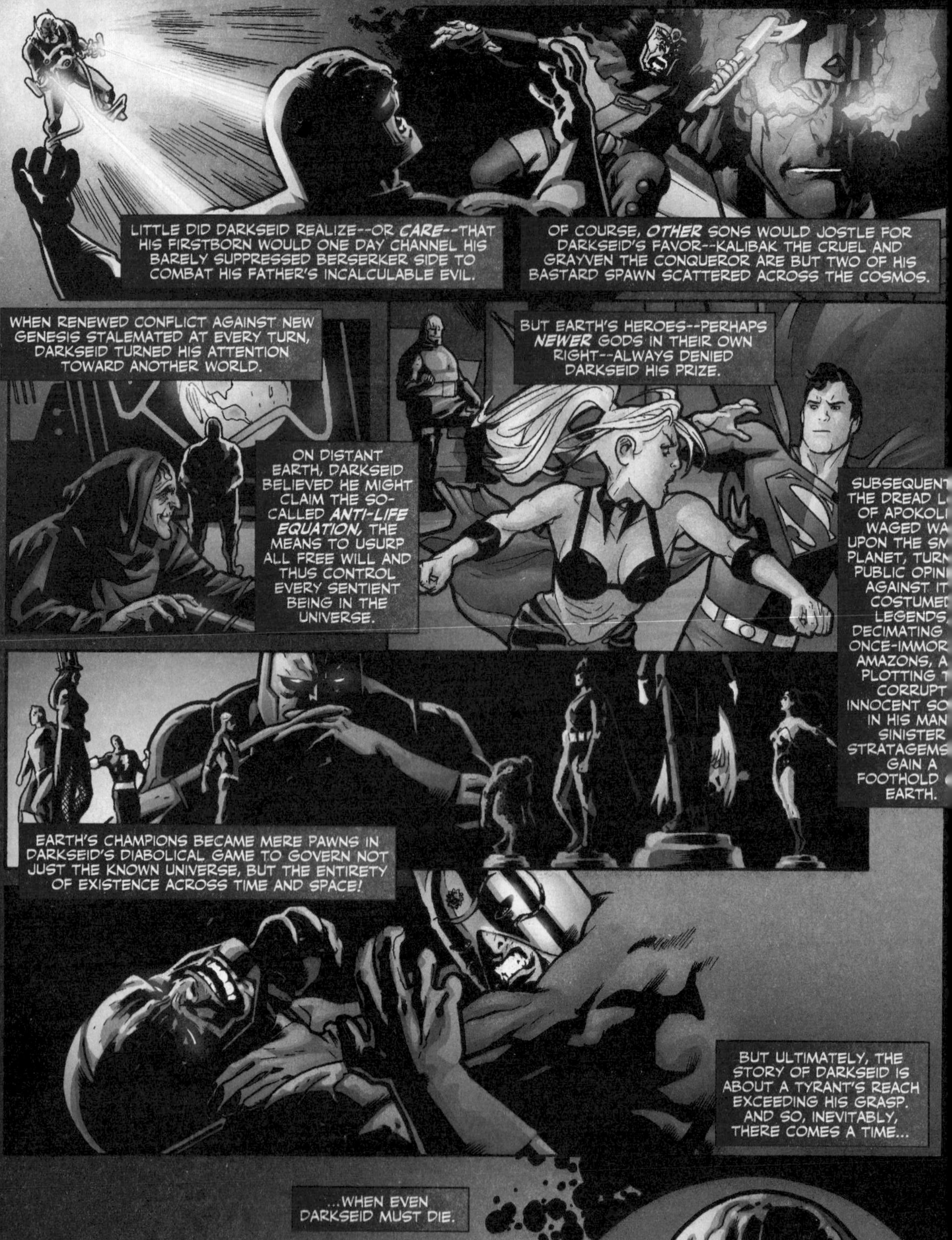
LITTLE DID DARKSEID REALIZE--OR CARE--THAT HIS FIRSTBORN WOULD ONE DAY CHANNEL HIS BARELY SUPPRESSED BERSERKER SIDE TO COMBAT HIS FATHER'S INCALCULABLE EVIL.
OF COURSE, OTHER SONS WOULD JOSTLE FOR DARKSEID'S FAVOR--KALIBAK THE CRUEL AND GRAYVEN THE CONQUEROR ARE BUT TWO OF HIS BASTARD SPAWN SCATTERED ACROSS THE COSMOS.
WHEN RENEWED CONFLICT AGAINST NEW GENESIS STALEMATED AT EVERY TURN, DARKSEID TURNED HIS ATTENTION TOWARD ANOTHER WORLD.
ON DISTANT EARTH, DARKSEID BELIEVED HE MIGHT CLAIM THE SO-CALLED ANTI-LIFE EQUATION, THE MEANS TO USURP ALL FREE WILL AND THUS CONTROL EVERY SENTIENT BEING IN THE UNIVERSE.
BUT EARTH'S HEROES--PERHAPS NEWER GODS IN THEIR OWN RIGHT--ALWAYS DENIED DARKSEID HIS PRIZE.
SUBSEQUENT THE DREAD L OF APOKOLI WAGED WA UPON THE SM PLANET, TURN PUBLIC OPINI AGAINST IT COSTUMED LEGENDS DECIMATING ONCE-IMMOR AMAZONS, A PLOTTING CORRUPT INNOCENT SO IN HIS MAN SINISTER STRATAGEMS GAIN A FOOTHOLD EARTH.
EARTH'S CHAMPIONS BECAME MERE PAWNS IN DARKSEID'S DIABOLICAL GAME TO GOVERN NOT JUST THE KNOWN UNIVERSE, BUT THE ENTIRETY OF EXISTENCE ACROSS TIME AND SPACE!
BUT ULTIMATELY, THE STORY OF DARKSEID IS ABOUT A TYRANT'S REACH EXCEEDING HIS GRASP. AND SO, INEVITABLY, THERE COMES A TIME...
...WHEN EVEN DARKSEID MUST DIE.

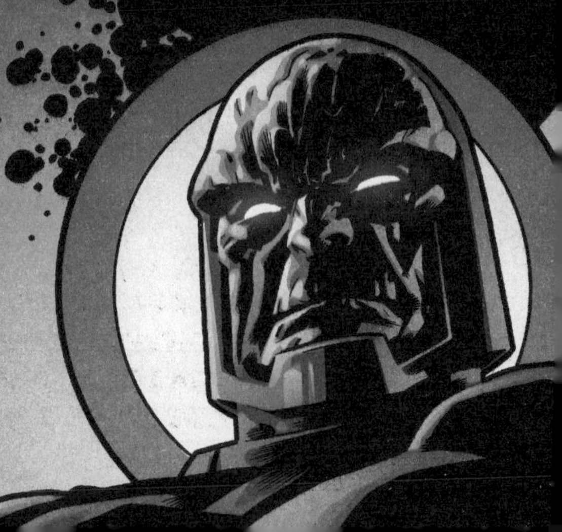

POWERS AND WEAPONS:

A being of unparalleled strength, Darkseid nevertheless preferred not to sully his gloves with hand-to-hand combat unless provoked to action. His eyes emitted the formidable Omega Effect, ray beams that could disintegrate, teleport, or resurrect depending on the dread lord's wishes.

ESSENTIAL STORYLINES:

- Jack Kirby's Fourth World Omnibus Vol. 1-4
- Legion of Super-Heroes: The Great Darkness Saga
- Legends
- Cosmic Odyssey
- Countdown